GRAND RAPIDS

AF700991

REPRESENTING PARENTS IN CHILD WELFARE CASES

Advice and Guidance for Family Defenders

FEB 2016
COOLEY LAW LIBRARY

MARTIN GUGGENHEIM AND VIVEK S. SANKARAN

Cover design by Elmarie Jara.

The materials contained herein represent the opinions of the authors and/or the editors, and should not be construed to be the views or opinions of the law firms or companies with whom such persons are in partnership with, associated with, or employed by, nor of the American Bar Association or the Imprint unless adopted pursuant to the bylaws of the Association.

Nothing contained in this book is to be considered as the rendering of legal advice for specific cases, and readers are responsible for obtaining such advice from their own legal counsel. This book is intended for educational and informational purposes only.

© 2015 American Bar Association. All rights reserved.

No part of this publication may be reproduced, stored in a retrieval system, or transmitted in any form or by any means, electronic, mechanical, photocopying, recording, or otherwise, without the prior written permission of the publisher. For permission contact the ABA Copyrights & Contracts Department, copyright@americanbar.org, or complete the online form at http://www.americanbar.org/utility/reprint.html.

Printed in the United States of America.

17 16 15 5 4 3 2 1

ISBN: 978-1-63425-297-3
e-ISBN: 978-1-63425-298-0

Library of Congress Cataloging-in-Publication Data

Sankaran, Vivek S., author.
Representing parents in child welfare cases : advice and guidance for family defenders / Vivek S. Sankaran, Martin Guggenheim.
pages cm
Includes bibliographical references and index.
ISBN 978-1-63425-297-3 (alk. paper)
1. Children—Legal status, laws, etc.—United States—Trial practice. 2. Custody of children—United States—Trial practice. 3. Child abuse—Law and legislation—United States—Trial practice. 4. Actions and defenses—United States. I. Guggenheim, Martin, author. II. Title.
KF8925.C45S26 2015
344.7303'27—dc23

2015034401

Discounts are available for books ordered in bulk. Special consideration is given to state bars, CLE programs, and other bar-related organizations. Inquire at Book Publishing, ABA Publishing, American Bar Association, 321 N. Clark Street, Chicago, Illinois 60654-7598.

www.ShopABA.org

CONTENTS

ACKNOWLEDGMENTS

This book is the product of a national movement aimed at recognizing the importance of parents' attorneys in the child welfare system. At the heart of this movement is the Steering Committee of the American Bar Association's Project To Improve Parent Representation, whose members drafted many of the chapters in this book. In particular, Mimi Laver, the project director, deserves credit for organizing and sustaining this movement. Without her tireless efforts and the work of the Steering Committee, this book would never have come into fruition. As such, all proceeds of this book will be donated to the work of the ABA Project.

The book is also a tribute to the lawyers who work in this field. Most of the authors of the chapters practice daily in court fighting to ensure that the law is faithfully followed. They are underpaid and overworked, with excessive caseloads. Despite this, they have shared their expertise by writing a chapter in this book to help lawyers everywhere get better at doing a very difficult job. This book could not have been written without their contributions.

We would also like to thank Jennifer Garrett and Misha Ross, who spent countless hours meticulously reviewing drafts of chapters, checking cites and ensuring that the book flowed smoothly from one chapter to the next.

Finally, we would like to thank the thousands of parents' attorneys across the country, who fight to keep families together under difficult conditions. Our hope in creating this book is to give them the tools they need to advocate successfully for their clients while also persuading stakeholders that the time has come to properly invest in parent representation throughout the country.

PREFACE

This book is written primarily for "family defenders"—lawyers and other advocates working with parents in court or administrative proceedings brought against them by the local child protection services agency. These proceedings are variously known as "dependency," "child neglect," "child abuse," or child protection," depending on the locality. In some of these cases, the local agency may be seeking nothing more than a protective order of some kind, directing that a caregiver do or refrain from doing something. In other cases, the agency may be seeking a child's removal from his or her family or the child's continued placement in foster care. In still other proceedings, the agency may be seeking permanent termination of parental rights. In all these proceedings, the state, through the exercise of its *parens patriae* or police powers, charges parents or other caretakers with being inadequate in the rearing of children.

It would be difficult to find a more important type of legal proceeding implicating an individual's rights. Many forms of state intervention potentially impact an individual's basic rights, interfering with someone's property or liberty. For many people, criminal proceedings are regarded as the form of state intervention that most threatens our most basic right: the right to remain free in society and avoid imprisonment. But child protection cases implicate rights that others would regard as even more fundamental. Many parents certainly agree with Justice Stevens's observation more than thirty years ago that depriving a parent of rights to raise one's child—"a deprivation of both liberty and property"—is "often . . . the more grievous" compared to sentencing someone to prison ("a pure deprivation of liberty"). *Lassiter v. Department of Social Services*, 452 U.S. 18, 59 (1981) (Stevens, J., dissenting).

All of this suggests that "family defense"—working on behalf of adults threatened by state intervention with the temporary and permanent loss of the custody and rights to their children—would be a well-known, highly prized legal field, at least comparable in status to criminal defense, and arguably, even more esteemed because of the importance of the threatened substantive rights. Sadly, this is anything but the case. Family defense is an outlier field, barely known to most lawyers and law school professors, let alone among Americans more broadly.

Why this is so is complicated. One reason has to do with its relative youth. Criminal prosecutions brought to punish law violators—well-known and feared by the Founding Fathers—are the focus of three specific Bill of Rights Amendments enacted when the country began. But the modern regime of state-initiated legal proceedings carrying the potential power to remove children from their families and to cut permanently children's ties with families only began in 1974 when Congress enacted the Child Protection and Treatment Act, federalizing much of the child welfare field. By that time, the Supreme Court had already interpreted the Sixth Amendment to require a lawyer for criminal defendants. *See Gideon v. Wainwright*, 372 U.S. 335 (1963); *see also Argersinger v. Hamlin*, 407 U.S. 25 (1972). But in 1981, when it was first asked whether parents in family defense cases also have a right to counsel, the Supreme Court held that there is no such automatic right. *See Lassiter v. Department of Social Services*, 452 U.S. 18 (1981).

No less important a difference between criminal prosecutions and child protection cases is their relative impact on society as a whole. Though criminal proceedings are disproportionately brought against poor people, many prosecutions are brought against rich and powerful people each year. Most Americans know somebody who has been a defendant in a criminal case. Film and television regularly tell stories involving criminal prosecutions in which the defendants' rights are commonly a prominent focus. Well ingrained in these stories is an understanding that even innocent people can become the target of prosecutions. Because of this, Americans have a widely shared understanding of the central importance of the right to a rigorous defense to prevent overreaching by state officials and to ensure the protection of individual rights.

Child protection cases are a very different matter. Rather than reaching into all parts of town, these cases tend to be prosecuted only against poor families. Although child protective services are very well known in poor communities (which often fear them), they are almost never seen in well-to-do communities. In New York City, for example, 96 percent of the foster care population is non-white. As a result, many fewer Americans know someone who has been accused of parental unfitness; even fewer know someone who has lost the custody of their children to the state.

Finally, even when Americans know about these cases, they are less likely to believe that family defense is as important as criminal defense. They have a greater confidence in child welfare officials to ferret out worthy cases from unworthy ones. Recognizing the good intentions of child welfare professionals, many believe that fewer roadblocks should be placed in their path because they would not prosecute cases unless they honestly believed it was appropriate to do so. In addition, many place a greater focus on the children, who stand to lose the most when cases are wrongfully dismissed. Many of the same people who believe in a vigorous criminal defense as the price of liberty, even when it results in the acquittal of a guilty person, are unable to feel the same way when wrongful dismissal of a case means exposing a child to risk of harm.

Law schools also have contributed to the outlier status of family defense in the United States. In sharp contrast with criminal defense, very few law schools even teach about child welfare. And when they do, they tend to stress the importance of child welfare as the means by which vulnerable children are protected from dangerous situations.

In those few schools that offer clinical experience in child welfare matters for students, the vast majority place law students with local agencies prosecuting child welfare cases or with law offices that represent children in those proceedings. Rarest of all are law school programs training the next generation of family defenders.

Much could be said in response. For some, including Justice Brandeis, the intentions of state officials are hardly a reason to be less vigilant to prevent overreaching. "Experience should teach us," he wrote in 1928, "to be most on our guard to protect liberty when the government's purposes are beneficent. . . . The greatest dangers to liberty lurk in insidious encroachment by men of zeal, well-meaning but without understanding." *Olmstead v. United States*, 277 U.S. 438 (1928) (Brandeis, J., dissenting).

And history, even in the field of child welfare, buttresses his concerns. Two of the most famous child welfare efforts in American history, both carried out by people of goodwill intending only to further children's well-being, have come to be seen in historical perspective as deeply flawed efforts. Charles Loring Brace's work in the mid-1800s eventually led to as many as 250,000 "orphans" being sent to the Midwest from New York on "orphan trains," even though many of the children were not orphans, none of them or their families were given the opportunity to seek official review of the decision to send them away, and many ended up working as indentured servants throughout their childhood. *See* DUNCAN LINDSEY, THE WELFARE OF CHILDREN 13–17 (1994). Those responsible for placing children on these trains were proud of their work. But the Catholic families whose children were taken from them had a very different grasp of the situation. *See* NINA BERNSTEIN, THE LOST CHILDREN OF WILDER: THE EPIC STRUGGLE TO CHANGE FOSTER CARE 197–98 (2001).

Another blight on American history is the extensive use of American Indian boarding schools established by the Bureau of Indian Affairs during the late nineteenth century. In the name of achieving assimilation, the United States government engaged in a planned effort to eradicate Indian culture. *See* ROBERT A. TRENNERT, JR., THE PHOENIX INDIAN SCHOOL: FORCED ASSIMILATION IN ARIZONA, 1891–1935 (1988). The plan was to extirpate Indian custom and culture from Indian children by denying them the opportunity to speak in their native languages and forcing them to dress in non-native clothing and to engage only in non-native habits. Nor was this merely a very old mistake. As recently as 1959, United States policy encouraged the removal of Indian children and placement in non-Indian families for the same purpose. H.R. REP. 104-808, at 16 (1996). This practice was regarded by the families whose children were seized as the "ultimate indignity to endure." DAVID FANSHEL, FAR FROM THE RESERVATION: THE TRANSRACIAL ADOPTION OF AMERICAN INDIAN CHILDREN (1972).

Perhaps least of all should the fear that insistence on fair procedures (of which a strong defender bar serves as the foundation) will endanger children be an obstacle to creating a highly competent defender system. For one thing, this fear entirely ignores the contrary danger: that children will be wrongly wrested from their families; forced to become temporary or long-term state wards; have their lives permanently negatively impacted; threatened with abuse and other dangers disproportionately associated with foster children; and suffer long-term costs of poorer grades in school, lower graduation rates, higher incarceration rates, and considerably lower income levels over the course of their lives.

For another, family defense is conceptually very different from criminal defense. In many cases, criminal defense is focused on advancing the rights of the accused to prevent a conviction for reasons apart from factual innocence. As a consequence, a widely understood characteristic of criminal defense is defenders striving to achieve a victory for "technical" reasons (such as the enforcement of constitutional norms, which require suppressing statements, eyewitness identifications, or items seized by the police) even when evidence points to the defendant's guilt. But there are no such technical defenses available in family defense. When parents' lawyers are able to secure dismissal, it is either because the agency itself was persuaded that dismissal was appropriate or because a court found that the agency lacked evidence of parental wrongdoing required to permit intervention in the first place.

This leaves only the question whether children's rights (or society's interests) are better served by a legal system designed to prevent state intervention unless independent judges are satisfied there is a legal basis for the intervention. Differently asked, the question is whether children's rights are served by living in a society devoted to the rule of law. To ask the question is to answer it. Children have reciprocal rights to be raised by their families, qualified, of course, by the important principle that they also have the right to be protected from parental misconduct. But the rule of law fully satisfies such rights and their limitations. It seeks to protect and implement children's rights by ensuring that children are allowed to remain with their families when the law requires that result *and* that children are protected from maltreatment when the law requires it. Family defense does not undermine the values of child protection; it advances them.

This is true in still another way that is misunderstood by many professionals involved in child welfare. Of all the differences between criminal prosecutions and child welfare cases, perhaps the greatest involves the purpose of the intervention and its corresponding impact on almost everything that follows. Criminal proceedings are brought to punish criminals. The state's interests and those of the accused are at odds when the case is first brought and when it ends with a conviction and sentence. The parties are true antagonists.

Though this is sometimes true in child protection matters, in the great majority of cases, the state's interests are entirely consistent with the parents'. This is because the state's purpose in virtually all cases is to help families find ways to be able to raise their children safely. In every state, the primary purpose of child protection intervention is to develop a plan that will allow children to be kept safely with their families of origin or be returned to them promptly. Instead of being punitive, the purpose is rehabilitative.

Rather than trying to prevent parents from getting a second chance to raise their children, child welfare professionals seek to assist families to overcome the obstacles to the safe return of their children and to do so quickly. Only when parents fail to change their ways or prove unable to raise their children safely for the foreseeable future do the state's interests and that of parents' truly diverge (with parents seeking to retain their parental rights and state officials seeking to terminate them).

But the time between the filing of a case until this fateful divergence is the critical time in all child protection cases when family defense can serve as a vital ally with child welfare personnel by focusing attention to the critical issues of what deficits exist in the family, what needs to be done to address them, and how it may be possible for children to remain safely at home or be safely returned there.

Many who have worked in the field, including the authors of this book, do not believe that the intentions of state officials are a sufficient protection against state overreaching. Nor do we believe that a vigorous defense system threatens anything worth preserving. A thriving family defense system is needed throughout the United States to protect vulnerable families from the loss of the most precious of American rights (for both children and their families)—the right of families to raise children and of children to be raised by their families except when the conditions at home are sufficiently harmful that children deserve to be removed. Nothing about family defense threatens those rights; only its absence does.

Despite all of this, family defense is still in its infancy in establishing itself as an important legal field. The publication of this book is the field's coming out statement: we exist and we do important work. Those committed to civil rights should want to join the field because it advances the rights of poor families and children to be protected by the rule of law. And those many lawyers who represent children in child protection cases may come to appreciate the value to children's interests served by ensuring that their parents have well-trained, highly skilled lawyers devoted to serving the parents' interests. As adults think back on their lives, who would not have wanted their parents to be represented by the best lawyer in town when their right to remain in their family was at stake? This book is devoted to persuading the best lawyer in town to become a family defense lawyer and we hope the book will help lawyers become excellent in their practice.

The book is very different from those written about criminal or juvenile defense work because the things family defenders need to do to successfully negotiate the child protection system are very different from what is needed to defend criminal cases. Much follows from what is so different about the purpose of prosecuting child protection cases. Because the prosecution's first goal is to strengthen families so that children can remain with or be safely returned to them, family defenders must pay a great deal of attention to this purpose. They must do considerably more than what is common to criminal defense work. Like criminal defense, family defense requires a careful investigation into the facts and circumstances of the events that led to the prosecution. But unlike in some criminal cases, in family defense, parents can achieve all of their objectives (gaining the return of their children) whether or not they were "guilty" of something in the past. When parents have not done something that justifies coercive intervention in their families, family defenders should ensure that their rights are upheld. But what matters most in most cases is whether parents are moving toward something the judge or caseworker is demanding. Parents who comply with their case plan are most likely to achieve their long-term objective of regaining their children's custody.

For these reasons, family defense requires careful attention to the present and the future. Lawyers representing parents should be actively engaged in fashioning the case plan by participating in its creation. Many case plans are flawed from the beginning because they were created without an accurate understanding of the parents' needs. Family defenders are able to advance the goals of child welfare intervention by helping to identify more accurately what is going on in the parent's life that should be addressed. When case plans call for parents to engage in services that will not make them better parents, no one wins. If parents do not complete services—even when those services would not be of real help to them—parents will often pay the price by being found noncompliant by the court. Courts and agencies weigh compliance heavily as a litmus test for a parent's concern and love for his or her child. For these reasons, eliminating from a case plan services that will not be of any real use to the parent serves everyone's interest.

To be an effective family defender requires getting to know each client, finding out what she thinks will be of help to her and what she most wants from the court intervention. This attention to the present and the future—the period of time the case will take to resolve—is the critical difference between criminal and family defense. The book will describe what family defenders should do to increase the chances of families remaining together. It is written by an experienced community of parents' lawyers and advocates who have joined together in a national effort headquartered at the American Bar Association's Center on Children and the Law to advocate for every locality to provide quality legal representation to parents at the earliest possible time when a child protection case is being considered against a parent. We believe that high-quality legal representation is a critical component of the child welfare field. This book is written to provide advice, guidance, and encouragement to lawyers and other advocates who wish to be a family defender.

CHAPTER 1

General Overview of Child Protection Laws in the United States

Martin Guggenheim

1.01 The Statutory Framework

Every state has laws that protect children from harm. Criminal assault laws protect persons of any age against physical assaults. Child abuse and neglect laws are special in protecting only children. States give their juvenile courts jurisdiction over children who have been denied proper parental care. Particular statutes may be phrased in terms of neglect, abuse, abandonment, dependency, or something else, but all contain provisions vesting broad discretion in the court to find appropriate substitute care.

Although there is considerable similarity from state to state in the definitions of child maltreatment, very few statutes use identical language. Counsel representing parents in child protection proceedings must familiarize themselves with the statutory scheme in their particular state. The general overview of the law provided by this chapter is no substitute for study of the language of the governing statute of the jurisdiction in which any given case arises.

"Neglect" ordinarily refers to a temporary lapse of care on the part of the parent, often involving some degree of willfulness. Statutes may be quite detailed, enumerating specifics such as moral unfitness of a parent, mental or physical incapacity of a parent, and failure to send the child to school; or they may be couched entirely in broad phrases, such as lack of proper parental care, control, or guardianship. Even statutes that set out numerous specific grounds of neglect usually include a catch-all phrase to cover other situations.

Although most acts of child abuse would come within the standard neglect provisions, many states have separate child abuse statutes. The allegedly abusive parent may be charged with a criminal violation as well as with neglect or possibly subjected to proceedings for termination of parental rights.

In addition to child abuse, abandonment and dependency are two common categories of neglect that may be the subject of separate legislation. Abandonment is shown by parental absence, usually required to be willful and, when separated from neglect findings, is ordinarily included in adoption codes as a ground for permitting the child to be adopted by another concerned adult. Dependency denotes a failure to provide adequate care without fault on the part of the parent; in some states, a finding of dependency must be made as a precondition to the provision of social services to the family.

States also treat unwed fathers very differently. In some jurisdictions, unwed fathers may not even be counted as parents with rights unless they take particular steps to secure such rights. Counsel is well advised to study carefully the laws regulating how men get to become parents with substantive rights.

Finally, states vary widely on the time frame within which agencies are encouraged or required to file a petition to terminate parental rights once children have entered foster care. Counsel should know the law on terminating parental rights before beginning the representation of a parent because the mere passage of time—which may be as short as three to six months—may result in parents permanently losing their rights.

1.02 Common Problems in the Operation of Child Protection Laws

Whatever their precise terms, child protection laws are almost universally administered in a fashion that gives rise to a common constellation of problems. Counsel representing parents can expect to confront the following problems in child protection cases:

- children are removed from the families' custody and placed in foster care despite laws that should forbid such placements;
- the families prosecuted in these proceedings are overwhelmingly poor and, in communities with high rates of minorities, very disproportionately of color;
- these families are brought to court to address concerns regarding parental decisions involving children's health or education that are not made the subject of court proceedings for middle and upper income parents;
- courts do not rigorously oversee the decisions of agencies;
- as a condition of regaining custody of their children, parents are required to secure services that are either unavailable to them or are not needed;
- many localities do not have adequate interpreters available to communicate meaningfully with parents;

- parents are often mislabeled in psychological evaluations as having conditions they do not have;
- services that would eliminate the need for foster care placements are not used;
- intervention exacerbates the challenges of parents with special needs;
- parents and children in foster care are not allowed sufficient time each week for visiting and the few visits made available often take place in inappropriate sterile environments;
- children remain in foster care long after they could be safely returned to their families;
- agencies and courts focus more on a parent's deficits than strengths in making placement decisions;
- parents do not regard caseworkers as allies, devoted to helping them and concerned for their, and their children's, well-being;
- parents do not understand what happened in their case when they were in court;
- parents do not get to speak with their lawyers between court appearances and do not regard them as fighting for their rights or interests;
- cases are increasingly fast-tracked for termination of parental rights when children remain in foster care for one year;
- thousands of family relationships each year are permanently extinguished despite the children wanting to remain part of their families and even when they gain nothing by becoming legal orphans; and
- counsel for parents are not appointed before significant decisions have already been made and, when appointed, are required to handle unacceptably high caseloads.

1.03 The Impact of Congressional Legislation on Child Protection Laws

For most of American history, protecting and caring for children was considered a matter of state rather than federal concern. That changed beginning in 1980 when Congress enacted the Adoption Assistance and Child Welfare Act of 1980, Pub. L. No. 96-272, 94 Stat. 500. It was enacted in the face of widespread evidence in the late 1970s that children were being needlessly separated from their families by child-care agencies. After conducting extensive hearings on the subject, Congress concluded that there was a need for federal action to effect change in local practices. The 1980 law mandates that states receiving federal money comply with specifications designed to prevent unnecessary separation of children from their parents, to assure a careful monitoring of children who are separated, and to provide an infusion of services into the family to speed the ultimate return of children to their parents.

The Act gives parents' lawyers an important weapon for attacking deficiencies in state processes. It constitutes a statement of national policy that they can invoke to curb some of the most oppressive features of state child protection proceedings. The Act was meant to ensure the following results:

(1) no child will be placed in foster care, except in emergency situations, either voluntarily or involuntarily, unless services aimed at preventing the need for placement have been provided or refused by the family;
(2) no child will be involuntarily removed from his or her home, except on a short-term basis in emergency situations, unless there has been a judicial determination that the child should be removed;
(3) no child will be placed in foster care by the voluntary action of his or her parents unless a "voluntary placement agreement" has been signed by parents and agency;
(4) a child who has been removed from his or her home will be placed in the least restrictive family-like setting in which any special needs may be met, within reasonable proximity to his or her family and with relatives where appropriate;
(5) reunification services are made available to the child and his or her parents after removal from the home; and
(6) there must be a written individualized case plan developed for each child placed in foster care, an administrative review of each case plan at least every six months, and a dispositional hearing by a court or court-appointed administrative body to be held regularly.

See H.R. Rep. No. 96-136, at 6 (1979).

The 1980 Act has been amended many times, most notably in 1997 by the enactment of the 1997 Adoption and Safe Families Act. *See* Adoption and Safe Families Act of 1997, Pub. L. No. 105-89, 111 Stat. 2115, 2121, 2129. One cannot know child welfare in the United States without knowing these laws. This section will explain them and their significance to local practice throughout the country. The most important provisions are codified at 42 U.S.C. §§ 671, 672, and 675 (2014). Among them are strict conditions for the removal of children from their homes. In order to be eligible for federal money to subsidize foster care services, agencies are required in most cases to identify and employ services that would eliminate the need for placing children in foster care. Federal law requires that courts oversee and approve the foster care placement of all children. Such removals are ineligible for federal reimbursement unless courts have found two things: that reasonable efforts to prevent the need for the placement were made or there were proper grounds for not making them and that continuation in the home would be contrary to the welfare of the child. *See* 42 U.S.C. § 672(a); *see also* 42 U.S.C. § 671(a)(15). Federal law also requires, unless there are reasons to the contrary, that agencies continue to employ reasonable efforts to make it possible for the prompt, safe return of children to their families. *See* 42 U.S.C. § 671(a)(15)(B). Although federal law exempts from these reasonable efforts requirements cases in which parents have previously lost their parental rights or committed certain crimes or acts of abuse, in most cases the reasonable efforts requirement is ongoing throughout the life of the case. *See* 42 U.S.C. § 671(a)(15)(D).

Federal law also regulates where children should be placed in foster care and other important aspects of the foster care placement. It requires that whenever children are placed in foster care that agencies "exercise due diligence to identify" and contact all adult relatives to alert them of the placement and to offer them the opportunity to take temporary custody. *See* 42 U.S.C. § 671(a)(29). Federal law also requires that agencies make reasonable efforts to place siblings in the same foster home and to provide for frequent visitation during their placement. *See* 42 U.S.C. § 671(a)(31).

The Adoption and Safe Families Act has had a powerful impact on practice throughout the United States. Federal policy today encourages adoptions once children have been in foster care for a certain length of time, even in cases where there was no compelling need for foster care placement or where no efforts were undertaken to reunify children with their birth families. It is one thing for Congress to excuse states from exercising reasonable efforts toward reunification when parents have previously inflicted serious harm on their children or even, perhaps, when the state has previously terminated parental rights to a sibling. *See* 42 U.S.C. § 671(a)(15)(D). But current law substantially shortens the amount of time within which parents may regain custody of their children before the state is authorized to initiate proceedings to terminate parental rights in many unexceptional cases.

Under federal law, termination petitions ordinarily should be filed after a child has spent fifteen out of twenty-two consecutive months in foster care. In too many places, however, agencies and courts treat federal law as requiring that termination petitions be filed based solely on the amount of time children have been in foster care. This is a very serious misreading of federal law, and lawyers for parents should become familiar with the "exceptions" written into federal law that eliminate the requirement that a termination petition be filed.

Federal law does not require, *or even recommend*, that a termination of parental rights petition be filed when the child is in the care of a relative, 42 U.S.C. § 675(5)(E)(i), when there are no grounds for termination under state law, 45 C.F.R. § 1356.21(i)(2)(ii)(B) (2014), when adoption is not the appropriate permanency goal for the child, *id.* § 1356.21(i)(2)(ii)(A), and when the child is an "unaccompanied refugee minor," *id.* § 1356.21(i)(2)(ii)(C), among a number of other situations, 42 U.S.C. § 675(5)(E)(i); 45 C.F.R. § 1356.21(i)(2)(ii)(D).

The penalty for a state's failure to abide by federal law regulating foster care is a fiscal one. States that place or keep children in foster care in violation of federal law are ineligible for an increase in federal funds above the amount they received in 1979. Counsel should become familiar with these federal provisions and with the regulations the Department of Health and Human Services have promulgated. *See* 45 C.F.R.

§§ 1355–57 (2014). Moreover, every state has codified significant parts of the federal law. Counsel should read the state statute thoroughly and its accompanying administrative regulations as well. They invariably contain numerous provisions that, if enforced vigorously, would make the initial separation of parent and child difficult to bring about and, if the child is removed, would require significant state efforts to reunite the family as quickly as feasible. State case law should also be reviewed to determine which features of the federal requirements are being judicially enforced, which have been held unenforceable, and which have not yet been litigated. For a discussion of the details of the federal legislation and strategies to assure its implementation, *see* Amelia S. Watson, *A New Focus on Reasonable Efforts to Reunify*, 9 CHILD L. PRAC. 113 (2012); *see also* Jeanne M. Kaiser, *Finding a Reasonable Way to Enforce the Reasonable Efforts Requirement in Child Protection Cases*, 7 RUTGERS J.L. & PUB. POL'Y 100 (2009).

Whenever Native American children are the subjects of child protection proceedings or proceedings for the termination of parental rights, the Indian Child Welfare Act, 25 U.S.C. § 1901 *et seq.* (2014), should be consulted. See Chapter 11 for more information. This law applies to any child who is either a member of an Indian tribe or the biological child of a member and eligible for membership in a tribe. When covered children are subject to jurisdiction in state juvenile courts, the Indian Child Welfare Act ordinarily requires that jurisdiction be transferred to the appropriate tribal court if the parent or the tribe so requests. And even when proceedings involving covered children remain in the state courts, the Act's procedural rules are applicable, including federal standards of proof that supersede those ordinarily used in state courts to test the showing made of a need for foster care placement or termination of parental rights. *See* 25 U.S.C. § 1912(e)–(f); *see also* Megan Scanlon, *From Theory to Practice: Incorporating the "Active Efforts" Requirement in Indian Child Welfare Act Proceedings*, 43 ARIZ. ST. L.J. 629 (2011). Attorneys for parents should determine early in the case whether the Indian Child Welfare Act is applicable. If it is, counsel should study the Act, discuss with the client the rights and choices that the Act provides, and effectuate those that the client wants to pursue.

1.04 The Nature and Status of Parental Rights Under the Constitution

Although the Constitution does not expressly confer upon parents the right to rear their children without undue interference by the state, since the 1920s, the Supreme Court of the United States has consistently and vigorously protected parental rights through the application of constitutional principles. Indeed, it has characterized the rights to conceive and to raise one's children as "essential," *Stanley v. Illinois*, 405 U.S. 645, 651 (1972) (quoting *Meyer v. Nebraska*, 262 U.S. 390, 399 (1923)), "basic civil rights of man," *Troxel v. Granville*, 530 U.S. 57, 65 (2000) (quoting *Skinner v. Oklahoma*, 316 U.S. 535, 541 (1942)), and "rights far more precious . . . than property rights,"

Wisconsin v. Yoder, 406 U.S. 205, 232 (1972) (quoting *May v. Anderson*, 345 U.S. 528, 533 (1953)). In 2000, the Court characterized "the interest of parents in the care, custody, and control of their children" to be "perhaps the oldest of the fundamental liberty interests recognized by this Court." *Troxel*, 530 U.S. at 65. As the Court once summarized, a parent's legal interest in his or her child is "established beyond debate as an enduring American tradition." *See Yoder*, 406 U.S. at 232.

American constitutional law allocates to parents very broad authority to raise their children as they see fit and many Supreme Court cases have established the rights of parents to raise children as they choose. As the Court expressed, there is a "private realm of family life which the state cannot enter." *Prince v. Massachusetts*, 321 U.S. 158, 166 (1944). In the absence of a compelling state interest, raising children, and teaching them the values of their family, is something "the state can neither supply nor hinder." *See id.*

In the first significant parents' rights case, *Meyer v. Nebraska*, 262 U.S. 390 (1923), the Court held that a statute forbidding the teaching of the German language impermissibly encroached on the liberty parents possess. The Court explained that the Due Process Clause of the Fourteenth Amendment protects this liberty, incorporating "the right to marry, establish a home, and bring up children."

Relying on *Meyer*, the Court two years later struck down an Oregon statute requiring children to attend public schools. The Justices found that this statute unduly interfered with the right of parents to select private or parochial schools for their children and that it lacked a reasonable relation to any purpose within the competency of the state. *See Pierce v. Soc'y of Sisters*, 268 U.S. 510 (1925). The Court wrote:

> The fundamental theory of liberty upon which all governments in this Union repose excludes any general power of the State to standardize its children. . . . The child is not the mere creature of the State; those who nurture him and direct his destiny have the right, coupled with the high duty, to recognize and prepare him for additional obligations?
>
> *Id.* at 535.

In several other well-known instances, the Court ruled that state officials exceeded their authority by interfering with parental child-rearing choices. These cases protected a parent's right to make decisions about their children even when state officials disagreed with them. In 1972, the Court held that Wisconsin's compulsory education law violated an Amish father's rights to take his fifteen-year-old children out of school to complete their education in Amish ways at home. *See Yoder*, 406 U.S. 205.

In 2000, the Court declared unconstitutional a Washington statute that authorized judges to order parents to permit more visitation between children and their grandparents than the parents desired. *See Troxel v. Granville*, 530 U.S. 57 (2000). The Court held in *Troxel* that parents' childrearing decisions are presumptively correct. As a result, it is not enough for judges to find that a different choice than the parents' would further the child's best interests. Explaining that "it cannot now be doubted that the Due Process Clause of the Fourteenth Amendment protects the fundamental right of parents to make decisions concerning the care, custody, and control of their children," the Court ruled that judges lacked the power to overrule fit parents' childrearing judgments. *See id.* at 66 (plurality opinion).

Troxel stands for the important principle that neither agencies nor courts may take positions regarding children because they regard them as furthering the child's best interests. A "best interests" inquiry unavoidably grants the decision maker a degree of discretion to overrule parental childrearing choices that is incompatible with the protection of constitutional rights. In *Troxel*, for example, the trial judge's decision to award the grandparents more visitation than the mother would have allowed, was based in part on the judge's own experience as a child and his recollection of fond memories of time spent with his grandparents. Justice O'Connor's plurality opinion condemned this exercise of judicial power as "contravene[ing] the traditional presumption that a fit parent will act in the best interest of his or her child." *See id.* at 69. The trial judge, the Court held, "failed to provide any protection for Granville's fundamental constitutional right to make decisions concerning the rearing of her own daughters." *See id.* at 70. As the Supreme Court wrote in 1978, "We have little doubt that the Due Process Clause would be offended '[i]f a State were to attempt to force the breakup of a natural family, over the objections of the parents and their children, without some showing of unfitness and for the sole reason that to do so was thought to be in the children's best interest.' *Smith v. Organization of Foster Families*, 431 U.S. 816, 862–863 (1977) (Stewart, J., concurring in judgment)." *Quilloin v. Walcott*, 434 U.S. 246, 255 (1978).

The Court has done much more than jealously guard a parent's right to make childrearing decisions. It has also protected the custodial rights of parents. Perhaps the most important case in this line was *Stanley v. Illinois*, 405 U.S. 645 (1972). *Stanley* declared unconstitutional an Illinois dependency statute that deprived unmarried fathers of the care and custody of their children on the death of the mother without any showing of the father's unfitness. The Court declared the law unconstitutional, holding that unless a parent is unfit, he has the constitutional right to the care and custody of his children. In reaching this conclusion, the Court observed that "[t]he private interest here, that of a man in the children he has sired and raised, undeniably warrants deference and, absent a powerful countervailing interest, protection." *Id.* at 651. The Court characterized the state's interest in caring for a fit parent's children as "*de minimis.*" *Id.* at 657.

The Court also held that the Constitution requires that a parent's substantive custodial right must be protected by rigorous procedural protections that preclude presuming the father's unfitness: "All Illinois parents are constitutionally entitled to a hearing on their fitness before their children are removed from their custody." *See id.* at 658.

Stanley followed the 1944 Supreme Court decision in which the Court first explained that the state has a legitimate interest in ensuring that children are not harmed by their families. In *Prince v. Massachusetts*, 321 U.S. 158 (1944), the Court held that states may prosecute parents when they expose their children to serious hazards to their well-being. In sustaining the conviction of a minor's guardian who, in the exercise of her religious freedom, violated a child labor law, the Court explained that "[p]arents may be free to become martyrs themselves. But it does not follow they are free . . . to make martyrs of their children." *See id.* at 170.

Both *Prince* and *Stanley* are the foundational cases for applying constitutional protections in child welfare cases. Combined, they stand for three simple propositions. First, parents have constitutionally protected rights to the care and custody of their children. Second, those rights are limited and may be attenuated or lost when they fall below the minimum standard of care for childrearing. Third, when state officials believe children need protection from their families, they must charge parents with unfitness and prove their case in court.

Although the Supreme Court has never had occasion to comment on the subject, a number of federal courts have also added the important idea that the right to resist coercive state intervention in the family belongs to all of its members, including children. As the Second Circuit explained almost forty years ago, "[T]he right of the family to remain together without the coercive interference of the awesome power of the state . . . encompasses the reciprocal rights of both parent and child." *Duchesne v. Sugarman*, 566 F.2d 817, 825 (2d Cir. 1977). The court explained that children have the constitutional right to avoid "dislocat[ion] from the emotional attachments that derive from the intimacy of daily association with the parent." *See id.* (internal quotation marks omitted); *see also Tenenbaum v. Williams*, 193 F.3d 581, 599, 600 (2d Cir. 1999) (parents and children alike share the "fundamental right" to "remain together without the coercive interference of the awesome power of the state"); *Nicholson v. Williams*, 203 F. Supp. 2d 153, 235 (E.D.N.Y. 2002) (liberty "interest in not being forcibly separated by the state is shared by parents and children"). Other courts that have expressed similar sentiments include *Suboh v. Dist. Attorney's Office of Suffolk Dist.*, 298 F.3d 81, 91 (1st Cir. 2002); *Brokaw v. Mercer Cnty.*, 235 F.3d 1000, 1018–19 (7th Cir. 2000); *J.B. v. Washington Cnty.*, 127 F.3d 919, 927 (10th Cir. 1997); *Franz v. United States*, 707 F.2d 582, 594–95 (D.C. Cir. 1983).

The constitutional right to raise children is also the corollary of another set of fundamental constitutional rights of Americans: the right to procreate. In 1942, proclaiming that procreation is "fundamental to the very existence and survival of the race" and "one of the basic civil rights of man," the Court held that an Oklahoma law that allowed the state to sterilize persons "convicted two or more times for crimes amounting to felonies involving moral turpitude," violated the Equal Protection Clause of the Fourteenth Amendment because it infringed upon the fundamental "right to have offspring." *See Skinner v. Oklahoma*, 316 U.S. 535, 536 (1942).

Ever since, the Court has advanced the reproductive rights of Americans. In a 1965 decision, *Griswold v. Connecticut*, 381 U.S. 479 (1965), the Court used the opportunity to declare unconstitutional a Connecticut law that, although still on the books, had not been enforced for many years. The law barred the use and distribution of contraceptives, even for married persons. The Court ruled that the Constitution protects various kinds of intimate privacy and that the marriage relationship fell well within a zone of privacy that protected couples from virtually all governmental regulation. In a concurring opinion, Justice Goldberg wrote:

> The home derives its pre-eminence as the seat of family life. And the integrity of that life is something so fundamental that it has been found to draw to its protection the principles of more than one explicitly granted Constitutional right. . . . The entire fabric of the Constitution and the purposes that clearly underlie its specific guarantees demonstrate that the rights to marital privacy and to marry and raise a family are of similar order and magnitude as the fundamental rights specifically protected.
>
> 381 U.S. at 495 (quoting *Poe v. Ullman*, 367 U.S. 497, 551–52 (1961) (Harlan, J., dissenting)).

Griswold's reasoning was broadly extended seven years later from a privacy right within a marriage to an individual's privacy right. In 1972, in *Eisenstadt v. Baird*, 405 U.S. 438 (1972), the Court reasoned that because the marital privacy recognized in *Griswold* protects two independent and distinct individuals, this protection should apply equally to a single person. The Court announced that "[i]f the right of privacy means anything, it is the right of the individual, married or single, to be free from unwarranted governmental intrusion into matters so fundamentally affecting a person as the decision whether to bear or beget a child." *Id.* at 453. Accordingly, the Court invalidated a Massachusetts statute that prohibited the distribution of contraceptives to unmarried persons.

Both *Griswold* and *Eisenstadt* were important foundational decisions for the Court's next, and most controversial, foray into the field of procreative rights. In 1973, the Court decided *Roe v. Wade*, 410 U.S. 113 (1973), declaring for the first time that part of a woman's constitutional right to privacy (including the fundamental right whether or not to beget a child) includes the choice to terminate an unwanted pregnancy (at least in the early stages of the pregnancy). In *Roe*, the Court restricted state power to forbid abortions, holding that a woman's decision whether to bear a child is within the sphere of privacy "founded in the Fourteenth Amendment's concept of personal liberty." *See id.* at 153. The Court noted that even though the word "privacy" cannot be found in the Constitution, a "guarantee of certain areas or zones of privacy" has been constitutionally recognized in connection with "activities relating to marriage, procreation, contraception, family relationships, and child rearing and education." *See id.* at 152. The next year, the Court invalidated a scheme of mandatory leaves for pregnant public school teachers because that scheme unnecessarily interfered with the decision to raise a family, declaring "freedom of personal choice in matters of marriage and family life is one of the liberties protected by the Due Process Clause of the Fourteenth Amendment." *See Cleveland Bd. of Educ. v. LaFleur*, 414 U.S. 632, 639–40 (1974).

The Court has decided only a small number of cases that began as child welfare proceedings in state court. In 1981, the Court held that the Fourteenth Amendment's Due Process Clause does not require the appointment of counsel for indigent parents in every parental status termination proceeding. Rather, parents have a due process right to a fundamentally fair procedure that may, but not invariably, require the appointment of counsel. *See Lassiter v. Dep't of Soc. Servs.*, 452 U.S. 18 (1981). Even in reaching this holding, however, the Court stressed that a parent's desire for and right to "the companionship, care, custody and management of his or her children" is an important interest that "undeniably warrants deference and, absent a powerful countervailing interest, protection," *id.* at 27 (quoting *Stanley v. Illinois*, 405 U.S. 645, 651 (1972)), and that "a parent's interest in the accuracy and justice of the decision to terminate his or her parental status is, therefore a commanding one," *id.*

The following year, the Court declared unconstitutional, a New York statute that authorized termination of parental rights based on a preponderance of the evidence. *Santosky v. Kramer*, 455 U.S. 745 (1982). *Santosky* is the first Supreme Court case to hold that even *after* parents are found unfit in a contested court proceeding, they retain constitutionally protected parental rights. As the Court explained, "[t]he fundamental liberty interest of natural parents in the care, custody, and management of their child does not evaporate simply because they have not been model parents or have lost temporary custody of their child to the state. Even when blood relationships are strained, parents retain a vital interest in preventing the irretrievable destruction of their family life." *Id.* at 753.

The upshot of this body of case law is that parents have a constitutional right to the care, custody, and control of their children. This right includes the right to be free from interference by the state in the rearing of children, so long as parents discharge certain obligations to provide for their health and safety and education. Because of the fundamental nature of these rights, state intrusion into the upbringing of children or the integrity of the familial relationship is permitted only if strict due process safeguards have been observed, *see, e.g.*, *Santosky v. Kramer*, 455 U.S. 745 (1982), and after a showing has been made that a weighty state interest justifies disturbance of the parent–child bond and cannot be achieved in a less disruptive manner, *see, e.g.*, *Troxel v. Granville*, 530 U.S. 57 (2000).

The government gets to set the boundaries at the outer limits of what is acceptable parenting. Thus, laws protecting children from neglect and abuse are a proper exercise of the state's police power (regulating the conduct of citizens that has the potential to harm others) or *parens patriae* power (protecting individuals incapable of protecting themselves). But, this means only that parents are obliged to exercise a *minimum degree of care* when raising their children. Unless parents fall below this standard and are found to be *unfit* in court proceedings charging them with abuse or neglect, parental childrearing decisions are virtually immune from state oversight.

This places considerable attention on the definition of unfitness under state law. To ensure against state officials using the power to protect children from harm through open-ended, value-laden judgments, state law must strictly define *neglect* (or its equivalent term). The draftsman's goal in defining neglect is to proscribe parental conduct in which no one is permitted to engage without intruding into conduct that, however, unacceptable it may be to some, is above the level of impermissible. Only when no parent is permitted to do something are state officials authorized to prevent a particular parent from exercising his or her parental rights.

Many states, however, use phrases of great breadth and vagueness to define the circumstances warranting state intervention. For example, they commonly give juvenile court jurisdiction over children who are denied "proper parental care," *see, e.g.*, NEB. REV. STAT. § 43-247 (2014); 42 PA. CONS. STAT. § 6302 (2014), are found in conditions injurious to their "physical or mental well-being or morals," *see, e.g.*, TEXAS FAM. CODE ANN. § 161.001 (2014), or are deprived of "other care or control necessary for a child's physical, mental, or emotional health or morals," *see, e.g.*, GA. CODE ANN., § 15-11-2(48) (2014).

In a variety of contexts, the Supreme Court of the United States has held that statutes authorizing the abridgment of fundamental liberties protected by the federal Constitution must set forth with specificity the conduct that will trigger the state's action. *See, e.g.*, *Papachristou v. City of Jacksonville*, 405 U.S. 156 (1972); *Shuttlesworth v. City of Birmingham*, 382 U.S. 87 (1965); *Herndon v. Lowry*, 301 U.S. 242 (1937). The Court has emphasized three related but distinct dangers that make vague legislation intolerable in areas bordering on important constitutional rights. First, when state intervention is broadly authorized and inadequately channeled in these areas, there is a grave risk that the constitutional rights will frequently be invaded and that the invasions will be difficult to detect and remedy. Second, individuals are deprived of fair notice regarding the conduct that will subject them to state intervention. Third, vague authorizations of state intervention lend themselves to arbitrary and discriminatory enforcement. *See, e.g.*, *Smith v. Goguen*, 415 U.S. 566, 572–76 (1974); *Thornhill v. Alabama*, 310 U.S. 99 (1940).

In addition, because child protection proceedings infringe on fundamental constitutional rights, the Constitution requires that courts carefully limit the means used. Each aspect of intervention must be viewed through the lens of restricting constitutional freedoms only as much as necessary to achieve the specific compelling state interest. States must show both that (1) their actions further a compelling state interest *and* (2) they have chosen the least restrictive means to advance it or they are violating the Constitution. *See City of Boerne v. Flores*, 521 U.S. 507, 534 (1997) ("Requiring a State to demonstrate a compelling interest and show that it has adopted the least restrictive means of achieving that interest is the most demanding test known to constitutional law."); *see also Dunn v. Blumstein*, 405 U.S. 330 (1972); *Shelton v. Tucker*, 364 U.S. 479 (1960).

A number of courts have applied the strict scrutiny required by these doctrines to child protection statutes and to statutes authorizing the termination of parental rights and have declared them unconstitutional. A federal district court in Iowa in 1975 declared an Iowa law unconstitutionally vague that authorized termination of parental rights for "refus[al] . . . to give the child necessary parental care and protection" or for parental conduct "likely to be detrimental to the physical or mental health or morals of the child." *See Alsager v. District Court*, 406 F. Supp. 10, 14 (S.D. Iowa 1975), *aff'd per curiam*, 545 F.2d 1137 (8th Cir. 1976). The court found the statute suffered from three vices: "the absence of fair warning, the impermissible delegation of discretion, and the undue inhibition of the legitimate exercise of a constitutional right." *See id.* at 18.

A year later, another federal court struck down an Alabama law, saying:

> When is a home an "unfit" or "improper" place for a child? Obviously this is a question about which men and women of ordinary intelligence would greatly disagree. . . . Because these terms are too subjective to denote a sufficient warning to those individuals who might be affected by their proscription, the statute is unconstitutionally vague.
>
> *Roe v. Conn*, 417 F. Supp. 769 (M.D. Ala. 1976) (three-judge court).

The Supreme Court of Arkansas applied a similar analysis to invalidate a law authorizing the termination of parental rights whenever parents were found not to provide their child with a "proper home":

> Using any of . . . [the possible] meanings does little to make the words "a proper home" clearly understandable, so that it doesn't mean one thing to one judge, something else to another, and something yet different to still another. What is a proper home? A correct home? A suitable home? A fit home? An appropriate home? A home consistent with propriety? Is propriety to be determined ethically, socially, or economically? Or on the basis of morality? Or prosperity? Is the standard a maximum, a minimum, a mean or an average?
>
> *Davis v. Smith*, 266 Ark. 112, 133, 583 S.W.2d 37, 43 (1979).

In the child protection field, the great danger of overly vague laws is that they permit implementers—caseworkers who may have minimal training—to invoke state power in circumstances under which no legislative body ever contemplated or approved state action. When the power is used to pass judgment on parents and when that judgment is made, as it usually is, about poor parents who frequently are members of minority groups, there is an inordinate danger that the judgment will be based on cultural biases and values of the professionals. This point was made by the Supreme Court when it pointed out that termination of parental rights proceedings are "often vulnerable to judgments based on cultural or class bias." *See Santosky v. Kramer*, 455 U.S. 745, 763 (1982). This is so, the Court explained, because the parents involved in these matters "are often poor, uneducated, or members of minority groups," and the "determinations [are] unusually open to the subjective values of the judge." *See id.* at 762–63; *see also Smith v. Org. of Foster Families*, 431 U.S. 816, 833–34 (1977).

Vague laws, in other words, allow arbitrary intrusions into the lives of families both by failing to limit beforehand the discretion of caseworkers to remove children from their families or to charge caregivers with neglect and by allowing judges thereafter to rule against parents in situations in which the legislature made no determination that state intervention is appropriate. As the *Alsager* court said, intervention "in any given case may thus turn upon which state officials are involved in the case, rather than upon explicit standards reflecting legislative intent. This danger is especially grave in the highly subjective context of determining an approved mode of child-rearing." *See* 406 F. Supp. at 18–19.

These arguments, though persuasive in theory, will rarely result in a declaration of the unconstitutionality of a child protection law at the trial level. Most juvenile court judges are not used to being asked to rule that a statute is unconstitutional and are not apt to take seriously any kind of facial challenge to a law. In addition, a number of state appellate courts have upheld the constitutionality of dependency laws that were rather broadly worded. *See, e.g., In re Cager*, 251 Md. 473, 248 A.2d 384 (1968); *In re William L.*, 477 Pa. 322, 383 A.2d 1228 (1978), *cert. denied sub nom. Lehman v. Lycoming Cnty. Children's Servs.*, 439 U.S. 880 (1978); *Custody of R.R.B.*, 108 Wash. App. 602, 31 P.3d 1212 (2001).

1.05 The Limited Role of Federal Judicial Oversight in Child Welfare Matters

Even though the field is embedded in constitutional doctrine, it rarely feels that way in dependency court. Constitutional discourse is uncommon in these courts. Several factors inhibit the expansive development of federal constitutional rights of parents in child protection proceedings despite the strong doctrinal bases that exist for recognizing that these proceedings affect parental interests of importance under the Constitution. First, individual rights other than the parents' are directly implicated in child protection cases. The proverbial principle that it is better to let ten guilty persons go free than to countenance one innocent person's conviction does not express the balancing of interests generally believed to be appropriate in this area of the law. Indeed, some prefer, and some of the state statutory schemes appear structured to assure, overbroad intervention in order to assure that all children who need protection will get it.

In addition, federal courts, especially the lower federal courts, have not been significantly involved in the child protection area. There was a brief period in the 1970s when the lower federal courts decided several important cases in the area. *See, e.g., Sims v. State Dep't of Pub. Welfare*, 438 F. Supp. 1179 (S.D. Tex. 1977) (three-judge court), *rev'd on other grounds sub nom. Moore v. Sims*, 442 U.S. 415 (1979); *Roe v. Conn*, 417 F. Supp. 769 (M.D. Ala. 1976) (three-judge court); *Alsager v. District Court*, 406 F. Supp. 10 (S.D. Iowa 1975). But the Supreme Court has since developed doctrines limiting the exercise of federal jurisdiction that make the lower federal courts practically unavailable as a forum for this kind of litigation.

By changing the doctrine involving standing and ripeness, *see, e.g., City of Los Angeles v. Lyons*, 461 U.S. 95 (1983), challenges to state intervention can rarely be made the subject of a federal lawsuit before state judicial proceedings against the parent have been initiated. Once those proceedings have commenced, the abstention doctrine precludes a parent's recourse to the federal courts throughout the pendency of the state proceeding. *See Moore v. Sims*, 442 U.S. 415 (1979). Finally, the habeas corpus jurisdiction of the federal courts ordinarily does not extend to reviewing the result of a state child protection proceeding after it is over. *See Lehman v. Lycoming Cnty. Children's Servs. Agency*, 458 U.S. 502 (1982). The interplay of these rules has largely excluded the federal district and circuit courts from any direct involvement in child protection cases.

This has not entirely kept federal courts from overseeing state child protection practices. Some innovative litigators have succeeded in filing claims challenging the constitutionality of various state court or agency procedures. And they have sometimes achieved remarkable results. In the 1990s New York, for example, caseworkers were routinely charging mothers with neglect and removing children from their custody when the mothers—victims of domestic violence—"allowed" the children to witness the violence. Lawyers for these mothers filed a federal class action seeking an injunction preventing caseworkers from removing children from parents except upon a showing that the parents fell below the minimum standard of care when raising their children. In *Nicholson v. Williams*, 203 F. Supp. 2d 153 (E.D.N.Y. 2002), the federal district court declared unconstitutional the practice of separating children from their mothers solely because the mothers were victims of violence. The court even ordered that the amount of payment for court-assigned parents be increased. After an appeal to the Second Circuit, *Nicholson v. Scoppetta*, 344 F.3d 154 (2d Cir. 2003), New York's highest court was asked to answer some certified questions issued by the Second Circuit. In answering those questions, the Court of Appeals issued a strongly worded condemnation of the original practice and carefully explained that the removals, which had gone on for several years and been routinely approved by the trial and intermediate appellate courts, violated the plain meaning of the controlling statutes and were forbidden under New York law. *See Nicholson v. Scoppetta*, 3 N.Y.3d 357, 820 N.E.2d 840, 787 N.Y.S.2d 196 (2004).

There is little doubt that the glare of federal judges upon the New York courts impacted the Court of Appeals' decision, which many longtime practitioners regard as the best decision ever issued by the court. Along the way, the New York legislature was inspired to give the first raise in almost thirty years in hourly rates for court-assigned parent counsel, obviating the need for the federal order to be enforced.

An additional important form of action in which the federal courts can consider constitutional issues arising out of the child protection process is a damages action brought against state officials under 42 U.S.C. § 1983 (2014) after the conclusion of the state proceeding. Many such cases have been successfully waged over the years. *See, e.g., B.S. v. Somerset County,* 704 F.3d 250 (3d Cir. 2013); *Austin v. Borel*, 830 F. 2d 1356 (5th Cir. 1987); *Darryl H. v. Coler*, 801 F.2d 893 (7th Cir. 1986); *Duchesne v. Sugarman*, 566 F.2d 817 (2d Cir. 1977).

1.06 The Role of Counsel Representing Parents

It is a truism that attorneys do a better job when they believe that their work is worthy and when they value the rights of the clients whom they represent. The excellent esprit de corps developed by the criminal defense bar has often enabled attorneys for indigent criminal defendants to achieve remarkable results for their clients against overwhelming odds and despite intolerable working conditions. Parents' lawyers need to find colleagues and supporters for their work to avoid the danger of participating in a process that pressures a parent to accept an unwanted result because the professionals involved believe that result protects the best interests of the children.

Some parents' lawyers may feel discomfort in advocating results desired by their clients that entail a risk of harm to the health and happiness of children. This may reflect the lawyers' understanding that the Agency's intentions in most cases are to serve the well-being of innocent children. These concerns are altogether natural. But that is all the more reason why defense attorneys in these cases must undertake a measure of self-examination. In a system in which the lawyer's job includes counseling his or her client—an activity that can shade imperceptibly into a process of manipulating the client—it is far too easy for a parents' lawyer to become enlisted in the righteous work of protecting children despite the parents' wishes. Beginning with doubts about the propriety of enforcing the parents' preferences when these may hurt a child, the lawyer is readily persuaded that the parents' preferences are unwise, thence that their achievement is undesirable, thence that it is legally infeasible. Unsurprisingly, s/he ends by counseling the parents to accept a result that contravenes the parents' preferences even when those preferences might well have been achieved through vigorous advocacy.

Among the best protections against it is a healthy confidence in the rightness of representing indigent parents accused of inadequacy in the rearing of their children. Consideration of the following points may help to bolster this confidence:

(a) Parents are entitled to the same zealous representation that is owed to all clients who are accused by the state of wrongdoing. In child protection cases, the parents face a loss that to many is more severe than loss of physical liberty: the loss of the care, custody, and companionship of their children.

(b) For a large number of parents accused of inadequacy in the United States, this means that they face the loss of one of the few precious things in their lives. The overwhelming majority of parents charged with neglecting their children live in poverty and are disproportionately members of minority groups. *See* DOROTHY ROBERTS, SHATTERED BONDS: THE COLOR OF CHILD WELFARE (2002).

(c) Poverty is the leading reason children end up in foster care. Studies show that families earning incomes below the poverty line are twenty-two times more likely to be involved in the child protective system than families with incomes slightly above it. *See* Mark E. Courtney, *The Costs of Child Protection in the Context of Welfare Reform*, 8 THE FUTURE OF CHILDREN 88, 95 (1998).

(d) Studies have consistently found that the great majority of children in foster care could remain safely at home. Experts estimate that 40 to 70 percent of children currently in foster care have not been abused and need not be separated from their families if society sufficiently assisted poor families in raising their children at home. *See* DUNCAN LINDSEY, THE WELFARE OF CHILDREN 141, 155 (1994) (finding 46 percent of the foster children did not need to be in foster care).

(e) When children are placed in foster care, children and parents face a very high risk of having their relationship permanently severed. Once children are removed from the custody of their parents, the functional—if not legal—burden of proof often shifts to the parents to show that the return of the children to their custody is both appropriate and consistent with the best interests of the children. When parents do not have custody of their children, it is difficult to show that under the current conditions in the home the parents can care adequately for them.

(f) Even when parents have made some serious mistakes in the raising of their children, foster care placement frequently does more harm than good. "Those placed in foster care are far more likely than other children to commit crimes, drop out of school, join welfare, experience substance abuse problems, or enter the homeless population." *See* Joseph J. Doyle, Jr., *Child Protection and Child Outcomes: Measuring the Effects of Foster Care*, 97 AM. ECON. REV. 1583, 1583–84, 1607 (2007).

(g) Taken from their parents' home, children can languish for years in state-supported foster care arrangements of marginal quality at best, feeling deserted, unloved, and alone. To justify this outcome should require an extremely solid prediction that, if left in the parents' care, the child will suffer serious damage. But accurate predictions of the future behavior of people in a family unit are difficult to make, and accurate predictions of the long-range consequences of that behavior for a child's development are still more difficult. Neither the child protection authorities who believe that the separation of a child from his or her parents is the wiser course nor the lawyer who fears that the child will be endangered if that course is opposed at the parents' behest has a crystal ball.

(h) Good intentions on the part of the state authorities and agencies involved in child protection proceedings are no guarantee that they will have prophetic powers or even good judgment. Even the highly touted "permanence" that children in foster care purportedly receive after their parents' rights are terminated is greatly exaggerated. Over the past decade, more than a 100,000 children who lost all legal connection to their families never benefited by being adopted. *See* Cynthia Godsoe, *Parsing Childhood*, 17 Lewis & Clark L. Rev. 113, 115 & n.9 (2013); Josh Gupta-Kagan, *Filling the Due Process Don't Hole: Abuse and Neglect Cases between Disposition and Permanency*, 10 Conn. Pub. Int. L.J. 13, 57 (2010). They simply "aged out" of the foster care system, the metaphorical equivalent of stateless persons. Nor does adoption assure any kind of permanency. Each year thousands of children who were adopted by foster parents end up without their adoptive families and, more than occasionally, back with their families of origin—only now, legally unrelated to them. *See* Dawn J. Post and Brian Zimmerman, *The Revolving Doors of Family Court: Confronting Broken Adoptions*, 40 Cap. U. L. Rev. 437 (2012).

(i) Parents are more likely to take advice from an advocate who is vigorously fighting for their rights to make their own decisions for their families and are more likely to endure the process when they feel they have had a strong defense and a caring professional who listens to and respects them.

One final consideration. The poor families exposed to judicial and agency scrutiny in the child welfare system are reviewed through a lens that looks at the worst thing that has happened. In families of privilege, where unfortunate events are expectable, the bad things are invariably framed against the wonderful things that happen in families every day. The hugs, emotional support, and love that take place within families are always in the back of one's mind even when bad things happen to children. Families that do not end up in the child welfare system are judged as part of a moving picture of their families, even when children break bones or their parents use drugs or drink alcohol to an excess. The families that enter the child welfare system—parents and children included—deserve the right to be treated no differently from the way families living in wealthier parts of town are treated. The role of a parent's lawyer is to fight for this fundamental human right: to be treated the same way the most important members of the community are treated.

CHAPTER 2

Changing the Narrative in Child Welfare Cases

Matthew Fraidin

Women. The poor. People of color.

Those are the parents ensnared in the child welfare litigation process. Those are the respondents in dependency court.

What would it mean to ask them questions like these?

- "Who are you?"
- "What do you do?"
- "What do you know?"
- "Whom do you love?"
- "What was your greatest success?"
- "What is your dream?"
- "What is your favorite food?"
- "What's the most frivolous thing about you?"
- "What makes you laugh?"

If lawyers asked these questions, we would learn things about parents accused of inadequacy that never get revealed in court, in part because those topics are not even regarded as relevant. This chapter suggests that those questions can make a difference.

Lawyers for parents in child welfare cases face many challenges, but none more daunting than helping parents overcome the stereotypes, assumptions, and false expectations that smother them, and which pervade child welfare decision-making processes. Indeed, in child welfare cases, parents and their lawyers can be forgiven for believing that the die are cast before the litigants even walk into the courtroom. Parents in child welfare are infused with unattractive stereotypes that blind decision makers to the qualities and characteristics of the individuals actually before them. As a result, judges and social workers—and their lawyers, too—make judgments and decisions based on assumptions, rather than facts. And parents are separated from their children unnecessarily and to the children's detriment. Children remain in foster care far longer than they should, enduring more harm than good, often punishing them for being the children of parents no one gets to know.

This chapter describes the unfair, inaccurate, dehumanizing, and harmful stories told about parents in child welfare, and suggests ways for parents' lawyers to reframe their clients and cases. The questions listed above, and others like them, are designed to unearth more about parents than simply the acts captured in the Petition. They are tools to help lawyers discover all parts of a family's reality, including the admirable ones. By doing so, lawyers can deepen their investment in their clients and their commitment to them, and rewrite the stories they tell the social workers and judges.

* * * * *

The assumptions and stereotypes that govern child welfare cases cumulatively function as a "grand narrative"—a unifying, overarching story that seems to explain everything about its subject. In the context of child welfare, the accepted narrative is of terrible parents who inflict unfathomable terrors on children. According to the narrative, parents of children involved in child welfare are bad people, who are too dangerous to be allowed to raise children.

The narrative functions as a filter affecting the way child welfare participants understand information in every case. It is filled with harsh, inaccurate beliefs about parents of children in child welfare, rooted in racial, gender, and class-based stereotypes. As a consequence, parents are unreflectively regarded unsympathetically and punitively. This narrative—our unconscious, collective beliefs—is driven by relentless media coverage. Over 90 percent of news stories about children are about violence by and against children focused on a discrete incident. One researcher found that 70 to 95 percent of stories about child welfare are "horror stories." *See* John M. Johnson, *Horror Stories and the Construction of Child Abuse, in* IMAGES OF ISSUES: TYPIFYING CONTEMPORARY SOCIAL PROBLEMS 5 (1989). Psychological anthropologist Axel Aubrun and linguist Joseph Grady found that the most common child welfare media story frames depict murders or violent crimes committed by "brutal," "monstrous" parents. *See* AXEL AUBRUN & JOSEPH GRADY, HOW THE NEWS FRAMES CHILD MALTREATMENT: UNINTENDED CONSEQUENCES 3 (2003). These are stories about gruesome, brutal injuries inflicted on children by beastly parents such as beating, raping, maiming, and torturing.

According to the conventional story of child welfare, children in foster care have been rescued from parents who chained them to furnaces, starved them for years, burned them with cigarettes, sold them to sexual predators, and abandoned them in squalid apartments while out seeking drugs to fuel their addictions. But this is untrue.

The true picture of child welfare is dramatically different. Even more, the grand narrative of child welfare harms children because it encourages officials to place them in foster care as a perceived necessity to protect them from dangerous parents.

A large number of children in foster care, however, should never have been removed from their families. According to the federal government, more than 86,000 children removed across the country in 2009 were later found not to have been maltreated at all. *See* CHILDREN'S BUREAU, U.S. DEP'T OF HEALTH AND HUMAN SERVS., CHILD MALTREATMENT 2009: REPORTS FROM THE STATES TO THE NATIONAL CHILD ABUSE AND NEGLECT DATA SYSTEM, Table 6.5.

Moreover, more than 70 percent of the children in foster care are there because of allegations that they were neglected, not abused. *See* CHILDREN'S BUREAU, U.S. DEP'T OF HEALTH AND HUMAN SERVS., CHILD MALTREATMENT 2012: REPORTS FROM THE STATES TO THE NATIONAL CHILD ABUSE AND NEGLECT DATA SYSTEM 20. According to researchers, for example, "[U]p to 30% of children in foster care could be reunited with their parents if safe, affordable housing were available." Anne F. Farrell et al., *Supportive Housing for Families in Child Welfare: Client Characteristics and Their Outcomes at Discharge,* 32 CHILDREN YOUTH SERVICES REV. 145, 146 (2010) (citing Y. A. DORRE & LISA K. MIHALY, HOME SWEET HOME (1996)). Countless children end up in foster care because they miss school without an adequate explanation, because they are left alone by their parents for excessive periods of time, or because of "death of a parent, parental incarceration, parental chemical addiction, or homelessness" without maltreatment. *See* Catherine R. Lawrence et al., *The Impact of Foster Care on Development,* 18 DEV. & PSYCHOPATHOLOGY 57, 61 (2006).

The narrative also obscures another side of child welfare. Not only are far too many children needlessly separated from their families, but foster care is dangerous and harmful to children. A 1997 study of infants born to substance-abusing mothers found that the language development of children placed in foster care was delayed compared to that of children who remained with their mothers. *See* Suzanne Dixon et al., *Early Language Development in Children with Prenatal Exposure to Stimulant Drugs,* 13 DEV. NEUROPSYCHOLOGY, 371–72 (1997). A 2006 study concluded that children in foster care developed more significant behavioral problems than similarly maltreated children who remained at home. *See* Lawrence et al., *supra.* And an economist from the Massachusetts Institute of Technology who studied 15,000 children found that children taken from their families and placed in foster care fared worse in life than similarly maltreated children simply left with their families. *See* Joseph J. Doyle, Jr., *Child Protection and Child Outcomes,* 97 AM. ECON. REV. 1583, 1584 (2007).

But because of the master narrative relentlessly conveyed, Americans believe that the only children who end up in foster care are victims of terrible deeds inflicted on them by their parents and the only cases brought to court are prosecuted against terrible, unloving parents. These beliefs affect judges and caseworkers—and they also affect parents' lawyers. Like judges and caseworkers, parents' lawyers also unavoidably carry unconscious biases. They, too, have absorbed lessons that glorify class-, gender-, and race-based hierarchies, and which justify injustice and inequality. To represent clients successfully, lawyers must tell accurate stories about them. And to do that, lawyers first have to find out who their clients are.

How can parents' lawyers reframe their clients for themselves and for others? How can they depict their clients as human, to begin with? And how can they go further to retell the story of their relationships with their children as positive, constructive, and nurturing? How can they reconstruct the judge and social worker's constructed reality, to help them understand that the parents are *exactly* the people whose kids should be in their care?

First, lawyers must believe it themselves. Parents' lawyers have learned about the world in the shadow of the false narrative of child welfare. They, too, have read the sensational stories. They, too, are affected by the nearly unavoidable racial biases that flow unseen through every institution in society. So they, too, must unlearn. They must acknowledge their own assumptions about their clients and challenge them. Only then—when parents' lawyers see their clients differently and can tell themselves new stories about them, unchained from the false, harsh, stereotype-laden master narrative—can they tell new stories to others.

Here's how.

To challenge the narrative of child welfare, parents' lawyers will have to start by challenging their approach to serving clients. Parents' lawyers often see clients as no more than the sum of their needs. Clients and litigants come to lawyers with their problem. Indeed, they only get our attention because they *have* a problem. The first thing lawyers ask is "What is your problem? What do you need? How can I help you?" And they try to solve the problem.

But what is the result? In child welfare, lawyers representing parents are used to unhappy outcomes in too many cases.

Here is a different model. Instead of merely asking, "What is your problem? What is the disease, the defect that brought this mother—and by extension, her child—into my life," parents' lawyers can ask a different question. Not what is she lacking, but what does she have? Not only "what can I do?" but (directed toward a client or litigant) "what can *you* do?" What are her abilities, her strengths, her assets?

How can parents' lawyers reenvision their clients as rich, powerful, and capable?

Well, can the mother whose child is taken away braid hair? Can she cook a meal? Can she smile at an elderly person in a nursing home? And let's think about that person in the nursing home. Can she watch a child recite a poem and clap for the child? Can she read a story? Can she share her own story about life "in the old days?" Does she know by heart, perhaps, a recipe for the best fried turkey ever?

Parents' lawyers can see with different eyes, and look for successes. Did the child's mother pull her neighbor's weeds last week? Or change a light bulb? Or pick up litter? These are things she did, not things she didn't.

Can she shop for groceries? Can she throw a party, or drive a neighbor to the doctor? Can she paint a room or clean a house or walk a dog?

The answers will be yes, yes, and yes.

So again, how do parents' lawyers get there?

Start with a paradigm shift. The low-income people parents' lawyers meet in this line of work? They should suspend disbelief for a moment, and convince themselves their clients are rich. The crummy neighborhoods the children come from and broken-down communities parents' lawyers see all around them? Think of those as strong and healthful, instead of shabby and pathologized.

Indeed, there is evidence that this different perspective on the world is accurate. In Chicago, eighth graders in special education tutor first graders in math. In Washington, D.C., returned prisoners escort children to school.

In Washington, D.C., kids arrested for juvenile delinquency offenses run the Youth Court. In the Youth Court, the same children are judges and jurors. Youth Court is a diversion program, in which the very youth who come through the court as defendants sit as jurors, reviewing infractions of other youth. They hear facts, deliberate, and impose sentences of community service, restitution, counseling, or an apology. Appreciating the achievements of these youth helps reframe them, and helps others begin to see the strengths and talents of others whom many are accustomed to overlooking or even maligning.

Research is clear, for example, that women in violent relationships are the best judges of their own safety, better than the police, lawyers, caseworkers, or even judges. In Washington, D.C., when the highest court ruled there was no statutory right to custody for non-parents, low-income grandmothers submitted statements and testified about the necessity that the law be amended. In Washington, D.C., a homeless advocate led a successful campaign to restore funding for homeless services.

Developing an understanding that a parent and her family have assets and internal wealth, power, and strength, permits her lawyer to see her differently. The lawyer learns from her, gets to admire her, and grows from knowing her.

And then, the lawyer can turn outward, to the case workers and judges who perceive the parent as a deviant, monstrous black hole of problems, needs, and pathologies. Once parents' lawyers can tell themselves the stories of their client's competence, they can tell those stories to others. Instead of defensively trying to explain away problems and needs, parents' lawyers can tell a story of strength, power, and admirable qualities. Rather than begging the court and caseworker for scraps—an extra hour of visitation, for example—parents' lawyers can proudly and confidently argue that separation is unnecessary, or that reunification should come quickly.

Parents' lawyers must move beyond the stereotypes that comprise the accepted narrative of child welfare to know the true individual who is their client. And this is the starting point for challenging the narrative of child welfare.

The beginning of this chapter included a list of questions that may start the process of thinking about a client in a more expansive way than the depiction of her in the Petition. The list is far from exhaustive, and counsel's efforts to learn and understand their individual clients are limited only by their imagination and curiosity.

Does the client have hobbies? Does she have friends? Who are they, and why does she like them? What is the most recent favor she did for a friend, relative, or neighbor? And the one before that? Parents' lawyers who ask these questions will get to know their clients in a way that emphasizes their humanity and talents. In addition, they may acquire information that can be used in the litigation to strengthen others' perceptions of the parents' abilities and character.

Beyond finding out about the strengths of particular clients, parents' lawyers may also benefit from using the resources on the website of *Rise*, an online magazine written by parents involved in child welfare about their experiences in the system. The compelling, evocative, well-written stories in *Rise* exemplify the skills possessed by many clients, which may come as a surprise to many child welfare professionals. In addition, the parent-writers frequently publish stories reflecting significant achievements both within and outside the context of child welfare litigation. Finally, *Rise* makes available workbooks that provide useful suggestions and guidance for those seeking to uncover the real person beneath the stereotypes enfolding their clients.

* * * * *

It is a truism that there are at least two sides to every story. In child welfare, lawyers for parents often hear, and even retell, stories of sadness and failure, stories of disability and incapacity. They can be most effective, however, when they help their clients tell stories of happiness, success, strength, and achievement. The grand narrative of child welfare is state officials intervene in families only when children are found in dangerous, dysfunctional, and unloving homes. But as Professor Richard Delgado reminds us, "Counterstories . . . challenge the received wisdom . . . [and] open new windows into reality, showing us that there are possibilities for life other than the ones we live." Richard Delgado, *Storytelling For Oppositionalists,* 87 Mich. L. Rev. 2411, 2414 (1989).

Parents' lawyers can change the narrative of child welfare by telling counter-stories of strengths and successes.

CHAPTER 3

First Steps in Representing a Parent Accused of Abuse or Neglect

Matthew Fraidin

3.01 Building a Relationship with the Client

The challenges of representing parents in child welfare matters start right away. Because the vast majority of parents involved in the child welfare system have little income, most clients will not be privately retained, but instead will be assigned by court appointment. As a result, it is likely that counsel's first contact with a parent client will take place with a court hearing already scheduled and imminent. The client's child might have been removed from her care with little or no warning. The child may have been placed in foster care, with caretakers unknown to the client and at a location unfamiliar to the child and kept secret from the client.

This may be the most stressful and difficult time in the client's life. She may feel frightened about the whereabouts and condition of her child. She may be disoriented by the abrupt and punitive-seeming disruption to her family's life. She may feel deeply humiliated at the harsh judgment of her parenting inherent in the state's actions of initiating a dependency case or taking the child from her care. The emotional circumstances of this time, along with the likely time pressures of a looming court hearing, can largely define the beginning of the lawyer-client relationship, and will have a significant impact on initial efforts by counsel on the client's behalf. Sensitivity to the client's experience and diligence in the early stages of representation can forge strong bonds with the client and set the stage for a constructive working relationship throughout the case.

The most important quality counsel can bring to the first meeting with the client who has experienced these events is empathy. What the client needs above all else at this moment in her life is a respectful professional who avoids all prejudgment and shows proper respect for the parent by listening carefully to what she has to say and demonstrating a commitment to work on her behalf going forward.

3.02 Gathering Information About the Case and Client

When a child has been removed from a parent's care, or the Agency seeks court approval to remove a child, courts typically must hold a "removal hearing" within twenty-four to seventy-two hours. Although statutory language varies from state to state, courts ordinarily must allow a child to remain in, or return to, his parent's custody unless the Agency proves that the child is in "imminent" or "immediate danger," or the equivalent. In many cases, counsel will be appointed to represent a client on the day the removal hearing is scheduled. This places counsel and the client in an extremely challenging situation. The results obtained in the initial "removal hearing" (see Chapter 4) may establish the long-term course of the case itself. In many states, the longer children are in foster care, the less likely they will be returned home. This means counsel needs to work extremely hard on the case almost immediately.

The Agency's knowledge of the family is almost always limited to a very discreet event—a snapshot of a family's (and child's life). The more one looks only at the state's depiction of the child's experience, the stronger the claims for the state will seem. Because the state has initiated a dependency case, we can be certain that the state has drawn negative inferences from an event or series of events in the child's life. The state's investigation may have generated inaccurate facts, however, causing the conclusions—for example, that a child is in danger—to be wholly mistaken. The state's inferences also may be rooted in misinterpretation of facts, or facts taken out of context. Counsel's job is to uncover accurate information and expand the focus beyond the incident or condition on which the state may be focused with a broader perspective that places the situation in a more complete context. Counsel needs to get to know the circumstances of the family well beyond what the Agency knows.

As soon as the appointment is made, counsel should secure the Petition and all supporting papers. Counsel should specifically request all documents provided to the Court. Counsel should also ask for all other records in the Agency's possession regarding the client, such as services provided to satisfy the state's "reasonable efforts" requirement, *see* 42 U.S.C. § 672 (2014), and any school, medical, or other records collected by the Agency investigating the parent and her family.

In addition, counsel should seek any available information that will help her learn more about the client and the overall situation. Substantial information may be available in the courthouse. For example, counsel should search for files of cases involving the client in such matters as landlord-tenant proceedings, divorce and child custody, domestic violence, criminal, and prior dependency proceedings. Counsel should also search for cases involving other individuals who may be included in the case, including the other parent, a caretaker, relative, or friend.

When counsel obtains these files, she should review them and photocopy whatever seems relevant. They may contain information that will support the client's case. For example, in a case alleging "failure to protect," domestic violence case files may contain evidence of past efforts the client made to keep a batterer at bay. Counsel may also uncover harmful information, such as a parent's past criminal activity. Counsel must know this history to avoid being blindsided later in the case when the Agency reveals it for the first time.

If the child was removed, counsel should find out where the child has been placed, how to contact the child's caregiver, and any other information about the child's current condition. Although the caseworker may be reluctant to share such information, jurisdictions vary on the amount of information a parent has a right to know about these matters. This information is often of great interest to the parent who is worried about her child's well-being.

As discussed in the next section, among the earliest tasks counsel should perform almost immediately after a child has been removed is to meet with the client and all potential substitute caregivers the client suggests. With their permission, counsel should consider visiting their home and taking photographs and video footage to be used as persuasive evidence that the child can be safely placed there. In some jurisdictions, courts have the power to direct the particular placement resource for the child; in others, this is the Agency's responsibility. In either case, counsel will usually want to seek the Agency's agreement first, seeking court intervention only if necessary.

When the Agency has a policy to defer such placements until certain background checks are completed, counsel should take all steps necessary to accelerate the process, including securing the forms and helping fill them out with the parent or proposed caregiver. Treat the matter as the emergency it is; every day a child is separated from a parent matters.

When the court or Agency is reluctant to place the child with a recommended resource, counsel should take steps to persuade them. This requires some investigation and trial-prep-like steps. Get the names of people—including doctors, teachers, and day care providers—who can attest to the proposed resource's strengths and capability to take good care of children, speak with them, and share the information with the Agency or court. Arrange a prompt meeting with the resource or bring her to court to testify.

3.03 The Client Interview

3.03(a) The First Meeting

As soon as counsel has the client's telephone number or other contact information, arrange a meeting. To the extent possible in light of time constraints, counsel should meet with the client in a quiet and private location. In many instances, counsel may have no choice but to meet in the courthouse's hallway, and may have as little as a few moments to talk prior to the initial hearing.

When this is the case, counsel should consider whether to seek a delay of the hearing until counsel has had adequate time to meet with the client and assist the client in preparing to participate meaningfully in the court appearance. Depending on the allegations and counsel's sense of the need for preparation, the costs of putting the hearing off for a day or more may be outweighed by the benefits. Counsel's role is to help the client assess the pros and cons of a decision to proceed immediately or to seek a delay. Some parents will be willing to wait until their odds are strongest. Others will regard any delay as too costly. This decision may have significant short- and long-term consequences for the client, and should be made by the client after the lawyer has provided information and assisted the client's decision-making process.

3.03(b) Building Rapport

The quieter the setting for a first meeting with a client, the better. This is a very important meeting for the client. It is not an easy thing to build rapport and trust in a rushed meeting. But counsel cannot avoid trying. Counsel should consider the likely stress the client is experiencing and ask in what ways counsel can be helpful simply by meeting with the client. What is the client most likely feeling? What are her immediate needs? One can never know, of course, without meeting her. But counsel can anticipate that the client may be scared, feeling alone, full of questions, as starters. Use even this short meeting as an opportunity to address the client's immediate needs, postponing other components of the meeting for a few minutes. Ask about how the client is holding up. Explain what is going on in the case and what lies immediately ahead. Counsel should clarify counsel's role and aspirations for the case. Counsel will need to elicit facts from the client soon enough; but that does not require starting with them.

Clients may harbor suspicions of the justice system and even of lawyers, perhaps having had negative experiences in the past. Clients may know that lawyers commonly are appointed by the judge before whom the lawyer and client will appear, and are paid by the court for which the judge works. They may be wary that a lawyer's own interest in procuring future case appointments will restrain the lawyer's advocacy. And clients may quickly learn counsel has preexisting relationships with other child welfare system professionals, such as the state's attorney, caseworker, judge, and courtroom staff.

Accordingly, it is very important for counsel to assure the client that it is to her that counsel is solely responsible, and that counsel's loyalty to the client is unequivocal. State this directly. Counsel may also be able to build a strong relationship with the client by listening to her actively and non-judgmentally. One easy way to distinguish oneself from the myriad others who may have interviewed the client in connection with the case is to make statements and ask questions reflecting favorable assumptions about the client's parenting and her contributions to the community.

3.03(c) Explaining the Initial Hearing

Be sure to explain the decisions that the court will make at the preliminary hearing. Depending on the jurisdiction, it may decide whether to authorize the Petition, a finding there is probable cause to believe there are grounds for the Petition. Second, if the court authorizes the Petition, the court will then decide where the child will live while the case proceeds.

3.03(d) Eliciting Information About the Case

Explaining the decisions to be made at the initial hearing will provide a useful frame for the lawyer's efforts to gather factual information about the case. Counsel should acquire basic factual information about the case and advise the client on the decisions that the client must make immediately. Counsel will want to know how to contact the client between court appearances.

Some information about the case can be postponed to a second meeting with the client. Depending on the allegations in the Petition, counsel may want to know immediately how the family became involved with Children's Protective Services, any previous family involvement with the courts or the Agency, whether the family currently receives services, and whether the child has special needs. Other times, some of these inquiries can be postponed, with the predominant focus placed on avoiding the child's placement in a non-relative foster home.

In preparing for the aspect of the hearing relating to the sufficiency of the Petition, the contours of the interview will be determined largely by the allegations. Carefully review the charging document and other paperwork setting forth the Agency's concerns. There may be no grounds on which to challenge the Petition on its face, in which event a detailed "retrospective" inquiry into the merits of the Petition should ordinarily be postponed, especially when there is limited time for the interview.

In that circumstance, the main focus of the interview will be on the "prospective" issue of the child's safety going forward. If the Agency is seeking the child's removal or continued placement, it must prove that the child cannot be maintained safely in the parent's home. Counsel should interview the parent about information supporting the claim that the child can be safely kept at home.

Assuming the parent wants the child home, counsel should explore whether the parent will accept conditions for the placement, such as random drug testing or in-home reunification assistance. If the parent is not alleged to be the active wrongdoer, will she help enforce a court order requiring the other parent to leave the home? Is the parent willing to take the children to services such as counseling and medical appointments? Counsel should explain that the court may be more willing to return the child with such conditions in place and that accepting them does not require admitting to any wrongdoing. The question of whether the Petition can be sustained is saved for a later time.

Counsel should also discuss the parent's options if the court does not immediately return the child to the parent's custody, especially other placement possibilities that the parent considers more acceptable than foster care. There is a federal mandate to place children in the "least restrictive (most family like) and most appropriate setting available and in close proximity to the parents' home. . . ." 42 U.S.C. § 675 (2014). Placing children with an adult caregiver suggested by the parent falls solidly within this mandate, the purpose of which is to impose a placement least likely to disrupt the child's life. In light of this federal mandate, and likely counterparts in counsel's state statute, regulations, and case law, counsel should prepare to argue that the burden lies heavily on the party opposing the parent's recommended resource to show why the placement is too dangerous to allow.

There is also a federal mandate to prefer placing children with relatives over others when children enter foster care. *See* 42 U.S.C. § 671(a)(19) (2014). Identify relatives, friends, and others who could care for the child temporarily. When considering them, counsel should tell the parent that the court will want to know such things as the proposed caregiver's prior criminal or child protective history, the family's resources, and the proposed caregiver's previous involvement in this child's life.

Counsel should also address parenting time issues with the client. What type of parenting time would the client like? Where should the visits take place? How frequently should they occur? If parenting time must be supervised, does the client know someone who is willing to supervise the visits and can pass the Agency's background checks? When evaluating all these things, counsel should help the client develop creative solutions and assess the pros and cons of the available options.

3.04 Advising a Parent Who Is Under Investigation but Is Not Yet the Subject of a Court Proceeding

Counsel may be contacted by a parent under investigation by the local child welfare agency, but who is not the subject of a court proceeding. The parent may seek to retain counsel for assistance navigating the investigation process hoping to avoid the child's removal and the filing of a court case. This section discusses factors to address in assisting the client in deciding how to respond to the investigation.

Typical issues confronted by parents in these circumstances include a request by the investigating agency to inspect the home, interview the parent or a child or the child's siblings, to authorize the release to the Agency of confidential educational or medical records, to agree to a "safety plan," and to grant a relative or friend temporary custody of the child. Although the parent cannot be compelled to do any of these things without a court order, the parent may believe that she has no choice but to comply.

The lawyer's role at this stage is to counsel the client about whether and to what extent to cooperate with the Agency's investigation. Because child services agencies typically have unchecked power to remove a child in emergency circumstances, without judicial review for twenty-four hours or more, a lawyer counseling a parent considering the most effective response to a child welfare investigation must help the client navigate a hazardous passage.

On one hand, a parent who provides information to the state inadvertently may provide sufficient grounds for concern about the child that causes the removal. On the other hand, the Agency may believe that a parent who refuses to participate in the investigation, or who limits her participation, may be hiding evidence of maltreatment and demonstrating a consciousness of guilt; in response, the Agency may remove the child. Just as the parent must avoid providing the state with evidence that gives cause for the child's removal, the parent needs to know that the Agency may remove a child because the parent refuses to provide information. In either event, the first opportunity to persuade a court to order the child's return home may not occur until the "removal hearing" several days later. In the interim, the parent and child may experience fear, disorientation, shame, and trauma. Moreover, when judicial review does take place, the parent's likelihood of success is unpredictable and may be poor in jurisdictions in which judges are known to "rubber-stamp" removals.

The client's decision about how much to cooperate should take into account what the Agency already knows or likely knows. Often, the Agency has little evidence of abuse or neglect. When that is the case, it may be wisest for the client to remain relatively unforthcoming, to avoid assisting the state in building the case against her. For example, many investigations are undertaken in response to a report conveying an anonymous source's concern or suspicion about the parent's treatment of her child. The Agency's contact with the parent may well be the first step in the Agency's investigation. Under these circumstances, the Agency has little evidence that the parent maltreated her child or that the child is at risk of maltreatment. A parent who cooperates unreservedly with the investigation may provide the Agency with information that it otherwise would not have acquired but may be construed in a worse light than the parent anticipated. Many practitioners report that facts alleged in petitions commonly were obtained through statements made by parents during the early investigation—without which there would have been no basis to file a petition.

The client's decision may be influenced by the gravity of the Agency's concern. When parents do not know why they are being investigated, it may be appropriate for the parent to cooperate, at least enough to learn the nature of the allegations. Counsel may then advise whether the client should cooperate further, weighing the inconvenience and indignity of compliance against the risk that the Agency worker will file a petition.

When the allegations against the client are very serious, or supported by substantial evidence already possessed by the Agency, it may be damaging for the parent to provide additional information and support for its concerns, such as by admitting to actions or omissions alleged by the Agency. When grave or inflammatory allegations have been made, such as sexual abuse, a client's admission to involvement or culpability may limit her ability to have the child returned home, to have visits during placement, or to defeat the charges at trial. The agency is likely to ignore or find unpersuasive explanations of her conduct, even when bolstered by mitigating or contextualizing information. When the Agency seems likely to remove a child and the chances of defeating that effort seem poor, counsel should shift the focus to finding a trusted relative or friend to take temporary custody of the child. This may provide the Agency assurance of the child's safety and encourage it not to file a petition in court.

3.05 Advising a Parent Who Is Currently the Subject of a Court Proceeding Whether to Exercise the Privilege Against Self-Incrimination

The Fifth Amendment to the Constitution provides protection against self-incrimination. *See* U.S. Const. amend. V. ("No person . . . shall be compelled in any criminal case to be a witness against himself."). A witness in any case, including a civil child protection case, may decline to testify to avoid providing information that might incriminate him- or herself. The court can make an adverse inference against a parent who declines to testify, even when the reason for declining to testify is to avoid self-incrimination. *See Baxter v. Palmigiano,* 425 U.S. 308, 318 (1976).

In counseling a client about whether to testify in a child welfare proceeding, a lawyer must help the client balance the potential risks and rewards associated with the options available to the client. On one hand, the client may testify to important factual information about the child welfare case that could exonerate her, or explain or provide context for her actions. In addition, she may feel unjustly maligned by the child welfare proceeding and want an opportunity to tell her side of the story. Testifying may provide the client with a sense of control or influence over the proceedings. However, the lawyer must inform a client that self-incriminating testimony can harm not only the client's interests in the immediate proceedings but can also expose her to collateral criminal charges where abuse or neglect has been alleged. In helping the client balance all of these important concerns, the lawyer should seek to understand the client's motivations, one or more of which may be in tension with others. Finally, it is counsel's duty to help a client understand that a judge may not believe the client (no matter how truthful her testimony may be) even where other considerations mitigate in favor of the client giving testimony. Where necessary, the lawyer should explain to the client that this is so regardless of the merits of the choices she has made as a parent, and that a fact-finder's perception of the truthfulness of the witness may be informed by personal or subjective biases, even where the testimony is true. Finally, there may be other ways—apart and aside from adducing the client's in-court testimony—for counsel to empower the involuntary party to child welfare litigation.

CHAPTER 4

Challenging the Removal of Children

Lauren Shapiro

4.01 Introduction

Perhaps the most important court decision made at the outset of a child protection case is whether to remove a child from his or her home or whether to approve a removal if one has been made extrajudicially. If counsel is able to prevent the child's removal, the risk of a parent losing parental rights is sharply reduced. But, particularly since the passage of the Adoption and Safe Families Act in 1997, Public Law 105-89, when children are placed in foster care, there is a substantial risk that the final outcome will be termination of parental rights. *See* Paul Chill, *Burden of Proof Begone: The Pernicious Effect of Emergency Removal in Child Protective Proceedings,* 42 FAM. CT. REV. 540 (2003).

With this much at stake, there is a good deal that parent's counsel must do. The good news is that there are important constitutional, federal, and state statutory and regulatory provisions upon which counsel may rely when challenging a removal. Even when counsel is unable to prevent removal, counsel can try to advocate for a placement that the parent wants, such as with family members. That question is second in importance to preventing removal altogether.

This does not mean it is strategically wise in every case to challenge removal. When there are no grounds for such a challenge, it will rarely be wise to raise one. But things can change during the pendency of the case, and counsel should take steps to ensure that the decision not to challenge the removal immediately does not waive the right to make such a challenge when circumstances change. In some states, there is a non-waivable statutory right to challenge a child's foster care placement at any time before the adjudicatory hearing. *See, e.g.*, N.Y. FAM. CT. ACT § 1028 (2013). In all cases, there is a strong constitutional argument that a parent has the right to challenge the child's continuing foster care placement at any time upon a showing of changed circumstances.

This chapter examines the grounds upon which the state may remove children from their parents' care without prior court authorization, the constitutional issues involved in these removals, the statutory rights accorded parents to challenge an Agency's efforts to place a child in foster care over parental objection, and various strategic decisions to consider when representing a parent whose child has been placed into foster care.

4.02 Grounds for Emergency Removal of Children from Their Parents' Care

Most state statutes authorize local child protective agencies to remove children from their homes in emergency circumstances before going to court. In some states, statutes carefully set forth the grounds upon which children may be removed from their families and the circumstances under which they may do so without prior judicial approval. In New York, for example, removals without prior court approval are lawful only when there is reasonable cause to believe that the failure to remove the child would create an imminent risk to the child's life or health and there is not enough time to seek a court order without subjecting the child to such risk. *See* N.Y. FAM. Ct. Act § 1024 (2014). Many states have comparable rules. *See, e.g.*, ARK. CODE ANN. § 9-27-313(a)(1)(c) (2014) (extrajudicial removals are permissible only when the child is in "immediate danger," "removal is necessary to prevent serious harm," and "there is not time to petition for and to obtain an order of the court prior to taking the juvenile into custody"); MO. ANN. STAT. § 210.125.2 (2014) (extrajudicial removal authorized where "imminent danger" and "reasonable cause to believe the harm or threat to life may occur before a juvenile court could issue a temporary protective custody order or before a juvenile officer could take the child into protective custody").

In many states, however, statutes that authorize police officers and child protective caseworkers to take children into protective custody without prior judicial approval contain considerably more open-ended language. For example, Oregon merely requires a caseworker's conclusion that "the child's condition or surroundings reasonably appear to be such as to jeopardize the child's welfare." OR. REV. STAT. ANN. § 419B.150(1)(a) (2014).

4.02(a) Constitutional Issues Involving Emergency Removals

The Supreme Court has never decided a case involving the legality of a child's removal without a court order for protection purposes. Federal courts are divided on whether the Constitution ordinarily requires judicial approval, unless exceptional circumstances justify forgoing such approval. At least three circuits, the Second, Ninth, and Tenth, have held that, in the absence of special justification, state officials act illegally when they remove children from their parents' care without a court order. In these circuits, "exigent circumstances" are required for non-judicially approved removals to be lawful. *See Roska v. Peterson,* 328 F.3d 1230, 1246 (10th Cir. 2003); *Mabe v. San Bernardino Cty. Dep't of Pub. Soc. Servs.,* 237 F.3d 1101, 1106 (9th Cir. 2001); *Tenenbaum v. Williams,* 193 F.3d 581, 594 (2d Cir. 1999). The First and Eleventh Circuits have held that the Constitution allows for special rules when officials seek to protect children from neglect or abuse. In these circuits, it is lawful to remove children without securing judicial approval, even when there would have been time to do so. *See Doe v. Kearney,* 329 F.3d 1286, 1296 (11th Cir. 2003); *Tower v. Leslie-Brown,* 326 F.3d 290, 299 (1st Cir. 2003). Other circuits have discussed the issue but have not made a definitive ruling on the question. *See, e.g., Brokaw v. Mercer Cty.,* 235 F.3d 1000 (7th Cir. 2000); *Weller v. Dep't of Soc. Servs. for Baltimore,* 901 F.2d 387 (4th Cir. 1990).

Even if the Constitution prefers judicial approval for the removal of children, all courts recognize the state's strong interest in protecting children from abuse and, therefore, allow officials to take children into custody without a court order in "emergency circumstances." But courts more insistent on traditional application of Fourth Amendment principles have held that when "the danger to the child is not so imminent that there is reasonably sufficient time to seek prior judicial authorization . . . there is no reason to excuse the absence of the judiciary's participation in depriving the parents of the care . . . of their child." *See Tenenbaum,* 193 F.3d at 594. *See also Southerland v. City of New York,* 680 F.3d 127, 142 (2d Cir. 2012).

If counsel practices in a jurisdiction in which children are routinely removed from families without court orders, counsel should consider meeting with local authorities to alert them to the risks associated with continuing unconstitutional practices. A few years ago, lawyers who represent parents in New York City were able to persuade local child welfare officials to change their removal practice. In New York City, family defense is a relatively new field. In 2007, the city agreed to fund institutional providers that employed lawyers, social workers, and parent advocates to represent parents in child welfare proceedings. Lawyers in these new offices noticed that New York City child welfare officials routinely removed children from homes, schools, and hospitals in non-emergency situations without seeking prior judicial approval even when there was time to do so. These actions were plainly illegal under state law and controlling precedent in the United States Court of Appeals for the Second Circuit. In 2011, several of these new offices met with local officials and threatened to sue them unless they agreed to change their practice. The advocates brought with them numerous case examples in which children were removed without a court order, only to be returned to their homes after immediate judicial review at emergency hearings. This practice caused children the unnecessary harm of being removed from their families, which would have been prevented had the Agency sought judicial approval prior to removal.

In response, child welfare officials agreed to issue a new protocol for conducting removals without a court order and to train its entire workforce on the protocol. The revised procedure permits removal without a court order only when "the imminent danger to the child's life or health is so immediate that leaving the child with the parent while obtaining a court order will likely result in immediate harm to the child and there is no other safety intervention available." *See* N.Y.C. Admin. for Children's Servs., Conducting Emergency Removals, Policy #2011/01 (2011).

In addition to addressing when to remove children without prior judicial authorization, the New York City policy also clarified when removals should be sought in the first place. The policy states that removals "should never be based solely on the parents' failure to effectively engage with services unless there is a clear link between the parent's behavior and immediate danger to the child. The critical focus in assessing the need for a removal is always whether the child is in immediate danger." *See id.* This informal advocacy has helped reduce the number of emergency removals without prior authorization.

Whether parents live in states with a large or small number of constitutional protections, a parent's remedy for a constitutionally illegal seizure of one's child is limited to a damages action in federal court pursuant to 42 U.S.C. § 1983 (2014). Counsel should contact local civil liberties groups and law offices that seek damages in federal court for constitutional violations to challenge illegal removals through damages actions. If these removals do not violate state law, counsel should consider advocating for legislative change. At present, parents are unable to challenge a removal in juvenile court on the grounds that it was unconstitutional because the Agency did not first seek court approval. Once children have been removed from their home against their parents' wishes, counsel's focus should turn to considering how to secure their prompt return. That will be the focus of much of the remaining chapter.

4.02(b) Right to Judicial Review and a Removal Hearing

Whatever the statutory language authorizing emergency removals, all such removals constitute a seizure for purposes of the Fourth Amendment *and* a deprivation of liberty under the Due Process Clause. This means that the United States Constitution and the thousands of state and federal court decisions that have interpreted it place a significant constraint on the power of state officials to wrest children from their families. The Constitution provides parents with extremely important legal protections in removal cases, which counsel should integrate into everyday juvenile court practice.

The Constitution requires that courts review and approve removals after the fact. This review might be of two kinds. First, the Supreme Court has held that the Fourth Amendment requires that when individuals are arrested without a warrant (without a pre-seizure hearing), ordinarily there must be judicial review of the seizure within forty-eight hours. *See City of Riverside v. McLaughlin,* 500 U.S. 44 (1991). This review focuses on whether there is probable cause to justify the seizure. There is nothing about child welfare removals that changes this requirement. State officials may not seize individuals (of any age) without prompt judicial review of the circumstances of the seizure. But the *City of Riverside* review required by the Fourth Amendment is an inquiry into whether there is probable cause to believe the child is endangered.

Second, parents and children enjoy the substantive right to live together, absent a compelling state interest justifying a different result. Parents have substantive due process rights when the state seeks to interfere in the management, care, and custody of their children. *See Troxel v. Granville,* 530 U.S. 57, 65–66 (2000) (parents have a right to decide who visits their children, citing cases concerning the "fundamental right of parents to make decisions concerning the care, custody, and control of their children"). Likewise, children have a constitutionally protected liberty interest in the preservation of their family. *See Kia P. v. McIntyre,* 235 F.3d 749, 759 (2d Cir. 2000), *cert. denied,* 534 U.S. 820 (2001); *Ram v. Rubin,* 118 F.3d 1306 (9th Cir. 1997), *cert. denied,* 522 U.S. 1045 (1998); *Duchesne v. Sugarman,* 566 F.2d 817, 825 (2d Cir. 1977). The Constitution protects substantive rights with the procedural right to prompt judicial review of state action after the deprivation.

The Fourteenth Amendment, which protects a parent's substantive right to his or her child's custody and the child's right to remain with his or her family, requires a different inquiry than the Fourth Amendment's probable cause inquiry. The question that must be addressed under the Fourteenth Amendment is whether there is a compelling state interest in keeping the child in placement. This inquiry goes beyond the question of probable cause to believe the child is endangered and focuses on whether the child is sufficiently at risk that removal is an option and, even if it is, whether it is the least restrictive means to advance the state's child protection interest. *See, e.g., Berman v. Young,* 291 F.3d 976, 985 (7th Cir. 2002); *Nicholson v. Scoppetta,* 3 N.Y.3d 357, 820 N.E.2d 840, 787 N.Y.S.2d 196 (2004).

4.02(c) Time Frames for Removal Hearings

State statutes provide time frames for hearings to determine whether children should be placed or remain in foster care. The time is measured from either the time of removal or the time that a parent requests a hearing. The time frames vary by jurisdiction. For example, both Michigan and New Jersey require judicial review of a child's removal within twenty-four hours of the removal. *See* Mich. Comp. Laws § 712A.13a(2) (2014); N.J. Stat. Ann. § 9:6-8.31(a) (2014). In Colorado, parents have a right to a court hearing within seventy-two hours after a child is removed. *See* Colo. Rev. Stat. § 19-3-403(3.5) (2014). In Montana, parents have the right to a contested removal hearing only within ten days after they request one. *See* Mont.

CODE ANN. § 41-3-427 (2014). In Connecticut, courts must review removals within ten days and hold a hearing upon the parent's request within another ten days. *See* CONN. GEN. STAT. § 46b-129(b)–(c) (2014).

4.03 Factors Courts Must Consider in Deciding Whether to Place Children in Foster Care or Return Them to Their Families

Cases involving removals get before a judge in one of three ways: First, the Agency may seek judicial approval for a removal before a removal has occurred. These applications are usually made *ex parte* and are the child welfare equivalent of a prosecutor securing a search or arrest warrant before any criminal case has been brought. In such circumstances, counsel would not be involved. A second way the case gets before a judge is when the Agency seeks judicial authorization for either continuing the child's placement or requesting permission to remove the child. But in many states, counsel will not necessarily have been assigned when the Agency makes either of these requests, which should be made when the case is first before the court after a removal. If counsel practices in a jurisdiction that does not appoint counsel for parents as soon as the case is filed (or the parent first appears), there will be no one to oppose the application. Thus, a third way to secure judicial oversight of a removal is for the parent's lawyer to challenge the court order that found placement was necessary.

Because the typical case will likely involve a child who has been removed before counsel's involvement, counsel should remember that the correct question for the court is not whether there was any need for a removal when it was made. The critical question will always be what should be done with respect to the child now and in the immediate future.

State statutes provide the standard by which courts must determine whether children should be placed in foster care. Most states require the showing that removal is necessary to prevent danger, harm, or risk to the child (and, even if they do not, such a showing is required by the Constitution). In New York, for example, the court must determine "whether removal is necessary to avoid imminent risk to the child's health or safety." N.Y. FAM. COURT ACT § 1027 (b)(i) (2014). If the court decides removal is necessary, its order must include the findings that support the reasons. *See id.* § 1027. Unless the court finds that returning the child would pose an imminent risk to the child's life or health, the child must be returned home. *See also* ARK. CODE ANN. § 9-27-328(e)(1) (2014); KAN. STAT. ANN. § 38-2243 (2014).

Counsel should be intimately familiar with each factor that the court in the jurisdiction must consider in deciding whether to remove children. Moreover, counsel should ensure that the court takes these factors into account and applies them to the facts of the case. This will form the framework for the parent's defense or "theory of the case" at the removal hearing.

4.03(a) *Whether the Children Face an Imminent Risk of a Certain Degree of Harm if They Remain in the Home*

As mentioned, once the child has been removed, the question before the court shifts to a future-looking inquiry of whether there is a need now and in the immediate future to keep the child from the parent's custody. States are ineligible to receive federal matching funds to pay for the foster placement of a child unless the removal was reviewed and approved by a court that found that "*continuing*" the child at home "would be contrary to the welfare of the child." *See* 42 U.S.C. §§ 672(a)(1), 673 (2014) (emphasis added). In practice, this finding is routinely made *pro forma* without much inquiry into the harm of removal. Counsel should resist and insist that the court take the language seriously, particularly because placing children in foster care subjects them to known risks.

The first constitutional question raised when the state coercively removes a child from his or her family is whether the state has a sufficiently compelling state interest for its actions. Because a removal violates a parent's (and child's) substantive right to remain together—a "fundamental" right protected by the Due Process Clause of the Fourteenth Amendment—the state must have a compelling interest to override the fundamental right being threatened. In many state laws, this principle is articulated in two dimensions: (1) the *severity* of the problem (what the likely consequences would be if the threatened harm occurred); and (2) the imminence of the risk (how *likely* it is that the harm would occur). *See, e.g.*, N.Y. FAM. CT. ACT § 1027(b); COLO. REV. STAT. § 19-3-401 (2014) (requiring compelling reasons for removal).

These separate inquiries provide counsel with the opportunity to focus on how much actual harm the child would likely suffer if the child were to remain in the home exposed . On this point, counsel should stress that the grounds for finding neglect or dependency are significantly broader than the grounds to remove a child who has been neglected. Agencies should not be able to successfully argue that a child needs to be separated from his or her family because there are grounds to sustain a petition alleging neglect. The much more narrow question involves the severity of the harm that is to be avoided. Many removals are unreasonable because the Agency has sought to prevent an insufficiently grave harm to justify such drastic action.

In addition, counsel should be prepared to argue that the level of harm that might occur if a child is kept at home is insufficiently high to justify removal. Virginia, for example, requires the Agency to prove that the "child would be subjected to an imminent threat to life or health to the extent that severe or irremediable injury would be likely to result if the child were returned to or left in the custody of his parents." VA. CODE ANN. § 16.1-252 (2014). Counsel should also push back against a claim that the Agency believes there is a "possibility" of imminent risk. As New York's highest court explained, in interpreting the controlling New York statute, "Imminent danger . . . must be near or impending, not merely possible." *Nicholson v. Scoppetta*, 3 N.Y.3d at 369, 820 N.E.2d at 845, 787 N.Y.S.2d at 201.

4.03(b) Whether the State Made Reasonable Efforts to Prevent Foster Care Placement

Even when there is a basis for removing a child under state, federal, and constitutional law, an additional critical inquiry asks whether removal is the least restrictive means to protect the state's interests to keep the child safe. Federal law requires as a condition of receiving federal payment for foster care that a court specifically find that the Agency made "reasonable efforts" prior to the placement "to prevent, or eliminate the need for removal" *and* "to make it possible for the child to safely return to the child's home." *See* 42 U.S.C. § 671(a)(15)(B) (2014).

Many states have codified the requirements imposed by Congress for foster care payments. In these jurisdictions, the petitioning Agency must prove as part of its prima facie case that either preventive efforts have been made or that there are sufficient reasons to excuse the Agency from using them in the particular case. Although the Adoption and Safe Families Act of 1997 creates exceptions to this requirement when a court makes findings of "aggravated circumstances,"—such as the parent subjecting the child to abandonment, torture, unexplained serious injuries, chronic abuse, or sexual abuse, *id.* at 671(a)(15)(D)—in the vast majority of cases the Agency must provide reasonable efforts. If the Agency fails to prove one of these conditions, the court is obliged to order that the child be returned home.

Moreover, many state statutes have codified the federal preference for keeping children with their families. The introductory purpose clauses of many State's statutes contain language similar to New York's, setting out the State's purposes in terms that are extremely helpful to parents. *See, e.g.,* COLO. REV. STAT. § 19-3-100.5 (2014) (emphasizing the state's preference to prevent removing children and keeping families together); KAN. STAT. ANN. § 38-2201 (2014) (recognizing the importance of a child's relationship with child's family and keeping families together); N.Y. SOC. SERV. L. § 384-b(1)(a)(i)(iii) (2014) (identifying the state's "first obligation" as helping families remain together because of the general desirability of keeping children with their families). It was with this strong legislative set of principles in mind that New York's highest court clarified the duty of courts reviewing removals into foster care:

> [t]he court must do more than identify the existence of a risk of serious harm. . . . [It] must weigh, in the factual setting before it, whether the imminent risk to the child can be mitigated by reasonable efforts to avoid removal. It must balance that risk against the harm removal might bring, and it must determine factually which course is in the child's best interests.
>
> *Nicholson v. Scoppetta,* 3 N.Y.3d at 378, 820 N.E.2d at 852, 787 N.Y.S.2d at 208.

Courts that have interpreted the federal reasonable efforts requirement have held that they must be tailored to the particularized needs of the family. *See, e.g., H.H. v. Baldwin Cty. Dep't of Human Res.,* 989 So. 2d 1094 (Ala. Civ. App. 2008); *In re*

James G., 178 Md. App. 543, 943 A.2d 53 (2008). In one New York case, the court found that the Agency failed to provide the mother with sufficient services or referrals in response to her significant psychiatric needs. Even though the mother was receiving mental health services, the Agency "had a duty to ensure that the services were appropriate and to expand her services if necessary, to prevent the need for the children's removal." *See Matter of Jamie C.*, 26 Misc.3d 580, 889 N.Y.S.2d 437, 443 (Fam. Ct. 2009). When courts find a lack of efforts, the court often has the power by statute to order the Agency to arrange for the services to be provided. *See, e.g.*, N.Y. FAM. CT. ACT §§ **1015**, 1027, 1028 (2014).

Federal law does not forbid courts from placing children in care despite the failure to provide efforts to prevent their placement. Rather, the consequence of that failure is the possible loss of federal funding for that case. Many judges, however, are loath to punish the locality by increasing its financial costs for foster care placements. For this reason, judges rarely make findings that agencies did not provide reasonable efforts, at least when judges are inclined to approve the foster care placement. Even so, establishing that there are services the family would benefit from creates the opportunity to ask for an order returning children home with those services in place.

4.03(c) Whether There Are Court Orders That Could Eliminate the Risk of Harm to Children Remaining at Home

An early question counsel should always explore is whether there are orders that the court could put in place that would mitigate risk to the children. Before asking for services, counsel should discuss with the parent what services, if any, she would accept as a condition to keeping custody. Some services may be too intrusive for the parent and others may set the parent up for failure as the case progresses if the parent is unable to comply. With the parent's consent, counsel should request that the Agency be ordered to make referrals for whatever services would be beneficial to the family, keeping in mind the need for locating services near the parent's home to make compliance easier.

Identifying suitable services for a parent often requires specialized expertise or knowledge. Lawyers who work in interdisciplinary offices with social workers on staff are in a better position to identify such services. Lawyers without such colleagues should strive to become familiar with services in the community—where they are, what they do, eligibility criteria, and whether they accept Medicaid payments. Over a period of time, counsel should become sufficiently familiar with what is available in the community to identify services that are suitable. These services may include family shelters, intensive case management, and medical and mental health services, among many others. One of the most important roles counsel can play in a child protection case is to help shape the court-ordered service plan that will be developed to assist the family to keep or regain custody of their children. That process begins at the earliest stages of the case. The court will not find all efforts to be "reasonable."

Apart from services that may eliminate the need for a child's placement, counsel should consider the range of court orders that might be made that do not involve ordering services. Court orders that could eliminate risk to the children, depending on the allegations in the case, include orders directed against the parent forbidding him or her from leaving the children alone, using excessive corporal punishment, or being in the children's presence under the influence of drugs or alcohol. With the client's permission, counsel may also request an order of protection that excludes the person from the home accused of mistreating the children so that the children do not have to be removed. These kinds of orders should be regarded as examples of less restrictive actions that may be taken to meet the state's legitimate interest in a minimally intrusive manner. Such actions are consistent with the constitutional requirement that state action infringing on a fundamental right be undertaken in the least restrictive manner and are consistent with best practices in child welfare.

4.03(d) Whether the Harm of Removing the Children from Their Homes Outweighs Any Possible Risk

Counsel should help the court grasp, as Congress and many state legislatures understand, that the choice is never between safety and risk. Rather, it is between exposing children to one kind of risk (risks associated with entry into foster care) in order to eliminate another kind (risks associated with keeping children at home). It is impossible for the court to enter a risk-free order. The risks to children from entering foster care are considerable and can be devastating. *See, e.g.*, Joseph J. Doyle Jr., *Child Protection and Child Outcomes: Measuring the Effects of Foster Care,* 97 Am. Econ. Rev. 1583 (2007) (suggesting that children removed and placed in foster care tend to have poor life outcomes, such as lesser earnings, higher rates of juvenile delinquency, and higher teen birth rates). These harms may include the emotional trauma of removal, neglect, or abuse in the foster home, instability due to being moved among multiple foster homes, inconsistency and gaps in the receipt of mental health treatment and other services, school transfers, disruption in school attendance, less contact with siblings and families, and the stigma of being in foster care.

There is a wealth of child development literature establishing that a continuity of relationships, surroundings, and environmental influences are essential for a child's healthy development and should be disrupted only when there is no reasonable alternative. *See* JOHN BOWLBY, A SECURE BASE: PARENT-CHILD ATTACHMENT AND HEALTHY HUMAN DEVELOPMENT (1988); JOSEPH GOLDSTEIN, ANNA FREUD & ALBERT SOLNIT, BEYOND THE BEST INTERESTS OF THE CHILD 31–39 (1979).

In deciding whether children should be placed or remain in foster care, New York State's highest court ruled in 2004 that courts must balance the risk to the children of remaining in their parents' care with the harm of removing them. *See Nicholson v. Scoppetta*, 3 N.Y.3d 357, 820 N.E.2d 840, 787 N.Y.S.2d 196 (2004). Although New York law does not mention "harm of removal" as a factor for courts to take into account, the New York Court of Appeals explained that "[t]he plain language of the section and the legislative history supporting it establish that a blanket presumption favoring removal was never intended." *See id.* at 378. As a result, many factors are material to the inquiry, including children's attachments to their parents, the importance of parent/infant bonding, the children's special needs, that the children would be placed with strangers or in a congregate setting, that newborns would be unable to breastfeed, that siblings would be separated from each other, or any actual harm that has already befallen the children if they have already been placed in foster care and that is likely to continue if they are not returned home. Being faithful to this ruling, many trial judges in New York have returned the children or denied a removal application despite finding possible risk at home because the risk is outweighed by the harm that removal or continued foster care would cause.

Family defense attorneys outside of New York may rely on *Nicholson* to encourage courts to consider not only the risk to the children of remaining in the home, but also the harm of removing them from their families. This balancing test dramatically changes the equation and provides counsel with a strong argument that the court should disapprove the removal where there is strong evidence about the harm of removal.

4.03(e) Where the Child Will Be Placed

Congress has long had a preference for children being raised temporarily by extended family. *See* 42 U.S.C. § 675(5)(A) (2014); *Miller v. Youakim*, 440 U.S. 125 (1979). Federal and state laws impose on courts the duty to ensure that children placed in foster care are placed "in the least restrictive (most family-like) setting available and in close proximity to the parent's home," consistent with the child's well-being. *See* 42 U.S.C. § 675(5)(A). To implement these principles, courts are expected to strive to find relatives to care for children on a temporary basis. *See, e.g.*, CAL. FAM. CODE § 7950(a)(1) (2014) (making relative placement preferential, when appropriate); KAN. STAT. ANN. § 38-2286 (2014) (requiring that grandparents be considered as a placement option).

Counsel should find out from the parent the names of any resources the parent can identify to become temporary caregivers in order to minimize disruption in the child's life. Ensuring the child's placement in a home suitable to the parent may be the key to a successful outcome in the case. A caregiver close to the parent may be less willing to adopt the child and more likely to remain committed to working with the parent to maintain his or her parental rights. Visits may be more frequent and more natural when children are living with caregivers who have the parent's blessing.

4.04 Strategic Considerations for Deciding Whether and When to Request a Hearing to Challenge Removal and Seek Return of the Children

Whether to request a removal hearing is a particularly vexing question; so, too, is when to request one. The stakes are high. Cases can worsen during the time children are separated from parents. As time passes, it becomes that much more difficult to secure their return. If the parent proves unable to comply with the numerous conditions commonly included in the case plan, the chances of regaining custody are diminished. Although the children may have been removed for a particular reason, other concerns may become the focus of attention once the case is ongoing, including such technically irrelevant factors as the parent's level of degree of cooperation with the Agency.

Another factor to consider in determining whether to have an emergency hearing is that, unlike at the full adjudicatory hearing where only competent evidence will be admissible, hearsay is almost always admissible at removal hearings. If counsel believes harmful hearsay evidence will be admitted at the removal hearing which the judge might otherwise never learn about, that is a factor to take into account when considering whether to forgo the hearing.

Sometimes, hearings are requested to learn more about the opponent's theory and to discover the evidence upon which the Agency is relying. When using the hearing for discovery purposes, counsel should ordinarily conduct extensive questioning of the witnesses called by the Agency with an eye toward a possible trial on the merits in the future. But often, it is wise to forgo the hearing until the client is in the best position to win. It will rarely be worth the effort to hold a hearing for discovery reasons alone when the evidence against the parent is very strong and likely to negatively influence the judge's opinion about the parent. Discovery can often be achieved without these extra costs. Thus, it may be strategically wise to delay requesting a hearing until the client has engaged in services or has taken other remedial measures, such as moving into a domestic violence shelter, which should ameliorate the court's concerns. Sometimes, it is important to complete one's investigation into the case before having the removal hearing in order to present evidence that counsel would otherwise not be in a position to secure.

Counsel should also consider a strategy for getting the children back without a hearing. Parents need to know that very damaging information may come out at the hearing that might not otherwise be disclosed—such as prior criminal convictions, prior domestic violence history, or the existence of pending criminal cases—making it even harder to get the children home. In addition, the parent may have to testify to information that could be used against him or her in a criminal proceeding or in later stages of the child protection case (such as a motion for summary judgment in an adjudicatory hearing based on the testimony at an emergency hearing, or to impeach the parent if the parent testifies differently at the fact-finding stage). This risk may strongly outweigh the potential benefits of having a hearing when counsel concludes that the chance of winning the hearing is very small.

An additional complicating circumstance is when the parent is being prosecuted in criminal court for the events that led to the Petition in family court. This topic is discussed in much greater detail in Chapter 5. Counsel should be in close touch with the client's criminal lawyer in an effort to coordinate strategies across both jurisdictions. If the parent has a pending criminal case involving the same allegations that led to the Petition in family court, evaluating whether to challenge a removal is a much more complicated assessment because of the risk that the testimony will be used against him or her in the criminal proceeding. Balancing the risk to the parent of testifying in the removal proceeding against the risk of having a negative impact on the criminal case is an important challenge, but it can be overcome.

One way to try to avoid a parent waiving the privilege and testifying to potentially incriminating facts at the removal hearing is to call the parent on the stand for a very limited purpose. The parent could testify to his or her willingness to accept services or to comply with various court orders as a condition of keeping or regaining custody of her children without discussing any of the underlying facts that form the basis of the charges. Counsel should carefully explain to the parent the limited purpose of having him or her testify and prepare the parent to invoke the Fifth Amendment right not to answer particular questions about the merits of the charges.

In some cases, counsel will not be in a position to argue that the parent is not responsible for the maltreatment without engaging an expert. In *res ipsa* injury cases, for example, which often involve analyzing complicated medical evidence, counsel may not be able to present a cogent case against removal or continued foster care placement without the testimony of an expert to explain why the injuries are consistent with accidental infliction. Although it may be possible to win a removal hearing because the Agency failed to prove that the injuries were caused by child abuse, often an expert is needed to prove the injuries were accidental.

An important question in deciding when to request a hearing is whether there is a strategic advantage to gain by waiting. There may be no point in waiting if there is no likelihood that the chances of prevailing at the hearing will improve over time. It may be easier to persuade the court at the beginning of the case that the allegations do not warrant removal even when the court would reject an application to return a child from foster care once there is evidence that the parent is not sufficiently engaging in services. In many cases, the longer the parent waits to request a hearing for the return of the children, the more progress the court will expect to see. Furthermore, judges who understand the trauma of removing children from their homes may be less likely to remove a child from a home than to deny a parent's application for the return of a child already removed, because in the latter case the trauma of removal has already taken place.

In making the decision when to request the hearing, counsel should also take into account the harm to the child of remaining in foster care. If the child is placed with family that is facilitating the client's relationship with the children, counsel might be more inclined to request the hearing when the client is in a better position to prevail. If the child is in a licensed foster home with a stranger, this may call for an earlier hearing.

Participating in a removal hearing can be extremely stressful. For this reason, a particularly important conversation between counsel and parent is whether to seek a contested hearing. Ultimately, of course, it is the client's decision whether and when to have a hearing. Clients may have an opinion about whether it is better to wait while they secure services or get their lives together and it is important to listen to their instincts even though counsel may have more information about the law and the court process. Although the decision whether and when to request an emergency hearing could be considered a "legal strategy," it is much better for the attorney-client relationship if counsel and client reach an agreement about the strategy even when it means taking a risk counsel would not choose to take when the client is prepared to do so.

This analysis becomes much more difficult if counsel has concerns about the client's competence. Simply because a client insists on having a hearing even though counsel has advised differently does *not* mean the client is incompetent. If the client understands the advice counsel has offered but chooses to have the hearing anyway, that is his or her choice. However, when counsel believes a client is incapable of understanding advice and the consequences of different options and thinks the hearing will prejudice the client, one available option is to request that a guardian ad litem be appointed; however, this option should be used very sparingly because once a parent has been assigned such a guardian, the prospects for regaining custody of his or her children are diminished. For more information about representing a parent with a disability, see Chapter 12.

4.05 The Importance of Having a Theory for the Hearing

Before deciding whether to request a removal hearing, consider how it will further the client's goals. Ask how can it be won? What will be the hook for the judge? In developing a theory of the case, counsel should carefully review the allegations in the underlying Petition and any discovery, including agency case notes and medical records, to determine the case theory at the emergency hearing. Use whatever discovery devices are available to get discovery quickly. If the hearing was not held early in the case, counsel will be in a position to know many facts about a client's progress and other matters that may not be in the Agency's case records.

Think about the dynamics of the case. Are the caseworkers supportive? Imagine the client as a witness. Will s/he be able to explain him- or herself clearly? If counsel's theory is that circumstances have changed to eliminate or mitigate any risk to the children, the court will probably want the parent to recognize the seriousness of the allegations and show insight about the situation that led to the removal and how to prevent a recurrence. The parent may need to make certain admissions to convince the court s/he has gained insight, and counsel will need to advise the parent of the potential consequences of these admissions, including how they could be used against the parent in both family and in criminal court. Many parents will take such a risk to get their children back quickly, but it is important that the parent is aware of the risks when deciding to make such admissions, especially when there are collateral consequences such as potential loss of a job, jail time, or deportation.

It is wise to draft the argument to support the claim that the Agency has failed to show that the children are facing the kind of risk to justify removal or that, whatever risk there may be, removal is inappropriate for other reasons (the risk can be addressed by less intrusive means than removal or the risk of placement is greater than the risk of keeping the children in their family). Drafting the argument will help clarify the theory of the case and ensure that all the facts counsel brings out at the hearing are consistent with this theory. Counsel should also draft a closing argument that incorporates the testimonial and documentary evidence anticipated at the hearing.

The case theory may be that there is no imminent risk based on the allegations in the petition. This may be advanced by arguing that the facts in the Petition are untrue or, even if true, do not constitute imminent risk. Admitting that the facts are true will, of course, make it difficult or impossible to contest the charges in the Petition later in the case. Counsel should pay particular attention to the date the child protective worker first learned of the facts in the Petition. If the caseworker knew about facts for some time but did not seek a removal until recently, this would strengthen the argument that there is no current imminent risk now unless there has been a significant and recent change. If the child has lived safely at home during the time the case was being investigated, there rarely would be a reason to remove the child at the time the Petition is filed, particularly because the Agency may now secure a court order directing the parent to take certain steps or refrain from doing certain things as a condition of keeping custody of the child.

As discussed above, counsel may also choose to argue that whatever imminent risk arguably exists could be attenuated or avoided by ordering that services be put in place. Counsel should always consider calling the parent as a witness in the removal hearing to have the parent say (when the parent is willing to do so) that the parent is willing to engage in certain services or to refrain from certain behavior as a condition of keeping custody of the child. Humanizing the parent by having the court hear firsthand how strongly the parent loves his or her child and is committed to doing what the court requires may go very far toward persuading the court to allow the child to remain at home. Prepping the parent for this testimony is an extremely important task that counsel must engage in carefully and thoroughly.

When counsel's theory is that any possible risk of remaining in the parent's care is outweighed by the harm of removal, it is important to present evidence of the specific harm of removal. For example, if the children have been in foster care and suffered harm as a result, it is important to introduce evidence of this harm. One New York appellate court, for example, found that children should have been returned to their parent, even though there may have been grounds for removing the children without further consideration, because the children's special needs could not be adequately met in foster care. *See In re Alexander* B., 28 A.D.3d 547, 814 N.Y.S.2d 651 (N.Y. App. Div. 2006). *See also In re Yve S.*, 373 Md. 551, 819 A.2d 1030 (2003); *In Interest of A.B.*, 444 So. 2d 981 (Fla. Dist. Ct. App. 1983). Evidence of the harm of such disruption may be presented by calling an expert witness, including the child's therapist.

As with any hearing, counsel should ensure before the removal hearing starts that the parent understands the risks associated with having the hearing, the theory on which counsel will rely, and the implications for the parent of advancing the theory. When the parent doesn't agree with the theory or approach, it may not be the best one. When the parent is not on board with counsel's theory, the parent may intentionally or unintentionally undermine it when s/he testifies at the hearing. Counsel should prevent the case from collapsing in this way.

Among the most important factors counsel should consider in deciding whether to go forward with the removal hearing is how the parent will present at the hearing. The court's opinion of the parent's credibility will have short- and long-term implications for the case. When parents make a good impression on the judge at this hearing, the good impression may go a long way toward the judge giving the parent the benefit of the doubt. But the converse is also true. To place counsel and the parent in the best position to predict how the parent will present at the removal hearing, counsel should prepare as much as possible with the parent for the hearing and be willing—if the preparation phase reveals that the hearing will likely go poorly—to abandon the plan.

As with any hearing, counsel should consult with the lawyer for the children or guardian ad litem to assess his or her position and how it will affect the prospects of prevailing at the hearing. Find out the lawyer's concerns in advance and let the information help shape counsel's theory of the case.

4.06 Litigating the Hearing

An emergency hearing itself is much like any other hearing. Preparation will be similar to other hearings: (1) obtain necessary discovery, (2) carefully review all records, (3) develop a theory of the case, (4) try to find out what witnesses the Agency will call, (5) consult with the children's lawyer and seek his or her support, (6) prepare cross-examination of any potential witnesses, (7) prepare the client's testimony, and (8) gather evidence counsel wants to introduce. Subpoena any documents or witnesses needed as soon as possible. Speak to potential witnesses—such as service providers, supportive foster parents, or family members—to discuss their testimony and see if they are willing to testify on behalf of the client.

The main difference in litigating an emergency hearing is that the evidentiary rules are lax—hearsay is admissible. Another difference is that counsel will have less time to prepare and less knowledge of the facts of the case. At emergency hearings unanticipated issues are more likely to come up and will require quick thinking on one's feet. The more preparation counsel does in advance, the better able counsel will be to deal with any surprises at the hearing.

4.07 Conclusion

Removal hearings are a critically important stage of the proceeding. The decision made by the court will have enormous impact on almost everything that follows. Representing a parent at a removal hearing requires some of the most complicated decisions counsel must make; it also provides counsel with the opportunity to make his or her most important contribution: keeping the child and parent together.

CHAPTER 5

Special Considerations Representing Clients Involved with the Criminal Justice System

Joanna Woolman

5.01 Introduction

Over the last twenty years, disrupting families because of the incarceration of parents has become an increasingly serious problem in the United States. Never before has the United States had more people, both men and women, in state and federal prisons. With only 5 percent of the world's total population, the United States is responsible for incarcerating 25 percent of the world's total prison population and has the highest incarceration rate in the world. As a result, more children are affected by parental incarceration than ever. In 2010, there were 2.3 million people in jail or prison, compared to just five hundred thousand in 1980. The incarceration of that many adults affected 2.7 million children. Having a parent incarcerated makes children four times more likely to encounter the child protection system. *Parental Incarceration and Child Well-Being in Fragile Families*, 42 FRAGILE FAMILIES RESEARCH BRIEF 1-2 (2008). In 2009 at least fourteen thousand children were in foster care in the United States due in part to a parent being incarcerated. *See* U.S. GOV'T ACCOUNTABILITY OFFICE, GAO-11-863, CHILD WELFARE: MORE INFORMATION AND COLLABORATION COULD PROMOTE TIES BETWEEN FOSTER CARE CHILDREN AND THEIR INCARCERATED PARENTS (2011).

Even though rates of incarceration have skyrocketed, most people are in prison for committing non-violent offenses. *See* E. ANN CARSON & WILLIAM J. SABOL, PRISONERS IN 2011, U.S. DEPARTMENT OF JUSTICE, BUREAU OF JUSTICE STATISTICS, NCJ 239808 (2012). Men and women are serving longer sentences for drug offenses. At the federal level, prisoners serving time on a drug charge comprise half of the prison population.

At the state level, drug offenders have increased even more dramatically and reflect changes in drug sentencing practices rather than an increase in criminal activity. Women's incarceration rates have risen at especially alarming levels. According to the website of The Sentencing Project, the rate of women in prison has risen 646 percent since 1980, to a point where one in one hundred African American women are currently in prison, two-thirds of whom are mothers. The current average prison sentence in the United States is over five years. *See* LAUREN E. GLAZE & ERINN J. HERBERMAN, CORRECTIONAL POPULATIONS IN THE UNITED STATES, 2012, U.S. DEPARTMENT OF JUSTICE, BUREAU OF JUSTICE STATISTICS, NCJ 243936 (2013).

The vast majority of men and women serving time in state or federal prison will be released. Indeed, in recent years the number of releases from state and federal prisons exceeded the number of admissions. These released prisoners return to their communities, families, and their children's lives.

Incarcerating parents affects children's well-being, but, unlike other separations resulting from divorce, death, or military deployment, a child's loss of a parent because of incarceration is often unacknowledged. Compounding the problem is the difficulty children have in maintaining a relationship after their parents enter prison. In particular, the lack of collaboration between child welfare agencies and corrections departments—the two agencies that control the relationship between an incarcerated parent and his or her child—can inhibit visitation and regular communication between parents in prison and their children.

The most significant barrier that incarcerated parents face in the child protection system is the rigid set of timelines mandated by federal and state laws to achieve permanency. Between 1997 and 2002, termination of parental rights proceedings for incarcerated parents doubled. *See* WHEN A PARENT IS INCARCERATED, A PRIMER FOR SOCIAL WORKERS 9 (2011). This increase was due in large part to the implementation of the Adoption and Safe Families Act (ASFA), enacted in 1997 to promote permanency for children in foster care. Under ASFA, a petition to terminate parental rights must be filed if a child has been placed outside the home for fifteen of the previous twenty-two months, absent compelling circumstances such as child's placement with kin. *See generally* Chapter 14. In recent years, however, several states have moved to expand judicial discretion to delay termination of parental rights proceedings if the parent's incarceration or former incarceration is a significant factor for the child's continued stay in foster care.

Nonetheless, many incarcerated parents whose children are in the child protection system are at high risk of permanently losing their parental rights. Advocates for parents must be mindful of this reality. For many parents, a prison sentence will result in a loss of physical and legal custody and will require a temporary or permanent alternative custody arrangement in order for the incarcerated parent to retain parental rights (for example, transfer of legal custody to a relative). Zealous advocacy for these clients requires a comprehensive understanding of the child protection system, including legal protections for parents, the child welfare agency's duty to make reasonable efforts to reunify the family, and the accessibility of services in the correctional system. A parent's continued involvement in his or her child's life during incarceration is essential in preventing the termination of his or her parental rights.

This chapter provides suggestions for parents' attorneys representing clients involved with the criminal justice system. Section 5.02 lays out the basic architecture of child protection proceedings as they relate to incarcerated parents, including termination of parental rights proceedings. Section 5.03 discusses special considerations for clients with concurrent criminal charges. Section 5.04 focuses on the constitutional and statutory rights of incarcerated parents. Finally, Section 5.05 is a step-by-step guide through the child protection process for parents' attorneys.

5.02 The Child Protection System and Incarcerated Parents

The permanent loss of parental rights during incarceration can occur in one of two ways. The first scenario takes place outside the child protection system when a child who is not in foster care gets adopted. These cases commonly arise when the custodial parent who is not incarcerated marries or remarries. The new spouse, the child's step-parent, then wishes to adopt the child, which requires terminating the rights of the incarcerated parent. State laws provide that, with certain exceptions, a child cannot be adopted unless the child's parent consents to the adoption. Exceptions to the consent requirement may include situations where the parent has abandoned the child, abused or neglected him, or failed to support or visit him.

The second context in which parental rights may be permanently lost is when a child is already in the custody of the state's foster care system. The state may acquire custody of the child by filing a dependency petition prior to incarceration due to alleged neglect or abuse, or because of the parent's incarceration if there is no relative or third party to assume care for the incarcerated parent's child. Once a child is placed in foster care, the ASFA timelines are invoked.

State laws pertaining to termination of parental rights and adoption were historically aimed at parents who intentionally abandoned their children and disappeared from their lives. The laws are poorly suited to deal with parents involuntarily separated from their children because of incarceration. Involuntary absence and institutional barriers to contact—both factors beyond an incarcerated parent's control—are too often misconstrued as abandonment. In both termination contexts, abandonment is a sufficient justification for terminating parental rights. At least nine states allow incarceration alone to be considered as a ground for termination. *See* Grounds for Involuntary Termination of Parental Rights, Child Welfare Information Gateway (listing Alabama, Arizona, Arkansas, Colorado, Idaho, North Dakota, Ohio, Tennessee, and Texas).

It is important to note that termination of parental rights does not always result in creating new permanent families for the children of incarcerated parents. The increase in parental rights terminations over the past generation has not led to a corresponding increase in adoptions of terminated children. When compared with other children in state care, children of incarcerated parents are more likely to remain in foster care until they "age out" of the system at age eighteen, even if their parents' rights are terminated. *See* Marilyn C. Moses, *Correlating Incarcerated Mothers, Foster Care, and Mother-Child Reunification*, 68 CORRECTIONS TODAY 98, 98 (2006) ("[C]hildren of incarcerated mothers were four times more likely to be 'still in' foster care than all other children."); *see also* Diane H. Schetky et. al., *Parents Who Fail: A Study of 51 Cases of Termination of Parental Rights*, 18 J. AM. ACAD. CHILD PSYCH. 366, 367 (1979).

To address the "legal orphan" problem, some states have passed legislation allowing for reinstatement of parental rights where parents are now in a position to care for their children. *See generally,* Lashanda Taylor, *Resurrecting Parents of Legal Orphans: Un-terminating Parental Rights*, 17 VA. J. SOC. POL'Y & L. 318 (2010). For parents who were once unable to care for their children because of their incarceration, this may provide an avenue for family restoration post-release.

5.03 Advising Parents Facing Concurrent Criminal Charges

In some cases, the events that led to a child's foster care placement also result in a criminal investigation. Representing parents in the child protection system who are also facing concurrent criminal investigations presents unique challenges. Parents risk incriminating themselves in a criminal case by making statements and admissions in the civil case. When possible, counsel should try to resolve the criminal case first so the parent can fully participate in the child protection matter with no fear of self-incrimination. However, the pendency of a criminal case has no tolling effect on the strict timelines in a child protection case. Therefore, opting to resolve the criminal matter first is often not realistic. By the time the criminal matter is resolved, the parent may have lost the necessary time and opportunity to work with the child welfare agency to demonstrate what the juvenile court must see to reunify the family.

Parents' attorneys must consider the strategic implications of a client's decision to invoke the Fifth Amendment right against self-incrimination in a child protection proceeding. The Fifth Amendment provides that no person shall be compelled to testify as a witness against himself in a criminal trial. A defendant's invocation of this right in a criminal case cannot be used to infer the defendant's guilt. This right is absolute and protects defendants at all stages of a criminal proceeding.

In civil matters, including child protection cases, the protection against self-incrimination is also available; a party may refuse to answer questions when doing so may result in incriminating the individual. However, unlike in criminal cases, a negative inference may be drawn from the decision not to testify in a civil case. *See, e.g., Mitchell v.*

United States, 526 U.S. 314, 328 (1999). In child protection proceedings, the court may consider a party's assertion of the Fifth Amendment privilege and refusal to answer questions when evaluating the party's testimony and position.

In *Baltimore City Department of Social Services v. Bouknight*, the Supreme Court carved out an exception to a parent's otherwise absolute right to invoke the Fifth Amendment privilege in a child protection case. 493 U.S. 549 (1990). In *Bouknight*, an infant was removed from his mother's care due to allegations of physical abuse, including broken bones. After being adjudicated as a child in need of protection or services, the child was returned to his mother. For eight months, the mother failed to comply with the conditions of the protective order, and the court ordered the child to be removed again. In response, the mother refused to produce the child, or reveal where the child could be found, invoking her Fifth Amendment right against self-incrimination.

The Court grappled with whether the mother could invoke the Fifth Amendment privilege against self-incrimination to resist an order of the juvenile court to produce the child. The Court concluded that she could not. The government's right to information and to access the child superseded the mother's right against self-incrimination. *Id.* at 561. Thus, although parents generally maintain a right to invoke the Fifth Amendment in civil cases, narrow exceptions may exist when the child's safety is in question.

When a parent has committed the acts alleged in both the child protection Petition and the criminal complaint, the parent may want to admit to the allegations in the child protection Petition and move forward with services in order to eventually be reunited with his children. This may occur in cases of physical abuse, sexual abuse, or the failure of a parent to protect a child from serious abuse by another person. In these cases, parents' attorneys must be cognizant of how an admission to facts in the child protection Petition will affect the parent's concurrent criminal charges. Sometimes, when a parent pleads guilty to the criminal charges, cooperation with the child protection agency and completion of the case plan may actually help mitigate the parent's criminal sentence.

It is critical to remember that a criminal conviction for abuse or neglect alleged in a child protection Petition establishes the abuse or neglect in the child protection proceeding because the standard of proof in a criminal case is higher than the standard in a civil case. The converse, however, is not true. An admission to allegations of abuse or neglect in the child protection proceeding cannot prove the allegations in a criminal trial. Such an admission often will not meet the statutory elements needed to prove the crime. But statements made during a child protection hearing may be used against a parent in a criminal case. Some prosecutors may agree not to use admissions concerning the charged crime if they were made in therapy or as part of reunification services. Parent's counsel will want to negotiate these issues with the prosecutor or agency attorney.

One strategy to limit a parent's potential exposure to criminal liability is to amend the child protection Petition to remove problematic language. To move forward with the child protection case, the attorney for the child welfare agency may be willing to compromise. To the extent possible, counsel is advised to support the finding in the child protection case on statements by someone other than the parent, such as a caseworker or police officer. Statements directly admitting to the crime should be removed. When amending a Petition, counsel should be strategic in selecting statutory provisions (as part of a negotiated deal with opposing counsel). For example, admitting to a statutory provision about general neglect or an inability to parent appropriately rather than a provision that includes language about physical abuse or injurious behavior can make a significant difference in the criminal case. Parents' attorneys should confer with their clients' criminal defense counsel when considering how to amend language in the child protection petition to minimize potential liability for the client in the criminal case.

In addition to amending the Petition, parents' attorneys may limit a client's statements at the admission or plea hearing. Counsel may also consider having a "paper trial" based solely on the allegations in the Petition in order to avoid the need for a parent to make admissions on the record. This will usually allow the parent to move forward with the court-ordered case plan. In cases involving allegations of physical violence such as assault or criminal sexual misconduct, it may be necessary to delay any admission in the child protection case until the criminal matter is resolved. Such serious charges often result in a petition requesting the immediate termination of a parent's rights, in which case reasonable efforts may not be required. For these parents, having all options available at the criminal trial (with no interference or findings from the child protection case) will put them in the best position to contest the criminal charges.

5.04 Rights of Incarcerated Parents

Like all parents, incarcerated parents maintain the right to direct the "care, custody, and control of their children" which "does not evaporate simply because they have not been model parents." *Santosky v. Kramer*, 455 U.S. 745, 753 (1982). Courts across the country have afforded both constitutional and statutory rights specifically to incarcerated parents. Some of these are detailed below.

5.04(a) Right to Participate

Incarcerated parents have a right to participate in child welfare proceedings. Whether an incarcerated parent has the right to be physically present at the proceedings varies by jurisdiction. In making this determination, courts have considered such factors such as the delay resulting from securing the incarcerated parent's attendance; the need for a prompt disposition; the amount of time the proceeding has been pending before the juvenile court; the expense to the state of transporting the parent; the inconvenience or detriment to the parties or witnesses; the potential danger or security risk posed by the parent's release from custody or confinement to attend the hearing; the reasonable availability of the parent's testimony through means other than attending the hearing; and the best interests of the children. *See, e.g., In re R.G.*, 165 Ill. App. 3d 112, 518 N.E.2d 691, 166 Ill. Dec. 69, *app. denied*, 119 Ill.2d 557, 522 N.E.2d 1256 (1988); *In re B.L.E.*, 768 S.W.2d 86 (Mo. Ct. App. 1988); *In re A.B.*, 239 Mont. 344, 780 P.2d 622 (1989).

Denying an incarcerated parent the right to be physically present raises two distinct procedural issues: whether the alternative to physical presence adopted by the courts permits the parent to participate meaningfully and effectively at the hearing; and whether the fact-finder is given adequate evidence to be able to assess the parent's demeanor and credibility, the quality of the parent-child relationship, and other intangible factors in determining whether the parent is unfit.

Even where courts have found that incarcerated parents lacked an absolute right to attend a hearing, courts have consistently held that parents must have an opportunity to meaningfully participate in each hearing. Alternative ways for a parent to participate include by phone, submitting deposition testimony, having an opportunity to review the records and transcript and to present rebuttal evidence, and having the opportunity to consult counsel about cross-examining witnesses.

The bottom line is that counsel must protect the parent's right to meaningfully participate in all hearings, whether in person or through other means.

5.04(b) Right to Visit

Barring a finding of harm to the child, incarcerated parents retain the right to visit their children. Visiting with incarcerated parents is presumed to be in the child's best interest. *See, e.g., McCurdy v. McCurdy*, 173 Ind. App. 437, 441, 363 N.E.2d 1298, 1301 (1977). Yet many parents in prison never receive the opportunity to visit their children who are in foster care. The distance between the prisoner and his family, along with the high costs of transportation, food, and lodging, and the time involved, make it difficult for families to take children to visit their parents. These problems are exacerbated when parents are incarcerated long distances from their homes. Unfortunately, state correctional officials are not required to consider how an inmate's placement will affect family relationships when determining where he or she will be detained. In addition, penal institutions have the authority to limit or prohibit visitation where doing so is deemed necessary for prison security.

Statutes, case law, and agency policies govern visits between incarcerated parents and children. Several states have enacted laws that specifically address visitation with incarcerated parents. For example, in Oklahoma, visitation must be offered to incarcerated parents through the correctional system. *See* OKLA. ADMIN. CODE § 340:75-6-45 (2013) ("When the child's parent is incarcerated, services and visitation, when appropriate, are attempted through the correctional system."). In New Hampshire, visitation decisions are made after decision makers consider the best interests of the child, the reason for and length of the incarceration, and any unique issues arising because of the incarceration. N.H. Rev. Stat. Ann. § 461-A:1. Of all the states, California and New York offer the most extensive and specific statutory guidance for the rights of incarcerated parents. In these states, unless the court determines by clear and convincing evidence that visitation would be detrimental to the minor child, visitation between incarcerated parents and their children is mandated. *See* Cal. Welf. & Inst. Code § 361.5(e)(1)(2013); N.Y. Soc. Serv. Law § 384-b (2013).

Parents' attorneys may face judges who believe that visits between an incarcerated parent and his child are inherently harmful. Counsel can rebut those assumptions by noting that visiting rooms are often full of families and children, are heavily monitored, and are similar to a crowded restaurant or airport waiting terminal—places we frequently bring young children. Faced with arguments that visiting a prison will be too traumatic for a child, a parents' attorney can argue that visits can help mitigate the effects of the separation trauma children are already experiencing. Research on visits in prison suggests that visits can have positive outcomes for children but that children should have support before and after the visits. Support can include preparing for visits with child-appropriate reading materials, encouraging the child to prepare a list of things to talk about ahead of time, and making sure the child visits with a trusted adult who can discuss the experience with them afterward.

5.04(c) Right to Services

States are split on the types of efforts child welfare agencies must make to reunify the incarcerated parent with the child. One group of states provides no specific statutory guidance as to whether agencies must make reasonable efforts to reunify incarcerated parents. Presumably, in these states, child welfare agencies must make the same efforts for incarcerated parents as they would for any other parent. *See, e.g., In re Mason*, 486 Mich. 142, 153, 486 N.W.2d 747, 752 (2010) (finding that the court is required to facilitate the father's participation in each proceeding via phone and the agency is required to discuss with prison officials the services available in prison that would meet the requirements of a case plan).

In a second group of states, a parent's incarceration itself, the severity of the offense, or the length of incarceration may be considered as an aggravated circumstance that relieves child welfare agencies of their reasonable efforts requirement. *See, e.g.*, Colo. Rev. Stat. §§ 19-1-115(7)(a), 19-3-604(1)(b)(III) (2013) (reasonable efforts are not required when a parent has subjected a child to aggravated circumstances, which can include a parent's long-term confinement (not eligible for parole for at least six years, or three years if the child is younger than six years-old)); Fla. Ann. Stat. § 39.806 (a conviction and incarceration for a felony, and failure of the parent to arrange for the child's care is grounds for terminating parental rights). *See also* Alaska Stat. §§ 47.10.011; 47.10.080; 47.10.086; 47.10.088 (2013).

Finally, a third group of states enacted laws that mandate agencies to make reasonable efforts to reunify incarcerated parents with their children. In California, for instance, statutes specify that reasonable efforts must be provided to incarcerated parents. California recognizes the unique position that incarcerated parents are in, and creates concrete, workable options for incarcerated parents. Specifically, when counseling or other treatment services are ordered as part of a case plan, an incarcerated parent cannot be penalized for failing to participate in those services if the correctional facility does not provide access to the treatment services ordered by the court. CAL. WELF. & INST. CODE § 361.5(a)(3) (2013).

Besides mandating that services be offered to incarcerated parents, California law allows courts to extend the time for an incarcerated parent to complete services for up to eighteen months if the court finds there is a substantial probability that the child will be returned to the parent within the extended time period, or reasonable services have not been provided. In making the decision about whether to extend the time for reunification, courts must consider special circumstances of incarcerated or institutionalized parents, including any barriers to the parent's access to services and the ability to maintain contact with the child. Additionally, court-ordered reunification services may be extended for up to twenty-four months for parents recently discharged from incarceration who are making significant progress in establishing a safe home for the child's return. This extension can be granted if the court finds it in the child's best interest and there is a substantial probability that the child will be returned to the parent within the extended time period. *Id.* at §§ 361(a)(4), 366.22(b) (2013).

New York statutes take a similar approach and ask courts to consider how a parent's incarceration affects his ability to participate in case plan requirements and how special consideration may need to be given to overcome obstacles posed by incarceration. *See* N.Y. SOC. SERV. LAW § 384-b 7(f)(5) (2013). The agency must arrange for a child to visit the parent within the correctional facility, including transporting the child to the facility and providing services to resolve any issues that may impair the parent's ability to maintain contact with the child. The agency must also provide information to the incarcerated parent on his legal rights and obligations and on services available in the community to help develop a meaningful parent-child relationship, including whenever possible, transitional and family support services in the community to which the parent shall return.

Laws like those in California and New York create models for how jurisdictions should address the rights of incarcerated parents. In states with similar laws, parents' attorneys can use the language of the statute to advocate for services for their incarcerated clients. However, in states without such statutes, attorneys must rely on general reasonable efforts statutory provisions to ensure that their clients receive the services they are statutorily entitled to.

5.05 Helping Incarcerated Parents Navigate Multiple Systems

Representing parents involved in both the child protection and criminal justice systems can be challenging given the multiple governmental agencies with control over the families, the different courts involved, strict case processing time frames, and statutory nuances. What follows is a step-by-step guide through the different phases of both cases, with tips for parents' counsel at each one.

5.05(a) Arrest Phase

Typically, parents' attorneys meet their clients after there has been an arrest; often the parents' children will have already been removed from the arrested parent's care. After a client has been arrested, both the criminal defense and child protection attorney must advise the client not to discuss the pending criminal charges with anyone, including child welfare agency employees, the child's lawyer or guardian ad litem, and jail staff.

Some parents' time in jail or prison after an arrest will be brief. In these situations, attorneys for parents can advocate for family group conferencing or other informal mechanisms to develop safety plans for the children. These plans may include placing children temporarily with extended family through an informal arrangement or power of attorney or having family members temporarily live in the parent's home to care for the children while the parent is in custody. Identifying family or kinship placements for children at the time of arrest can prevent a child's placement in foster care and promote stability and familiarity for the child. Both sides of a child's family should be explored as kinship placements.

Counsel should advocate for immediate visitation between parent and child, which may be possible in some facilities. Additionally, parent's counsel must immediately explore options for services for the incarcerated client since some jails may offer services like Narcotics Anonymous or Alcoholics Anonymous meetings or mental health treatment.

5.05(b) Sentencing Phase

Because of the strict timelines that apply in child protection cases, parent's counsel must work with the defense attorney to try to shorten the length of a criminal sentence. This may include providing information to the criminal defense attorney to use in a sentencing proceeding that explains to the judge that the parent needs to be back in the community as soon as possible to care for their children. An example of this would be including specific information about the impact of parent's incarceration on the family and children in the pre-sentencing report. Alerting the defense attorney and sentencing judge to the parent's case plan in the dependency case and the need to complete services quickly may help reduce the criminal sentence. Evidence of the parent's compliance and cooperation with the case plan may also be helpful during the criminal sentencing phase.

For parents who may be sentenced to prison for a longer period of time, advocating for placement at a facility as close to their children as possible is important. Again, parent's counsel should work with the defense attorney to ensure that the court or corrections department knows of the impact that the incarceration will have on the children and the need for continued contact.

5.05(c) Incarceration Phase

After the parent enters prison, counsel should immediately contact the parent's prison caseworker, either via letter or phone call, to let them know about the ongoing child protection case. Counsel should follow up by sending the caseworker a release of information form for the incarcerated parent to sign so that counsel can have regular contact with the prison caseworker, to update him about the status of the child protection case and to confirm the availability of and compliance with services in the prison.

Counsel should also ensure that the names of potential visitors are on the approved visitor's list. If relatives, friends, or case workers will be transporting the children to the prison for visits, these individuals must be pre-approved to be placed on the list. It may take months for individuals to receive the approval to visit the incarcerated parent, so this process must be started immediately.

Counsel should ensure that their clients can visit with their children as soon as possible. For young children, this may prove challenging, depending on the visiting arrangements at the prison. While some women's prisons have child-friendly visitation areas, many men's facilities do not. Parent's attorneys must be persistent in advocating for regular visitation and phone contact throughout the pendency of the child protection proceedings.

Finally, when a parent enters prison and has a pending child protection matter, the parent's attorney must identify what relevant services are available to the parent at the prison. This will require obtaining lists of potential services and ascertaining when the services will be provided. An attorney can obtain information about the services by calling a prison caseworker or speaking with a deputy warden for programming or another staff member at the facility. Many prisons offer educational services and employment training that will benefit the parent in the short and long term. Informing the judge and other parties to the case about the visiting policies and available services at the prison is essential during the early court appearances in the child protection case.

5.05(d) The Dependency Court Proceeding

While a parent is incarcerated, the attorney must maintain regular contact with the parent. Typically, prisons will allow attorneys to have regular contact with their clients outside of the scheduled visitation times at the facility. Attorneys can maintain contact with their clients in person, by phone, or in some facilities, via email. Deciding how communication will occur, setting up a communication schedule, and maintaining constant contact with the client is crucial.

In addition to having regular contact with their clients, parents' attorneys must ensure that the parent is able to fully participate in all court proceedings. In some jurisdictions, judges prefer for inmates to appear via phone. However, appearing in person for a hearing puts parents in the best overall position to advocate for themselves and fully participate in their case. Therefore, using the laws and policies in their jurisdiction, counsel should push systems to arrange for their clients to be physically present at all hearings.

Parents' attorneys must also advocate for regular contact between agency caseworkers and parents. Such contact is vital in ensuring that the agency knows about the progress the incarcerated parent is making in prison and is knowledgeable about the services that are available. *See* Office of the Assistant Secretary for Planning and Evaluation Research Brief, The National Evaluation of the Responsible Fatherhood, Marriage, and Family Strengthening Grants for Incarcerated and Re-Entering Fathers and their Partners Parenting from Prison: Innovative Programs to Support Incarcerated and Reentering Fathers (U.S. Dep't Health & Human Services 2010). This brief provides examples of innovative parent engagement and visitation programs for incarcerated fathers and their families. If an agency caseworker is not maintaining regular contact with the parent, and not making reasonable efforts to reunify the family, the parent's attorney must notify the court and other parties about this on the record or in writing.

In court, parents' attorneys must create a detailed record to support their client's position with regard to case planning services and visitation in prison. This record is important throughout the proceeding but is critically important at the dispositional phase of the case, where orders related to the case plan and visitation are entered. The information that the parent's attorney has gathered from the prison should be presented to the court at all stages of the case, but particularly at the dispositional phase.

When the prison cannot offer services to the parents, counsel must raise this issue in the dependency proceeding. Parents' attorneys should prevent their clients in prison from agreeing to complete services in a court-ordered case plan when those services are not offered at the prison. Agreeing to a case plan that contains services that are unavailable will only set the parent up to fail. Conversely, counsel should let the court know what services are available and request that those services be made a part of the court-ordered case plan.

Advocating for court-ordered visitation for a parent in prison can be challenging because the judge or the agency may not support it. However, maintaining parent-child relationships is critical in preventing the termination of the incarcerated parent's rights and increasing the likelihood of successful reunification after release. Parents' attorneys should stress the positive benefits for the client's children. Visits can help maintain the parent-child relationship and reduce a child's sense of abandonment. Visitation can also help preserve the child's sense of belonging as part of a family.

Even when in-person visits cannot occur, the availability of new technology has led to a significant improvement in the ability of incarcerated parents to stay in touch with their children. Once restricted to sending letters and making expensive phone calls, incarcerated parents can now use email, Skype, and video and audio recording to stay connected with their children. Across the nation, programs provide incarcerated parents with the opportunity to select a donated children's book and record themselves reading the book aloud. The book and tape are then mailed to the inmate's children. These are but a few examples of the types of increased contact incarcerated parents can have with their children because of improved technology.

Some judges and county workers may remain unconvinced about the need for any contact between children and their incarcerated parents. In these situations, it is especially important to advocate for regular visitation to create a detailed record of a parent's desire for contact and visitation with his or her children, which may become important if the matter is appealed.

5.05(e) Concurrent Planning Phase

If a parent faces a lengthy prison sentence or cannot be reunified with his or her child after prison for other reasons (including those situations when the child or another child was the victim of a crime the parent committed), the parent's attorney should develop and advocate for a concurrent plan other than reunification. To do so, the parent's attorney must identify family members or friends who may be able to care for the parent's children in the long term through a custody arrangement, a guardianship, or an adoption.

Incarcerated parents may be reluctant to give caseworkers or the court the names and contact information of family or friends who may be able to care for the child. Parents may be distrustful of the agency and courts or may not want their family to know about the child protection case. In these situations, the parent's attorney must help the client understand the benefits of identifying extended family members or friends as possible placements of their children. When reunification is not possible, parents can maintain relationships more easily if the children are placed with family. If children are placed with relatives, the termination of their parental rights is not required under ASFA, even if the child has been in foster care for fifteen out of the preceding twenty-two months.

5.05(f) The Permanency Phase—The Termination Trial

When a termination of parental rights Petition is filed and the parent remains incarcerated, a parent's attorney faces a significant challenge in preventing the court from terminating the client's parental rights. As previously discussed, in most jurisdictions, although incarceration alone may not be enough to terminate a parent's rights, a parent's incarceration in addition to other enumerated factors may be.

Chapter 14 discusses strategies to defend clients facing termination of their parental rights. Parents' counsel should focus on four overarching issues when representing an incarcerated parent at the termination of parental rights stage. First, was the parent sufficiently involved in the child protection process? Did the court provide him with proper notice of all proceedings and was he able to appear at hearings? Second, did the agency make reasonable efforts to reunify him with his child? Third, did the parent make arrangements for the child to live with a relative during his period of incarceration? If so, in some jurisdictions, this is an affirmative defense to a termination of parental rights petition. Finally, is there a sufficient bond between the incarcerated parent and the child to warrant a finding that termination is not in the child's best interest? Other factors relevant to the best interest determination may include the age of the child, the offense committed by the parent that led to the incarceration, and the financial support that the parent is providing to the child, which may be cut off if parental rights are terminated. Counsel must explore all arguments that termination may not be in the best interests of the child.

5.06 Conclusion

The prevalence of parental incarceration is taking its toll on families. Parents who are in prison are at risk of losing custody of their children because of their involvement with the child protection system. In situations involving extreme physical or sexual violence, it is clearly not in the best interests of the child to remain with a perpetrator. But the vast majority of child protection cases are not so straightforward. Lawyers representing parents facing criminal charges or parents who are already incarcerated must understand the unique challenges present and zealously advocate for the parents' rights and interests.

These attorneys must remember the ultimate goal of family reunification but also recognize that in cases involving lengthy period of incarceration, a concurrent goal other than reunification may be necessary. The challenges and difficulties involved in this representation are many: multiple agency coordination and interaction; institutional resistance and a dearth of services for incarcerated parents; deadlines, distances, and unfavorable nuances in the law. However, the potential for preserving the sacred bond of family is equally impressive. All parents in prison deserve zealous representation in the fight to preserve relationships with their children.

CHAPTER 6

Achieving the Client's Objectives to Shorten Foster Care Stays and Reunify the Family: Advocating for Supportive Placements, Appropriate Services, Parenting and Visiting Time, and Leveraging Opportunities for Advocacy at Conferences and Meetings Outside the Court Process

*Center for Family Representation**

6.01 Advancing the Client's Goals Beyond Defending the Petition

Respondents in neglect or dependency proceedings commonly have multiple objectives that go well beyond defending the allegations against them. Many recognize their need for help and, at least temporarily, that they cannot parent their children in the way they would hope. Especially when children are ordered into foster care, the parents' goals commonly include remaining meaningfully involved in their children's lives even when they are not in their custody, securing services they feel are helpful, and ensuring that they will not find themselves in family court again. In these situations, parents deserve a particular kind of representation in addition to the traditional one that investigates the

* *Richard Barinbaum, Jillian Cohen, Michele Cortese, Payal Dalal, Elizabeth Fassler, Maura Keating, Jennifer Miller, Sandy Rosin, and Christine Zielinski*

legal and factual claims to identify the strongest basis for defeating the Petition. They deserve a set of professionals who will work closely with them throughout the process.

This chapter, written by several of the staff at the Center for Family Representation in New York City (CFR), describes what we have learned from our interdisciplinary practice. Three things, in particular, stand out:

A. Parents' attorneys need to develop creative legal and advocacy strategies to pursue their clients' objectives that are not exclusively allegation-based. Usually, they can formulate these strategies by relying on statutes, regulations, and policy directives issued by state and city child welfare agencies.
B. When parents' attorneys defend the allegations and focus on these additional objectives, they often help parents engage with the child welfare and family court systems in a way that proves productive for the families. It helps the parents stay better engaged with their attorneys and it allows the "system" to view them more fairly. Their cases progress more quickly, and they often achieve shorter time frames to reunification and even total avoidance of the removal of their children from their care.
C. When children return home more quickly and parents can access meaningful resources, attorneys often achieve litigation settlements that are more favorable than initially offered by the child welfare agency. Additionally, parents are less likely to have a repeat case.

Since 2007, we have been tracking the results of our work. From that year on, the median time the children of CFR's clients have been in foster care is just over 4.5 months; this compares with a New York City median of 11.5 months before CFR began its high-volume practice of representing indigent respondents. Thirty-seven percent of the children of CFR's clients returned home within six months compared to 28 percent statewide; 52 percent returned home within one year compared to 43 percent statewide. Eight percent of our client's children reentered care at one point, compared to 15 percent statewide. CFR annually achieves an average dismissal rate of 33 percent compared to 11 percent before we began our high volume practice. The majority of these dismissals are on consent, without an adjudication of neglect (referred to as "adjournments in contemplation of dismissal" in New York State), and as a result of the family's stability over time.

This chapter will focus on advocacy strategies that practitioners can pursue both in and out of court. It will stress the importance of (i) ensuring that when a child is initially placed, the foster parent (or other alternative custodian) is supportive of the child's attachment to the parent; (ii) advocating that parents whose children are in foster care can visit often and for as long as possible, with as little supervision as possible; (iii) ensuring that these visits progress over time and are organized around activities that mimic family life; (iv) leveraging every opportunity to advocate at out-of-court conferences for the parent based on his or her multiple objectives; and (v) ensuring that recommended services are based on the parent's strengths, abilities, and needs, and are not duplicative, formulaic, or otherwise inappropriate.

6.02 Using Administrative Regulations and Policies to Help the Client, Paying Careful Attention to All That Is Being Done by the Child Welfare Agency

Attorneys and all members of the parent representation team (e.g., social workers and parent advocates) need to become well versed in the administrative rules and regulations and the official policies of the child welfare agency. These less-studied regulations can be invaluable tools when advocating for services, supportive placements, and better visits for a parent. Judges and agency case planners want to be confident they have the authority to grant applications and requests made by parents, especially when they may be rare in local practice. Although it may be daunting to cut a path through often dense regulations, being able to cite them as a source for the authority to secure something a parent wants will make it more likely that the decision maker agrees to abide by the request, which, in turn, will reap rewards for clients. Administrative regulations and policies of child welfare agencies address a broad set of areas that are of great importance to parents in dependency cases, including visiting, placement, housing benefits, and preventive services.

Regulations typically detail the obligations that government agencies owe to families and set forth not only the duties of foster care and child protective agencies in executing the law, but also the source of the money for them to do so. Whether in an oral application or written motion in court, or at an out-of-court conference, explicit reference to regulations by parents' attorneys and advocates supports a legal architecture for arguments regarding placement, visiting, services, conferences, and other areas of critical importance in dependency matters. It also often leads to a deeper understanding of particular issues. There is no substitute for knowing, for example, what the Agency's legal obligations toward the parent are when parents need suitable housing. Attorneys and advocates should be creative with all regulations a jurisdiction has to offer and should research the extent to which regulations are considered to have the force and effect of law in their particular state.

Although administrative directives, memos, policies, and guidelines do not have the force of law, they represent the state or local social services district's interpretation of best practices and legal obligations, and they can be as useful and persuasive as statutes and regulations in convincing a judge or a caseworker to move on an application. Such policies can be found on many state and county social service department websites, and cover an array of topics such as visiting, working with parenting youth, consenting to the administration of medication, assisting parents and children with mental health diagnoses, and housing subsidies.

Regulations and administrative directives narrow the broad statutory concepts, such as "reasonable efforts" from the federal Adoption and Safe Families Act (ASFA) and "diligent efforts" or "preventive services" from state statutes. These concepts are generally defined not only as services that may prevent entry or reentry into foster care but also that minimize time in foster care. Although they commonly expand on what a social services district or agency has the authority to do rather than what it must do, these regulations and directives provide the means by which an attorney or advocate may develop and fine-tune case theory regarding litigation or in seeking orders for a client's benefit. For instance, regulations regarding the provision of therapy as a preventive service may help an attorney formulate a case theory regarding what constitutes "reasonable efforts" by the Agency to advance a permanency goal of return to parent. They may further assist in determining what evidence is needed to support applications made in court or at a conference, for preparation for the examination of witnesses, and for the writing of an affirmation or affidavit. Applying regulations and guidelines to advocate at agency conferences is not so different than in court. Despite a local district's efforts to train its many actors, conference participants may not have a detailed understanding of their authority or obligations, and many case planners are open to diplomatically presented arguments regarding the complicated legal construct in which they operate.

In crafting applications and queries based on regulations, administrative directives, policies, guidelines, and memos, parents' attorneys and advocates should bear the following in mind:

1. Start with the "reasonable efforts" language in ASFA and the sections of the local dependency statutes. Under most circumstances, "best interests of the child" language can be included. Also look to statutes in the jurisdiction that give the court broad authority to fashion remedies or direct social services officials to take action to promote the family's interests.
2. Argue that the act contemplated by the regulation is a reasonable effort that the Agency must make toward the statutory goal. For example, regulations may support a parent's preference for his or her children to be placed with their godparent rather than a relative due to the godparent's proximity to the children's afterschool program, and if this program is one in which the child would continue upon return, pursuing the placement should be deemed a necessary reasonable effort. Likewise, when a very young child goes into care, assigning a visit host who can ensure that a parent can visit multiple times per week is a reasonable effort to further that child's developmental ability to stay bonded to the parent.
3. Be ready to present evidence in support and always have copies of any relevant regulations and guidelines to submit to the court, opposing counsel, agency personnel, and conference participants. In the example above, this might include regulations regarding efforts the Agency must make to maintain a continuity of services for

children, who have been removed from their parent. It may also require an affidavit from the godparent or even having him or her come to court to testify.

4. Provide documentation that supports the factual scenario the parent is promoting. In the placement scenario regarding the godmother, distributing copies of a letter from the director of the afterschool program along with cited authority will assist in promoting the parent's position, whether in a conference or in court.
5. Consider supplying a prepared draft of an order to the court that cites the authority for the relief sought. If the judge appears uncertain how to proceed, ask that the Agency be given the time to "explore" the provision of the service or accommodation and report back to the court by a set date, close in time. Very often, if the application is deemed reasonable, the Agency uses this extra time to find ways to agree.

In combination with broader statutory authority, regulations and administrative policies and guidelines can help make effective applications regarding the myriad needs of parents, including housing, visitation, transportation to visits and appointments, foster care placements, and services. Begin by becoming comfortable with the argument architecture for one or two areas covered by regulations and other policies. Then create a brief script that will facilitate obtaining successful outcomes for clients. Often, advocacy based on regulations and non-statutory authority leads to clients obtaining more natural parenting time and services truly tailored to their needs. Such results exponentially increase the chances of a favorable outcome, such as a desired settlement or a speedy reunion.

The assistance—or lack thereof—that agency and district personnel provide parents and their families is critical at all stages of dependency matters. Attorneys and advocates cannot afford to wait until the adjudication stage, permanency hearings, or filing of termination petitions to obtain updates from their clients and institutional actors. Counsel should regularly seek updated case records from opposing counsel, and advocates should consistently check in with case planners. Anyone working with a parent should routinely ask him or her what the Agency or district personnel has been doing to effectuate the service plan. Conferences present an ideal opportunity to assess whether "reasonable efforts" are being exerted by the Agency.

Practitioners should regard an Agency's ASFA obligations as far more than the mechanism by which it and the local district receive federal funding; efforts that are "reasonable" under ASFA assist clients and their families in achieving their ultimate goals. Arguments based on regulations and other administrative guidelines increase the odds of obtaining legal findings of "no reasonable efforts," and this may thwart the Agency from successfully alleging the diligent-efforts prong of a termination of parental rights cause of action.

6.03 Exploring and Securing a Placement Option That Is Supportive of the Parent's Relationship with the Children and Keeps the Children Well Connected to People and Services in Their Community of Origin

Finding an appropriate placement for children entering foster care is vital in dependency cases. Attorneys and advocates for parents, along with children's attorneys and case planners from child welfare agencies, should invest significant time, effort, and creativity to locate and secure placements that minimize the disruption to children's lives and help the children stay connected to parents, extended family, friends, teachers, and their communities. Moreover, when a parent's attorney (as opposed to a case planner or guardian ad litem) stresses the importance of minimizing disruption for the child, it reminds the court and every actor that the parent is always the person most invested in the child's well-being.

When children enter foster care, parents' attorneys and social workers should advocate for a placement that is supportive of the parent's relationship with the children and keeps the children well-connected to people and services in their community of origin. Families experience multiple disruptions when children enter foster care, and children are often confused as to why they have been moved to a new home. During this fragile time, it is crucial that children maintain as much continuity in relationships and routines as possible. Placement in the same community or neighborhood will ease the transition by making it more likely for children to remain in the same school, day care, or community groups and with the same physicians, therapists, and other service providers. Although these community supports cannot erase the painful experience of removal, they can help maintain a sense of normalcy for children and ease the transition to foster care and the transition home.

Importantly, such placements not only support children but also help keep parents engaged in the court and child welfare process. When parents fear that a foster parent is not attending to their children's needs or is changing cherished routines, they can become overly distracted by these concerns. Parents may understandably be invested in keeping their children in the same school or day care and connected to familiar adults, even when they are in foster care. When this is not possible, parents may experience heightened anxiety and anger. Every parent knows that disruption in a child's life can cause great stress, but when a child is placed in a home or environment with which a parent is wholly unfamiliar, the parent may develop acute concerns about the child's care and safety and the child's level of attachment to the foster family. Any or all of these concerns may impede a parent's progress in various critical aspects of the case, such as productively participating in mandated services or engaging well at visits.

For these reasons, from the onset of a case, parents' attorneys and social workers should advocate for placing children with people who have a significant relationship with the family and a significant investment in supporting the child and parent's attachment. Counsel should ask their clients who in their families and community networks may be a resource for placement. When contemplating resources, parents should look beyond blood relatives:

- Is there a godparent, neighbor, teacher, or parent of a child's friend who may be available?
- Who is most willing and able to permit the parent and child to spend time together in a way that is most natural and family-oriented?
- Is there a non-biologically related adult ("fictive kin") who can receive foster care subsidies that will enable him or her to take temporary care of the child?

Parents and their advocates should consider the following:

- Does the person have room in his or her home to accommodate the child or children?
- Can the respondent parent move out of his or her home so children may remain under the temporary care of a different adult with whom they are familiar?
- Does the person have child protective or criminal history?
- Does the person have the ability and willingness to support the reunification of the parent and children?
- Will the person host visits with the parent in his or her home?
- What is the person's relationship with the child?
- Does the person require foster care funding or can they maintain children in their home without financial assistance?

Whenever considering possible placement resources, parents' advocates should strive to ensure that these potential caregivers understand and can fulfill their responsibilities as foster parents or placement resources. For instance, they should know that their home will be subject to increased scrutiny and that they will be expected to transport children to visits, services, and possibly to court appearances and appointments with the children's attorneys.

When the family court determines that children cannot return home within a time frame in accordance with permanency guidelines, ensuring that children are placed with kin (fictive or otherwise) may lead to an outcome far preferable to a termination of parental rights, such as custody or guardianship. Because of the importance of placing children with family in their community, focusing on potential placement resources should not be limited to the beginning phase of a case. Even when children cannot be placed with someone committed to the parent's long-term interests when the case starts, counsel should keep speaking with appropriate and supportive resources throughout the life of the proceeding, in case someone's capacity or willingness to care for the child has changed. By the same token, the relationship between a parent and a caregiver can deteriorate over time, and for this reason, counsel should always ask the client whether the client believes there is some change that needs to be considered.

Regardless of whether children are placed in kinship settings, regular meetings between parents and foster parents are useful tools to promote healthy transitions into and out of foster care. Parents can offer valuable information to the foster parents regarding the children's needs and care. Mutual feedback and communication can lead to consistency for the children in both homes. Often, when parents develop a relationship with the foster parents, they are less uncertain and fearful about their children's care and can better focus on other aspects of their case.

When respondent parents are young and in foster care themselves, advocates should know that many jurisdictions allow for multiple placement options. The child may be released to the care and custody of the parenting foster youth, who maintains legal and physical custody of his or her child under the supervision of child welfare personnel while residing in a foster home, residential facility, or inpatient mother-child treatment program. The court may also order a joint placement in which the parenting foster youth and his or her child are placed in the same foster home. Although the foster parent retains responsibility for both the young parent and child, a joint placement provides opportunities for bonding and parenting. When a joint placement is not feasible for a teenaged parent who is a respondent in the case, advocates should always explore the possibility of kinship placements for them.

6.04 Advocacy on Behalf of the Parent at Conferences and Other Agency Meetings That Take Place Outside of Court: Preparing the Parent

Family-centered child welfare practice has become the norm in many jurisdictions. Child protective investigators and service providers increasingly involve families directly in meetings to formulate the safety and service plans that courts then often adopt as mandates for parents in dependency proceedings. These out-of-court agency meetings provide important opportunities for parents, caregivers, and children to give meaningful input into the important decisions contemplated by child welfare workers and courts, such as:

- Will the family remain together?
- Is there a viable "kinship" foster parent?
- How frequently will visits occur and who will supervise them?
- What services are necessary for the family to achieve reunification?

Much critical decision making occurs outside of the courtroom in the social work and child welfare sphere. Counsel can maximize the potential benefits of having clients participate in these meetings by preparing them for meaningful involvement and by ensuring that parents do not attend these meetings without someone who can support them and help them advocate for their wishes and needs. Interdisciplinary legal representation, where attorneys and social workers or advocates work together on the legal case, allows parents to have knowledgeable advocates with them at meetings. However, an attorney does not need a social worker on staff to guarantee that clients have support at out-of-court meetings. Counsel can advise their clients and other advocates they identify, such as relatives, friends, or pastors, about what to expect and what can safely be discussed.

To prepare for the client's participation in agency meetings throughout a case, here are preliminary steps to take:

- Find out if the Agency holds family team meetings, team decision-making conferences, or other out-of-court planning meetings involving parent respondents.
- Research state regulations and administrative memos issued by the social services district to find out if counsel may attend agency conferences or what type of staff, such as a social worker or paralegal, is permitted to attend.
- Ask about the agencies' protocols for out-of-court meetings, including what documents these meetings generate.
- Ask the attorney for the social services district or Agency to notify counsel before any meetings to which the client will be invited, or ask the court to make an order that the Agency does this.
- Discuss with the client what will happen in between court appearances and make sure the client knows who may accompany him or her to conferences, what documents to bring, and the necessity of notifying counsel of the time and place of the conference so that counsel can prepare him or her before the meeting.
- Provide the client with copies of all important court orders such as orders of protection/restraining/exclusionary orders, orders about the children's placement, and orders regarding visits or services. Encourage the client to bring them to agency meetings.
- If counsel's office has social workers, advocates, interns, or other non-legal staff available to attend agency meetings, have the non-legal staff regularly contact social services district and agency personnel to find out when meetings have been scheduled.
- Help ensure prior or current service providers are also notified of meetings. If necessary, ask the court to direct that service providers be included in notifications of meetings. Families may distrust their child welfare workers, especially following the removal of children. Involving supportive service providers and family members or advocates from the community in the decision making may help address those concerns early in a case. Consider arguing that the inclusion at conferences of any other adult the parent regards as a support constitutes a "reasonable effort" toward reunification.

- Keep clients informed of mandated reporting laws so they know with whom they have confidentiality.
- Consider providing a checklist to clients when counsel first meets them so they have information regarding who can attend conferences with them, what to bring, when to call counsel with questions or for advice, and any other written information that may prepare them to maximize their participation in out-of-court events affecting their case.

6.05 Participating in and Attending Agency Meetings with the Parent

Parents' attorneys or other advocates who plan to attend agency meetings with clients should prepare in advance just as they would for a court appearance. The goals of the agency meetings include: (i) determining risk to a child who is in a parent's care; (ii) developing placement options including the exploration of placement resources; (iii) identifying services like drug programs, mental health assessments, and crisis intervention counseling for parents and family members; (iv) determining a visiting plan and the appropriate level of supervision for children placed in out-of-home care; (v) troubleshooting obstacles like lack of medical insurance and transportation; (vi) assigning tasks and timeframes for completion; and (vii) providing a blueprint for the court to determine what will be its orders. These meetings often result in a written agreement that all participating parties are asked to sign and which become part of the child welfare agency or court record.

Whether a parent attends an out-of-court meeting with an attorney, advocate, family member, friend, or alone, the following are suggestions for maximizing the likelihood that the meeting will be productive for the parent:

- Be sure that the parent knows the meeting's purpose and agenda, format, invited players and any important legal advice counsel wants the client to retain for the discussion, such as how to address any pending concurrent criminal charges or whether to submit to a drug screen.
- Discuss strategies for handling a tense meeting, a difficult worker, or for a service or visit plan that the parent feels is not helpful for his or her family.
- Prepare the parent for a candid discussion of the "allegations" or the concerns that brought the family to the attention of the child welfare system, including what counsel or the parent should say in the many instances when the parent should not discuss the allegations.
- Anticipate a reasonable service plan and know what the parent is able and willing to do so that both counsel and the parent can respond to the agency's suggestions about services.

- Help parents productively present their service needs. Often, when parents need help, they can frame the request without compromising their legal case.
- Hold the agency workers accountable for concrete tasks and time frames by asking for specific referrals and dates for completing those referrals.
- Take advantage of the meeting to ask for assistance with concrete problems, for example, medical insurance information, shelter referrals, and travel vouchers.

In our experience, the following guidelines yield productive experiences when the parent's attorney or advocate can attend conferences:

- Be knowledgeable and respectful about what is happening legally, including the current status of court orders, as this will help inform conference participants about what solutions and strategies are allowable at any stage of a case. In a social-work-focused meeting, child welfare workers may perceive attorneys as combative or unwilling to acknowledge safety concerns. Consider strategies that help facilitate the planning around services and that ensure the smooth execution of visiting plans. Model how counsel would want clients to participate without an advocate present.
- Ask clarifying questions but keep the meeting about the client and not about larger agency policies, which may be more appropriately addressed in a different venue.
- Set a date by when counsel wants to follow up to verify that the service plan is moving forward. For example: Did the agency worker make the appropriate parenting program referral by the date she committed to at the meeting? Was the client's sister explored as a placement or visiting resource in the two weeks following the meeting?
- Use counsel's experiences at the meetings to inform future clients, to create client checklists, and to hone the legal advice to give to a client attending on her own.

Traditionally, child welfare professionals made important decisions without meaningful parent or child input, and with no input from parents' attorneys. Recent national trends toward family engagement have forced jurisdictions to adopt models in which families participate in every stage of the case, most often through out-of-court agency meetings. In addition, as parents' attorneys are increasingly focused on out-of-court practices, more children are being placed with family members, more visits are happening outside of agencies, and more service plans are being tailored to families' needs.

6.06 Negotiating the Terms of Service Plans Including Services for the Child

As discussed above, more and more parents are being asked to participate in out-of-court meetings to discuss many critical issues pertaining to their cases. Services are regularly discussed at these meetings, and the *right* services play an important role in reunifying the family and possibly preventing future involvement in the child welfare system. For services to be effective, it is important that at the outset of the representation, counsel ask the parent about his or her service needs and his or her availability and willingness to participate in services. For a service plan to have a positive impact on the entire family, the plan must be meaningful, realistic, and attainable and must also build on the family's strengths. Child welfare professionals who attend these meetings might not have had an opportunity to get to know the family, especially early on, and it is therefore necessary to think critically about what is being offered and ask the question "why." Consider the following scenario.

Ms. Ortiz is a forty-five-year-old single parent of two children, Yvonne, age twelve, and Natasha, age sixteen. Child protective services removed Yvonne and Natasha from Ms. Ortiz's care after the school reported that Natasha came to school with a bruise on her leg. The report counsel has been provided also states that Ms. Ortiz abuses marijuana daily. When counsel meets with Ms. Ortiz, she explains that Natasha has been skipping classes and spending time with a twenty-year-old boy from the neighborhood. She tells counsel that on the night of the incident Natasha came home after midnight and would not tell Ms. Ortiz where she had been. The two argued and Ms. Ortiz hit Natasha with a belt. Ms. Ortiz says that she smokes marijuana once in a while and could stop using without the assistance of a program.

Ms. Ortiz has many questions and concerns about her case and is eager for her daughters to come home. Yvonne has developmental delays and attends special education classes at school. Ms. Ortiz has been actively involved in Yvonne's school. She wants to ensure that Yvonne will continue her attendance and receiving of services there. Ms. Ortiz also wants to maintain her own involvement at the school. Besides concerns regarding Yvonne's school, Ms. Ortiz, who is employed full time, is worried about losing her job due to upcoming court dates and the possibility of participating in several different services. She is willing to engage in individual therapy and family therapy with Natasha and tells counsel that she already went to see the pastor at her church to discuss the case and the issues that led up to it with him.

At the initial conference to discuss services, the foster care agency asks Ms. Ortiz to participate in parenting skills and anger management classes, an outpatient substance abuse program, and individual and family therapy with her daughters. The following are questions to consider when negotiating the terms of this service plan:

- Why are multiple services being offered to Ms. Ortiz? Are these formulaic services the Agency asks all parents to complete or are they services that will help Ms. Ortiz reunify with her daughters? Do they seem duplicative or unnecessary?
- Are the services appropriate given the family's specific issues? Why is the Agency recommending parenting skills classes and have they provided concrete reasons

for its necessity? If the class is necessary, is it specifically geared toward parenting adolescents?

- Does Ms. Ortiz need to attend an outpatient drug treatment program? Could she first receive an assessment to determine whether a program is necessary? Could she submit to random drug testing before a program is considered?
- How do these services build upon the strengths of the family? Ms. Ortiz has been actively involved in Yvonne's school and maintaining that connection is important to both Ms. Ortiz and Yvonne. Will Ms. Ortiz be able to attend meetings at school? What about school plays and field trips? Is that something that could continue?
- Could the services be consolidated? Is it possible for an individual therapist to incorporate anger management and parenting skills in individual sessions with Ms. Ortiz? Could this same therapist have collateral sessions with Natasha and Yvonne? If Ms. Ortiz is already comfortable with her pastor, is it possible for her to continue to meet with him individually? Could this also apply for family therapy if the pastor is willing to meet with the family?
- Are the service referrals in locations easily accessible for Ms. Ortiz? Since Ms. Ortiz is employed full time, could the referral for services be made to a provider who has evening or weekend hours in her community or near her job? Does Ms. Ortiz have insurance, and, if she does but it will not pay for a service, could a provider be located who provides low-cost, sliding scale, or free programs?
- Will the caseworker from the Agency make the referral for services? How will Ms. Ortiz be notified? Does the agency caseworker have Ms. Ortiz's insurance information?
- What will the service plan for the children be? How much input will Ms. Ortiz have in her children's plan? Will the girls be able to continue to participate in the same activities they were engaged in prior to their removal? Will Ms. Ortiz be able to attend any of those activities with the children?
- Are the recommended services culturally competent and sensitive? Are they in Ms. Ortiz's primary language?

Starting a dialogue with the child welfare professionals about a family's strengths would allow them to get to know a particular family better; a parent and his or her children will not just be another "case" but an individual family unit with specific strengths and needs going through a difficult time. Adding services that are not meaningful or productive would only risk making the family members less interested in participating. Talking about what is important to a family and how its members wish to move forward in their service plan would most likely lead to faster reunification.

In addition, though an attorney, advocate, or parent may propose that services be consolidated or take place at a more convenient time for the parent, child welfare personnel may disagree and continue to make referrals that interfere with work schedules and other existing obligations. Remember, even if services have not yet been ordered by the court, attorneys and advocates may make referrals to services in which their clients will engage.

Once referrals have been made, it is important that parents sign appropriate releases so that counsel can communicate with the service providers. Therapists and other providers may not understand the court process and what kind of progress the court and child welfare personnel are expecting parents to make before considering a change in placement or the visiting plan. Speaking with providers early in a case, informing them of the allegations in the legal proceeding, and explaining the kind of information that will be most effective for the court process may be hugely beneficial as the case proceeds. Letters and other reports from service providers may also save valuable time for the attorney and speed up or resolve litigation by providing the court with the needed tools to move cases toward resolution.

6.07 Advocating for Parenting Time and Visitation: Exploring Visit Hosts

Besides services, the Agency will discuss the visiting plan during the initial out-of-court meeting and at all subsequent meetings. If not explicitly raised by the court, counsel should raise visitation issues often throughout the court process, especially if visits between parents and children are agency-supervised only or otherwise restricted at the outset of a case.

Visitation plays a crucial role for the family throughout the life of a case, and research has shown that meaningful and frequent visits between parents and their children are the single best predictor of safe and lasting reunification. *See, e.g.*, Sonya J. Leathers, *Parental Visiting and Family Reunification: Could Inclusive Practice Make a Difference?*, 81 CHILD WELFARE 595 (2002). Visiting plans that allow parents to attend medical appointments and school meetings enable parents to continue to play a parenting role in their children's lives, which, among other things, may help keep them engaged in their own services. Unfortunately, the standard time allotted for visits in many jurisdictions—once every two weeks for two hours—is not nearly sufficient for parents and children to maintain meaningful and consistent relationships. Parents' attorneys and advocates should have in-depth discussions with their clients about what constitutes a meaningful visiting plan for the family. Ideally, visits should:

- *Occur with as little supervision as necessary to maintain the safety of the children.* For every visiting plan proposed by the Agency, question whether this is an appropriate plan for the parent. Visits should be unsupervised if they would not pose a risk of harm to the children. Older children may be able to visit without supervision even if the Agency feels supervision is necessary for younger children. If visits must be supervised, question why they have to take place at the Agency.

Request that visits be held in the community or under the supervision of a visit host (someone approved by the Agency to host visits between a parent and child). A visit host might be a family member, friend, teacher, pastor, or neighbor. Ask the parent to think about people in his or her life who may be a visit host and provide that information directly to the Agency so that the case planner may run a clearance of the proposed visiting resource. In New York City, the Administration for Children's Services (ACS) continues to promote a move toward increasingly reasonable and meaningful visitation for families with dependency cases. As part of these efforts, ACS undertook discussions with Agency providers and a variety of practitioners, including CFR, and promulgated guidelines that deal with visits generally as well as visit hosts specifically. *See* N.Y.C. ADMIN. FOR CHILDREN'S SERVS., A BRIDGE BACK HOME: VISIT HOST (2007) (excerpted in Appendix A to this chapter); N.Y.C. ADMIN. FOR CHILDREN'S SERVS., BEST PRACTICE GUIDELINES FOR FAMILY VISITING ARRANGEMENTS FOR CHILDREN IN FOSTER CARE (2013) (excerpted in Appendix B to this chapter).

- *Take place as frequently as possible and outside the Agency when possible.* In many jurisdictions, it is standard practice for visits to take place once a week or every other week for two hours at a time. The Agency may say they do not have the resources to supervise additional visits. Question whether there are alternatives to agency-supervised visits. For example: Do the children engage in any extracurricular activities in which the parent could participate without agency supervision? Could the parent attend medical or school appointments for the children? If the children are young, is there a plan that allows the parent to have frequent visits during the week? Is there a community organization whose services include supervising visits? Are any of the children old enough that they could safely meet their parents out in the community for a limited period without supervision?
- *Be flexible.* Explore with agency personnel whether parents may call their children or even video chat with them at an agreed upon time and location to allow for more frequent contact. If a visit host has been identified, consider whether the parent and the visit host can work out their own schedule that may allow for contact beyond the usual hours of the Agency.
- *Progress to longer visits with less supervision.* If visits start out supervised, ask the case planner about the Agency's plan for them to become less restrictive. How many supervised visits does the Agency want to assess before considering less restrictive visits? May the parent have unsupervised day, weekend or even overnight visits?
- *Be organized around activities that mimic family life.* Child welfare personnel and parents' advocates should always look for visits to take place around activities that mimic family life. If the child plays a sport or is in a school play, the parent should be allowed to attend the activity. If visits must be supervised and a visit host has been identified, could the parent go out to the movies with the child and the visit

host? These activities are not only important for the parent but also are extremely important for the child; seeing and interacting with a parent only at a child welfare agency does not allow for the bonding and attachment that an activity closely resembling family life will. This interaction is important for all children, but especially important for young children who may have had fewer opportunities to spend time with their parents in natural, non-agency settings.

Expanding the amount and length of visits should be raised at every out-of-court meeting, even if the meeting has not been convened specifically to talk about visitation. If the visiting plan has not progressed, there are many strategies a parent's attorney or advocate can use to promote more and better visiting time:

- Make clear to everyone involved that routine visiting practices amounts to preciously little time for a family. For example, a single visit once a week for one hour is fifty-two hours a year, allowing a family to be together for only a total of two days each year. This should hardly count as a reasonable or minimum amount of time.
- Argue that expanded and progressive visiting is a "reasonable effort" in support of reunification.
- Talk about visiting from a child's perspective. A younger child may not understand why he or she is only spending two hours a week with his or her parent and may have a harder time adjusting after each visit. If the child is in therapy, find out what the child's therapist thinks about increasing visits between child and parent or encourage the child welfare staff to speak to the child's therapist. Remind others in the case that a child's "negative" emotions following a visit may indicate a need to see a parent more often, not less.
- If visit hosts still have not been explored, remind others that visit hosts are often also mandated reporters, which may comfort the child welfare staff. Counsel should also strive to allow parents visiting time whenever other mandated reporters, including teachers and medical personnel, would be monitoring the visit.
- An agency may have discretion to increase or expand visiting time. If it has not exercised that discretion, find out why. Perhaps the Agency has not spoken with the parent's therapist or another service provider. Bring necessary documentation including letters from service providers, copies of relevant court orders, and printouts of helpful regulations and administrative guidelines to out-of-court meetings. If this is impossible, email any relevant information to agency staff after the meeting and consistently follow up about increasing visiting time.
- Perhaps the Agency simply has not figured out the logistics of expanding visiting time. For example, the Agency may feel stymied because the visit host works full time. Is the visit host willing to have the parent come over in the evenings or on

the weekends? These are questions the child welfare staff may not have asked, and therefore it is important that parents' advocates raise them.

If for any reason visits are not taking place because the Agency is not coordinating them, a foster parent is not bringing the children to visits, or the Agency has not approved an identified visit host, counsel should immediately contact opposing counsel and consider whether it is necessary to file a motion asking that visits resume immediately and that the parent receive makeup visits. Similarly, if the Agency is not allowing expanded visits despite a client's progress with services and despite a lack of safety concerns to the children, the attorney should file a motion to bring the matter to the court's attention.

6.08 Motion Practice and Litigation Directed Toward Improving Placement Options, Services, and Parenting and Visiting Time

6.08(a) Type of Application

Motion practice in child protective cases is a valuable and often overlooked tool. A motion is simply a written request for the court to enter an order. Each jurisdiction has specific requirements regarding the form, substance, and service, and counsel should consult the appropriate statutes or court rules before writing or filing any papers.

Written applications can take the form of a "notice of motion" or an *ex parte* motion to the court often known as an "order to show cause." A notice of motion provides the other parties with the most notice and an opportunity to be heard by the court at the same time as the moving party. A notice of motion requires the moving party to describe the relief sought supply supporting factual and procedural history and legal arguments, and assign a future court date on which the court will decide the application according to statue or court rule. Although filing the notice of motion provides notice to the other parties and places the matter on the court's calendar, it generates no order until heard by the court. In contrast, an order to show cause is an *ex parte* request for immediate interim relief. The court—not the moving party—assigns the return date at which all parties must appear to argue or litigate the ultimate relief, often the same as the requested interim relief. If the court grants the interim relief, that relief remains in effect until the adjourn date even prior to notice or the opportunity to be heard by any other party. The court will set a date by which the filing attorney must serve the order to show cause.

The decision to submit notice of motion or order to show cause depends on the following questions:

1. Does the application require the court to act quickly?
2. Does the application require prompt attention from the court or anyone else?

3. Does the client need time-sensitive relief between the date the papers are filed and the date on which the application will be heard?
4. Is the court likely to hear oral argument or rule on only the papers and those of the other parties?
5. Is the guarantee that the parent's application will be heard within a set number of days with a notice of motion more important than the possibility of the court granting the interim relief sought in an order to show cause?
6. What other issues in the case might be affected by the timing of the motion?
7. How is counsel's own schedule affected?
8. What affirmation, affidavits, or exhibits should be attached to the papers?

6.08(b) Deciding to File

Prior to putting time and energy into negotiation or motion practice, counsel must assess whether the client's position is supported by the law. In some cases, negotiation may be the best option due to a client's circumstances. Suppose the client becomes excessively anxious around court appearances or some negative development recently occurred in the client's life, like a relapse or an arrest, but the caseworker is especially supportive of the parent and likely to agree to a settlement without appearing in court. Motions are most needed when the law and facts support the parent's position but counsel is unable to get the Agency to move quickly enough. Just as in negotiation, the dynamics between parents and their caseworkers may influence the attorney's decision to file a motion. For instance, if agency personnel are overly critical or excessively disagreeable toward a parent, it is often best to ask the court for an order rather than wait for the caseworker to consent.

Creative and respectful negotiation can be a faster, more efficient strategy to advance a parent's goals than filing a motion. Negotiation can occur among caseworkers and social workers for the parents or among the attorneys. It may occur in or out of court, by email or on the phone, among the attorneys only, or with all clients present. However it is done, negotiation should be a discussion about why a party is entitled to the relief sought and whether a compromise can be reached. In the negotiation, counsel should be prepared to propose solutions that may not be precisely the requested relief in court, if the parent agrees that getting something less is acceptable. For instance, if a parent is requesting three visiting days per week instead of two, the following questions could also be entertained in reaching a resolution: Can the current weekday visits can be longer? Will someone from the Agency transport the child on a third day if the foster parent cannot do so? Can the parent visit at the foster parent's home? Can someone else approved by the Agency supervise the visits on the third day? Does the current court order allow for three visits rather than two?

Although family court practitioners may regard filing motions as too adversarial or burdensome, when negotiation efforts are unproductive, bringing a matter back to court reminds the parents, attorneys, and case planners that the court—not the case planner or the Agency—has the power to make decisions about the best interests of the children and the family.

6.08(c) Best Practices for Written Applications

Never waste time! If another attorney in the office has written a similar motion, use it as a template.

Specificity makes a motion persuasive, and counsel should avoid making vague or broad requests. For instance, if an attorney requests "unsupervised day visits," the Agency might interpret that as three hours per day while the parent believes it means eight hours. Ensure that the requested relief is such that, once granted, all parties will ascribe to it the same meaning.

A parent's attorney must have one or more conversations with the client to discern his or her precise wishes. While a parent may request more time with his or her child, the attorney must know if the client can increase visits with the children and, if so, under what parameters. In any motion, counsel should provide as much positive information as possible about the client even if it is not directly related to the disputed issue.

A motion or order to show cause should include an attorney affirmation, which is made upon personal knowledge and upon information and belief, the sources of which should be listed, and a memorandum of law supporting the request. Because the affirmation is submitted under penalty of perjury, the attorney must be clear about which statements are derived from the observations or knowledge of others. The attorney affirmation should include a general introductory statement, a factual and procedural history section, an argument section, a short conclusion, and, when filing an order to show cause, a section about the necessity for the interim relief sought.

Supporting affidavits are often either required or recommended, and counsel should consult court rules or relevant statutes to be certain what is required. Affidavits typically have an introductory paragraph to identify the affiant and his or her relation to the case. They need not restate procedural or historical facts.

Depending on the jurisdiction's rules, a parent may also submit an affidavit, prepared with counsel, about why the motion should be granted. When considering whether to attach an affidavit to a motion—especially from a client—counsel should remember any sworn statement may be used for impeachment. If a parent is requesting expanded visitation, his or her affidavit might include:

- A description of activities he or she plans to do with the children during the expanded time, such as going to the park or library, helping with homework, preparing and eating meals together, playing games, changing diapers or working on potty training, engaging children in learning to walk, talk, or count to ten.

- A statement about what the parent would agree to as a condition of the unsupervised time, such as negative drug tests, pick up and drop off at the Agency, and signing releases for the case planner to speak to service providers.
- A description of the parent's progress in his or her service plan and what he or she is learning from the services.
- A statement about why the parent believes it is best for the children to spend more time with the parent, such as the supervised visitation has been positive, the child repeatedly asks for the parent, and the parent can assist with homework.

Counsel should make motion papers user-friendly. If there are several exhibits, tab them and make sure that references to the exhibits are correct throughout the papers. In addition ask someone to read the papers to assess for technical precision and the logic and breadth of the argument. Similarly, be sure the citations comply with Bluebook or commonly used citation rules in the jurisdiction.

6.08(d) Litigating a Motion

Whether or not a motion will result in an evidentiary hearing depends on the judge and jurisdictional rules. If a motion is not settled, some judges may routinely schedule an evidentiary hearing on the matter at a later date. Other judges may ask parties to orally argue the matter on the return date. The preparation, time, and thoughtfulness that go into the affirmation, affidavits, and exhibits of a motion are rarely wasted, even when the motion is unsuccessful. At minimum, the time and effort helps counsel become more prepared for whatever contested hearings are in the future, and makes a complete record on an issue for an interim or final appeal.

6.08(e) Other Benefits of Motion Practice

One main benefit of motion practice is that it encourages settlement. Motions may make it more likely that the contested matters will be resolved by reference to legal norms, which often are helpful to parents. Additionally, motions are likely to lead to a focused conversation about the merits of the requested relief because some judges require the parties to conference the relief sought in a motion before scheduling any hearing.

An additional but often unrecognized benefit of motion practice is that seeing the argument in writing instills confidence in parents. Depending on the parent's wishes and abilities, the attorney may provide a copy of the motion to the parent, who may be inspired by the language of the law and by seeing it applied to his or her family. The parent benefits from seeing that counsel is fighting for him or her, which may positively affect the attorney-client relationship.

6.09 Working Toward Systemic Change in Practice: Building Relationships with Social Services Department and Foster Care Staff

The most important question in many child welfare cases is not whether a parent "neglected" his or her child, it is whether and when children can safely live at home with their parents. Case planners are central to determining how and when that happens. They make referrals, observe visits, and generate court reports that detail a family's progress and struggles. An effective way to achieve success in individual cases while slowly changing the child welfare landscape in the jurisdiction is by building collaborative relationships with agency case planners, supervisors, directors, managers, and policy makers.

Building relationships with front-line staff can be challenging; agency staff may not trust an attorney who advocates for a parent. Traditionally, child welfare professionals have made decisions without input from parents' attorneys, and initial reception may be cold. However, maintaining positive relationships with case planners ultimately helps the client and counsel achieve their goals.

The following are basic steps counsel can take in building positive relationships with case planners:

- Early in the case, get introduced to the case planner. If the agency lawyer does not allow communication between attorneys and case planners, explore whether counsel can reach either a formal or informal agreement that guides communication in particular areas such as visitation, services, conferences, and placement resources. In New York City, discussions among all the professionals in the system led to the development of formal rules allowing for certain kinds of communication between parents' lawyers and caseworkers, so long as the topics discussed only address details regarding the service plan and avoid discussion of the merits of charges in the petition. *See* N.Y.C. ADMIN. FOR CHILDREN'S SERVS., PROTOCOL FOR COMMUNICATION BETWEEN ACS AND PROVIDER AGENCY CASEWORKERS AND ATTORNEYS REPRESENTING CHILDREN AND PARENTS (2012) (Appendix C to this chapter).
- Find out how the case planner prefers to communicate, such as by email or phone, and act accordingly.
- Ask questions rather than directing the case planner to take certain actions. If the visits are not going well, ask why and what he or she has observed. Similarly, if a referral has not been made, ask if counsel can provide assistance. Avoid making assumptions and instead ask questions to trouble shoot challenges.
- Develop a referral list and offer information about services to case planners. If a particular therapist helped a client on another case, provide the therapist's contact information to the case planner on this case.

- Be knowledgeable about services that counsel thinks are appropriate for the family and be able to explain why they are the best services.
- If counsel attends meetings with case planners, debrief afterwards with the case planner about how the meeting went, clarify any ambiguities, and highlight the positives.
- Use plain language and stay away from legal terms, acronyms, or other terms of art with which the case planner may not be familiar.
- Attend out-of-court conferences and focus on issues that are often the most critical to successful reunification, such as visitation, placement, and realistic services that suit the family. Counsel's attendance and participation (or that of someone from counsel's office) show that counsel is thinking outside the parameters of court and is concerned about the needs of the family.
- Reframe a parent's negative behavior and build on his or her strengths. Sometimes case planners experience the worst of a parent, who may appear angry or uncooperative. Look for opportunities to point out a parent's resiliency in the face of adversity, willingness to receive help, love for his or her children, openness to new parenting techniques, or improved insight. If the parent is not participating in his or her service plan, explain to the case planner why he or she should not conclude that the parent is resistant to change. If the parent is saddled with too many appointments or tasks or there is some other explanation, find out what it is and help the case planner better understand what the parent is going through.
- Frame situations from the perspective of the needs of the children as this demonstrates counsel is thinking about the entire family. Talk about ways to improve the attachment between parent and children, including by introducing specific activities at visits and addressing the therapeutic needs of the children. Underscore how the parent desires to assist in that process.
- Do not gloss over allegations or pretend they do not exist, but talk about safety and safety planning and how the family may be reunified if certain steps are put in place.
- Keep case planners in the loop. If the parent's contact information changes and counsel has permission from the client, give that information to the case planner right away. When the parent completes a program and tells counsel but not the case planner, relay that information to the Agency or opposing counsel right away rather than waiting until court.
- Within reason, give case planners the benefit of the doubt if they make no referral or fail to schedule a visit as quickly as counsel would like. There may be many reasons for the delay including a large caseload, crises with other parents, emergency removals, non-working phone numbers, and more. When counsel contacts a case worker or his or her supervisor, focus on the needs of the family and enlisting help rather than only addressing the case planner's negligence. Zealous advocacy and holding the case planner accountable in a reasonable way are not mutually exclusive.

On a broader level, systemic changes can happen by collaborating with the department of social services in targeted areas. In New York City, there are several examples of family court practitioners coming together with the department of social services to create systemic change. In one instance, attorneys for parents and children identified mental health as an area of concern to focus collective efforts. Stakeholders across child welfare and New York City's ACS held a series of meetings and worked with attorneys and social workers for parents, children, and mental health practitioners to create a guide for child welfare professionals. *See* N.Y.C. ADMIN. FOR CHILDREN'S SERVS., PRINCIPLES TO INFORM CHILD WELFARE DECISION-MAKING REGARDING MENTAL HEALTH ISSUES (2013).

A similar process occurred with the creation of ACS's "Visitation Guidelines and the ACS Visit Host Guidelines." Parents' attorneys were crucial in developing best practices with the department around visitation and gave feedback about those policies once they were implemented. Similar efforts resulted in guidelines regarding working with young parents in out-of-home foster care, communication protocols between case planners and attorneys for parents and children, and visit hosts. These collaborations create opportunities to implement new policy and build relationships among attorneys, case planners, supervisors, and managers. They also enhance work on individual cases.

Taking the following steps can help launch the process toward larger systemic change:

- Find opportunities to connect. If there are policies being implemented by the department of social services, offer to give feedback during the development stage and again several months after implementation.
- Schedule a meeting with the department of social services to discuss common issues of concern such as visitation, domestic violence, immigration, and mental illness and make a plan of action together. Try to include professionals outside of child welfare that can improve the practice. Encourage the department to include parents and families affected by the child welfare system in policy discussions.
- Use every opportunity not only to share the parent's perspective but also to ask questions about the perspective of the department of social services and other stakeholders.
- Offer to share training opportunities with department heads or to present the "parent advocate perspective" with their new staff.

Try to develop a routine meeting with caseworkers and managers to talk about collective work on individual cases, to trouble shoot challenges, and to acknowledge success. This creates an opportunity for broader and deeper conversations about the practice.

6.10 Conclusion

In addition to vigorously investigating and defending allegations against clients, advocacy directed to achieving their multiple additional objectives serves them well. Achieving these objectives should be central to any family defense practice, especially when children enter foster care. Advocacy directed to well-suited services, meaningful visits, and placements that support family bonds is strengthened when attorneys make reasonable efforts arguments bolstered by regulations and state and county policies on best practices. Outside of court, at family team meetings or case planning sessions, attorneys can and should focus on making sure parents are well supported in conversations about what they need and what must happen for children to return home. A focus that goes beyond the allegations often leads to faster reunification, favorable court settlements, and fewer repeat investigations or court involvement for our clients. This focus has yielded many fruitful opportunities to influence child welfare practice in the areas of family visiting, teenage parents, and mental health issues, to name a few. Whether an attorney is a solo practitioner or practices with other professionals such as parent mentors or social workers, it is important to incorporate some of the approaches discussed in this chapter to help parents achieve the many goals they have for themselves and their families.

APPENDIX A TO CHAPTER 6

A Bridge Back Home: Visit Hosts New York City Administration for Children's Services Division of Family Support Services Office of Family Visiting (2007)

Background

Visiting is critical to children in foster care. Frequent and ongoing contact with family members reduces the trauma of removal for children, improves their adjustment to placement, and helps expedite permanency, regardless of whether the goal is reunification, adoption, independent living, or adult custodial care.

Visiting is also a critical element in the child welfare system's response to the Adoption and Safe Families Act (ASFA). Passed by Congress in 1997, ASFA was designed to ensure that children in foster care are either reunited with their families or found other, permanent, stable homes in a timely manner. In order to meet ASFA's time frames for permanency, it is critical that children maintain frequent contact with their families whenever it is safe for them to do so.

In August of 2006, Children's Services reissued the "ACS Best Practice Guidelines for Family Visiting Arrangements for Children in Foster Care." The guidelines addressed the increasing recognition that improved family visiting reduces the confusion and anxiety of children in foster care; is a critical factor in the safe reunification of families; and supports the achievement of another permanency arrangement when reunification is not possible. The guidelines are intended to make visiting a fruitful, family-specific, child-focused opportunity to sustain and strengthen family relationships.

The visiting guidelines direct that, whenever possible and in the child's best interest, agencies should:

(a) offer weekly visits of *at least* two hours in duration;
(b) arrange for visiting in a location *outside* the agency that is convenient for all parties;
(c) provide the *minimal* level of supervision necessary to ensure the well-being of the child; and
(d) increase the visit frequency and length in anticipation of reunification. Visits should evolve from weekly to more frequent visits of greater length, to overnight and weekend visits, leading to trial and then final discharge.

The guidelines introduce an intermediary category of supervision termed "monitored visiting," designed to offer caseworkers more options and assist the progression from a higher to a lower level of supervision. The guidelines also clarify that (contrary to common practice) *the presumption is that visits are unsupervised* unless supervision is warranted. Supervision must be justified by a safety concern and/or need for assessment. Finally, the guidelines direct agency workers to identify "significant relatives (or others)" who "can and should be considered resources for the case planner . . . they can help . . . by *hosting* parent-child visits." Research shows that visit arrangements significantly influence the quality of visits. One recent study suggested, for example, that agency visiting spaces may be the least reliable venue in which to make difficult and critical assessments about family attachment and a parent's abilities to meet his/her child's needs.

Introduction

Foster care agencies have cited insufficient resources and high caseloads as barriers to implementing frequent and quality visits. The practice of utilizing Visit Hosts offers a potential solution to these barriers on appropriate cases. These guidelines are intended to assist foster care agencies in recruiting and integrating **Visit Hosts** into routine family visiting practice for children in foster care. A **Visit Host** is someone identified by the family (parents, youth, or relatives) or by the foster care agency who can monitor family visits for children and their parents or siblings *in lieu of* the agency worker. The use of Visit Hosts is a promising approach because:

- frequent and high-quality visiting between parents and children in appropriate cases is a vital predictor of safe reunification;
- visits that are fun and permit a family to feel supported and engage in normal family activities support a child's overall well-being and adjustment to foster care;
- visits that are frequent and meaningful contribute to parents feeling empowered and motivated;
- it allows visits to be taken out of the agency earlier but still provides a level of supervision needed on the case.

- agencies often need additional resources to consistently provide frequent and high quality visits, particularly visits that occur outside the agency or for extended time periods;
- visit Hosts can be this additional resource on appropriate cases.

A Visit Host is someone who can assure the safety of the child(ren), is invested in the well-being of the child(ren), and is supportive of the parent and the family's attempts to reunify or maintain strong relationships. A Visit Host can accompany the family in settings that are more comfortable than the typical agency visiting room. She can bring participants together more frequently and for longer periods of time than an agency caseworker who has responsibility for multiple families. For example, Visit Hosts can hold regular family dinners, accompany the family to the library or zoo, or go with the parent to a child's medical appointment.

These guidelines should serve as a reference in recruiting, assessing and training Visit Hosts in order to provide more frequent, consistent and rewarding visits for children and their families.

What Situations Are Appropriate for Visit Hosts?

There are many situations in which Visit Hosts can enable families to spend more productive and meaningful time together. While the practice makes the most sense for those families with a goal of reunification, Visit Hosts may also be appropriate where reunification is not the goal but where there is a need to maintain a child's connections to parents, siblings, extended family or others. Visit hosts can be integrated at any point during the life of a foster care case. Examples of family situations which may be ideal for consideration of a visit host include:

- large sibling groups where all the children do not reside together;
- older teens, regardless of the permanency goal, who wish to spend more time with each other, with parents, extended family, or other people identified by the teens themselves;
- families for whom the visiting plan should progress to more natural, less closely supervised visits, to support the transition to unsupervised visits;
- families who would benefit from a combination of unsupervised and supervised visits;
- families for whom more frequent visits outside the agency are appropriate but the agency lacks resources to facilitate such visits;
- families who can identify people with whom and/or places where they would like to spend time as a family outside the agency;
- families who can identify activities and events that they would like to participate in together or that the caseworker feels would be helpful for them to engage in together (i.e., parent attending early intervention appointments with a child or shopping for school clothes);

- families who are able to identify a person who could host visits;
- families in which a parent is isolated and a Visit Host could play an important role in building a support network for that parent.

Families who are homeless or otherwise lack appropriate housing or space in which to spend time together during the day or for overnight visits.

Identifying a Visit Host

In many cases, simply asking parents and youth about people who might be able to host visits will yield several options. A good starting point is to meet with the parent to gather psychosocial information and develop a genogram (i.e., resource map) including family members and other important people in his/her and the child's life. Relatives who are identified but unable to be foster care resources are often good candidates. Places and activities that are important to the parent and family should also be explored. School-age children may have been involved with coaches and guidance counselors; families may have been involved with churches, local community groups, or preventive agencies. These outside agencies often include people who not only know the family but who are also willing to help the family stay connected. Because these hosts would only be working with the particular family they know, they may be able to provide additional opportunities for visits, and have experience to draw from in supporting the family.

Visit hosts can also be identified by the agency, and can include existing staff or volunteers, parent advocates, prior adoptive parents, or others who may be willing or interested in hosting visits. Though not initially known to the family, these hosts can offer support and connections for families who may otherwise be isolated and in need of a greater support network. In other words, the benefits of exploring hosts even when families cannot identify one can be enormous. Use of Visit Hosts can be explored at family team conferences, and at any casework meeting where service planning is discussed.

Use of a Visit Host should be considered whenever the provider reviews the level or type of supervision that is necessary for a family. Certainly, a desire to have visits outside the agency or organized around more family-friendly activities should prompt a discussion of visit hosts.

The following are examples of questions to ask parents, and often youth as well, in the effort to identify potential visit hosts:

1. Who are the people who are important to you and have been important and supportive to you and your family?
2. Does your child have a godparent or other adults he/she is close to? What other adults did your child spend time with prior to foster care?
3. How, and with whom, do you celebrate birthdays and holidays? What were fun activities that you did together prior to foster care? Who else participated in those

activities? Are there school, church, or recreational activities that are important to you or your children?

4. Are there people in your community who know your child, who you trust and feel are supportive and reliable?
5. Who else did you spend time with before you came into foster care? Would you feel safe if this person were at a visit with you and your parents? Who are other adults you like or respect? (for a child/youth)

Assessing Whether a Person Is Appropriate to Be a Host

A Visit Host's primary responsibility at a visit is to ensure the safety and well-being of a child. Visit Hosts are not generally trained visit coaches or experts in child development. Nonetheless, in each case, you will have to determine if you feel this person is reliable and willing to work with the agency to support visiting, while at the same time attending to concerns about visits that you may have in a particular case. Some general criteria for potential Visit Hosts are outlined below to guide agency staff in making these assessments.

General Criteria for Selecting a Visit Host

An appropriate candidate to be a Visit Host is a responsible adult who:

1. has a connection to the family *or* is identified by an agency as someone who has demonstrated a commitment to supporting family reunification, mentoring, and so on, such as a parent advocate or prior foster parent;
2. is willing and able to host visits on an ongoing basis;
3. is willing to maintain consistent contact with the foster care agency and respond to agency inquiries in a timely manner;
4. will intervene appropriately if any problem occurs during a visit and is willing to report back to the agency;
5. agrees to be honest and forthcoming about the quality and content of the visits;
6. is knowledgeable about the original placement circumstances, ongoing family issues, and current goals of the family;
7. is invested in helping the family to have safe, productive, positive visits;
8. is willing to participate in a home assessment (if relevant), interview, and background check for child abuse history;
9. is willing to discuss any of his/her own relevant child protective services history with the agency;
10. is willing to participate (if necessary) in training or orientation to learn more about the responsibilities of being a visit host or to learn how to meet the family's needs during a visit;
11. is willing to sign an agreement (if considered necessary) to the above expectations.

What to Discuss with a Parent, a Child, and the Host Candidate

Most of the time, when a parent proposes someone to host a visit, that person will be someone with enough history with the family that s/he will be aware of at least some of the circumstances that led to the child's placement. Many relatives and community supports, for example, were close to the family prior to placement and it may be just this intimate relationship that makes them a good candidate in the first instance. However, this may not be the case, and parents should be asked about whether and how much the potential host knows about their child welfare case. *Parents should always be given the option of sharing information with the Visit Host, and the case planner and the parent should come to agreement about how much information needs to be shared with the Host.*

Prior to considering a visit host candidate (and certainly prior to meeting with a candidate), you should be sure to discuss with the parent that you will need to share with a Visit Host any information about the case that is pertinent to the child's safety on a visit (which may include sharing the allegations that brought the child into foster care). For example, you may want to share with the host that the case involved substance abuse so that you can communicate to the host your expectation that the parent will be sober on a visit.

Children, particularly older children, may also be able to propose a visit host, or at the very least tell you about other people with whom they spent time prior to care. Children are often able to tell you whether they feel safe with such a person and why. You should be sure to let a child know that s/he will have the opportunity to talk privately with the caseworker about how visits are going with the host once they begin.

How to decide whether someone is appropriate on any given case will vary with the circumstances. At a minimum, you should always have at least one meeting with the proposed Host individually and one meeting with the parent and the Host. More meetings may be necessary at first, including a meeting with the child(ren). Strengths-based information including progress and changes since the child's entry into foster care should be shared, as well as expectations and concerns.

As suggested, you should get a sense of how the person would handle particular situations if child safety became a concern during a visit they were hosting; you should also ask the person to describe his/her relationship with the child(ren) or the parent to see if it coincides with the description provided by the parent and/or child.

Possible Additional Activities to Include in the Assessment

- Ask the person to come to some of the visits currently being held at the agency so that you have a chance to see the person interact with the parent and child.
- Ask the person for pertinent references.

- Show the person redacted portions of any Visit Host agreements you have used on prior cases or would like to use on the identified case to see if it raises questions or concerns.
- If you have a Visit Host working on another case, ask the candidate to speak with that Host.

Approving a Visit Host

Within your agency, you should have some discussion about whether you wish to consider a Visit Host a "volunteer" in the same way that you do other people who assist the agency without compensation, such as volunteers who help with transportation, putting on parties or events, and so on. Because most visit hosts will work with only *one* family as opposed to being available to work with multiple families, they are not "volunteers" in the typical sense. It is unclear whether, and to what extent, state regulations governing agency volunteers would apply to every visit host situation; however, **these recommended steps for approving visit hosts are reflective of and based on those regulations:**

- Obtain an SCR clearance: It is critical that you determine whether the Visit Host candidate has ever had allegations of abuse or neglect made against him or her. *The mere existence of an SCR history should not automatically preclude the person from hosting visits; rather, as with potential foster parents, it should be one factor that the agency uses to determine if the Host is appropriate.* In reviewing prior SCR history, agencies should consider how much time has passed since the report as well as the type and severity of the allegations.
- Address criminal background: Criminal background checks are usually accomplished in one of two ways: either by finger printing or by asking a candidate to execute a sworn written statement attesting to any prior criminal record. **State regulations do not require fingerprinting for volunteers** and in addition, fingerprinting can be costly and time consuming. *As is true of SCR clearances, the circumstances of any prior criminal record should be viewed with discretion as one factor, but not the only determinative one in approving a visit host.*
- Provide for orientation, training, and ongoing work with a Visit Host: Orientation and training for a Visit Host can be informal, that is, individual meetings you have with the host to discuss expectations. *In particular, a host needs to understand what s/he is expected to do if a child's safety or well-being appears to be at risk at a visit.*
- Conduct a home assessment if the Host intends to monitor visits at his or her home: Whenever the host will have the child and his/her family to the host's home, you should conduct the same safety assessment you do when initially investigating the home of a potential resource. This is particularly important when someone is hosting extended or overnight visits.

- *In addition to* these *steps, programs may consider the following steps, depending on the circumstances of the case.*
- Conduct an SCR clearance on any adult residing in the Host's home: If a child will be spending time at the host's home or if other adults may accompany the host at visits, you should conduct an SCR clearance on those people. You should always be clear with the host that s/he is responsible for the visit and no other adult should be at the visit without the parent's consent and the agency's knowledge, or if prior agreements regarding the visit have precluded that person (i.e., someone who is considered a risk to the child or the parent). You should also talk with the child about additional adults who may participate.
- Ask the host and/or the parent to establish a written agreement about the visits: Written agreements can function in the same way that other service "contracts" do in child welfare practice. While these agreements do not guarantee that a problem will never arise, they can help clarify the ground rules of the visit and provide guidance for both the host and the parents.
- Have the Visit Host appear in court: In those cases where the Court has made specific directions regarding visits in the past, you may wish to have the Visit Host appear with the worker in court to discuss with the attorneys on the case, as well as the judge, the plans and expectations for visits.
- Have the Visit Host meet other pertinent actors on the case: The foster parent, other extended family, and others may be able to help the Visit Host appreciate the importance of their role and can help parents appreciate that a Visit Host is an integral part of a service plan to help them reunify successfully with their child.

Orientation, Training, and Ongoing Work with the Visit Host

Every case will be somewhat different in terms of the level of orientation or training a Host will need to begin supporting a family on visits. As suggested, you may accomplish this in casework meetings that include the parent and/or the child. It is valuable to make your expectations about the visit clear to the host and the parent together. Certainly, a host needs to know what you would like them to do if they feel a visit is not going well, which should always include the expectation that the host will end the visit and return the child to the foster home or the agency, depending on the arrangements you make. In advising the host, you may want to draw on expectations and guidance you provide to kinship foster parents who have visits in their home with a child's parents.

The assigned caseworker or supervisor should always be present for the first few visits that take place with the host as a means to identify additional issues that may be important for assuring a safe, productive, positive visit for the family. Over the life of a case, it is recommended that the caseworker be present with the Visit Host from time to time to assess the arrangement. You should regularly check in with the Visit Host to find out about the progress of visits as well as to address any of the host's concerns, in much the same manner as you would check in with a kinship foster parent who monitors visits in his/her home. Less frequent check-ins should be possible as the case progresses, if visits continue to go well.

Conclusion

With proper exploration and application, Visit Hosts offer a promising approach to improving family visits, meeting the needs of children and families in foster care, and enhancing the network of support families can continue to rely on outside of the child welfare system. We strongly encourage agencies to utilize these guidelines and to integrate Visit Hosts into standard case practice.

APPENDIX B TO CHAPTER 6

New York City Administration for Children's Services Best Practice Guidelines for Family Visiting Arrangements for Children in Foster Care

I. Introduction

Congress passed the Adoption and Safe Families Act (ASFA) in 1997 to expedite the process by which children in foster care are either reunited with their families or find other permanent, stable homes.

In order to meet ASFA's accelerated time frames for making permanency decisions, it is critical that children maintain frequent contact with their family when it is safe for them to do so. Frequent and ongoing contact with family members reduces the trauma of removal for children, improves their adjustment to placement, and helps expedite permanency, regardless of whether the goal is reunification, adoption, independent living, or adult custodial care.

For children who will be reunited with their parents, frequent and consistent parent-child contact supports reunification by preserving parents' emotional attachment to their children and by allowing parents to share in the day-to-day responsibility of parenting their children in care. When visiting is expanded to include "shared parenting" responsibilities such as accompanying the foster parent to medical and school appointments, or assisting in supervising the child's homework or meal preparation, it offers parents a realistic sense of what will be involved in caring for their child after their discharge from care.

For other children, frequent parent-child contact may help reveal, early on, cases where reunification may not be the appropriate permanency goal. When a parent expresses little interest in shouldering some of the responsibilities involved in the daily care of his or her child and consistently disappoints a child by failing to participate in visits, this may be an important signal that the child's permanency goal should be changed.

As ASFA makes clear, the child's health and safety must be our "paramount concern" in scheduling or expanding visits. But for the many cases where child safety is not an issue, these Guidelines set forth a framework for expanding and intensifying parent-child contacts in order to expedite the permanency process.

II. Best Practice Guidelines for Family Visiting Arrangements for Children in Foster Care

From the time of removal throughout placement and up to the achievement of a permanency outcome (and even after), contact between children and their family members is critical. Although safety and protection are always paramount concerns, it is also critical to continue the child's existing relationships and to maintain family ties. For all children in foster care, the importance of contact between children and their parents and other family members should not be underestimated, and should be facilitated, as appropriate, in a manner which is timely, frequent, and of high quality.

The ACS Guidelines outlined here address the various and complex aspects of visiting with the aim of offering **clarity** and **guidance** in this area. Case-specific decisions concerning a child's visiting plan should be consistent with the ACS guidelines detailed below. Note that while this document makes reference to the role of foster parents in facilitating and supporting visiting, these guidelines also apply to child care workers employed in congregate care settings.

Parent-Child Contact Immediately Following Removal

The moment of a child's removal from his/her family is a traumatic event, often involving urgent efforts on the part of casework staff to gather information, contact relevant parties, and clarify the reasons for removal to both the child and the parents. At this time, the need for children to see their parents can be lost in the mix of other important and pressing concerns. However, the importance of discussing and scheduling parent-child contact immediately after removal should not be overlooked. Timely parent-child contact can serve to: (1) provide continuity and reassurance for children, (2) send a vital message of responsibility to the parent, while supporting him/her to immediately begin to address the reasons for their child's removal, and (3) allow for a casework assessment of the likelihood of reunification to begin as soon as possible.

For the above reasons, visiting plans and arrangements should be discussed and put into place and/or revised at both the 72-Hour Child Safety Conferences and 30-Day Family Permanency Conferences (ACS Family Team Conferences). Parent-child contact should be arranged as soon as possible, with the level of supervision deemed necessary and appropriate given the circumstances of the case and the relationship between the child and the parent, or as directed by court order. Reasons for and purposes of supervision should be clearly identified.

Sibling Contact

Recognizing the importance of the sibling relationship and consistent with the Family Court Act, the Social Services Law and OCFS regulations (18 NYCRR 431.10), ACS requires that all siblings and half-siblings be placed together whenever possible unless placement together would be detrimental to the child's best interests. In the event it is not possible to place siblings together in the same foster boarding home or agency boarding home on an emergency basis, they must be reunited within 30 days.

When siblings are placed separately, foster care agencies are required to exercise diligent efforts to facilitate biweekly face-to-face contact between siblings and half-siblings, unless it would be harmful to their health or safety or unless geographic proximity precludes visiting. Additionally, regular telephone contact and other forms of correspondence should be arranged between visits. When in the best interests of all children involved, every effort should be made to coordinate parent-child visits so as to include the entire sibling group and the parent.

OCFS regulations also require that siblings and half-siblings who are freed for adoption be placed together in a pre-adoptive home, unless placement together is contraindicated to one or more of the children.

It is strongly recommended that visiting among siblings continue after the final adoption of one or more of the sibling group, and cooperation among the adoptive parents should be encouraged.

The importance of sibling visits for older children and youth in care should not be overlooked or underestimated. This includes facilitating visits and regular sibling contact for youth with permanency goals of Independent Living.

Responsibility for Visits

It is always the foster care agency's responsibility to arrange and facilitate visits and other forms of contact between the child and parents, and among separated siblings. This responsibility applies to both planning and non-planning agencies. Although foster parents can escort children to visits, or host visits in their homes, and actively participate in visit arrangements, the ultimate responsibility for ensuring that visits take place lies with the agency itself. In most situations parent-child and sibling contact as soon possible after removal is in the child's best interest. If upon removal from the home, a child is *not* placed in a foster care facility or in a Department of Mental Hygiene facility and there is no specific foster care agency responsibility for the child (e.g., the child is placed in a hospital), it is DCP's responsibility to arrange/facilitate visits and other forms of contact. Facilitating parent-child and sibling contact includes not only arranging face-to-face visits, but also arranging regular phone contact and other forms of correspondence between visits.

Quality of Visits

The quality of the interaction and relationship between a child and his/her parent post-removal will depend in part on the circumstances surrounding their time together. Decision making about visit circumstances should always be guided by what is in the child's best interest and what is specified in any existing court orders. Visit arrangements should take into account factors such as the child's age and developmental level, the circumstances of placement, the child's previous relationship with the parent, and the parent's concern for and commitment to the child, the parent's level of cooperation with the service plan, and level of personal responsibility/accountability toward the reasons for placement. The lowest level of supervision that safeguards the well-being of the child should always be chosen in order to allow the parent to resume/assume the maximum amount of parenting responsibility possible. [See "ACS Guidelines for Decision-Making Concerning Supervised Parent-Child Visiting."]

Scheduling

Visit arrangements should take into consideration the schedules and circumstances of all those involved, including the parent, the child, and the foster parent. For example, in scheduling visits, caseworkers should factor in other obligations the parent may have in complying with the service plan (such as participating in a drug treatment program, attending medical appointments, job search, income maintenance appointments, etc.). Case planners should also be mindful of the schedules and commitments of youth in care (such as school attendance, after-school activities, etc.), as well as the fact that many foster parents have full-time jobs.

Travel distance and cost, and safety considerations (such as in cases involving domestic violence), as well as cultural, religious, and language issues should all be considered when scheduling visits.

Frequency and Length

Current OFCS regulations require that children with goals of "return to parent" visit their parents at least once every two weeks, but it is expected and recommended that more frequent contact be arranged and facilitated. Whenever possible and in the best interests of the child, it is recommended that: visits occur on a weekly basis; visit length be at least two hours; visits occur in sites identified by participating parties as comfortable, supportive, and convenient.

Activities and Location

When the goal is reunification, child-parent visits should serve as preparation for reunification, allowing parents to resume as much parental responsibility as possible and safe for the child. With this in mind, and whenever possible, visits should be integrated into the already scheduled activities of children, and activities which the parent will be involved with post-reunification. This type of visiting arrangement maximizes the naturalness of "visits" for children and parents, (re)integrates the parent into the child's life, supports the continuation of the visit activities post-reunification, and eases the burden on foster parents to make special scheduling arrangements for visits.

Suggested activities for child-parent visits: school plays and after-school programs, parent-teacher conferences, medical/dental appointments, shopping, haircuts/appointments, birthday celebrations, school trips, supervising homework, preparing meals in the foster parent's or parent's home, local community events, sports, and games. Suggested locations for visits: local public libraries, parks, recreational centers, community and youth centers, foster parent's home, parent's home, local churches or other places of worship, and facilities of other service providers (such as drug treatment programs), if appropriate space is available. Agencies should develop a listing of local resources available for parents and children, with consideration of suggestions from parents, children, and foster parents.

Preparation

For both children and parents, preparation before visits is critical throughout the life of a case, and particularly immediately after removal. It is also important to prepare foster parents for visits, as this will help them to support children after visits and additionally, help them to understand the meaning of children's post-visit reactions.

Prior to visits, children, parents, and foster parents should all be provided with information regarding: (1) each party's rights and responsibilities regarding visits; (2) the circumstances of the visit (where, when, for how long, who will be there); (3) what is planned for the end of the visit (e.g., children should not expect that they will go home with the parent, unless this is actually the case), and (4) when the next visit will be.

Agency case planners (or other qualified staff and foster parents) should meet with the parent prior to the first visit and subsequent visits as necessary to convey the importance of visits, explain the visit circumstances, help the parent prepare visit activities, and address any questions or anxiety the parent may have. "Visiting" between a parent and his/her child may feel awkward and unnatural, and case planners should not assume that parents will automatically understand the importance of visits and know how to make the most of them. Parents should be helped prior to visits to understand the importance of visiting, both for the child's emotional health and the achievement of the goal of reunification.

Preparing the parent for visits should also include helping the parent to understand a child's sense of time and need for attachment. Particularly in the cases involving younger children, case planners (and others) can help the parent understand that the longer their children stay in foster care the greater the children's attachment may become to the substitute caregiver. Although the parent may always see the child as their child, the child may come to see another caretaker/provider as their parent (Beyer, 1999, p. 8). This information should not be conveyed in a threatening way, but in a way that emphasizes, motivates, and supports a parent to visit frequently and progress in complying with the service plan. Supporting parents to visit with their children also includes scheduling visits at times and places that are reasonable for the parent.

Children also need to be prepared for visits with their parents. Children's own feelings about the visit and their placement in foster care, in general, should be explored carefully (ideally by a mental health professional). Visits should be arranged so as to minimize children's anxiety, maximize safety, and support the maintenance of the parent-child bond. See the attached article, "Parent-Child Visits as an Opportunity for Change" [Beyer, 1999], for examples of ways to empower children, while also supporting parents, so that visits both preserve safety and address children's attachment and developmental needs.

Debriefing/Processing

Debriefing/processing after the visit can be equally as important as preparation before a visit. Particularly toward the beginning of a case when all parties—parent, foster parent, case planner—are becoming familiar with one another, debriefing/processing after visits can help build the communication, trust, and understanding vital to the safe and timely achievement of the permanency outcome that is in the child's best interest. Processing visits with children (in age and developmentally appropriate ways, either verbally or through play, art, and other activities) often serves to greatly reduce negative behavioral reactions sometimes seen in children. Reducing these reactions will in turn make it easier for foster parents to support children in spending time with their parents.

Processing with the parent includes helping him/her to understand the needs of the child, and providing him/her with guidance and information about effective parenting techniques for addressing these needs. Processing the visit with foster parents is also important, especially in helping them to understand and handle children's reactions to visits.

Ideally, processing should occur directly after the visit. When this is not feasible, a follow-up phone call (or face-to-face contact) should be made with the various visiting participants as close to the time of the visit as possible.

Effective processing after each visit also serves as preparation for the next visit. This is particularly true for parents, for whom each visit represents an opportunity to practice better parenting and strengthen the parent-child relationship.

Interpreting Children's Reactions to Visits

An important part of post-visit processing for the case planner, the foster parent, and for the parent as well, is interpreting and understanding the child's reaction after the visit. Children's reactions to visits are often misunderstood. When children exhibit regressive behavior, "act out," or demonstrate other negative behaviors, the parent is often blamed as being an "unfit," "ineffective," or even harmful parent. Adults often respond to children's visit reactions by moving to limit, suspend, or even terminate visits. This can be very harmful to children whose seemingly negative reactions to visits may be caused by their attachment to the parent and may actually be the child's way of expressing the desire to spend more time, not less, with the parent. For this reason, case planners and foster parents should carefully explore the nature of children's reactions to visits and in many cases, may want to increase a child's contact with the parent (through phone calls, letters, having a photo of the parent, finding out more from the parent about what the child likes, eats, wears, etc.) before limiting a child's time with the parent.

Although a child's safety is always of paramount concern, interpretations of children's negative visit reactions must also take into account the nature of attachment and separation, and the fact that children will act out their feelings of loss, sadness, and disrupted attachments, all of which may subside with increased contact with their parent. It is always advisable to seek professional guidance (from a qualified mental health expert) before making any decisions to limit or terminate visits solely based on the child's reactions.

Interpreting Parents' Reactions to Visits

When interpreting parents' reactions to visits, it is important for case planners and foster parents to place these "visits" in the context of foster care and remember that: (1) having a child removed from the home is a traumatic event, even when the removal is a result of the parent's own behavior; (2) "visiting" can be an initially uncomfortable way for parents and children to spend time together; and, (3) parents' own feelings (which may include guilt, confusion, sadness, anger, helplessness, and despair) about their child's placement may manifest themselves in different ways before, during, and after visits.

Parents often feel enormous pressure surrounding visits. Many parents realize that interpretations of the nature of their interaction with their children during visits will heavily inform casework decisions about whether reunification is in the child's best interest. The pressure to have visits "go well" can increase when the visits are supervised in a manner that leaves the parent feeling judged rather than supported by the visit supervisor. When visits end with sadness on the part of the child and/or difficulties in separating from the parent, parents themselves may be so disturbed by their children's emotional reactions that they decide the visits are not good for the children. In these cases, case planners should help parents understand their children's reactions, including providing information about attachment and separation, the importance of continuous parent-child contact, and the fact that children's negative reactions at the end of visits often subside over time when regular contact is maintained.

For all of the above reasons, communicating with the parent before, during (as appropriate), and after visits is critical to ensuring that the visits go well and that the visit plan responds to the needs of the children, the parents, and the achievement of the chosen permanency goal. When parents feel supported by the case planner and foster parent, they are more likely to ask questions about parenting techniques, feel more comfortable during visits, and communicate more openly. When parents feel judged, this can increase the awkwardness of the visits and inhibit the parent's ability to resume parental responsibility for the child and address the reasons for placement.

In all cases, if a parent does or says anything before, during, or after a visit that appears to place the child in danger, acts inappropriately, or violates agency rules, this should be addressed immediately.

Progression of a Visiting Plan

Best case practice dictates that a child's visiting plan will progress and evolve according to and in conjunction with the parent's compliance with the individualized service plan and as deemed beneficial to the child's well-being, health, and safety. When reunification is the permanency goal, it is understood that visit frequency and length will increase over time, with the level of any supervision deemed necessary decreasing over time as consistent with the safety of the child. In general, a visiting plan should evolve from weekly to more frequent visits of greater length, to overnight and weekend visits, leading to trial and then final discharge.

Although the variation in case circumstance renders it difficult to set forth specific time frames for the progression described above, it is expected that visiting plans will be evaluated regularly and should have significantly progressed during the six months between service plan reviews. *If a child's visiting plan has **not** progressed over a six-month period, the reasons justifying the lack of change must be clearly documented in the case record.* At a minimum, the visiting plan and level of supervision should be reviewed at all Family Team Conferences (including ACS 72-Hour Child Safety Conferences and 30-Day Family Permanency Conferences), service plan reviews, dispositional and permanency hearings, and at any other court dates. Court orders pertaining to visiting can only be modified in court.

When considering a change in visiting plan, case planners should arrange to be present at all or part of a visit to assess case circumstances and progress, in order to ensure that the proposed change in visiting plan is appropriate. Also, as a general rule, children should not be trial or final discharged without first having experienced successful overnight and weekend visits with the parent over a period of time. In cases where there is a court order for an immediate discharge, the court order must be obeyed and implemented accordingly, regardless of whether or not there have been prior overnight and/or weekend visits.

Decision-Making and Authority over Changes in a Visiting Plan

There is often confusion and misunderstanding over who has the authority to implement changes in a child's visiting plan. It is vital that all those involved in these decisions understand how visiting plans may evolve in order that reunification not be delayed unnecessarily.

The following describes who has authority over specific decisions regarding visit plans, and details the decision-making process.

Increasing the Frequency of Parent-Child Visits

If there is a **court order** concerning the frequency of visits, and the agency would like to increase the visit frequency, it can do so without returning to court so long as the language of the court order does not limit the frequency of the visits. **Or**, the agency can return to court to request that the court order be modified so that the more frequent visits can occur.

If the previous court order also specified a particular level of supervision, the court modification should also address the issue of supervision (e.g., the modification can include a change to monitored or unsupervised visits, or supervision at the agency's discretion, or another creative and appropriate plan).

In pre-disposition Article 10 cases, the agency must notify the ACS attorney prior to returning to court. In all cases, agencies must submit to the case manager a form CS-853C prior to the court date. After the court hearing, the attorney will forward copies of the Court Action Summary to the case planner and the case manager.

If there is **no court order** for supervision on a case or other court specifications regarding visit arrangements, and the agency would like to increase the visit frequency or move to unsupervised visits, it can do so without returning to court provided that any existing court orders are complied with. The authority to increase visit frequency or have unsupervised visits lies with the planning agency, and must be approved by agency staff at least one level above the case planner. In pre-disposition Article 10 cases, the agency must notify the ACS attorney prior to returning to court. In all cases, this change must be documented in the Uniform Case Record (UCR).

Decreasing the Level of Supervision

When there is a **court order** regarding the level of visit supervision, agencies wanting to decrease the level of supervision should contact their agency attorney to return to court to modify the order. In pre-disposition Article 10 cases, the ACS attorney must also be contacted prior to returning to court. After the court hearing the attorney will forward copies of the Court Action Summary to the case planner and the case manager. Changes to the visit plan must be documented in the Court Involvement and (Re)Assessment sections of the UCR.

When there is **no court order** regarding the level of visit supervision, agencies have the authority to decrease the level of supervision on a case, including moving to unsupervised visits, provided that this decision has been approved by an agency staff person two levels above the case planner. In pre-disposition Article 10 cases, advance notification to the ACS attorney is required. The change in visiting plan should be documented in the UCR.

Decreasing the Frequency, Limiting, Suspending, or Terminating Parent-Child Visits

In cases **with or without court orders** pertaining to visit arrangements, the decision to decrease, limit, suspend, or terminate parent-child visits lies with the court. For all children in foster care whose parents' rights have not been terminated, the decision to limit visits to less than the minimum requirement for visiting requires either court approval or written parental consent (which must then be included in the case record). Note that this applies to children with goals of adoption who have not yet been legally freed.

In emergency situations when the agency believes that a visit will place the child in imminent danger, the individual visit may be suspended or controlled. If the agency feels that parent-child visits in general pose a threat to the child's well-being, and that as a result the visits should be limited or terminated, agencies must contact their agency attorney immediately and return to court to change the visiting plan. On the same day as the decision to limit the visit plan is made, agencies must send a CS-853C to the case manager (ACS Foster Care Standards, p. 41). In all cases, ACS attorneys must be notified in advance of the decision to limit the visit plan. Once the agency has returned to court, the Court Action Summary must be sent to both the case manager and the case planner.

If there is no court order, written parental consent to limit the visits may be sought, and would allow the agency to limit the visit arrangement without returning to court. If the written consent applies only to a specified timeframe, this agreement is only valid between these dates. When the agreement expires, the agency must resume the minimum requirements for visits, pursue a court order, or have the parent sign another consent agreement. The parent's written consent must be included in the UCR.

Any change made in the visiting plan must be documented in the (Re)Assessment section of the next UCR that is due. If a planning agency goes to court for an order to change a child's visiting plan, this must be documented in the "Court Involvement" section of that UCR.

Permanency Goal Changes from Reunification (01) to Adoption (04)

Unless the Court has ordered otherwise, parents of children whose permanency goal has been changed from reunification to adoption maintain the right to visit with their children until their parental rights have been terminated, i.e., the children are legally freed. A goal change to adoption does not in and of itself change the visiting plan. If an agency feels that parent-child visits are no longer in the child's best interest and wishes to limit, suspend, or terminate visits between the child and the parent at the time of goal change, the agency must follow the steps outlined above for limiting the visit plan. Without a court order or the parent's written consent, parents retain the right to visit with their children until the TPR is finalized, that is, the children are legally freed.

Child Contact with Non-Resource Parents, Relatives, and Other Significant Parties

In addition to facilitating parent-child contact, case planners should keep in mind that there may be other significant relatives (or others) in the lives of children with whom contact should be facilitated. These people can and should be considered as resources for the case planner—they can help lessen the trauma of removal and placement for children, help to provide support for the parent in complying with the service plan, and may be able to provide respite for or help to the foster parent by assisting with transportation, taking the children to appointments, hosting parent-child visits, or participating in activities with children. Particularly for older children and youth in care, relationships with those whom they identify as important to them should be explored and, when deemed safe and appropriate, visiting and other contact arrangements should be facilitated and supported.

Child Contact with Foster Parents Post-Reunification

Children in foster care may develop strong attachments to the foster parents and/or others who care for them during their placement in foster care. Although ACS and planning agencies do not have authority over a child after final discharge, case planners can work with parents as their children near final discharge to help them understand their child's need for continuity of relationships. Depending on the circumstances, parents should be encouraged to consider ways to allow their children to maintain a relationship, with their child's primary caretaker during the stay in foster care. Although this may be difficult for some parents, the focus should always be on what is best for the child.

Children with Goals Other than Reunification

For children whose goal is adoption, independent living, or another permanent living arrangement, a careful individualized assessment should be made before moving to terminate parent-child visits. Unless such visits pose safety or health risks to the child/youth, visiting with parents and other family members often remains vital to his/her well-being, sense of continuity and connectedness, and can help to provide a sense of reassurance to children/youth at a time of transition. Contact (including visits, phone calls, and letters) with parents, siblings, relatives, and others identified by the child/youth in care, should be facilitated as required and appropriate.

III. ACS Guidelines for Decision-Making Concerning Supervised Parent-Child Visiting

In developing a child's visiting plan, one of the critical decisions that must be made concerns the issue of supervision. In many cases, this decision will be made by the court. In others, it will be left up to the discretion of the planning agency and/ or ACS. ACS has developed the principles and guidelines outlined below in order to clarify and offer guidance on case-specific decisions in this area. These principles and guidelines are effective immediately.

Principles Concerning the Application of Supervision

The ACS principles outlined below should be applied as general rules, consistent with best casework practice and individualized case assessment. Case managers will apply these principles and the guidelines that follow, as they review visiting plans. Additionally, since Family Court judges often play an important role in determining visiting practice on individual cases, ACS attorneys and case planning staff will refer to these principles and guidelines concerning the appropriate levels of supervision at supervised visits prior to and at the time of court hearings.

1. Decisions concerning the appropriate and necessary level of supervision should start from the premise that family and sibling visits are important to the healthy growth and development, and in the best interests of, **all children** in foster care. Family and sibling visits should be facilitated regularly and **at the least** in accordance with ACS minimal requirements. Decisions concerning supervised visiting should be consistent with the best practices outlined above and clearly documented in the case record. Any decision to limit a child's visit plan requires court approval (or written parental consent) and should be clearly documented in the case record.
2. Consistent with the Guidelines listed below, visits should be unsupervised if there is no reason for supervised visiting on a particular case and, when supervision is necessary, should be supervised at the lowest level of supervision consistent with the reasons for supervision. When there is no court order for supervised visiting, and none of the reasons justifying supervision listed below exist, it is expected that unsupervised visiting will be the rule unless circumstances justifying the need for supervision are distinctly identified in the case record.
3. If the goal for the child is reunification and one of the reasons for supervised visiting listed below exists, there should be a timely progression from a higher level of supervision to a lower level of supervision, and from supervised to unsupervised visits, consistent with the case situation.
4. If there is a court order directing supervised visits with specific directions concerning the level of supervision, case planning staff must follow the court's directions, using the Guidelines listed below to define the meaning of the court's chosen level of supervision.

5. If there is a court order that directs supervised visiting without specific directions concerning the level of supervision, it is up to the planning agency to determine the appropriate level of supervision that should be applied.
6. In appropriate cases, ACS attorneys, in consultation with case planning staff, will ask family court judges to include language in supervised visiting orders that will give the planning agency, with ACS input as appropriate, the discretion to move to a lower level of supervision and/or to permit unsupervised visiting, at a future date without returning to court to do so. Such requests will help to ensure that children's visit plans evolve according to a timeline based on case circumstances and best interest determinations, rather than according to scheduled or available court dates.
7. If there is a court order containing conditions that the agency believes are no longer appropriate, the agency attorney must be informed as soon as possible so that motions to modify the court order can be made in appropriate cases. In pre-disposition Article 10 cases, the ACS attorney must also be notified prior to returning to court. In all cases, a CS-853C must be sent to the case manager as notification. Agency case planning staff should present their attorneys with a clearly developed recommendation for modifying the court ordered visiting plan and be able to justify the recommendation with up-to-date case information.

   The question of whether orders relating to supervised visiting should continue or whether a request for modification should be made should be reviewed on an ongoing basis, but no less frequently than at Family Team Conferences, service plan reviews, dispositional hearings, or permanency hearings. Although the court ordered visit plan will be described at the latter two hearings, court orders may actually be modified whenever the case is in court.
8. If there is no court order concerning visiting, the planning agency, with ACS input as appropriate, has discretion to determine the level of supervision that may be justified by case circumstances. If the reasons for supervised visiting listed below do not exist on a particular case or for an individual visit, visits should be unsupervised. As with any change in the visiting plan, any changes in the level of supervision should be clearly documented in the UCR.

Guidelines for Decision-Making Concerning Supervised Visiting

Reasons Justifying the Application of Supervision

(1) to ensure the safety of the child; (2) to avoid undue influence on the child's potential testimony; (3) to permit an appropriate assessment of the case situation so that planning decisions can be made; (4) to teach and model new parenting behaviors for parents and provide immediate feedback to parents regarding appropriate

responses to children's behaviors; (5) to comply with court orders requiring supervised visiting.

ACS Defined Levels of Visiting Supervision (from the highest to the lowest)

(1) Strictly supervised visiting; (2) Monitored visiting; (3) Unsupervised visiting.
ACS has established guidelines concerning the levels of supervision—**strictly supervised, monitored**, and **unsupervised**—which may be applied when one or more of the reasons justifying supervision exists. These levels are defined below.

Strictly supervised visiting

The purpose of strictly supervised visiting is to provide a high level of supervision when one or both of the following reasons apply:

- There is a reasonable basis to believe that the child may be at serious risk; and/or
- There is a reasonable basis to believe that the parent may attempt to interfere with, manipulate, or coerce the child's potential testimony in court.

These visits must be supervised by professional-level staff, preferably the assigned case planner or supervisory staff.

Where strict supervision is required, it is the visit supervisor's responsibility to be present during the entire visit, and be able to hear all verbal communications and observe all physical contact between the parent and the child. The visit supervisor will assess the factors listed below under **monitored visiting,** but will also assess:

- the safety of the child, paying close attention to the nature of any physical contact between the parent and child;
- the reaction of the child to any physical contact between the parent and the child;
- whether the parent attempts to interfere with, manipulate, or coerce the child's potential testimony.

Because of the concern for the child's safety in these cases, the visit supervisor cannot leave the parent and child alone at any time during the visit. Although present at all times, the visit supervisor will generally not interfere in the relationship between the parent and the child at the visit, except in instances where the emotional or physical safety of a child is threatened, or if the parent tries to interfere with the child's potential testimony in Court, or if the parent requests assistance or support. These visits can take place either at the agency or at alternative visiting sites, so long as strict supervision can be maintained.

Monitored visiting

The purpose of monitored visiting is to provide a lower level of supervision than in strictly supervised visits when one or more of the following reasons apply:

- To ensure the safety of the child when it is felt that parent-child contact presents a low to medium level of risk.
- To serve the function of case assessment, including monitoring case progress and ensuring that visiting plans evolve appropriately.
- To teach and model appropriate parenting behaviors, and support the parent in working toward achieving reunification.

During monitored visits, the visit supervisor can come and go, but should observe from a distance, and assess the following factors:

- Timeliness of the arrival of parents and children.
- Greeting between child(ren) and visiting adult.
- Preparation for the visit made by visiting adult.
- Proximity of adult and child during visit.
- Activities during the visit, including level of participation of both parent and child indicators of child's level of comfort during visit (child's demeanor, physical contact with parent, excessive requests to leave visit room, crying, etc.).
- Parent's ability to establish appropriate boundaries for child's behavior.
- Separation behaviors of parent and child at visit's end.
- Children's reaction to the visit (resistant, eager, ambivalent).

Depending on case circumstances, monitored visits may be supervised by other qualified staff or foster parents, but careful assessment of case circumstances and the nature of the relationship between the parent, child, and the person supervising the visit should always be made. This holds true for kinship placements, as well as non-relative foster care. If someone other than the case planner is monitoring the visits, the case planner should periodically monitor a visit in order to stay abreast of case circumstances. Documentation in the progress notes and UCR should include information about the visit supervisor (who, how often, relationship to parent, etc.).

The visit supervisor will generally not interfere in the relationship between the parent and child at the visit, except in instances where emotional or physical safety of a child is threatened, or if the parent tries to interfere with the child's potential testimony in court, or if the parent requests assistance or support. It is the visit supervisor's responsibility to remain impartial and to observe and hear the interaction between a parent and child. Depending on the specific case circumstances and the reason for the application of this level of supervision, the practical meaning and actual arrangements of monitored visits will vary. When the primary function of monitoring is assessment of case progress, the visit plan can include a mixture of monitored and unsupervised visits, and/or an individual visit may be partially monitored. When considering a change in visiting plan, there should always be a monitored visit (where the case planner is present for at least part of the visit) to ensure that the case planner is up to date on the case circumstances and progress, and the proposed change in visiting plan is appropriate. Whenever possible, monitored visits should take place in locations that support and promote the relationship between parent and child. The safety of the child should always be considered when determining appropriate visiting locations.

Unsupervised visits

When none of the reasons listed above justifying the presence of a visit supervisor exist and are clearly identified in the case record, visits between children and their parents should be unsupervised. Cases with unsupervised visits will still require occasional monitored or partially monitored visits for assessment purposes, and this should be clearly explained to the parent. As stated above, prior to a change in the visiting plan—including moving to overnight and weekend visits, and to trial discharge—there should always be a monitored visit (where the case planner is present for at least part of the visit) to assess case progress and circumstances, and ensure that the proposed change is appropriate.

Unsupervised visits should take place in locations that support and promote the parent-child relationship, and that are identified by participating parties as comfortable, supportive, and convenient.

In all cases, ACS attorneys should be contacted for specific questions about any court orders concerning visiting, including modifying court orders, or other concerns related to the issue of visiting.

APPENDIX C TO CHAPTER 6

Protocol for Communication Between New York City Administration of Children's Services and Provider Agency Caseworker and Attorneys Representing Children and Parents (2012)

I. Introduction

A. It is the policy of Children's Services to encourage communication regarding families' and children's needs, the provision of individualized services, and optimal family visiting plans. Attorneys for parents and children can work with caseworkers to facilitate the sharing of information that will allow us to meet families' needs. This new protocol is intended to provide guidance to Children's Services Child Protection Specialists (CPS) and provider agency case planners to enhance communication with attorneys for parents and children.

B. It is anticipated that both CPS and provider agency case planners and parents' and children's attorneys will consistently keep the FCLS attorney apprised of their mutual discussions. CPS and case planners shall memorialize these conversations in Connections.

II. Who Represents Parents, Children, and Youth in Family Court?

A. In addition to the provider agency and CPS, there are likely to be many other players involved in the family's case. These players include the Family Court Legal

Services (FCLS) attorney, the provider agency attorney, the parent's attorney, and the attorney for the child.

B. If the parent has an attorney, he or she may be court-appointed (from the 18B panel), privately retained, or from an organization which provides legal assistance in Family Court, such as the Center for Family Representation, Bronx Defenders, Brooklyn Family Defense Project, and others.

C. Every child who is the subject of a family court petition has a court-appointed attorney called an attorney for the child, usually from the Legal Aide Society's Juvenile Rights Practice, Lawyers for Children, or the 18B panel.

D. Attorneys representing children and parents are often assisted by social work, parent advocate, and paralegal staff. For the purposes of this protocol, the term "parent's (or child's) attorney" includes the non-attorney staff assisting with the parent's or child's case.

E. In all abuse and neglect cases, including permanency hearings the FCLS attorney will represent the CPS and case planner; the provider agency attorney will appear on most termination of parental rights cases; and at times both the FCLS and provider agency attorney will appear to represent the ACS/provider agency position.

F. There may also be preventive services workers, CASA (Court Appointed Special Advocates) representatives, and/or other service providers involved with the case who appear in court. **If you are unfamiliar with someone's role and are asked to share information, consult with the FCLS attorney before discussing the case or responding to any requests made by that person.**

III. Prior to Every Court Appearance

A. The FCLS attorney shall speak with the CPS and provider agency case planner to prepare for the court appearance.

B. The CPS and provider agency case planner shall provide the FCLS attorney with updated information about the services provided to the parents and child(ren) and inform the FCLS attorney of any changes in status, including changes in the child(ren)'s placement or visitation schedule.

C. The FCLS attorney shall inform the attorneys representing the parent(s) and child(ren) about the status of the services provided and any changes in the child(ren)'s placement or other relevant issues.

IV. The Initial Court Appearance

At the initial court appearance, the FCLS attorney should introduce the CPS and foster care agency case planners to the parent's and child(ren)'s attorneys to clarify and facilitate anticipated communication outside of court, including a discussion about the appropriate parameters of the communication, as discussed further below.

V. Family Team Conference

Attorneys for parents and children, and the social workers affiliated with these attorneys have a right to attend Family Team Conferences. The provider agency case planners should inform parents' and children's attorneys of the dates of upcoming Family Team Conferences.

VI. Child Safety Conferences

Social workers working with attorneys for parents and children are permitted to participate in the Initial Child Safety Conference, if previously assigned to represent the parent or child, and the Follow-up 20 Day Child Safety Conference. The CPS should let the FCLS attorney know if any Initial Child Safety Conference is going to be held concerning a parent or child who has an open Family Court case. The assigned FCLS attorney will then inform the attorneys representing the parent and child of the date, time, and place of the conference so that the social worker can attend. Case planners and CPS staff should let the attorney for the child or the assigned social worker know if the date for the Follow-Up 20 Day Child Safety Conference has changed since the date was selected at the Initial Child Safety Conference.

VII. Appropriate Communication

A. CPS and foster care agency case planners, and parents' and children's attorneys are permitted and encouraged to communicate on certain topics with the goal of maximizing family engagement. Sharing relevant factual information and trouble-shooting service and visiting issues are encouraged.

B. Examples of appropriate communication include:
   (1) Pick-up and drop-off times, schedules and locations for family visits, as opposed to discussions regarding the quality of the visits.
   (2) Information regarding programs with family involvement.
   (3) Relatives' contact information as visiting or caretaking resources.
   (4) Discussions of court-ordered services without interpreting orders.
   (5) Dates, times, and locations of Family Team Conferences or other meetings.
   (6) Requests for copies of service plans.
   (7) Information regarding a child's medical and educational progress (e.g., report cards, medical updates), notice of doctor's appointments and school meetings that the parent can attend.
   (8) Updates on changes in the child's placement or other service plan issues.
   (9) Information on programs that could assist the parent and inquiries about the status of pending referrals.
   (10) Clothing allowances, enrollment of a child in school, establishing Medicaid and housing programs.

(11) Communication of parents' requests for letters for public housing, public assistance (e.g., to request visiting allowance) or for other social service programs.

VIII. Inappropriate Communication

A. The CPS and provider agency case planners shall not discuss the following areas with an attorney representing the parent or children:
  (1) Interpretations of court orders.
  (2) Allegations of abuse or neglect.
  (3) A position regarding the outcome of the court case including modifications in visitation.
  (4) Requests for orders against Children's Services.
  (5) **If a Children's Services caseworker or provider agency case planner is asked about any of the items listed above, then he/she should ask the parent's or child(ren)'s attorneys to contact the FCLS attorney directly. In addition, any and all reports prepared in anticipation of a court appearance must be provided to the FCLS attorney and have FCLS approval to distribute before they are provided to any other parties.**

IX. Issues Specific to Working with Children's or Youth's Attorneys

A. The child's attorney on a neglect or voluntary placement case has a right and obligation to meet with the child privately at his/her office and/or foster care placement, and to communicate about how to best make these arrangements.
B. If a child has been brought to court, the Children's Services caseworker or provider agency case planner should inform the child's attorney as soon as possible.

CHAPTER 7

Discovery and Pretrial Proceedings

Kenneth Krekorian

7.01 Pretrial Proceedings

Pretrial proceedings should be a routine feature in child welfare matters. Depending on the jurisdiction, either the general civil discovery rules apply in dependency proceedings or there are specific discovery rules in the statute or rules governing practice in dependency court. However, in many places, discovery is handled informally. Similarly, motion practice before a trial may be based upon rules for courts of general civil jurisdiction, specific rules applicable only to dependency court, or, most commonly, a combination of general and specific rules.

7.02 Discovery: An Overview

Discovery is an available tool in all legal proceedings including civil, criminal, and juvenile matters. It gives counsel the opportunity to learn the evidence on which the other side is relying and is an essential tool for enabling parties to assess the strength of their case. This information commonly forms the basis for deciding whether to settle the matter, and on what terms, or to take the case to trial. It also allows the parties to make strategic decisions on such basic matters as what witness to call, whether to call an expert witness, and what the trial strategy should be.

Discovery is no less invaluable in child welfare cases and is especially useful to parents' attorneys in determining the strength of the case brought by the Agency. Counsel should be familiar with the rules governing discovery in the state's court of general civil jurisdiction and should make liberal use of the devices they provide. Child protection cases typically proceed very rapidly from the filing of the Petition to the adjudicatory hearing, making the need to engage in discovery promptly all the more imperative. Counsel should give priority to being fully prepared for trial, which often means using discovery techniques available in ordinary civil actions. Most of these can be undertaken without involvement of the court unless the adverse party fails to comply with requests for discovery.

Many states mandate that the Agency provide relevant information to respondents; in practice, however, agencies too often get away with providing incomplete information to parents and their lawyers. In many jurisdictions, much of the information that is given to parents' attorneys and is considered discoverable in child welfare matters comes from the social worker who conducts the initial investigation to determine whether a Petition should be filed and whether or not the child should be removed. In other jurisdictions, parents' counsel needs to take affirmative steps to secure the agency case file. Counsel should always secure this file before making critical strategic decisions. This is particularly true in more complex cases dealing with injuries to children where medical issues are commonly involved and material medical records may not be in the Agency's possession.

Counsel should obtain all relevant documents in the course of preparing for trial. These may include hospital records, police reports, agency investigation records, the notes of any expert who interviewed the parent or child, and court records of any related proceedings or previous cases involving the family. As discussed in Chapter 3, in the first interview with the client, counsel should routinely obtain his or her written permission to enable counsel to examine and copy all documents and records pertaining to the client or the family, with an express waiver of any right to confidentiality as against counsel.

7.03 Meeting with the Agency Attorney

Counsel should arrange to meet with the attorney for the Agency and try to find out as much as possible about the case. This meeting should be conducted informally. Counsel should strive to obtain information about the Agency's objectives and what the attorney for the Agency thinks about the overall direction of the case. The more information counsel can secure from this conversation, including getting access to the records in the Agency's possession, the quicker counsel can be prepared for trial without going through the effort of using formal discovery.

7.04 Formal Discovery Efforts

Pretrial discovery includes the traditional forms of discovery such as interrogatories, depositions, requests for admissions, and requests for the inspection and copying of documents. Pretrial discovery may be initiated by any party in juvenile dependency proceedings but will vary depending on state law. Formal discovery requests should be made on notice to all parties when any party is seeking information. Several states, including Michigan, California, and Pennsylvania, have rules regarding informal requests for discovery. *See* CAL. R. CT, 5.546; PA. R. JUV. CT. P. 1340; MICH. CT. R. PRAC. § 3.922(A)(1). In these jurisdictions, when the parties are in dispute regarding compliance with the informal request, the filing of motions may follow informal discovery. Other states, including Florida, have a comprehensive and formal discovery process setting forth strict rules of discovery. *See* FLA. R. JUV. P. 8.245.

Time constraints in dependency cases may limit the type of discovery that can be relied upon. Many jurisdictions regulate the time limits for cases to go to disposition when children are in foster care. In some jurisdictions, the jurisdictional or adjudicatory hearing must be held within fifteen days when the child is in foster care or within thirty days if the child is released to a parent or guardian, unless the parent agrees to extend the time frames. *See, e.g.*, PA. R. JUV. CT. P. 1510. Similarly, in many jurisdictions, the dispositional hearing must be held within sixty to ninety days of filing the Petition, unless waived. *See, e.g.*, CAL. WELF. AND INST. CODE, § 352 (b) (sixty days); OHIO JUV. R. 34 (ninety days). These extremely attenuated pretrial periods make it difficult to use discovery procedures that, by their nature, take time to resolve. *See, e.g.*, ORE. REV. STAT., § 419B.305 (2001); WASH. REV. CODE § 13.34.110 (2007). Counsel needs to be prepared for a contested hearing very quickly after the Petition is filed.

Texas uses a formal system of discovery but does so by a "discovery control plan." *See* TEX. R. CIV. P. 190.1. By using a control plan, the court may limit or expand the manner and amount of discovery conducted. In dependency cases, this allows the court to tailor the discovery to fit the circumstances of dependency cases. Thus, the discovery control plan takes into account the accelerated setting of hearings in dependency cases.

California and Pennsylvania employ an informal discovery process designed to be completed in an accelerated manner so that the mandatory timelines to disposition of the case are accomplished. These discovery processes are also designed to encourage a minimally adversarial process. The California process, for example, places an affirmative duty on the Agency to disclose police reports relevant to the pending matter and any evidence or information within petitioner's possession or control that is favorable to the child, parent, or guardian. CAL. R. CT. 5.546. Although not all inclusive, this Rule establishes eight categories of information that, unless privileged, must be turned over to the requesting party upon a timely request.

Pennsylvania's process is very similar to California's. In Pennsylvania, discovery and inspection are expected to be informal, but the rules require that the petitioner give to parent's counsel the names of all witnesses in addition to their written statements, scientific evidence, including expert opinions, police reports, physical and mental examinations, and tangible objects, including documents. PA. R. JUV. CT. P. 1340.

Whether or not the Court will be willing to extend the time to trial to allow different forms of discovery to be completed will play a role in helping counsel choose which discovery method to use, with the goal of ensuring that counsel obtains all needed information within the time period needed to be prepared for trial. Cost is another variable to keep in mind. Although depositions allow counsel to ask questions of live witnesses—an invaluable aid for trial preparation—it costs both time and money. (Although the capacity to videotape depositions makes it significantly less expensive than it once was when a court reporter was needed for every deposition. When using video, counsel needs only to make a written transcript of the portions of the transcript that will be used at trial. In many instances, the information counsel secures during the deposition is more important than the written transcript.) However, even such mundane acts as photocopying records costs money when counsel must pay for the copying fees charged by the records holder.

Depending on the jurisdiction, counsel may be able to access certain funds available to indigent clients to be tapped for case-related outlays. More commonly, there are no such funds for this purpose. Nonetheless, in every state that has a statutory right to counsel for indigent respondents in child welfare proceedings, there is a corresponding statutory right to an adequate lawyer. It is impossible to be thoroughly prepared for trial without engaging in some form of pretrial discovery. When a particular kind of discovery is needed for adequate preparation and the locality does not have funds set aside for such expenses, counsel should consider filing a motion seeking funds for the discovery and base the motion on the client's right to an effective lawyer, a right that would be denied in the case unless counsel can secure the needed pretrial information.

In many courts, such a motion will be denied without much consideration because judges commonly regard their job as husbanding budgets for the county. When there is a clash between the cost needed to represent a client adequately and the willingness of the state to pay for it, the right to an effective lawyer must prevail. When the court denies the motion for needed discovery funds, counsel should seek an interlocutory appeal, if such appeals may be brought in the jurisdiction. Where there is no possibility of appeal from anything other than the final order in the case, counsel should raise the pretrial motion order as one of the errors in the record requiring reversal on appeal.

7.05 What Is Discoverable?

In criminal proceedings, the Constitution imposes on prosecutors the duty to disclose all material to defendants that fits the category "exculpatory," defined by the Supreme Court to include "evidence favorable to a defendant which is material to guilt." *Brady v. Maryland,* 373 U.S. 83, 87 (1963). Prosecutors in criminal cases must disclose such evidence without a request. *United States v. Agurs*, 427 U.S. 97, 107 (1976). This requirement extends to evidence that the investigative or prosecutorial agency possesses or has the right to possess. *See In re John George Brown*, 17 Cal. 4th 873, 879, 72 Cal. Rptr. 2d 698, 952 P.2d 715 (1998).

To be discoverable in civil cases, the information sought must generally be known and in the possession of the party from whom it is being sought. In child welfare cases, the petitioner is the social services agency. The Agency's attorney may attempt to preclude discovery of information by claiming the social worker, who does not yet hold the records, is a party and the attorney-client privilege precludes discovery of the information. The petitioner may attempt to claim that material sought through discovery is not in its possession because it may not have physical custody of the evidence. The evidence may not yet have been turned over to the social services agency from the entity holding the evidence, such as a medical provider. This claim would not be successful in criminal cases. *See Kyles v. Whitney*, 514 U.S. 419, 437 (1995) (extending *Brady* to "any favorable evidence known to others acting on the government's behalf"). As the California Supreme Court explained, in criminal matters "[c]ourts have consistently 'declined to draw a distinction between different agencies under the same government, focusing instead upon the "prosecution team" which includes both investigative and prosecutorial personnel.'" *In re John George Brown*, 17 Cal. 4th at 880, 72 Cal. Rptr. 2d at 702, 952 P. 2d at 719 (quoting *United States v. Auten*, 632 F.2d 478, 481 (5th Cir. 1980)).

In a number of ways, dependency proceedings are more like criminal prosecutions than ordinary civil cases. The agency representing the social services department is part of the government and is using its powers to infringe on protected rights of citizens. As the prosecutorial agency that it is, the petitioner in these cases should have the duty to secure all evidence in the hands of some governmental agencies on which the Agency is relying in gathering information. A common example would be the Agency relying on the opinions of medical personnel at a public hospital regarding a child's physical condition allegedly caused by abuse. It should not matter whether the agency lawyer physically gathers the medical records or leaves them with the hospital. Counsel should argue—and the court should find—that this information belongs in the petitioner's hands and must be made available to the respondent.

Dependency cases, however, are considered civil proceedings virtually everywhere in the United States. The good news is that, except for *Brady*-related purposes, labeling a proceeding as "civil," rather than "criminal," is advantageous to the respondent because civil proceedings are dramatically more forthcoming in providing litigants with an opportunity to discover information than are criminal proceedings.

In civil proceedings, all information not objectionable or privileged is discoverable. For example, "[p]arties may obtain discovery regarding any matter, not privileged, that is relevant to the subject matter of the pending action, whether it relates to the claim or defense of the party seeking discovery or the claim or defense of any other party." FLA. R. JUV. P. 8.245. In California, where prehearing discovery is construed to favor informal disclosure, "informal disclosures, (are) subject to the right of a party to show privilege or other good cause not to disclose specific material or information." CAL. R. CT. 5.546(a).

In many civil proceedings, however, the information being sought must be in the possession of the adverse party. The petitioner in juvenile dependency cases is the social services agency, and its initial response to a report of abuse or neglect often comes by way of a person calling in to the agency "hotline." Neither the informant's name nor the actual statement made is discoverable in many jurisdictions because this information is deemed confidential. If the law enforcement agency involved in the initial response also opens a criminal case, it may attempt to withhold information because giving out information on a case subject to an ongoing investigation would compromise law enforcement's ability to investigate.

Often agency attorneys claim they do not have the information being requested, for example, medical records, or complete medical records. Issuing a subpoena *duces tecum* directly to the medical provider or the entity from which the information is being sought in order to copy and inspect the records is often the quickest way to secure the desired information. To be assured that one gets the desired information, the request should be detailed and specific.

As with all discovery inquiries, specific objections to requested material may be made by asserting that the material is irrelevant, immaterial, or confidential. Certain material may be protected as within the attorney-client privilege, physician-patient privilege, the psychotherapist-patient privilege, or other privileges. When faced with such an objection, counsel must conduct research to determine whether the objects are legally valid.

7.06 Ethical Duty to Conduct Discovery

As previously mentioned, parents in dependency proceedings have the right to the effective assistance of counsel, at least in those jurisdictions that assure parents a right to counsel. In the words of the Supreme Court of Texas, "the statutory right to counsel in parental-rights termination cases embodies the right to effective counsel." *In re M.S.*, 115 S.W.3d 534, 544, 46 Tex. Sup. Ct. J. 999 (2003). Almost every state that has considered the question has agreed that the right to assigned counsel, whatever its origins, carries with it the right to an effective lawyer. *See, e.g., In re E.D. v. State Dep't of Human Res.*, 777 So. 2d 113, 115 (Ala. 2000); *In re Rushing*, 9 Kan. App. 2d 541, 543, 684 P. 2d 445, 448 (1984); *State v. A.H.* (*In re E.H.*), 880 P.2d 11, 13 (Utah. App. 1994).

Counsel has a duty to fight for the client's right to an effective lawyer. Accepting conditions that make it impossible for counsel to be effective makes lawyers for indigent clients partners with the government. Unfair rules need to be challenged by lawyers for respondents in child welfare proceedings so that lawyers are able to protect the clients' rights. Such challenges will not make counsel popular with the court, but current rules in many places make it practically impossible for court-assigned lawyers to perform the amount of pretrial preparation that would be regarded as a minimum amount in any proceeding in which the rights at stake are as important as they are in these matters.

A major problem for parents' lawyers, however, is that courts rarely will impose sanctions on the Agency for failing to comply fully with discovery requests or rules. Certainly, the remedy that may be available in some proceedings—dismissal of the Petition or prohibiting the introduction of certain evidence or calling a particular witness—is practically unheard of in child welfare cases due to the importance of the state's interests in protecting children. Because that interest is commonly expressed in speedy trial requirements, parents' lawyers are often placed in the position of not having received material to which they are entitled and nonetheless pressured to participate in the contested hearing that the court is loath to postpone. Delay in juvenile dependency cases is disfavored and many courts will work hard to keep to the mandated time requirements imposed by statute or court rules. All of this makes it particularly important for counsel to focus on securing discovery promptly.

Undertaking routine discovery in every case is a minimum obligation of lawyers. There can be no strategy in failing to do so. Counsel will never know what s/he failed to learn through discovery and no privately retained lawyer would forgo this invaluable tool designed to place the lawyer and client in an adequate position to make sound strategic choices in the case.

7.07 Traditional Forms of Discovery

Traditional forms of discovery include depositions, interrogatories, and requests for admissions and the production of documents.

7.07(a) Depositions

Depositions are widely used in most general civil proceedings. However, time constraints and costs associated with taking a deposition usually prohibit the practical application of this discovery tool in juvenile dependency cases. Unless a motion to shorten time can be procured from the judicial officer, a deposition is a notice proceeding and usually requires thirty days' notice. The other practical consideration is the cost of a deposition. It is a reported proceeding, and unless the court allows an audio or video recording of it, a certified court reporter is expensive.

7.07(b) Interrogatories

Interrogatories—another form of traditional discovery in civil proceedings—are written questions submitted to a party or witness. They are commonly limited to a specific number. Texas, for example, has a twenty-five-question limit on interrogatories, and Illinois limits written interrogatories to thirty questions, including subsections, in most cases. Ill. Sup. Ct. R. 213. In California, parties served with written interrogatories usually have at least thirty days to respond, which may be too long when contested evidentiary hearings are supposed to begin before then. This thirty-day period is common in many jurisdictions.

Civil discovery rules ordinarily provide for both written interrogatories addressed to the opposing party and examinations (or depositions) of witnesses before trial. Counsel should consider serving written interrogatories to be answered by the caseworker and perhaps other agency personnel. These can be served within days of picking up the case after developing a bank of standard interrogatories, which are easily adaptable to the circumstances of the particular case and served without much effort. Among the questions to ask routinely include:

- the qualifications of the caseworker, including his or her educational background, degrees earned, licensure, work experience, and number of years of employment at the Agency;
- the caseload of the worker, including the number and types of cases the worker is currently handling;
- the specific facts giving rise to the charges in the Petition; how the matter was originally called to the Agency's attention; what steps the Agency has taken to investigate the case; whether the worker visited the respondent's home and, if so, when; whether the worker spoke with the respondent and, if so, when and under what circumstances; what the respondent was asked; what the respondent said;
- whether the worker spoke with the child and, if so, when and under what circumstances; what the child was asked; and what the child said;
- all information pertaining to the case that was in the possession of the Agency at the time of filing of the Petition; the sources of each item of information; when, where, and under what circumstances conversations were had between the agency personnel and persons having knowledge of the case; and the precise words spoken in those conversations. Counsel should also request copies of all notes or summaries of those conversations.

7.07(c) Requests for Admissions

Requests for Admissions are a rarely used discovery device in dependency cases.

7.07(d) Request for Production of Documents

The most important discovery tool in dependency cases may be a *Request for Production of Documents*. If the jurisdiction does not require that documents be given to respondents in dependency cases, it is incumbent on counsel to request documents in every case. California, and some other states, have informal discovery rules and require that certain documents be shared in every case. For example, California requires disclosure by the Agency, through its attorney, of any evidence or information within petitioner's possession or control favorable to the parent and also requires that the social worker's and police reports be given to the respondent as well. CAL. R. CT. 5.546.

There is a natural temptation to skim records that appear at first glance to have no bearing on counsel's present conception of the case, particularly when—as is all too frequent—the records consist mainly of vacuous work and tedious jargon. Nonetheless, they should be read carefully.

In practice, such evidence is not usually made available in the way the law requires. When counsel is aware that discovery requirements are not being adhered to and is unable to secure compliance by requesting the information informally, counsel's only option is to make a motion in court. Although the duty to disclose favorable information is a continuing one, it is rarely practiced. Once the initial requested information is turned over, counsel should periodically renew a request for such information.

If informal discovery is the local practice, requests are effective by sending a discovery letter at the beginning of every case. If formal discovery is used, counsel should prepare a template motion to use in every case. The motion may be adapted for specific inquiries when necessary to request important subsequent documents as they are produced. For example, law enforcement may generate an initial report based on detaining contact with the family, and this will be turned over to parent's counsel. However, oftentimes follow-up interviews will take place; unless parent's counsel re-requests information, counsel may be surprised at the time of hearing with this new information.

Below is a list of frequently requested documents that greatly assist counsel in their defense of the parent. Except for the procurement of medical reports, the cost of gathering the information is negligible.

- All social workers' reports, whether or not said report is in connection with the pending matter or a previous matter regarding the child subject to this filed petition, a sibling, or parent.
- All records of statements, admissions, or conversations by the child, parent, or guardian taken by any person, whether or not said statement, admission, or conversation is in connection with the pending matter or a previous matter.
- All records of statements, admissions, or conversations by a co-participant taken, whether or not said statement, admission, or conversation is in connection with the pending matter or a previous matter.
- Names and addresses of all witnesses interviewed by an investigating authority, including law enforcement agencies, in connection with the pending matter, whether or not counsel intends to call the person as a witness.
- All written records of statements, and the identity of the person making said statement, given to an investigating authority in the pending matter or any previous matters investigated by the Department of Children Services, whether or not counsel intends to call the person as a witness.
- All photographs or physical evidence relating to the pending matter.
- Records of prior felony convictions of the witnesses counsel intends to call.

- All case notes, log notes, and handwritten notes.
- The names, addresses, and curriculum vitae of all expert witnesses counsel intends to call as an expert witness.
- All hospital records of child(ren) relating to the pending matter including, but not limited to, admissions summary, discharge summary, nurses notes, physician notes, reports, results of examinations, including x-rays, MRI, CT, eye examinations, other examinations, summaries, diagnosis, and prognosis.
- All police reports regarding (child) or (parent) relating to the pending matter.

7.07(e) Investigations

On-site investigations are often necessary to complete preparation for trial. In many cases, it is crucial for counsel to personally visit the parent's home. When counsel inspects the home or any site whose physical characteristics may be important, counsel should arrange to have pictures taken of the site that can be produced in court, if relevant to a contested issue. Interviewing neighbors and friends as potential witnesses is also important. Finding a reason to call them as witnesses may be helpful even when their role is largely peripheral. Their very presence can be a signal to the judge that the parent is sufficiently well-regarded in his or her community that neighbors and friends are willing to appear in court to testify on the parent's behalf.

7.07(f) Discovery by the Petitioner

Among the most common and important means by which petitioners rely on the court to secure discovery after the Petition has been filed is to request an examination of the respondent by medical or other professionals. Counsel should always request the right to be present during these court-ordered examinations. Some courts have held that a parent has a constitutional right to counsel at these examinations because they are critical stages of the litigation and because counsel cannot effectively cross-examine the professional at trial if s/he was not present during the interview itself to observe the interaction between the parent and the professional. *See, e.g., In the Matter of Alexander L.*, 60 N.Y.2d 329, 457 N.E.2d 731, 469 N.Y.S.2d 626 (1983) (holding that a parent has the right for an attorney to observe the court-ordered psychiatric examination in absence of a demonstration as to how such presence would impair the validity and effectiveness of the particular examination). If counsel is able to obtain the services of a defense expert consultant, the consultant may be able to attend this interview instead of counsel.

7.08 Pretrial Motions

7.08(a) Demurrers or Motions to Dismiss for Failure to State a Cause of Action

Demurrers or motions akin to a demur may be made to challenge the sufficiency of the Petition. Demurrers address a failure of a Petition to state a cause of action or the vagueness and uncertainty of the allegations against the parent.

In every jurisdiction, a Petition is defective unless it contains a concise statement of facts, separately stated, to support the conclusion that the child upon whose behalf the Petition is being brought is a person within the definition of the statute under which the proceedings are being instituted. When a Petition fails to identify with clarity the exact behavior by the respondent that is asserted to warrant the jurisdiction of the court, counsel should file a motion to dismiss the Petition for failure to state a cause of action, a motion to make the pleadings more definite and certain, or any similar motion that is authorized by the state's general civil procedures as a means of challenging the facial sufficiency of an initial pleading or requiring the pleader to clarify it. Counsel will find it considerably easier to prepare for a trial in which discrete acts allegedly committed by the parent on designated dates are the matters to be tried as opposed to when the client is charged generally with being an unfit parent or neglecting the needs of the child.

A demurrer must be made prior to entering a plea. However, in the name of expeditiously resolving a case, courts sometimes allow a plea to be entered and the setting of a demurrer. If the demurrer is not sustained, the court is then ready to go forward with the case.

The grounds for a demurrer must appear on the face of the pleading or from judicially noticeable matters. *See, e.g.*, CAL. CIV. P. CODE § 430.30(a) (1972); WIS. STAT. § 802.06(2)(a) (2007); W. VA. CODE § 56-4-36 (1997); *Blank v. Kirwan*, 39 Cal. 3d 311, 318, 703 P. 2d 58, 62, 216 Cal. Rptr. 718, 722 (1985). When the demurrer is based on the legal sufficiency of a pleading, the sole issue will be whether the facts pleaded, if true, state a valid cause of action (does the Petition plead facts entitling the petitioner to relief?). *See, e.g., Limandri v. Judkins,* 52 Cal. App. 4th 326, 339, 60 Cal. Rptr. 2d 539, 545 (1997); *Larson v. City of Tomah*, 193 Wis. 2d 225, 233, 532 N.W.2d 726, 729 (1995). A general demurrer admits the truth of all material allegations properly pleaded in the challenged pleading, regardless of possible difficulties of proof. *See Blank*, 39 Cal. 3d at 318, 703 P. 2d at 62, 216 Cal. Rptr. at 722. No matter how unlikely or improbable, petitioner's allegations must be accepted as true for the purpose of ruling on the demurrer. *See, e.g., Del. E. Webb Corp. v. Structural Materials Co.*, 123 Cal. App. 3d 593, 604, 176 Cal. Rptr. 824, 830 (1981); *Evan v. Cameron*, 121 Wis. 2d 421, 426, 360 N.W.2d 25, 28 (1995). However, this rule does not apply to allegations expressing mere conclusions of law, allegations contradicted by the exhibits to the complaint, or matters of which judicial notice may be taken. *See, e.g., Vance v. Villa Park Mobile homes Estates,* 36 Cal. App. 4th 698, 709, 42 Cal. Rptr. 2d 723, 729 (1995); *Krings v. Haberman*, 136 Wis. 2d 555, 402 N.W.2d 389 (1987).

There may be certain costs to failing to file a demurrer (beyond the obvious one of losing the opportunity for the court to dismiss the Petition). Some courts have held that the failure to file a demurrer or other motion addressed to the sufficiency of the Petition constitutes a waiver of any claim that the Petition was facially defective, denying counsel on appeal the chance to make that argument. *See, e.g., In re Shelly J.,* 68 Cal. App. 4th 322, 328–329, 79 Cal. Rptr. 2d 922, 926 (1998).

Counsel should not be deterred from filing demurrers even when there is no formal provision for them in dependency cases. Appellate courts often will rule that such pleadings challenging the sufficiency of the Petition are available even when no explicit rule permits them. *See, e.g., In re Fred J.*, 89 Cal. App. 3d 168, 176, 152 Cal. Rptr. 327, 330 (1979). In Florida, for example, rules specifically promulgated to regulate juvenile court practice apply. These rules allow for general motions and motions to dismiss, but do not mention demurrers. *See* FLA. R. JUV. P. 8.235(a), 8.235(b). Despite this omission, the notes accompanying the rules state that the controlling rules "allow any party to move for a dismissal based on the grounds that there are no material facts in dispute and that these facts are not legally sufficient to prove dependency." FLA. R. JUV. P. 8.235 Committee notes (2010).

7.08(b) Motions to Affect the Pleading or Motions for Summary Judgment

Motions directed at affecting the pleadings are motions to strike a count or a portion of a count in the Petition, motions for a judgment on the pleadings, motions for directed verdict, and motions for summary adjudication. Not all jurisdictions have codified these types of motions for juvenile dependency cases. In some jurisdictions, motions for summary judgment are an important tool available to parents' attorneys. These motions are based on the claim that uncontested evidence requires ruling for the respondent without the need to conduct an evidentiary hearing. Closely related in concept to a demurrer or motion to dismiss for failure to state a cause of action, a motion for summary judgment focuses not on what is alleged in the Petition that is insufficient as a matter of law but on what remains as a contested fact after discovery has been completed. When the uncontested facts require judgment for the respondent if those facts were adduced at an evidentiary hearing, counsel should consider filing a motion for summary judgment on all of the charges in the Petition or on particular charges. For example, the Agency may have pled that an injury occurred both intentionally, and, in the alternative, negligently. There may be enough evidence to go forward with an adjudication based on the theory of negligence, but not enough evidence to prove abuse by intentional, inflicted means. Counsel should attach to the motion the statements of witnesses secured through discovery or affidavits that demonstrate there are no contested facts that could support a finding against the respondent.

This motion is a very useful tool for counsel because it provides an opportunity to set forth in writing all of the good facts in the case. Having the judge read them before the adjudicatory hearing begins often pays dividends even when the motion is denied. It is an invaluable way to reframe the case more favorably to the parent before the trial starts.

These motions may be difficult or impossible to file in some jurisdictions due to time restrictions. A successful motion to strike a portion of the Petition prior to the adjudicatory hearing makes defending the Petition considerably more focused by limiting information received by the court, often changing the entire tenor of the case.

7.08(c) Motions in Limine

Motions *in limine* may be made on the date of the adjudication hearing or even prior to the hearing date. Notice should be given to all parties so as to provide the other side with the ability to respond.

1. *A Motion to Exclude Evidence* is a common Motion *in limine*, and is usually made after discovery has been completed. The best practice is to marshal all of the evidence and be prepared to bring a Motion to Exclude Evidence, usually based on lack of foundation, relevance, hearsay, lack of authentication, or to exclude evidence based on the assertion of a privilege.
2. *Motions to Compel Discovery* or *Motions to Continue* for failure to produce discovery or evidence are also common pre-adjudication motions. Often the Agency's attorney will refuse to provide specific requests for discovery, such as a medical report, based on the assertion that the information is not within his or her possession and control. But some States, like Texas, may require parties requesting enforcement of a request for discovery to include a certificate that reasonable efforts to resolve the dispute prior to court intervention were made. TEX. R. CIV. P. 191.2. A party may then seek a court order to compel compliance, as well as sanctions. Sanctions may include precluding admission of evidence; however, courts are usually reluctant to impose this sanction on the Agency or child because it could create an outcome that may be contrary to the best interest of the child, that is, dismissal of an allegation.
3. *Motions to Take Judicial Notice* of various kinds of evidence should be made by a Motion *in limine*. The most commonly used judicially noticed evidence includes decisional, constitutional, and statutory law of any State of the United States, and of the United States, Rules of Court, the true signification of all English words and phrases and of all legal expressions, and facts and propositions of generalized knowledge so universally known that they cannot reasonably be the subject of dispute. Counsel must be careful where opposing counsel will seek to have the legal file of previous cases pertaining to the parties, or the legal file of the open case admitted into evidence by judicial notice. Although these files contain information that can be judicially noticed, such as previous orders of the court, they also contain information that may have been previously excluded because of other considerations such as hearsay. At a minimum, before the court takes judicial notice of any document, counsel should receive a copy of it and thoroughly review it.
4. *Motion to Exclude Testimony* may also be made by way of a Motion *in limine*. It is not uncommon for a party to attempt to qualify a witness who is an expert in one field as an expert in another filed. For example, the Agency's attorney may have a report in which a pediatrician made opinions on ophthalmological matters and this physician is scheduled to testify as a witness. Counsel should make

a motion to exclude not only the opinions in the report that are outside of the pediatrician's field of expertise but also to exclude him as an expert witness on ophthalmological matters.

7.09 Conclusion

In too many dependency proceedings in the United States, local practice is so informal that it stands alone among all courts adjudicating important rights as a court that does not take seriously the general rules of practice that have been designed to ensure fairness to all parties. Counsel for parents in these proceedings can be an important force to upgrade the standard of practice by using standard means of pretrial practice employed in all other courts. Though there is sure to be pushback from experienced practitioners on the other side and from judges who are not used to efforts to formalize court procedure, the advantages that come from utilizing the tools discussed in this chapter will far outweigh the temporary discomfort that will come from improving court practice.

CHAPTER 8

Negotiating for Services for the Family in Court; Admissions to the Petition

Kara Finck

Services to parents and children in abuse and neglect proceedings can make the difference between a timely reunification of the family and a child's extended stay in foster care. Focusing on services from the beginning of the case, especially throughout permanency hearings, gives counsel a wider range of options to contest the original Petition, to argue for alternative dispositions, and to advocate for the goal of a child's return to his or her parent at the permanency hearing. This chapter will focus on the role of the service plan in abuse and neglect proceedings, strategies for negotiating services on behalf of parents, and an overview of the process for enforcing services through out-of-court advocacy and contempt orders.

The chapter also discusses how to determine whether to make an admission in a case and how to counsel clients about admissions and no-contest pleas. Counsel will have to consider whether an admission to the Petition is warranted to resolve the case or obtain services. Since services are a part of a parent's case both pre- and post-adjudication, legal advice about making an admission must take into account the ongoing nature of a neglect or abuse case and the impact on services. Understanding the particular consequences to making an admission or no-contest plea in family court will assist parents' attorneys in fully advising clients about their options when resolving the case.

8.01 Identifying When Services Are Not Provided or Needed by Using Out-of-Court Measures

In abuse and neglect cases, the service plan is one of the most critical aspects of the case, and can be an integral part of a successful resolution. Counsel should understand the federal and local laws detailing the requirements for developing and recording service plans. With that foundation, counsel will be in a better position to (1) determine when service plans are not being properly implemented, (2) to enforce the service plan, and ultimately, (3) to ensure that the parent is receiving necessary services.

Initially, a parent's attorney must determine whether services are necessary at all in the case, and if so, which services are appropriate. Although the traditional default may be that services are always necessary if a case has come to family court, there should be an independent assessment conducted by the parent's attorney to determine the appropriate and individualized services in that particular case. Ideally, this determination is done in collaboration with the parent and any collateral sources that the parent identifies as supports. If counsel has access to an independent social worker, counsel should include them in the assessment of service needs, as his or her training will be helpful in determining the service plan that is most likely to succeed.

In all states, child welfare laws require that services be provided to parents and children to address the allegations that brought the family into the child welfare system. Services may include mental health counseling, parenting skills classes, substance abuse treatment, individual counseling, group counseling, and independent living skills. In addition to the better-known services that address drug abuse and mental health issues, there are concrete services that may be particularly helpful for the client. These services include assistance with obtaining food, transportation, financial assistance, and housing. The services provided should be linked to promoting the best interests of the child, and at the outset of the case, to furthering the goal of return to parent if a child has been placed in foster care.

The range of services available will vary by jurisdiction, and it is important for counsel to become familiar with the local service providers, including drug treatment programs, community-based mental health clinics, and social service agencies. Service providers can be helpful sources of information, such as by providing updates on services, providing additional recommendations, and testifying in support of the client in court. Sometimes, a foster care agency will be responsible for providing the parent with services within the agency, in addition to supervising the case or making referrals to a third-party provider. For example, a foster care agency charged with supervising the case may also conduct its own parenting skills classes. The parent's service plan might include attending a parenting skills program at the agency and engaging in individual therapy through a referral to a community-based mental health clinic.

Counsel should remember that services are not limited to cases involving an out-of-home placement or where children are in foster care. For parents whose children remain in their care, there are home-based services, including intensive case management, individual counseling, and parenting and life skills training. Additionally, counsel may request transition or post-reunification services for a client and his or her family if counsel thinks those would ensure a successful transition plan or reunification.

8.02 The Service Plan Review in a Child Welfare Case

One of the most common mechanisms for identifying services is through the service plan review meeting. Jurisdictions use different terms for this process including family service plan meetings, case staffing, service plan reviews, family team conferences, and case planning meeting.

The service plan or case plan is an integral part of all child welfare cases and plays a large part in the court proceedings. Federal law requires that the child welfare agency develop a written case plan when any child is placed in foster care. *See* Adoption Assistance and Child Welfare Act of 1980, Pub. L. No. 96-272, 94 Stat. 500. States are responsible for determining whether the specific standards for the case plan are articulated in statutes or regulations. The relevant law should specify the following: the time frame for developing the case plan, whether a case plan is required for all children receiving services or only those children placed in out-of-home care, whether the child is involved in creating the case plan, and whether any other stakeholders are included in developing the case plan. Additionally, the case plan should set out any goals or objectives for the parents to fulfill during the case and the projected time frame for achieving those goals and objectives. Often, the case plan also covers the visitation schedule for the parents, including the frequency, level of supervision, and time frame for visits.

The terminology for the case plan meeting will differ from state to state. In North Carolina, the case plan meeting is referred to as a "permanency planning child and family team" and in Missouri the plan meeting is the "family support team meeting." *See* Case Planning for Families Involved with Child Welfare Agencies, Child Welfare Information Gateway 3 (2010). Parents' attorneys should become familiar with the terms used in their jurisdiction. The court or the local child welfare agency might have this information available on a website or in brochures. Nationally, this information is compiled by the federal Department of Health and Human Services through the Child Welfare Information Gateway.

In California, the written case plan must be completed within sixty days of the child being removed from the parent's care or the date of the dispositional hearing if the child has not been placed in out-of-home care. *See* Cal. Welf. & Inst. Code § 16501.1 (2014). California law also requires that "the case plan shall be updated as the service needs of the child and family dictate." *Id.* at § 16501.1(d). The content of the case plan is explicitly laid out in the code and must include the "specific goals and the appropriateness of the planned services in meeting these goals." *Id.* at § 16501.1(f)(2).

Louisiana has a similar provision requiring the case plan to state "a plan for assuring that the child receives safe and proper care and that services are provided to the parents, child and foster parents in order to improve the conditions in the parents' home, facilitate the safe return of the child to his own home or other permanent placement, or both, and address the needs of the child while in foster care, including a plan for visitation." LA. CHILD. CODE ANN. art. 675 (2014).

New Jersey requires the case plan to include "the needs of the child, the parent, and the child's care provider in order to meet the case goal; the behavioral and other changes expected from each person; the services or actions intended to meet the identified needs and who is responsible to provide the services and complete the activities, with projected timeframes." N.J. STAT. ANN. § 30:4C-55 (2014).

While the mechanisms for conducting case plan meetings will vary depending on the particular policies of the state and the local child welfare agency, the ultimate goal of the meetings is threefold: (1) to develop a service or case plan for the parent, the children, and any other parties; (2) to specify who is responsible for implementing the service plan; and (3) to record the service plan in accordance with local, state, and federal regulations. It is important to consider each of these goals when counseling a parent about his or her participation in the service plan review meeting. Attorneys for parents will need to be familiar with the case plans for all of their clients. Advocating for a successful case plan can pave the way for a quicker reunification of the family or resolution to the case.

8.02(a) Creating the Service Plan: The Service Plan Review Meeting and Its Role in the Case

In order to develop the case plan, the child welfare agency holds a service plan meeting with the parent and other stakeholders. This meeting includes a review of the allegations in the Petition and a discussion of what, if any, services should be included in the service plan for the parents, children, and family as a whole. Commonly, the meeting includes a child welfare agency caseworker, a foster care agency caseworker if applicable, the parents and children over the age of twelve, and any other persons suggested by the parent or the Agency.

Although the allegations in the Petition are certainly discussed, there is nothing to prevent the child welfare agency or child advocate from seeking services designed to address issues not alleged in the Petition. Therefore, counsel should inform the client in advance that the meeting may include questions or requests that go beyond the Petition and services that are not directly responsive to the allegations in the Petition. For example, suppose a Petition alleges that a parent has failed to meet the minimum degree of care because of a dirty house and lack of supervision. At the service plan meeting, the agency caseworkers may suggest that the parent undergo a mental health evaluation or drug test, even though the allegations do not include substance abuse or mental illness as a ground for neglect. Additionally, evidence that was not included in the Petition may be referenced in the service plan meeting, including information from collateral sources or the caseworker's observations.

Counsel should also make clear to the parent that the service plan meeting is an extra-judicial meeting that is not confidential. Therefore, anything said in the meeting is not only admissible in court, but will be permanently included in the agency records also. As a consequence, if the parent admits to something that would constitute an admission during the service plan review, it will be treated in the same manner as an admission in court. Because these meetings typically happen before trial, counsel must take pains to explain this to the parent. Parents may not understand, unless advised by counsel, that they do not have to discuss the specific allegations in the Petition but can limit their discussion to the need for or agreement to services going forward. This is especially important in jurisdictions where parents attend service plan meetings by themselves without counsel or parent advocates present.

In all jurisdictions, the service plan meeting will identify the services for the particular case and who is responsible for providing those services directly or making a referral to an outside agency for the service. The service plan meeting will also discuss the visitation plan or parent-to-child contact, including the level of supervision, location of the visitation, and frequency. Referrals for the services identified at the meeting are often made contemporaneously or soon thereafter. It is important to keep track of the referrals made for the client, including how those referrals were communicated. For example, if counsel has a non-English speaking client, counsel would want to request that written referrals are written in the client's native language and service providers with translation or foreign language capabilities are identified. In some cases, parents' attorneys request that copies of all written referrals are provided to them as well to ensure both that the referrals are being made and that the parent has the accurate information to follow through on the referral. Counsel can make the request for all written referrals in the formal discovery demand, advise the parent to request copies, request an order to that effect from the court, or send the parent with a written request for copies of all referrals.

At the conclusion of the service plan meeting, the Agency generates a record of the meeting including any agreement to engage in services, a visitation plan, and a description of the plan for the next period of time, generally anywhere from two to six months. In most jurisdictions, the parent will be asked to sign this report and to note whether they consent to the service plan. Ideally, the parent's attorney should be provided with a copy of any document originating from the service plan review as a matter of course, but counsel might need to specifically request this document in court on the record or through the means described above for obtaining copies of service referrals.

It is critical to keep track of the service plan meetings and any reviews made in writing, given the important role that services play in an abuse and neglect case. First, the service plan will often be incorporated into the court's order. Therefore, counsel should make clear to the parent that the terms and conditions in the case plan include responsibilities imposed on the Agency and obligations imposed on the parent. When the services are incorporated into a court order, the parent could be held in contempt for any alleged violation of that order. It is critical to underscore the difference between the service plan review and a court order, so that the parent is fully aware of the liability that attaches for failure to fulfill the order.

Second, service plans are generally reviewed or discussed at every court appearance. To advocate effectively for the parent, counsel needs to understand the rationale behind the service plan so that counsel can demonstrate compliance and success or to raise objections to the service plan. This also requires counsel to remain updated throughout the case as to the client's progress with services, especially if there is the possibility of advocating for a change in custody or court order as a result of compliance.

Finally, the service plan is often used explicitly as a measure of the progress the client has made in working on the issues that brought his or her family into the child welfare system. As a result, the service plan might take on more importance than the visitation schedule or relationship between the parent and children. Counsel should discuss with the parent how important the service plan is, especially in light of the individual judge on the case and the particular practices in the jurisdiction.

8.02(b) Collaborating with Social Workers on Service Plans

Whether counsel is fortunate to have a social worker in-house or is interacting with the agency caseworker assigned to the parent, collaboration with social workers is an integral part of representing parents in abuse and neglect proceedings. As such, it is important for parents' attorneys to understand the roles, expectations, and ethical codes of social workers. This cross knowledge is especially critical as part of counsel's responsibility to assess the requirement and provision of services to the parent and his or her children. As the parent's attorney, counsel should take a critical eye to the assessment and provision of services in the case. It is helpful to collaborate with a social worker who has experience working with local service providers and clients in crisis, especially when counsel is unfamiliar with the services in question.

Even if caseworkers from the child welfare agency do not have a master's degree in social work, the general principles and ethics of social work should apply in child welfare practice. It is important to be aware of social work ethical obligations, especially since the parent will interact with social workers and caseworkers far more frequently than with anyone else in the case. Social workers follow the National Association of Social Work ("NASW") Code of Ethics, which explicitly supports interdisciplinary collaboration; "[s]ocial workers who are members of an interdisciplinary team should participate in and contribute to decisions that affect the well-being of clients by drawing on the perspectives, values, and experiences of the social work profession."

See CODE OF ETHICS § 2.03 (Nat'l Ass'n of Soc. Workers 2008). However, counsel should be mindful of social workers' independent responsibility to clients and, if employed elsewhere, to their own organization or employer. As the parent's attorney, counsel should also be clear about why collaboration with a social worker is necessary and what role counsel envisions the social worker playing on the case, particularly if the social worker is part of the legal team or retained as a consultant to the case.

Some questions that may be helpful in setting expectations for the collaboration include: Who does the social worker see as the client? Are there any conflicts that can and should be anticipated? What are the limits of confidentiality in the social worker's relationship with the client? Is the social worker willing to come to court or prepare letters of support for the client? What concerns, if any, does the social worker have about sharing information about the client's services and case plan? It is important to clarify these expectations and roles early in the case. When those roles have been clarified, it is more likely that the parent will understand the collaborative but separate roles of the attorney and the social worker. Additionally, the parent will have no doubt that both professionals are advocating for their interests.

8.02(c) Establishing Trust with the Client Around Services

Services can make a huge difference when contesting the Petition on its face is not a viable strategy. In order to have a better sense of which services will be appropriate and successful, it is critical to have a trusting relationship with the client that includes open lines of communication. Counsel is in a stronger position to advocate for the client if counsel understands his or her strengths and challenges. Additionally, since these cases are not fixed in time and often last for many months or years, the open lines of communication ensure that counsel has the most current information to advocate effectively.

To the extent possible, counsel should communicate with clients not only to prepare for court hearings and status appearances, but also to obtain regular updates on cases in between court dates. In abuse and neglect cases counsel is the only person charged with zealously advocating for the parent and maintaining confidentiality. This is in sharp contrast to the various service providers and agency caseworkers who are not bound by confidentiality and may be called to testify against the parent in court. Emphasizing the special nature of the attorney-client relationship will help parents understand the importance of being honest and upfront with counsel about engagement with services, setbacks, and goals.

In many states, parents involved in the child welfare system may lack consistent methods of communication or be transient, so it is especially vital that counsel has multiple means of contacting a client. This could include finding collateral supports who are relatives or friends willing to share their contact information with counsel when it becomes impossible to get in touch directly with a client. With advances in technology, some attorneys implement a system of regular email or text communications with clients to remain updated on their engagement with services and the visitation plan. Ensuring a trusting and consistent relationship creates a solid foundation for counseling parents on service plans, case strategy, and admissions.

8.02(d) Advising Clients on Keeping a Record of Their Services and Attempts to Get Services in Place for Themselves or Their Children

In addition to developing open lines of communication to remain abreast of services and progress, counsel should encourage parents to maintain their own independent record about services and visitation. This record-keeping process could be important for court hearings when counsel may wish to challenge the Agency's position or argue whether a court order for services is needed. If parents document their interactions with all service providers, including foster care agency staff that may be providing services internally, they could provide critical information for counsel to determine whether a court order is needed for services. For example, many drug treatment agencies will provide clients with a letter when they come for a counseling or treatment session. Counsel should recommend that clients obtain documentation of their engagement with services in anticipation of a challenge from another party or a misrepresentation of the parent's participation.

The importance of current and updated information cannot be understated in these proceedings. For example, a caseworker might receive incomplete information from the service provider, perhaps indicating that the client has missed multiple appointments. The caseworker may report to the court that the client is out of compliance with the service plan and is not engaged in working toward reunification with her children. If the parent can demonstrate the opposite through letters or proof of attendance, counsel is in a stronger position to argue in court that the parent is in compliance with the service orders.

If service providers are unable or unwilling to provide clients with a record of their attendance and participation in advance of court, counsel should strongly encourage parents to create their own logs. This log should include the following information: (1) date of the service, (2) location or agency name, (3) time of appointment, and (4) a summary of what happened during the service, including the names of specific services provided whenever possible. This will assist counsel in determining whether there is a basis to challenge any issues regarding the parent's participation.

In many cases, the parent should also record any phone calls with the caseworker or other service providers. This practice empowers the parent to take an active role in his or her case and often serves as a helpful means of organizing the multitude of players involved in child welfare cases. The log should also include information on the services geared toward the children to document the parent's ongoing involvement in the child's care and services.

Ex. A Case Log for Client

Service	Date	Contact Person for Service	Notes
Individual Counseling	2/26/14	Sarah Martin	Counselor was out sick that day.
	3/1/14	Sarah Martin	Attended.
	3/8/14	Sarah Martin	Missed session. Called before to reschedule for 3/10.
	3/10/14	Sarah Martin	Attended session. Got certificate.
Parenting Class	2/25/14	Ms. Jones	Attended.
	2/28/14	Ms. Jones	Went to class.
	3/1/14	Ms. Jones	Went to class. Late by 15 minutes because of train.
	3/8/14	Mr. Wilson	Missed class. Left message for Wilson.
	3/12/14	Ms. Jones	Make-up class.

8.03 Seeking Court Orders for Services

8.03(a) Determining If Counsel Needs a Court Order to Get the Services

Prior to requesting an order for services from the court, counsel must determine why the service has not been provided by the Agency. The possible reasons could include a jurisdictional issue with the provision of a specific service, a financial prohibition, or simple negligence on the part of the child welfare agency. An example of a jurisdictional problem would be a parent seeking a special education service for her children who have been placed in foster care. Although the court may have a legal obligation to provide educational and medical services to address the child's special needs and to ensure that the placement is in the children's best interests, the court may not have the jurisdiction to order another government agency—whether federal, state, or local—to provide a particular service. In other words, the court may not have the power to order the local Department of Education to provide a specific special education service to the parents' children. The court may be limited to ordering the child welfare agency to investigate and assist the Department of Education in obtaining the specific service.

Once counsel has determined why the service has not been provided, counsel might want to attempt obtaining the service without a court order by contacting the caseworker. Additionally, if counsel has social work support or staff, counsel can often negotiate for a specific service without obtaining a court order by advocating for the client at the service plan meeting.

Whenever possible, out-of-court advocacy for the parent can be a helpful means of getting services in place without having to involve the court. In some instances, a court may be reluctant to order a particular service or, in the other extreme, will be very active in determining the type of service appropriate for the client. Of course, whenever a service is included in a court order, as opposed to simply the family service plan or the case plan, the parent may be held liable for contempt of that order if he or she fails to comply. Counsel must be mindful of the substance of any court orders and carefully assess whether a court order is absolutely necessary for that service.

If the determination is made to seek a court order, counsel should consider whether to bring service providers to court when determining which evidence to present at dispositional and permanency hearings. Often, service providers have the most current and substantive information about the parent's progress. Since the court is required to make specific findings at most hearings, the service provider who supports the parent and can testify to his or her progress is a uniquely helpful witness when arguing for a change in visitation or placement.

Service providers might be reluctant to testify in court. This reluctance might stem from a concern about how their testimony would affect the treatment relationship with the parent or about not being compensated for their time in court. In these instances, counsel would have to consider whether it is possible to get a letter of support admitted or used before a hearing to negotiate a settlement. Of course, counsel could always subpoena the service provider to testify. Before doing any of this, however, counsel should attempt to speak to the service provider about his or her position on the issue at hand. Additionally, counsel should request the release of any records relating to the parent in advance of the court appearance, presuming that counsel has previously provided the service agency with a release signed by the client.

8.03(b) Obtaining the Immediate Provision of Services by Seeking a Court Order

When counsel cannot obtain services for the parent or his or her children through extra-judicial measures such as the service plan meeting or informal advocacy, counsel should seek relief directly from the court. There are several ways to seek services through a court order, including filing a motion for the immediate provision of services and requesting services as part of the dispositional or permanency hearings. Arguably, parents are entitled to services from the beginning of the case, although the court order may only be enforceable or mandated once there has been an adjudication of abuse or neglect.

Since the Adoption and Safe Families Act (ASFA) mandates that state courts review the status of any case involving foster children at least once every six months, counsel is assured to have an opportunity to advocate for services on numerous occasions. *See* 42 U.S.C. § 675(5)(B) (2014). During the review hearings, the court must determine that the Agency has made "reasonable efforts" to reunify the child placed out of home.

See id. § 675(5)(C). As part of this inquiry, the court is to determine whether the Agency's case plan is appropriate for the family and children. For example, in Georgia, the court is charged with determining at a permanency hearing whether "reasonable efforts were made by the division to preserve and reunify the family prior to the placement of the child in the custody of the department to prevent or eliminate the need for the removal of the child from that child's home, and to make it possible for the child to return safely to the child's home." GA. ANN. CODE § 15-11-58 (2014). Therefore, the service plan and all efforts made by the Agency to engage and refer the parent will be included in the court's determination of reasonable efforts.

Some states, such as Illinois, direct the court to inquire whether "services, including placement services, are necessary, relevant, coordinated, and appropriate." *See* IL. ADMIN. CODE tit. 89, § 316.30 (2014). As a result, counsel has multiple opportunities to raise the issue of services on behalf of the parent at court appearances.

8.03(b)(1) Oral Applications for Services at Status Appearances

The frequency of court appearances varies from state to state and sometimes from county to county. While every court has adjudicatory, dispositional, and permanency review stages, the number of court appearances in between those hearings and the length of time between hearings depends on the particular court and perhaps the individual judge. Regardless of the number of listings, each appearance should be treated as an opportunity to advocate for the parent, including the provision of new or different services. Since court orders are ongoing, the parent's attorney and all other parties may raise modifications or terminations to those orders at any time. Therefore, the parent's attorney must consider the orders regarding services and visitation as ongoing orders, subject to revision throughout the pendency of the case.

Prior to filing any emergency order, there are several strategies to ensure that any order for services is implemented within the appropriate time frame. Initially, counsel could request that the court include the date by which a service must be implemented on the court order. Counsel could also request that the order include the condition that all parties receive written confirmation of a referral to a service or a written update on the service by a certain date. It is often important to reduce any oral orders from the court to written orders, especially if the order at hand implicates any party or organization that is not present in court at the time of the order.

First, counsel would need to determine the substantive content of the order sought from the court. Counsel should think broadly when considering the potential range of services to request in an order. Since most laws regarding the provision of services require that the service provided be related toward the goal of the case, there is wide latitude for creative arguments on behalf of the parent. Examples include requesting a specific provider of the service, a specific service, increased or decreased frequency of a service, and even a motion for the assignment of an independent social worker to the case if warranted. Whenever counsel is making an argument for a service, it is helpful to work with the parent and social work staff (if available) to document the need for the service and the reasons why this service would improve the safety plan or permanency goal. In order to do this, counsel should make the explicit link between the services and the best interests of the child as articulated through the service plan or goal. If counsel is able to obtain consent from all parties in advance, then counsel could present the motion as a proposed order on consent by all of the parties. If counsel is unable to obtain consent from all of the parties, counsel should be prepared to argue and to elicit testimony on both the legal basis and the rationale for the desired service. This might include calling the client to testify or subpoenaing service providers to testify in support of the motion.

Second, counsel should consider the timing of the request, either in writing or orally at a court appearance. Besides filing motions for a service to be provided through normal civil practice timelines, counsel may need to move for the immediate provision of services. Often, this will be done through an emergency order or an order to show cause, allowing the case to be brought back before the court prior to the next court appearance. Counsel should be mindful of the timelines dictated by ASFA when determining whether or not to bring an emergency motion. A case where the children have been in foster care for longer has different ramifications than a case at the beginning or where the children are at home with the parent.

8.04 Holding the Agency Accountable for Implementing the Service Plan

The first step in holding the child welfare agency accountable for the service plan is to create a system for both counsel and the client to document and record the provision of services. This can be similar to the recordkeeping described in §8.02(d). Counsel should have an ongoing discovery demand that includes updates and records from any service providers identified in the court order and/or family service plan. Often, the court order will specify a service, for example, substance abuse treatment, but not the specific provider of the service. Implicitly, the court order has mandated the child welfare agency to make a referral for that service. It is critical that counsel request in the court order that a copy of the referral be provided to counsel and the parent. This way, counsel may keep track of referrals that have not been made by the Agency as evidence supporting the request or motion to hold the Agency accountable.

Counsel could also obtain records and ongoing updates from service providers by having the parent sign an authorization for the release of confidential information from the service provider organization at the start of the program. Once the release has been signed, it may assist in creating a relationship with the service provider staff. The relationship with service providers can facilitate the timely receipt of records, updates, progress letters, and testimony at future hearings when appropriate. In the best case, the service provider becomes a collateral source for the case that will contact counsel when there are issues or concerns before there is a report to the Agency. When that happens, counsel has the opportunity to speak with the parent earlier and to try to remedy the problem prior to coming to court.

In addition to requesting copies of written referrals, counsel should also request a copy of the written family service plan or case plan as part of the court order. In many jurisdictions, all counsel and parties are provided with a copy of the case plan per the Agency's protocol. If that is not the case in a jurisdiction, then counsel should make an ongoing demand to receive both notice of any upcoming service plan meetings and a copy of any final service plans.

In many jurisdictions, clients and counsel are not provided with written orders at the end of a court appearance. It is important for clients and counsel to have the written court order after all appearances where services were ordered. Requesting that a court's order regarding services be reduced to a written order is appropriate for all counsel and especially critical for parents' attorneys. Without the written order, there might be confusion over what has been ordered of the Agency, the parent, or another service provider. The order may be provided to third-party service providers also who were not present in court to ensure that the appropriate services are provided.

Finally, counsel should provide the parent with the court order at every appearance. The written court order is helpful to explain what services are required as part of his or her court case, and it provides parents with support for their efforts to secure services. If it is not the practice in the jurisdiction to provide written orders in all instances, counsel should request that the order be reduced to writing at the end of an appearance or offer to prepare the order for the court's signature. This is another important way of holding the Agency accountable for its actions and ensuring transparency and full participation of the client.

8.04(a) Enforcing Court Orders Through Contempt Proceedings

When a client informs counsel that there is a problem with getting services, counsel has multiple strategies available to enforce the court order. Initially, counsel should confirm that the client and all relevant parties, including the service provider, have a copy of the court order in question. Counsel should also try to resolve the dispute with the caseworker and attorneys for the opposing parties out of court. Many of the same negotiation strategies discussed earlier could be used in this situation as well, including highlighting a parent's compliance or attempts at engaging with the service provider.

If out-of-court efforts to enforce a court order are unsuccessful, counsel should consider a written motion to hold the Agency in contempt of the court order or an oral motion to the court to hold the Agency accountable. Depending on the length of time before the next court date, counsel may need to consider writing a formal motion, or order to show cause, for contempt or to enforce the court order. The written motion will be heard within a shorter period of time under the jurisdiction's rules of civil procedure. This is often a successful strategy for getting the case back before the judge in advance of the next appearance, which could be as many as three to six months away. As noted earlier, the provision of services is critical to the parent's ability to reunite with his or her children and there are significant timelines in ASFA if children are placed in foster care. Therefore, counsel should not simply wait until the next scheduled court date when considerable time will elapse in the interim. The consequences to the parent's case of waiting might be too significant.

Contempt proceedings may be brought against any of the parties in the case, and any third parties that may be under the jurisdiction of the court through a court order or otherwise. Counsel will need to consult local rules to determine whether any distinction is made for moving for contempt under general civil practice rules or raising contempt as a potential remedy in family court. In Michigan, there is a specific provision for contempt in child abuse and neglect proceedings: "If the agency fails to implement court orders in a timely manner despite requests from the parent and attorney, then the attorney should file a motion requesting that the court hold the agency in contempt of court." MICH. COMP. LAWS § 712A.26 (2014).

In New York, by contrast, "[t]he provisions of the judiciary law relating to civil and criminal contempts shall apply to the family court in any proceeding in which it has jurisdiction under this act or any other law, and a violation of an order of the family court in any such proceeding which directs a party, person, association, agency, institution, partnership or corporation to do an act or refrain from doing an act." N.Y. FAM. CT. ACT § 156 (2014). Although the language suggests a broad-based contempt power, Section 156 is limited by the provision "unless a specific punishment or other remedy for such violation is provided in this act or any other law." *See id*. Therefore, if a remedy already exists in a subsection of the New York Family Court Act, contempt should not be sought as a remedy. This underscores the general principle that contempt is a last resort, particularly when other remedies, although less powerful, are available. *See, e.g.*, Merrill Sobie, PRACTICE COMMENTARIES TO THE DOMESTIC RELATIONS LAW AND THE FAMILY COURT ACT § 156 (2014).

A successful motion for contempt documents the range of out-of-court efforts made by counsel to deal with the breach of the order. These efforts might include contacting the service provider directly, providing the service provider or opposing counsel with copies of the court order, and reaching out to opposing counsel to remedy the contempt. Counsel should keep detailed records of attempts to remedy the violation without court involvement and, when appropriate, advise the parent to record any efforts as well.

8.05 Obtaining Services for the Family Without Admitting to the Petition

For many parents, one of the most frustrating and confusing parts of a court case is the need to engage in services prior to a hearing on the allegations in the Petition. It is important to stress to clients the benefits of engaging in services quickly, especially in jurisdictions where the time from the filing of the Petition to adjudication is lengthy.

Often, counsel for the city or state and the court will look at the parent's participation in services from the inception of the case, or lack thereof, when determining the level and frequency of supervised or unsupervised visits, and when negotiating a resolution to the case.

Services available prior to adjudication might not differ substantially from services available to the parents and children after adjudication. The pre-adjudication services must still be geared toward achieving the case goal of return to parent. Since they are in the pre-adjudication stage, the court, arguably, does not have the authority to mandate that the parent participate in services. A notable exception to this rule is when courts tie participation in a program to a safety determination with regard to visitation or placement. For example, a court may require, pre-adjudication, that the parent participate in a substance abuse treatment program if the child is to remain at home. Alternatively, the court may tie the level of supervision during visits with the parent's children to his or her participation and success in the substance abuse program. As a result, the order, while not technically mandating the parent to attend substance abuse treatment, might carry the same weight from the parent's perspective.

When the case is pre-adjudication, it is wise to counsel clients about the exchange of information related to their services given ongoing discovery and the common practice of asking parents to sign releases for information from service providers. Often, the petitioning Agency will request or even require a parent to sign a release of information from the service provider to the petitioner. A limited release of information might be preferable, focusing only on potentially uncontested facts, including attendance at programs or results from testing for substance abuse.

8.06 Obtaining Services for the Family by Admitting to the Petition

When counsel and the client have determined that the client will make an admission to all or part of the Petition, counsel should discuss with the client which, if any, services would likely be requested as part of the dispositional phase that follows the admission. The discussion of services should be tailored to the specific admission that the client will make in court. For example, if the client is making an admission to neglect as a result of an addiction, counsel must discuss with the client the inevitable request that the client engage in substance abuse treatment as a condition to having his or her children returned. Counsel should make clear that any admission would form the basis for the requirement of mandated services to address the substance of the admission. In some jurisdictions, the case will proceed to disposition immediately, thereby mandating the services in the dispositional order.

8.06(a) Determining Whether to Admit to the Entire Petition or a Particular Charge

A client may make an admission to all or part of the Petition alleging abuse, neglect, or dependency. When counseling a client about whether to make an admission, counsel should review whether there are allegations in the Petition that do not need to be included in the admission. This determination should be based on several factors, including the parent's statements about the veracity of the allegations in the Petition and counsel's independent assessment of their weight. Prior to counseling a client on making an admission, counsel should review the entire discovery packet in the case, including the case record, any investigatory documents, and counsel's own conversations with the client and collateral sources or witnesses about the allegations. In some cases, counsel might be able to negotiate with the petitioning attorney to limit the admission. If the parent has a collateral criminal or immigration case, counsel should always consult with the client's attorney in those proceedings to determine whether there are any collateral consequences to the admission.

8.06(b) No-Contest Pleas in Family Court

Many states allow parents to make the equivalent of a no-contest plea in criminal court in their abuse or neglect proceeding. Generally, the no-contest plea is specified in the statute delineating the requirements for entering an admission. In California, a parent "may elect to admit the allegations of the petition, plead no contest, or submit the jurisdictional determination to the court based on the information provided to the court and waive further jurisdictional hearing." CAL. R. CT. 5.682(e). As required when entering an admission, the Court must find that the "plea of no-contest . . . is freely and voluntarily made." *Id.* at 5.682(f)(5). Some jurisdictions specify the court's colloquy when accepting a no-contest plea. The court might be required to advise respondents of their rights and the consequences of the no-contest plea, similar to an admission to the Petition.

In Michigan, the court must "advise the respondent on the record or in a writing that is made part of the file" of their right to counsel and the multiple consequences of entering a plea, including trial waiver and that the plea could be used as evidence against the parent in a subsequent termination of parental rights, prior to entering a no-contest plea. *See* MICH. CT. R. 3.971(B)(1)–(4). The Michigan statute specifically states that the court is not permitted to question a respondent entering a no-contest plea, but still needs to "obtain support for a finding that one or more of the statutory grounds alleged in the petition are true." *See id.* at 3.971(C)(2). Additionally, Michigan courts are required to state on the record the reasons justifying a plea of no-contest. *See id.*

Courts in California have interpreted the validity of a no-contest plea and the counseling required to accept a no-contest plea under the same due process requirements when entering a guilty plea in criminal court. For example, when a mother appealed her no-contest plea entered in a dependency proceeding, the court found that she had knowingly and voluntarily entered the no-contest plea because she signed a written waiver form and acknowledged the no-contest plea and waivers in open court. *See In Re Patricia T.*, 91 Cal. App. 4th 400, 406 (2001). As New York law clarifies, "prior to accepting an admission to an allegation or permitting a respondent to consent to a finding of neglect or abuse," the court must advise the parent of the consequences of the order of abuse or neglect that will result from the admission or no-contest plea. *See* N.Y. FAM. CT. ACT § 1051(f). If the specific notice about these consequences, including that placement in foster care may lead to a termination of parental rights, is not provided by the court, then the finding based on the admission or no-contest plea "shall be vacated upon motion of any party." *See id.* at § 1051(f)(iii).

New Mexico has also codified the court's obligation "address[] the respondent personally in open court, determining that" the respondent understands the allegations, waiver and consequences of making an admission or no-contest plea. *See* N.M. CHILDREN'S CT. R. 10-342(C).

Whether counsel is advising a client about an admission or a no-contest plea, it is critical to underscore the waivers and consequences that follow from entering the admission or plea. Although the specific statutory language will vary by jurisdiction, the common elements are that the client is waiving their right to a full trial on the allegations and that the court will have jurisdiction to assume custody or to place the client's children. When advising a client, it is helpful to include counsel's own assessment of any specific consequences that might follow the finding. For example, if a client is making an admission or a no-contest plea to substance abuse allegations, counsel should advise the client about the potential ramifications of not completing the substance abuse treatment program once the court has entered a finding of neglect. Taking care to link the client's individual service plan with the generalized requirements for entering an admission or no-contest plea will ensure that the client truly understands not only the consequences of entering a plea but also the next steps in his or her case.

8.07 Procedure for Entering an Admission

8.07(a) Requirements for Admission

A parent or caregiver may make an admission to the allegations in the Petition to resolve the adjudicatory phase of the case. In all jurisdictions, the court will require that the parent be counseled about the consequences of the admission, including the possibility that the court orders the removal of the child from the parent's care. Therefore, it is critical that parents' attorneys discuss all of the possible outcomes from making an admission, including children remaining in foster care or potentially being adopted.

The court may also engage in a colloquy on the record when considering whether to accept an admission. The colloquy will include questions about whether the parent is willingly making the admission and whether the admission meets the statutory minimum to find neglect or abuse. For example, West Virginia's Rules of Procedure for Child Abuse and Neglect state that "the court shall determine that the parties understand the content and consequence of the admission or stipulation, the parties voluntarily consent, and the stipulation or uncontested adjudication meets the purposes of these rules and controlling statue and is in the best interests of the child." W. VA. R.

P. 26. Since the admission has to meet the statutory threshold for abuse or neglect, a parent would not be permitted to make an admission to a petition that did not contain sufficient allegations to prove abuse or neglect. This is another reason to consider carefully whether the client is making an admission to all or part of the Petition.

Similarly, New York's Family Court Act has specific guidelines for entering an admission, which require that "prior to accepting an admission to an allegation or permitting a respondent to consent to a finding of neglect or abuse, the court shall inform the respondent that such an admission or consent will result in the court making a fact-finding order of neglect or abuse, as the case may be, and shall further inform the respondent of the potential consequences of the order." N.Y. FAM. CT. ACT § 1051(f) (2014). The statute then specifies the consequences of the admission including that the court will enter a disposition that may result in the child being placed in foster care, that the placement in foster care may result in a termination of parental rights proceeding if the parent fails to comply with the case plan, and the length of time that the initial report of abuse and neglect remains accessible to employers through the state central registry. *See id.* at § 1051(f)(i–iii). Emphasizing the importance of the colloquy when accepting an admission to abuse or neglect, the statute makes clear that "any finding upon such an admission . . . without such notice being given by the court shall be vacated upon motion of any party." *See id.* Counsel's obligation to advise the client full on the consequences of the admission is clear and a thorough understanding of the client's service plan and current engagement will assist in describing the individual consequences to a parent.

In addition to the issues discussed above, counsel should also explain to the client that entering an admission means that the client is waiving his or her right to appeal. Additionally, if the client makes a specific admission, those facts in a stipulation or admission may be used against them in a criminal case. The Superior Court Rules of the Family Division in the District of Columbia require judges to inform the parent or caregiver of those two consequences and others before accepting the admission or stipulation to the petition. *See* SUP. CT. R. FAMILY DIVISION § 18(c)(1)–(5). As noted earlier, counsel should be in contact with a parent's criminal defense attorney, if there are concurrent criminal charges to ensure that an admission in family court will not compromise any options in criminal court.

8.07(b) Counseling Clients on the Consequences of Entering an Admission

At a minimum, every jurisdiction requires the court to determine that the admission is voluntary and intelligent. Therefore, counsel should explain to the client the consequences of making an admission and clarify his or her rights to contest the charges in the Petition. These rights include the right to testify, to call witnesses, to cross-examine the Petitioner's witnesses, and to otherwise present a full defense to the allegations. In order to advise the client about giving up his or her right to trial, it is important to return to the original Petition and provide an assessment of the strength of the client's case and the evidence that may be brought forward by the opposing parties. It is also important to inform the client that the determination as to abuse and neglect is based on the original Petition, and not, as some clients may mistakenly believe, about consequent participation or compliance with services.

If there is a written stipulation or admission, counsel should give a copy to the client and review it together in person prior to entering the admission. If the client must make an oral admission in court, counsel should discuss the general process for making the admission and what the client will be expected to say. These admissions go more smoothly when counsel practices the court proceeding with the client before it takes place. In many jurisdictions, if the client decides not to make the admission at the last minute or the court refuses to accept the admission, the case will proceed immediately to trial. In light of this, it is especially important to counsel the client on all aspects of the admission so that there are no surprises and the client is comfortable engaging in the colloquy with the court.

8.07(c) Determining Which Section of the Petition to Admit

The first step is to determine which sections of the Petition will form the basis of the admission. After counsel has reviewed all of the documents obtained through discovery and conducted a thorough investigation into the merits of the case, counsel is in a position to determine which charges in the Petition would most likely be upheld after a contested trial. Often, there is sufficient proof for one charge, but not for all charges in the Petition. For instance, in a case in which a parent is accused of educational neglect and misusing drugs, counsel might conclude that there is no hope of prevailing on the educational neglect charge because the school records document a very high number of unexcused absences. In these circumstances, when the client denies misusing drugs or there is insufficient proof of substance abuse in the file, counsel should advise the client that it is important to admit only to educational neglect, but not to substance abuse.

It is often important to negotiate the specific admission with the Petitioner's attorney and the lawyer for the child before the court appearance, since some jurisdictions permit these parties to raise objections to the admission. In this negotiation, counsel should include counsel's assessment of the case after reviewing the discovery and also counsel's current information on the client's services and visitation plan. Often, a client's participation and compliance with services can be marshaled as evidence supporting a more favorable resolution in the case. Therefore, it is important that counsel has the most current and substantive information about a client's participation, so that counsel can advocate for the best resolution. It can be helpful to determine what the other parties would request at the dispositional hearing. Once counsel knows their positions, he or she can begin advising the client on the potential admission and strategy around disposition after the finding of abuse or neglect.

8.07(d) Counseling the Client on the Admission and Subsequent Disposition

As noted earlier, the court will engage in a colloquy with the parent to ensure that the admission is knowing and voluntary. Many jurisdictions spell out the colloquy in a statute, which makes preparing the parent for the court appearance easier. At a minimum, the court will inquire whether parents understand what they are giving up by making the admission, whether they discussed the admission with their attorney, and whether they are under any disability that would render them incapable of making the admission, such as being under the influence of medication. If counsel is unsure of the specific language required in court, it is often helpful to ask the judge's court clerk or other counsel to get a better sense. The process of making an admission in court can vary widely depending on the judge and the jurisdiction. Counsel will need to prepare the parent if the judge is going to detail all of the collateral consequences that stem from making an admission, such as a termination of parental rights and adoption. Counsel does not want the parent to hear those consequences for the first time when he or she is in the middle of making an admission to the petition.

Once the admission to the Petition is made, the case will move to the disposition phase. Many jurisdictions schedule the dispositional hearing to follow immediately after the admission. Other jurisdictions will postpone it until another court date. When considering whether to proceed directly to the dispositional hearing, counsel needs to assess how the specifics of the admission will affect the content of the dispositional order. If counsel thinks that the client might be in a position to request a return of his or her children as part of the dispositional order, it might make sense to delay the disposition if additional time will ensure that result. As a general matter, counsel should think carefully about the strategy in making an admission and either postponing the disposition or proceeding quickly. For example, counsel should consider the impact of additional time to complete services, participate in more visitations, and be viewed by the court and other parties as engaging in the process.

8.08 Conclusion

The process of counseling clients about services, negotiating for services, and enforcing appropriate and meaningful service plans through court orders requires parents' attorneys to step outside of their courtroom advocacy and engage with the extra judicial processes that often define the clients' experiences of a family court case. Counsel's willingness to think critically and strategically about services from the beginning of the case supports the development of a trusting relationship with clients and ultimately a richer and more substantive counseling when educating clients about case milestones, such as an admission to the Petition.

CHAPTER 9

The Adjudicatory Hearing

Darice Good-Dworak and Diana Rugh Johnson

9.01 Introduction and Overview: The Nature of the Adjudicatory Hearing

Although adjudicatory hearings (or trials) are not the way most dependency cases are resolved, lawyers representing parents must be confident that they can perform well in such hearings. Although most cases settle, parents' lawyers can better negotiate for a settlement when they are comfortable participating in a trial. Lawyers can convince themselves (and then their clients) that a particular settlement is good. But sometimes, lawyers regard a settlement as good because they are afraid of going to trial. When that fear is based on the merits of the case and the lawyer's assessment that the trial is unwinnable, all is fine. But when lawyers conclude the risk of going to trial is high because of their lack confidence as trial lawyers, lawyers are doing their clients a great disservice.

This chapter is written for both the novice and seasoned trial lawyer. As will be explained, the two most important ingredients for successful trial practice are careful preparation and developing a successful theory of the case. Respondents in dependency proceedings deserve lawyers who are willing to go to trial if necessary.

9.02 Influencing and Changing the Culture of a Non-Adversarial System

Across the country, courts that handle child welfare cases expect non-adversarial practice in which attorneys for the various parties always resolve the allegations in the Petition without contesting the charges and, almost always, on terms favorable to the state. In these courts, practice is exceedingly relaxed and informal. Such an atmosphere may work well for agencies and courts, but in some instances will not serve the interests of parents, who face the potential permanent loss of their children. Often, a parent's best defense to the charges requires contesting the charges in a trial. When this is the case, counsel must work toward shifting the court atmosphere from one that may be too informal to a more respectful, formal setting. Striving to accomplish this even before the trial begins will often facilitate the creation of the ideal atmosphere for successful trials.

Among the steps parents' attorneys may take to increase the formality of the process is to pay careful attention to dressing appropriately, similar to how counsel would dress in federal court or any court in which the parties are respected as important members of the community. Counsel may also consider advising clients how to dress for court and might want to maintain a clothing closet at the office that clients may wear for their court appearance when, as a result of poverty, they lack suitable clothing. A small lightweight wrap and belt is easy for attorneys to carry in their briefcase and use when a parent comes to court inappropriately dressed.

Counsel should also focus on how parties are addressed. Everyone should address each other formally and by last name. In courts where common practice is to refer to parents as "mother," "father," or by their first name, counsel should object to the practice and request that clients be treated with the same dignity and respect that is accorded parties in the most important courts in the country. Changing the culture in this way not only enhances respectful treatment of parents, but also helps create an atmosphere more conducive to conducting fair trials, the ultimate focus of this chapter.

9.03 Developing the Theory of the Case

Preparation for trial is crucial to successful outcomes. Less obvious, perhaps, is the central role counsel's theory plays in trial preparation. Without having developed a coherent theory of the case (which commonly includes multiple theories, but will be referred to throughout this chapter in the singular) trial preparation is difficult. After having developed it; however, and after the investigation has been completed, the crucial work is still left to be done.

From the case theory comes everything else: the evidence themes for witnesses, an assessment of what evidence will be helpful to the defense, what evidence will be harmful, and what evidence is irrelevant to the case theory. The theory of the case should be well-framed before counsel develops his or her exhibit list, organizes the evidence, and drafts examinations of witnesses developed to support the theory.

An important aspect of case preparation is carefully researching the substantive law that will control the legal issues. Often, counsel's strongest claim will be that the facts are insufficient as a matter of law to constitute neglect, abuse, or dependency. Thorough knowledge of controlling case law is essential in developing any defense.

Counsel must begin by thoroughly reviewing the Petition. Counsel should make a short list of each allegation in the Petition. This list allows counsel to filter through evidence and decide what needs to be admitted and what should be excluded. Moreover, the list also helps to formulate a theory of the case. See the following case example as illustration.

Child is removed at the end of May. She is removed for unstable housing, lack of food, and the parent's mental health issues. Parent and child moved three times in the last year. Child is not school age. When the Agency went to the parent's house at the end of May, there was very little food in the home. The parent is diagnosed with depression and refills her prescriptions late each month, so she has a few days at the end of the month that she goes without medications.

Dependency Allegations

(1) Unstable housing
(2) Lack of food
(3) Mental health issues

After creating the list of allegations, counsel should make two columns besides each allegation. One column is for the Agency's evidence and the other for the parent's.

Dependency Allegations

Allegation	Agency	Parent
Unstable Housing	Three apartments in one year	• Child always had a roof. • No evidence that three moves affected welfare of child.
Lack of Food	Very little food when Agency went to home	• Agency only visited once. • Food runs low at end of month because Mother only gets paid the first of each month. • Receipts of groceries each month. • No evidence child is malnourished or hungry.

After completing the list, patterns in the allegations emerge. In the above example, there are at least two patterns. The first is the impact of the parent's poverty on the family. The second is the lack of evidence of harm to the child. From these patterns, two possible theories emerge. The theory can range from one word, to a short phrase, a sentence or a paragraph. The first possible theory is poverty. Poverty is not dependency; despite being poor, the parent cares for her child and there is no evidence that the child is harmed. The theory can take a serious, funny, or aggressive tone. The importance is to create something that triggers what the case is all about and something that sticks with counsel throughout the litigation.

It is also important to develop a case theory that has similar facts to the parent's story and ends with the outcome the parent wants. The parent's attorney can then prepare the parent's story and use it in closing argument.

The theory of the case should trickle down to the evidence presented. Counsel should identify each piece of evidence (testimony and documents) expected to be admitted at trial, regardless of which party will be introducing it. For each witness and document, counsel should determine how the witness supports the theory.

In the above example, the case manager's testimony will be vital. To support the parent's theory of the case, counsel will want to elicit the following testimony from the case manager. *Whenever case manager visited the home, the child was properly nourished; the parent had receipts for recently purchased groceries; the apartment was safe and adequate for the child's needs; the parent was taking her medications.* The theme of this witness's testimony, in counsel's mind, might be grouped into one of two categories: "no case," meaning the testimony shows there is no issue of dependency, or "good mother," meaning the evidence shows that the parent cares for the child and there is no harm to the child.

9.04 Pretrial Conferences

Depending upon the jurisdiction, the court may require a pretrial conference. Such conferences commonly address dates and timelines for the exchange of discovery, pretrial motions and trial-related issues, including a discussion of the issues to be tried and the trial's expected length. These conferences are also where evidentiary issues may be raised and resolved, including the possible stipulation to particular facts and the admission of evidence. Counsel should always consider using stipulations to reduce the trial's length and to help focus the court on the contested issues at the trial (which, invariably, are the issues on which cases win or lose). Judges appreciate lawyers who work hard not to waste the court's time.

When lawyers have a good handle on the theory they wish to advance at trial, often there are only a few matters that are in dispute and many matters that both sides can agree upon. Eliminating the uncontested matters from the trial helps everyone focus on the issues that will decide the outcome. Shorter trials, better focused on what is disputed, increase the possibility of successful outcomes.

9.05 Witness Preparation and Examination

Once counsel determines what evidence to present at adjudication, she must prepare for the evidence and prepare for the Agency's and child attorney's evidence. Witness testimony will include direct examination and cross-examination. Counsel must prepare each witness for both. Even when counsel does not plan to call the parent, counsel should prepare the parent for possible witness examination because the Agency may call him or her.

Counsel must meet with the parent to discuss the case theory and what testimony is important to the theory. Counsel should also discuss with the parent any testimony that the parent wishes to present. If the testimony is not relevant to the theory or is detrimental to the parent, counsel must explain why it should not be presented. While counsel should walk the parent step by step through the testimony, it is important to avoid doing this too much at the risk of the witness appearing to be rehearsed.

Another aspect of witness preparation is to alert the client to certain aspects of the trial that are likely to occur. For example, counsel should explain to the client the importance of not continuing to answer a question when an objection is made until the judge tells the client to continue. Counsel should also advise clients to seek clarification of the question whenever they are unsure what is being asked. Witnesses should also be advised to try hard to answer the questions asked only and not to elaborate beyond the question unless prompted to do so by counsel.

An important aspect of trial preparation is to prepare the client for cross-examination. Counsel must explain to the client that often the Agency attorney's goal will be to upset the client before the judge so that the client will display anger or some behavior the judge will use against her. Counsel should work hard in the courtroom to prevent the agency lawyer from doing this.

Lay witnesses should also be prepared for their testimony. When doing so, counsel should avoid having these witnesses appear to be too well rehearsed. All witnesses should be prepared for cross-examination and the potential that other attorneys may become aggressive with the witnesses. Finally, witnesses should keep a calm and attentive demeanor during all examinations as it credits their testimony as being objective and truthful. Witnesses should only be asked once or twice to explain their testimony and how it is helpful to the parent.

9.06 Preparing the Exhibit List

Documentary evidence is also essential to the parent's story. Prior to the trial, counsel should prepare the parent's proposed exhibit list. The exhibit list is proposed because the documentary evidence may or may not be admitted. Documents in the proposed exhibit list may be inadmissible but still available for refreshing recollection or impeachment. Counsel should number each document and should provide the court, parties, and court reporter with the proposed exhibit list. The proposed exhibit list and numbering of documents prior to the trial will help counsel seamlessly present the parent's story. The list will also make it easier to access documents quickly. Additionally, it will avoid frustrating the court when time is wasted at trial looking for critical documents. The list also allows everyone, including the court reporter, to know which document is being introduced, helping to create a clean record. Finally, preparing this exhibit list reflects well on trial counsel, adding credibility to the parent's case.

9.07 Critical Features of the Adjudicatory Hearing

9.07(a) Burden of Proof

In dependency trials, the Agency carries the burden of proof; but burden is not the same everywhere. In a majority of states, the Agency needs to prove the allegations in the Petition by a preponderance of the evidence. *See, e.g.*, ARK. CODE ANN. § 9-27-325(h)(2)(B) (2014); CAL. WELF. & INST. CODE § 355 (2014); VA. CODE ANN. §§ 16.1-252 (2014); WASH. REV. CODE § 13.34.130 (2014). In the rest, and in cases controlled by the Indian Child Welfare Act, the burden of proof is clear and convincing evidence. *See, e.g.*, 25 U.S.C. § 1912(e) (2014); GA. CODE ANN. § 15-11-180 (2014); IOWA CODE § 232.96 (2014); KAN. STAT. ANN. § 38-2250 (2014).

9.07(b) Bench or Jury Trial

Only a small number of states, including Colorado and Michigan, recognize a parent's right to a jury trial in dependency cases. *See, e.g.*, COLO. REV. STAT. § 19-3-505 (2014) (jury of 6); MICH. CT. R. 3.911 (2014). If counsel is involved in a jury trial, counsel should use local rules for voir dire in jury selection as an opportunity to introduce the critical features of counsel's theory and begin sensitizing the jurors to the critical issues for the parent. In the vast majority of states, however, dependency cases are tried without a jury. In some jurisdictions, the initial finder of fact may be a referee or magistrate and the case may be reviewed by a judge.

Preparing for bench trials can be extremely challenging for lawyers who practice before judges who rarely conduct trials and who sometimes frown upon lawyers who insist on having a trial. Equally challenging is practicing in a jurisdiction in which few can recall the last time the judge dismissed a case based on insufficient evidence. Lawyers who practice in such places, along with lawyers who appear in courts with a better track record of deciding cases on the merits, should consider using the trial process to vindicate a client's rights when the Agency is offering a settlement that is unfair to the client and when a defense to the charges in the Petition exist. Counsel should also regard litigating cases as part of a longer term effort to constrain the power of agencies that are used to winning everything they file in court. Part of a longer vision of reform is to invigorate in the judiciary a sense of its role of meaningfully overseeing executive branch power, rather than serving as an ally of the child welfare department by allowing it to do whatever it believes is appropriate.

A successful trial is often the result of knowing the judge. Counsel must understand the procedures of the courtroom and any practices the court requires during trial. Counsel should observe how the judge acts during a trial. Counsel can also speak with attorneys who have tried adjudications before the judge and can read appellate cases that were taken from the court. Knowing the court will help in developing a theory of the case, preparing for trial, and trial strategy.

9.08 Special Note About Corresponding Criminal Charges

In cases involving physical injuries to a child, the parent may face criminal charges based on the same events or injuries that are the basis of the dependency case. Because timelines in dependency court move much faster than in criminal court, the parent's civil adjudication will most likely precede the criminal adjudication. For this reason, it is very important for the parent's attorney in the dependency case to work closely with the attorney defending the parent in the corresponding criminal case. While the parent's goal in the dependency case is most often the reunification of the parent and child, it is important to take into account that this reunification will be delayed if the parent is convicted of the criminal charges and sentenced to incarceration. In consultation with the client, the criminal defense attorney's approach will inform how counsel should proceed at adjudication. In some cases, the criminal attorney may want a preview of the testimony of the medical experts and other witnesses, so s/he may ask that counsel try the dependency case. If the dependency case moves forward first and if the case is dismissed, the criminal charges may also be dismissed. If the Agency was unable to prevail when the standard of proof was either preponderance of clear and convincing evidence, it is unlikely that the state would be able to prevail when held to the reasonable doubt standard. However, the criminal defense attorney may prefer that the parent not exercise the right to an evidentiary hearing in the dependency case. In these cases, counsel should discuss with the parent the risks and benefits of negotiating a stipulation in the dependency matter.

Many sex abuse cases also include concurrent criminal prosecutions. In these cases, counsel should confer with the criminal defense attorney and remember that statements made in the dependency case may be used against the parent in criminal court. For more information, *see* Chapter 5.

9.09 Once the Trial Begins

9.09(a) Courtroom Behavior

When addressing the court, questioning witnesses, and making objections, counsel should always stand up. Counsel's client should be advised to stand when addressing the court also. Standing signifies that what the speaker has to say is significant and signals others to listen. When making objections, counsel should stand, state the basis of the objection (e.g., hearsay, cumulative, etc.), and then, if need be, explain the objection in more detail. Standing during objections signals to the court and others to stop the proceeding (which is vital to a clean record of the adjudication), and it signals to the court that the objection is critical and possibly a point of appeal if overruled. Stating the basis of the objection first, shows the judge there is a legal basis. Standing and firmly stating the legal basis for the objection can throw the other agency attorney off and potentially disrupt negative evidence.

Counsel should pay attention to behavior at counsel's table in the courtroom. Actions such as slouching, leaning on one's face on elbows, tapping pens or legs, showing reactions to evidence such as anger, disbelief, disgust, or pleasure, folding arms across chest, should be avoided by counsel and the client. If the parent has difficulty maintaining a calm demeanor, consider offering him or her a stress ball that can be easily hidden in the parent's hand and held beneath counsel's table without being seen by the court.

Another way to create an atmosphere most conducive to fair proceedings is to request permission from the court prior to taking steps such as approaching a witness or moving around the courtroom. Demonstrating respect for the court may be rewarded by raising the level of respect for everyone.

Appearance, actions, and demeanor in the courtroom work to increase the formality of the proceedings and remind the parties and the court that the separation of child and parent is a constitutionally significant decision that must be respected at all levels.

9.09(b) Opening Statements

An opening statement is rare in family court due to the pace of calendars and the historical lack of treating these proceedings as normal trials. When choosing to make an opening statement, counsel risks losing the goodwill of the judge even before the first witness is called. However, an opening statement is the first opportunity to introduce the theory of the case and the parent's story to the court before the Agency presents its evidence.

In some cases, however, forgoing the opening statement will deprive counsel of a crucial opportunity to alert the judge to the parent's theory of the case before the first witness is called. This is particularly true in cases in which the theory will not emerge clearly during cross-examination of the Agency's witnesses and will first become evident from witnesses called by the respondent. In these cases, counsel should insist upon the right to present an opening, explaining that counsel intends to be brief. If the local custom is such that an opening is truly an extraordinary event, counsel should consider adding that s/he understands that openings are unusual but that the particular case before the court is so unusual that an opening is essential. (Of course, counsel will then have to deliver on the promise to demonstrate that the case is, in fact, an extraordinary one.)

This means, even when used, opening statements should be brief. For example, in the scenario discussed in § 9.03, the opening statement could be: "Ms. Jones, though impoverished, provides her child with stable food, shelter, care, and love. She does so despite suffering depression, which she regularly treats with medication. Her child is happy and healthy and therefore, the Petition must be dismissed."

It is also effective in the opening statement to refer to case law that controls the legal principles. For example, a recent appellate decision in Georgia expressed the law as follows: "The State has no right to irrevocably sever the natural parent-child relationship simply because a parent is incapable of providing her children with an idyllic middle-class lifestyle." *See CJV*, 323 Ga. App. 283, 291, 746 S.E.2d 783, 791 (2013). Counsel could use this principle in the opening statement as follows: "Although Ms. Jones cannot provide her child with an idyllic middle-class lifestyle, she consistently provides her child with food, shelter, care, and love despite suffering depression, which she regularly treats with medication. Her child is happy and healthy. Therefore, the State cannot sever that right and the Petition must be dismissed."

9.09(c) Presenting Document Evidence

To present documents, counsel should remember these five steps: (1) Mark, (2) Show, (3) Approach, (4) Identify, and (5) Admit. The five steps can be illustrated using the case example referred to earlier. The respondent parent wishes to admit grocery receipts to show she regularly bought food for the child. When she is on the stand, counsel should use the five steps to admit the grocery receipts into evidence.

> *Let the record reflect I marked [Mark] this document for the purpose of identification as Respondent's #1. Let the record reflect I am showing [Show] Respondent #1 to the Agency and child attorney. May I approach [Approach] the witness. Ms. Ogletree, do you recognize [Identify] what has been marked as Respondent's exhibit #1? How do you recognize it? What is it? How did you obtain them? What do they show? At this time, I would like to admit [Admit] Respondent's #1 into evidence.*

Counsel should always refer to documents by the exhibit number to keep the record clean.

9.09(d) Direct Examination

Conducting direct examination involves more than questioning a witness. The organization and form of questions, as well as the voice intonation, cadence, and demeanor of counsel are also important. Counsel should be prepared to respond to objections during direct examination by anticipating potentially objectionable questions or answers and being prepared to defend them. The better prepared counsel is in responding to objections, the less likely that objections will interrupt the witness's testimony. Counsel's overall purpose in calling each witness should be to have that witness add something to the case. Often this will be something new that otherwise would not be made known to the finder of fact. Sometimes, the witness's substantive contribution is to corroborate testimony given by the parent, anticipating that the witness may be more credible.

Direct examination should be organized to tell a story. When examining witnesses in a bench trial, emotion matters and counsel must bring testimony to life even when that means using some theatrics to emphasize the significance of the testimony. Judges are humans, too, and can be swayed by emotion. In addition, the more entertaining the story, the more likely the judge will pay attention to it and remember it when the trial ends. One of the most important challenges when conducting bench trials is conducting an exciting trial that stands out from the countless events the judge attends to over the course of a long week. This challenge is best met by bringing life and character to the evidence being presented. In direct examination, counsel should use voice intonation and cadences to emphasize important points. Counsel should also stand where the witness can see and hear counsel, but the witness should direct the testimony to the court, not the attorney.

9.09(e) Cross-Examination

Cross-examination involves as much skill and technique as direct examination. First, counsel must become familiar with common objections. Counsel should prepare a list of common objections and use them during the direct examinations of the agency witnesses. Part of the strategy of cross-examination is to disrupt the Agency's story. Counsel should not object to everything, but instead should use the objections strategically to exclude testimony and evidence that is harmful to the parent's story.

A good cross-examiner controls the witness. This is accomplished by the form of the question, counsel's body language, and voice. The point of cross-examination is to extract testimony from the witness needed to support the parent's story. The testimony extracted will then be connected during closing arguments. Counsel should not make the mistake of attempting to connect the extracted testimony to the parent's story during cross-examination. Doing so almost always ends in giving the witness the opportunity to explain away the points counsel intends to make in closing. Also, counsel must be very careful in the scope of testimony extracted to avoid opening the door to any testimony excluded during the direct examination of the witness.

9.09(f) Expert Witnesses

Expert witnesses must be thoroughly prepared. They are a challenge for attorneys unfamiliar with the expert's area of know-how. Counsel should try to learn as much about the expert's area of knowledge. This will help in preparing the expert and organizing the case. Developing an expertise in one case often will pay dividends down the line because dependency cases often involve similar charges and fact patterns.

Counsel should craft the expert's testimony to allow the court to follow it. Counsel should not assume that the court is familiar with the area of expertise. Counsel should try to break down the expert's explanation of complex terms and definitions so that an average person would understand it. Using charts and demonstrative evidence to illustrate the expert's testimony is often extremely useful.

In states in which the admissibility of evidence is regulated by statutes or a set of rules, there is often a section or group of sections that covers expert testimony. In states that have not codified this aspect of the law of evidence or adopted a set of rules of evidence, local case law commonly prescribes the standards for presenting expert testimony.

Until the Supreme Court's decision in *Daubert v. Merrell Dow Pharmaceuticals, Inc.*, 509 U.S. 579 (1993), the standard for admission of expert testimony in the federal courts and in the vast majority of states was the so-called "*Frye* test," drawn from *Frye v. United States*, 293 F. 1013, 54 App. D.C. 46 (1923). Under the *Frye* test, scientific evidence (or, more precisely, scientific evidence of a novel type) was admissible only if the scientific technique was "sufficiently established to have gained general acceptance in the particular field in which it belongs." *See id.* at 1014. *See also Daubert*, 509 U.S. at 585–86 & n.4 (discussing the *Frye* test). In *Daubert*, however, the Court established a new standard for the federal courts, interpreting the Federal Rules of Evidence to provide that the admission of "novel scientific evidence at trial" (*id.* at 585) turns upon a trial judge's finding that the "scientific knowledge" to which "the expert is proposing to testify . . . will assist the trier of fact to understand or determine a fact in issue." *See id.* at 592. The Court explained that the question to be addressed by the trial judge "entails a preliminary assessment of whether the reasoning or methodology underlying the testimony is scientifically valid and of whether that reasoning or methodology properly can be applied to the facts in issue." *Id.* at 593.

In *Kumho Tire Co. v. Carmichael*, 526 U.S. 137 (1999), the Court wrote that "*Daubert's* general holding—setting forth the trial judge's general 'gatekeeping' obligation [under the Federal Rules of Evidence]—applies not only to testimony based on 'scientific' knowledge, but also to testimony based on 'technical' and 'other specialized' knowledge." *Id.* at 141. The Court reiterated in *Kumho* that "the test of reliability is 'flexible,' and *Daubert's* list of specific factors neither necessarily nor exclusively applies to all experts or in every case." *Id.*

Although *Daubert* was concerned only with what the Federal Rules of Evidence require in federal trials and is not binding on state courts, quite a few state legislatures and courts have replaced their former tests for admissibility of some or all kinds of expert testimony with a standard modeled on *Daubert*. *See, e.g.*, ARIZ. R. EVID. 702 & cmt (2014); MISS. R. EVID. 702 (2014); TEX. R. EVID. 702 (2014); *State v. Foret*, 628 So. 2d 1116 (La. 1993) (adopting standard set forth by *Daubert*). *But see* PA. R. EVID. 702 (2014) (requiring general acceptance); *In re O.D.*, 221 Cal. App. 4th 1001, 1006 n.3, 164 Cal. Rptr. 3d 578 (2013) (California Supreme Court has declined to adopt *Daubert* standard for admissibility of expert testimony that relies on a new scientific technique); *People v. LeGrand*, 8 N.Y.3d 449, 457, 835 N.Y.S.2d 523, 867 N.E.2d 374 (2007) (New York follows *Frye* standard).

When preparing to present an expert witness or to cross-examine an expert, counsel should carefully consult any potentially applicable evidentiary requirements in the jurisdiction's statutes, rules, or case law. Even when local practice treats certain rules of expert evidence as well-accepted, counsel should consider the possibility that a novel challenge could produce a different rule.

9.09(f)(1) Subjects to Cover in Qualifying an Expert

Before an expert witness is competent to give an opinion, s/he must be qualified to the satisfaction of the court. There are no categorical standards of qualification; the matter is left essentially to the trial judge's discretion. If the expert's profession is licensed by the state, it is obviously desirable that s/he meet state standards for licensing. Eminence in the field will impress the trier of fact, but juries (and even many judges) prefer hometown experts. Counsel should attempt to form some impression of the credentials that are regarded as prestigious within the profession; handwriting experts, for example, usually become such by experience more than by formal training. A present or prior position with a law enforcement agency enhances the appearance of dispassion of the expert. In the same vein, counsel is ordinarily permitted to bring out, where applicable, the fact that an expert who has testified in other delinquency or criminal cases has predominately testified for the prosecution.

To qualify an expert, the following questions should be asked, when appropriate:

(1) Please state your name for the record.

(2) What is your profession [employment]?

(3) Would you tell the court, please, what is the subject matter of that profession? (Counsel and the expert should have rehearsed a short, general, nontechnical description.)

(4) Do you specialize within the field?

(5) What is your specialty?

(6) Where are you employed?

(7) What degree, if any, do you hold?

(8) Are you licensed as a . . . in the state of . . . ?

(9) How long have you been licensed?

(10) How long have you been in practice?

(11) Are you also certified as a specialist in the field of . . . ?

(12) What are the duties and functions of your present position, please?

(13) In the course of your work, have you had occasion to conduct examinations of . . . (stating the kind of examination involved in this case)?

(14) How many such examinations would you say you have conducted?

(15) Have you published any works that appeared in professional journals in the field of . . . ?

(16) Are you a member of any professional associations? Do you hold any special positions in those associations? What are the positions that you hold?

(17) Have you ever previously testified as an expert witness in court?

(18) On how many occasions, if you remember?

(19) And have you also been appointed by the court to testify [or, serve] as a neutral and impartial expert witness dependency cases?

Counsel should conclude with: "If the court please, I ask the court to accept [the expert witness] as a qualified expert in the field of [the expert's expertise]."

9.09(f)(2) Stipulating the Qualifications of the Expert

If counsel's expert is known to the Agency, the Agency may be willing to stipulate to the witness's qualifications. Counsel has a right to decline the stipulation and to make his or her record. Generally, it is advisable not to agree to stipulate to the witness's qualifications unless (1) there is some doubt whether s/he will qualify as an expert, (2) the witness's qualifications are less impressive than those of the Agency's expert, or (3) the qualifications of the experts for both sides are equally impressive, and the parties are agreeing to stipulate to the credentials of both witnesses.

9.09(f)(3) Structure of the Expert's Testimony

An expert can give opinion testimony. An expert describes the studies s/he has performed, the conditions under which they were performed, and the reliability of the studies under these conditions. After describing the data that the expert has examined or observed, s/he must be asked whether s/he has formed an opinion, based upon these data, concerning a legally relevant issue. To be admissible, the opinion usually must be of "reasonable certainty."

After the expert has stated his or her opinion, counsel should ask the expert to explain the reasoning that led to the opinion. This portion of the expert's testimony should emphasize each item of factual information that supports his or her ultimate conclusion and indicate that the expert has considered every item of factual information in the case that might tend to cut against his or her conclusion. The expert can deal best with the latter facts by either (1) describing how they can be reconciled with his or her conclusion if they can or (2) admitting that they cut against his or her conclusion and explaining why s/he gives greater weight to other facts that support his or her conclusion. Either sort of testimony tends to be more convincing on direct examination than on cross.

The direct examination of the expert should be concise. If at any time the expert witness uses technical terms, s/he should be asked to explain them. Expert testimony must be carefully prepared to assure that the expert witness will speak to the level of understanding of the trier of fact. Before trial, counsel should point out to the expert the terms and concepts that will need explanation in everyday language. The expert should have formulated these explanations to the satisfaction of counsel before coming to court. An expert should never be put in the position of having to coin a definition for the first time on the stand. The expert is not necessarily used to explaining his or her specialty in terms that are not its own.

Counsel's questioning of an expert at trial should show the witness's expertise, not counsel's. Simple questions drawing on the experience and knowledge of the expert will impress upon the trier of fact that the witness possesses the knowledge and understanding necessary to testify authoritatively in his or her specialty.

9.09(f)(4) Hypothetical Questions

When an expert's opinion is based on knowledge gained through his or her professional investigation of the matters at issue in the trial, the expert may testify in response to a hypothetical question that asks the expert to assume the requisite facts. These facts, of course, must be established by independent proof. It is not necessary that the hypothetical question include all of the facts of record, but it is necessary that all of the facts which it does include be facts that could be found on the basis of the record.

As a practical matter, counsel should include as much of the evidence as possible without making the question tediously long; otherwise the expert will likely be asked on cross-examination whether his or her opinion would change if each of the omitted facts were added—one by one. Even if the expert says that the opinion would not change, s/he is cast in the posture of appearing to explain away matters and to defend his or her opinion more than is desirable.

The form of the hypothetical question normally is: "I ask you to assume the following set of facts to be true and correct: [stating facts]. Assuming those facts to be true and correct, can you express an opinion with reasonable certainty as an expert whether [stating the problem]?" Following an affirmative answer to this question, counsel should ask: "What is that opinion?" When the opinion is given, counsel should ask for an explanation of the reasoning on which it is based.

9.09(f)(5) Preparing the Expert for Cross-Examination

In preparing an expert to testify at trial, counsel should have been careful to give the expert literally all the facts at counsel's disposal without editing or screening. Some of the facts may be unimportant, but it is for the expert witness to make this judgment on the basis of his or her expert knowledge, not for counsel.

When facts are contested, counsel should fully inform the expert concerning the Agency's version of the facts as well as the defense version. It is predictable that the other side will ask the expert at trial whether his or her opinion would change with different facts. Counsel should have asked the expert these questions in preparation sessions and the expert should have a ready answer at trial.

9.09(g) Closing Argument

Although closing arguments may not be expected because they are not always asked for by courts, counsel must work to create an opportunity, after the close of evidence, to argue counsel's case. Using case law in closing arguments is very important. Case law is powerful for several reasons. It reminds the court that if it decides against the parent, counsel will appeal and the court stands to be overturned.

Case law is emotionally moving and can inspire a court. Judges are human and experience human emotions. Like jurors, judges can be persuaded by powerful language. Counsel should remind the court that the Supreme Court has often reiterated that the parent-child relationship is protected as a basic, fundamental constitutional right. *See, e.g., Lassiter v. Dep't of Soc. Servs.*, 452 U.S. 18, 27 (1981) ("[A] parent's desire for and right to the companionship, care, custody, and management of his or her children is an important interest that 'undeniably warrants deference and, absent a powerful countervailing interest, protection.'") (internal quotation marks and citations omitted); *Stanley v. Illinois*, 405 U.S. 645, 651 (1972) ("The integrity of the family unit has found protection in the Due Process Clause of the Fourteenth Amendment, the Equal Protection Clause of the Fourteenth Amendment, and the Ninth Amendment.") (internal citations omitted). State appellate courts have also reiterated these basic truths. *See, e.g., State in Interest of A.V.*, 14-465, p. 5 (La. App. 5 Cir. 10/29/14); *In re Dependency of G.G.*, 338 P.3d 887, 894 & n.18 (Wash. Ct. App. 2014). When they do so, counsel should quote them.

The above sections provide a basic overview of the trial process. What follows is a discussion of specific types of cases that may arise in practice and how parents' attorneys should approach them.

9.10 Medical Child Abuse

9.10(a) Failure to Ensure That Children Are Properly Treated for Medical Conditions

Parents have a legal duty to protect their children from harm. A common basis for charging parents with unfitness is that they failed to ensure that their children received necessary medical care. Although the Constitution protects religious freedom, the Supreme Court has stated that "parents are not free to make martyrs of their children" by endangering their health to further religious beliefs. *See Prince v. Massachusetts*, 321 U.S. 158, 170 (1944). This means, absent statutory language to the contrary, a parent's failure to provide needed medical care for a child because of the parent's religious beliefs is not a defense in dependency or neglect cases. More specifically, if a parent is found to have failed to provide a child with required care, it will not matter that the parent deliberately failed because of religious beliefs. Child protection cases are prosecuted on the theory of child protection, not punishment of inadequate parenting.

Despite the absence of a federal constitutional right to defeat these cases based on religious beliefs, in many states there is a statutory exemption from charges of medical neglect based on a parent's good-faith religious practices, as a result of lobbying efforts by certain religious groups. *See, e.g.*, WIS. STAT. ANN. § 948.03(6) (2014). This is particularly pertinent to parents who belong to the Church of Christian Science. *See* Scott St. Amand, *Protecting Neglect: The Constitutionality of Spiritual Healing Exemptions to Child Neglect Statutes*, 12 RICH. J.L. & PUB. INT. 139, 147 (2009). If counsel is representing a parent charged with failing to provide her child with necessary medical care and the explanation for the failure is reliance on religion, counsel should carefully study the controlling statute and case law to determine whether the good-faith defense is available.

Apart from special considerations involving religion, the critical inquiry in all of these cases will be the same: Did the parent fall below the minimum standard of care parents must meet to thwart coercive state intervention? A key concept in all charges involving a child's health is that parents are not guarantors of their child's health nor may they be held strictly liable for injuries sustained by their children. The critical question in all cases involving medical neglect, once the correct diagnosis of a child has been determined, is whether the parent may be held legally accountable for the condition. In other words, did the parent do something that parents may not do or fail to do something required of parents, which caused the condition?

Children commonly get hurt, fall, break bones, and get sick. Although an unavoidable inquiry in child protection cases is into the precise condition of the child, the ultimate focus of attention is on the parent's conduct. Even when parents are responsible for the child's condition, such as when a child is injured in a car accident when the parent was driving, that does not mean there would be any basis for finding the child to have been neglected or abused. Parents are not required to be perfect; even negligent acts by parents do not, by themselves, prove parental unfitness.

9.10(a)(1) Failure to Thrive

One common type of charge of medical neglect is "failure to thrive." There are two types of failure to thrive. One is caused by a medical condition; the other is caused by the child's environment. *See* AM. ACAD. OF PEDIATRICS, CHILD ABUSE MEDICAL DIAGNOSIS & MANAGEMENT 44 (Robert M. Reece & Cindy W. Christian eds., 3rd ed. 2008) [hereinafter REECE].

Counsel should find out (1) the parent's understanding of the child's medical needs; (2) what steps, if any, the parent took to address them; and (3) why the parent took those steps and not others. These cases are often about why the parent acted or failed to act as much as they are about what the parent did or did not do.

Often, a parent avoids bringing a child for medical checkups because of a lack of health insurance. Children without medical insurance "often have compromised health because they receive less preventive care, are diagnosed at more advanced disease stages, and, once diagnosed, receive less therapeutic care." Jack Hadley, *Sicker and Poorer—The Consequences of Being Uninsured: A Review of the Research on the Relationship Between Health Insurance, Medical Care Use, Health, Work, and Income*, 60 *Med. Care Res. & Rev.* 3 (2003).

Indigent parents are less likely to ensure their children are regularly treated for reasons beyond limited or no health insurance. They may be unable to take work off as often as necessary to bring their children for follow-up treatments or are unable to take their child for treatment because they are unable to find child care for their other children. They may not be able to pay for transportation needed for the treatment, especially when they live in a rural area where there is limited access to medical care. This may be true even when children are covered by Medicaid or otherwise covered under the Affordable Care Act. Appointments may be missed even when parents meant to keep them because transportation is unreliable. Parents may also fail to follow treatment advice because of language barriers that prevent them from fully understanding what they were supposed to do.

On the opposite side of the spectrum, parents may understand but disagree with the recommended medical care. Parents do not always trust health care professionals. The recommended medical care may scare the parents. Depending upon the medical issue, the child may not exhibit immediate signs of illness and therefore the parents do not agree the medical care is necessary. The parents may have other children with similar issues who are doing well and thus believe this child will be fine without further medical care.

Alternatively, the case may be more reasonably characterized as a disagreement between the parents and the Agency over what kind of care is needed. Parents may prefer homeopathic treatment or other medical care that the Agency believes is inappropriate. An important case decided by New York's highest court many years ago well illustrates the legal principals involved in this kind of dispute. In *In re Hofbauer*, 47 N.Y.2d 648, 419 N.Y.S.2d 936, 393 N.E.2d 1009 (1979), parents of a three-year-old child diagnosed with leukemia rejected the advice of a doctor to put their son through a very difficult regime and painful chemotherapy that offered only some hope for recovery. Instead, the parents found a doctor willing to treat the boy with laetrile, a highly controversial treatment at the time, but not illegal under state law. The local child protective agency, having learned that the parents refused the first doctor's advice that the child receive chemotherapy, charged them in family court with medical neglect. The Court of Appeals unanimously dismissed the Petition, emphasizing that parents are free to choose medical care for their children that is not illegal. The court explained that the proper question is whether the parents fell below the minimum standard of care, not whether their choice of care is better than what the Agency prefers. In dismissing the Petition, the court held that whenever parents are following a licensed physician's advice, they could never be charged with unfitness, even when most experts would reject that advice. Child protection cases, the court explained, are not the place to litigate what is the best treatment for children.

Special consideration is required when the problem concerns an older child who refuses to comply with the treatment. Many treatments can cause children great pain and discomfort, even making their condition worse. Sometimes, children simply refuse the treatment; other times, they may pretend to take medication but not do so. In these cases, once again, the question is whether the parents fell below the minimum standard of care required by law. Parents may find themselves in an impossible position when efforts to force children to do something can result in their being charged with neglect because their efforts were too severe. Recognizing this, parents who refuse to force their children to do something against their will should not be subject to neglect charges for doing too little. They may lack the capacity to make their children do what they refuse to do.

Counsel should always thoroughly investigate the case to determine whether one or more of the above defenses apply. Counsel may need to know the parents' income, employment history, access to transportation, health care and health insurance, education, and knowledge of children's medical needs. Counsel should search for witnesses to testify to the parents' ability to care for the children's daily needs. Counsel should try, if possible, to win the case at trial and have the court dismiss the Petition. But counsel should also be looking beyond dismissal and establish facts that will persuade the court to permit the parents to keep the children in their care by entering a protective order requiring the parents to comply with whatever the court wants the parents to do going forward.

Counsel's theory of why the Petition should be dismissed should be developed by carefully tracking the controlling statutory language and case law interpreting it. Where the evidence supports the claim, counsel should stress that the parents love their child and are willing to do what is needed to ensure their health and well-being and that any misunderstanding regarding the child's health before the Petition was filed has now been cleared up and the parents are fully committed to ensuring that the child receive all appropriate care going forward.

A different theory might be that the child did not suffer from the condition alleged in the Petition or that it was reasonable for the parents not to recognize the child's condition.

9.10(b) Factitious Disorder by Proxy (or Munchausen Syndrome by Proxy)

In almost complete contrast with the kind of medical abuse described in the previous subsection, Munchausen Syndrome by Proxy involves cases in which parents are alleged to harm their children by subjecting them to damaging, invasive, and unnecessary medical treatment. This category is also highly controversial with many experts believing it should not be recognized. It was only as late as 1994 that it was first recognized by the American Psychiatric Association as an official diagnosis, when it was included in the Diagnostic and Statistical Manual of Mental Disorders ("DSM"). *See* AM. PSYCHIATRIC ASSOC., DIAGNOSTIC AND STATISTICAL MANUAL OF MENTAL DISORDERS (4th ed. 1994). In the more recent DSM-V, the condition was renamed Factitious Disorder by Proxy ("FDP") or Factitious Disorder Imposed on Another. *See* AM. PSYCHIATRIC ASSOC., DIAGNOSTIC AND STATISTICAL MANUAL OF MENTAL DISORDERS (5th ed. 2013).

This condition is currently defined as a caretaker who makes another appear sick by fabricating or falsifying symptoms or actually causing harm to another for the purpose of gaining attention from medical providers and others. In a number of jurisdictions in the United States, parents have been charged with maltreating their children in this way.

In an attempt at clarifying when a parent with this condition is harming a child, the American Professional Society on the Abuse of Children distinguishes between the behavior and the motive of the caretaker behind the behavior. *See* John Stirling, Jr. et al., *Beyond Munchausen Syndrome by Proxy: Identification and Treatment of Child Abuse in a Medical Setting*, 119 PEDIATRICS 1026 (2007). When a parent who suffers from FDP raises a child, the child's diagnosis is called "pediatric falsification condition." *See id.* Regrettably, two researchers, Drs. Thomas Roesler and Carole Jenny, argued in a book published in 2009 that these classifications should not be used in the child abuse context and that "medical child abuse" is a sufficient label to describe children whose parent suffer from FDP. *See* THOMAS A. ROESLER & CAROLE JENNY, MEDICAL CHILD ABUSE: BEYOND MUNCHAUSEN SYNDROME BY PROXY (2009). This reasoning is flawed because it renders the parent's motive in seeking treatment irrelevant. Even when the parents' motive is to seek the best medical treatment with no intent to harm the child, the parent could still be accused of medical child abuse in some jurisdictions.

Parents with FDP risk being charged with endangering their children by wrongfully requiring them to undergo unnecessary and invasive medical treatments. These parents can succeed in securing multiple treatments often by bringing the child to different doctors or hospitals without revealing the prior interventions and hiding contrary conclusions that doctors may have reached. The parent may be accused of exaggerating or making up the child's symptoms. In worst case scenarios, the parent may have deliberately made the child ill.

More should have to be proven than that the parent disagreed with treating physicians by continuing to insist the child is ill. Parents who fit the profile of FDP have additional characteristics than disagreement with treating physicians over whether a child needs medical care. They are usually very interested in the medical condition or a closely related condition to the one the parent insists the child has. Often these parents suffered numerous illnesses themselves. Known cases involve parents who have used social media to obtain funds for treating the child.

When the only basis to charge a parent is disagreement between the doctor and the parent, counsel's job is to find a medical expert who agrees with the parent. The diagnosis should not be left to the primary physician or a child abuse pediatrician. *See* Stirling, *supra*. Sometimes, the parent is charged with seeking treatment when the child has no medical condition simply because the attending physician is unable to find a condition. Parents may be vindicated long into a case when a better doctor is able to discover the problem that was missed before.

If counsel represents a parent accused of FDP, available defenses include the treatments were medically necessary or that the parent's motive was to seek the best medical care for the child's illness. If there is reason to believe the parent has FDP, then the best course of action is to seek immediate psychiatric treatment.

If counsel is representing a parent accused of acquiescing to the child's treatment based upon the other parent's representation of the child's need for such treatment, whether or not the other parent is diagnosed with FDP, the defense should straightforwardly be that the parent did not fall below the minimal standard of care necessary to adjudicate the parent unfit. The parent accepted in good faith the other parent's assertion that the child needed continued medical treatment. Counsel should help the court see that the parent could just as easily have faced charges of neglect had the parent wrongfully interfered with the other parent's efforts to seek medical treatment for the child.

The investigation of a case involving allegations of FDP can be considerable. Discovery should produce medical and mental health records. If the child is receiving dosages of medicine when the Petition is filed, courts often will remove the child and place him or her in a hospital so that the child can be taken off medications and treatments to establish a "baseline" for the child's condition. Medical records, along with all ongoing medical visits, are vital so that counsel can test any claims that the child has improved since being removed from the parent's care.

Counsel should also seek other records such as the child's health insurance and school records. Counsel should know whether the child was found by the school to have special needs. Schools often use their own medical providers to determine if the child had special needs and if so, what educational accommodations should be made. These records may be used to show that an independent medical provider concluded the child has a particular diagnosis.

The records also allow counsel to cross-examine agency witnesses to show the testing that was performed to determine whether the child needed the treatment. If the child underwent invasive treatment, counsel will want to prove that doctors performed independent testing and observation and reached the conclusion that the treatment was appropriate before it was performed. Rarely are invasive procedures performed without such independent observations.

Finally, the records may be used to impeach physicians and other witnesses regarding the child's symptoms. A critical claim in most FDP cases is that the parent fabricated or exaggerated symptoms or, in the worst cases, created the symptoms. Medical and school records may show documentation of the symptoms exhibited by the child and independently observed. The records may show that the parent was consistent in disclosing symptoms to physicians and the school. Counsel can use records prepared by the physician or physicians who diagnosed the child with pediatric falsification condition to discredit Pediatric Falsification Condition based upon the controversy surrounding the diagnosis within the medical community.

Unlike in other dependency cases, health insurance records are essential in FDP cases. Health insurance companies will rarely cover extensive treatments without documentation from the physicians showing the treatment is medically necessary. Therefore, insurance companies require an "Affidavit of Medical Necessity" for each treatment that is beyond general child health care. Normally with a medically fragile child almost every treatment is outside general child health care. The affidavits require the physician to verify why the treatment is needed. Since the physician will not be paid without the insurance company, the physician will list every reason for the treatment and it will not normally be solely based upon the parents' report. The affidavit can then be used to impeach the physician. Counsel may also want to call the insurance agent as a witness because insurance agents work with the family to coordinate the child's care and sometimes communicate with the different physicians in deciding about the child's care.

In most FDP cases, counsel should expect that the court will order that the parent undergo a psychological evaluation. Depending on the jurisdiction, counsel may be able to prevent the court from doing so over objection. But in most jurisdictions, courts have the authority to order such evaluations when there is reason to believe the parent is suffering from a condition that places the child at risk. Rather than fight the effort, counsel should conclude that having it done quickly may expedite completing the case even if the court finds against the parent if the parent is undergoing treatment by the time the case is finished.

If possible, counsel should choose the psychologist for the evaluation. Experts chosen by the Agency in too many jurisdictions fail to undertake a thorough evaluation. Too often, the psychologist chosen by the Agency obtains limited information about the case, commonly only from the case manager and parent. An independent evaluator will be more used to conducting a more thorough investigation. In these cases, review of medical records, insurance records, mental health records, and the interview of collateral contacts are essential for accurate diagnoses. In addition, counsel will want a psychologist who understands the controversy surrounding the FDP diagnosis. If counsel cannot use the psychologist of choice, counsel should request that the parties agree to one that the court chooses from a list accepted by the parties. When the expert is selected, counsel should speak with the expert and ensure that the expert will review all appropriate documents before completing the evaluation.

If the psychologist who was chosen by the Agency rules out FDP, it is very likely that a settlement will be reached favorable to the parent. If the Agency's expert finds that the parent has FDP, a crucial aspect of the trial will be the cross-examination of counsel's expert. To prepare for that, counsel will need to determine the evaluation's weaknesses. Consulting with counsel's own expert will be helpful for this purpose. The weaknesses could be that the psychologist failed to collect and consider collateral information, has no experience with FDP, or administered the wrong tests or interview. The expert may also be impeachable because virtually all of the psychologist's practice is writing evaluations at the Agency's request.

If the psychologist chosen by counsel returns with an evaluation that rules out FDP, but the Agency insists on continuing with the case anyway, counsel should prepare the expert for direct examination by including the psychologist's qualifications and a detailed explanation for the expert's findings. If the Agency attempts to stipulate to the psychologist's qualifications, counsel should accept the stipulation but request to continue to establishment of the psychologist's expertise "for the record." Eliciting the psychologist's qualifications in court will influence the judge to credit it. Doing so also makes it more difficult for the Agency to suggest through cross-examination that the psychologist is unqualified or inadequately prepared the evaluation.

For each diagnosis or illness, counsel must present witnesses who observed the symptoms exhibited by the child. Teachers, pastors, day care providers, other parents, coaches, and medical providers (who disagree with the Agency) are the most appropriate witnesses. Family members may be used, but witnesses who have no personal connection to the client are better. Counsel should avoid using witnesses who know the client through support groups for parents with medically fragile children, unless the witness is vetted and will appear credible to the court. Though it is common and even recommended that parents join support groups, the Agency will often use it against the client as proof that the client wants attention and uses support groups to garner it.

Depending upon the child's diagnosis, counsel may want to present independent experts to explain the diagnosis, what symptoms the diagnosis exhibits, and the recommended treatment. For example, parents with children diagnosed with Mitochondrial Syndrome have recently been in the public spotlight. Mitochondrial Syndrome is a diagnosis in which a child could do well one day and then find themselves unable to walk the next day. Having an expert explain the idiosyncrasies of the diagnosis may be needed to undercut the Agency's witnesses who testify that when they saw or examined the child, the child was doing well or that the child was improving in foster care.

If there are two parents, the Agency may choose to call both. If neither is called, counsel must assess if the parents' testimony will be helpful. The non-offender parent should almost always testify to reassure the court that s/he can protect the child. The decision to present the offender parent's testimony will depend on counsel's assessment judgment of the parent's demeanor when discussing the child's medical issues. If the parent has a history of using social media to discuss the child's medical health, has a serious mental health diagnosis, or appears too knowledgeable about medical issues, counsel might reasonably conclude that the parent would not make a good witness.

Even if it is determined that the parent medically abused the child, counsel should stress the parent's good-faith intention in seeking the treatment. Although the parent's motive is no longer legally relevant, courts can be swayed to deny the Agency's Petition based upon intentions. This is particularly so when the parent is fully cooperating with medical personnel and promises to do so going forward. Even if the parent's intention does not persuade the court to dismiss the case, it may move the court to return the child under a protective order.

9.11 Defenses to Physical Injury to Child

9.11(a) Physical Abuse

Defending parents in cases involving allegations of physical abuse is particularly challenging because many tragedies reported in the media involve horrific physical abuse of children. For this reason, when preparing a case involving physical injuries to a child, it is important to take a calm, factual approach to the defense. Often, the Agency will focus primarily on the seriousness of the injuries, but failing to tie them to any evidence of parental culpability, the Agency will often rely solely on expert medical witness testimony. It is counsel's job to fill in the blanks in the prosecution's case with evidence that is favorable to the parent and supportive of family reunification.

9.11(b) Corporal Punishment

Visible marks on a child resulting from corporal punishment often trigger a report to child protection agencies. Parents have the right to punish children corporally in every state, although the right is not absolute. *See, e.g.*, *Nixon v. State*, 773 So. 2d 1213, 1215, 25 Fla. L. Weekly D2862 (Fla. Dist. Ct. App. 2000) ("[O]ne in parental authority . . . enjoys a privilege of corporal punishment."); *People v. Green*, 2011 Ill. App. 2d 091123, ¶ 14, 354 Ill. Dec. 440, 444, 957 N.E.2d 1233, 1237 (2011) ("A parent's right to corporally punish his or her child is derived from the right to privacy, which is viewed as implicit in the United States Constitution. This right encompasses the right to care for, control, and discipline one's own children."). Because parents have the legal and moral responsibility to shape children's values, corporal punishment is a legitimate form of discipline of children by parents. Many school districts even authorize state employees (principals or teachers) to punish students corporally for violating school infractions. *See, e.g.*, ALA. CODE § 16-28A-1 (2014) ("Teachers are hereby given the authority and responsibility to use appropriate means of discipline up to and including corporal punishment as may be prescribed by the local board of education."); S.C. CODE ANN. § 59-63-260 (2014) ("The governing body of each school district may provide corporal punishment for any pupil that it deems just and proper."); *Ingraham v. Wright*, 430 U.S. 651 (1977) (Florida scheme of corporal punishment in public schools not unconstitutional under Eighth or Fourteenth Amendment).

What parents may not do is inflict *excessive* corporal punishment, even though no two states define the term identically. In most jurisdictions, excessive force is measured by the marks left on the child that constitute serious physical injury. *See, e.g.*, CAL. WELF. & INST. CODE § 300(a) (2014); GA. CODE ANN. § 19-7-5(b)(4)(A) (2014). In other states, a determining factor will be the method of punishment used. For example, striking a child with a closed fist or in the face may be sufficient to prove the parent engaged in prohibited conduct.

Counsel should prepare for a corporal punishment case by learning what prior cases have said in allowing or dismissing charges of excessive corporal punishment. Rarely will the statute say enough to clarify whether the facts warrant a finding against the parent. *See, e.g.*, ALA. Code § 13A-3-24 (2014); ARIZ. REV. STAT. § 13-403 (2104) (parents may use only reasonable and appropriate physical force); HAW. REV. STAT. § 703-309(1)(a) (2014) (force will be measured with due regard for age and size of minor).

At the outset, counsel should determine whether the punishment was a single incident or part of a pattern. If it was a single incident, it should be easier to fight for the child to remain at home throughout the case. Even if corporal punishment is administered regularly, unless the child was harmed by the punishment, the Petition should be dismissed.

In either case, the critical inquiry will be whether the parent engaged in impermissible conduct. Because parents have the right to punish their children, counsel may want to defend the case on the theory that the parent did not intend to harm the child and meant to do something good for the child. Sometimes, defending the case by taking it to trial will provide the court with a chance to evaluate the parent's conduct based on the parent's demeanor and testimony in court. This can be a hazardous undertaking in some cases, however. If the court concludes that the parent's conduct was unreasonable, it may lose faith in the parent if s/he continues in court to try to justify the behavior. Depending on the severity of the injuries or the method used to punish, counsel may prefer to shift focus to settling on favorable terms to the parent. The court may be more willing to return children to a remorseful parent than to a defensive one. If parents express a willingness to adjust their disciplinary style, counsel should seek the child's return home with services such as parenting instruction and family counseling.

9.12 Injuries That Can Be Accidental or Intentional

9.12(a) Burns

Thermal burns to a child's skin can be intentional or accidental. Accidental burns to a child can trigger allegations of neglect or inadequate supervision; burns believed to be intentional can lead to serious allegations of child abuse.

9.12(a)(1) Accidental Burns

Types of accidental burns include those caused by brief contact with a hot object such as an iron, stove top, seat belt buckle, or lit cigarette. These burns tend to have ill-defined borders because they involve more glancing contact with the hot object as opposed to the sharp borders of an inflicted burn. Accidental burns caused by hot liquids often are the result of a liquid being accidentally spilled on the child or when the child tips a container of hot liquid over on him or herself. When this happens, the liquid cools relatively quickly and the burn is less severe than an immersion burn. The presence of a non-scald burn from a container coming in contact with child's skin and splash marks that showing the direction the liquid was traveling may confirm the accidental nature of these burns. *See* CHILD WELFARE LAW AND PRACTICE 21–22 (Donald N. Duquette & Ann M. Haralambie eds., 2d ed. 2010).

If the burn in question is determined to be accidental, the case will turn on whether the burn was either unforeseeable or the result of poor parenting due to neglect or inadequate supervision. Even when properly supervised, a toddler can reach up to touch a hot surface or grab a container of hot liquid. An unforeseeable accident should never support a finding of parental unfitness. Counsel should enlarge the focus of the proceeding from the single occasion on which the child was injured by putting it in a broader context. This was the *only* injury the child has ever sustained. The parent has gone out of his or her way to create a happy, safe home environment and has an excellent record of raising the child safely and well. If the parent makes a good witness, it is important to have the parent tell the court in his or her words how s/he felt when the child was hurt, what s/he did immediately upon discovering the injury, and why s/he should not be held legally responsible for it. Counsel should buttress this testimony with testimony from other witnesses who can establish the parent's reputation as a conscientious parent who provides good supervision for the child. Counsel should also present pictures showing the condition of the home.

9.12(a)(2) Intentional Burns

When the Petition alleges that the parent intentionally burned a child, and the parent denies the allegation, there are only two possible defenses: (1) either someone other than the parent inflicted the injuries and the parent should not be held responsible for them or (2) the burns were not inflicted intentionally. To develop the first defense, counsel should try to establish when the injury happened and who was with the child at the time. Counsel will want to show why the parent should not be held responsible for the actions of the person who burned the child.

If the defense is that the burns were not intentionally inflicted, counsel may need an expert to examine the burns or pictures of them to explain to the court why they were not intentionally inflicted. Several skin conditions can be confused with intentional burns, including pressure injuries, car seat burns from upholstery or buckles, impetigo, sunburn, allergic contact lesions, and staphylococcal scalded skin syndrome. *See* REECE, *supra*, at 44. Cross-examination of the state's medical expert should focus on the failure to effectively rule out the medical mimic or accidental cause that is the parent's explanation.

9.12(b) Bruises

Bruises on children are not necessarily indicative of intentionally inflicted trauma. Bruises can be the result of normal play and movement. When defending a parent accused of bruising, it is important to differentiate between accidental and inflicted bruising. As a general rule, children who are not yet walking or pulling up to a standing position should not have bruises, whereas accidental bruising is common in children who are walking or learning to walk. *See* CHILD WELFARE LAW AND PRACTICE, *supra*, at 19. Such bruises normally occur over bony prominences such as the shins, lower arms, prominences of the spine, forehead, under the chin, or on the iliac crests of the hips. However, bruises on the upper arms, trunk, upper anterior legs, sides of the face, ears, neck, genitalia, and buttocks are more likely to be the result of inflicted trauma. *See* AM. PROF'L SOC'Y ON THE ABUSE OF CHILDREN, THE APSAC HANDBOOK ON CHILD MALTREATMENT 191 (John E. B. Myers, 3rd ed. 2010). Abusive bruises can also be differentiated by shape such as oval or round bruises arranged in a pattern indicating grabbing or pinching, hand-shaped bruises, or those consistent with a belt, electrical cord, angle of a wire hanger. *See* CHILD WELFARE LAW AND PRACTICE, *supra*, at 19–20.

When defending a parent who asserts that the bruising on the child was not the result of child abuse, it is important to have an alternative theory of the bruising. There are many scenarios in which a child can acquire an accidental yet atypical bruise. A bruise on the buttocks can result from a backward fall onto an object and a genital bruise can result from a straddle injury. When presenting such a defense, it is essential to show pictures of the scene, to present a clear picture of the mechanism of the injury, and to correlate the two with witnesses who can attest to the incident or the fact that the incident is typical of the child's activities or behavior.

It is also important to rule out medications that the child is taking as contributing to the severity of the child's bruising. Medications that may cause a child to bruise easily include blood-thinners such as warfarin and heparin, as well as aspirin and other non-steroidal anti-inflammatory drugs. *See* Adrian M. B. Minford and E. M. Richards, *Excluding Medical and Haematological Conditions as a Cause of Bruising in Suspected Non-Accidental Injury*, 95 ARCHIVES DISEASE CHILDHOOD EDUC. & PRAC. 2 (2009).

There are also underlying medical conditions that can mimic abusive bruising or can cause children to bruise excessively from relatively minor trauma. These medical conditions include von Willebrand disease, hemophilia, idiopathic thrombocytopenic purpura, and other coagulopathies. *See* Martha E. Laposata & Michael Laposata, *Children with Signs of Abuse: When Is It Not Child Abuse?*, 123 AM. J. CLINICAL PATHOLOGY 119 (2005).

9.12(c) Fractures

A defense based on failure to rule out a non-accidental cause for a fracture begins with a thorough review of the medical record. Counsel should carefully read the child abuse pediatrician's report. The diagnostic section of this report should list differential diagnoses and whether these diagnoses were ruled out before the non-accidental trauma diagnosis was made. It is also important to read the reports from any specialists whose evaluation of the child informed the child abuse pediatrician's assessment. It is not uncommon for one specialist to suggest that a non-accidental cause be considered before assigning a diagnosis of non-accidental trauma and for that suggestion not to be followed. For example, a radiologist may identify a corner fracture or classic metaphyseal lesion on an infant's wrist, which is suspicious for inflicted trauma, and will suggest that lab work be performed to rule out metabolic bone disease as a cause.Unexplained fractures in a non-mobile child are difficult cases to defend. If the cause of the fracture is unknown to the parent, the doctor who examines the child will typically assert that if the parents cannot cite an accidental cause for the fracture, the fracture must be the result of inflicted trauma. Sometimes, the cause of the injury is known to the parent, but the doctor who evaluates the child refuses to accept the explanation and concludes that the injury was intentionally inflicted. In either instance, the burden may have unofficially shifted to the parent to prove that the parent did not inflict the injury.

Although the state should carry the burden of proof at adjudication, it is very difficult to win a case involving an unexplained fracture without presenting an alternative theory of the injury. This explanation can be medical, mechanical, or both. If the mechanism of injury is known to the parent, but not accepted by the investigating physician, a successful defense depends on investigating the scene combined with effective cross-examination of the Agency's medical expert to determine exactly which parts of the parent's account the physician found implausible. Counsel must then present evidence to show that the physician's assessment of the parent's credibility is incorrect.

Before diagnosing a fracture as non-accidental trauma, the investigating physician should consider and rule out possible non-abusive causes for the injury. *See* REECE, *supra*, at 147–57. Defenses based on alternative medical explanations for fractures will usually focus on the investigating physician's failure to rule out underlying conditions that can cause or predispose a child to fractures. These include obstetric trauma, prematurity, nutritional and metabolic disorders, medication toxicity, infection, neuromuscular defects, skeletal dysplasia, and neoplasm. If it appears from the medical record that the investigating physician failed to properly rule out a non-abusive cause for the child's injury, counsel should seek further evaluation of the child by an independent physician.

In order to plan an effective defense based on failure to rule out an alternative medical explanation, counsel needs to become conversant with the diagnostic protocols for unexplained fractures. There are several excellent resources available that explain the diagnosis of non-accidental trauma and discuss the conditions that must be ruled out before the diagnosis is made. One of the best resources is AM. ACAD. OF PEDIATRICS, CHILD ABUSE MEDICAL DIAGNOSIS & MANAGEMENT (Robert M. Reece & Cindy W. Christian eds., 3rd ed. 2008). Also useful is AM. PROF'L SOC'Y ON THE ABUSE OF CHILDREN, THE APSAC HANDBOOK ON CHILD MALTREATMENT (John E. B. Myers, 3rd ed. 2010). Many other valuable resources can be found on the website of the American Academy of Pediatrics. Counsel should consult these resources to gain an understanding of the standard of care applicable in the evaluation of injuries in children. These resources may provide a good basis for cross-examination of the state's medical expert.

The hours leading up to the diagnosis of non-accidental trauma are not always the most important. Therefore, it is important to gather the child's entire medical record, not just the records regarding the injury in question. These records include prenatal records, records from the child's birth, pediatric records, records concerning any previous injuries or illnesses, and records from urgent care facilities. Also important are records generated in the weeks and months after the injury in question, including those from continued hospitalizations, subsequent hospitalizations, follow-up radiology records, and records from any therapies the child may require. Note that not all records generated in a hospital will be included in the child's medical record. Some departments maintain their own records that have to be obtained separately. This is often true for radiology, pathology, and emergency transports.

It is critical that counsel not become so involved with the medical aspects of the case that the practical aspects of parent defense are forgotten. In medically complicated cases, it is still essential to take pictures of the scene, interview the client, interview family members, friends, the child's pediatrician, and any other potential witnesses, and investigate any criminal or social services history of the family. It is essential to paint a broad picture of the parent.

Although opening statements are not usually made in child welfare hearings, an opening statement is very important in cases involving unexplained fractures. Counsel should use the opening statement to introduce the non-abusive explanation for the child's injury. The opening statement is counsel's opportunity to talk about everything the parent did right, including recognizing something amiss and seeking medical treatment for the child.

9.12(d) Head Trauma

Abusive head trauma, formerly known as shaken baby syndrome, is characterized by a triad of injuries consisting of subdural hematoma, retinal hemorrhage, and cerebral edema. This diagnosis has undergone a series of name changes as well as changes related to its features. What began as "whiplash shaken infant syndrome" in the 1970s was later renamed "shaken baby syndrome." *See* John Caffey, *The Whiplash Shaken Infant Syndrome: Manual Shaking by the Extremities with Whiplash-Induced Intracranial and Intraocular Bleedings, Linked with Residual Permanent Brain Damage and Mental Retardation*, 54 PEDIATRICS 396 (1974) (whiplash shaken infant); Steven Gabaeff, *Challenging the Pathophysiologic Connection Between Subdural Hematoma, Retinal Hemorrhage and Shaken Baby Syndrome*, 12 W. J. EMERGENCY MED. 144 (2011) (shaken baby).

In the 1980s, faced with scientific challenges regarding the capacity of shaking alone to cause brain injury, the definition of shaken baby syndrome was expanded to encompass "shaken impact." *See* Gabaeff, *supra*, at 154. Most recently, in 2009, the term "abusive head trauma" was adopted by the American Academy of Pediatrics as a label inclusive of all mechanisms of injury that can be associated with shaking. *See* Cindy W. Christian & Robert Block, *Abusive Head Trauma in Infants and Children*, 123 PEDIATRICS 1409 (2009).

Despite the shifting landscape and controversy surrounding the so-called "syndrome," courts have tended to allow experts to testify about it, whether using the tests established in *Frye* or *Daubert*. Even in criminal cases, judges tend to find sufficient general acceptance in the medical community, despite recognizing ongoing scientific challenges to the underlying methodology of shaken baby syndrome and abusive head trauma. *See* Deborah Tuerkheimer, *The Next Innocence Project: Shaken Baby Syndrome and the Criminal Courts*, 87 WASH. U. L. REV. 1 (2009).

Even if counsel is unable to exclude expert testimony describing shaken baby syndrome or abusive head trauma, there is plenty of room to attack the reliability of an expert's opinion through cross-examination, presentation of contrary evidence, and closing argument.

Many of the same lessons that apply to unexplained fracture cases also apply to cases involving allegations of abusive head trauma. Child abuse physicians often rush to label an injury "abusive head trauma" without properly considering any different diagnoses. This tendency to over-label diagnoses as "abuse" is partially reinforced by policy. Although the American Academy of Pediatrics advocates that pediatricians consider alternative hypotheses when evaluating a patient with findings suggestive of abusive head trauma, the organization also suggests that physicians make a working diagnosis and take the legally mandated steps for further investigation where indicated. *See* Christian & Block, *supra*. For this and other reasons, the risk of confirmation bias in the initial medical investigation is very high and, as a result, many innocent parents are accused of having shaken or otherwise wrongfully abused their babies.

9.12(d)(1) Abusive Versus Accidental Head Trauma

If a child previously suffered head or cranial trauma, even one documented as caused by an accident, it is very likely that the second injury will be diagnosed, at least initially, as abusive head trauma. This is not only because whenever a child twice suffers a serious injury the treating physician's suspicions are aroused, but is also because many doctors do not believe that simple accidents can cause head trauma. In particular, many doctors believe that falls from a short height almost never cause serious or head injuries. The abusive head trauma literature is replete with studies supporting this idea and physicians are routinely advised to disbelieve a parent's explanation that the child fell from a short height when the child has suffered a severe intracranial injury. *See* Reece, *supra*, at 67–70. But this is highly contested and parents' lawyers should become familiar with the growing literature explaining even severe head injuries as fully compatible with accidents not involving any kind of child abuse.

There are a number of disorders that can cause a child to present with symptoms suggestive of or consistent with abusive head trauma. Below is a list of differential diagnoses for abusive head trauma. These disorders may cause a child to present with one or more symptoms of the triad and should be ruled out before a diagnosis of abusive head trauma is made. Unfortunately, in the rush to medical judgment, differential diagnoses are often ignored or overlooked. Counsel needs to review the child's full medical and family history in search of information that any of differential diagnoses are indicated, but were inadequately investigated.

9.12(d)(1)(A) Coagulopathies

Coagulopathies are bleeding disorders that impair the blood's ability to clot effectively. They can affect the formation both of subdural hematomas and retinal hemorrhages. Common pediatric coagulopathies include hemophilia, von Willebrand disease, neonatal alloimmune thrombocytopenia, and disseminated intravascular coagulation. Coagulopathies can be ruled out by laboratory testing only. *See* Reece, *supra*, at 73–75.

9.12(d)(1)(B) Metabolic Disease

Manifestations of previously undiagnosed metabolic diseases can sometimes be mistaken for abusive head trauma. One of these is Glutaric Aciduria Type I, an autosomal-recessive disease, which can lead to comatose episodes, subdural hematomas, and retinal hemorrhages. *See* Luis C. Gago et al., *Intraretinal Hemorrhages and Chronic Subdural Effusions: Glutaric Aciduria Type I Can Be Mistaken for Shaken Baby*

Syndrome, 23 RETINA 724 (2003). Another is Menkes Disease, a recessive disorder, which affects copper levels in the body and can cause massive subdural hematomas as well as metaphyseal bone changes that resemble fractures. Children with this rare disorder are very likely to be suspected of being the victim of abuse. *See* Marie-Cecile Nassogne et al., *Massive Subdural Haematomas in Menkes Disease Mimicking Shaken Baby Syndrome*, 18 CHILD. NERVOUS SYS. 729 (2002). Both of these metabolic diseases can be diagnosed through genetic testing.

9.12(d)(1)(C) Congenital Malformations

Sometimes infants are born with malformations such as intracranial arteriovenous malformations, aneurisms, or other cerebral vascular malformations of the brain and meninges. These malformations can rupture resulting in subdural hemorrhage, brain swelling, and retinal hemorrhages. *See* Waney Squier, *The "Shaken Baby" Syndrome: Pathology and Mechanisms*, 122 ACTA NEUPATHOLOGICA 519, 527 (2011). *See also* REECE, *supra*, at 73.

9.12(d)(1)(D) Venous Thrombosis and Sinus Thrombosis

Cortical vein thrombosis and sinus thrombosis are associated with subdural and other types of brain bleeds. Blood flowing through the parietal veins, which empty into the superior sagittal sinus, become clotted, which leads to hemorrhage and localized brain swelling. Approximately 10 percent of infants do not show symptoms of this condition, while others present with non-specific symptoms such as depressed consciousness, lethargy, poor feeding, vomiting, or seizures. *See* Squier, *supra*. Cortical vein thrombosis and sinus thrombosis are best diagnosed by an MRI with venography and are associated with clinical risk factors such as infection or dehydration. *See* REECE, *supra*, at 73.

9.12(d)(1)(E) Birth-Related and Chronic Subdural Hematomas

Subdural bleeding occurs after birth in up to 46 percent of infants, is usually asymptomatic, and resolves without further complication in most cases. *See* Gabaeff, *supra*, at 153; Squier, *supra*, at 528. However, in a small percentage of infants, the subdural bleeding either continues or restarts, resulting in non-specific symptoms such as failure to gain weight, refusal of feedings followed by frequent vomiting, irritability, progressive enlargement of the head, and seizure. Diagnosis of chronic subdural hematomas requires a careful review of obstetric and birth records, changes in head circumference, and current and prior brain scans.

9.12(d)(1)(F) Increased Intercranial Pressure

There is a correlation between increased intracranial pressure and retinal hemorrhage that is independent of abuse. Specifically, there is a relationship among increased intracranial pressure, optic nerve sheath hemorrhage, and retinal hemorrhage. The increased intracranial pressure can be the result of impact trauma, extreme coughing, or choking episodes. *See* Gabaeff, *supra*, at 151.

9.12(d)(1)(G) Enlarged Extra-Axial Spaces

In some infants, cerebrospinal fluid accumulates in the space between the brain and its covering. This condition is believed to be the result of delayed development of the channels in the brain that reabsorb cerebrospinal fluid. Although the condition usually resolves on its own, it may also predispose infants to subdural hematomas that are either spontaneous or the result of minor trauma. The exact mechanism for development of subdural hematomas is not known, but one hypothesis is that enlargement of the cerebrospinal fluid spaces stretches the bridging veins, causing them to leak. *See* P. Daniel McNeely et al., *Subdural Hematomas in Infants with Benign Enlargement of the Subarachnoid Spaces Are Not Pathognomonic for Child Abuse*, 27 AM. J. NEURORADIOLOGY 1725 (2006); Squier, *supra*, at 528–29.

9.12(d)(2) Available Strategies in Defending Head Trauma Injuries

One cannot succeed in defending a parent accused of shaking a baby and inflicting abusive head trauma without an alternative theory that explains the child's symptoms and medical findings. Unlike cases involving unexplained fractures, it is not enough to show that a physician failed to consider and rule out a differential diagnosis. Although the abusive head trauma diagnosis is deceptively straightforward (triad = abuse), refuting the diagnosis is incredibly complex. As outlined above, the disease and disorders that can mimic some or all of the triad symptoms are complex in their presentation and require additional laboratory testing, imaging, and medical history review to properly diagnose.

Further complicating matters is the interrelatedness of some of these conditions. For example, a chronic subdural bleed resulting from a subdural hematoma that was present shortly after birth can lead to an increase in intracranial pressure that results in retinal hemorrhages. Effective presentation of this defense theory requires testimony from a radiologist, a pediatric neurologist, and either an ophthalmologist or a pathologist.

Despite the difficulties of presenting a thorough medical defense to abusive head trauma, it is possible to mount a successful defense. This begins, as always, with counsel carefully reading the child abuse pediatrician's report with an eye toward differential diagnoses. Counsel should pay particular attention to what the child abuse pediatrician said as compared to what the specialists said. Counsel should also take note of what records were reviewed (and what records were not reviewed) by the child abuse pediatrician and any other specialists. For example, without reviewing the child's birth records, post-birth hospitalization records, pediatric records, or prior imaging studies, it would be impossible for a physician to rule out a chronic subdural hematoma or the re-bleed of a subdural hematoma present at birth and thought to be resolved.

In preparing the defense involving abusive head trauma case, counsel must also consider and understand the very specific arguments developed by those who regularly prosecute these cases. Many of these arguments are summarized in *Overcoming*

Defense Expert Testimony in Abusive Head Trauma Cases, which is available on the website of the National District Attorneys Association.

9.13 The Charge of Exposing a Child to Domestic Violence

Many child welfare cases are prosecuted when officials become aware that the child was exposed to domestic violence. Counsel might defend the parent accused of inflicting the violence or the parent who was its recipient. Obviously, the defense to the two cases will differ.

Representing a parent who inflicted domestic violence on the other parent is not easy. Many courts will presume that a parent who engaged in intimate violence is per se a danger to the child. Counsel should regard this thinking as creating de facto a rebuttable presumption that the parent poses a danger to the child. To successfully defend the parent in this situation, counsel will have to present evidence to rebut the presumption. The evidence might include proof that the domestic violence was a one-time incident, took place when the child was not present, and should not be used to conclude that the parent would ever hit the child. Counsel should present evidence of a strong parent-child relationship to buttress the claim that there is no reason to believe the child is in danger.

Representing the parent who was the recipient of violence is, to say the least, an easier task. Some jurisdictions charge parents with "allowing the children to be exposed to domestic violence" when this means nothing more than the fact that the child was present when the parent was hit by a domestic partner unexpectedly. This does more than blame the victim. It misunderstands the law. *See Nicholson v. Scoppetta*, 3 N.Y.3d 357, 787 N.Y.S.2d 196, 820 N.E.2d 840 (2004) (charging a parent with neglect based merely on a child's presence when the parent was hit does not state a cause of action because it fails to show how the parent fell below the minimum standard of care due the child).

At minimum, counsel should insist that the children remain in the non-abusing parent's care during the pendency of the proceeding. This is usually accomplishable by issuing an order of protection forbidding the other parent from going near the parent or children. Sometimes, this is not what the client wants; but it may be an arrangement the client will have to accept to keep custody of the children pending the outcome of the case. Counsel should advise the client of what there is to gain by seeking a temporary protective order prohibiting the abuser from contact with the parent or children. This may be the only way to keep the family together until the trial.

Counsel should argue at trial that the court should not punish the victim parent for not ending the relationship or escaping the abuser sooner. Rather the court should focus on the children's current safety and well-being. If there was evidence presented at trial to show that the children suffered harm from the exposure to domestic violence, counsel should argue that the harm should not be compounded by placing them in foster care, thereby turning an incident of domestic violence into the destruction of a family and one victim of violence into several. If the children suffered some harm already, that is all the more reason they should be allowed to secure the emotional support of the one person who understands what they have been though.

Fortunately, many states have updated their laws to reflect the complexity of domestic violence situations and the need to protect children rather than punish the victim parent. For example, Florida requires child protective services responders to know how and when to use the injunction process to remove a perpetrator of domestic violence from a home as in intervention to protect the child. *See* FLA. STAT. § 39.301 (2014). In Utah, the Department of Child and Family Services must provide domestic violence services to families and provide protective services to victims of domestic violence and their families. *See* UTAH CODE ANN. § 62A-4a-105(3) (2014). In Alaska, the child welfare department must make "reasonable efforts to protect the child and prevent the removal of the child from the parent or guardian who is not a domestic violence offender." *See* ALASKA STAT. § 47.17.035 (2014).

9.14 Defenses to Substance Abuse

With some exceptions, drug use alone is insufficient to establish dependency. *See, e.g., L.P. v. Dep't of Children and Family Servs.*, 962 So. 2d 980, 32 Fla. L. Weekly D1830 (Fla. Dist. Ct. App. 2007) (mother's cocaine use alone, without evidence of specific harm to children, did not support adjudicating children dependent); *State of N.M. ex rel CYFD v. Amanda H.*, 154 P.3d 674, 680, 141 N.M. 299, 305 (2006) ("[A]n unfavorable personal status of a parent, such as incarceration, mental illness, prior convictions, or addiction, is alone insufficient to support an adjudication that a child is neglected."). Rather, a finding of dependency usually must rest on evidence that the parent has used drugs in the presence of the child, has provided inadequate care or supervision while under the influence of drugs, has exposed child to drug trafficking and its associated dangers, or evidence of access or exposure to parent's drugs. As with other allegations against parents, a finding of dependency should be based on a finding that the child has suffered or will suffer harm as a result of the parent's drug use. A successful defense to dependency based on parental drug use focuses the court on the needs of the child rather than on the mere fact of parental wrongdoing.

Across the states, appellate court rulings generally support the notion that drug use alone is insufficient to support a finding of dependency absent a showing of neglect or other harm to the children. For example, a California appellate court found that evidence was insufficient to support a finding of dependency where a mother tested positive for marijuana and methamphetamines because there was no evidence that the mother's drug use caused her to neglect her child or that the child had been harmed by the drug use. Even the child's statements that she could sometimes smell marijuana did not reach the necessary level of harm. In its findings, the court took into account that the child, because she was eleven years old, was able to avoid certain hazards within the home. *See In re Destiny S.*, 210 Cal. App. 4th 999, 148 Cal. Rptr. 3d 800 (2012).

Similarly, an Oregon appellate court found that evidence did not support a finding of dependency where a mother tested positive for marijuana, but the department did not show that this created a harmful environment for the children where the mother did not use marijuana in the home or in the presence of the children. *See Dep't of Human Servs. v. C.Z.*, 236 Or. App. 436, 236 P.3d 791 (2010). Conversely, a New Hampshire appellate court found that evidence supported a finding of dependency where large quantities of illegal substances were discovered in the home, the children were exposed to both drugs and to monetary exchanges for drugs, and the children had unfettered access to drugs. *See In re P. Children*, 149 N.H. 129, 816 A.2d 982 (2003).

Appellate court rulings regarding prenatal exposure are less consistent. A New Jersey appellate court found that evidence was insufficient to support a finding of dependency where an infant tested positive for cocaine at birth, but appeared healthy. The mother also tested positive for cocaine earlier in the day and had tested positive for marijuana during her fifth month of pregnancy, but there was no evidence regarding the severity of the mother's drug use or the severity of harm to the infant. *See New Jersey Dep't of Children and Families, Div. of Youth and Family Servs. v. A.L.*, 213 N.J. 1, 59 A.3d 576 (2013). However, an Ohio appellate court affirmed a finding of dependency where an infant was born with cocaine in his system, finding that a child born with illegal substances in his or her system is per se abused. *See In re Baby Boy Blackshear*, 90 Ohio St. 3d 197, 736 N.E.2d 462 (2000).

At trial, counsel must hold the Agency to its burden to show that the children have been harmed by parental inability resulting from the parent's drug use. If these items reflect favorably on the client, counsel should consider presenting pictures of the home, the children's report cards or progress reports from school, and their attendance and disciplinary records. Other favorable evidence might be the children's vaccination records showing that they are up-to-date on all immunizations. Counsel should consider cross-examining the Agency's investigator about the condition of the children upon removal from the home, especially if the children were clean, well nourished, and dressed appropriately for the weather.

In cases involving allegations of drug use by the parent, it is important to consider the validity of any drug tests administered to the parent. If the test on which the Agency is basing its allegation of illegal drug use is an instant test in which the sample is tested on-site using a dipstick or cup-testing method, it is important to know the exact test that was used and what the capabilities of the test really are. Drug testing products, like over-the-counter medications, have a package insert that contains a wealth of information about the test. Some package inserts even disclaim the reliability of the test. As the package insert for the popular ECO Cup One Step Drug Test explains, its test results may not prove anything determinative.

The ECO Cup One Step Drug Test package insert warns that because of "technical or procedural errors," and other reasons, the results may be erroneous. In addition, the insert warns that the test "does not distinguish between drugs of abuse and certain medications." Instead, it "provides only a qualitative, preliminary analytical result." Once there is a positive result, the insert further warns, a "secondary analytical method must be used to obtain a confirmed result" and it specifically recommends that the confirmatory method use a "gas chromatography/mass spectrometry" test.

Another very common test—the Alfa Rapid Medical Tests Multi-Drug Dip Card—also disclaims acting on any result the test might yield. It explains a positive result is merely "a preliminary positive test" that requires further testing to confirm the results.

Sometimes, the results of an instant drug test are reported as a "faint positive," meaning that the test line contained some color, but was not as dark as the control line. In this situation, counsel must educate the court about the correct interpretation of such a result. It is essential to obtain a copy of the package insert for the drug test used and to read the parameters for interpreting results. Most package inserts contain a note about how the intensity of the test line will vary, but that the test should be considered negative whenever there is even a faint distinguishable color line.

The admissibility of the drug test is also an important consideration. When representing a client accused of drug use where the client denies use, it is possible to prevent the results of a positive drug test from being entered into evidence. Because the rules of evidence are often treated very casually in child welfare cases, the Agency is used to relying on hearsay or other inadmissible evidence to prove parental drug use. When the rules of evidence are strictly applied, the results of a laboratory drug test cannot simply be entered into evidence without accompanying testimony from the technician who performed the test. *See Melendez-Diaz v. Massachusetts*, 557 U.S. 305 (2009) (sworn affidavits are testimonial in nature and do not meet the business records exception to the hearsay rule).

Although there are many effective techniques that prevent children from being adjudicated dependent based on parental drug abuse, when counsel has reason to believe that the parent is experiencing serious addiction issues, counsel should begin a conversation with the parent about what is best for him or her. Although it is easy to think only in terms of the short-term goal of winning the case at trial, counsel may wish to focus the parent on the long-term goal of remaining a family. If the parent is suffering from an addiction, the abrupt loss of the children to state custody might serve as a triggering event for the client to seriously consider rehabilitation, potentially accelerating the recovery process. It should go without saying, of course, that the final decision of the client will control counsel's strategy in all phases of the case.

9.15 Defenses to Neglect Predicated upon the Mental Illness of Parent

When the allegation of abuse or neglect is based upon the mental health of the parent, the law in most states requires a determination that the effects of the parent's illness result in an inability to provide proper care for the child. Even where the law does not specifically require such a determination, counsel can argue that the definition of dependency, no matter the basis, requires evidence of a negative effect on the child or of the child's basic needs not being met.

When representing a parent whose mental health is central to the case, it is important to hold the Agency to its burden to prove not only the harm to the child, but the mental illness itself if the diagnosis is not supported. Too often, allegations regarding the mental illness of a parent arise from hearsay or speculation by third parties. Statements such as "she doesn't take her meds" or "she's bipolar" are often assumed by the Agency to be true and are used as the basis for an allegation of dependency due to mental illness. Such statements regarding a parent's mental health are hearsay and lack foundation because the layperson making them is not qualified to make such a diagnosis.

If the Agency has obtained an actual psychological evaluation of the parent and that evaluation serves as the basis of the allegation of mental illness, counsel must consider both the admissibility and the validity of the admissibility of evaluation. Counsel should not allow the Agency to admit the parent's psychological evaluation into evidence unless the psychologist is present to authenticate the document and to be cross-examined regarding its contents.

Counsel should review the psychological evaluation and consider the validity of the diagnoses. If the diagnoses are not accurate, counsel must be prepared to discredit the evaluation. Counsel should first consider the qualifications and background of the evaluator. Does the evaluator hold a doctoral-level degree? Has the evaluator received specialized training in conducting forensic evaluations? Is the evaluator qualified to administer the tests and measures used in the evaluation? Finally, what percentage of the evaluator's work is devoted to conducting forensic evaluations for the Agency? How much of the evaluation was actually performed by the evaluator (as opposed to clinical staff or assistants) and how much time did the evaluator actually spend with the parent?

In assessing the evaluation itself, counsel should also consider whether the evaluator operated in full compliance with the ethical guidelines set forth by the American Psychological Association. These guidelines are available on the association's website. The general code for the profession is the Ethical Principles of Psychologists, also available on the association's website. Of particular interest to parents' lawyers are the Specialty Guidelines for Forensic Psychologists ("SFGP"), which provide additional guidance for practitioners who perform forensic evaluations such as the ones used in child welfare cases.

One common problem with psychological evaluations ordered by the Agency is the degree to which the evaluator relies on one-sided and often inaccurate background information given by the Agency's case manager. There is a risk that this information, if it is the evaluator's sole source of collateral information, will prejudice the evaluator against the parent. This could lead to inaccurate diagnoses and recommendations for treatment that are more demanding than they may have been otherwise. If this happens, counsel should cross-examine the evaluator regarding his or her compliance with SGFP Guidelines 8.03 and 9.02, which direct evaluators to strive to access information or records from collateral sources, to avoid relying solely on one source of data, and to corroborate important data whenever feasible.

Counsel should also look carefully at the assessment techniques, tests, and instruments used by the evaluator. SGFP Guideline 10.02 requires that forensic practitioners use assessment procedures whose validity and reliability have been established and that the procedures used be appropriate to the examinee's language preference and competence. Counsel should be alert to problems with the administration of written measures to parents with limited literacy or the administration of interviews or tests in English if that is not the parent's preferred language. In evaluating the validity, reliability, and proper application of the tests employed by the evaluator, counsel should also consider obtaining and consulting the most recent Tests in Print publications from the Buros Center for Testing in Lincoln, Nebraska. These guides contain vital information regarding all of the commercially available tests including what each test is designed to measure, the intended test population, and critical reviews. Tests in Print are available for sale on the Buros Center's website.

Even if a valid or unassailable evaluation provides a mental health diagnosis for the parent, that is only part of what the Agency must prove at trial. It must also prove that there is a nexus between the parent's mental health diagnosis and an inability to provide for the physical, mental, and emotional needs of the child. If the parent's diagnosis results in strange or idiosyncratic behavior that does not pose a danger of abuse or neglect to the child, the evidence is insufficient to prove neglect. Nor is the evidence sufficient if the parent's symptoms are controlled by a medication regiment with which the parent is compliant. Counsel should be alert for allegations that are based on speculation that the parent's condition may worsen or that the parent may not remain medication compliant. When faced with such allegations, counsel should argue that the evidence must demonstrate a current risk to children and that potential future dependency does not meet the legal definition of a dependent child under state law.

9.16 Defenses to Allegations of Sexual Abuse

Allegations of sexual abuse in dependency proceedings against parents appear in two forms: either the parent is alleged to be the direct offender or is alleged to have failed to protect the child from sexual abuse (often referred to as the non-offender parent). The defenses to allegations of sexual abuse for these different types of respondents depend on the position they will take at trial. When one parent is accused of being the active offender and the other as the non-offender, each requires separate counsel.

The non-offender's defense to the charge of failure to protect is built on the claim that the parent did not fall below the minimum standard of care parents must meet to retain their right to raise their children. As with all calamities that may befall children, the critical inquiry when a parent is accused of failing to prevent an injury sustained by a child which no one suggests the parent inflicted is whether the parent should be held accountable for the injury. Raising children is not a strict liability undertaking. Children get hurt all the time. Parents may not be held responsible for a child's injury merely by proving the child was injured. The critical, additional charge must include that the parent is legally accountable for the injury because she failed to take steps that a reasonable parent would have taken to prevent the injury. A parent who did not know and could not have known that abuse was occurring and who did not place the child in an unsafe environment based on what the parent knew beforehand is not legally responsible for the abuse. Often in these cases, proof of what the parent did after learning of the abuse is powerful evidence supporting the claim that the parent should not be held accountable for the abuse. When, for example, the parent took immediate steps to address the sexual abuse by taking the child for medical attention, notifying the authorities, or removing the offender from the home, counsel should present these facts to bolster the claim that the parent is exactly the kind of parent child welfare officials want a child to have.

When the alleged offender is the other parent, the non-offending parent may be placed in a very difficult position. S/he could defend the charges on the ground that no abuse happened, but this is a sink or swim defense that often results in a finding against both parents if the court finds there was abuse. Courts often will find fault with a parent who refuses to believe what the court has found occurred. But if the non-offending parent offers an alternative defense—either it did not happen or the parent is not responsible for it—the court is often more interested in seeing where the parent's allegiance lies. Non-offending parents are often placed in the position of having to choose to reject the other parent or risk losing custody of the child.

To successfully defend allegations of sexual abuse, counsel must conduct a thorough investigation by securing all documentation—including the child's school records, medical records, therapeutic records and psychological evaluation, police investigation records, and the forensic interview records and all recorded written and the child's statements, as well as researching the most recent psychological and scientific information surrounding allegations of sexual abuse.

The most important material to obtain promptly is the complete statement of the child, together with any recording of the statement that may have been made. Counsel will be interested in ascertaining whether there is any possible reason for a false report.

Counsel should inquire whether there is any record of prior false or substantiated allegations made by the child or the person who reported the child's disclosure. It is also important to visit the site of the alleged sexual abuse to determine whether it is likely that the abuse occurred as the child described. If someone was allegedly present when the abuse allegedly occurred, counsel should interview that person.

Lastly, counsel should investigate whether the child was sexually abused by someone else and is blaming the offender or is mistaken in the abuser's identity. In this vein, counsel should look beyond the time immediately prior to and after the disclosure. Counsel should request all records concerning the child, particularly therapeutic records and any psychological evaluations. Counsel should also request the Agency's protocols and policies for investigating allegations of sexual abuse, the resume or curriculum vitae of all experts who interviewed the child or assisted in the preparation of the Agency's cases, and a list of the Agency's witnesses and a summary of their testimony.

In defending a non-offender parent, counsel should obtain all records, documentation, and witnesses that reflect that the non-offender parent has a history of protecting the child, why the non-offender was unaware of the sexual abuse, and the actions the non-offender took to protect the child when the outcry was made. Information that shows the non-offender's history of protecting the child is very important.

In many instances, the case against a non-offending parent is circumstantial. Lacking direct evidence of wrongdoing, the Agency's theory is that the parent failed to do what a reasonable parent would have done under the circumstances. In some cases, of course, the Agency has direct proof of the non-offending parent's misconduct. But more often such direct proof is lacking. Instead, the Agency seeks a finding of neglect or dependency because the parent did not do enough to prevent the abuse. In these cases, the best defense often is a rebutting circumstantial case.

Counsel's theory should be that the non-offending parent has a track record of being a caring protector of his or her children, and that this record is incompatible with the parent having wrongfully allowed the child to be abused. Counsel should gather evidence to show that the parent has created a safe environment for the child and has taken steps throughout the child's life to protect the child from harm. This defense can focus on the various ways the parent has been responsible, such as ensuring that the child has regular health checkups, good school attendance, and the like.

The condition of the home is also something counsel should investigate. If the parent created a safe home environment for the child by keeping the home in repair, clean and clutter-free, posting emergency numbers and having emergency equipment, and employing working security precautions, counsel should consider proving these facts in court. Counsel should also want to learn what steps the parent may have taken to protect the children from harm, such as a parent who moved the family after learning that there was some danger in the immediate environment. In addition to finding evidence that demonstrates good parenting before the abuse occurred, evidence of what the parent did upon learning of the abuse is especially important. If the non-offending parent took steps that the court would agree are what good parents who want to protect their children would do, counsel should stress those facts before the court. Establishing the non-offender parent's history of protecting the child will overcome any presumption by the court that the parent cannot continue to protect the child.

Once counsel has obtained, investigated, and reviewed all records, it is important to become familiar with the latest research on child sexual abuse allegations. This information may be accessed through the Internet and the public library. A number of organizations including the American Society of Professionals on the Abuse of Children, the American Bar Association Center on Children and Law, National Center on Child Abuse and Neglect, the Department of Health and Human Services' Administration for Children and Families, Children's Bureau Child Abuse and Neglect, and the American Academy of Child & Adolescent Psychiatry are excellent places to start the research.

In most jurisdictions, forensic interviewers are used during the investigation of child sex abuse inquiries. When these professionals are used, they are commonly the most important witness at the trial. In many jurisdictions, there is an exception to the hearsay rule allowing the out-of-court statements of children to be admitted as substantive evidence in dependency trials. *See, e.g.*, Md. Code Ann., Crim. Law § 11-304 (2014); N.Y. Fam. Ct. Act § 1046(a)(iv) (2014); Wash Rev. Code Ann. § 9A.44.120 (2014). In these states, the forensic interviewer will be allowed to testify to what the child said during the interview, even if the child is not called as a witness and made subject to cross-examination. In other jurisdictions, the interviewer may be allowed to testify to what the child said, but the child will have to be made available for cross-examination. *See, e.g.*, S.C. Code Ann. § 19-1-180(B)(1) (2014) (child must testify unless found unavailable under S.C. Code Ann. § 19-1-180(B)(2)).

One need not be qualified as an expert to testify to what the child said in an out-of-court interview. But most forensic interviewers are also asked to give their opinion on one of two different matters: whether, in the interviewer's opinion, the child was abused or whether the child behaved in a manner consistent with an abused child.

Counsel should be prepared to challenge the interviewer's expertise, seeking to prevent him or her from being qualified as an expert. If counsel succeeds, the interviewer may not testify to any opinions. To prepare for challenging the interviewer as an expert, counsel should consult a local expert in child sexual abuse and in proper interviewing techniques of allegedly abused children.

If counsel decides to challenge the witness as an expert, the proper procedure would be to voir dire the witness before the witness is qualified by the court. In many jurisdictions, the decision whether to challenge a witness as an expert needs to be made at a pretrial conference. Counsel should prepare accordingly.

Deciding whether to challenge a witness's qualification as an expert is a complicated inquiry. One advantage of doing so is that counsel gets to ask the witness questions before the witness has had a chance to say anything harmful to the defense. Even where counsel expects that the witness will be qualified as an expert, counsel might wish to use voir dire as an opportunity to alert the fact-finder to something useful to the defense. If, for example, counsel's theory is that the child falsely reported to the expert that s/he was abused, counsel may choose to use voir dire as an opportunity to test the witness's expertise by asking the witness whether the witness is aware of examples of false assertions by children. No answer to this question could hurt. If the witness answers "no," that s/he is unaware of such cases, counsel can argue that the witness should not be qualified as an expert. If the answer is "yes," the witness may be qualified but counsel will have planted the seed in the fact-finder's mind that just because a child tells someone s/he was abused is not proof that abuse occurred.

Counsel should not assume because the witness testifies often in court that the witness is qualified, although having been qualified as an expert in prior cases is a factor in favor of qualifying the witness again. Depending on the witness's education and experience counsel may be able to elicit answers suggesting either that the witness is unqualified or that the witness is barely qualified. That said, counsel should never presume that the smart thing to do is to challenge the witness's expertise. Some expert witnesses are so obviously qualified that counsel would do well to steer clear of any opportunity to have the witness remind the court of just how qualified s/he is. In those cases, stipulating to the witness's qualifications is the way to go.

If counsel decides to conduct a voir dire, among the topics counsel should consider exploring include the witness's education and degrees, licensure, work experience, membership in associations, and publication record. If counsel is able to consult with a defense expert, counsel should ask the expert for advice on whether to challenge the witness's credentials and, if so, on which particular grounds. The field of child sex abuse is constantly changing, and proving that the witness is unaware of important recent developments may be very helpful to the defense, even if the court ultimately qualifies the witness.

To be qualified as an expert witness, the forensic interviewer should be a professional trained in child sexual abuse with specific knowledge of child development, family dynamics related to sexual abuse, effects of sexual abuse on children, and be trained in diagnostic evaluation of children and adults. *See* THE AM. ACAD. OF CHILD & ADOLESCENT PSYCHIATRY, POLICY STATEMENT, GUIDELINES FOR THE CLINICAL EVALUATION OF CHILD AND ADOLESCENT SEXUAL ABUSE (1990).

If the interviewer is qualified as an expert, jurisdictions differ on what the expert may testify to. Counsel should carefully research the relevant statutes and case law and be prepared to cite controlling law in support of the claim being made. Even when an interviewer is allowed to testify to what the child said—thereby eliminating counsel's opportunity to object to such testimony on hearsay grounds—counsel may be able to prevent the statement from being introduced or to persuade the court not to give it weight based on the interviewing method used to extract the statement. This is an especially important area for inquiry by counsel, either during voir dire to determine whether the statement is admissible or during cross-examination to support the argument that the statement should be given little weight.

Among the most important factors in determining the admissibility or weight of a child's statements are the interviewer's methods during the interrogation. Many infamous cases have demonstrated the ease with which children can make false statements of their abuse because the questions suggested to the children what the "right" answers are. *See, e.g., Idaho v. Wright*, 497 U.S. 805 (1990) (affirming conclusion of Idaho Supreme Court that use of blatantly leading questions, in addition to children's susceptibility to suggestive questioning, indicated potential for elicitation of unreliable information); *State v. M.Z.*, 241 N.J. Super. 444, 575 A.2d 82 (1990) (ruling child's out-of-court statement inadmissible because investigator could not distinguish between what child said and what was suggested to her). Because children can be coached into giving false answers or encouraged to "admit" they were abused when they were not, experts have developed careful protocols for interviewing children in a manner that avoids the danger of suggesting any particular answer. Best practices and guidelines for forensic interviews of children can be found on the websites of the National Children's Advocacy Center and the Eunice Kennedy Shriver National Institute of Child Health and Human Development.

To ensure reliable interviews, the forensic interviewer must create an atmosphere in which the child feels comfortable speaking. *See, e.g.*, NAT'L CHILDREN'S ADVOCACY CTR., FORENSIC INTERVIEW STRUCTURE (2011). The child's comfort level can be determined by the child's behavior toward the interviewer during the interview. Children may be uncomfortable disclosing intimate details to an interviewer of the opposite sex. They may feel more at ease with an interviewer of the same race, especially if the offender is the opposite race. For this reason, the child's cultural background should be considered when choosing a forensic interviewer, particularly if the child does not speak English. *See* Michael E. Lamb et al., *Structured Forensic Interview Protocols Improve the Quality and Informativeness of Investigative Interviews with Children: A Review of Research Using the NICHD Investigative Interview Protocol*, 31 CHILD ABUSE & NEGLECT 1201 (2007). There are extra complications whenever a child is interviewed through an interpreter because of the heightened possibility of details being lost in translation. *See generally* CHILD ABUSE TRAINING AND TECHNICAL ASSISTANCE CTR., GUIDE FOR SPANISH-SPEAKING FORENSIC INTERVIEWING OF CHILDREN (2d ed. 2011). Some children may respond better to forensic interviewers closer to their parents' age and some children respond better to interviewers their grandparents' age. Children have been known to feel intimidated when the interviewer resembles the offender in height, weight, or stature. *See, e.g.*, Michael E. Lamb & Michelle E. Garretson, *The Effects of Interviewer Gender and Child Gender on the Informativeness of Alleged Child Sexual Abuse Victims in Forensic Interviews*, 27 LAW & HUM. BEHAV. 157 (2003).

These interviews should always be videotaped so that courts and others will be in a position to determine whether the interview was conducted appropriately. *See* Ralph Underwager & Hollida Wakefield, *Special Problems with Sexual Abuse Cases*, *in* COPING WITH PSYCHIATRIC AND PSYCHOLOGICAL TESTIMONY 1315 (Jay Ziskin ed., 5th ed. 1995).

Best practices call for the video camera to capture the entire room, including the face and body of the child and the interviewer. This is important because the child's body language, expressions, and actions can reveal the child's feelings about the sexual abuse allegation. Seeing the interviewer allows a subsequent assessment of whether, by words or actions, the interviewer influenced the child's responses.

Counsel should always obtain the videotape of the interview. Ideally, counsel should give the videotape to an expert to review so that counsel can be advised whether the interview could be attacked on cross-examination. Depending on what counsel is advised, the cross-examination should attack the method of the interview or avoid the topic entirely. When counsel concludes there is no basis to attack the interview, the focus of the cross might shift to reasons children are known to report falsely that they have been abused, apart from poor interrogation techniques.

Counsel should pay careful attention to the instructions given to the child by the interviewer. The recommended instructions to the child are telling the child that "it is okay if you do not know the answer to a question, it is okay if you do not remember, do not guess the answer if you do not know, if you do not understand the question ask me to explain it, I may ask the same question more than once and if I do, it is not because you gave the wrong answer, but because I may not have remembered everything and it is okay to correct anything I say." *See* CTR. FOR CHILD ABUSE AND NEGLECT, THE DIFFERENCES BETWEEN FORENSIC INTERVIEWS AND CLINICAL EVALUATIONS (2000). The interviewer should not place importance on the interview, such as by telling the child this is a very important meeting and the child should always tell the truth. The interviewer may then participate in rapport building with the child before beginning the interview questions.

The interviewer must be objective. Counsel should determine, for example, whom the forensic interviewer works for, who paid him or her, and whether the expert always works for the Agency. Counsel should not ask the forensic interviewer whether every child they interviewed was found to be sexually abused because the invariable answer will be "no." But counsel should ask, particularly when counsel knows the answer, whether the forensic interviewer has ever testified for the defense and, if so, the percentage of times compared with how often the interviewer has testified for the Agency.

The location of the interview is a particularly important topic of inquiry. Current protocol, almost everywhere, is to interview children in a neutral setting, avoiding such sites as police stations, foster homes, agency offices, and prosecutor's offices. Beyond the place and characteristics of the interview room, interviewers should also appear neutral. This means interviewers should not be uniformed police officers or persons wearing a badge of any kind. Even revealing to the child that the interviewer works for the police or prosecutor can improperly influence the child. In addition to considering these factors, counsel should find out who was in the room at any time during the interview and whether the interviewer informed the child that others were watching from another room.

As with all state-initiated investigations, counsel should be attuned to the possibility that "the interview" about which the expert is testifying is actually the third or fourth interview the child underwent that day. Counsel should seek to find out the name of every person who was near the child from the time the investigation began. The child may have been interviewed in the car driving to the interview site, in another office by an intake officer, or in a medical treatment facility. Counsel should learn what the child might have said before the interview that could serve as the basis for the admissibility of the child's statements because those antecedent statements may well have influenced the child's "official" statement. And if the child did not make any prior statement, despite having been asked to make one, there is always the possibility that the "official statement" is the product of coercion and is made by the child to end a seemingly unending process of questioning.

Some experts believe that obtaining information about previous disclosures may unknowingly influence the interview or result in the interviewing leading the child. Despite this, the common practice is for interviewers to obtain as much background as they can before interviewing the child. This history includes: (1) the child's initial disclosure, what allegedly happened and who was present at the time; (2) the name of the person who reported the abuse, including what, if any, relationship the reporter has with the alleged abuser; (3) the medical evaluation, if any, including where it was made, by whom, and what was found; (4) all prior interviews with the child, including where one interrogated the child and what the child may have said; (5) the time lapse between the alleged event and the interview; (6) what, if any, prior history of sexual abuse might exist in the family; (7) what, if any, prior history is there between the alleged offender and the child with a particular focus on whether this history might explain the false reporting of abuse; (8) what, if any, history is there between the alleged offender and the child's parent with a particular focus on whether this history might explain the false reporting of abuse; (9) any information about the child's behavior that might be an indicator of abuse (such as fear of going home, bed wetting, eating problems, sleeping problems, and nightmares); and (10) any prior psychological evaluation of the child including any signs of Child Sexual Abuse Accommodation Syndrome. *See* Roland C. Summit, *The Child Sexual Abuse Accommodation Syndrome*, 7 Child Abuse & Neglect 177 (1983).

There are also some actions that forensic interviewers should take after they have interviewed the child. These include: (1) going to the scene of the incident to see if the incident described by the child could have happened as the child reported; (2) gathering social and demographic information about the child's family; (3) learning whether the child has made prior allegations of sexual abuse, what was the result of those allegations, if any, and what is the child's reputation for truthfulness.

An effective way to cross-examine a forensic interviewer is for counsel to become familiar with the literature involving the memory and suggestibility of children. A child's memory is more suggestible than an adult's. Consequently, whenever a child is interviewed, and particularly when a child is interviewed about the same subject more than once, there is a danger that the interview process itself can change the child's recollection of the underlying event, leading to the child entering a "state of false belief." *See* Amy H. Morton, The Successful Barlow Defense Examining Interview Techniques with Child Witnesses (2003). *See also* Stephen J. Ceci & Maggie Bruck, Jeopardy in the Courtroom: A Scientific Analysis of Children's Testimony (1995); Debra A. Poole & Michael E. Lamb, Investigative Interviews with Children: A Guide for Helping Professionals (1998). One researcher explains a state of false belief as one "where the child comes to believe the story to the extent that the story no longer bears markers of a false accusation because the child does not believe they are lying." *See* Maggie Bruck, *Reliability and Credibility of Young Children's Reports: From Research to Policy and Practice*, 2 Am. Psychologist (1998).

To help counsel determine whether the forensic interviewer used appropriate language during the interview, counsel should consult Anne G. Walker, Julie Kenniston & Sally S. Inada, Handbook on Questioning Children: A Linguistic Perspective (3d ed. 2013). Questions should be age and developmentally appropriate. Leading questions are inappropriate. So, too, are complex, compound, or confusing questions. *See* Ctr. for Child Abuse and Neglect, *supra*.

Counsel should be alert for certain particularly egregious questions in the interview. Children should never be told what other children have already revealed or label the alleged offender as "bad." See Morton, *supra*. Nor should the interviewer provide "selective enforcements" such as reacting positively when the child says what the interviewer wants or offering gifts in exchange for certain answers. *See id.* In one case, a worker at an advocacy center in Georgia was seen in the video giving a child a choice of stuffed animals. The video showed that after the child finished the interview she asked if she could have the stuffed animal she was promised after she told the interviewer what happened. This is known as "co-opting." *See id.*

The forensic interviewer should be aware of inconsistencies in the child's statements. The interviewer's responsibilities include exploring any inconsistencies. The most common places for inconsistencies are the scene of the incident and the content and timing of the outcry.

Although anatomical dolls remain in use as a device to find out from the child precisely what happened, their use has no scientific support and is, accordingly, highly controversial. Whether or not it is used, it is not regarded as a reliable scientific tool. *See* Allan Tasman & Stephen M. Goldfinger, *Sexual Abuse of Children and Adolescents*, 10 Am. Psychiatric Press Rev. Psychiatry 281 (1991). Some courts have held that testimony of what a child did with a doll is hearsay. *See State v. Bratt*, 250 Kan. 264, 824 P.2d 983 (1992), *overruled on other grounds*, *State v. Davis*, 283 Kan. 569, 158 P.3d 317 (2006).

Interpreting a child's drawings is also suspect as a diagnostic tool. Two types of drawings are used in forensic interviews of children who allege sexual abuse. First are anatomical drawings of the male and female body both front and back that are used to help the child identify the body parts touched during the sexual abuse. Anatomical drawings of the male and female are often pre-printed by the interviewer and the interviewer allows the child to write on the picture what happened and where, or the interviewer writes on the drawing as explained by the child. Second are drawings the child creates in response to being asked either to describe the sexual abuse or to draw anything, mainly family members including the alleged offender. These drawings are often used when children have difficulty verbally describing the sexual abuse. Both are suspect because there is little research that shows the drawings of a child who has been sexually abused differ from those of children who were not. *See* Underwager & Wakefield, *supra*.

The forensic interview must also look for signs the child was coached or influenced. A child may be intentionally or unintentionally coached or influenced by family members, friends of family, prior interviewers, police officers, attorneys, or case managers. The forensic interview should discuss with the child whom the child spoke with about the sexual abuse and what was said to the child to determine whether the child was coached or influenced.

One of the vexing issues involving allegations of child sex abuse is the understanding that there have been many cases of false reports. Experts have identified certain factors as increasing the probability that there has been a false report. They include when there is an ongoing custody dispute between the parents. *See* Tasman & Goldfinger, *supra*. Adolescents sometimes "make false allegations out of vindictiveness or to cover their own sexuality." *Id.* As a consequence, the interviewer should explore with the child whether the child has a motive to lie. Also, because of the serious consequences of sexual abuse allegations and the known record of false reports, it is critical that the interviewer "remain neutral, keep an open mind, be non-judgmental, and obtain corroborating information." *See id.*

If the interview was not videotaped, counsel should file a motion to exclude all references to the child's out-of-court statements because those statements were improperly preserved for review. *See, e.g., Idaho v. Wright*, 497 U.S. 805 (1990) (failure to videotape interview contributed to inadmissibility of child's statements); *State v. Michaels*, 136 N.J. 299, 642 A.2d 1372 (1994) (failure to videotape interview may trigger a taint hearing). If the interview was audio recorded, but not videotaped, counsel should still object to the use of any out-of-court statement. *But see State v. P.S.*, 202 N.J. 232, 997 A.2d 163 (2010) (no per se rule that child sexual abuse victim's out-of-court statement is inadmissible in absence of a video or audio recording of statement).

Sometimes, the Agency will call as its expert a differ kind of expert than a forensic interviewer. The Agency might instead call the expert who serves as the child's therapist or clinical evaluator. This very different kind of expert is used to determine the treatment for the child and, sometimes, will be the child's therapist. *See* Ctr. for Child Abuse and Neglect, *supra*. Counsel should object to testimony of a clinical evaluator or therapist at the dependency trial where the question to be decided is *whether* the child was abused (and by whom), not what kind of intervention the child needs or is receiving (a question material to the dispositional phase of the case, but not the adjudicatory or trial phase). In addition, clinical evaluators or therapists are very rarely certifiable as experts regarding the validity of the allegations in the Petition. Their expertise only concerns treatment for abused children.

Depending on the jurisdiction, the Agency may be able to prove its case without having to produce the child. In other jurisdictions, the child has to be available for cross-examination. Even in criminal cases, where defendants enjoy an express Sixth Amendment to confront adverse witnesses, the Supreme Court allows courts latitude to protect child witnesses from being forced to make eye contact with the accused when testifying. *See Maryland v. Craig*, 497 U.S. 836 (1990). Even when children are called as witnesses, counsel should proceed cautiously. Judges often feel highly protective of children in their courtroom and counsel should attack a child's credibility only when there is good reason to do so.

In cases where the investigation had begun because the child disclosed the incident to someone, counsel should attempt to learn the name of the first person to whom the child spoke. Counsel should interview this person before trial and obtain a full description of what precisely the child said, if possible. Comparing this original version with what the child later said may support the claim that the incident never happened or did not happen in the way the child claimed.

Counsel should also obtain local police or agency protocols and guidelines for investigating allegations of child sexual abuse. Guidelines are written to avoid investigative bias in which investigators seek information supporting their initial understanding of what happened. Proper procedure calls for trying to uncover all evidence, leaving the meaning of the evidence to be resolved after the facts have been uncovered. These guidelines may help counsel discredit an investigator who did not follow the guidelines.

When counsel's theory is that the incident was fabricated by an adult who wants to hurt the alleged wrongdoer, counsel should cross-examine that person and try to reveal a motive that s/he may have had to hurt the accused. When counsel wants to present character witnesses to testify to the accused's good character, two things should be kept in mind. First, witnesses who are very close to the alleged wrongdoer are often expected by the fact-finder to be prepared to say good things about the alleged wrongdoer. With this in mind, counsel should try to find character witnesses who would not necessarily be expected to testify favorably, such as a prior spouse, particularly one who has children. Pastors and church members are also effective character witnesses, as are physicians, therapists, coaches, and teachers. Second, many people with good reputations have shocked people in their communities, and character witnesses do not, by themselves, disprove that the abuse occurred. For this reason, character witnesses are far more important when called after counsel has presented evidence that casts doubt on the Agency's claim that any abuse took place.

Preparing the parents to testify is vitally important. In some jurisdictions, agency attorneys routinely call the parents in their case-in-chief. For this reason, counsel must prepare the client to take the stand. If a criminal investigation was dropped, counsel should find a way to bring this out through the parent's testimony.

When representing the non-offending parent, counsel has a choice to try to support the offending parent and argue the abuse did not take place. As noted above, unfortunately, sometimes this defense carries with it a sink-or-swim characteristic. If the court finds against the offending parent, the court will commonly find against both parents, particularly because once the court finds the abuse occurred, the court will be reluctant to trust the child to someone's care who refuses to believe the truth. This places the non-offending parent in a difficult dilemma. Sticking by the alleged offending parent may be perceived by the judge as indifference to the child's well-being.

A different defense for the non-offending parent is to focus on all the good things the parent has done in raising the child. This can include the time period prior to and after the disclosure of alleged abuse. If the non-offending parent's defense is that the abuse occurred, but when disclosed the parent took all appropriate steps, counsel should focus on what the parent did to make sure this does not happen in the future. If the parent was co-dependent upon the alleged offender, counsel should present evidence that the parent is in therapy for co-dependency and will be able to prevent any abuse going forward.

Counsel may also wish to present the testimony of a psychologist. In some jurisdictions, the results of a psychological evaluation cannot be admitted into evidence except by stipulation of the parties. If the psychological evaluations are positive for the parents, counsel should have the psychologist testify since testimony is often more persuasive than when the court reads the evaluation. The psychologist could testify to the lack of mental health disorders that affect the ability of the parents to care for the child. The psychologist could testify to the non-offender parent's past and present capability to protect the child from harm. If the parents completed the recommendations in the evaluation, the psychologist could explain how doing so increased parental ability to care for and protect the child. The psychologist may also be able to explain how the family created or ended up in this situation and how what the parents have learned will reduce the risk of continued allegations.

In addition, counsel may wish to present evidence through other expert witnesses. An independent forensic interviewer could testify to the forensic interview of the child, whether the interviewer used improper questioning techniques or failed to obtain a full history of the child and family. Moreover, the forensic interviewer can testify to the harm associated with multiple interviews and inadequate interview techniques by others who interviewed the child. An obstetrician could be presented to discredit any medical findings or lack of medical findings of the physicians during the medical examination of the child ("the rape kit").

9.17 Requesting Findings of Fact, Conclusions of Law, and Disposition in the Adjudication Order

At the conclusion of the trial, counsel should request an order that accurately states the finding of facts, conclusions of law, and disposition. Most jurisdictions already include the facts, conclusions of law, and disposition in the order announcing the outcome of the trial. However, in some jurisdictions, counsel must request these findings on the record at the end of the adjudication or they are deemed waived for appeal.

The finding of facts should state the facts made by the court to support its decision. Simply because evidence was admitted or testified to at a trial does not mean that the court relied on it to make the decision. Evidence on which the court did not rely would not be a finding of fact. Evidence may have been disregarded by the court for credibility reasons. Finding of facts should not include facts introduced at other hearings, unless the court took judicial notice of prior orders and then the facts should be those referred to in the prior order only, not at the prior hearing. The facts that establish jurisdiction and venue should also be included in the finding of facts.

Conclusions of law should include how the facts found by the court established the legal requirements. Additionally, conclusions of law are essential because if any conclusions are absent in the order the adjudication may be reversed on appeal.

Disposition in most jurisdictions is held either immediately after the adjudication or set to a later date. The most common disposition after a finding of dependency or neglect is made against the parent is the child's placement in foster care or the child's return to the parent's custody under a protective order.

Depending upon the jurisdiction, the court, the Agency, or the parent's attorney will prepare an adjudication order. If counsel prepares the order, the order should be sent to all parties for review prior to submitting the order to the court. Counsel should allow the parties at least two business days to review the order. Counsel should request that the parties submit recommended changes to all parties prior to submission to the court. When counsel disagrees with the submitted changes, counsel should notify the parties of the changes sought and set a short time period to address the changes. Putting a deadline on the submission of changes is important to ensure that the parent has an order to follow or use going forward. If the parties agree on the changes, counsel should submit the proposed order to the court. If the parties cannot agree, counsel should notify the parties that the proposed order will be submitted as approved and notify all parties when this is done so they will have an opportunity to raise any objections or propose their own orders to the court. If the court does not sign counsel's prepared order or changes it in a manner counsel opposes, counsel should file an objection to the order. In addition, counsel may consider filing a "Motion to Set Aside the Order" and, if the changes are not in accordance with the transcript of the hearing, requesting a copy of the transcripts. Filing an objection to the order creates a record in case the parent wishes to file an appeal.

If the Agency prepares the order, counsel should carefully review it. If counsel is not allowed an opportunity to review the proposed order, and it contains something objectionable, counsel should file a "Motion to Set Aside the Order" explaining that one of the parties could not review the proposed order. If counsel is allowed to review the proposed order and recommends changes not accepted by the Agency, counsel should make sure to be notified when the Agency submits the order to the court. Counsel must then submit the parent's proposed order. If the court signs the Agency's order and not the parent's, counsel should file an objection. Counsel should then follow the steps to file a "Motion to Set Aside the Order" as outlined above.

If the court prepared the order, counsel still must review the order to make sure it accurately reflects the adjudication. If need be, counsel should request a copy of the transcript to compare to the adjudication order. If there is a conflict and that conflict is important to the parent and the case, then counsel should consider pursuing a correction to the order. The correction can be done by filing a "Motion to Set Aside the Order" or on appeal. If counsel plans to file a motion and not appeal, counsel must first consider how the motion may affect the court's position toward counsel and the parent. If the motion creates controversy or animosity toward the parent, then counsel should weigh the consequences of filing the motion first. If the conflict is such that it could be detrimental to the parent down the road in a termination of parental rights hearing, then the better option may be to file an appeal. On appeal, counsel can argue reversal of the trial court's decision or the conflict between the transcript and the evidence. These decisions are best addressed by knowing the court beforehand. If the only argument on appeal is that the order does not reflect the transcript, then the trial court may have been less offended had counsel filed a "Motion to Set Aside the Order." Most likely, if the only argument on appeal is the conflict, the appellate court will remit the order to the court to correct it.

Ultimately, the importance of accuracy in orders that include finding of facts and conclusions of law stems from the need to avoid inaccurate information damaging the parents later, such as in subsequent cases on other children. This consideration should be carefully decided before deciding to correct adjudication orders.

9.18 Representing Non-Adjudicated Parents

What should happen when counsel is representing a parent who has not been adjudicated or even accused of abusing or neglecting a child? The rights of non-offending parents (sometimes referred to as "non-respondent" or "non-adjudicated") is constantly changing. For this reason, counsel must track case law and statutory enactments on this issue, as they should do with any child welfare topic.

9.18(a) Constitutional Framework Governing the Rights of Non-Offending Parents

Counsel representing non-offending parents must understand that their clients have constitutionally protected rights to care for their children. Like all parents, non-offending parents have a substantive due process right to direct the care, custody, and control of their children. In *Stanley v. Illinois*, 405 U.S. 645 (1971), the Supreme Court held that a parent's constitutional right to direct the care of his children extends to non-offending parents. At issue in *Stanley* was an Illinois law that permitted the state to place the children of unwed fathers automatically in foster care upon the death of their mothers without having to make any finding that the fathers had harmed their children. *See id.* at 646. The state argued that proof that an unmarried mother of a child was dead was enough to separate the children from their father. The state sought to shift the burden of proving parental fitness onto the non-offending father, whom it said could prove his ability to care for the child by filing for guardianship or adoption, proceedings in which he would be treated as a legal stranger to the child. *See id.* at 647.

The Supreme Court rejected the argument and held that the Constitution required, as a matter of due process, that the father have a "hearing on his fitness as a parent before his children were taken from him." *See id.* at 649. The Court found that the state's interest in presuming the unfitness of all unmarried fathers and efficiently disposing of their rights did not outweigh the constitutional interests of the father. The Court stated:

> Procedure by presumption is always cheaper and easier than individualized determination. But when, as here, the procedure forecloses the determinative issues of competence and care, when it explicitly disdains present realities in deference to

> past formalities, it needlessly risks running roughshod over the important interests of both parent and child. It therefore cannot stand.

Id. at 656–57. The Court made clear that infringing upon a non-offending parent's right to custody of his children is strictly forbidden under the Constitution absent a judicial determination of parental unfitness.

Other decisions have made clear that the constitutionally required unfitness finding cannot be satisfied if a court makes an unfitness finding against the other parent. In *Parham v. J.R.*, 442 U.S. 584 (1979), the Court noted that "[t]he statist notion that governmental power should supersede parental authority in all cases because some parents abuse and neglect children is repugnant to American tradition." *Id.* at 603. Federal appellate decisions have made similar findings. *See, e.g.*, *Burke v. Cnty. of Alameda*, 586 F.3d 725, 733 (9th Cir. 2009) (holding that a reasonable jury could find the noncustodial parent's constitutional rights were violated when the noncustodial parent was not accused of wrongdoing and the State failed to investigate the possibility of placing his daughter with him rather than the government); *Wallis v. Spencer*, 202 F.3d 1126, 1142 n.14 (9th Cir. 2000) ("The government may not, consistent with the Constitution, interpose itself between a fit parent and her children simply because of the conduct—real or imagined—of the other parent."). These decisions make clear that as a matter of federal constitutional law, non-offending parents have a substantive due process right to care for their children that cannot be interfered with by the state absent a finding of unfitness.

9.18(b) Statutory Framework Involving the Rights of Non-Offending Parents

Despite this case law, across the country, states vary on whether and how they safeguard the rights of non-offending parents. In fact, many states have enacted statutes or created practices that disregard the constitutional rights of non-offending parents in some way. For example, several states permit courts to strip non-offending parents of legal and physical custody immediately upon a finding that the other parent has abused or neglected the child. *See, e.g.*, *In re C.R.*, 108 Ohio St. 3d 369, 843 N.E.2d 1188 (2006). In these jurisdictions, immediately upon a finding against one parent, a trial court can obtain temporary custody of the child and can issue any order it deems is in the child's best interest. Even without a finding of unfitness against the non-offending parent, the court may place the child in foster care, compel the non-offending parent to comply with services, and order the termination of that parent's rights based solely on the parent's failure to comply with those services. These systems treat non-offending parents as legal strangers to their children, and place the burden on them to prove to the court that it is in their children's best interest to be placed with them. In these jurisdictions, Supreme Court precedent has played little impact in shaping the jurisprudence involving non-offending parents.

Other jurisdictions have adopted a more nuanced approach while continuing to deprive non-offending parents of their full custodial rights. *See, e.g., In re Jeffrey P.*, 218 Cal. App. 3d 1548, 267 Cal. Rptr. 764 (1990); *J.P. v. Dep't of Children and Families*, 855 So. 2d 175, 28 Fla. Weekly D2101 (Fla. Dist. Ct. App. 2003). In these states, judges recognize that parents have the right to care for their children but only apply that right with regard to physical custody.

Absent a finding of unfitness, non-offending parents are granted physical custody of their children, but the court still retains legal custody, that is, the authority to make decisions regarding the child, and can order the non-offending parent to comply with services. Although safeguarding the physical custody rights of non-offending parents, these systems intrude on their right to make decisions regarding their children.

Two states, Maryland and Pennsylvania, have recognized that non-offending parents have constitutionally protected rights, and have adopted a very different approach. *See In re Russell G.*, 108 Md. App. 366, 672 A.2d 109 (1996); *In re M.L.*, 757 A.2d 849 (Pa. 2000). In these states, if a non-offending parent steps forward and requests custody of his child, the court may not assume jurisdiction over the child for any purpose, even to offer services to the offending parent or the child. The juvenile court must dismiss the case and the only limited action it may take is to grant custody to the non-offending parent before dismissal. Once the transfer of custody is made, all court involvement or oversight must be terminated.

Finally, in Michigan and in Nevada, the highest courts have held that while a court can obtain jurisdiction over a child based solely on findings against one parent, it cannot use its dispositional authority to order the non-offending parent to comply with services or place his child in foster care absent a finding against that parent. *See In re Sanders*, 495 Mich. 394, 852 N.W.2D 524 (2014); *In re Parental Rights as to A.G.*, 295 P.3d 589 (Nev. 2013). This approach allows the juvenile court to issue orders pertaining to the abusive parent while protecting the constitutional rights of the non-offending parent.

This brief overview reflects the different ways in which child welfare systems treat non-offending parents. Advocates must become familiar with the rights their state affords non-offending parents to both guide their clients through the trial court process and to determine when issues must be appealed.

9.18(c) Strategies for Services: Visitation and Custody

Counsel representing a non-offending parent must first conduct a comprehensive interview of the client to identify the client's goals. Does the client want immediate placement of the child? Does the client want the right to see his or her child? Or does the client wish to release his or her parental rights? Without knowing answers to these and other related questions, counsel cannot develop a strategy to further the client's goals.

In addition to identifying the client's goals, the interview should further the fact investigation that must occur to learn more about the client's circumstances. Was the client involved in the child's life previous to the abuse or neglect case? In what way? What are the client's strengths? Who are individuals in the community who can speak on the client's behalf? What concerns exist? How will counsel address those concerns? Counsel must investigate the facts of the case, beyond just the interview of the client, to ensure that counsel is well positioned to advance the client's goals.

If the client wishes to remain involved in the child's life—either by caring for the child full time or by visiting the child—then counsel should consider adopting a dual strategy. First, counsel should pursue a traditional litigation strategy to persuade the trial court to safeguard the constitutional rights of the client. Counsel should consider filing a motion for immediate placement or visitation, highlighting the fact that no findings of abuse or neglect have been made against the client. The motion should rely on constitutional case law, such as *Stanley v. Illinois*, 405 U.S. 645 (1972), and should seek to convince the court that the Constitution mandates an immediate return of the child to the non-offending parent absent a finding of unfitness. As noted above, recent decisions in Michigan and in Nevada may be helpful to review. *See In re Sanders*, 495 Mich. 394, 852 N.W.2D 524 (2014); *In re Parental Rights as to A.G.*, 295 P.3d 589 (Nev. 2013). Counsel should also explore state law grounds to support this position. Filing such a motion is also important to preserve issues for appeal.

In addition to relying on legal arguments in the motion, counsel should also establish in the motion how placing the child with the non-offending parent is good for the child. Detailing the previous relationship between the child and the parent, highlighting the strengths of the parent, and addressing any weaknesses are crucial. Counsel should consider attaching affidavits from respected members of the community, such as teachers, clergy, and employers, in support of the motion and any reports that reinforce the client's commitment to the child. Pure legal arguments, divorced from a factual claim that placing a child with the non-offending parents would be in the best interests of the child, are unlikely to succeed at the trial court level.

If the trial court denies the motion for immediate placement, counsel should consider appealing the decision. Whether to do so will rest on a number of variables including the likelihood that the child will be returned to the client quickly, the length of time of the appeal, and any negative consequences that may be incurred by pursuing the appeal, including a loss of momentum in the case. Ultimately, the client will have to weigh those factors and make a decision.

While pursuing this litigation strategy, counsel should also consider a "softer" approach to demonstrate to the court that the client is committed to the child and to develop a concurrent plan in the event that the court refuses to immediately place the child with the client. This approach may involve facilitating supervised parenting time between the child and the client. It may also require the client to engage in services, such a participating in parenting classes, or submitting to drug screens. While the law may not require the non-offending parent to take such steps, voluntarily cooperating with the child welfare agency may expedite the reunification process and may be the most effective way to achieve the client's goals quickly. Ultimately, the specific approach to recommend to the client will depend on the facts of the case.

In short, counsel representing non-offending parents must recognize that (1) their clients have constitutionally protected relationships with their children, (2) such relationships must be safeguarded using traditional litigation tactics, but (3) that concurrently adopting a "softer approach" may also be an effective way of quickly achieving the client's goals.

CHAPTER 10

Representing Parents at Disposition and Permanency Hearings

Richard Cozzola and Lee Shevell

10.01 Introduction

In most jurisdictions, the adjudication that a child has been abused or neglected occurs in the first six months of the case. But the series of disposition and permanency hearings that follow the adjudication hearing can stretch on for years, continuing until a child is returned home, a court terminates the rights of the parents or awards guardianship to a relative, or until the child ages out of the foster care system. Although these hearings often employ relaxed evidentiary standards and use written reports instead of direct testimony from professionals, they are the hearings where a court makes many of the major decisions about the ultimate direction of a case. These decisions include: what services parents must complete to regain custody of their children, whether the services an Agency is offering are reasonable, whether a parent is making progress to regaining custody, and whether an Agency should discontinue providing services to a parent in favor of terminating the child and parent relationship.

The post-adjudication stage of the case has two unique features. The first is the parent's ability, through her conduct, to develop the evidence for the case that the court will hear. The second is the lawyer's use of advocacy skills to gather facts, work with social workers and other professionals involved with the family, and advocate a theory of the case that assists the client.

10.01(a) Theory of the Case

To be an effective advocate a lawyer must develop a theory for why her client should prevail. Experts in advocacy call this the "theory of the case." The theory of the case is the lawyer's integration of the client's story with the relevant legal issues. It combines the law and facts in a way that leads to the conclusion that the counsel's client should win. *See* STEVEN LUBET, MODERN TRIAL ADVOCACY 8 (2004). For example, in a criminal case, a defense theory might be, "The state's witnesses are inconsistent about time, place and person. Because the facts don't add up, you cannot find the defendant guilty beyond a reasonable doubt."

The parent's theory in a child protection case is an evolving theory because the legal issues and facts might change from hearing to hearing. The legal issues at adjudication focus on the past events, whereas the disposition, review, and permanency planning hearings occur after a court has already determined that the parent was responsible for the abuse or neglect of a child. A theory at adjudication in an excessive corporal punishment case might be a choice between two options: (1) that no corporal punishment occurred or (2) that corporal punishment occurred but a question exists about its severity and whether it rises to the legal standard for child abuse. However, when the trial court finds that the corporal punishment occurred and constitutes abuse, the theory must evolve at the disposition hearing. Given the court's finding, the theory must focus on whether the parent can care for the child now, having learned better ways to manage behavior, and whether the child's best interests support returning the child home to the parent's care.

Additionally, because the lives of parents and their children are not static, the facts on the ground can change. The parent who used a ruler to hit a child may learn new methods of child discipline. When that kind of change in the client's life occurs, the theory will likely change at disposition. The client's story (and her lawyer's theory) now becomes the story of the parent who made a mistake, hurt her child, but has now taken positive steps toward becoming a better parent.

While disposition and permanency hearings usually involve different issues, they all focus on the parent's progress and the best interests, safety, and well-being of the child. Thus, it is critical that the parent's attorney develops a theory that her client has been focusing on those issues. The overall goal of a parent's attorney at these hearings is to use facts to help develop a persuasive theory, and then employ advocacy skills to advance that theory both in and out of court.

10.01(b) Outline for the Chapter

To demonstrate how an attorney can create a workable case theory at this juncture of the case, this chapter begins with an overview of disposition and permanency hearings, but assumes that the reader knows her state's law regarding these hearings. The chapter then discusses fact gathering. Fact gathering is both a legal necessity and a process that enables the lawyer to develop a theory of the case. Fact gathering begins with the client, moves on to family members and significant others, and concludes with the caseworker and other professionals. The chapter looks at interactions with professionals at child and family meetings, as well as other informal advocacy settings. Finally, the chapter examines work in the courtroom itself.

One word of caution before moving to these issues: Although the outline of this chapter seems to present the lawyer's work as linear—first gather facts, then advocate—these activities are often simultaneous and interrelated. Parents' lawyers advocate out of court and in court to get clients the services they need, to increase visitation, and to motivate clients to try to achieve their goals. Fact gathering never ends. Parents' lawyers learn new information about their cases constantly, in the hallway outside of a courtroom and in the courtroom itself as a hearing occurs. Each court appearance provides the opportunity to fine-tune the case theory and adjust how the lawyer presents it to the court based on new facts. Remember, throughout the process the goal for representation remains the same—to use the ever-evolving theory of the case to help the client achieve her goals—whether that goal is return home, permanent placement with a relative, adoption by a non-relative, residential placement for a child with profound disabilities, or any other goal achievable under the law.

10.02 The Legal Elements and Issues at Disposition and Permanency Planning Hearings

10.02(a) Disposition Hearings

Although the exact terminology of disposition hearings varies from state to state, the process courts follow and the issues they decide are similar. The initial disposition hearing usually takes place shortly after the adjudication. By the time of the initial disposition hearing, the adjudication finding has given the court the jurisdictional authority to make orders at disposition about who should have custody of the child and the services the child and family should receive.

At disposition, the court must first decide whether the child will live in the custody of the parents, relatives, or in non-kinship foster care while the case is ongoing. In many states, the critical inquiry whether to permit the child to live with his parent is based on the ability of the parent to care for the child safely. If the court decides the child cannot live in the custody of one or both of the parents, it must then decide who will be the child's custodian or guardian. The options are usually placement with a relative, placement with a foster parent, placement in a group setting, or placement with an Agency or "state guardian" with the authority to decide where to place the child.

At the disposition hearing, the court will also order the parent to comply with the case service plan which details the services that must be completed to effectuate reunification. Typically, the Agency will draft the case service plan and present it to the court. The court will decide whether to adopt the document in its entirety, or amend it based on the information provided by the parties.

Some states also use the term "disposition hearing" to refer to situations after the initial disposition hearing, when the court considers whether to return a child home at a later date. At such times the court usually considers the same issues as at the initial one, whether the parent is able to care for the child safely and whether the child's best interests are consistent with a return home. In this chapter the term "disposition hearing" will refer to the initial disposition hearing.

10.02(b) Permanency Hearings

Unlike disposition hearings, which have been a component of juvenile court hearings since the inception of the juvenile court, permanency hearings were added to these proceedings by federal legislation designed to encourage courts to place children into "permanent" homes expeditiously. To do this, the federal government requires, as a condition of federal money for foster care, that states conduct a permanency hearing no later than twelve months from the date the child enters foster care and then at least once a year thereafter. *See* 45 C.F.R. § 1356.21(b)(2) (2012).

At these hearings, federal regulations require courts to determine the long-term goal for the child's placement, the services to achieve that goal, and the progress made since the last court review. Goals range from returning the child home to terminating parental rights so that children may be adopted. Other permanency options include legal guardianship or permanent placement with a relative. If none of these options is appropriate, the court must seek a different permanent living arrangement, such as independent living for an older adolescent. All of these decisions are to be based on the child's safety, health, and well-being. *See* 42 U.S.C. §§ 621, 672(a)(2)(ii) (2014).

At the annual review hearings required by federal law, states are supposed to determine whether the Agency is making reasonable efforts to achieve the permanency goal and whether the child's placement is safe and consistent with the goal. *See* 45 C.F.R. § 1356.21(b)(2). Federal regulations allow these review hearings to be conducted by courts or administrative agencies. Because of the similar issues in review and permanency hearings, this chapter will use the generic term "permanency hearing" to cover the issues that occur at both.

The establishment of permanency hearings brought new terminology to abuse and neglect proceedings, but in many ways the issues have remained the same: How much progress has the parent made to become better able to parent safely and to resolve the issues that brought the case to the attention of the court? Is it in the child's best interest to return home? Were the services reasonably provided to achieve that goal? Is the child's placement safe and appropriate? Perhaps the most important change permanency hearings brought was a formal structure to investigate client progress in services and to reexamine the goals to align services to best meet them.

Because the focus of permanency hearings is on the present and future, it is important for attorneys to work with parents to keep them from re-litigating whether abuse or neglect occurred. When helping prepare a client for a disposition or permanency hearing, explain that the central issue will be the client's progress with services and the strength of the parent-child relationship during the review period. Listen to what the parent says about that progress and the relationship with his or her child. Additionally, find and listen to other people who can shed light on these issues.

Parents might want to focus on other matters: complaints about a caseworker who never has a positive word to say or a judge who does not seem to understand the challenges of being poor, for example. The lawyer's job is to listen to the complaints, evaluate them, and then refocus the client on critical issues of the client's progress and her relationship with the child. The next section discusses ways to do that.

10.03 Communicating with the Client about Disposition and Permanency Hearings

10.03(a) Understanding the Client's Point of View

Communications with parents in child welfare cases are often overshadowed by the frustrations that clients have faced. By the time counsel discusses a disposition hearing with the client, the client has already lost (in the traditional sense) several hearings at court. The court has found reason to take temporary or protective custody of the child at the beginning of the case and to hold the parent responsible for his or her child's abuse, neglect, or dependency.

Moreover, permanency hearings usually occur only if the child has been in foster care for some period of time *after* disposition. This means that a parent at a permanency hearing "lost" the disposition hearing. The court has already found that the parent should not have custody of the child.

Even parents who have made progress in services can be overwhelmed by what appears to be a persistent stream of bad results from previous court hearings and by the challenges of trying to complete required services. They may regard their attorney as part of that system and blame him or her for the overall frustrations they face.

Still, not all parents are full of frustrations. Some have made significant progress in overcoming addiction or other afflictions. Some have established positive relationships with caseworkers, social workers, or therapists and are proud of their progress and thankful to be where they are. Counsel's job is to get a sense of where the client stands on this continuum of progress, frustration, and hope, and respond accordingly.

10.03(b) Talk with the Client Early and Often Enough to Make a Difference

Counsel's discussions with the client at this stage should be a continuation of the conversations that have taken place since the beginning of the case. From the beginning, counsel should explain the importance of demonstrating progress at every opportunity. Conversations should occur early and often so the parent understands that her everyday actions can affect the hearing's results. Parents have the power to use their day-to-day actions to create the evidence the court will consider at the disposition hearing. If a parent engagingly attends ten therapy sessions, that may sway the court to enter an order favorable to the parent. Correspondingly, if a parent tests positive for drugs in the days before an upcoming hearing, the result would almost assuredly sway the court to enter a very different kind of order. Counsel should ensure that parents realize the extent to which the actions they take between court appearances influence the court's determinations.

In an ideal world, immediately after the conclusion of a disposition or permanency hearing, counsel and the parent would work on what needs to be accomplished to persuade the court at the next appearance. The real world is different. It is difficult for parents to plan for the next court date when they are still absorbing and sorting out what just occurred. If a judge decided not to send the child home with the parent at disposition, the parent might be angry and frustrated, and not interested in learning about another hearing. Additionally, at times of high frustration and anxiety, a client may not be able to absorb and integrate new information well. Thus, counsel should schedule a time with the parent to discuss the upcoming disposition or permanency hearing at a later time to allow the parent to process the present hearing's outcome and next steps.

If setting a date for a meeting is impossible, and the only realistic time for talking about the next hearing is in the courthouse immediately after the hearing, counsel should work to structure the meeting to give the client some control. To do this, organize the meeting with the client. Ask that they spend five minutes talking about the next hearing, and get the client to agree to that. Then ask the client something that gives the client some control. "Do you want to talk here standing up, or over there on the bench? Do you want to get some water first, or shall we talk now?" Then move to the content of the meeting.

At the meeting, counsel should listen to the client's frustrations and anger about court, and play them back to her. Ask about the progress the client believes she has made. Reiterate that the next hearing provides an opportunity to show the judge she has made more progress. Remind the client that between now and the next phone call or meeting she should follow through with whatever services and visitation she needs to do. Be concrete and focused. "We are going to talk next Thursday. Between now and then you need to make your two Narcotics Anonymous meetings and the Friday visit with John. Do you think you can do that?" Don't be afraid to ask the client to commit or to challenge the client. One experienced attorney tells clients, "Your actions tell the judge how much you care for your children. If I am working harder than you are, we're in trouble."

In order to stay as informed as possible and to problem-solve issues before they escalate, counsel should be in communication with the parent about service attendance, completion, and any issues. It is important to hear from the parent-client immediately when problems with services occur. Some example of the challenges parents routinely face include a job schedule that conflicts with visits, a therapist who cannot meet regularly, a laboratory that fails to report clean drug tests, or a transportation problem that makes visitation nearly impossible.

10.03(c) Ask What the Client Wants and Listen to What the Client Says

Regardless of where or when the meeting occurs, counsel must understand the relevant legal issues at the specific stage of the case. At permanency hearings one of the issues the judge must decide is the goal for the child's permanency. The two most common goals for younger children are polar opposites: reunification with a parent or termination of parental rights. Counsel must remind the parent that deciding what the goal will be will determine how often the parent sees the child, under what circumstances the contact will occur, and what services the child and parent will receive.

Next, focus the conversation and advocacy based on the client's desires. Ask the client what she wants. Does she want her child to return home? Does she want the placement to be with a different substitute care provider? What does she think she has to do to achieve that goal? If she is the parent of an older child who needs considerable help (such as teen parenting services or a group home) before returning home, explain which goal fits with those services. Approaching the parent and asking what she wants helps to achieve several objectives. First, it forces the lawyer to listen to the client; when a client feels listened to, the conversation is easier. Second, it gives the client a sense of control. Third, it provides an opportunity for the lawyer to reinforce positives: that the client can understand her next steps and what some of the challenges may be.

At this stage of the conversation, rather than challenging the client on her story, begin the conversation by playing back what the client says. "So you're saying two things. First you are saying that you want John to come back to live with you. And you are saying that you understand you have to continue to stay clean and make your N.A. meetings." Then reinforce the client's feelings about the child and whatever she got right about achieving her goal. "I can tell how important it is for you to have John back with you. And you are right. You will have to stay clean and make your N.A. meetings."

Before moving on to challenging the client on points, or providing a list of tasks, continue to ask the client if there's anything else she believes she must do to accomplish her goal. Again, reinforce the steps the client identifies: exercising her visitation rights consistently, attending therapy, remaining calm when disappointed, learning how to better attend to her child on visits. Repeat this conversation until the client cannot think of other issues. Then add whatever the client has left out. "You've talked about N.A. meetings, staying clean, and going to therapy every week, but there are a couple of other things that are important. Remember, showing up for every visit on time and focusing on John when you are on a visit help him and your connection with him."

Next, summarize the list of tasks for the client. Counsel can empathize about how much there may be to accomplish and can ask the client if she still wants to take all those steps to get the child back. Having the client affirm that she wants to take those steps may be helpful.

At some point in the conversation, a client might ask about services she does not think she needs to complete. A parent's lawyer may be tempted to tell the client she needs to do whatever is in the service plan. But instead, first listen and play back what the client says. "You don't think you need to go to N.A. services, because you were only an occasional marijuana user." Rather than telling the client that it'd be easier to just follow the services and not dispute them, consider whether the client is suggesting that more research should be done to determine whether the service is necessary. If counsel thinks that consulting with an expert on the issue would be helpful, let the client know. Decide with the client about whether it is better for the client to follow through with the services until the question is resolved or whether she should wait. If the decision is to wait, figure out with the client how this decision will be communicated to the caseworker, and whether the communication will come from the attorney or from the client.

10.03(d) Explain in Simple Terms How What the Client Does Will Affect the Next Court Date

Clarify that at the next court hearing counsel will elicit testimony describing all the positive steps the client has taken toward reunification. Counsel should explain that the more positive things that occur—learning how to set limits without corporal punishment, staying clean, and so on—the more positive things counsel can present to the judge. Counsel should explain to the client that the goal at each hearing is to show the judge that the client loves her child and is making progress at being a better parent.

10.03(e) Work with the Client to Come Up with a Plan for Achieving the Client's Goals

After explaining that the goal of each hearing is to show progress, have the client identify what she can do herself to achieve her goals. If her goal is to get closer to having her child return home, then have the client again list the things she can do between the time of the conversation and the next court date to achieve those goals, such as following through with visitation and continuing to learn new parenting skills from a parenting coach.

10.03(f) Review a Genogram of the Client. Find Out if There Is Someone on the Client's Genogram to Talk to Now or Later

Lawyers sometimes forget that clients' lives and their relationships with others, particularly family members, constantly evolve. Mental health and substance abuse treatment can bring about some of that change. A relationship with a parent, aunt, or uncle can become closer or more distant. Relatives who once wrote the client off can become supporters and potential child-care providers. Even if a thorough assessment of relationships was done at the beginning, counsel must go over those relationships again. Some questions that might help include: Who has seen the client interact with the children and do they have positive things to say? If a possibility exists of a change of foster placement from non-relative to relative, where might potential placements be? Are any of the people the client values available as persons who can help her get to visits or provide backup childcare if the child should be returned home? Counsel should not presume that a client's past relationships with certain family members have not changed.

10.03(g) Set Expectations for Communication

At the conclusion of the conversation, counsel should discuss when the next conversation will occur, and whether it will be in person or over the phone. Consider whether the parent wants to communicate via email or text messages and the risks to confidentiality of such communications. Whatever decisions are made about communicating, counsel should establish realistic expectations about how quickly she can respond to requests. Set a date for the contact, but remind the client that if something comes up, she should immediately make contact. Counsel should consider giving the client an example of what might constitute an emergency. "If the worker does not have your unsupervised visit set up by Thursday, call me." But, an attorney must define the scope of the attorney's role. Counsel should not create an expectation that allows the client to rely on the lawyer as a therapist. Being empathetic differs from providing treatment. The client's mental health professional should be the person the client seeks for therapeutic aid. Similarly, the client should know how to communicate with the attorney if she has a legal emergency.

10.03(h) Be a Reality Check

Listening to a client's goals, hopes, and frustrations is critical. Equally as critical is the lawyer's role in providing the client with a reality check. For example, a client may be convinced she has beaten an addiction problem without N.A./A.A. or other substance abuse treatment. Even if the lawyer believes the client may have beaten the problem, the lawyer needs to let the client know the downside of trying to prove such a claim without a treatment provider to support this claim. The lawyer and client need to plan a course for the client based on both the client's wishes and the realities of demonstrating recovery to the court.

10.03(i) Follow up as Agreed

One common complaint clients have about their attorneys is that their attorneys fail to communicate with them. This complaint is even more valid when an expectation is created that regular communication will occur. If a time is scheduled to meet with a client, then the attorney must stick to that schedule, or inform the client about the conflict ahead of time. If the lawyer will be late to a meeting, the lawyer must relay that information to the client.

10.04 Working with Caseworkers, Service Providers, and Third Parties

10.04(a) Know the Law

Prior to collaborating with caseworkers and service providers, counsel must have a working knowledge of all laws that may be implicated at disposition and permanency hearings. For example, counsel needs to know the law on the confidentiality of medical and mental health information and records in order to know how to get such records and how to have other professionals use them for consulting or expert witness purposes. Counsel should know the guiding ethical rules also, to determine whether and how to communicate with caseworkers, who are often government employees represented by a lawyer.

To know what to expect of caseworkers and other service providers, counsel must also research administrative laws and regulations and internal child welfare agency policies. These often outline the responsibility of the state agency regarding placements, visitation, and services. Familiarity with these laws and regulations will make it easier to resolve issues when dealing with other professionals and to advocate for clients both in and out of court.

10.04(b) Develop a Working Relationship with Caseworkers and Service Providers

Among the most important relationships a parent's attorney can cultivate is with the caseworker. This should begin as early as possible. With other service providers, such as a therapist or a parenting class instructor, counsel should initiate contact with the professional early, ideally within a month of the beginning of the provider's work with the client. Prior to these conversations, counsel must have secured all necessary releases by the client and may need a court order to waive privileges.

Counsel should establish a protocol when calling a caseworker or service provider. It is wise to begin by acknowledging the limited time the professional may have and ask whether the professional has time for a short conversation. If the professional does not have the time, set up another time to call back. Once the substantive conversation begins, counsel should explain her role in terms of the child and the client. "One of the big issues in this case is what's best for little John. I need your help in understanding what's going on, so that I can know how to work with the court and John's mother." Then, counsel can ask the necessary questions, but respect the professional's time constraints.

Once counsel initiates contact with a professional, she should keep in regular touch, not just in the days preceding a court hearing. Parents' attorneys are in touch with caseworkers far more regularly than the other service providers and, as such, should attempt to foster a good relationship with this very important player in their clients' cases.

The following sections focus on issues specific to the different roles caseworkers and other professionals play in child welfare.

10.04(b)(1) The Caseworker

The agency caseworker is the primary point of contact for clients. In most states, the caseworker is an employee of the state agency. In other states, the caseworker works for a private agency that contracts with the state. In either case, counsel should review whether conversations with caseworkers are subject to ethical rules that govern communications with persons represented by counsel.

The caseworker and the caseworker's supervisor are usually responsible for arranging services for the parent and the parent's children, supervising visits, evaluating the parent's overall progress, informing the court and the attorneys about the parent's progress, and making recommendations to the court concerning all of the above. Judges often call them the eyes and ears of the court. As noted above, counsel should contact the caseworker early in the case to establish a working relationship. If a worker changes, counsel must do this again. Let the worker know that she will be in contact regularly.

Counsel's conversation with the caseworker should focus on the parent's progress in visitation, treatment, and other services, and the parent-child relationship. Here is a simple checklist for the information counsel should gather from the caseworker:

1. How is the client doing in his/her services?
2. How is the child doing in his/her services (e.g., early intervention, early childhood, school, counseling)?
3. What is the caseworker's assessment of the parent's progress? How did the caseworker make that assessment?
4. Are there additional services that the caseworker or service provider recommends? Why?
5. How are visits going? What are the strengths of the client on visits? Where does she need improvement?
6. Can visits be expanded? Why or why not?

Between court appearances, counsel should communicate with the Agency in writing to ensure documentation is available when counsel raises the claim of lack of reasonable efforts in court. When communicating with the Agency on these issues, do not overstate a problem the client has encountered with the Agency, for example, by saying the Agency "never" provides meaningful help with visits, even though that is how the client feels. Such overstatements might antagonize an agency against the parent and reinforce a view that the parent focuses on the Agency's problems through exaggeration while ignoring his or her own challenges.

In communications with the Agency, make clear that the parent wants to do what is necessary to make progress, and recognizes the Agency's efforts to do more to help. The Agency will be more likely to respond favorably if counsel demonstrates an understanding of agency rules and roles, the caseloads workers face, and the implications of a finding of no reasonable efforts. For example, counsel can get positive results by letting a caseworker know that state rules requires the Agency to schedule therapy at reasonable times and locations, and then asking the worker how that will be accomplished.

When communicating client concerns, counsel should not share client information from the client without consulting the client and considering how the information may influence the caseworker. Counsel should discuss with the client the advantages and disadvantages of providing information to the caseworker, especially when the client is frustrated or angry. When talking to the worker, if a strong concern about the caseworker's action emerges, counsel should frame the concern to the worker so that the attorney, not the client, draws any anger from the worker.

Counsel should use solution-based problem solving in her interactions with the caseworker. When talking with the caseworker, counsel should focus her conversations on solutions rather than complaints. This will help the caseworker to feel part of the resolution of the issue. Counsel can use the client's suggestions to help frame the solution. For example, if a client's primary language is not English and the Agency failed to provide treatment in her native language, a discussion might include the following: the lawyer can remind workers that courts must find that the Agency has made reasonable efforts, and that in this case it is reasonable for treatment to be in a client's native language. The lawyer can then outline a solution for such therapy, such as a program that has openings and provides such treatment or an individual therapist in an underserved area who is willing to become involved.

A lawyer does not have to agree with the caseworker; but listening and acknowledging that counsel understands what the caseworker is saying will help develop a positive working relationship. This lets the caseworker know that counsel understands what the caseworker said, and allows the conversation to continue so counsel can learn more about the case.

If, despite counsel's best efforts, a caseworker is persistently unwilling to do what the parent wants or is unavailable, counsel may need to speak to the caseworker's supervisor. To do this, know the chain of command at the Agency and the administrative rules and procedures that govern it. If all else fails, counsel should consider filing a motion in court seeking to change the caseworker, arguing that the relationship between the parent and the caseworker is incompatible with the Agency's duty to provide reasonable efforts to the parent.

10.04(b)(2) Relative

Federal and many state laws contain preferences for placement with relatives. *See* 42 U.S.C. § 671(a)(19). This follows social science research showing that children do much better when placed with relatives compared with non-relatives. *See, e.g.*, Jed Metzger, *Resiliency in Children and Youth in Kinship Care and Family Foster Care*, 87 CHILD WELFARE 115, 124–26 (2008); Marc A. Winokur et al., *Matched Comparison of Children in Kinship Care and Foster Care on Child Welfare Outcomes*, 89 J. CONTEMP. SOC. SERV. 338, 341–43 (2008). It is also what many parents prefer. Counsel should never assume what a client wants and should forgo asking for a placement with relatives when the parents do not want it.

To find out about a parent's wishes regarding relatives becoming temporary caregivers, counsel should learn about extended family and other family figures. A genogram is a good visual aid for this process and aids counsel's understanding of the client's views about who are the best relatives and why. Once a relative is identified, counsel should speak with him or her about several subjects. Some suggestions for that discussion follow.

For a child already placed with the relative, begin by explaining why her stepping forward to take on the care of the child is so important to the case. Explain counsel's role. Then move to the following areas:

1. What do you like about the child living in the home?
2. What are your hopes for the child?
3. How did the child come to live with you?
4. How is the child doing in whatever programs the child is enrolled?
5. Are there services the child needs that you think he or she is not getting?
6. What have you tried to do to get those services?
7. Tell me about parent and child visits you have observed.
8. Does the child tell you anything about missing his or her parent?
9. What positive things do you think the parent is doing?
10. Where do you think the parent still must improve?
11. If the parent had the child living with her, would you be able to help with child-care. Why? Why not?

For a child not placed with a relative:

1. Explain the importance to the case of becoming the temporary caregiver.
2. Would you like the child placed with you? Why? Why not?
3. Explain the state requirements regarding background checks for the household and the reasons.
4. Would you be able to meet those standards?
5. Have you tried to become a placement resource? What is your prior relationship with the children?

Then move to any of the questions above that relate to the case.

10.04(b)(3) Foster Parents

Developing a good relationship with the foster parents can be helpful, but remember that foster parents are potential adversaries if their relationship with the parent breaks down. It is important to clarify counsel's role. Strive to make all communication with the foster parent friendly, focus on the parent and child relationship, listen respectfully to any complaint the foster parent may have about the parent, and respect their wishes not to talk to parents' counsel.

10.04(b)(4) Service Providers: Therapists, Psychologists, Doctors, Teachers, Parenting Coaches, and Others

Keep in mind the particular expertise and ethical duties each professional in this category has. Determine how their expertise, knowledge, and experience can contribute to the development of the theory of the case. Remember that these professionals may have many clients, with extensive time commitments. Because of this, these professionals may not have the time or the interest in talking with a lawyer unless they have an understanding of how that discussion may benefit their patient, client, or student. Forging a good relationship with these professionals is important both in this case and for building counsel's knowledge base for other clients. Keeping promises helps with building such a relationship. A fifteen-minute, planned phone conversation should be kept to fifteen minutes. If more time is needed, counsel should not presume the individual has it available. Make strategic decisions whether to take written notes of these conversations based on the discovery rules of the jurisdiction.

The following is a brief template for these conversations using an expert on early childhood attachment as an example. Begin by asking about her expertise. Explain why the expert's information and assessment is important. Explaining the purpose of the court proceedings is very important because many service providers do not understand how their opinions bear on the court's or Agency's decisions. "I need to know about the mother's progress because the court is going to decide the future direction of the case. If it finds that the goal of the case is to terminate the mother's parental rights, the Agency will likely end her treatment and her visits with her son John will decrease substantially. If the court eventually terminates the mother's parental rights, her son would not have the right to visit with his mother and his mother would not have the right to visit with him. On the other hand, if it finds that she is making enough progress, the court will keep the goal of returning John to his mother, and she would continue to get services like therapy to help with John's return home." With this background, counsel is ready to ask what the expert thinks and why. Counsel's goal is to find out what the expert has observed and what these observations say about the parent's progress and the parent's connection to her child.

Since many observations will include negative and positive information, probe for ways to improve the situation. Does the expert recommend that the Agency or parent do something different? Are there services that are not being used that would help? Where and how can more services be accessed? It is often important to secure these answers in writing, either in letter or affidavit form.

In terms of the positives, counsel should explore what the expert believes is good about the parent-child relationship. For example, if the expert believes that a positive parent-child attachment is important to his assessment, ask why such attachments are important generally, and why it is critical in this case. Explain to the expert that examples of the strengths in the relationship are very helpful to informing the court of the parent-child relationship. Remind the expert that the judge will make critical decisions about what the future holds for the mother and her child. A description of a positive interaction showing a close relationship, such as a parent and toddler enjoying each other's company, often shows far more about the relationship than a simple conclusion that someone is making progress. It gives the court a concrete example of positive parenting and shared intimacy between the parent and child. It paints a compelling picture for the court at a hearing.

10.05 Advocacy at Family Team Meetings

The "Family Team Meeting" is a process for engaging for families in child welfare cases. In a growing number of states, agencies are using this process under a variety of names, including family team conferencing, family team meetings, family group conferencing, family team decision making, family unity meetings, and team decision making. *See, e.g.*, U.S. DEP'T OF HEALTH AND HUMAN SERVICES, ADMINISTRATION FOR CHILDREN AND FAMILIES, FAMILY GROUP DECISION-MAKING (2014).

Depending on the model, the team might include children, parents, extended family, current caregivers, other important adults identified by the parties, caseworkers, therapists, children's attorney or guardians, and/or parents' counsel. Sometimes these meetings happen informally. At other times, they take place based on agency regulations that require a meeting with parents before the Agency may change the case plan, services, visitation, the child's placement, or the permanency goal. Whichever model the jurisdiction uses, parents' counsel should formally request from the caseworker or Agency to be informed before all meetings. Parents' counsel should also tell the client to let counsel know of these meetings. The more counsel attends these meeting with their clients, the greater likelihood of successful advocacy.

10.05(a) Plan for the Meeting with the Parent

Planning with the parent can both empower her and lead to better results. Planning enables the parent to be part of the process instead of a role player at a pre-orchestrated event. Figure out a strategy for the meeting: What information should the Agency know? What are the best responses to concerns the Agency or others are likely to have? Planning for these things with the parent helps her comprehend that if her attorney chooses not to bring up a particular concern in the meeting, it is for strategic reasons.

Make a list of the parent's key concerns and those counsel believes are important. Prepare the client to answer particular questions counsel intends to ask at the meeting. The more the parent understands the process, the more likely she will be able to help herself at the meeting. For example, consider explaining to the parent something along these lines: "Sometimes it helps to tell the story about you and the boys and how important their toy trucks are to them. Even though you have heard me tell the story a million times, I am going to talk about it again. It helps them understand how much you focus on your children."

Finally, develop a plan for how the parent can signal during the meeting that she wants to say something. Sometimes social services staff might interpret negatively a parent's request to talk to the lawyer privately. To avoid this, when the parent gives the signal, her counsel can tell the other participants that counsel needs a moment with the parent. It is far better for the workers to draw negative inferences about the parent's counsel than the parent.

When parents may bring supportive friends or relatives to a meeting, encourage them to do so. Sometimes the mere presence of someone on the parent's side of the table helps parents feel less isolated. Discuss with the person before the meeting how she can help. When the purpose of the meeting is to consider a new placement resource, bring the person to the meeting. This will help initiate a change-of-placement decision.

10.05(b) Conducting the Family Team Meeting

Once the meeting begins, counsel should draw a diagram listing the names and roles of the persons at the table. Counsel's checklist of important points and goals should be in a readily accessible place. Also keep the genogram of the family handy. Use a notepad, but only record what is important (such as a commitment by the Agency to provide a particular service or something that should be brought up later).

Choose a place to sit where counsel can communicate with the client easily and directly. Most often this is next to the client. From the beginning, align and stay with the client. The client must understand counsel is there for the client, not as another part of the "system."

When the meeting begins, the person leading the meeting might outline ground rules. If the people present refer to the parents by titles such as "parent" or "bio-mom," suggest that everyone use proper names such as Ms. Bentley. Focus on listening at the beginning.

10.05(b)(1) Possible Roles to Play at the Family Team Meeting

Counsel may play several different roles for the parent. What follows are five of the most important roles.

1. ***Translator.*** Child and Family Team meetings, like meetings on special education, can be full of jargon. These include short-hand terms for hearings, rules, forms,

and types of services. Some are words that only exist in the unique world of child welfare. At one meeting, the convener asked a parent if she had any "anecdotes" about her child. The mother's lawyer could tell that the mother was confused, and asked the convener what an "anecdote" was. This made the lawyer, not the client, appear confused and forced the convener to explain that she was looking for incidents that illuminated the child's condition. This provided the lawyer with the opportunity to say, "Oh you want stories about the times he has trouble paying attention." Once the mother understood this, she could rattle off story after story about the child's challenges in staying on a task in a way that showed she understood the issues her child was facing.

2. ***Advocate.*** Lawyers receive training to be courtroom advocates. Advocacy at family team meetings involves many of the same skills as in court: listening, staying focused on the issues consistent with counsel's theory, and having a checklist of things counsel wants to accomplish.

   Meetings are not controlled by rules of evidence, but those rules exist for good reason. When a question or statement is vague, confusing, or conclusory, draw on evidentiary rules. Clarifying when and where something happened according to whom, is just as important at meetings as in the courtroom. When someone reports that a visit did not go well, counsel should ask for the source of the report, when the event took place, and what specifically did not go well.

   Counsel should focus on the child's needs both in services and in developing a positive relationship with the parent. If the Agency has not followed through on transportation for visits, point out that missed visits disappoint both the child and the parent. Focus on solutions. When someone failed to follow a rule, point it out in a polite but firm way and open the door for fixing the problem. "I know that the Agency's rules require transportation to be arranged two days in advance. Is there a way we can ensure, going forward that this will happen?"

3. ***Facilitator.*** Look for opportunities for the client to show her strong points and to explain her concerns. Then give the client the opportunity to do so. One such opportunity is when counsel responds to something said by a caseworker. Rather than answering the question, ask the client about the particular issue that gives the client the chance to answer the question phrased by counsel. For example, the worker might repeat a request that the client attend a new service at a particular day and time. Counsel might know the client is upset about this because she has to work at that time. The goal should be to set a different day and time for the service and to do so without the client displaying anger. This might be accomplished by asking the parent: "Could you tell the caseworker about your work situation on Wednesdays and let her know the other days that work for you?" This does more than fix the problem; it creates a record of why counseling began later than it might have. ("Do you remember the parent being at the April 6 staffing?

On that date didn't she tell you that she could not do therapy on Wednesday evenings, because she had to work late?")

To identify client strengths, focus on the case theory, the client's progress, and her connection with her child. Look for opportunities for the client to demonstrate these. For example, if a child has feeding issues, and the client has learned new techniques for dealing with the eating problems, ask her about a positive incident rather than an abstract principle. "Tell the caseworker about how you got Jessica to eat last week when she was pouting." If counsel and the client have discussed the incident previously, the client should be more able to provide the information at the meeting. Her story of success shows the progress she made far better than merely saying, "I learned X skill that I will apply to my parenting."

Counsel could also use the facilitator's role to get other professionals at the meeting to describe incidents that further demonstrate the improved parenting and commitment to the child. If counsel's preparation led to knowledge that a therapist has identified something that is both significant and helpful to the theory of the parent's case, bring this out. "You observed that the child and parent said something really important when they were drawing pictures of each other. What was it? Why is that important for their relationship?" Frame the question to focus the witness on the critical issue or incident.

4. ***Storyteller.*** "If we are to be successful in presenting our case we must not only discover its story; we must become good storytellers as well. Every trial, every . . . argument for justice is a story." GERRY SPENCE, WIN YOUR CASE 86 (2005). Stories are one of the ways we tell each other about our lives. They are persuasive when they are real and make a point. One of the reasons for this is that a good story demonstrates a point while allowing the listener to draw her own conclusion, even when the arc of the story leads to that conclusion. *See* Sonya Dal Cin et al., *Narrative Persuasion and Overcoming Resistance*, *in* RESISTANCE AND PERSUASION (E. S. Knowles & J. A. Linn, eds. 2004).

   Some clients are good at identifying stories that exemplify a point; others have trouble doing so, especially when they are under stress. Sometimes it is easier for counsel to tell a story about their client than it is for the client. Regardless of who tells the story, it is important to remember that the story should focus on the parent and child. The story should show a skill the parent has learned that demonstrates an improved knowledge or ability, or highlight the parent's ability to advocate for and connect with the child. For example, a parent's lawyer might explain that when he or she attended an IEP with the parent, the school staff appreciated the parent's ability to outline a way for school staff to respond to the child's school problems. This demonstrates the parent's knowledge and skill by showing her awareness of her child's needs and attention to finding a positive solution. If her child is in foster care, her attendance at the IEP shows her increased commitment to her child.

5. ***Negotiator.*** At a certain point in a meeting, counsel should try to reach a desired outcome. Look at the list of outcomes counsel wants to achieve. Think about what has been said at the meeting that advances them and propose something. If the Agency hesitates or offers a different solution, consider it. If counsel needs time to talk with the client alone, ask for a few minutes. If possible, put the onus on counsel rather than the client. "I need to speak alone with Ms. Benton." When alone, ask the client about what she wants and whether she can follow the solution proposed by the Agency. Ask her if she has other solutions. When back in the meeting, don't be afraid to be the tough negotiator to the client's good one. "I think you are asking too much here, four different services on two days, even if Ms. Benton were to say she would try. It would be better to do them on the following schedule."

10.05(c) Closing the Meeting

Ideally, all the meeting participants should confirm their understanding of the results of the staffing before leaving. If this cannot be done, go over the points and write them down. Then immediately after the meeting, follow up with a letter that confirms the agreements and outlines whatever remaining disagreements exist. The letter should be firm and friendly, not confrontational. ("Thank you for agreeing to increase Ms. Benton's visits to two days a week because of the progress she has made, and the child's desire to see her more. Thank you also for understanding that her work conflicts with scheduling a parent coach for Wednesday evenings. We agree to work with you to find another date and time, or parent coaching agency if necessary.")

If the meeting creates or amends a case plan or other written document, be sure the client agrees that it furthers her goals. Also be sure that the client can comply with the newly imposed tasks. When counsel disagrees with a proposal, frame the disagreement in terms of the child's and parent's interests. ("From the perspective of a three-year-old child, the visits should be in a location where the child and parent can focus on each other and play together, not at a table in a busy McDonald's.") If the parent is asked to sign a document, take time with the parent, apart from the others. Ask if she can follow the steps outlined, and emphasize this is the time to ask for changes, if she wants them. If the client and counsel disagree with the outcome described in the document, consider drafting a concise statement outlining the disagreement in terms that show the client's commitment to the child.

10.06 Preparation for Disposition and Permanency Hearings

10.06(a) Considering Reasonable Efforts by the Agency and Utilizing Motions Concerning Reasonable Efforts

As the time for the next court appearance approaches, counsel should gather the written communications with the Agency. An email chain works as well for this purpose as does a series of letters. A "paper trail" outlining requests for services or accommodations that were either ignored or refused, goes a long way to laying a foundation for a claim of no reasonable efforts. Counsel may decide to raise the no reasonable efforts issue at a hearing without a motion (where reasonable efforts is a required element of a hearing) or by drafting a motion on the issue. If using a motion, the motion should follow these same guidelines: identify the needed service, the reason for it and its availability, the requests made for it, and the absence of results. The motion should identify what the Agency could have, but has not, done and why the missing steps matter.

Use the opportunity to offer a solution-based approach when drafting and presenting the motion. Instead of simply asking for a negative finding, outline a way to fix the problem. If visits have not been held because the Agency lacks the staff to supervise visits, begin with facts: that visits cannot occur without supervision, that many visits were canceled because the Agency was unwilling or unable to supervise them, and that visits are vital to the parent and child and are a critical component to reuniting the family. Then use the law to promote a solution. Explain that state rules allow relatives to supervise visits, and then propose a relative. It is wise to add that the Agency's failure to use the relative is evidence of a lack of reasonable efforts on the Agency's part. Whether counsel asks the court to find that the Agency has not made reasonable efforts or only asks to certify the relative as eligible for supervision is a strategic choice counsel must make.

One reason to ask for a finding that the Agency failed to use reasonable efforts is the speed at which any case can move from a goal of reunification to termination of parental rights. If the state initiates a termination proceeding, a finding of no reasonable efforts by the Agency will be helpful in defending the case. But unless counsel can identify something to be gained from such a finding, it may be strategically more advantageous to focus on moving the case in the right direction. To accomplish this, counsel should ask the court to amend the case plan to include the supervision being sought.

Whatever claim is made in court should correspond to what was claimed out of court. Being able to show the court the care with which the parent and counsel have communicated with the Agency can make a very positive impression on the court in several ways. It demonstrates that the parent has tried her best to secure needed services, bolstering the critical point that the parent cares about her children and wants them back. It also strengthens the claim that the Agency has failed to do what it had to. It is considerably easier to prove that an Agency failed to do something it should have done when counsel has a paper trail proving that they were asked to do it several times and ignored the requests. Finally, the court is very likely to have sympathy for the parent when the record shows that the parent is helpless in forcing the Agency to do what it refuses to do.

10.06(b) Preparing the Client for the Initial Disposition Hearing

The case plan and counsel's notes should act as a road map for the disposition hearing. If throughout the case, counsel has been in regular communication with the client and caseworker, there should be few surprises during the hearing about the parent's participation in services and visitation. This hearing is the first time the court will be formally evaluating the parent's efforts, as it must determine whether the parent is ready to regain custody of the child. Discuss with the client before court the probability that the court will conclude that the client has made enough progress at this point to have the child returned home.

Prepare the parent for the hearing by explaining that courts do not commonly return children from foster care at the first disposition hearing. Accordingly, counsel should forewarn the parent not to be defeated emotionally if the court continues the foster care placement. Let the parent know the timetable the court tends to use; if the child returning home is more likely six months from now, the parent should know this.

Parents will often be important witnesses at these hearings. Prepare the parent well for this appearance. Plan to present the information using leading questions to set the stage, giving the parent a chance to talk in a narrative, and emphasizing how much she loves her children and that she is willing to do what the court asks to get them back.

Also, prepare to use the information gathered at agency meetings in court, such as agreements about visitation or services. Because the parent was present, she can confirm these conversations even if there is disagreement about what was said. Introduce the confirming letter counsel wrote after the meeting or written agreements. This is an example of some short testimony that might productively be adduced:

> Mr. Thomas, you were at the staffing with your therapist and the caseworker and me on January 8th?
>
> And you heard your therapist say that a parenting coach could help you with learning how to better deal with Jacob's attention deficit disorder?
>
> Tell the court whether you would like help in that area and why it's important to you and your son.

10.06(c) Theory of the Case

The advocacy that counsel provides at disposition and permanency hearings should build on the work done throughout the case. Counsel's goal is to continue to present the client's theory through the events occurring in real time, in her life and the life of her children. If the story is about making a recovery from addiction and learning to be a better parent, the evidence gathered from professionals and meetings may give counsel the events that tell that story. But the reality is sometimes more challenging. The client may have taken steps that demonstrate improved parenting and her commitment to her children, or she may have faltered. A father committed to fostering a relationship with his child just two months ago may have followed through on a visitation plan or he may have missed the last month. The first step in planning is to return to theory. Begin by fitting the facts with the legal standards and rules of evidence for the upcoming hearing. Make a list of the positive and negative facts as they fit with the legal issues at the upcoming hearing. Then determine whether the theory still makes sense and is persuasive. If not, then counsel needs to modify the theory. What follows is an example of how to develop a theory first for the initial disposition and then how that theory would differ at the permanency hearing.

As the disposition hearing begins, suppose the mother recently relapsed in substance abuse recovery. Because the legal standards at disposition focus on the ability to parent safely, it is almost certain that the court will order that the child remain in foster care. Counsel's goal is to demonstrate any positive steps made by the client despite the problem.

First, counsel needs to check his or her own feelings about the client and the system. The relapse may lead counsel to feelings of sadness, frustration with the client, or anger toward the system for failing the parent. It is important to be aware of the feelings but not to let them interfere with counsel's ethical duty to continue to advocate for the client despite the relapse.

Second, counsel should talk to the client when he or she learns about the relapse, and work with the client to refocus her efforts on getting back on track soon. Tell her that counsel's goal is to present something positive to the court despite the relapse. Explain to the client that ideally counsel would tell the judge she is getting back on track and, for that to happen, the client needs to return to or stay in treatment and maintain her visiting schedule. Ask her and her treatment provider if there is some service that might help her. If one is available, encourage the client to participate.

As the disposition hearing approaches, counsel should review the information she has gathered and figure out what story emerges regarding why the client relapsed, what the client has done since relapse, and the Agency's actions in providing her reasonable services to address the relapse. Again, return to the list of negative facts (e.g., the relapse, missed appointments or visits) and positive facts (e.g., acknowledging the relapse, returning to treatment, desire to become a better parent). Out of these facts, a theory may emerge. One possible theory is that while the parent would like her son back, she realizes that because she has relapsed recently, return home is unlikely at present. The theory acknowledges the present reality and sets the stage for further progress.

The theory focuses facts and analysis on the same themes as it has throughout the case: the client's goal of resolving the problems that brought the case to court and providing care for her children. Presenting the theory will not keep the judge from ordering the child to remain in foster care, but it might demonstrate that the client has a level of maturity and is focusing on making positive steps to be a better parent.

Next, identify facts that support the theory, such as a conversation with a therapist or a positive interaction with the child on a visit. These may already be included on the list of negative and positive facts. Plan how to introduce the information—through the caseworker or possibly the client herself—acknowledging her relapse and showing the court she wants to get back on track. Outline a brief closing statement to highlight the present realities and the hope for a better future.

At a permanency hearing, counsel's theory might be slightly different. Now the desired end is to keep the goal of return home despite the setbacks. In many states, if a court changes a goal to something other than return home, the child welfare agency will stop providing services and visitation will be reduced. Once that happens, the prospects of a good outcome diminish substantially. To keep return home as the goal may require something more than just an acknowledgment of a problem. The theory might be that relapse is a setback, but also a step in recovery, and that the client's response to the relapse (e.g., perhaps she reengaged in inpatient treatment) demonstrates that she is making progress, and therefore the goal should remain return home. That theory might require testimony about recovery from a substance abuse professional. Identify all the facts that support that the parent has focused on positive steps despite the relapse: establishing consistency in visits, participating in domestic violence treatment, or attending treatment with her child. If there is a service that counsel believes has been missing from the client's services or service plan, incorporate that into the theory. All of this helps to present a client theory that makes a goal of return home possible.

Finally, consider several strategic choices at both disposition and permanency hearings.

First, think about active steps counsel can take to get the client's story of progress across to the court in the best way. States differ in how quickly the disposition hearing must take place. Know what the rules are in the jurisdiction. For each client, think of the timing of the disposition hearing as part of legal strategy. If a parent is in substance abuse treatment, and the treatment will be completed soon, try to delay the disposition if it gives the client enough time to complete that stage of treatment. Counsel's goal should be to have the first major hearing that focuses on progress be one that includes completion of one of the most critical services needed for reunification. Let the court and the client know this is the reason for the continuance request. Doing so shows the client that counsel is focused on the best way for her to present her case to the court. It also tells the court about the progress and that there is a good reason for the delay. If completion is impossible by the disposition time limit, consider whether the progress made is enough to support a motion for increased visitation at disposition. Remember the goal of showing progress at every court date.

If a court report includes documentation of substance abuse or therapy, make a strategic choice about whether to call the service provider. If a client in the early stages of recovery is still testing positive for PCP because it stays in the system for longer than thirty days, and not because the client is using, figure out a way to get that information to the court. Counsel should make a judgment on who will testify.

If the Agency is not putting services in place and the client is ready and willing for them, do not push off the disposition. Consider whether it makes sense to present evidence of lack of reasonable efforts. Decide whether to use a carrot or a stick: The carrot approach is demonstrated below in 10.07(b) and focuses on using the reasonable efforts issue to get services put in place. The stick, seeking a finding that the Agency has failed, should be used when an Agency has refused to provide an important service or when it is needed as a prevention strategy for termination of parental rights possibilities. Once counsel decides on the approach, file the motion to outline the issues. *See* 10.06(a) above.

Finally, where the facts support it, file a motion for increasing visitation, even if the disposition hearing is being strategically delayed. Progress of any kind helps clients to see that good work results in good outcomes from the court.

10.06(d) Securing the Necessary Documents

Counsel for parents often receive reports from caseworkers or other professionals as a matter of course. Unfortunately, the reports often get delivered on the day of a hearing when almost no time exists to review them. Strive to get the reports ahead of time: call the caseworker or therapist, get a court order at the prior hearing setting a date, encourage court rules that ensure that reports get to counsel in sufficient time. Do whatever is needed to get the reports other than at the last minute.

Consider other documentation. Review the local court rules and the Agency's administrative code to identify what information parents have a right to see. A caseworker's daily notes contain a wealth of information, often in short vignettes about the child's life or parent-child interactions. "She stopped playing with the dolls at the visitation center and ran to her mother, when her mom arrived." In some jurisdictions it is possible to get copies regularly, by agreement, order, or subpoena. Similarly, if the Agency uses agents or employees to observe visitation, get those notes by the same means.

10.06(e) Consider Who Will Make the Best Witnesses

In most cases, the witness who has the most information is the caseworker. However, always consider whether the service providers would make a stronger case for reunification. While the caseworker can testify that the parent attended and is making progress in therapy, the therapist may articulate something more critical. She can focus on how progress is measured, whether the parent has achieved treatment goals, and what additional work is needed. The therapist can also testify whether the parent's work can be completed with the child in the parent's custody. Consider the limitations of the therapist—she may not be able to give an opinion about whether it is in the child's interest to return home because the child is not her patient, or she may have ethical concerns about whether it is appropriate in her role to offer a best interests opinion. Also, consider whether the client will testify and if it may sway the court toward more rapid reunification.

Again, if the issue is substance abuse recovery, consider whether testimony from the client's treatment provider is important in helping the court understand a major point, such as how relapse fits in with recovery for this client. Having a caseworker relate a summary of a substance abuse counselor by saying "relapse is part of recovery" may be enough to "make a record" but it may not be enough to prevent a goal change. Testimony directly from an expert about how common relapse is in treatment, and how relapse can lead to recovery, may do both.

10.07 Conducting the Court Hearing

Disposition hearings tend to focus on a snapshot of the client's progress up to that point, but may include elements of permanency determinations depending on state law. Permanency hearings have specific goals, in part because of the federal regulations requiring them. Courts must set a permanency goal, then monitor services, placement, and other efforts to ensure that they are being administered properly to advance the permanency goal, and monitor the placement of the child. Courts need information presented concisely to meet these goals.

One important overall strategy is to use each court appearance as an opportunity to make a forward step. Present something that shows progress. Make a list of things the court should learn about the parent. These might include attendance at school events, new insights into an issue in therapy, the plan to present a relative as a placement option, or clean drug screens. Child welfare cases take a long time; let the judge know the positives about the parent at every opportunity.

Continue bringing information about the parent to the court's attention. Use a permanency or status hearing to detail the good things happening in the case. Even when the parent's progress is not formally on the agenda for the court appearance, find a way to bring it up. Look for reasons to have a parent testify. If a case is scheduled for discovery status, consider telling the court: "Judge, I just wanted to let you know that Mr. Wilson was at his son's IEP meeting last week. Because he was not the foster parent, he did not have final say on the plan, but could provide input. If you want testimony on the issue he can provide it."

Caseworkers will commonly be called as witnesses to give a report. Prepare all questioning thinking about how to get the important information out through a combination of leading and open-ended questions. Counsel's preparation should include leading questions to get out the important information efficiently. It can then move to open-ended questions about why some issues or events are important:

> You said the feeding sessions were influential to your recommendation?
> Why are those sessions important in demonstrating Ms. Abernathy's growth as a parent?

Then, if the expert gives three reasons, outline them for the court.

> You said reasons A, B, and C.
> Let's start by discussing A.

10.07(a) Substantive Issues to Consider

10.07(a)(i) Ability to Parent and the Child's Best Interest

Regardless of other factors, courts are always concerned about a parent's ability and the child's best interests. Know the jurisdiction's definition of what constitutes best interests—and tailor the questioning to align with reunifying the child and the parent. General questions on best interests are important, such as: the child's wishes, safety, sibling relationships, the parent's progress in services, and most influentially, the child's attachment with the parent. As counsel prepares, keep the definition prominently in mind. Look for facts that specifically fit the definition. Some require little explanation. For example, if attachment is one of the elements of best interest, what names does the child use for the parent ("Mommy" or "Daddy")? Does the child ask about the parent? Other areas may require a discussion with a professional. For attachment issues, counsel may want to prepare by meeting with a child development specialist or child therapist to learn more about how children demonstrate attachment at different ages. A two-year-old may demonstrate attachment in a variety of ways, snuggling with a parent, being upset when she leaves the room, sharing a cupcake, or even by getting angry because she knows that the parent will stay connected to her despite the anger. A ten-year-old may show it in a very different way. If counsel is knowledgeable about these matters, tailor questions to the caseworker to bring them out. Counsel should examine the caseworker after reviewing the case notes, which likely contain examples of attachment or the child's desire to be with her parent.

Counsel should also insist that "best interests" is supposed to be weighted in favor of children being with their families absent legitimate safety concerns to the contrary. In many cases, safety can be a factor favoring reunification when the original condition requiring removal is no longer a concern. If a worker identifies safety as a concern, counsel should use leading questions to list the safety concerns, and then to provide positive examples of how those concerns were resolved, by asking questions that demonstrate what would reduce those concerns, and what the Agency has done to reduce the concerns. Counsel could also elicit facts suggesting that the parent has paid close attention to safety concerns over the recent months.

Counsel should be prepared at the hearing to demonstrate that the parent currently possesses the ability to care for her child safely. If the local law has specific parenting standards, do the same thing with the standards as with best interest factors. These standards commonly are expressed in terms of the minimum things required of parents: the need to provide adequate food and clothing, for example. Use the language required of parents to prepare questions that demonstrate that she could meet them if given the opportunity.

Questions demonstrating that the parent provides adequate food and proper clothing for the child when the parent is with the child are facts from which counsel and the court can reason inductively that the parent would continue to make safe and appropriate parenting choices if given the opportunity to do so. Counsel may be able to argue that the parent's progress during the placement period may very well have eliminated or attenuated the safety concerns and that increasing the parent's unsupervised access to the child is a sound way to determine whether the risks remain high.

Be ready to switch to leading questions when the caseworker does not remember or turns hesitant. "On January 4, the day of the big snow, Ms. Benson brought a new set of boots that she bought at Salvation Army for the child. They were clean and they fit the child, correct? "

10.07(b) Role of Child Protective Services and Reasonable Efforts

Reasonable efforts by the Agency to reunite parent and child can be a critical area of inquiry, particularly when the child is likely to remain in placement. Making a record that the Agency has not done as much as required under the law is important as a possible defense in a future termination of parental rights case and will serve as a basis for a court order that the Agency do something going forward that it has not done already.

Know what constitutes reasonable efforts under controlling law. If the Agency has been less than diligent, prepare questions to illustrate the parent was ready and willing to do more services, but the Agency failed to refer the parent or did not refer her soon enough. If there are services that could be provided to assist with reunification, be prepared to prove it. Think of this part of the examination in three steps. First, determine the missing services. Second, demonstrate their importance to the client's progress or the parent-child relationship. Third, show what the court or Agency could do to ensure their implementation. The following is an example:

> Now, Mr. Caseworker, in addition to monitoring the placement, you also supervise Ms. Turner's progress in services, don't you?
> Two months ago she began one-on-one therapy, isn't that right?
> Her therapy takes place on the north side at (location) at 3:00 in the afternoon, doesn't it?
> She also began a job training class last month, right?
> The job training class is on the west side at . . . ?
> It was at 10:00 A.M. on Mondays.
> It's now at 10:00 A.M. on Tuesdays, isn't that correct?
> She has made six out of her eight therapy appointments?
> And one of the missed appointments was because of an illness?
> The therapist called that an excused absence?
> The other was on a day when Ms. Turner had a job training class, isn't that right?
> She told you she could not get from the west side to the north side on time?
> And she said she could not call the therapist because her phone was out of power?
> After that you and Ms. Turner changed the job class to Wednesdays?

Ms. Turner has also gone to eight out of ten visits?
The two visits she missed occurred on days when she did not receive a bus card?
She called your Agency about that issue?
You now arrange for her to pick up her transit pass at your Agency the first of each month?
Since obtaining the tokens, she has made all of her visits?

These questions are fact-based, without broad opinion statements that might draw an objection or negative opinion from the worker. They paint a straightforward picture of a client working to become a better parent, and they support a goal of return home. They also reveal how hard complete compliance with required services can be.

The style and form of cross-examination of a worker regarding the lack of reasonable efforts by the Agency will follow from counsel's purpose in exploring the subject. When the goal is to secure an agreement going forward on what a parent needs to make progress, rather than to embarrass the worker, avoid emphasizing the worker's failures and point toward a solution. The following examination follows the traditional cross-examination technique of recommitment, accrediting, and confrontation. However, it does so in a way that provides a solution for the court and leaves the worker the opportunity to be the solution provider, rather than the object of criticism:

Recommitment:
You said on the last court date that you did not know of any kinship placement options, correct?

Accredit:
Your Agency has a goal identifying possible kinship options for foster children?
And you would consider the placement if the relative could provide a safe and positive home for a child?
In fact, that is in your best practices guide/rules/procedures, isn't it? (Ask this question only if the worker knows of the particular reference or if you have a copy of the document on hand.)

Confrontation:
Do you remember that last Tuesday, Ms. Benton's mother came to a staffing with her at the office?
And I was at that meeting, along with you and your supervisor, correct?
Ms. Benton, Sr. could not come into the staffing because of confidentiality rules?
But she was waiting in the waiting room, right?
After the meeting, when the three of us were in the waiting room, Ms. Benton said that she would be happy to be a caretaker for Jerome, didn't she?

Solution:

I realize that was only last week, but you have now begun exploring Ms. Benton, Sr. as a placement option, haven't you?

And you agree to know within the next two weeks if she is such a resource?

And if she is, you will ensure that a team meeting is scheduled right away to change the placement?

10.08 After the Hearing

Meet with the client after the hearing. The after-court conversation will go one of two ways: (1) now that you have your children home, it is advisable to . . . or (2) although your children are not yet home, it is important that you continue to . . . .

When the court has ordered the children returned home, parents should be reminded of the importance of following all court orders, which often include an order of protection. Parents should be advised to keep the Agency informed of anything involving the children that they, as parents, would want to know. If a child goes to the park and injures himself, the Agency should know if a scrape or bruise forms. If the child goes to the doctor for a cough, the Agency should receive a phone call that day and a copy of the medical records. If the child will be with a babysitter, the Agency should be kept informed. At this stage, the parent should be overly cautious and informative with the Agency. Advise parents to watch for certain elements of the order of protection that may seem overly involved. If the children were placed with the other parent (i.e., not with the client), discuss the way custody courts will address this issue and how visitation will work.

Failing to secure the children's return home can be devastating to parents. Counsel's job is to help the parent survive the moment and appreciate that she is in a marathon. What matters most once the court hearing is over is what happens over the coming months. To boost the parent's spirits, counsel should reinforce all the things the parent has done well, including whatever favorable things the court may have said about the parent. Remind the client that progress is being made little by little and that regaining custody of the children is still very much in play (when that is true). Remind the parent of the continued importance to stay in touch with the caseworker and counsel. Discuss any barriers to attending services and the importance of steady participation in services, especially visitation. Remind the client of good progress and encourage her to keep up the good work. Set up a time to talk again and make a plan for ensuring that any missing services get added.

If evidence at the court hearing revealed that the parent has not followed through on visitation or treatment, counsel should reinforce the importance of doing better going forward. Once again it may be necessary to be a reality check. Among counsel's responsibilities are to ensure the client understands that the court will interpret the parent's failings as evidence that she does not want custody of her child. Listen to the parent's response. Explain that counsel's responsibility includes clarifying what the parent needs to do to secure custody. Remind her that not showing up at visits or therapy sends the wrong message. Saying that she wants to regain custody is one thing, showing that she wants it by working on becoming a better parent is more important. Remind the parent that an important part of counsel's job is to bring all the positive steps the parent has taken to the judge's attention and that, when she has not taken those steps, there is too little to tell the judge.

When the parent is doing very little to comply with the case plan, try to leave space for the parent to talk about a different result. Some parents find it too difficult to acknowledge that they do not feel up to the task of caring for their child. Counsel must help parents understand that counsel's role is to serve the client, not to tell her how to live her life. Whatever the parent's goal, even if it involves releasing parental rights, explore the concrete steps needed to achieve that goal, and have the parent decide if she will take them.

CHAPTER 11

The Indian Child Welfare Act

David Meyers

11.01 Introduction

In 1978, Congress passed the Indian Child Welfare Act (ICWA), 92 Stat. 3069, 25 U.S.C. §§ 1901–1963 (2014), in response to "abusive child welfare practices that resulted in the separation of large numbers of Indian children from their families and tribes through adoption or foster care placement, usually in non-Indian homes." *Mississippi Band of Choctaw Indians v. Holyfield*, 490 U.S. 30, 32 (1989). "[T]he primary mischief" Congress intended to prevent by enacting the law was "to counteract the unwarranted removal of Indian children from Indian families due to the cultural insensitivity and biases of social workers and state courts." *Adoptive Couple v. Baby Girl*, 133 S. Ct. 2552, 2561 (2013). ICWA established "minimum Federal standards for the removal of Indian children from their families and the placement of such children in foster or adoptive homes." *Id.*

The law was enacted after Congress conducted extensive hearings leading it to find that "an alarmingly high percentage of Indian families are broken up by the removal, often unwarranted, of their children from them by nontribal public and private agencies and that an alarmingly high percentage of such children are placed in non-Indian foster and adoptive homes and institutions." 25 U.S.C. § 1901(4) (2013). To address the tragic destruction of Indian families, the law established minimum federal standards for the removal of Indian children from their families so that the "unique values of Indian culture" could be protected. *Id.* § 1902. Many have praised ICWA's standards as being the "gold standard" which should guide decision making in all child welfare cases.

Despite ICWA, the child welfare system's discriminatory treatment of Indian children still persists. Numerous studies have found that a disproportionate number of Indian children enter and remain in foster care despite ICWA's intent to prevent this precise outcome. *See* Child Welfare Info. Gateway, U.S. Dep't of Health & Human Servs., Addressing Racial Disproportionality in Child Welfare 3 (2011). The best way to ensure rigorous adherence to ICWA is for parents' counsel across the country to become familiar with its provisions.

This chapter provides an overview of ICWA's key protections. It details these protections as applied to placing children into foster care or terminating parental rights. Lawyers representing parents in child welfare matters should possess a comprehensive understanding of ICWA because it provides Indian families with substantial protections beyond what is available to non-Indian families.

11.02 When Does ICWA Apply?

The law applies in all proceedings involving the foster care placement, potential termination of parental rights, or an adoptive placement of an "Indian child," defined as anyone under eighteen who is a member of, or eligible for membership in, a federally recognized Indian tribe *and* the biological child of a member of an Indian tribe. 25 U.S.C. § 1903(4). State law may use a more expansive definition. The Secretary of the Interior, through the Bureau of Indian Affairs (BIA), publishes an annual list of federally recognized tribes in the Federal Register. Because ICWA only protects children who are members of or eligible for membership in federally recognized tribes, children belonging to Canadian tribes, other foreign tribes, and non-federally recognized tribes are excluded, though state laws may protect such children. *See, e.g.*, Iowa Code § 232.7 (2014) (enforcing that child custody proceedings for Indian children comply with ICWA); Minn. Stat. § 257.0651 (2014). Whether a particular child is a member of or eligible for membership is ultimately a tribal determination; membership requirements differ from tribe to tribe. *See, e.g.*, *In re A.G.*, 326 Mont. 403, 401, 109 P.3d 756, 759 (2005); *In re A.L.W.*, 108 Wash. App. 664, 671, 32 P.3d 297, 301 (2001).

Based on this understanding, parent's counsel should investigate whether his or her client's child is a member of or eligible for membership in an Indian tribe. At a minimum, this investigation should include interviewing the client and his or her family members about possible Indian ancestry and reviewing all the documents in the case to see whether there is a possibility that the child is Indian. These steps should be taken at the outset of the proceedings, preferably in the first client interview. Counsel should promptly inform the Agency and court when there is reason to believe the case is covered by ICWA.

11.03 Requirement to Provide Notice to the Tribe

Because a tribe makes the ultimate decision whether a child is eligible for membership, tribes must receive prompt, written notice when a court "has reason to know that an Indian child is involved." 25 U.S.C. § 1912(a). If the identity of the tribe cannot be determined, notice must be given to the Secretary of the Interior.

The Bureau of Indian Affairs' guidelines set forth the most common circumstances giving rise to a reasonable belief that a child may be an Indian. *See* Guidelines for State Courts; Indian Child Custody Proceedings, 44 Fed. Reg. 228, 67586 (Nov. 26, 1979). The regulations call for notice when "[a]ny party to the case informs the court that the child is an Indian child," "[a]ny public or state-licensed agency . . . has discovered information which suggests that the child is an Indian child," or "[a]n officer of the court involved in the proceeding has knowledge that the child may be an Indian child." *Id.* As the Vermont Supreme Court explained, federal law prefers "to err on the side of giving notice and examining thoroughly whether the juvenile is an Indian child." *In re MCP*, 153 Vt. 275, 288-89, 571 A.2d 627, 635 (1989). Many states have made the inquiry into a child's Indian status a continuing obligation. *See, e.g.*, CAL. WELF. & INST. CODE § 224.3 (2014); COLO. REV. STAT. § 19-1-126 (2014); IOWA CODE § 232B.4 (2014).

The notice requirement is so central to the statutory scheme that courts may not conduct any hearings concerning a foster care placement or termination of parental rights until "at least ten days after receipt of notice by the parent or Indian custodian and the tribe or the Secretary." 25 U.S.C. § 1912(a). Parent's counsel should insist that the court comply with this law and not enter orders regarding placement or termination of parental rights during the ten-day period. Only after the ten-day period has expired, and the tribe or the Secretary of Interior has not responded or has informed the court that the child is ineligible for membership, may the case proceed as any other. If the court receives notice that the child is eligible for tribal membership, then ICWA applies. If the child is an Indian child, federal law gives parents and tribes up to twenty additional days to prepare for a hearing after receiving notice. *See id.*

Not all states have embraced ICWA's full reach. A minority of state courts have limited ICWA's reach by creating an "exception" to ICWA's reach—the "Existing Indian Family Exception." States that recognize the exception deny ICWA's protection to children who have not been living with an Indian parent or who were not closely connected with the tribe prior to the court proceedings. *See, e.g.*, *Rye v. Weasel*, 934 S.W.2d 257, 261 (Ky. 1996); *C.E.H. v. L.M.W.*, 837 S.W.2d 947, 952 (Mo. Ct. App. 1992); *In re K.L.D.R.*, 2009 WL1138130 (Tenn. Ct. App. 2009). Counsel should learn whether this exception applies in their jurisdiction and should work with appellate attorneys to challenge it because it contravenes ICWA's plain language.

11.04 Tribe's Right to Intervene and to Transfer Jurisdiction

Once a determination is made that the case involves an "Indian child," the proceedings change dramatically. ICWA grants an Indian "custodian" and the Indian child's tribe a non-waivable right to intervene in the child protection proceeding. *See* 25 U.S.C. § 1911(c). A "custodian" refers to someone to whom a tribe has granted custody. This right can be exercised at any point in the proceeding. *See id.* § 1914.

Intervention allows Indian tribes and custodians to participate fully in all phases of the case. They have the right to receive discovery, present evidence, cross-examine witnesses, and be heard on every issue. Technically, these intervenors become formal parties entitled to access to the full court record. When a tribe intervenes, parent's counsel should strive to work closely with the tribal representative to achieve a mutually acceptable outcome.

Upon intervention, the tribe may proceed in several ways: the tribe may choose not to participate, it may participate fully in the state child welfare proceedings, or it may request that the case be transferred to tribal court.

Whether the court must transfer to tribal court upon a proper application hinges on a number of factors. ICWA establishes dual jurisdictions for tribes and state courts. Tribes have exclusive jurisdiction over child custody matters when the Indian child resides or is domiciled on an Indian reservation, or when the child is a ward of the tribal court, unless federal law provides otherwise. *See* 25 U.S.C. § 1911(a). Even when an Indian child resides with the tribe, a state court can assert emergency jurisdiction to prevent the child's imminent physical harm. *See* 25 U.S.C. § 1922. However, when the Agency removes a child residing with the tribe, federal law requires that it "expeditiously initiate a child custody proceeding . . . [and] transfer the child to the jurisdiction of the appropriate Indian tribe, or restore the child to the parent or Indian custodian, as may be appropriate." *Id.*

When an Indian child does not live with the tribe and is not a ward of the tribe, either court may hear the matter. If a party requests that the case be transferred to tribal court, the parents will be given an opportunity to support or oppose the request. In the absence of an objection by the parent, the court must transfer the case to tribal court unless there is "good cause" not to. *See* 25 U.S.C. § 1911(b). ICWA is silent on what constitutes good cause. The Bureau of Indian Affairs guidelines, however, set forth several factors that constitute such cause:

(1) if the Indian child's tribe has no tribal court as defined by the Act to which the case can be transferred;

(2) the proceeding is at an advanced stage when the petition to transfer is received and the petitioner did not file the petition promptly after receiving notice;

(3) the Indian child is over twelve and objects to the transfer;

(4) the evidence necessary to decide the case could not be adequately presented in the tribal court without undue hardship to the parties or the witnesses;

(5) the parents of a child over five are not available and the child has had little or no contact with the child's tribe or members of the child's tribe. Guidelines for State Courts; Indian Child Custody Proceedings, 44 Fed. Reg. 67,584, 67,591 § C.3 (Nov. 26, 1979).

Courts interpreting these guidelines apply them in light of the strong legislative purpose behind ICWA to protect the rights of tribes. Many go so far as to place the burden on the party opposing the party opposing the transfer to show there is good cause not to do so by clear and convincing evidence. *See, e.g., In re Armell*, 550 N.E.2d 1060, 1064 (Ill. App. Ct. 1990); *In re M.E.M.*, 195 Mont. 329, 339, 635 P.2d 1313, 1317 (1981); *In re S.W.*, OK CIV APP 26, 41 P.3d 1003, 1013 (2001).

One of the most important tasks for counsel in these cases is to discuss with the client in depth the advantages and disadvantages of transferring the case to tribal court. Some tribal courts may be more reluctant to terminate parental rights than state courts, a powerful reason for parents to prefer tribal court. But tribal courts may have fewer resources to offer parents and may be located far from where the parent resides. To help parents make an informed decision, counsel should contact the tribe directly to find out as much as possible about the tribe's approach to child welfare cases. The determination of which court will resolve the underlying case is a particularly critical decision in ICWA cases.

Once a case is transferred to tribal court, the laws enacted by the tribe governing child welfare proceedings will govern. The protections in ICWA detailed below do not apply when a case is being heard in tribal court. If counsel remains on the case in tribal court, she will have to become an expert on the laws of the tribe. These are commonly available on the Internet. Although tribal laws tend to be similar to state law, they are rarely identical.

If the case remains in state court, ICWA provides a set of robust protections to safeguard the rights of parents and children. The protections applicable to state-initiated child welfare proceedings are explained in the following sections.

11.05 Protections Involving the Child's Removal from the Home

ICWA seeks to protect Indian children from being improperly removed from their families. If a child is voluntarily placed into foster care by his or her parents, the child must be returned to parental custody if that voluntary consent is subsequently withdrawn. 25 U.S.C. § 1913(b).

ICWA also prohibits the involuntary placement of a child into foster care unless there is clear and convincing evidence, including testimony from a qualified expert witness, that the continued custody of the child by the parent or Indian custodian is likely to result in serious emotional or physical damage to the child. 25 U.S.C. § 1912(e). This is a very substantial protection for parents and children, requiring a greater showing than in non-ICWA cases before a court may approve the continued placement of an Indian child. Even after showing clearly and convincingly that there are statutory grounds for removal, federal law requires that the Agency show that "active efforts" were made to prevent the removal. *See id.* § 1912(d).

These legal requirements raise several questions: (1) what is a foster care placement under ICWA; (2) what type of evidence would meet the clear and convincing evidence threshold; (3) what is a qualified expert witness; and (4) what type of efforts constitutes active efforts. These questions are discussed below.

11.05(a) What Is a Foster Care Placement?

ICWA's definition of a "foster care placement" is very expansive. It includes all court-ordered placements in which the parent cannot demand the child's return, even including private causes of action. *Id.* § 1903(1)(i).

11.05(b) What Type of Evidence Can Meet the "Clear and Convincing" Threshold?

To sustain its case for removal under ICWA, the state must clearly and convincingly prove that the child's removal is necessary to prevent serious emotional or physical harm. The evidence must show the nexus between the conditions and the damage and cannot simply be generalized allegations about community or family poverty, crowded or inadequate housing, or nonconforming social behavior. *See* Guidelines for State Courts; Indian Child Custody Proceedings, 44 Fed. Reg. 67,584 § D.3 (Nov. 26, 1979).

11.05(c) What Is a Qualified Expert Witness?

To place a child in foster care in an ICWA case, the state must present testimony from a qualified expert witness. According to the BIA, the following may testify as such an expert: (1) a member of the Indian child's tribe who is recognized by the tribal community as knowledgeable in tribal customs and how they pertain to family organization; (2) a lay expert having substantial experience in the delivery of child and family services to Indians and extensive knowledge of prevailing social and cultural standards and child rearing practices within the Indian child's tribe; or (3) a professional having substantial education and experience in the area of her specialty. *See id.* at 44 Fed. Reg. 67,584 § D.4 (Nov. 26, 1979).

State courts have varied in implementing the expert witness requirement. Some states require the witness to "provide the Court with knowledge of the social and cultural aspects of Indian life to diminish the risk of any cultural bias." *In re N.L.*, 1988 OK 39, 754 P.2d 863, 867 (1988). Others, however, allow a person to qualify as an expert even if he or she has no knowledge of, or experience with, Indian culture. *See, e.g.*, *Rachelle S. v. Ariz. Dep't of Econ. Sec.*, 191 Ariz. 518, 520, 958 P.2d 459, 461 (1998); *In re Tucker*, 76 Or. App. 673, 682, 710 P.2d 793, 798 (1985). Similarly, states vary as to whether a social worker at the Agency can be qualified as the ICWA expert witness and whether the testimony of the witness must be based on actual interactions with the family. *See, e.g.*, *In re Kreft*, 148 Mich. App. 682, 688, 384 N.W.2d 843, 846 (1986) (allowing qualification where the social worker possessed additional qualifications); *In re A.N.*, 325 Mont. 379, 383, 106 P.3d 556, 559 (2005) (allowing expert witness to testify based on review of the file).

Even more than with ordinary experts, counsel in an ICWA case should carefully review a putative expert witness's credentials before conceding that the witness qualifies under federal law. In non-ICWA cases, it may not be crucial to prevent a witness from being found an "expert." In ICWA cases, however, the state must present an expert or it cannot prevail. The law is clear that the state's failure to present a qualified expert witness deprives a court of authority to remove an Indian child and requires reversal on appeal. *See* 25 U.S.C. § 1914(f); *In re N.L.*, 754 P.2d at 867. Accordingly, counsel should litigate this issue thoughtfully. Ordinarily, counsel should request the opportunity to *voir dire* the witness, carefully review the witness's resume, and attempt to demonstrate that the witness possessed very limited special knowledge. Counsel should inquire into the putative expert's knowledge of the tribe and its customs.

Counsel should also consider countering a qualified expert witness by calling an expert witness for the parent. The best way to find qualified expert witnesses is to contact members of the tribe, including tribal social workers, to locate a suitable person with knowledge of tribal customs.

11.05(d) What Are "Active Efforts"?

ICWA requires state agencies, prior to involuntarily removing children from their parents, to make "active efforts" to prevent the breakup of the Indian family and to demonstrate that those efforts were unsuccessful. *See* 25 U.S.C. § 1912(d); *see also D.J. v. P.C.*, 36 P.3d 663, 672 (Alaska 2001) (holding that ICWA requires "active efforts" be made to prevent breaking up Indian families); *In re N.B.*, 199 P.3d 16, 24 (Colo. App. 2007); *In re Nicole B.*, 175 Md. App. 450, 461, 927 A.2d 1194, 1200 (2007). This requirement imposes a heightened obligation on agencies to take steps to prevent placements than exists in cases involving non-Indian children (requiring "reasonable efforts"). *See In re Nicole B.*, 175 Md. App. at 472, 927 A.2d at 1206.

Several courts have captured the essence of this requirement. The Montana Supreme Court observed that "[t]he term active efforts, by definition, implies heightened responsibility compared to passive efforts." *In re A.N.*, 325 Mont. at 384, 106 P.3d at 560. Similarly, the Alaska Supreme Court distinguished between active and passive efforts: "passive efforts entail merely drawing up a reunification plan and requiring the 'client' to use his or her own resources to . . . bring . . . it to fruition. . . . Active efforts, on the other hand, include 'tak[ing] the client through the steps of the plan rather than requiring the plan to be performed on its own.'" *A.M. v. State*, 945 P.2d 296, 306 (Alaska 1997) (internal citations omitted).

When making active efforts, the Agency must take into account "the prevailing social and cultural conditions and the way of life of the Indian child's tribe and must use the available resources of the extended family, the tribe, Indian social services agencies, and individual Indian care givers." *See* Guidelines for State Courts; Indian Child Custody Proceedings, 44 Fed. Reg. 67,584, 67,592 (Nov. 26, 1979). Ultimately, the "active efforts" requirement imposes a duty on the Agency to engage the family.

Unlike the Adoption and Safe Families Act, which contains exceptions to the ordinary requirement imposed on agencies to make reasonable efforts to reunify a family, ICWA contains no exceptions. As a result, in every case involving an Indian child, agencies must make active efforts to prevent the removal of the child. *See In re J.S.B. Jr.*, 2005 S.D. 3, ¶ 19, 691 N.W.2d 611, 617 (S.D. 2005); *D.J. v. P.C.*, 36 P.3d at 674. Nor does the fact that a parent is incarcerated excuse the Agency from making active efforts. *See, e.g., In re D.G.*, 2004 S.D. 54, ¶ 19, 679 N.W.2d 497, 502 (2004).

11.06 Placement Preferences

If a court removes an Indian child from his or her home, ICWA requires that the child be placed in the least restrictive setting which most approximates a family and in which his special needs, if any, may be met. The child also must be placed within reasonable proximity to his or her home, taking into account any special needs of the child. *See* 25 U.S.C. § 1915(b).

In addition to these general requirements, ICWA requires the court, absent a showing of good cause by clear and convincing evidence, to utilize the following hierarchy when placing a child in foster care: (1) a member of the Indian child's extended family; (2) a foster home licensed, approved, or specified by the Indian child's tribe; (3) an Indian foster home licensed or approved by an authorized non-Indian licensing authority; or (4) an institution for children approved by an Indian tribe or operated by an Indian organization which has a program suitable to meet the Indian child's needs. *See id.* § 1915(b).

The BIA Guidelines set out three factors that may, either singly or together, constitute good cause to deviate from the placement preferences: (1) the request of the biological parents or the child when the child is of sufficient age; (2) the extraordinary physical or emotional needs of the child as established by testimony of qualified expert witnesses; or (3) the unavailability of suitable homes that meet the preference criteria. *See* Guidelines for State Courts; Indian Child Custody Proceedings, 44 Fed. Reg. 67,584, 67,594 (Nov. 26, 1979). Some state courts have applied criteria other than these as good cause not to follow the placement preference of ICWA, including a child's bonding to a particular caregiver. *See In re Baby Boy Doe*, 127 Idaho 452, 462, 902 P.2d 477, 487 (1995); *In re B.G.J.*, 281 Kan. 552, 557, 133 P.3d 1, 5 (2006). Other courts have treated the BIA Guidelines as limiting what constitutes good cause. *See In re S.E.G.*, 521 N.W.2d 357, 363 (Minn. 1994), *cert. denied sub nom*, *Campbell v. Leech Lake Band of Chippewa Indians*, 513 U.S. 1127 (1995). Counsel should be prepared to argue that the BIA Guideline's definition of good cause is binding on the court.

A few points should be emphasized about the placement preferences. First, a parent's desire not to apply the placement preferences constitutes "good cause" to deviate from the specified preferences. *See In re Baby Boy Doe,* 127 Idaho at 461, 902 P.2d at 486; *In re Baby Girl Doe*, 262 Mont. 280, 285, 865 P.2d 1090, 1095 (1993); *In re Child of Indian Heritage (Indian Child II)*, 111 N.J. 155, 170, 543 A.2d 925, 932 (1988). Second, ICWA defers to the tribe to determine who is an "extended family member." As such, any member of the tribe could qualify as a relative in an ICWA case, even if state law offers a more restrictive definition of a relative. Third, the Agency cannot refuse to approve placement of an Indian child within the tribal community because of preconceived notions about conditions within the tribal community being inadequate. *See In re M.E.M.*, 195 Mont. 329, 338, 635 P.2d 1313, 1318 (1981). If the tribal social services agency approves a placement, the inquiry about the adequacy of the home should end. In fact, the court must consider the prevailing social and cultural standards of the Indian community in which the parent or extended family members reside, or with which the parent or extended family members maintain social and cultural ties, when determining placement. *See* 25 U.S.C. § 1915(d). Finally, the placement preferences apply any time a child's placement changes, unless the child is being returned home.

Despite the placement priorities specified in the law, the tribe still retains the ability to change the placement preferences by passing a resolution so long as the placement is the least restrictive setting appropriate to the particular needs of the child. *See id.* § 1915(c). For example, a tribe could determine that a child should be placed in a licensed Indian foster home as opposed to with a family member. In determining whether to adopt the different placement preferences of the tribe, the court shall consider the preference of the Indian child or parent where appropriate. *See id.* § 1915(a).

11.07 Termination of Parental Rights

A primary reason for ICWA's passage was to prevent the unnecessary permanent destruction of Indian families. Accordingly, ICWA employs the most exacting proof, combined with the highest standard of proof required for terminating the parental rights of an Indian child. To prevail in a termination case, the state must demonstrate beyond a reasonable doubt that the continued custody of the child by the parent or Indian custodian is likely to result in serious emotional or physical damage to the child. *See* 25 U.S.C. § 1912(f). As part of its burden, the state must also show that it made active efforts to reunify the family and is required to introduce the testimony a qualified expert witnesses—two requirements that are discussed in section 11.05. In addition to meeting all of these requirements, the state must also meet the requirements to terminate a parent's rights under state law. Chapter 14 provides more detailed guidance on how to litigate termination of parental rights cases.

11.08 Remedies

Federal law allows "any Indian child who is the subject of any action for foster care placement or termination of parental rights under State law, any parent or Indian custodian from whose custody such child was removed . . . to petition any court of competent jurisdiction to invalidate such action upon a showing that such action violated any provision of sections 1911, 1912, and 1913." 25 U.S.C. § 1914.

When there has been an ICWA violation which is in the client's interest to raise, counsel can raise the issue in the trial court, asking that the order be set aside, appeal the court's order in state court, or file a separate federal action claiming a violation of ICWA. *See* 25 U.S.C. § 1914; *see also Doe v. Mann*, 415 F.3d 1038, 1047 (9th Cir. 2005).

Upon a finding that ICWA was violated, any order that resulted from the violation should be set aside. 25 U.S.C. § 1914. However, when the violation was simply a failure to provide notice to an Indian tribe, then the matter will likely be remanded to the trial court for proper notice to be provided to the relevant tribe. If the child is found to be a member of the tribe or eligible for membership and the child of a member, then the case would begin anew with the ICWA protections applying. However, if, after notice is provided, the child is found not to be a member of the tribe, then the order in question will likely be affirmed. *See, e.g.*, *In re I.E.M.*, 233 Mich. App. 438, 447–48, 592 N.W.2d 751, 757–58 (1999); *In re M.S.S.*, 86 Wash. App. 127, 137, 936 P.2d 36, 28 (1997).

11.09 *Adoptive Couple v. Baby Girl* and Its Impact on Child Welfare Proceedings

In 2013 the Supreme Court decided *Adoptive Couple v. Baby Girl*, only the second case ever to interpret ICWA. *See* 133 S. Ct. 2552. The decision interpreted a very small piece of ICWA regarding private placement adoptions. This section explains the holding and why it is not material to child welfare or involuntary terminations of parental rights.

Adoptive Couple involved a child born out of wedlock voluntarily placed by her mother to live with an adoptive resource shortly after her birth. The birth mother was non-Indian; the birth father was Indian. Before the child's placement, the birth father had never had custody of the child and had abandoned her within the meaning of controlling state law.

Adoptive Couple held that when "the adoption of an Indian child is voluntarily and lawfully initiated by a non-Indian parent with sole custodial rights, the ICWA's primary goal of preventing the unwarranted *removal* of Indian children and the dissolution of Indian families is not implicated." 133 S. Ct. at 2561. As applied to a non-Indian birth mother voluntarily placing her out-of-wedlock child for adoption, the Court interpreted the meaning of three ICWA provisions: §§ 1912 (d), (f) and § 1915(a).

Section 1912(d) conditions involuntary termination of parental rights with respect to an Indian child on a showing that remedial efforts have been made to prevent the "breakup of the Indian family." The Court held that for adoptions of newborns born out of wedlock, the provision "is inapplicable when, as here, the parent abandoned the Indian child before birth and never had custody of the child." 133 S. Ct. at 2563. The Court stressed that its decision is limited to the facts of the case before it. *See id.* at 2562.

The critical statutory interpretation the Court made was that "Congress did not extend the heightened protections of § 1912(d) and § 1912(f) to all biological fathers" when their children are voluntarily placed for adoption at birth. *See* 133 S. Ct. at 2562. The Court expressly limited its holding to a particular kind of adoption: "only in the case of a parent who abandoned his or her child prior to birth and never had physical or legal custody." *Id.* at 2563, 2579 n.8.

Comparably, the Court read § 1912(f), requiring a heightened showing that a child would suffer serious harm if allowed to remain in the parent's continued custody before terminating parental rights as inapplicable where the mother voluntarily placed her child at birth and the Indian father had abandoned the child and never had custody. In the Court's words, "[i]n sum, when, as here, the adoption of an Indian child is voluntarily and lawfully initiated by a non-Indian parent with sole custodial rights, the ICWA's primary goal of preventing the unwarranted removal of Indian children and the dissolution of Indian families is not implicated." 133 S. Ct at 2561.

Finally, the Court held § 1915(a)'s requirement of giving a preference "to a placement with (1) a member of the child's extended family; (2) other members of the Indian child's tribe; or (3) other Indian families" also is "inapplicable in cases where no alternative party has formally sought to adopt the child." 133 S. Ct. at 2561. Because no extended family member or other tribal member came forward to seek to adopt the child, no preference to another person was required.

The Court not only expressly limited the holding to cases in which the sole custodial non-Indian parent of an Indian child voluntarily initiated the adoption proceeding, but also endorsed Congress's "sensible requirement" that states undertake remedial efforts to prevent the needless breakup of a family "when applied to state social workers who might otherwise be too quick to remove Indian children from their Indian families." 133 S. Ct. at 2563.

What most concerned the Court in *Adoptive Couple* was if federal law, through § 1912(d), mandated measures such as "attempting to stimulate [Biological] Father's desire to be a parent," that would mean that "prospective adoptive parents [would be] required to engage in the bizarre undertaking of 'stimulat[ing]' a biological father's 'desire to be a parent.'" *Id.* The Court stressed that such a requirement "would surely dissuade some [potential adoptive parents] from seeking to adopt Indian children." *Id.* This would not only reduce the potential pool of adoptive parents, but it "would, in turn, unnecessarily place vulnerable Indian children at a unique disadvantage in finding a permanent and loving home, even in cases where neither an Indian parent nor the relevant tribe objects to the adoption." *Id.*

None of these concerns has any application when state officials are responsible for the placement of Indian children into foster care. First, such placements are quintessentially "removals"—the precise focus of ICWA. In contrast, the Court stressed in *Adoptive Couple* that there was no removal of any kind in the case. Second, when children are removed by state officials and placed in temporary foster care, the goal of all such placements is striving to reunite the child with his or her family of origin. *See* 42 U.S.C. § 671(a)(15)(B) (requiring states receiving federal funds for foster care and adoption assistance to make "reasonable efforts . . . to preserve and reunify families" prior to foster care placement or removal of a child from its home). This goal serves as the central theme of child welfare practice whose first principle, under both federal and state law, is to offer services to parents whose children are in foster care so that the children can be safely returned to their families if such return can be accomplished in a reasonable period of time. *See* Adoption and Safe Families Act, Pub. L. No. 105-89, (codified at 42 U.S.C. §§ 620–79 (2014)). As a consequence, there is no danger of "plac[ing] Indian children at a unique disadvantage in finding a permanent and loving home" as the active efforts requirement of ICWA furthers this goal. *Adoptive Couple*, 133 S. Ct. at 2564.

Third, there is no comparable worry of reducing the potential pool of adoptive parents because foster parents, unlike the prospective adoptive parents in *Adoptive Couple*, always participate in child welfare matters on the understanding that the foster child may appropriately be returned to his or her family of origin. To the extent the "active" (or "reasonable") efforts requirement in federal and state law deters potential foster parents from coming forward, it has been deterring such persons for a generation. Of course, that is the very point of child welfare. Foster agencies do not wish to engage foster parents who step forward to accept foster children into their homes on the condition that the children must be available for adoption. Deterring potential foster parents who do not wish to relinquish foster children temporarily placed with them furthers the principles and values of child welfare policy.

Fourth, the Court expressly explained that § 1912(d) is inapplicable only because "'the breakup of the Indian family' has long since occurred" when a child is voluntarily placed for adoption by the mother and "an Indian parent abandons an Indian child prior to birth and that child has never been in the Indian parent's legal or physical custody." 133 S. Ct. at 2562. In the child welfare context, however, "the breakup of the Indian family" is continuing during the foster care placement phase of the case.

Fifth, the Court acknowledged Congress's purpose "to help preserve the cultural identity and heritage of Indian tribes," but stressed that its interpretation of ICWA was based in part on its concern that a contrary interpretation of the law "would put certain vulnerable children at a great disadvantage solely because an ancestor—even a remote one—was an Indian." 133 S. Ct. at 2565. In the Court's words, the interpretation the Court placed on ICWA as applied to the adoption case before it was necessary to prevent "a biological Indian father [from] abandon[ing] his child in utero and refus[ing] any support for the birth mother—perhaps contributing to the mother's decision to put the child up for adoption—and then [ ] play his ICWA trump card at the eleventh hour to override the mother's decision and the child's best interests." *Id.* None of these considerations has any pertinence to child welfare cases. There can be no eleventh-hour intervention by Indian birth fathers. Their presence is called for from the beginning of the case by requiring active efforts to identify them. When those efforts are unavailing, the case may proceed in the direction that furthers the child's best interests.

Despite this, in 2014, the Alaska Supreme Court in *Native Village of Tununak v. State*, 334 P.3d 168 (Alaska 2014), applied *Baby Girl* to a child welfare case. The case involved the adoption of an Indian child by her non-Indian foster parents after the parents' rights had been terminated. The child's Indian grandmother opposed the adoption and unsuccessfully invoked 25 U.S.C. § 1915(a)'s preference for Indian relatives over non-Indian potential adoptive parents. The court held that the grandmother could benefit from this preference only if she had filed a competing petition to adopt. This ruling goes beyond *Baby Girl's* requirement that an Indian relative must have "come forward" to express a desire to adopt the child (without clarifying what precise steps the relative must take to meet this requirement). The Alaska court stressed the continuing vitality of 25 U.S.C. § 1915(b)'s requirement that a preference be given to placing an Indian child with a member of the extended family or a foster home specified by the child's tribe. But it also made clear that if the child is placed with a non-Indian foster family, the Indian relative must formally seek to adopt the child to benefit from the statutory preference that the child be adopted by an Indian relative over a non-Indian relative.

11.10 Conclusion

As in all cases, attorneys representing parents in cases involving Indian children must counsel their clients and ascertain where they want their children placed. They should then use the protections in ICWA to further those goals. ICWA provides powerful tools for attorneys to get children placed with extended family members or members of the Indian tribe, if the parent desires. At the same time, ICWA gives parents the tools to block actions by the tribe to which they do not agree. Thus, having a strong knowledge of the placement preferences, how to deviate from those preferences, and how to block the application of those preferences is crucial.

CHAPTER 12

Representing Parents with Disabilities

Joshua B. Kay

12.01 Introduction: Scope and Nature of the Problem

Parents with disabilities are more likely than other parents to become involved in the child welfare system, and once involved, their cases are more likely to end in termination of parental rights. This chapter covers basic information about parents with disabilities and child welfare involvement, including the prevalence of disability among parents generally and the frequency with which parents with disabilities are involved in child welfare cases. It discusses why these parents are disproportionately involved in child welfare proceedings and the biases of professionals that contribute not only to this frequent involvement but also to the poor outcomes in many of these cases. The chapter also covers the legal framework specifically applicable to these cases and key elements of effective advocacy, including how to raise claims under the Americans with Disabilities Act ("ADA"), 42 U.S.C. § 12101 (2014) to ensure that these parents' disabilities are reasonably accommodated when reunification services are provided.

12.01(a) Prevalence of Disability Among Parents and Frequency of Child Welfare Involvement

Many parents have a disability of some type, whether physical, sensory, cognitive, or psychiatric. National estimates indicate that at least 8.4 million and possibly more than 10 million parents with disabilities have children under the age of eighteen living in the home. *See* Megan Kirshbaum & Rhoda Olkin, *Parents with Physical, Systemic, or Visual Disabilities*, 20 Sexuality & Disability 65 (2002); Rhoda Olkin et al.,

Comparison of Parents with and Without Disabilities Raising Teens: Information from the NHIS and Two National Surveys, 51 REHABILITATION PSYCHOL. 43, 44 (2006). Child welfare issues are a significant concern for parents with disabilities, because these parents are disproportionately involved in the child welfare system. Once entangled in the system, they are far more likely than parents without disabilities to have their parental rights terminated. Parents with psychiatric and cognitive disabilities appear to be especially at risk of child welfare involvement and eventual termination of their parental rights. The problems that parents with disabilities encounter in the child welfare system are so severe that the National Council on Disability released an extensive report substantially dedicated to these issues. *See* NAT'L COUNCIL ON DISABILITY, ROCKING THE CRADLE: ENSURING THE RIGHTS OF PARENTS WITH DISABILITIES AND THEIR CHILDREN (2012).

Parents with cognitive or psychiatric disabilities are more likely than non-disabled parents to access state services, inviting close scrutiny by state personnel, and they have considerable contact with professionals who are mandated reporters of suspected child abuse and neglect. *See* Susan Kerr, *The Application of the American with Disabilities Act to the Termination of the Parental Rights of Individuals with Mental Disabilities*, 16 J. CONTEMP. HEALTH L. & POL'Y 387, 403 (2000). These professionals are often the source of a Children's Protective Services (CPS) referral, and they have considerable credibility with CPS, so their reports are likely to prompt the Agency to intervene in the matter. *See id.* This situation contributes to the high rate of child welfare involvement for these parents and eventual termination of their parental rights. It is estimated that among mothers with mental illness, 40 to 75 percent lose custody of one or more of their children, a range of rates substantially higher than for mothers without mental illness. *See* Colby Brunt & Leigh Goodmark, *Parenting in the Face of Prejudice: The Need for Representation for Parents with Mental Illness*, 36 CLEARINGHOUSE REV. 295, 297–98 (2002). Even higher percentages have been found among parents with intellectual disabilities, which may be the group most likely to become entangled in a CPS matter and eventually lose their parental rights. A prominent researcher has found in his sample groups that upward of 80 percent of parents with intellectual disabilities have experienced a termination of parental rights. *See* Maurice A. Feldman, *Parents with Intellectual Disabilities: Implications and Interventions, in* HANDBOOK OF CHILD ABUSE RESEARCH AND TREATMENT 401, 415 (John R. Lutzker ed., 1998). Rates of child welfare involvement for parents with physical and sensory disabilities also exceed those in the general population.

12.01(b) The Role of Poverty in the Involvement of Parents with Disabilities in the Child Welfare System

A significant contributor to the disproportionate involvement of parents with disabilities in the child welfare system is poverty. It is well established that poverty is among the strongest predictors of child welfare involvement, and parents with disabilities are twice as likely as other parents to be living in poverty. *See* Olkin, *supra* at 44. Whereas people with greater financial resources can purchase services privately to help them with family problems, those who live in poverty are more likely to come to the attention of the state by accessing public assistance. *See, e.g.*, Rosemary Shaw Sackett, *Terminating Parental Rights of the Handicapped*, 25 FAM. L.Q. 253, 290 (1991). This reliance on the public system of care contributes to the close scrutiny experienced by parents with disabilities. For example, parents with a cognitive or psychiatric disability are likely to obtain services from a publicly funded mental health clinic while also getting other public benefits, such as Social Security or cash assistance. These parents have a great deal of contact with various caseworkers and other professionals who may refer them to CPS.

12.01(c) Common Biases and Assumptions about Parents with Disabilities

Negative assumptions about parents with disabilities appear to be common among various professionals, including CPS caseworkers. The combination of frequent contact with professionals, close scrutiny by state workers, and negative assumptions about the parental fitness of people with disabilities can be devastating. For example, the belief that people with psychiatric conditions are dangerous and largely beyond help is widespread in the child welfare field and may motivate lackluster service planning. *See* Theresa Glennon, Symposium, *Walking with Them: Advocating for Parents with Mental Illness in the Child Welfare System*, 12 TEMP. POL. & CIV. RTS. L. REV. 273, 292 (2003). In contrast, high-quality research suggests that most parents with a psychiatric disability—or a cognitive disability—can provide appropriate parenting for their children with proper treatment and support.

Many caseworkers and other professionals, including psychologists who perform evaluations of parents in CPS cases, believe that a mental illness or, especially, a cognitive disability, cannot be changed, so no amount of treatment or support would allow the parent to provide adequate care for a child. Faced with this assumption, caseworkers are not motivated to engage in careful service planning with these parents, and psychologists are less likely to develop detailed treatment recommendations to address identified problems. In turn, the lack of treatment and other services increases the likelihood of eventual termination of parental rights.

The nature of disability varies a great deal within categories such as "cognitive," "psychiatric," "physical," and "sensory." There is wide variability even within subcategories, such as specific psychiatric diagnoses like schizophrenia or bipolar disorder, or cognitive disabilities such as intellectual or memory impairment. Placing a parent in a general disability or diagnostic category contributes little to an understanding of that individual parent's strengths, weaknesses, and needs. A categorical view of disability, in which the criteria for a particular category are emphasized instead of the person's actual capacities, contributes to the assumption that a disability is pervasive and static, because a caseworker may believe that a parent in a given category must have some set of characteristics assumed to be common to that category. *See* Alexander J. Tymchuk, *The Importance of Matching Educational Interventions to Parent Needs in Child Maltreatment: Issues, Methods, and Recommendations*, *in* HANDBOOK OF CHILD ABUSE RESEARCH AND TREATMENT 421, 422–23 (John R. Lutzker ed., 1998). In other words, caseworkers and other professionals may assess the category into which they have put the parent rather than the parent him- or herself. Once a person is categorized as disabled in some particular way, assumptions about what that means for parenting can dictate further actions by professionals. The child welfare system generally takes this approach to people with disabilities, which undermines service planning and increases the chances of termination of parental rights. *See id.*

In contrast, a "functional" perspective emphasizes what an individual person—rather than a broad category of people—can do and learn, and the circumstances under which the person successfully learns or applies what is learned. *See id.* at 22. A focus on abilities and contexts allows for a better fit between individual needs and educational methods and services. *See id.* The functional perspective on disability leads to a thorough assessment of relevant skills and deficits, which leads to the provision of high-quality services. This perspective fits well with the legal requirement that reasonable efforts include treatment plans tailored to the specific needs of parents and children.

Agency assumptions about disability are often reflected in petitions filed against parents with disabilities. When reviewing a termination Petition, it is especially important to determine whether the Petition indicates a nexus between the disability of the parent and actual parenting ability and any risk to the child. Does the Agency allege problems with actual parenting? Is a risk to the child articulated in the Petition? Or is there merely a recitation of disability-related facts, such as psychiatric symptoms that the parent may have? If no nexus to parenting ability is made clear, or the risk to the child is not described, it may be possible to get the Petition dismissed or challenge the Agency's request for removal. For strategies regarding removal hearings, *see* Chapter 4.

12.02 The Need for Appropriate Family Services

In nearly all cases, child welfare agencies must make "reasonable efforts" to prevent removal or reunify a family. Much of what constitutes reasonable efforts is included in a case service plan, which identifies family needs and services to address those needs. Although case service plans must be tailored to the specific needs of an individual case, in reality many are "one-size-fits-all" plans that list identical services for almost every case. These services may include parenting classes, training about domestic violence and anger management, a psychological evaluation, psychotherapy or counseling, drug testing, and substance abuse evaluation and treatment. Few parents, whether or not they have a disability, are well served by cookie cutter case service plans, but parents with disabilities may be most vulnerable to the ineffectiveness of the low-quality, generic services so often provided. It is difficult for parents with disabilities to demonstrate any benefit from services not provided in a manner that accommodates their disability, and this difficulty can put them on a path to termination of their parental rights.

For example, a parent with mental illness is likely to require psychiatric and psychotherapeutic care, yet there may be a long waiting list for public clinics. This problem is especially serious given the short time frames allowed in child welfare cases, time frames that courts may be reluctant to extend. Even once services are provided, they may be of low quality or otherwise a poor fit for the parent's needs, slowing any improvement. Furthermore, many public mental health services are structured as brief interventions, yet more intensive, long-term intervention may be necessary to give the parent adequate support and keep psychiatric symptoms at bay. Besides psychotherapeutic and psychiatric care, many parents with disabilities need concrete services, such as cash assistance, help with housing, medical care, food aid, and transportation. To develop, maintain, and make needed adjustments to an individualized package of services to make it effective, excellent assessment and thorough case reviews are needed. Too often, those elements are missing from child welfare cases, particularly when a parent has a disability and caseworkers and other professionals lack the expertise to work successfully with that person. For a more detailed discussion of case service planning for parents with disabilities, *see* Robert F. Kelly, *Family Preservation and Reunification Programs in Child Protection Cases: Effectiveness, Best Practices, and Implications for Legal Representation, Judicial Practice, and Public Policy*, 34 FAM. L.Q. 359, 380 (2000); Glennon, *supra* at 282–83, 296.

Tailored services can be effective for improving the parenting skills of parents with disabilities, including intellectual disabilities, contrary to the assumptions of many caseworkers and courts. For parents with intellectual disabilities, a group particularly vulnerable to inappropriate service provision and eventual termination of parental rights, Maurice Feldman has found that in-home interventions are best, particularly if they include techniques such as simplified instructions, pictorial prompts, modeling, feedback, role-playing, and positive reinforcement. He has further found that gains made by parents during these interventions are maintained for a longer term and that the rates of termination of parental rights were greatly reduced in the cases that received interventions compared to what the same parents had experienced in prior cases and to comparison groups. When in-home programming is not feasible, several hallmarks of these interventions can still be implemented, including one-on-one work, simplified instructions, modeling, visual cues, and the like. *See, e.g.*, Feldman, *supra*.

In cases involving parents with disabilities, obtaining appropriate services is among an attorney's greatest challenges, yet without them, there is little chance that the case will end favorably for the client. Unfortunately, there are relatively few professionals with adequate expertise in working with parents with disabilities, and fewer still work on contract with child welfare agencies. However, service provision is the area of a child welfare case most readily addressed by the ADA, which provides significant protection for these parents.

12.03 Applicability and Operation of the ADA in Child Welfare Cases

To obtain appropriate services for parents with disabilities, advocates must bring to bear more than just the reasonable efforts standard required in most child welfare cases. Services to prevent removal or reunify a family must comply with the ADA, which requires that a service recipient's disabilities be reasonably accommodated by the Agency. Title II of the ADA states that "no qualified individual with a disability shall, by reason of such disability, be excluded from participation in or be denied the benefits of the services, programs, or activities of a public entity, or be subjected to discrimination by any such entity." 42 U.S.C. § 12132. Reasonable accommodations under the ADA may include modifications to programs, extension of time limits, access to more specialized services, and the like. In essence, reasonable accommodations are designed to make services as effective for people with disabilities as they are for those without a disability such that similar results are likely to be achieved.

12.03(a) Raising an ADA Claim: Timing, Reasonable Efforts, and Reasonable Accommodations

The timing of an ADA claim in a child welfare case is crucial. Advocates must not wait to raise a claim for ADA protections until a supplemental Petition for termination of parental rights is filed. Numerous courts have declared that the ADA provides no defense to termination of parental rights. The reasoning for this holding has varied. Some courts have decided that termination of parental rights is not a service, program, or activity within the meaning of the ADA. *See, e.g., S.G. v. Barbour Co. Dep't of Human Res.*, 148 So. 439 (Ala. Civ. App. 2013); *In re Anthony P.*, 84 Cal. App. 4th 1112, 1116, 101 Cal. Rptr. 2d 423 (2000); *In re Antony B.*, 54 Conn. App. 463, 472, 735 A.2d 893 (1999); *Interest of B.K.F.*, 97-572, p. 5 (La. App. 5 Cir. 11/25/97), 704 So. 2d 314, 317; *Adoption of Gregory*, 434 Mass. 117, 121, 747 N.E.2d 120 (2001); *In re Terry*, 240 Mich. App. 14, 25, 610 N.W.2d 563 (2000); *Matter of La'Asia S.*, 191 Misc. 2d 28, 41–42, 739 N.Y.S.2d 898 (Fam. Ct. 2002); *Matter of Chance Jahmel B.*, 187 Misc. 2d 626, 632, 723 N.Y.S.2d 634 (Fam. Ct. 2001); *In re Kayla N.*, 900 A.2d 1202 (R.I. 2006), *cert. denied*, *Irving N. v. R.I. Dep't of Children, Youth & Families*, 549 U.S. 1252 (2007); *In re B.S.*, 166 Vt. 345, 351–52, 693 A.2d 716 (1997).

Other courts have decided that by the time termination of parental rights is sought, a parent can only bring a separate case alleging discrimination, but such a case would not constitute a defense to termination of parental rights. *See, e.g., In re Anthony P.*, 84 Cal. App. 4th at 1116; *In re Antony B.*, 54 Conn. App. at 472; *In re Doe*, 100 Haw. 335, 343, 60 P.3d 285 (2002); *In re E.E.*, 736 N.E.2d 791, 796 (Ind. Ct. App. 2000);

Interest of B.K.F., 97–572, p. 5 (La. App. 5 Cir. 11/25/97), 704 So. 2d at 317; *Matter of Chance Jahmel B.*, 187 Misc. 2d at 632; *In re Harmon*, No. 00-CA-2693, 2000 WL 1424822 (Ohio Ct. App. Sept. 25, 2000); *In re B.S.*, 166 Vt. at 351–52 (noting that juvenile court is of limited jurisdiction and may not consider claim under ADA); *In re Torrance P.*, 187 Wis. 2d 10, 522 N.W.2d 243 (Wisc. Ct. App. 1994). Instead, the parent would seek damages for discrimination in the provision of services, and termination of their parental rights would unlikely be affected.

Still other courts have held that allowing an ADA claim as a defense to termination would improperly elevate the rights of parents over those of children in child protection proceedings. *See, e.g., J.T. v. Ark. Dep't Human Servs.*, 329 Ark. 243, 258, 947 S.W.2d 761 (1997); *People in Interest of T.B.*, 12 P.3d 1221, 1224 (Colo. Ct. App. 2000); *In re Guardianship of R.G.L.*, 344 N.J. Super. 418, 441, 442, 782 A.2d 458 (2001). Finally, some courts have decided that the ADA was not intended to change obligations imposed by unrelated statutes, so the ADA cannot be used to avoid termination of parental rights. *See, e.g., Interest of T.B.*, 12 P.3d at 1224 (finding nothing in ADA indicates that a violation of the statute would interfere with the right of the state to terminate parental rights); *In re Antony B.*, 54 Conn. App. at 472; *In re Doe*, 100 Haw. at 343 (finding nothing in ADA or legislative history suggests it was intended to be grafted onto state statutes for purpose of supplementing remedies already provided for in such statutes); *In re Torrance P.*, 187 Wis. 2d at 16. Regardless of the reasoning, the holding remains the same: Waiting too long to raise an ADA claim in a child welfare case is fatal, because the ADA provides no defense to termination of parental rights.

There is broad agreement that an ADA claim may be brought when services provided by the Agency are so inadequate that they discriminate against parents with disabilities. Such a claim does not attack the termination of parental rights, nor does it wait until that late in a case; instead, it targets the Agency's provision of inadequate services and seeks an order that appropriate services be provided. Courts have found that the reasonable accommodation requirement under the ADA is consistent with the reasonable efforts requirement such that if the Agency does not make reasonable accommodations, the court cannot find that reasonable efforts were made to reunite the family. *See* Chris Watkins, Comment, *Beyond Status: The Americans with Disabilities Act and the Parental Rights of People Labeled Developmentally Disabled or Mentally Retarded*, 83 CAL. L. REV. 1415, 1473 (1995). *See also J.H. v. State Dep't of Health & Soc. Servs.*, 30 P.3d 79, 86 n.11 (Alaska 2001); *C.W. v. State Dep't of Health & Soc. Servs.*, 23 P.3d 52, 55 (Alaska 2001); *Cassidy v. Ark. Dep't Human Servs.*, 76 Ark. App. 190, 196–97, 61 S.W.3d 880 (2001) (Vaught, J., dissenting); *In re Antony B.*, 54 Conn. App. at 473 n.9; *In re E.E.*, 736 N.E.2d 791, 796 (Ind. Ct. App. 2000); *Stone v. Daviess Cnty. Div. of Children & Family Servs.*, 656 N.E.2d 824, 830 (Ind. Ct. App. 1995); *Adoption of Gregory*, 434 Mass. at 122–25; *In re Terry*, 240 Mich. App. at 25, 26; *In re Guardianship of R.G.L.*, 344 N.J. Super. at 8; *Matter of La'Asia S.*, 191 Misc.

2d at 42 (noting ADA guidelines are helpful supplement to State's diligent efforts standard); *Matter of Chance Jahmel B.*, 187 Misc. at 632; *In re Welfare of Angelo H.*, 124 Wash. App. 578, 587, 102 P.3d 822 (2004).

It is crucial to determine whether courts in the jurisdiction have decided the issue of the reasonable accommodation requirement and whether they have put any parameters in place (e.g., Can the ADA be used to require the creation of new services or merely modifications to existing services or provision of additional services?). If the issue has not been decided in the jurisdiction, research whether nearby jurisdictions have considered it, as findings from nearby states may be persuasive.

A claim for reasonable accommodations under the ADA—or, similarly, a claim that the Agency has failed to make reasonable efforts because the provided services have not reasonably accommodated a parent's disability—must be made as soon as possible. Basically, once the ADA violation is or should reasonably be apparent, a parent's attorney should raise the claim. Better yet, the parent's attorney can raise the issue of disability in the initial disposition hearing, invoke ADA protections, and demand reasonable accommodations. It may be fruitful to discuss the claim with the Agency ahead of time, when case services are being planned, as the Agency may provide the accommodations, preventing a court battle (though it is important to put the applicability of the ADA on the record in court). Thus, it is critical that parents tell the Agency about their disability as soon as possible and request accommodations accordingly so that any ADA issues can be raised early in the case.

If the Agency does not make reasonable accommodations despite the court finding that the ADA applies, a court may later find that reasonable efforts were not made. This finding threatens the Agency's access to federal funds to help pay for the case and also could slow any eventual effort to terminate the parent's rights. There are incentives on all sides to deal squarely with disability issues: Parents cannot afford to waive an ADA claim by failing to inform the Agency and the court of their disability and demand accommodations, the Agency cannot afford to ignore the parent's disability, and the child cannot afford the delay that may occur if disability issues are not addressed.

12.03(b) Raising an ADA Claim: Proving Disability

The threshold for whether the ADA applies in a child welfare case is whether the parent has a disability. That question was the focus of much litigation for many years in ADA cases, but the ADA Amendments Act of 2008, P.L. 110-325, clarified the definition of disability and the intent of Congress in passing the ADA. Disability is defined as "(A) a physical or mental impairment that substantially limits one or more major life activities of [the] individual; (B) a record of such an impairment; or (C) being regarded as having such an impairment." 42 U.S.C. § 12102(1). Whether a person is disabled is to "be construed in favor of broad coverage." 42 U.S.C. § 12102(4)(A). The ADA Amendments Act of 2008 clarified that the focus of an ADA case should be on whether covered entities have complied with their obligations under the law, not on whether the claimant has a disability. P.L. 110-325 § 2(a)(7), (b)(5). The ADA lists numerous "major life activities" that may be limited and thus fall under ADA protection. These activities include many physical and cognitive tasks. 42 U.S.C. § 12102(2)(A). The non-exhaustive list in the statute includes, among other activities, learning, reading, concentrating, thinking, communicating, and working. In other words, the list includes tasks that may well be impaired for parents with disabilities, and these impairments may interfere with a parent's ability to benefit from the standard services provided by the Agency.

Although the ADA Amendments Act of 2008 made it easier to qualify for ADA protection, evidence of disability is still needed to trigger protection under the statute. Evidence might include facts found in medical and mental health records, Social Security determinations, and educational records. Importantly, even where a parent lacks evidence of a disability, agency caseworkers may have made written or verbal statements that indicate that they regard the parent as having a disability, which may be the key to gaining ADA protection for the parent. Often, the allegations within the Agency's Petition include assertions that a parent has a mental illness that interferes with parenting, is intellectually impaired in a manner that affects parenting, or lacks the capacity to parent effectively or to learn new parenting skills. Similarly, court reports filed by the caseworker may contain statements that demonstrate the caseworker's doubts about capacity or concerns about mental illness, cognitive impairment, or many disability-related issues. These statements can trigger ADA protection for a parent because they indicate that the Agency regards the parent as having an impairment that is a disability under the law. *See* 42 U.S.C. § 12102(1)(C).

Under the ADA, people may be regarded as having a disability and thus protected if (1) they have an impairment that does not actually substantially limit a major life activity but are treated by a public entity as being substantially limited in a major life activity; (2) they have an impairment that substantially limits a major life activity because of the attitudes of others toward the impairment; or (3) they are simply treated by a public entity as having an impairment that substantially limits a major life activity. 28 C.F.R. § 35.104. *See also* 42 U.S.C. § 12102(3)(A). Many commentators have noted with concern that caseworkers and other professionals in child welfare cases often focus on the disabilities of parents. *See, e.g.*, NAT'L COUNCIL ON DISABILITY, *supra*, for a detailed overview. Yet this very focus can trigger ADA protection thanks to the "regarded as disabled" provision.

12.03(c) Raising an ADA Claim: "Qualified Individual" and "Public Entity"

Protection under the ADA applies to a "qualified individual with a disability," which is defined as a person who, "with or without reasonable modifications," "meets the essential eligibility requirements for the receipt of services or the participation in programs or activities provided by a public entity." 42 U.S.C. § 12131(2). Parents with disabilities in child welfare cases meet these criteria, because they are eligible for family preservation and reunification services in most cases regardless of any modifications. It is their parenthood that makes them eligible for services, not their disability or associated accommodations. It is worth noting, however, that where aggravated circumstances are alleged, so that a parent would not be entitled to family preservation or reunification services, and the Agency has denied services based on those grounds, having a disability does not entitle the parent to services. *See* 42 U.S.C. § 671(a)(15)(D) (aggravated circumstances provision of the Adoption and Safe Families Act of 1997 stating that reasonable efforts are not required in such cases). For a similar provision codified in state law, *see*, e.g., MICH. COMP. LAWS § 712A.19a(2) (2014)). In such cases, parents are not entitled to services regardless of disability, because ADA protections do not provide an exception to aggravated circumstances statutes. Furthermore, parents are no longer "qualified individuals" for reunification services if the Agency and court determine that reasonable efforts are not required due to aggravated circumstances.

As for the "public entity" requirement for protection under the ADA, this is not a part of an ADA claim that is likely to be litigated in the child welfare context. Under the statute, a "public entity" includes any department of a state or local government. 42 U.S.C. § 12131(1)(B). Child welfare agencies—and the private agencies that work under contracts with governmental child welfare agencies—qualify as public entities.

12.03(d) Raising an ADA Claim: The Need for Specificity

Another important part of an ADA claim is specificity about which accommodations are needed. Counsel must articulate why the services offered do not reasonably accommodate the parent's disability and suggest to the court and Agency how the disability may be reasonably accommodated through modifications to the services. Generally, both the court and the Agency will lack expertise about disability issues, so it is incumbent on counsel to propose options for accommodations. A combination of knowledge, connections with experienced professionals, and, most importantly, close consultation with the client about the disability and the parent-child relationship is essential to successful advocacy.

Sometimes, even after consultation with the client and other steps, counsel will not know what accommodations might be most effective, often because the assessment of the client by the caseworker and other professionals has been inadequate. In that case, the first accommodation may be for the Agency to arrange a thorough assessment by an expert familiar with parents with disabilities. Such experts may include occupational therapists, speech and language therapists, psychologists, physicians, rehabilitation consultants, and other professionals. Also, clients may have worked with professionals they trust who might be in an excellent position to provide a thorough assessment and ongoing treatment services.

Remember that accommodations may vary considerably from case to case, and there are many options. Accommodations can address where, how, when, and for how long a service is provided. Specialized services, or services from providers with particular expertise in disability as opposed to the Agency's usual roster of providers, can be ordered. Instead of class or large group formats, one-on-one or small group approaches can be used. Think broadly and creatively and consult closely with the client and professionals with expertise in the field. It may be possible to negotiate with the Agency outside of court to obtain many accommodations, and then a plan can be presented to the court. This approach has the added benefit of allowing all of the players time to put together an individualized package of services, creating a sense of "buy-in" and well-tailored interventions. Some child welfare offices may have certain caseworkers with specialized training in disability issues who can be assigned to the case as a consultant or as the primary caseworker.

12.03(e) Raising an ADA Claim: Summary

A parent may claim ADA protection regarding services provided by the Agency by demonstrating that he or she is a qualified person with a disability who requires a reasonable accommodation of that disability by a public entity. This claim must be raised as early in the case as possible and cannot first be raised when termination of parental rights is sought or on appeal. Courts have rejected the ADA as a defense to termination of parental rights but have supported its use to guarantee that the services provided by the Agency reasonably accommodate a parent's disability. Because courts have equated reasonable accommodations with reasonable efforts, such that they may find that reasonable efforts have not been made if a parent's disabilities have not been reasonably accommodated, a timely ADA claim can cause a later reversal of a termination of parental rights if the parent shows that the trial court failed to timely address the disability issue or the Agency failed to make required accommodations, and thus reasonable efforts were not made. The key is to make the ADA claim early and, if the court or the Agency does not address it properly, be persistent so the record repeatedly reflects that the claim was made.

Finally, it may be worth using ADA noncompliance to challenge an order that the Agency initiate termination of parental rights proceedings under the Adoption and Safe Families Act's fifteen-of-twenty-two-months provision. Under that provision, if a child has been in foster care for fifteen of the past twenty-two months, the court shall order the Agency to initiate termination of parental rights proceedings unless an exception to the requirement applies. *See* 42 U.S.C. § 675(5)(E). One of the exceptions is a failure to make reasonable efforts. *See* 42 U.S.C. § 675(5)(E)(iii). Because a failure to provide reasonable accommodations may preclude a finding that reasonable efforts were made, ADA noncompliance may trigger this exception to the fifteen-of-twenty-two-months rule. Again, practitioners must raise the applicability of the ADA early and cannot wait until the

Agency seeks termination of parental rights. If the court has ordered the Agency to make reasonable accommodations, and the Agency has failed to do so, the court may be reluctant to order the Agency to initiate a termination of parental rights proceeding.

For technical assistance, practitioners may want to consult their state Protection and Advocacy office or Through the Looking Glass, a national center dedicated to serving families in which a parent, child, or grandparent has a disability. Also, in its ROCKING THE CRADLE report, the National Council on Disability provides a list of ADA requirements, which is reproduced here:

Pursuant to Title II of the ADA, child welfare agencies must:

1. Provide parents with disabilities an equal opportunity to participate in programs, services, and activities. To implement this mandate, the agencies must make reasonable modifications in policies, practices, or procedures, unless such modifications would fundamentally alter the nature of the service, program, or activity.
2. Administer services, programs, and activities in the most integrated setting appropriate to the needs of qualified people with disabilities.
3. Not impose or apply eligibility criteria that screen out or tend to screen out any person with a disability from fully and equally enjoying any service, program, or activity, unless such criteria can be shown to be necessary for the provision of the service, program, or activity being offered.
4. Furnish auxiliary aids and services when necessary to ensure effective communication, unless an undue burden or fundamental alteration would result.
5. Provide, as needed, benefits, services, or advantages beyond those required by the regulation to people with disabilities.
6. Not impose surcharges on people with disabilities to cover the costs of measures to ensure nondiscriminatory treatment, such as making modifications required to provide program accessibility or providing qualified interpreters.
7. Not deny the benefits of programs, activities, and services to people with disabilities because entities' facilities are inaccessible.
8. Provide services, programs, and activities that, when viewed in their entirety, are readily accessible to and usable by people with disabilities.

NAT'L COUNCIL ON DISABILITY, *supra* at 88–89 (internal citations omitted).

12.04 Key Elements of Advocacy: Client Counseling, Strategies, and Building Expertise

It is important that counsel ask their clients about any disabilities and accommodations that might be needed. Counsel should guide the client through the likely phases of the case, including a discussion of what the courthouse is like and the places in which a client might receive services, as various accommodations might be needed in these settings. Clients often have considerable expertise about their disability, how it affects them in different contexts, how it might affect parenting, and how services and accommodations of all types might best be provided to them. The client is counsel's best resource.

Client interviewing and counseling can provide detailed information about the parent, the child, the parent-child relationship, family and other supports that have been in place or could be arranged, any services that the parent already receives, and whether any allegations against the parent that refer to disability are accurately linked to actual parenting skills or the home situation. For clients with cognitive disabilities, including learning or intellectual impairments, lawyers may need to take longer to explain the legal situation and should check in with clients to ensure that they have a good understanding of the case.

Clinical knowledge and professional contacts should be cultivated in areas such as mental health, medicine, social services, and rehabilitation. Attorneys should take the time to learn basic information about mental health treatment, social work practice with parents with disabilities, and issues such as Social Security or other public benefits, and common barriers in areas such as housing or employment. Interview any service providers the client may already have and get their ideas for what might be helpful. The services of these professionals may be included in the case service plan, and these providers may also have opinions and advice about how other parts of the plan can be implemented most effectively. Again, it is best if the client can play an active part in these discussions. Client counseling and consultations with service providers who have worked with the client and/or are knowledgeable about disability contribute a great deal to the ability of lawyers to argue for specific accommodations under the ADA, as discussed above.

In court, counsel must educate the judge about the client's disability, because otherwise the judge is left only with assumptions about what a parent with that disability can and cannot do. Emphasizing the actual parent-child relationship can be effective to counteract biases about parents with disabilities, which may include that a child would be better off with a non-disabled parent or that children of parents with disabilities do not love their parents or have as much of a bond with them as other children do. If the parent will need support in the home to provide care for the child, put together a plan of care. Even a partially formed plan of care can show the court that the parent is actively working to address any identified issues, decreasing the possibility that the court will see the case as one in which there will be no positive change. Case service plans must be scrutinized for specificity and to ensure that appropriate, measurable outcomes are identified. Often, requesting a more frequent hearing schedule can force the Agency to act more swiftly in developing and providing services and fight agency inaction. Sometimes, agency caseworkers pressure parents with disabilities to relinquish their parental rights, because the caseworkers believe that the parents will not be capable of caring for their children. Counsel must shield clients from such pressure and provide caseworkers with a different narrative that emphasizes their clients' abilities and positive aspects of the parent-child relationship.

12.05 The Problem of Expert Testimony

In many child welfare cases, and perhaps especially those involving parents with cognitive or psychiatric disabilities, agency workers often seek—and courts order—assessments of parents by mental health professionals. These assessments carry tremendous persuasive weight in many courts. Judges have little contact with the families before them, and often little expertise with disability issues, so they are likely to rely on expert reports and testimony. Experts too often go unchallenged as they offer their opinions about the parent's present level of psychological and cognitive functioning, capacity for change, and prognosis. Yet these experts may not have expertise in parenting with a disability and instead rely on what amount to class-based declarations about parents. Experts in child welfare cases may make blanket statements about the ability of people with intellectual impairment to parent children with little regard for how *this* parent takes care of that child or what supports might be effective to improve parenting in a particular case. Coupled with this tendency—and contributing to it—is the common reliance of mental health experts on psychometric testing, such as IQ testing, that has little to no direct connection to parenting skills. Similarly, experts may rely on the fact of a given psychiatric diagnosis to state that the parent lacks the ability to take care of his or her child, rather than thoroughly assessing an individual's actual parenting skills. Few observe the parent and child together.

In the face of this testimony, many courts and even attorneys fail to take a skeptical approach to expert testimony and often ask about the expert's qualifications and not the empirical basis for the expert's conclusions, even though qualifications alone are insufficient to establish expertise. *See* Daniel W. Shuman, *What Should We Permit Mental Health Professionals to Say About "The Best Interests of the Child"?: An Essay on Common Sense,* Daubert, *and the Rules of Evidence*, 31 FAM. L.Q. 551, 564–65 (1997). There is little assurance that the methods employed by the expert are reliable and valid for the purpose for which they were used. Absent reliable and valid methods, what experts are really relying on are their subjective beliefs, biases, and extrapolations, which may not be supported by research in their field.

Ideally, a parent's attorney can obtain an evaluation from a different, trusted expert with which to challenge the conclusions of the Agency's expert. Too often, though, funds are not available, and these requests are denied. If counsel cannot secure her own expert, the only tool available to refute expert testimony may be vigorous cross-examination. When challenging expert testimony, the attorney should insist that the expert show that any assessments are actually relevant to parenting. Attorneys should also try to keep experts from testifying about behavior, test results, and clinical impressions not related to parenting. Read expert reports carefully, learn about the procedures used, determine whether the psychometric tests employed by the evaluator are up-to-date and considered valid for the assessment, and check the licensing status of the expert.

It may be useful to research the scope of practice for a particular profession to determine whether the expert has exceeded his or her bounds, and attorneys for parents would do well to be familiar with the American Psychological Association's Ethical Principles of Psychologists and Code of Conduct, to be in a position to discredit a psychology expert who did not complete an assessment in an ethical and professional manner. Psychologists are bound by their code of ethics and are vulnerable to licensing complaints for violations. All psychologists receive training in psychology ethics, and their licensing examination covers ethics requirements. These background facts are useful to bring out when cross-examining a psychologist who has failed to conduct an evaluation ethically. The American Psychological Association has also created several relevant best practice documents that are available on its website. *See* AM. PSYCHOLOGICAL ASSOC., GUIDELINES FOR ASSESSMENT OF AND INTERVENTION WITH PERSONS WITH DISABILITIES (2014); AM. PSYCHOLOGICAL ASSOC., GUIDELINES FOR PSYCHOLOGICAL EVALUATIONS IN CHILD PROTECTION MATTERS (2013); AM. PSYCHOLOGICAL ASSOC., SPECIALTY GUIDELINES FOR FORENSIC PSYCHOLOGY (2013). Although aspirational rather than binding, these documents illustrate the state of the art in the areas of child protection psychological evaluations, forensic evaluations, and how psychologists should work with people with disabilities. Practitioners should become familiar with them not only to facilitate challenging expert testimony, but also to know what to look for in a good independent evaluation.

12.06 Guardians ad Litem for Parents

In some cases, the possibility of appointing a guardian ad litem ("GAL") to represent a parent's best interests is raised because of indications that the parent is unable to direct his or her counsel. A request for a GAL by a parent's lawyer is drastic, as the need for the GAL is likely to be seen by the Agency and court as undermining any claim that the parent can provide adequate care for the child. Less drastic steps should be attempted first, such as use of a support person of the client's choosing to help the client participate in meetings with the lawyer, understand the case, and make decisions; using shorter meetings that cover less material more slowly; soliciting the client's understanding of what the lawyer has explained; giving the client enough time to discuss a decision in the case thoroughly with the lawyer and with others whom the client trusts; allowing the client enough time to make decisions; and using multiple modes of communication, after consultation with the client and professionals who have worked with the client about preferred modes of communicating.

Attorneys must be mindful that discussions about the case with third parties may jeopardize attorney-client privilege, but steps sometimes can be taken to mitigate the concern, such as having the third party enter into a confidentiality agreement. The concern about attorney-client privilege may be less pressing than the need to avoid appointment of a GAL. Besides the impression given to the court by a request for a GAL, any GAL appointed by the court may have no particular expertise in working with people with disabilities. Little may be gained by their appointment, and much may be lost.

Nevertheless, attorneys who represent parents with disabilities must also be cognizant of Model Rule of Professional Conduct 1.14(a), which requires lawyers to, "as far as reasonably possible, maintain a normal client-lawyer relationship" with a client who has diminished capacity to make adequately considered decisions about the case. Again, steps should be taken consistent with this rule to try as much as possible to avoid appointment of a GAL. However, if those steps are not adequate, and a lawyer believes that a client's diminished capacity places him or her "at risk of substantial physical, financial or other harm," and the client "cannot adequately act" in his or her own interest, Model Rule 1.14(b) requires the lawyer to "take reasonably necessary protective action," which may include "seeking the appointment of a guardian ad litem, conservator or guardian." In such cases, it may be possible to identify a guardian who could provide care for both the client and the child, but again, the drastic step of enlisting a guardian—or a GAL—should be avoided if possible because it undermines the client's argument that he or she is a competent parent.

CHAPTER 13

Representing Out-of-State and Non-Citizen Parents

Annick I. Lenoir-Peek

13.01 Introduction

In our mobile society, it is not unusual for a child welfare case to involve parents or relatives who live in another state or country. This chapter, in two parts, will discuss some of the things counsel should know and do when representing such clients. Part I (Sections 13.02–13.06) focuses on representing parents who are living in another state than the one in which the Petition has been filed. For these cases, the most important law to become familiar with is the Interstate Compact on the Placement of Children (ICPC), a uniform law designed to ensure that a child can be safely placed in a home in another jurisdiction and to enable child welfare agencies to monitor those placements when necessary. These sections are designed to help counsel navigate the ICPC in order to advocate for the best possible outcome.

Representing parents who are not citizens or residents of the United States presents unique challenges that can be overcome with good advocacy. Part II (Sections 13.07 to 13.09) is intended to assist counsel in advocating for their non-citizen clients, whether they are located in this country or abroad.

PART I

13.02 Structure of the Interstate Compact on the Placement of Children (ICPC)

The Interstate Compact on the Placement of Children ("ICPC" or "Compact") is not a federal law. Rather, it is a uniform law that has been enacted in all fifty states, the District of Columbia, and the U.S. Virgin Islands. The Compact establishes a framework on how children will be placed across state lines when a child welfare agency or court is making the placement. The Compact does not apply when parents are making a placement across state borders unless it is for purposes of adoption. The goals of the ICPC are to ensure: (1) the safety of the child, (2) that the child receives needed services, and (3) that the sending state retains responsibility for the child. In general terms, the ICPC requires the state to which the child is being sent (the receiving state) to conduct and approve a home study of the proposed placement before the child can be sent there by the court in the state that has jurisdiction over the case (the sending state).

The ICPC is divided into ten articles. The most relevant articles for child welfare-related matters are Articles II, III, and V. The full text of the articles can be found on the web and is attached in the Appendix to this chapter.

13.02(a) Regulations

The ICPC is administered by the Association of Administrators of the Interstate Compact on the Placement of Children (the "Association"), a division within the American Public Human Services Association. The Association, created by Article VII, requires every state to designate a Compact Administrator who will, as part of the Association, "promulgate rules and regulations to carry out more effectively the terms and provisions" of the ICPC. These regulations provide detailed guidance on how the ICPC process works, but several courts have held that they are not binding because many states have not formally adopted them. *See, e.g., H.P. v. Dep't of Children & Families*, 838 So. 2d 583, 28 Fla. L. Weekly D203 (2003).

Counsel must determine how their jurisdiction regards the Association's regulations and whether they are legally binding. A copy of the regulations is attached in the Appendix to this chapter. Because they are subject to change, counsel should always be sure what the current regulations say. They are easily found through the Association's website.

13.03 The Applicability of the ICPC to Child Welfare Proceedings

When facing a potential interstate move of a child in foster care, counsel must first determine whether compliance with the ICPC is required. The ICPC governs the interstate placement of "any child for placement in foster care or as a preliminary to a possible adoption." ICPC art. III(a). The regulations broadly define "foster care" to include care "by a relative of the child, by a non-related individual, or . . . by the child's parent(s) by reason of a court-ordered placement." ICPC reg. no.3. Only placements of children with noncustodial parents over whom the court does not retain jurisdiction are exempted from this broad definition. *See id.* According to the regulations, the Compact also applies when a family who is under ongoing court oversight wishes to move to the receiving state, unless the stay will last for ninety days or less. ICPC reg. no. 1.

Many courts have rejected the broad language in these nonbinding regulations and have limited the ICPC's reach in important ways. Although a majority of courts have held that the Compact governs placing foster children with relatives in another state, many courts have held that the ICPC does not apply when children are sent to live with their birth parents in another state. A strong argument can be made both that the ICPC does not apply when children are sent to live with their birth parents and that it would be unconstitutional if it did. The right of parents to the care, custody, and control of their children is recognized as a fundamental liberty interest. *See Troxel v. Granville*, 530 U.S. 57, 65 (2000). Advocates should read the appellate case law in their jurisdiction as well as that in the receiving state on the applicability of the ICPC to parents and relatives. A list of the current case law on this issue can be found in the Appendix at the end of this chapter.

All of the courts that have addressed the ICPC's applicability to placements with birth parents have limited their analysis to the ICPC's text and purpose. No court has yet addressed the constitutionality of the statute when applied to placements with parents. When so applied, the ICPC raises serious constitutional concerns because it transfers decision-making authority from courts to child welfare agencies and allows parents to be stripped of their right to care for children based solely on a finding by the Agency that the placement is contrary to the child's interests. For a thorough analysis of these constitutional arguments, *see* Vivek S. Sankaran, *Out of State and Out of Luck: The Treatment of Non-Custodial Parents under the Interstate Compact on the Placement of Children*, 25 YALE L. & POL'Y REV. 63 (2006). Counsel practicing in jurisdictions that have already held that the ICPC applies to out-of-state placement with parents are encouraged to argue that the Constitution forbids such an interpretation. An ultimate appeal to the state Supreme Court should be considered when lower courts rule that the ICPC does apply in these placements. No court has yet upheld the reach of the law to such cases.

The placement of children across state lines in violation of the ICPC regulations renders many services in the receiving state unavailable. For example, there would be no Agency that would be responsible for monitoring or reporting on the placement or the child's welfare. Additionally, if the child or family was in need of therapeutic or mental health services, the parent or family could have problems accessing such services in the receiving state.

If counsel decides to argue that the Compact is inapplicable, it is also important to provide the court with sufficient reassurances that the placement will be in the child's best interest. Testimony from the proposed caregiver, along with evidence demonstrating his or her suitability (e.g., proof of employment, information regarding care of other children, pictures of where the child would reside, and criminal or child protection history), may provide the court with enough information to determine that the placement serves the child's interests. Additionally, counsel may have to clarify how the child would be monitored if the proposed placement were made and how the child would receive services, if necessary. Some courts have suggested that private child welfare agencies in the caregiver's state could perform these functions if the local public agency is unwilling. *See, e.g.*, *In re Johnny S.*, 40 Cal. App. 4th 969, 979, 47 Cal. Rptr. 2d, 94, 64 USLW 2399 (1995) ("If DFCS determines that monitoring by an agency in Texas is needed, it may choose to enter into an agreement for such services.").

13.04 The Home Study Process—Advocacy Suggestions

If the court determines that the ICPC applies, then counsel usually will want to try to expedite the home study process. Having a basic understanding of how the process works helps. The following steps explain this process:

1. A party suggests an out-of-state parent or relative as a placement.
2. The court orders the Agency to request an ICPC home study.
3. The caseworker prepares the paperwork and submits it to the sending state's ICPC administrative office.
4. The sending state's ICPC administrative office sends the request to the receiving state's ICPC administrative office.
5. The receiving state's ICPC administrative office sends the request to the local agency's office.
6. The receiving local agency caseworker conducts the home study and conducts necessary background checks.
7. The receiving local agency forwards the completed home study to the receiving state's ICPC administrative office.
8. The receiving state's ICPC administrative office makes a recommendation whether to accept or deny the home study based upon the "best interest" of the child.
9. The receiving state's ICPC administrative office forwards the home study decision to the sending state's ICPC administrative office.
10. The sending state's ICPC administrative office forwards the home study decision to the sending local agency.
11. The sending local agency submits the home study decision to the requesting (sending) court.

12. If the home study has been approved, the requesting court makes a decision on whether to place the child in the receiving state.
13. If the home study has been denied, the requesting court has no authority to make the placement, unless it determines that the ICPC does not apply.

This process can take months, if not years, to complete. Home studies are regularly not completed within a reasonable time period. Federal law mandates that interstate home studies be completed within sixty days. *See* 42 U.S.C. § 671(a)(26). However, rare is the case that is done within this period. *See* Vivek S. Sankaran, *Foster Kids in Limbo: The Effects of the Interstate Compact on the Placement of Children on the Permanency of Children in Foster Care*, A Report To The Annie E. Casey Foundation (Univ. Mich. Law Sch. Child Advocacy Law Clinic), 2013. Even the Association's regulation calling for home studies to be completed in six months is commonly ignored. *See* ICPC, reg. no. 2. The reasons for long delays in completing home studies are too numerous to list, ranging from mistakes made in filling out the paperwork, missing information on the original requests, lack of personnel to conduct the necessary studies, or lack of follow-through by family members.

A very useful role counsel can play in these matters is to help expedite the home study process. These are among the first things to consider.

13.04(a) Can it Count as an "Expedited Placement"?

Counsel should first determine whether the placement can be considered an "expedited placement." *See* ICPC, reg. no. 7. When a case is so designated, courts and agencies commonly give it high priority. The Regulation authorizes expediting cases when the child is to be placed with a relative (including a parent) *and* one of the following has occurred: (a) unexpected dependency due to a sudden or recent incarceration, incapacitation or death of a parent or guardian; (b) at least one of the children being placed is younger than four years old; (c) any child in the sibling group sought to be placed has a substantial relationship with the proposed placement resource ("substantial relationship" means the proposed placement has a familial or mentoring role with the child, has spent more than cursory time with the child, and has established more than a minimal bond with the child); or (d) the child is currently in an emergency placement. *See id.*

When any of these factors apply, counsel should file a motion seeking a court order expediting the home study and further directing that the receiving state provisionally approve the home immediately. In the order, the court should specify the reasons the placement requires expedited consideration and detail the next steps in the case. Regulation No. 7 spells out the specific steps that must be followed once such an order is issued. It requires the sending state to send to the receiving state the completed home study request within five business days of the order and also requires that the home study be completed within another twenty business days. *See id.* A request for provisional approval must be completed within seven days. Clarifying these steps in the court order dramatically helps speed the process.

13.04(b) Submit the Home Study Paperwork

Whether or not the court orders that the home study be expedited, once the request for the ICPC home study is made, the next step is to ensure the sending state agency transmits the correct paperwork promptly. Counsel should work with the caseworker assigned to the case to ensure that s/he has all the needed documentation and will be sending the necessary papers promptly. Counsel is also well-advised to get to know the professionals who work in the state's ICPC office who often are invaluable allies to speed things up. If, for some reason, there are unnecessary delays in the transmission of the paperwork, counsel should consider filing a motion seeking an order that the sending state submit the request immediately. Failure to comply with such an order can be enforced through the contempt powers of the court.

13.04(c) Contact Receiving State Administrators

Once the paperwork requesting the home study is transmitted to the receiving state, the advocacy strategy becomes more complicated because the sending court has no jurisdiction over the child welfare agency in the receiving state. Counsel now needs to shift the focus to informal advocacy with the administrators in the receiving state responsible for conducting the home study. Each state child welfare agency has an ICPC office and an individual designated as the compact administrator. This office should be able to provide counsel with information about the caseworker assigned to conduct the home study in the local office.

13.04(d) Contact the Receiving State's Home Study Caseworker

Contacting the caseworker responsible for conducting the home study will humanize the client and remind the worker of the importance of conducting the study promptly. Often, the worker performing the assessment will not have met the child and her only contact with the case will be paperwork from the sending state. She may not know the urgency of the situation. Counsel can bring these facts and stories to the worker's attention and can also provide information to ensure the study is completed quickly. Counsel should also work with the proposed caregiver to collect all necessary information, which may include proof of income, copies of the lease, and health certificates. Checklists of what is required by the home study worker to complete her assessment may be available. Missing information and incomplete paperwork is a leading cause for delay under the ICPC.

13.04(e) Address Delays

If there is unnecessary delay in the home study process, counsel should contact the ICPC compact administrator in the sending state to follow up with their counterpart in the receiving state to identify the causes for delay. Additionally, counsel should request that the court order the sending state compact administrator to file monthly reports detailing the status of the home study's completion and convene frequent hearings while the process is being completed.

13.04(f) Advocate for Continued Contact Between the Placement and the Child

While the caseworker in the receiving state is completing the home study, counsel should advocate for continued and increasing contact between the child and the parent or relative in the receiving state. In-person contact, in addition to contact via Skype or the Internet, is a possibility. Nothing in the text of the Compact prohibits visits while the home study is pending. All that the Regulations say is that out-of-state visits with caregivers who are the subject of a home study should be presumed to be for the purpose of a placement. But that presumption is rebuttable. Alert those involved that visits are occurring but that visits are not a placement and ask a court order to reflect this finding.

13.05 Challenging Home Study Denials

If the receiving state denies the placement, then counsel faces a steep obstacle. The ICPC makes plain that the placement cannot take place without the consent of the receiving state. *See* ICPC art. III. The ICPC is completely silent, however, regarding what further steps may be taken to challenge the rejection of the placement. By its terms, sending courts lack the authority to order the interstate placement absent the consent of the receiving state. *See id.* Very few states have any kind of established process to review or challenge ICPC denials administratively.

The apparent absence of any procedure to challenge the decision is made all the more acute because (a) the consequences of refusing to consent are so grave and (b) the substantive bases upon which the decision is reached are so broad. Receiving states seem to have unlimited discretion when deciding whether or not to approve the placement. The Compact requires the receiving state only to determine whether the proposed placement "does not appear to be contrary to the interests of the child." ICPC art. III. But the standard itself is not defined. Thus, an almost unlimited number of factors can be used to deny a planned placement, even if they would not be justified in denying an intrastate placement. These factors include barring a caregiver because they have a dated criminal record or a particular health condition that may be debilitating, life threatening, or interfere with their capacity to raise the child. The size of the living space is commonly used as a basis for denying the planned placement, even when there are no minimum space requirements in the jurisdiction. Sometimes caregivers are explicitly rejected because, in the words of the home study worker, the caregiver "failed to cooperate" appropriately with the worker. *See* Sankaran, *supra, Foster Kids in Limbo.*

What can be done when negotiating a system that applies arbitrary and subjective decision making and fails to provide any opportunity to contest those decisions? Counsel in such situations must be creative in their strategies. What follows are some suggested tools.

13.05(a) Address the Issues Underlying the Denial

Counsel should work with the ICPC offices in both states to see whether the issues that led to the denial can be addressed. For example, if the proposed caretaker's house was too small, perhaps the juvenile court could order the sending state agency to help the caretaker find a bigger place. If the caretaker has prior child protective history, counsel can work with the caretaker to see whether the findings can be expunged. Often, the decisions denying placements are made by the receiving state with very limited information and providing more information about the placement to the home study worker may address any concerns. Key to this process is having an open, cooperative dialogue with those in the receiving state responsible for making this decision.

13.05(b) Explore Administrative Remedies

Counsel should explore whether any administrative processes exist in the receiving state. If so, inform the caretaker how to navigate that process or locate counsel to represent him or her. For example, Massachusetts law permits "any person aggrieved by any action or inaction of the Department involving the placement of children across state lines" to have a fair hearing on the matter. *See* 110 MASS. CODE REGS. 7.523 (2014). Similar statutes may exist elsewhere. Even if state law in a jurisdiction does not explicitly provide this right, counsel should look at the administrative procedures acts in the receiving state to determine whether an argument can be made that the acts covered encompass agency denials of home studies under the ICPC.

13.05(c) Request a Placement Hearing

Counsel should consider filing a motion with the dependency judge requesting a placement hearing to determine whether the child's best interests will be served by the placement. Although the ICPC explicitly bars judicial review of placement decisions, advocates could argue the entire framework violates the constitutional rights of children and parents by depriving them of protected liberty interests without any opportunity to be heard. Courts have repeatedly held that once children are placed in foster care, the state has a heightened obligation under the Fourteenth Amendment to protect them from physical and emotional harm, which includes the responsibility to maintain familial relationships absent compelling circumstances. *See, e.g., Marisol A. v. Giuliani*, 929 F. Supp. 662, 677 (S.D.N.Y. 1996) (finding that the Fourteenth Amendment obligates the state to protect foster children's associational rights with their family).

Forcing children to remain in temporary placements for months if not years while a home study is completed and then denying the placement without any opportunity to contest the decision implicates their liberty interests. When the proposed placement is with a birth parent, additional constitutional interests arise since the parent, too, has a protected interest in maintaining his or her relationship with the child. By divesting children and parents of the right to a hearing, the ICPC fails to recognize these basic constitutional rights. To preserve the constitutionality of the statute, counsel should argue that courts must afford a hearing to those aggrieved by negative decisions and must have the authority after such a hearing to order the placement if it furthers the child's best interest.

13.05(d) Help the Caregiver File for Custody or Guardianship

In cases where evidence clearly shows the caretaker is a suitable long-term placement for the child, counsel could also encourage and assist the proposed caretaker to file for guardianship or custody of the child in either the receiving or sending state. Since the Compact only covers placements of children "in foster care or as preliminary to a possible adoption," counsel could argue that placements made in guardianship or custody proceedings are not covered by the Compact. Therefore, in those collateral proceedings, the court arguably has authority to grant the Petition despite the negative home study. This option could be pursued in lieu of pursuing a placement via the Compact. This argument may be more successful if the juvenile court judge is willing to dismiss the child protective case immediately upon the granting of the custody or guardianship petition. If the custody or guardianship court determines the ICPC does apply to these proceedings, counsel can still argue that the framework is unconstitutional and that a best interests hearing is required based on the arguments above. The common thread of all of these potential arguments is that the Constitution, as a matter of due process, requires that children and parents be given the right to a placement hearing before the state can infringe upon their liberty interests.

Counsel need not lose hope when confronted with a negative home study. Through persistence and cooperation, state officials often reconsider their decisions, especially when presented with new evidence. The arguments described above protect basic due process rights of children and parents and are grounded in fundamental constitutional principles supported by case law.

13.06 Final Thoughts about Interstate Placements

Counsel must ensure that their out-of-state client is an active and vocal participant at every stage of the proceedings. Counsel should use legal arguments based on the text of the Compact and the Constitution along with factual arguments, resting on reassuring the court that the placement is safe and in the best interests of the child. If the court insists on following the ICPC, counsel should take steps to gather all the necessary information and establish working relationships with caseworkers in both the sending and receiving states. Although the process can be time consuming, the extra telephone calls will be worth the effort.

PART II

13.07 Representing Non-American Parents in Child Welfare-Related Proceedings

The remainder of this chapter addresses issues involving representing non-citizen parents, whether living within or outside the United States. Immigration law is complicated and involves potential ramifications that require specialized knowledge. Counsel should always consult with an immigration lawyer when she has specific questions and should establish referral agreements or links with organizations that may be able to assist clients in specific situations. In many communities, there are lawyers working in indigent legal services offices or affiliated with various charity organizations or law school clinical programs with expertise in immigration law who may be willing to answer questions from lawyers who have an immigration-related question.

13.08 When the Parent is Living in the United States

13.08(a) Establishing the Parent's Immigration Status

One of the first steps counsel should undertake when representing non-citizen parents is ascertaining their immigration status. Some parents are fearful of discussing their immigration status because they believe that they will be reported to the authorities and that they will be deported because of their involvement with the court system. Counsel should reassure them that involvement with the child welfare system is not a deportable offense and emphasize with them the need to stay involved in the dependency case if they wish to regain or keep custody of their children.

United States law recognizes four kinds of non-citizens:

- *Legal Permanent Residents* may live and work permanently and legally in the United States. Some immigrants are afforded conditional permanent resident status before achieving permanent status.
- *Refugees or Asylees* have established that they would suffer or have suffered persecution in their country of origin. Refugees are accorded refugee status before they arrive in the country; asylees seek protection upon entering the United States.
- *Nonimmigrant Visa Holders* possess temporary visas authorizing presence in the country for a specific period under conditions. Common examples of these visas are tourist, student, temporary work, and diplomatic.
- *Undocumented immigrants* are individuals without current lawful immigrant statutes. They may never have had lawful status or the lawful status may have expired.

In addition to learning the parent's immigration status, counsel should find out the immigration status of the parent's family members, including the children involved in the court matter. The parent may want to suggest one of these family members as a placement for the child. However, family members who offer to become a placement resource sometimes fail to return social worker phone calls when it is time for a home study due to fear of reprisals or being reported if they are not properly documented. Awareness of the family members' immigration status will assist counsel in advising these family members about the confidentiality of juvenile proceedings and how they will not encounter trouble with the law by participating in a home study. Having this discussion in advance will expedite the home study process by ensuring that relatives who are comfortable participating in the process come to the court's attention quickly.

A family member may have an immigration status that allows her to sponsor another family member, such as the parent, either to remain in the country or to come for an extended visit if the parent is not present. These are important considerations to remember as the case progresses. Obtaining copies of visas or special status documentation should be done early because applying for official copies of these documents can be time consuming.

A good resource to help explain basic issues concerning the intersection of immigration and child welfare issues is the Migration and Child Welfare National Network website.

13.08(b) Determining Rights and Entitlements of Parents

Even if the parent is undocumented, she may be entitled to some rights or entitlements and may even be able to apply for a special visa depending on her situation. For example, victims of domestic violence may qualify for a U Visa. Obtaining a U Visa is time consuming and counsel should assist the client in locating a resource that can request such a visa on the client's behalf as soon as possible if she qualifies. There are a limited number of U Visas issued every year and when the quota is exhausted, the client must wait to reapply the following year. The limited availability of such visas can affect a parent's ability to access services or obtain employment.

Depending on the parent's status, both the parent and child may be entitled to access certain services and programs, under both federal and state schemes, which may assist in either alleviating the conditions that brought them within the sphere of attention of the child welfare agency or which may provide services that will assist in meeting goals set out by the child welfare agency or the court. The National Immigration Law Center maintains "A Quick Guide to Immigrant Eligibility for ACA and Key Federal Means-tested Programs," which is updated frequently. Important information concerning eligibility for federal programs for immigrants can be found by searching the National Immigration Law Center's website. It contains information regarding medical assistance and food assistance programs, as well as eligibility for state-funded TANF and SSI replacements.

13.08(c) Placement with Undocumented Parents or Family Members

Counsel should object to efforts made by courts and child welfare agencies to bar placements of children with parents or family members due to immigration status. Agencies and courts occasionally refuse to place a child with a parent or other undocumented family members because if deported, the child's placement will be disrupted. *See, e.g., In the Interests of V.S.*, 249 Ga. App. 502, 506, 548 S.E.2d 490, 493 (2001) (reversing an adjudication of parental unfitness based largely on a finding that the father was an illegal alien and subject to deportation). But other courts have rejected the possibility of deportation as a valid consideration in determining placement or the termination of a parent's rights. *See, e.g., In re M.M.*, 263 Ga. App. 353, 587 S.E.2d 825 (2003) (finding that termination must be based on clear and convincing evidence of parental misconduct or inability and not speculation about "the vagaries or vicissitudes that beset every family on its journey through the thickets of life"); *In Re Dependency of M.R.*, 166, Wash. App. 607, 270 P.3d 607 (2012) (holding it an error to remove children from undocumented grandparents based solely on their immigration status when the children were bonded to them and the risk of deportation was low). Counsel should look to state law to determine the law in her jurisdiction.

13.08(d) Language, Cultural and Legal Barriers to Overcome in Helping the Parent

If the parent does not speak English well, counsel should immediately seek to secure an interpreter for the court proceedings and, if counsel needs one, for out-of-court communications with the parent. An interpreter that works in the court proceedings will translate everything happening during the court hearing. The courtroom interpreter may or may not be the same person who will translate client communications with counsel. Counsel should check the rules that apply in the jurisdiction regarding confidentiality of communications between counsel and parent if the same interpreter is being used for both attorney-client communication and courtroom interpretation. While an interpreter is used for oral communications, a translator will also work with written documents. Most courts have a procedure for requesting both, as needed.

Federal law protects the right to such an interpreter. *See* Title VI of the Civil Rights Act of 1964, 42 U.S.C. § 2000d (2014). The right is implemented through extensive regulations found at 45 C.F.R. §§ 80.1-80.13 (2014). Federal law prohibits discrimination on the basis of national origin, which includes protecting individuals with limited English proficiency. This protection extends to the right to receive services and documents in an individual's native language from any agency or department that receives federal financial assistance. Because individuals are entitled to receive meaningful access to services, the Office for Civil Rights (OCR) of the

U.S. Department of Health & Human Services has required both oral and written communication to be available to those with limited English proficiency. This right entitles parents to receive copies of summonses, petitions, safety plans, and any documents in their native language. Furthermore, if the court order requires them to obtain psychological services or parenting classes, these services must be made available in their native language as well.

If the case or defense involves a cultural issue, consult an expert, such as an anthropologist at a university, about how some of the cultural issues may be a barrier to complying with the case plan. This assistance can also be useful in explaining behaviors that may have been misinterpreted as dangerous or neglectful or which will influence how the family reacts to reunification efforts. Use the expert to assist in crafting an appropriate plan that addresses the court's safety concerns in a culturally appropriate context.

13.08(e) Working with ICE Holds

The U.S. Department of Homeland Security, through the Immigration and Customs Department (ICE), is responsible for removing individuals who are not properly documented or have violated their documented status. ICE commonly learns of individuals subject to deportation through two primary methods: raids of locations in which undocumented persons may assemble and law enforcement arrests.

When a parent is in the custody of law enforcement, he or she may be placed on an ICE detainer. Counsel should first verify that a detainer has been issued (DHS Form I-247). A detainer is an instruction to law enforcement agencies to hold an individual for forty-eight hours (excluding Saturdays, Sundays, and holidays) to give the Department of Homeland Security time to determine whether to assume custody of the individual. At the end of forty-eight hours, unless DHS has acted, the individual is supposed to be released. Many immigrants who get arrested are not on a detainer at the time of their arrest. Nevertheless, ICE may be interested in the individual being held pending trial and may ask local authorities to notify them when he or she is released so that ICE can issue a detainer if it chooses. But this request is voluntary and should not be confused with a detainer.

Once ICE assumes custody of the parent, the individual is known in the parlance to be on an "ICE hold." They will be sent to an ICE facility and proceedings will be started to determine whether the parent will be deported. If the parent has been detained by ICE, counsel will need to ascertain where he or she is being held. For many years, trying to ascertain where a parent was being detained and having him or her participate in a court proceeding concerning the child was very difficult. But in August 2013, a new ICE policy on family preservation took effect. The text of the policy is found in the Appendix and can be found on the ICE website. An ICE Contact Sheet for each facility is found in the Appendix.

Of particular note for those representing parents, under the new policy:

- The detained parent has a right to participate in court proceedings and to be kept informed of the proceedings.
- The detained parent has a right to participate personally (i.e., be transported) or via teleconferencing (i.e., via Skype) at each hearing.
- The detained parent has a right to have visits with the child while in custody (preferably in person but via teleconferencing if the distances are too great).

Counsel should ask ICE to exercise their discretion to not detain the parent if the parent will be responsible for caring for her children or to move them nearby if the case plan is reunification. Counsel should consider asking the court in the dependency proceeding to enter orders directing ICE to facilitate the parent's participation in all aspects of the case such as:

- Transporting the parent to hearings, or at least allowing participation by telephone or video.
- Allowing participation by the parent in meetings concerning the child, such as child and family team meetings, therapeutic team meetings, and so on.
- Allowing in-person visits between parent and child, or at a minimum through video or teleconferencing.

Counsel should insist that these rights be enforced for detained parents as a preventive measure to having their parental rights terminated. Before this policy took effect, some courts treated a parent's placement in immigration detention as an abandonment of the children. *See, e.g.*, *In Re Adoption of C.M.B.R.*, 332 S.W.3d 793, 820 (Mo. 2011) (reversing a termination of parental rights order that had been based on abandonment because the mother was in ICE detention and criticizing the trial court for failing to provide the mother with notice and an opportunity to be heard).

The Women's Refugee Commission has a toolkit for undocumented parents and practitioners who represent them that can be found on their website. One of the considerations that must be made is what should happen with the undocumented parent's children in the event of the parent's deportation. A plan should be made for locating children's identification and travel documents and whether or not the children will remain in the United States or accompany their parents if the parents are deported.

13.08(f) Legal Advocacy for Non-Citizen Parents

When representing a non-citizen parent, counsel should treat the case indistinguishably from any other case. Immigrant parents have a constitutionally protected right to the care and custody of their children unless they are found to be unfit by a court.

The constitutional protection applies to undocumented immigrants whose status in the dependency case is unchanged merely because of their immigration status. *See, e.g., In re Diaz/Orozco (In re B and J)*, 279 Mich. App. 12, 23, 756 N.W.2d 234, 241 (2008) (quoting *Zadvydas v. Davis*, 533 U.S. 678, 693 (2001)) ("The fundamental liberty interest in the companionship, care, custody, and management of their children pertains to citizens and aliens alike because the Due Process Clause applies to all persons within the United States, including aliens, whether their presence here is lawful, unlawful, temporary, or permanent."); *In re Adoption of Male Infant L.*, 61 N.Y. 2d 420, 430, 474 N.Y.S. 2d 447, 452, 462 N.E.2d 1165, 1170 (1984) (reversing a trial court for using the fact of the parent's immigrant status as a basis for determining parental fitness and holding specifically that the parent's alienage and poverty associated with her status were irrelevant and impermissible considerations).

Counsel should consult other chapters of this book for constitutional arguments to protect a parent's right to direct the care of her child.

13.09 Working with Parents and Relatives Living Outside of the United States

Counsel may be appointed to represent a parent who does not reside in the United States. This may be a parent who has never been to this country, who left voluntarily, or who was deported.

13.09(a) Service on Parents Residing in Another Country

Counsel must first determine whether or not the out-of-country parent has been properly served with the Petition and other documents. There are several methods for obtaining service on a United States citizen living abroad or a foreign national. Until the parent has been properly served with the documents in a case, they are not a proper party to the proceedings unless such a defect is waived. Counsel should protect the parent's rights by advising the parent whether to waive proper service and how to effectively participate in actions from abroad.

13.09(a)(1) Service by Foreign Central Authority Pursuant to Multilateral Treaty or Convention

There are two primary treaties concerning international service. They apply both to United States and non-U.S. citizens living outside the country: the Hague Convention on the Service Abroad of Judicial and Extra-Judicial Documents in Civil or Commercial Matters, 20 U.S.T. 361; 658 U.N.T.S. 163, T.I.A.S. No. 6638, and the Inter-American Service Convention on Letters Rogatory and Additional Protocol ("IACAP"), January 30, 1975, S. TREATY DOC. No. 27, 98th Cong., 2d Sess. (1984).

Countries must be a party to both the Convention and the Additional Protocol for a treaty relationship to exist. Replacing the traditional letters rogatory process, the

IACAP provides a mechanism for service of documents by a foreign central authority. The Department of Justice is this country's central authority. Requests from the United States are transmitted through a private contractor carrying out the service functions on behalf of the Department of Justice.

The Inter-American Service Convention is currently in force between the United States and Argentina, Brazil, Chile, Colombia, Ecuador, El Salvador, Guatemala, Mexico, Panama, Paraguay, Peru, Uruguay, and Venezuela. Additional information about the IACAP can be found on the website of the Organization of American States.

13.09(a)(2) Service by International Registered Mail

State rules of civil procedure may allow for the service of documents through international registered mail. However, not all foreign countries recognize service by international registered mail. If a country has objected to such service in a treaty signed by the United States, then such service is not available in that country. A complete list of these countries may be found on the Hague Conference on Private Law website.

13.09(a)(3) Personal Service by Agent

In countries allowing personal service by an agent, the agent would execute an affidavit of service at a U.S. consular office or in front of a local notary. Countries will have specific rules as to who may serve as an agent if they allow such service.

13.09(a)(4) Service by Letters Rogatory

Letters rogatory are a formal request by a court to a foreign court for assistance. Letters rogatory can be used for obtaining service and evidence available in another country. In some countries, letters rogatory are the only acceptable service method for a United States action. A step-by-step explanation of how to obtain and use letters rogatory is available on the United States State Department website.

13.09(a)(5) Service by Publication

State rules of civil procedure may allow service by publication as one way to secure jurisdiction over a parent, if the parent cannot be located. When the parent is in another country, the publication must be effectuated under the rules of that country, which may be nonexistent or preclude its use in a particular case. Counsel should check the treaty and laws of the country in which service is being sought to determine whether and how service by publication is permitted.

13.09(a)(6) Waiver of Service

State rules of civil procedure commonly describe how a foreign party may waive service issues. These waivers usually must be signed before a United States consular official abroad who will then sign an affidavit or acknowledgment. Not all countries recognize waivers, so counsel should check the law of that country.

13.09(a)(7) Language in Documents Served Abroad

Counsel should also insist that whatever documents are served on the parent have been translated into the parent's language. Although the treaties listed above do not require this, state courts have held that untranslated documents are inadequate because it will not be clear whether the parent was actually informed of the importance of the underlying proceeding. *See, e.g., In re P.S.S.C. and P.D.S.C.*, 2011 Pa. Super 253, 32 A.3d 1281, 1286 (2011) (termination order reversed because father was not properly notified when the papers served on him were only in English, a language he did not speak).

13.09(a)(8) Subpoenas for Parents Living Abroad

Some attorneys may contemplate issuing subpoenas to obtain the parent's presence at a hearing. Whether subpoenas served on parents abroad are effective depends on whether the parent is a United States citizen or lawful permanent United States resident. When the parent is an American citizen or permanent resident, federal law establishes how to serve the subpoena. *See* 28 U.S.C. §§ 1783–84 (2014); Fed. R. of Civ. P, 45. There are no provisions for service upon other persons. *See* 22 C.F.R. §§ 92.86–92.89 (2014).

13.09(b) Establishing Contact with the Parent

It is important to locate and establish contact with the out-of-country parent quickly. Counsel should ask the child welfare agency, the other parent, and the child, if old enough, how to locate the parent. The first court hearing is a time to request the court obtain such information from the parties if it was not provided in the Petition or accompanying affidavit.

Counsel should be creative in searching for the parent. The Internet has become a remarkable tool for tracking someone down; counsel should consider accessing Facebook, Twitter, Instagram, and other forms of communication that families use to keep in touch even when living continents apart. Counsel should also try using specialized agencies that locate family members in the parent's country, such as "Find Families in Mexico."

13.09(c) Assistance from the Consular Office

As soon as the parent indicates that he or she wants to be considered for the child's placement, counsel should contact that nation's consular office responsible for the region. Some consular offices have developed Memorandums of Understanding (MOU) with the local social welfare agency that clarifies what the local agency has agreed to accept as services for that country's nationals.

If counsel needs birth certificates, marriage licenses, or other such documents, they can commonly be requested through consular offices or the Internet when it is too difficult to go to the consular office. In addition, Mexican consulates have been very helpful in assisting citizens in Mexico to obtain home studies (either for a parent or relatives) and in having those documents translated for court.

Counsel should request the completion of any foreign home studies early in the process and ask the court to be specific on the type of information they should contain, including photographs if those will be helpful to the court. Counsel should request that the social worker who performed the home study be available to testify by telephone to follow up on the court's questions about a home study and file a motion to allow such telephone testimony when necessary.

Counsel should arrange for a translator or interpreter to be available when appropriate. As discussed in the ICPC Section above, every effort should be made to provide the court with the information similar to information the court is used to receiving in the court reports provided by the child welfare agencies in the jurisdiction where the matter is pending. The home studies should provide criminal background checks, child protective services history, family structure and resources, resources available, education and health facilities. And, at a minimum, counsel should ask for contact between the child and the parent and family members at least telephonically, but also by Skype if available, to continue the familial bonds.

13.09(d) Parent Participation

Just as with parents who reside out of state, it is important for the court to view the parent who is not in the country as an active participant concerning his or her child. Even when the parent cannot travel to the hearings, ensure that participation occurs by Skype, telephone, or other electronic means. In some locations, a deposition may be appropriate, with the written transcript available in lieu of in-person testimony. Parents who have been deported will have a more difficult time being allowed to participate in person at a future hearing, but counsel should request a court order directing the parent to participate in all important court hearings. A copy of this order can be provided to ICE for the purpose of allowing the parent to participate in proceedings that may affect the termination of their parental rights, which arguably could include other hearings such as those ceasing reunification efforts or establishing the permanent plan as termination of parental rights.

13.09(e) Applicable International Treaties

There are several international treaties available to assist in advocating for clients not residing in the country. These treaties trump all other laws in this country. *See* U.S. CONST. art. VI, cl. 2.

13.09(e)(1) Vienna Convention on Consular Relations

The Vienna Convention on Consular Relations is a United Nations Treaty. The agreement requires the United States "to inform the competent consular post without delay of any case where the appointment of a guardian or trustee appears to be in the interests of a minor or other person lacking full capacity who is a national of the sending State." Vienna Convention on Consular Relations, art. 37, Apr. 24, 1963, 21 U.S.T. 77, 596 U.N.T.S. 261. Several state courts have recognized the relevancy of this treaty to child welfare cases. *See, e.g., In re Antonio O.*, 18 Neb. App. 449, 461, 784 N.W.2d 457, 467 (2010); *In re Angelica L.*, 277 Neb. 984, 1013, 767 N.W.2d 74, 97 (2009) (Gerrard, J., concurring); *In re R.W.*, 2011 VT 100, 191 Vt. 108, 39 A.3d 682 (2011). A more thorough discussion of these treaties is found at Caitlin Delphin, *Protecting the Interests of Foreign-National Minors in the United States Through Consular Notification*, 45 New Eng. L. Rev. 941, 953-54 (2011).

13.09(e)(2) The Hague Convention on the Civil Aspects of International Child Abduction

When the parent resides in a foreign country and has a custody order from that country, counsel should consider invoking the Hague Convention on the Civil Aspects of International Child Abduction, as implemented by the International Child Abduction Remedies Act, which establishes rules for determining when a second court (in this instance, a court in the United States) may enter an order that supersedes a custody order issued by another country. *See* 22 U.S.C.A. §9001(2014). Counsel should read this Convention and review applicable case law interpreting it to see whether invoking the Convention may require the court to transfer the case to the court that issued the original custody order. The State Department's website has information about the Convention for attorneys, judges, law enforcement, and others. It includes processes to be followed and lists the signatories and how the process might differ from one country to the other. Counsel should be aware that not every country is a signatory to this treaty.

13.10 Conclusion

All parents are entitled to the opportunity to parent their children and participate in the court processes whether or not they are living in the jurisdiction handling the child welfare case and regardless of their citizenship or immigration status. Representing such parents can present unique challenges. But they can be overcome through strong legal advocacy.

APPENDIX TO CHAPTER 13

Interstate Compact on the Placement of Children

Article I. Purpose and Policy

It is the purpose and policy of the party states to cooperate with each other in the interstate placement of children to the end that:

(a) Each child requiring placement shall receive the maximum opportunity to be placed in a suitable environment and with persons or institutions having appropriate qualifications and facilities to provide a necessary and desirable degree and type of care.

(b) The appropriate authorities in a state where a child is to be placed may have full opportunity to ascertain the circumstances of the proposed placement, thereby promoting full compliance with applicable requirements for the protection of the child.

(c) The proper authorities of the state from which the placement is made may obtain the most complete information on the basis of which to evaluate a projected placement before it is made.

(d) Appropriate jurisdictional arrangements for the care of children will be promoted.

Article II. Definitions

As used in this compact:

(a) "Child" means a person, who by reason of minority, is legally subject to parental guardianship or similar control.

(b) "Sending agency" means a party state, officer or employee thereof; a subdivision of a party state, or officer or employee thereof; a court of a party state; a person, corporation, association, charitable agency or other entity which sends, brings, or causes to be sent or brought any child to another party state.

(c) "Receiving state" means the state to which a child is sent, brought, or caused to be sent or brought, whether by public authorities or private persons or agencies, and whether for placement with state or local public authorities or for placement with private agencies or persons.

(d) "Placement" means the arrangement for the care of a child in a family free or boarding home or in a child-caring agency or institution but does not include any institution caring for the mentally ill, mentally defective or epileptic or any institution primarily educational in character, and any hospital or other medical facility.

Article III. Conditions for Placement

(a) No sending agency shall send, bring, or cause to be sent or brought into any other party state any child for placement in foster care or as a preliminary to a possible adoption unless the sending agency shall comply with each and every requirement set forth in this article and with the applicable laws of the receiving state governing the placement of children therein.

(b) Prior to sending, bringing or causing any child to be sent or brought into a receiving state for placement in foster care or as a preliminary to a possible adoption, the sending agency shall furnish the appropriate public authorities in the receiving state written notice of the intention to send, bring, or place the child in the receiving state. The notice shall contain:

   (1) The name, date and place of birth of the child.
   (2) The identity and address or addresses of the parents or legal guardian.
   (3) The name and address of the person, agency or institution to or with which the sending agency proposes to send, bring, or place the child.
   (4) A full statement of the reasons for such proposed action and evidence of the authority pursuant to which the placement is proposed to be made.

(c) Any public officer or agency in a receiving state which is in receipt of a notice pursuant to paragraph (b) of this article may request of the sending agency, or any other appropriate officer or agency of or in the sending agency's state, and shall be entitled to receive therefrom, such supporting or additional information as it may deem necessary under the circumstances to carry out the purpose and policy of this compact.

(d) The child shall not be sent, brought, or caused to be sent or brought into the receiving state until the appropriate public authorities in the receiving state shall notify the sending agency, in writing, to the effect that the proposed placement does not appear to be contrary to the interests of the child.

Article IV. Penalty for Illegal Placement

The sending, bringing, or causing to be sent or brought into any receiving state of a child in violation of the terms of this compact, shall constitute a violation of the laws respecting the placement of children of both the state in which the sending agency is located or from which it sends or brings the child and of the receiving state. Such violation may be punished or subjected to penalty in either jurisdiction in accordance with its laws. In addition to liability for any such punishment or penalty, any such violation shall constitute full and sufficient grounds for the suspension or revocation of any license, permit, or other legal authorization held by the sending agency which empowers or allows it to place, or care, for children.

Article V. Retention of Jurisdiction

(a) The sending agency shall retain jurisdiction over the child sufficient to determine all matters in relation to the custody, supervision, care, and disposition of the child which it would have had if the child had remained in the sending agency's state, until the child is adopted, reaches majority, becomes self-supporting or is discharged with the concurrence of the appropriate authority in the receiving state. Such jurisdiction shall also include the power to effect or cause the return of the child or its transfer to another location and custody pursuant to law. The sending agency shall continue to have financial responsibility for support and maintenance of the child during the period of the placement. Nothing contained herein shall defeat a claim of jurisdiction by a receiving state sufficient to deal with an act of delinquency or crime committed therein.

(b) When the sending agency is a public agency, it may enter into an agreement with an authorized public or private agency in the receiving state providing for the performance of one or more services in respect of such case by the latter as agent for the sending agency.

(c) Nothing in this compact shall be construed to prevent a private charitable agency authorized to place children in the receiving state from performing services or acting as agents in that state for a private charitable agency of the sending state; nor to prevent the agency in the receiving state from discharging financial responsibility for the support and maintenance of a child who has been placed on behalf of the sending agency without relieving the responsibility set forth in paragraph (a) hereof.

Article VI. Institutional Care of Delinquent Children

A child adjudicated delinquent may be placed in an institution in another party jurisdiction pursuant to this compact but no such placement shall be made unless the child is given a court hearing on notice to the parent or guardian with opportunity to be heard prior to his being sent to such other party jurisdiction for institutional care and the court finds that:

1. Equivalent facilities for the child are not available in the sending agency's jurisdiction; and

2. Institutional care in the other jurisdiction is in the best interest of the child and will not produce undue hardship.

Article VII. Compact Administrator

The executive head of each jurisdiction party to this compact shall designate an officer who shall be general coordinator of activities under this compact in his jurisdiction and who, acting jointly with like officers of other party jurisdictions, shall have power to promulgate rules and regulations to carry out more effectively the terms and provisions of this compact.

Article VIII. Limitations

This compact shall not apply to:

(a) The sending or bringing of a child into a receiving state by his parent, stepparent, grandparent, adult brother or sister, adult uncle or aunt, or his guardian and leaving the child with any such relative or non-agency guardian in the receiving state.

(b) Any placement, sending or bringing of a child into a receiving state pursuant to any other interstate compact to which both the state from which the child is sent or brought and the receiving state are party, or to any other agreement between said states which has the force of law.

Article IX. Enactment and Withdrawal

This compact shall be open to joinder by any state, territory or possession of the United States, the District of Columbia, the Commonwealth of Puerto Rico, and, with the consent of Congress, the Government of Canada or any province thereof. It shall become effective with respect to any such jurisdiction when such jurisdiction has enacted the same into law. Withdrawal from this compact shall be by the enactment of a statute repealing the same, but shall not take effect until two years after the effective date of such statute and until written notice of the withdrawal has been given by the withdrawing state to the Governor of each other party jurisdiction. Withdrawal of a party state shall not affect the rights, duties and obligations under this compact of any sending agency therein with respect to a placement made prior to the effective date of withdrawal.

Article X. Construction and Severability

The provisions of this compact shall be liberally construed to effectuate the purposes thereof. The provisions of this compact shall be severable and if any phrase, clause, sentence or provision of this compact is declared to be contrary to the constitution of any party state or of the United States or the applicability thereof to any government, agency, person or circumstance is held invalid, the validity of the remainder of this compact and the applicability thereof to any government, agency, person or circumstance shall not be affected thereby. If this compact shall be held contrary to the constitution of any state party thereto, the compact shall remain in full force and effect as to the remaining states and in full force and effect as to the state affected as to all severable matters.

CHAPTER 14

Termination of Parental Rights

Sarah Katz

14.01 Introduction: The Relationship between Neglect and Termination Cases

Representing parents in termination of parental rights (TPR) proceedings is one of the most challenging aspects of handling dependency cases. A termination decree ends a parent's rights to visit, communicate with, and have information about his or her child. As the Supreme Court has explained, "[T]erminating parental rights is *final* and irrevocable. Few forms of state action are both so severe and so irreversible." *Santosky v. Kramer*, 455 U.S. 745, 759 (1982). Lawyers representing parents in termination proceedings take on a huge responsibility.

Counsel is well-advised to be aware of the specter of a parent's loss of parental rights from the very beginning of the dependency or neglect case. Dependency and termination of parental rights cases are inextricably linked because of the time frames developed by Congress when it enacted the Adoption and Safe Families Act (ASFA). ASFA requires that, absent certain exceptions, states move to terminate parental rights so that the child is eligible for adoption whenever a foster child cannot be reunified with a parent in a fixed period of time. Under ASFA, termination petitions may be brought once a child has been in foster care for fifteen of the preceding twenty-two months, *see* 42 U.S.C. § 675(5)(E) (2014), and, if "aggravated circumstances" are present, even sooner. *Id.* at § 671(a)(15)(D)(i) (2014). Because the passage of time counts against parents when children are in foster care, case workers or agencies may "quit" on a parent early in the case and move mechanically toward the goal of termination (and adoption), with the assumption that is how the case will end. These are dangerous and self-fulfilling practices that counsel will want to prevent from being implemented.

Despite being the harshest penalty judges can impose in civil proceedings, termination of parental rights is conceived as a non-punitive disposition designed only to further a child's interests. Over the past twenty years, federal law has identified two children's interests as standing out above all others in importance: (1) child safety (which often results in children being removed from families and placed in foster care) and (2) permanency (which is a code word for adoption in many states). *Impermanency*, which usually means allowing children to remain in foster care for more than a year or two, is regarded as a far worse result for children than permanently banishing their families of origin from their lives. *See* Sacha Coupet, *Swimming Upstream Against the Great Adoption Tide: Making the Case for "Impermanence,"* 34 CAP. U. L. REV. 405, 412 (2005). This awesome state power is hailed as child-friendly, because children are supposed to gain something very valuable as the price paid for losing their family of origin: the creation of a new family. Termination of parental rights, for the overwhelming percentage of cases, is sought less to bar parents from their children forever (even if it has that consequence) than to free children to become the legal children of new parents via adoption.

Counsel who represent parents from the beginning of the dependency proceeding have the responsibility throughout the case to advocate aggressively for the most extensive and flexible visitation possible, and to work hard to ensure mandated services are actually provided. It is much safer and effective to fight for services needed to reunite a family than to lay back and complain at the termination stage that the Agency failed to do its job. Working hard to ensure that case plans are being implemented may not only help reunite the family, but may also prevent a termination petition from being filed, or help to mount a successful defense if one is filed.

When counsel is appointed only at the termination stage, it is often wise to focus on strategies aimed at convincing the Agency not to prosecute the termination petition because of various antecedent failures to assist the parent to comply with the case plan, or to refocus the goal of the case to one of the alternate dispositions discussed in section 14.06. If the case must proceed to trial, counsel's attention must turn to mounting a defense, as addressed in sections 14.07–08.

14.02 Whether and When to File a Termination Petition

ASFA allows the Agency to request findings in court that fast-track cases to termination where "aggravated circumstances" are present, such as abandonment, torture, chronic abuse, sexual abuse, or where the parent has committed murder or voluntary manslaughter of another child of the parent 42 U.S.C. § 675(a)(15)(D). Although these definitions amount to suggested grounds for termination, many states have expanded the bases for termination to encompass other definitions.

The amount of time children have been in foster care has become a primary measure for determining when to terminate parental rights. In too many jurisdictions, efforts to terminate are made mechanistically once children have been in foster care for the statutory minimum period of time. In these localities, petitions are filed without regard to other statutory or equitable considerations. Federal law was never designed to work that way. Built into ASFA's fabric are legal and equitable bases for foregoing a termination petition, and agencies faithful to federal law should assess every case individually to determine whether the law's exceptions are present.

ASFA identifies three exceptions to the fifteen-of-twenty-two-month rule. Whenever a relative is caring for children, federal law explicitly exempts states from seeking to terminate, and the federal government is committed to continuing to pay for foster care without a need to terminate parental rights. 42 U.S.C. § 675(5)(E)(i). Federal law also gives localities complete authority to conclude that a termination would not further the child's best interests. All that federal law requires is that agencies explain in the case plan "compelling reasons" for this determination. *Id.* at § 675(5)(E)(ii). Federal law also excludes situations in which termination should be sought where required reasonable efforts were not undertaken to seek a child's safe return to the family. *Id.* at § 675(5)(E)(iii). A majority of states have incorporated these or other exceptions into their laws. *See, e.g.*, Ala. Code § 12-15-317 (2014); Conn. Gen. Stat. § 17a-111a (2014); Mo. Rev. Stat. § 211.447 (2014); Neb. Rev. Stat. § 43-292.02 (2014).

Although ASFA does not define "compelling reasons," as discussed in § 14.05(b), federal regulations, state statutes, and case law have mapped out what may qualify as a compelling reason. Counsel should become familiar with these provisions, and with ASFA's history, to be equipped to explain to the Agency's lawyer and argue in court that there are federal and state statutory grounds not to terminate parental rights. Because "compelling reasons" are not defined by federal statute, counsel may also be able to make creative arguments that they exist. These reasons may avoid the need to defend against a termination action altogether or provide the frame for an effective defense.

In all events, when representing parents are trying to reunify with their children, time matters. In all states, most termination proceedings cannot be filed until a child has been separated from the parent for a specified period of time. In a few states, the child must have been separated from the parent for the entire fifteen month ASFA time frame. *See, e.g.*, Conn. Gen. Stat. § 17a-111a; Ind. Code § 31-35-2-4.5 (2014); N.M. Stat. Ann. 32A-4-29 (2014).

In many states, however, twelve months in foster care is an independent ground for termination of parental rights, as long as there is proof the Agency has been making reasonable efforts to reunify. *See, e.g.*, Ark. Code Ann. § 9-27-341 (2014); Miss. Code Ann. § 93-15-103 (2014); N.J. Stat. Ann. § 30:4c-15 (2014); N.Y. Soc. Serv. § 358-a (2014). In Florida, a showing of substantial failure to comply with the case plan for twelve months is sufficient for terminating parental rights of foster children.

See FLA. STAT. § 39.806 (2014). Other states add to this requirement that the child cannot be placed back with the parent within a reasonable time. *See, e.g.*, LA. CHILD. CODE ANN. art. 1015(6) (2014); MO. REV. STAT. § 211.447; N.C. GEN. STAT. § 7b-1111 (2014); OHIO REV. CODE ANN. § 2151.414 (2014).

However, many states authorize termination of parental rights when children have been in foster care for less than one year. Arizona permits terminating parental rights when children have been in foster care for only nine months; six months are sufficient for children under three. *See* AZ. REV. STAT. §8-533 (1996). Maine permits termination cases to be filed after children have been in care for nine months, during which the parent has made no significant effort to correct the situation that required the placement. *See* ME. REV. STAT. tit. 22, § 4055 (2014). Delaware permits termination cases involving infants after they have been in foster care for six months. *See* DEL. CODE ANN. tit. 13, § 1103 (2014). Kentucky, South Carolina, and Washington State allow petitions to be filed after children of any age have been in foster care for six months. *See* KY. REV. STAT. ANN. § 625.090 (2014); S.C. CODE ANN. § 63-7-2570 (2014); WASH. REV. CODE § 13.34.180 (2014). Oklahoma requires waiting a mere three months. *See* OKLA. STAT. tit. 10A, § 1-4-904 (2014). Finally, a few states appear to have no minimum time period before a termination petition may be brought. *See, e.g.*, ALA. CODE § 12-15-319 (2014); MINN. STAT. §§ 260.012, 260C.301 (2014); MONT. CODE ANN. §§ 41-3-423, 41-3-609 (2014); W. VA. CODE §§ 49-6-5, 49-6-5b (2014).

Although the specific statutory grounds for termination vary state by state, the focus of the termination proceeding generally is on the parent's efforts or success in remedying the circumstances that resulted in the child's placement in foster care, namely whether the conditions that resulted in the child's placement in foster care are still present. *See, e.g.*, ARK. CODE ANN. § 9-27-341(b)(3)(B)(i); IOWA CODE § 232.116(1)(d)(2) (2014); KAN. STAT. ANN. § 38-2269(b) (2014); OHIO REV. CODE ANN. § 2151.414(E)(1).

14.03 The Client Interview

Given the high stakes involved in termination cases, counsel meeting the client for the first time at the termination stage has a challenging task of developing a meaningful attorney-client relationship. The parent is facing an extraordinary trauma: the prospect of losing his or her child forever. Some parents may react with extreme hostility and anger, while others may not appear to grasp the finality of the proceeding he or she is facing. Effective preparation for a termination proceeding likely requires multiple interviews and counseling sessions with the parent.

Another barrier to developing a trusting attorney-client relationship is that the parent may have difficulty differentiating counsel's role from that of the agency caseworkers and other parties bringing the termination proceeding. By definition, the topics and questions that counsel must address may sound all too similar to the agency worker or judge's reproach regarding the parent's failures. If counsel has represented the parent throughout the dependency proceedings, the parent may blame him or her for the negative direction the case has turned. Counsel must communicate empathically with the parent, while also offering legal advice calculated to motivate the parent to take steps that may help defeat the termination petition or reach a favorable settlement.

Sometimes counsel's most effective strategy is to clearly delineate the attorney role and the attorney's responsibility to provide advice and counsel. Use of third-party reflection techniques may be fruitful, both to clearly communicate that counsel is loyal to the client, and to elicit important information, such as, "Why do you think the agency worker would say [that negative thing about you]?" and "When you say [that], the Judge may conclude you didn't try very hard."

Ideally, counsel will already know some of the important details of the case by having reviewed the court file. Whether counsel has had the chance beforehand or not, the initial interview is usually the place to establish (i) when and why the child was separated from the parent; the frequency and quality of the parent's visits and contact with the child since the separation (and any explanation of the parent for any lapses or difficulties with the frequency or quality); (ii) the parent's participation in all mandated services (and any explanation for any lapses or difficulties with following through with any mandated services); (iii) the parent's participation in any other relevant services not mandated; (iv) the nature of the parent's relationship with the agency caseworker(s); and (v) feelings about the Agency's and the parent's long-term plans for the child.

At this interview, counsel should also have the parent sign any releases for court documents and agency documents if the jurisdiction does not automatically allow access to these records for counsel. In addition, counsel should obtain releases for the client and the child for all relevant health records, mental health records, school records, substance abuse treatment records, or any other participation in services that relate to the case.

14.04 Pretrial Preparation

14.04(a) Discovery

After the initial interview, if not sooner, counsel should focus on obtaining all relevant records. First, counsel should always thoroughly review the court file, whether or not counsel has represented the parent from the beginning of the dependency proceeding. Counsel should carefully review the findings of fact and conclusions of law, if any were made in the dependency proceeding. Particular attention should be paid to the original reasons that the child was separated from the parent, to what visitation and services were court mandated, if any, and to any findings by the court concerning the parent's progress (or lack of progress) regarding visitation and participation in services.

Next, counsel should review the entire agency file. Counsel should insist on reviewing the entire unedited file, not just the portions the Agency seeks to introduce. Although the agency attorney may attempt to assert that the file is confidential, this is not a valid objection. Many state statutes make clear that parents may see the agency file; in jurisdictions that have not made this a statutory right, there still should be no reason to deny a parent access to the agency files once the client has executed a release for her attorney to see them. If counsel cannot gain prompt access to the agency file, a motion should be filed in court to gain such access. When special statutes or regulations protect the name of the reporter who initially contacted the Agency, redaction of that information will protect that interest. This limited redaction is acceptable if it does not impair the parent's ability to investigate and challenge the reliability of all the information used to establish the Agency's case against the parent.

Besides obtaining the Agency's case files, counsel should seek to obtain any manuals or operating procedures that the Agency may have. Many agencies have sets of formal directives, local, statewide, or both, that deal with such matters as the services to be provided to parents, the number and length of visitations to be allowed, the grounds on which termination proceedings are to be commenced, and the processes by which the decision to file a termination petition is to be made. The directives or agency manuals also commonly specify the records that the Agency must maintain. They will alert counsel to the types and names of other documents for which to look. Moreover, if the caseworker has not complied with the directives—a common phenomenon—counsel will gain leverage in settlement negotiations with the agency attorney and information for use at trial. Violations of agency rules may be introduced to show possible bias of the caseworker against the parent, the caseworker's incompetence, or both. Agency directives and manuals can ordinarily be obtained either by a demand to produce them for inspection and copying or by a subpoena *duces tecum*.

Finally, counsel should seek to obtain records from any agencies that have provided services to the parent and/or the child. Counsel can do this using the discovery methods available, such as using executed releases from the parent, or by serving subpoenas for relevant records. Because child welfare agencies frequently contract with a wide variety of service providers to provide services directly to the family, or make referrals for services provided outside the child welfare system (such as behavioral health or substance abuse treatment), it is important that counsel obtain these additional records. The parent may also have engaged in services not mandated by the court, but which will be helpful in mounting a case, such as therapy or domestic violence counseling, and securing these records may be very helpful to the case. To the extent permissible under the state's relevant rules of civil procedure, counsel may also make use of written interrogatories and/or depositions of adverse witnesses.

14.04(b) Investigation

After counsel has read all of the reports and records obtained through the discovery process discussed above, counsel should attempt to arrange an interview with each professional who wrote a report. The purpose of these interviews should be to clarify any inconsistencies in the reports and the recommendations of the provider. Perhaps the single most important set of materials counsel will want to know well is the case plan. Counsel should know how it was developed and when and where it was approved. If the Agency is receiving federal matching funds for the child's placement, federal law requires periodic case plan reviews. *See* 42 U.S.C. § 675(5)(C). If caseworkers testified at any of these reviews, counsel should seek a court order allowing counsel access to audio tapes of the proceeding or request that a written transcript is made of them. Knowing what agency personnel said under oath about the family is a vital part of preparing for the termination trial.

One of the particular challenges when defending against termination is that the full weight of the state's resources can go into mounting the case against the parent. Often the Agency has what seems to be a veritable mountain of documentation cataloguing each failure of the parent. Through the discovery and investigation process, counsel may come across particular witnesses, documents, or information that the Agency will choose not to present. A foster care agency worker who felt the visits with the parent were going well, and recommended an increase in visitation between the parent and child, is unlikely to be called as an agency witness. If that worker is called as a witness, she will now testify she is "on board" with the agency-recommended goal of termination and adoption. Through careful review of the record, counsel can identify witnesses who will be favorable to the parent, or who can testify on cross- examination to information that is useful to the parent. Because the Agency is charged with making "reasonable efforts" to reunify the parent with the child, effective cross-examination may result in an admission by the agency worker that s/he knew of the parent's failures but failed to take appropriate action. Further, counsel should strive to identify additional witnesses who can help bolster the parent's explanation for the parent's failures being alleged in the termination petition.

Counsel should also consider the possibility of retaining an independent expert witness. The Agency will frequently use their own expert to testify to parental incapacity and/or a lack of bond between parent and child. Using the mechanism available in the jurisdiction, counsel should ask the court to appoint an independent expert, or to provide funds to hire one. Sometimes an independent expert can evaluate the quality and accuracy of the Agency's expert's opinion.

Further, counsel should consider whether any of the fact witnesses who may be called might be certified as expert witnesses. For example, personnel from an intensive parenting program or a treating therapist may have the credentials to be qualified as an expert and offer their own opinion. Even if presented as fact witnesses, these witnesses can be helpful in counterbalancing a negative report from an agency expert.

14.05 Pretrial Motions

14.05(a) Filing a Written Answer to the Petition

Although it is rare that a jurisdiction requires a formal written answer to the termination petition, counsel should consider submitting one. By filing a written answer, counsel can include denials of facts alleged, but also affirmative defenses and/or counterclaims. This is particularly relevant where counsel will seek to prove the Agency failed to provide proper or necessary assistance to the parent. Filing counterclaims may also broaden the issues that can be raised at trial. Furthermore, filing a written answer draws the attention of the judge because it is an unusual practice in most jurisdictions.

14.05(b) Motion to Dismiss

Depending on the jurisdiction, the termination case may have been commenced by a separate petition, by a motion seeking judicial authorization to conduct a termination hearing, or by some other route. Whatever the method, counsel should consider challenging the effort by addressing the claims that justify moving to the termination stage. If the proceeding is brought by petition, counsel should review it carefully and consider whether there are grounds for a motion to dismiss. If the court previously granted a motion to move to the termination stage, counsel should consider bringing a motion to reconsider.

In all jurisdictions, courts must consider more than whether enough is pled to permit the court to terminate parental rights. Several equitable inquiries are invariably bound up in the question. Even when there may be grounds to terminate parental rights, courts are not supposed to do so, and may not even be supposed to conduct a hearing to consider doing so, when there are independent grounds to avoid that result. The child's wishes, the child's placement with relatives, failing to offer parents all appropriate services, and the best interests of the child, among other factors, are all things that can be considered not only to refuse to terminate parental rights but even to prevent the matter from going forward. *See* section 14.05(b)(1) below for a more complete discussion of compelling reasons not to terminate parental rights. Whenever it is possible to make an argument that compelling reasons under the law exist, counsel should consider taking steps to prevent the termination case from proceeding. Often the best form of this effort will be a motion in court.

14.05(b)(1) There Are Compelling Reasons Not to File

When a termination petition has already been filed, counsel may nonetheless inquire into whether there was a compelling reason not to have done so. If the court finds there was one, it may have the discretion to dismiss the petition, even when there are grounds under the law to grant it. The justification for this result is that the case never should have been brought in the first place.

14.05(b)(2) The Child Does Not Wish to Be Adopted

Under federal law, the child's preferences are supposed to have been considered when deciding whether to file the termination petition. *See* 42 U.S.C. § 675(5)(C)(iii). Counsel should seek to determine the child's preferences in the case. When there is reason to believe the child does not want to end all legal ties with his or her family, counsel should consider filing a motion to dismiss the Petition on that ground. In Colorado, New Mexico, and West Virginia, among many other states, the child's preference not to be adopted constitutes a compelling reason not to file the termination petition. *See* Colo. Rev. Stat. § 19-3-702(5)(a)(II) (2014); N.M. Stat. Ann. § 32A-4-29(G)(3); W. Va. Code § 49-6-5b(b)(2).

In some states, the child's preferences matter only upon reaching a certain age, commonly ranging from ten to fourteen years old. *See, e.g.*, Cal. Welf. & Inst. Code § 366.26A(C)(1)(b)(2) (2014); Colo. Rev. Stat. 19-3-702(5)(a)(II); Iowa Code § 232.111 (2014) (age ten); Me. Rev. Stat. tit. 22, § 4055 (age twelve); N.M. Stat. Ann. § **32A-4-29**; N.Y. Soc. Serv. § **384-b (2014)**; Va. Code § 16.1-283 (2014) (age fourteen). Other states leave it to the discretion of the judge to find whether the child is sufficiently mature to make an informed decision. *See, e.g.*, Nev. Rev. Stat. § 128.107 (2014); W. Va. Code § 49-6-5b.

14.05(b)(3) Adoption Is Not the Permanent Goal

In many states, when adoption is not the permanent goal, there may be a compelling reason for the Agency to be permitted or required to file a termination petition. *See, e.g.*, Colo. Rev. Stat. § 19-3-702(5)(a)(III). *See also* N.Y. Soc. Serv. § 384-b(3)(l)(ii)(B) (no need to file a termination petition when permanency goal is other than adoption).

14.05(b)(4) The Child Is in the Custody of a Relative

In many states, if a child is in the care of a relative, a termination of parental rights petition need not be filed. *See, e.g.*, Conn. Gen. Stat. § 17a-111a; Mo. Rev. Stat. § 211.447; Or. Rev. Stat. § 419B.498 (2014). Keep in mind that this is an exception, not a rule, so if the relative wishes to proceed with adoption, termination of parental rights may still be advanced as a permanency goal.

14.05(b)(5) The Child Is an Unaccompanied Refugee Minor

Federal regulations list cases for which termination petitions are not required to include children who are unaccompanied refugee minors. *See* 45 C.F.R. § 1356.21(2)(ii)(C) (2014).

14.05(b)(6) There Is a Positive Parent-Child Relationship

In several states the existence of a positive parent-child or sibling relationship is itself a compelling reason not to file a termination petition. *See, e.g.*, Cal. Welf. & Inst. Code

§ 366.26 (2013); IOWA CODE § 232.111 (2014); N.M. STAT. ANN. § 32A-4-29(G)(2); OR. REV. STAT. § 419B.498 (2014). These statutes require a determination that it would be detrimental for the child to lose any existing bonds with parents and/or siblings. Some statutes require a determination that a permanent plan other than termination of parental rights is best for the child. *See, e.g.*, OR. REV. STAT. § 419B.498(2)(b)(B) ("Another permanent plan is better suited to meet the health and safety needs of the child or ward, including the need to preserve the child's or ward's sibling attachments and relationships.").

14.05(b)(7) The Parent Has Maintained Regular Contact with the Child and the Child Would Benefit from Continuing Ties with the Parent

What a parent has done throughout the period in which the child is in foster care is also an important part of the inquiry into whether the termination petition should even be filed. If parents have maintained regular contact with the child throughout the time the child has been in foster care, their parental rights might not be terminated even if one of the grounds for termination exists. *See, e.g.*, CAL. WELF. & INST. CODE § 366.26(c)(1)(B)(i) (compelling reason defined as "parents have maintained regular visitation and contact with the child and the child would benefit from continuing the relationship"). *See also* COLO. REV. STAT. ANN. § 19-3-702(5)(a)(I); NEV. REV. STAT. § 128.107. Being in broad compliance with the service plan may serve as a compelling reason not to terminate, particularly when compliance is likely to lead to the child being able to safely return home. *See* N.M. STAT. ANN. § 32A-4-29(G)(1); OR. REV. STAT. ANN. § 419B.498(2)(b)(A). More generally, in some states, a compelling reason can be that the parent has demonstrated a willingness to adjust her circumstances in order for the child to return home, such as providing financial support or emotional support to the child. *See* NEV. REV. STAT. § 128.107.

14.05(b)(8) The Child's Continued Foster Care Placement Is the Result of Conditions Beyond the Control of the Parent

In a number of states, a compelling reason against filing the termination petition is that continued foster care was needed for reasons beyond the parent's control. *See, e.g.*, COLO. REV. STAT. § 19-3-604(2) (2014); IDAHO CODE ANN. §§ 16-2005, 16-1624 (2014); IOWA CODE § 232.111; N.M. STAT. ANN. § 32A-4-29; OKLA. STAT. tit. 10A, § 1-4-904; WASH. REV. CODE § 13.34.180. Poverty is the most common example. *See, e.g.*, FLA. STAT. § 39.806 (petition not to be filed based on parental failure to comply with case plan when failure is due to lack of money); NEB. REV. STAT. § 43-292.02 (petition not to be filed based on parental failure to provide health care when failure is due to lack of money); 23 PA. CONS. STAT. § 2511(b) (2014) (parental rights may not be terminated because of "environmental factors" such as inadequate housing or clothing that are beyond parent's capacity to offer).

14.05(b)(9) Children's Length of Stay in Foster Care Is Not the Parent's Fault

In some states, court delays and continuances that resulted in children being left in foster care for too long through no fault of the parent may serve as a compelling reason not to file. *See, e.g.*, COLO. REV. STAT. § 19-3-604(2)(k)(4).

14.05(b)(10) Parent Is in the Military or Is an Inpatient in a Substance Abuse Program

In some states, the time children spend in foster care when parents are in the military or enrolled as an inpatient in a substance abuse program should not count against the parent. *See, e.g.*, *id.*; IOWA CODE § 232.111; N.M. STAT. ANN. § 32A-4-29; N.Y. SOC. SERV. § 384-b; WASH. REV. CODE § 13.34.180.

14.05(c) Motion in Limine

Depending on local practice, this may also be the appropriate stage to file motions or petitions for alternative dispositions discussed in section 14.06. Counsel should also consider other relevant motions that should be filed. For example, motions in limine may be filed to prevent the presentation of particular evidence.

14.06 Settling the Case on Terms Favorable to the Parent

Because termination of parental rights permanently ends the parent's legal relationship to his or her child, counsel should investigate whether there is an acceptable way to reach a less drastic outcome which would preserve parental rights, or maintain some contact with the child. Once counsel has completed the discovery and investigation process described above, counsel may be prepared to approach the other parties to discuss settling the case. Alternatively, counsel may choose to file counterclaims asserting an alternative outcome such as guardianship or reunification.

14.06(a) Guardianship

In some cases, legal guardianship may be an alternative to termination of parental rights and adoption. Under ASFA, adoption is seen as the most permanent alternative for children after reunification, because it creates a new permanent family for the child. *See* DONALD N. DUQUETTE ET AL., U.S. DEP'T OF HEALTH & HUMAN SERVS., ADOPTION 2002: THE PRESIDENT'S INITIATIVE ON ADOPTION AND FOSTER CARE: GUIDELINES FOR PUBLIC POLICY AND STATE LEGISLATION GOVERNING PERMANENCE FOR CHILDREN, II-1, II-3 (1999). Legal guardianship, however, is also a very acceptable federal goal, seen as achieving an important measure of permanence by removing the children from foster care and awarding legal and physical custody to a third-party caregiver, but with the added benefit of maintaining the legal parental relationship between the child and his or her birth parents. *See id.* at II-1, II-10, II-12. Although legal guardianship has been used in most states for many decades, ASFA formalized its place as a permanency outcome in federal child-welfare law. *See* Mark F. Testa, *The Quality of Permanence—Lasting or Binding? Subsidized Guardianship and Kinship Foster Care as Alternatives to Adoption*, 12 VA. J. SOC. POL'Y & L. 499, 506 (2005). Legal guardianship also received major support when Congress enacted the Fostering Connections to Success and Increasing Adoptions Act of 2008 (Pub. L. 110-351), which authorizes states to provide kinship guardianship assistance payments for foster children when a relative is taking legal guardianship.

Legal guardianship is frequently an option where the child is placed with a family member (or friend of the family, known as "fictive kin") because the kinship exception to the ASFA fifteen-of-twenty-two-months rule may apply. However, not all states limit legal guardianship to kinship situations.

Legal guardianship is often an acceptable outcome to a parent at risk of losing the termination case because, in most states, parents maintain residual rights after legal guardianship is granted. The parent can often maintain communication or visitation with the child after the guardianship is granted. In the majority of states, parents may eventually file to vacate the legal guardianship, upon a sufficient showing of a "significant change of circumstances," and that it would be in the child's best interests to be returned to the parent's custody. For further discussion of legal guardianship orders under ASFA, and the modifiability of these orders, *see* Sarah Katz, *The Value of Permanency: State Implementation of Legal Guardianship Under the Adoption and Safe Families Act of 1997*, 2013 MICH. ST. L. REV. 1079 (2013).

Some agencies and judges may object to guardianship as the best outcome because of their concern that the parent may be able to eventually regain custody. To overcome this concern, counsel can agree to place on the record the reasons that the child cannot reunify and the condition that no modification of the guardianship order may be made without court approval.

14.06(b) Post-Adoption Contact (Open Adoption)

Counsel may also consider the possibility of negotiating post-adoption communication and visitation between the parent and child. Post-adoption contact agreements commonly allow the parent to continue to visit with and to receive phone calls and letters from the child after adoption. A majority of states provide for legally enforceable post-adoption contact agreements. U.S. DEP'T OF HUMAN SERVS., POSTADOPTION CONTACT AGREEMENTS BETWEEN BIRTH AND ADOPTIVE FAMILIES (2011). Where these agreements are legally enforceable, the parent may go to court to enforce the agreement when it is breached. In many states, adoptive parents may seek to modify or terminate the agreement if it is no longer in the child's best interest. Even where such agreements are not legally enforceable, nothing prevents a prospective adoptive parent from agreeing informally to allow post-adoption contact between the child and the parent.

Post-adoption contact would not be appropriate in every case. It works best where the parent and the adoptive parents are able to maintain a relationship, and the parent is prepared for someone else to become the child's legal parent. If counsel represents the parent in the underlying dependency case, it may be helpful to lay the foundation for a post-adoption contact agreement by encouraging the parent to cultivate a positive relationship with the foster parent. Although the parent may initially resent the foster parent, it may prove to be a wise long-term strategy should the case head toward termination.

14.06(c) Custody to the Other Parent

After completing discovery and investigation, counsel may conclude that although the client has a poor chance of defending against his or her termination of parental rights, the other parent's chances are much better. Although legally possible, it is unusual for courts to terminate parental rights of one but not the other parent when two parents are named in the termination petition. This is because the principal purpose of termination is to free a child for adoption, which would not happen unless the parental rights of both parents are terminated.

In these cases, counsel may want to collaborate on strategy with the other parent's attorney. This can be useful to both parents' cases. For example, the mother may be a fact witness regarding particular events or incidents that are relevant to the father maintaining parental rights, or vice versa. Successfully defending against the termination petition and carving the path toward reunification with the other parent almost always benefits the noncustodial parent, because his or her parental rights are preserved.

Counsel should be mindful that the risk to this strategy is that if the parents are differently situated, the parent with the stronger case for reunification may be hurt in the court proceeding if he or she is seen as too closely allied with the other parent, especially if the other parent is perceived as a safety risk to the child. In this situation, the parent with the stronger case for reunification may need to explain how he or she will keep the child safe if reunification is achieved.

14.06(d) Reunification

Counsel may also conclude that reunification is a viable goal for the parent to pursue. In such a case, counsel should explain to the agency attorney, the child advocate, or both, why they should seek to change the permanency goal to reunification. In some jurisdictions, counsel should file a counterclaim seeking reunification with the child. Sometimes, parents simply need a little more time to complete all of the mandates in the case plan, or they have not received key services that stand in the way of reunification.

14.06(e) Voluntary Relinquishment

Sometimes, after assessing the case, counsel may conclude that the parent has too weak a case to defend against termination. In this situation, counsel may want to advise the parent to voluntarily relinquish parental rights rather than going forward with a contested hearing. This becomes particularly relevant in the thirty-six states where an involuntary termination of parental rights can form the basis of a later finding of "aggravated circumstances" as to another child. *See* U.S. Dep't of Human Servs., Grounds for Involuntary Termination of Parental Rights (2013).

If the parent has other children in foster care, or is young and may eventually have other children, counsel should explain the risk of a later aggravated circumstances finding as a result of involuntary termination. This can be a very difficult conversation to have because the risks involved are predicated on a series of conditions. *If* the parent has another child, and *if* that child enters foster care, the children and youth agency *might* ask for a finding of aggravated circumstances and the court *might* find the Agency is relieved from making reasonable efforts. Nevertheless, because an aggravated circumstances finding can fast-track a case toward termination of parental rights, parent attorneys have an obligation to have this discussion with their clients.

The possibility of a finding of aggravated circumstances aside, a parent may conclude that voluntarily relinquishing rights is the best course of action. Although in most states voluntary relinquishment cannot be a condition of legally enforceable post-adoption contact, voluntary relinquishment may ease the relationship between the prospective adoptive parents and the natural parent. Or, if the parent has other children in foster care, the parent may conclude that his or her efforts are better spent focusing on reunification with those children. These are difficult decisions. In most states, relinquishment is not revocable absent a showing of cause, such as fraud or duress. *See* Ann M. Haralambie, Handling Child Custody, Abuse and Adoption Cases § 13:21 (3d. 2014). But going through a hopeless termination hearing will cause severe emotional harm to some parents. Other parents will elect to fight termination even when their lawyer has advised them they are unlikely to prevail. The parent will rely on the thoughtful advice of counsel in determining what strategy to pursue.

14.07 The Termination of Parental Rights Hearing

Termination proceedings provide an opportunity for creative lawyering. Counsel should identify one or more claims calculated either to argue that the legal bases for termination do not exist or that the court should not exercise its power to terminate because of other factors. Termination is a drastic remedy designed to serve the child's best interests. It should never be allowed without considering the broad swath of law and policy that serves as its background.

Counsel should always take advantage of preamble clauses attached to child welfare legislation because they commonly mention the importance of maintaining familial ties and clarify that the primary goal of child welfare intervention is to maintain the family relationship whenever doing so is consistent with children's safety and well-being. Consider the preamble in New York to see how much is contained within it that creative counsel can use to argue against either filing or granting a termination petition. The legislature's "statement of legislative findings and intent" introducing the legislative bases for termination parental rights emphasizes that "it is generally desirable for the child to remain with or be returned to the birth parent because the child's need for a normal family life will usually best be met in the home of its birth parent, and that parents are entitled to bring up their own children unless the best interests of the child would be thereby endangered;" and that "the state's first obligation is to help the family with services to prevent its break-up or to reunite it if the child has already left home."

See N.Y. Soc. Serv. Law § 384-b(1). Similarly, Pennsylvania's Juvenile Act has as its first purpose "[t]o preserve the unity of the family whenever possible or to provide another alternative permanent family when the unity of the family cannot be maintained." 42 Pa. Cons. Stat. § 6301 (2014). Minnesota explains that its child welfare scheme is built on the foundational principles of "preserv[ing] and strengthen[ing] the child's family ties whenever possible." *See* Minn. Stat. § 260C.001(b)(3).

Through these clearly articulated legislative values, counsel can build whatever argument is supportable by the facts that termination is inappropriate even though there may be grounds to terminate. In each case, the court should exercise its awesome power to destroy family ties cautiously and with a strong weight on the scale in favor of preserving them when there is some reason to do so. This greatly widens the focus of the case by allowing counsel to introduce any evidence that supports the claim that something too vital will be lost if termination is ordered.

14.07(a) The Agency's Burden of Proof

Termination proceedings are often both retrospective and prospective in focus. The statutory standard for termination of parental rights commonly requires that the petitioner present evidence not only of what the parent has affirmatively done or failed to do in the past, but also of what the parent will likely do in the future. The evidence presented may focus on events (e.g., the parent's alleged failure to attend visits scheduled with the child), or may be prognostic (e.g., the parent's expected ability to meet parental responsibility) or both. The Supreme Court has never directly held that the Constitution requires a factually based finding of unfitness, abandonment, or harm to the child as a precondition to termination of parental rights. However, the Court has indicated in *dicta* that this might be necessary. *See Smith v. Org. of Foster Families for Equal. & Reform*, 431 U.S. 816, 862–63 (1977).

In *Santosky*, the Court stated that "[a]ny *parens patriae* interest in terminating the natural parents' rights arises only at the dispositional phase, *after* the parents have been found unfit." *Santosky*, 455 U.S. at 767 n.17. This language suggests that the standard for termination of parental rights must not be vague or simply amount to "best interests of the child." *See also Quilloin v. Walcott*, 434 U.S. 246, 255 (1978) ("We have little doubt that the Due Process Clause would be offended '[i]f a State were to attempt to force the breakup of a natural family, over the objections of the parents and their children, without some showing of unfitness and for the sole reason that to do so was thought to be in the children's best interest.'") (quoting *Smith*, 431 U.S. at 862–63 (1977) (Stewart, J., concurring in judgment)).

In all termination proceedings, the burden of proof rests on the petitioner. The Supreme Court has held that the grounds for termination of parental rights must be proven by at least clear and convincing evidence. *See Santosky*, 455 U.S. at 746. One court explained the standard to require evidence "so clear, direct, weighty, and convincing as to enable the [factfinder] to come to a clear conviction without hesitancy of the truth of the precise facts in issue." *In re Adoption of Hamilton*, 379 Pa. Super. 274, 278, 549 A.2D 1291 (1988) (internal quotations marks omitted). *See also In re Adoption of James J.*, 332 Pa. Super. 486, 493, 481 A.2d 892 (1984), *rev'd on other grounds*, 511 Pa. 590, 515 A.2d 883 (1986). In New Hampshire, and in all cases involving children, courts must find sufficient evidence beyond a reasonable doubt to terminate parental rights. *See* 25 U.S.C. § 1912(f) (2014); *In re Jessica B.*, 121 N.H. 291, 294, 429 A.2d 320 (1981). *See also* Chapter 11, which discusses the Indian Child Welfare Act in greater detail.

Proof of past adjudication of parental wrongdoing is insufficient to terminate parental rights. Not only are past adjudications of dependency or neglect commonly supported by a mere preponderance of evidence, but the Supreme Court explained that a parent's fundamental constitutional right to the care and custody of their children "does not evaporate simply because . . . [the parents] have not been model parents or have lost temporary custody of their child to the State." *Santosky*, 455 U.S. at 753. *See also State in Interest of L.L.Z. v. M.Y.S.*, 620 So. 2d 1309, 1313 (La. 1993).

14.07(b) Grounds for Termination

All states have grounds for terminating parental rights that relate to their child protection or child welfare statutes. Federal law is silent on the substantive bases for terminating parental rights. State law will determine what those grounds are, limited, of course, by what the Constitution requires. Counsel should become familiar with the statutory grounds for termination in the jurisdiction and all case law interpreting those grounds.

14.07(b)(1) Abandonment

Abandonment, usually defined as a failure to contact, provide care, or support the child for a prescribed period of time, is a common ground for termination. *See, e.g.*, CAL. FAM. CODE § 7822(a)(3) (2014); FLA. STAT. § 39.806(1)(b); VA. CODE § 63.2-1202(H) (2014). Counsel should pay close attention to the definition of abandonment under state law. In some states, abandonment is a subjective inquiry: Did the parent intend to abandon her parental role? *See, e.g.*, MO. REV. STAT. §§ 211.447–511 (2014); *In re Trapp*, 528 S.W.2d 489 (Mo. Ct. App. 1975), *superseded on other grounds*, *In Interest of B.C.H.*, 718 S.W.2d 158 (Mo. Ct. App. 1986); *In re T.H.* 497 S.W.2d 210 (Mo. Ct.

App. 1973). *See also In re Jack H.*, 106 Cal. App. 3d 257, 165 Cal. Rptr. 646 (1980) (termination reversed where evidence insufficient to show mother's intent to abandon); *Matter of Adoption of a Child by D.M.H.*, 135 N.J. 473, 641 A.2d 235 (1994) (termination granted where intentional abandonment by mother).

More commonly, the inquiry is objective. Has the parent done particular things that count as steps toward developing or maintaining a parental relationship? *See State in Interest of Summers Children v. Wulffenstein*, 560 P.2d 331 (Utah 1977) (applying objective intent standard to uphold termination where, despite father's expressions of intent, his behavior disregarded the parent-child relationship). Evidence of a parent's efforts at visitation, phone calls, letters or other communication, as well as other behavior geared at maintaining the parent-child relationship, will usually be determinative of whether grounds are met for abandonment, and a single event that might count for the parent often is not enough. *See, e.g.*, *Copeland v. Todd*, 282 Va. 183, 715 S.E.2d 11 (2011) (abandonment found where parent visited on one occasion during six-month period preceding termination petition).

14.07(b)(2) Serious Criminal Misconduct or Abuse

In every state, certain criminal acts or proof of serious physical, sexual, or emotional abuse provide a statutory basis for terminating parental rights. Sometimes, the acts are broadly worded, involving the use of "intentional or willful infliction of serious physical injury." *See, e.g.*, ALA. CODE § 12-15-319 (same); ARIZ. REV. STAT. § 8-533 (2014) (same); NEB. REV. STAT. § 43-292 ("serious bodily injury"). Other times, the behavior is more specific, involving "torture," or "sexual abuse." *See, e.g.*, DEL. CODE ANN. tit. 13, **§ 1103(a) (torture)**; KAN. STAT. ANN. § 38-2269(b)(4) (sexual abuse); KY. REV. STAT. ANN. § 625.090(2)(f) (same); S.D. CODIFIED LAWS § 26-8A-26.1(4) (2014) (torture). Still other times, behavior that is "heinous or shocking" will form the basis for terminating parental rights. *See* OKLA. STAT. tit. 10A, § 1-4-904(B)(9).

If a parent has been criminally convicted of the abuse alleged in the termination petition, the parent will be collaterally estopped from re-litigating the underlying facts. *See, e.g.*, *State ex rel. S.L.J.*, 41, 808 (La. App. 2 Cir. 12/13/06), 945 So. 2d 304. When the criminal case is still pending, counsel must consider Fifth Amendment self-incrimination issues when crafting the defense in the termination case. *See* Chapter 5 for a more thorough discussion of what to do when there is a pending criminal case. In the absence of a criminal conviction, counsel's tactic often will be to attempt to show that the alleged abuse does not meet the statutory definition justifying termination.

Even when counsel is unable to challenge the charge underlying wrongful acts committed by the parent, counsel may be able to focus the court's attention on the efforts the parent has made to rehabilitate since the incident of abuse occurred, or other reasons, equitable in nature, that should give the court pause to terminate the parent-child relationship, even if there are statutory grounds to do so.

In many of these cases, the same statutory grounds for terminating parental rights will justify forgoing reasonable efforts to rehabilitate the parent. *See* § 14.02. These "aggravated circumstances" mean both that the court has already found that there are grounds to excuse the Agency from its ordinary duty to help the parent and that the case deserves to be fast-tracked for termination. This not only means the parent is unlikely to have been offered services, it also means the court is disinclined to care about the parent's rehabilitation. Nonetheless, counsel should present evidence that the child would benefit from maintaining a legal relationship with the parent, apart from the question of how likely it is that the parent will regain the child's custody. Especially where adoption is not a probable outcome in the case, counsel should press the claim that there is more to gain from maintaining the legal parent-child relationship than from destroying it.

14.07(b)(3) Incapacity, Such as Substance Abuse, Mental Illness, Intellectual Disability

Parental rights may also be terminated due to serious and ongoing incapacity of the parent, resulting from substance use, mental illness, or an intellectual disability. In a number of states, proof of ongoing or chronic substance use is sufficient grounds to terminate parental rights. *See, e.g.*, D.C. CODE § 16-2353(5) (2014); FLA. STAT. § 39.806(j). In Maine, chronic substance abuse is presumed when a parent is unable to provide safe care for her child for at least nine months. *See* ME. REV. STAT. tit. 22, § 4055(1)(A)–(C). And in Minnesota and Ohio, proof that a parent still using drugs has twice failed to complete a treatment program or twice refused to participate in one constitutes presumptive proof that reasonable efforts have failed. *See* MINN. STAT. § 260C.301(b)(5)(iv); OHIO REV. CODE ANN. § 2151.414(E)(9). Montana requires a showing that the use of alcohol or drugs "affects the parent's ability to care and provide for the child." *See* MONT. CODE. ANN. § 41-3-609(2)(c).

Similarly, proof of chronic untreated or unmanaged mental illness may be grounds for termination. *See, e.g.*, HAW. REV. STAT. § 571-61(b)(1)(F) (2014); NEB. REV. STAT. § 43-292(5). New Hampshire requires proof from at least two licensed psychiatrists or clinical psychologists that the parent's deficiency is likely to continue "for a longer period of time than would be wise or prudent to leave the child in an unstable or impermanent environment." *See* N.H. REV. STAT. ANN. § 170-C:5(IV) (2014).

A parent's intellectual disability is often also used as evidence to support grounds of ongoing incapacity. *See, e.g.*, HAW. REV. STAT. § 571-61(b)(1)(F); VA. CODE § 16.1-283(B)(2)(a) ("The parent or parents have a mental or emotional illness or intellectual disability of such severity that there is no reasonable expectation that such parent will be able to undertake responsibility for the care needed by the child in accordance with his age and stage of development."). A diagnosis of mental illness or intellectual disability is usually not *per se* evidence of grounds for termination; there must be specific proof that the parent's diagnosis renders him or her unable to parent.

What is required to prove ongoing incapacity is most often statutorily defined. Because the grounds vary from state to state, counsel must pay attention to the specific statutory language, as well as attendant case law in the jurisdiction, insisting that the agency present sufficient proof by clear and convincing evidence to support termination.

14.07(b)(4) Failure to Plan or Passage of Too Much Time

As discussed in section 14.02, the mere passage of time (that the child is in foster care), or a parent's failure to comply with a reunification case plan over a period of time, can sometimes be sufficient grounds to terminate parental rights. It can be particularly difficult for parent's counsel to craft a defense where the parent's alleged "flaw" is the passage of time. At least one court has held that a statute authorizing termination of parental rights merely because a child has been in foster care for fifteen months is unconstitutional because it is insufficiently narrowly tailored and does not further a compelling state interest. *See In re H.G.*, 197 Ill.2d 317, 259 Ill. Dec. 1, 757 N.E.2d 864 (2001).

14.07(c) The Impact of Termination on the Child

Terminating parental rights when the child and parents know each other in a meaningful way at the time of the termination proceeding exacts a high cost. Permanently banning a child from his or her parent(s) and other birth relatives may be a necessary act in some cases. But counsel should work hard to present evidence that it is rarely a cost-free act and that the destruction of these ties has severe, negative consequences for the child. Even in a case where the weight of the evidence in terms of grounds against the parent seems undefeatable, counsel for the parent should turn attention to evidence concerning the child's best interest, which may still weigh strongly against termination of parental rights.

Even when grounds for termination of parental rights have been proven by clear and convincing evidence, state laws commonly require that the petitioner also prove that termination would be in the child's best interests. This aspect of the inquiry usually focuses on the value of the parent-child relationship and what impact permanently ending it would have on the child. Florida, for example, requires inquiry into the "love, affection, and other emotional ties existing between the child and the child's parent or parents, siblings, and other relatives, and the degree of harm to the child that would arise from the termination of parental rights and duties." FLA. STAT. § 39.810 (2014). In some states, the question is whether the child would be harmed as a result of severing the parent-child relationship. *See also* ALASKA STAT. § 47.10.082 (2014); WIS. STAT. § 48.426(2)–(3) (2014).

Counsel should take full advantage of this additional inquiry. In many cases, counsel's strongest chance of preventing termination is to focus on the effect permanently ending the parent-child relationship will have on the child. Proof of grounds to terminate parental rights is necessary but insufficient to order termination. Frequently, even if the parent may never be in a position to regain custody, there is value in maintaining the parent-child relationship. *See, e.g.*, Matthew B. Johnson, *Examining Risks to Children in the Context of Parental Rights Termination Proceedings*, 22 N.Y.U. Rev. L. & Soc. Change 397, 405 (1996).

The Agency will often present an expert witness to testify about the quality of the parent-child "bond" and whether that bond is worth preserving, even if such an expert is not required. These experts, often paid by the Agency, commonly spend very little time with the parent. As discussed in section 14.07(e)(2), counsel should become familiar with the standards set out by the American Psychological Association for such forensic evaluations, and hold the evaluator to these standards through cross-examination. *See* Am. Psychological Assoc., *Guidelines for Psychological Evaluations in Child Protection Matters*, 68 Am. Psychologist 21 (2013). Whether not the Agency calls an expert, counsel should consider using an expert for the parent to testify to the strength of the relationship. This may be a treating therapist or someone retained only for the purpose of testifying in court. For more on these types of forensic evaluations, see section 14.07(e)(2).

In many states, it is sufficient to prevent termination by proving that the child would benefit from continuing the relationship with the parent. *See, e.g.*, Colo. Rev. Stat. § 19-3-702; Iowa Code § 232.111(2)(b)(2); Mo. Rev. Stat. § 211.447(7)(1); Tenn. Code Ann. § 36-1-113(i)(4) (2014). Particularly where parents have visited with their children in foster care, counsel should demonstrate that the relationship is worth preserving. This can be done by having the parent and other family relatives testify to their love for the child and the reasons the child would benefit from continued connections to the family, including siblings, cousins, and grandparents. Counsel should consider calling an expert to testify to the emotional harm associated with permanent loss of family and why such loss should be avoided unless necessary.

Courts in some states are also expected to consider the impact of termination on the child's siblings. *See, e.g.*, Md. Code Ann., Fam. Law § 5-323 (2013); Ohio Rev. Code Ann. § 2151.414(D)(1). When termination will substantially interfere with sibling relationships, counsel should argue that the price of termination is too high. *See* Cal. Welf. & Inst. Code § 366.26(E). In focusing on the child's best interest, the Agency will frequently try to focus the court's attention on the child's relationship with the foster parent or other caretakers. And in some states, courts are to consider if "a psychological parent-child relationship has developed between the substitute family and the child." *See* N.M. Stat. Ann. § 32A-4-28(3)(c) (2014).

However, a number of courts have found that the child's relationship with foster or pre-adoptive parents should not be a determinative basis to grant a termination of parental rights petition. *See, e.g., Interest of J.R.*, 478 N.W.2d 409 (Iowa Ct. App. 1991) (bonding with foster parent not sole determinative factor in termination of parental rights); *In re Alana S*, 2000 ME 126, 802 A.2d 976 (2002) (fact that a very young child may have bonded with the child's foster parents cannot control an evaluation of the parenting capacity or parental fitness of the natural parents; termination warranted based on weight of the evidence); *Matter of A.*, 277 N.J. Super. 454, 649 A.2d 1310 (1994) (child's bonding to foster parents not grounds for termination of parental rights where no irreparable harm caused by child's reunification with natural parent).

In addition to focusing on the negative impact that termination may have on the child, counsel should be prepared to address the Agency's or court's likely response that whatever harm a termination will exact is outweighed by the benefits that will accrue to the child in the long term. This counterargument is strongest when the child is in a pre-adoptive home and the plan is for the child to be adopted in the near future. For better or worse, American child welfare policy is wedded to the claim that adoption is the ideal outcome of a case when a foster child is unable to be reunited with his or her family in the near future. For this reason, efforts by counsel to oppose termination when adoption is the almost certain next step will rarely succeed once there are statutory grounds for termination.

When there is no adoption plan for the child, and the Agency seeks to terminate a meaningful, existing parent-child relationship, counsel should forcefully oppose the effort. It is one thing to create a legal orphan temporarily so that the child will be adopted. At least in such cases, the harm the child will suffer may be offset for a greater good: the permanency of an adoption. But it is an entirely different matter when the court enters an order that has a known harmful impact on a child and only a possibility of something better coming from it. That high-stakes gamble, at the expense of the child's well-being, is something counsel should strongly oppose. But in a great many cases, adoption is, at best, something the Agency hopes will happen. This is particularly true with respect to older children and children with disabilities. In these cases, the court is contemplating a result that has a clear cost but an unclear benefit. Counsel should assertively cross-examine the Agency's witnesses and call an expert to explain that, given the high cost of such a drastic result, it is appropriate only when the child will gain something tangible from it.

Courts are divided as to whether an adoption plan is required before termination is granted. In several states, courts are expected to inquire into the likelihood that the child will be adopted if the termination order is entered. *See, e.g.*, ARK. CODE ANN. § 9-27-341(b)(3)(A)(i); CAL. WELF. & INST. CODE § 366.26(c)(1). Others, however, permit courts to enter such orders with no requirement of an adoption plan. *See, e.g.*, 23 PA. CONS. STAT. § 2512(b). *See also In re Davonta V.*, 285 Conn. 483, 940 A.2d 733

(2008) (termination in child's best interest even in absence of adoption plan). Counsel should always oppose terminations in cases where no permanency plan exists and should not rest until the state's highest court rules that the practice is inappropriate.

Counsel should also know what the child thinks and wants. Depending on the child's age, his or her wishes may be controlling. As discussed in section 14.05(b)(2), in many states, children above a certain age must consent to being adopted. When these children are opposed to termination of their parents' rights, courts should refuse to terminate.

14.07(d) Admissibility of Records at the Hearing

Depending on the jurisdiction, the rules of evidence may or may not apply at the termination hearing. Counsel must ascertain this well before the start of the hearing in order to craft the strategy to defeat the termination petition and to determine what evidence the Agency can and cannot present. Even in jurisdictions where the rules of evidence do not apply at the termination hearing, counsel should be prepared to object to the admission of documents that are unreliable.

Commonly, the most important documentary evidence the Agency will introduce at trial is the case file maintained by the Agency. Often agency attorneys seek to have the case file admitted into evidence wholesale, as a business record. Counsel needs to be prepared to object to the whole record being admitted because many entries should be excluded as not meeting the criteria for the business-record exception to the hearsay rule. Case files frequently include notations by multiple personnel who lack personal knowledge of the events noted and incorporate multiple levels of hearsay (hearsay within hearsay). The agency file may also include documents not produced by the Agency, such as reports from other providers, mental health professionals, or doctors which may not meet any hearsay exception. Counsel cannot wait until the trial begins to prepare for this objection. Rather, it is essential for counsel to read the entire case file before trial and mark those portions counsel wants to be redacted from the original file. Coming to court prepared to object to the admission of the entire file with a substitute version containing only the portions to which counsel does not object significantly enhances the odds that the court will admit only the redacted version. The agency attorney is unlikely to do the work of redacting the file in this way, and may agree to the parent attorney's stipulated version, in lieu of battling over evidentiary objections.

There is no meaningful way to argue about the introduction of entries in the agency file without pointing to each entry and specifically demonstrating why each does not meet the hearsay exception for business records. Putting the amount of time into pretrial preparation required to carefully examine every page in the case record advances three broad purposes. First, proper preparation ensures that counsel will be fully familiar with the record, something that can be of enormous value during the trial and closing argument. Second, it increases the chances of excluding hearsay that would hurt the client. Third, it demonstrates to the court a level of professional competence and thoroughness that will often redound to the client's advantage.

It is also important for counsel to know both the rules of evidence and controlling case law in the jurisdiction, as well as the Agency's practices regarding how cases are handled and when notations are made in the file. Even without worker turnover, it is common for multiple workers to have responsibility for working on a case since most agencies divide responsibility for intake/investigation, family stabilization, foster care, and permanency planning among different units. Thus, the worker testifying at the termination trial may have little personal knowledge about the family. This is precisely why the Agency will seek to rely so heavily on the Agency's case file regarding the family.

Here are some common objections that will be helpful to parent's counsel in seeking to keep out various portions of a case record:

(1) *Objection, hearsay. . . . Counsel has not laid a foundation that this is the type of record kept in the ordinary course of business. Further, this witness (the agency worker) is not the custodian of these records and cannot testify as to what is the routine practice of the Agency.*

In most jurisdictions, before a business record may be admitted into evidence, there must be testimony that the notations in the record were made contemporaneously or shortly thereafter. This generally requires testimony that the notations were made in the routine course of business.

(2) *Objection, hearsay. . . . Counsel has not laid a foundation that this is the type of record kept in the ordinary course of business. Further, this witness (the agency worker) holds no supervisory role and cannot testify as to the Agency's practices and procedures.*

In most jurisdictions, before a business record may be admitted into evidence, there must be testimony about the circumstances under which such notations are made in the ordinary practices of the business.

(3) *Objection, hearsay. . . . The worker who made the notation did not have firsthand knowledge of the events he or she noted in the record.*

In many jurisdictions, in order to meet the requirements of the business record exception, the person making the notation must have direct knowledge of the events being described. If the worker who made the notation did not directly witness or experience the events described, the notation may not be admissible.

(4) *Objection, hearsay within hearsay. . . . This notation is based upon information that the case worker did not gain firsthand.*

Frequently the agency worker will attempt to testify to what other individuals (a foster care worker, a drug treatment counselor, a family member of the parent) told the worker. These statements are inadmissible hearsay, regardless of whether they were noted in the agency's case record regarding the family.

(5) *Objection, hearsay. . . . This worker did not produce this document or record.*

Frequently, the agency file includes records or reports from numerous other agencies or institutions, such as school records, hospital or other medical records, and mental health records. Just because these records are included in the agency file does not make them a business record. Absent a local or state rule to the contrary, the custodian of these records or the person who generated the report must be present for these records to be admitted into evidence.

14.07(e) Cross-Examining the Agency's Witnesses

14.07(e)(1) Cross-Examining the Caseworker

The agency caseworker is usually the Agency's most important, if not only, witness. Effective cross-examination of the agency caseworker is crucial to successfully defending a termination of parental rights case.

The Agency worker's testimony will likely focus on the parent's failures to comply with the service plan. As mentioned in section 14.02, because the Agency is charged with making "reasonable efforts" to reunify the parent with the child, effective cross-examination may cause admissions by the Agency worker that he or she knew of the parent's failures but failed to take appropriate action to help the parent. Counsel can effectively draw in the Agency worker on cross-examination, by seeking to pin down the details of the parent's poor behavior recounted on direct, and determining when precisely the worker learned of the behavior, and that it was contemporaneous to the events described. While the worker might think that the reliability of his or her testimony is being questioned, counsel would be establishing precisely when the worker became aware of the parent's failings. The questioning can proceed to clarify all of the possible actions (as specified in counsel's questions) that the worker did not take to help the parent remedy the problem.

To help prepare for this line of cross-examination, counsel should meet with an experienced social worker to find out what an excellent case worker would be expected to do whose goal was to offer parents all feasible assistance to overcome whatever obstacles exist in the case. The reasonable efforts requirement is an important subject for counsel to mine. The goal is to persuade the judge, not that the agency worker could have done more, but that a reasonable caseworker devoted to helping the parent *would* have done more. Offering the court specific examples of what might have been done will go a long way toward persuading the court that not enough was actually done.

Another common focus of agency worker testimony may be the child's apparent negative reaction to visits with the parent or subsequent to visits with the parent. However, this reaction may not indicate a bad relationship between parent and child. In fact, it may indicate a good relationship, and how upsetting it is to the child to be separated from the parent and have no control over the situation. Effective cross-examination on these issues can cause admissions by the agency worker that there are many reasons a child in foster care may be upset during or after visitation with a parent. To help prepare counsel for this cross-examination, counsel should meet with an expert on foster children's reactions after visiting with parents and weave questions of the caseworker based on the expert's advice.

14.07(e)(2) Cross-Examining Expert Witnesses for the Agency

Agencies frequently call psychiatrists, psychologists, or other expert witnesses to testify in termination cases. Usually these witnesses are called to testify to the parent's capacity to parent, and/or to the bond between the parent and child. Depending on the allegations in the termination petition and the answer, if an answer to the petition was filed (*see* section 14.05(a)), the expert's testimony regarding the adequacy of the parent's caretaking ability, plans for the future for the child, or the likely probability of reunification may or may not be relevant at the adjudicatory stage. Similarly, depending on the statutory grounds for termination and the law in one's jurisdiction, testimony regarding the best interests of the child may be relevant at the dispositional stage only, and parent's counsel should insist that best interests not be introduced into the trial before it is legally relevant.

Effective preparation for cross-examination of an expert witness requires that parent's counsel used pretrial discovery to obtain the expert report, and all of the materials relied upon for the expert to produce his or her examination and opinion. Ideally, counsel will have also obtained his or her own expert to review the agency expert's report and assist in developing a line of cross-examination. A pretrial interview with the agency expert and/or a pretrial deposition is invaluable to ensure that counsel will be fully prepared at trial. Most often, the agency expert will have only been brought into the case once termination is contemplated. Parent's counsel can use cross-examination to bring out the limited time the agency expert spent with the parent and/or child and the agency expert's limited knowledge of the parties or resources available.

Familiarity with recommended practices in forensic evaluations will help counsel prepare for cross-examination or rebuttal. One of the challenges for counsel in dealing with parenting capacity evaluations is "the lack of clinical tools available to adequately assess minimal parenting competence, and the absence of any clear criteria regarding what constitutes 'good enough' parenting." Fred Schmidt et al., *Assessing the Parent-Child Relationship in Parenting Capacity Evaluations: Clinical Applications of Attachment Research*, 45 FAM. CT. REV. 247, 247 (2007). Counsel should be familiar with the basic framework of the evaluation and prepared to challenge evaluations that do not meet basic assessment principles or are not grounded in adequate scientific bases. *Id.* The evaluation should emphasize a functional approach, "examining the parent's behavior and skills in everyday performances." *Id.* at 248. At a minimum, the evaluation should include "information about a parent's relationship history and mental health status, child protection history and concerns, quality of the parent-child relationship, family social supports, and the parent's ability to make changes and work with respective professionals." *Id.*

For both parenting capacity and bonding evaluations, the American Psychological Association's *Guidelines for Psychological Evaluations in Child Protection Matters* recommend that an evaluator employ "multiple methods of data gathering, including but not limited to, clinical interviews, interviews with collateral contact, clinical observations, and/or psychological testing that are sufficient to provide appropriate substantiation for their findings." Am. Psychological Assoc., *Guidelines for Psychological Evaluations in Child Protection Matters*, 68 AM. PSYCHOLOGIST 20, 27 (2013).

In addition to using multiple sources for data and multiple methods of gathering the data, the assessment should also include multiple sessions; compliance with these three recommendations creates a greater and presumably more reliable pool of information upon which the evaluator can base his or her findings. *See* Karen S. Budd et al., *Clinical Assessment of Parents in Child Protection Cases: An Empirical Analysis*, 25 LAW & HUM. BEHAV. 93 (2001). Although bonding evaluations more directly are meant to assess "attachment" of the parent and child, many clinicians feel that attachment theory is also a critical component of parenting capacity assessments. *See* Schmidt et al., *supra*, 45 FAM. CT. REV. at 248. Frequently, the agency expert evaluations will fail to meet these standards of practice, which can be brought out on cross-examination.

14.07(f) The Defense Case

The most effective way to counter a termination of parental rights petition is to show that the Agency has failed to meet its burden of proof to support statutory grounds for terminating the parent's rights. As addressed in section 14.07(a), the burden of clear and convincing proof is weighty. Even in a case where the Agency may have seemingly compelling evidence against the parent, counsel's job is to demonstrate what is missing or insufficient. At the end of petitioner's case, counsel should move to dismiss the petition on the grounds that the Agency has failed to meet its burden of proving statutory grounds for termination by clear and convincing evidence (or beyond a reasonable doubt).

The following section outlines possible defenses and counterclaims to a termination proceeding. Other defenses may be specific to the grounds and applicable case law in the jurisdiction where the termination case is filed.

14.07(f)(1) The Agency Has Failed to Make Reasonable Efforts to Support and Reunite the Family

The Adoption Assistance and Child Welfare Act of 1980 requires states that receive certain federal funds to make "reasonable efforts" to prevent out-of-home placement, and to make "reasonable efforts" to reunify families where out-of-home placement is necessary. 42 U.S.C. § 671(a)(15). Although the Adoption and Safe Families Act of 1997 creates exceptions to this requirement where a court makes findings of "aggravated circumstances," and the Agency is relieved of its responsibility to make reasonable efforts to reunify the family, in the vast majority of cases the Agency must provide reasonable efforts. *See id.*

When reasonable efforts are required by state law, the Agency's failure to provide appropriate services can be a defense to termination of parental rights. *See, e.g., In re Shaiesha O.*, 93 Conn. App. 42, 887 A.2d 415 (2006); *In re Children of T.R.*, 750 N.W.2d 656 (Minn. 2008); *In re Sheila G.*, 61 N.Y.2d 368, 474 N.Y.S.2d 421, 462 N.E.2d 1139 (1984); *In re Natalya C.*, 946 A.2d 198 (R.I. 2008). Although they are not required to exhaust every possible service, *See, e.g., In re Shirley B.*, 419 Md. 1, 18 A.3d 40 (2011), or offer services that would be entirely futile, *See, e.g., Matter of Appeal in Yuma Count J-88-201, J-88-202, J-88-203*, 172 Ariz. 50, 833 P.2d 721 (Ct. App. 1992); *In re Interest of S.R.*, 239 Neb. 871, 479 N.W.2d 126 (1992), agencies must implement a meaningful service plan designed to help parents overcome the obstacles to the child's safe return. If counsel can show that the Agency knew of the parent's difficulties or problems early in the case, and failed to provide services or referrals tailored to meet the needs of that parent, counsel has laid the foundation for an effective defense to termination.

It will often be the case that the court has previously made findings that reasonable efforts were made. This should not be a barrier at termination, however. In some jurisdictions, the record that matters for the termination case is limited to the evidence presented at the termination trial. Counsel should feel free to argue that efforts were unreasonable, regardless of antecedent findings at the dependency stage of the proceeding. The "reasonable efforts" findings at the earlier stages were made to allow federal funding to pay for foster care services. *See* 42 U.S.C. § 671(a)(15). The "reasonable efforts" requirement at the termination stage is for the very different purpose of meeting the substantive basis for termination. Due process requires that counsel have the opportunity at the termination stage to challenge the claim that the services provided were reasonable. Nor can the antecedent findings serve as any kind of estoppel. At the termination stage, the court must find by clear and convincing evidence that reasonable efforts were provided. Courts do not use this higher standard at permanency hearings. A court's finding by a preponderance of evidence that reasonable efforts were provided carries no weight when the court must decide this by clear and convincing proof.

Counsel should not hesitate to draw out evidence that the Agency knew of the parent's failings and neglected to develop an appropriate plan to effectuate reunification. Parent's counsel should be thoroughly familiar with controlling case law, especially decisions by the jurisdiction's highest court, addressing what constitutes reasonable efforts and tailor cross-examination accordingly.

Counsel may present evidence of any rehabilitative and reunification services that the Agency could have used but did not. A social worker or a former Agency caseworker can be called as an expert witness to describe available programs and resources and to explain how he or she might have helped the family. Agencies can often be shown to have been derelict in arranging visitation, obtaining benefits, therapy, or counseling for the parent or the child, or not doing other things that would have facilitated the return of the child to the parent. Depending on the jurisdiction, the services available may be codified, or may be set forth in regulations or policy. Many state laws are explicit in the kinds of services agencies are expected to offer parents. These expansive lists commonly include the requirement that agencies make reasonable attempts to assist, develop, and encourage a meaningful relationship between the parent and child, and that they work closely with the parent in developing a service plan. *See, e.g.*, N.Y. Soc. Serv. § 384-b(7)(f). States also spell out specific kinds of services agencies should be using, such as child care, day care, homemaker services, housekeepers, caretakers, respite care, in-home health care, crisis counseling, domestic violence counseling, parent education, cash assistance, transportation to obtain any services, family therapy, counseling and treatment. *See, e.g.*, Ark. Code Ann. § 9-27-303(25) (2014); D.C. Code Ann. § 4-1301.02 (2014); 325 Ill. Comp. Stat. § 5/8.2 (2014).

Starting with this list, counsel should be prepared to demonstrate services that were never offered to the parent. When these services are listed as among those agencies are supposed to offer, counsel's only remaining task is to offer evidence that the services may have been helpful to the parent. Ideally, the caseworker will acknowledge this on cross-examination. Counsel should also be prepared to call an expert for the parent—a social worker is sufficient for this purpose—to testify what the service is supposed to accomplish and why the parent would likely have benefitted from it had it been offered. Where, for example, a parent with a mental illness could have benefited from a treatment that was not offered by the Agency because it misdiagnosed the parent, the Agency failed to provide required services. *See I.R. v. Dep't of Children & Family Servs.*, 904 So. 2d 583, 587, 30 Fla. L. Weekly D1507 (Dist. Ct. App. 2005).

When counsel appears before a judge who expresses a disinclination to permit proof of a lack of reasonable efforts, counsel should explain that among the parent's statutory rights is the right to have been offered help from the Agency, and that the Agency's failure to offer such help is a material element in the case. When the court forbids a certain line of inquiry, counsel should consider making an offer of proof of what counsel would have shown had the court permitted the inquiry. Making a record in this way may be important to preserve the claim on appeal.

14.07(f)(2) The Parent Has Complied (Sufficiently) with the Case Plan

Counsel should try to offer evidence of compliance with case plans whenever possible. It is rare for appellate courts to have drawn a sufficiently precise line demarcating what degree of compliance is too little or just enough to defeat a termination petition. Whenever the facts involve the parent having done *some*thing, but not enough to satisfy the Agency, counsel should ensure that everything the parent has done is documented in the record. This may persuade the judge that, although the parent could have done more, the Agency failed to prove convincingly that the parent did too little. This evidence will also be important to make the necessary record for an appeal. Parents are not compelled to do everything required of them. Nor are they required to succeed at everything. They may lose their parental rights when they did too little; but what counts as "too little" will depend on a complete showing of what the parent did.

14.07(f)(3) The Parent Has a Valid Justification for Any Failure

A parent may defend against a termination petition by offering justification for why he or she could not meet certain obligations (such as maintaining contact with the child or planning for the child's return). This may be the result of the Agency's failure to clarify sufficiently what was required. An ambiguous statute that fails to clarify what parents must do to keep their children may even be unconstitutional because it delegates too much discretion to the Agency to decide what must be done. *See, e.g., In Interest of R.W.*, 495 So. 2d 133, 11 Fla. L. Weekly 427 (1986).

A parent's failure to comply may also be caused by factors beyond the parent's control, such as the parent's illness, incarceration, or lack of financial resources for transportation. Many courts across the states have reversed trial court orders because parents were blamed for failing to do something when the failure was reasonably explainable. *See, e.g., In re DeJohn B.*, 84 Cal. App. 4th 100, 100 Cal. Rptr. 2d 649 (2000) (parent deprived of fair hearing due to Agency's failure to notify her of six-month review hearing at which reunification services were terminated and case was referred to permanency hearing); *In re M.F.*, 304 Ill. App. 3d 236, 237, Ill. Dec. 889, 710 N.E.2d 519 (1999) (mother's failure to complete court-ordered counseling was reasonable where she had to suspend counseling to comply with drug treatment); *In re Parental Rights of J.L.N.*, 118 Nev. 621, 55 P.3d 955 (2002) (given parent's incarceration, parent had accomplished what could be accomplished while she was in prison).

Most parents facing termination of parental rights are poor. The case plans for many parents require them, in effect, to overcome their poverty. Appellate courts are generally loath to affirm a termination order that is the equivalent of condemning a parent for remaining poor. Thus, a California appellate court reversed a termination order because of the parent's inability to obtain housing. *See In re P.C.*, 165 Cal. App. 4th 98, 80 Cal. Rptr. 3d 595 (2008). Counsel should bring out the efforts the parent has made to locate suitable housing or employment. An expert witness may be helpful to clarify the systemic barriers that exist to the parent accomplishing these tasks without assistance from the Agency.

14.07(g) Termination Will Cause More Harm Than Good for the Child

Many state appellate courts in recent years have pushed back against terminating parental rights merely because there are technical grounds to do so. They are keenly interested in what the child will lose as a result of the termination order. Thus, an Iowa appellate court in 2003 reversed a termination order after finding that there was a close bond between the child and parent. *See In re M.M.*, 662 N.W.2d 372 (Iowa Ct. App. 2003). In 2014 a Nebraska appellate court found that termination was not in the child's best interests where, among other factors, the child and parent had a strong bond. *See In re Interest of Athina M.*, 21 Neb. App. 624, 842 N.W.2d 159 (2014). And in 2008, the New Jersey Supreme Court reversed a termination order finding that termination would do more harm than good where a twelve-year-old, psychologically fragile child had an enduring emotional bond with her mother. *See N.J. Div. of Youth & Family Servs. v. E.P.*, 196 N.J. 88, 952 A.2d 436 (2008).

It is unusual for the child to be called as a witness at the termination of parental rights hearing. Most often, the child has separate legal counsel or a guardian ad litem who may object to the child's testimony. If the child is represented, parent's counsel will need to seek permission of the child's attorney or guardian ad litem to interview the child before the hearing, or use discovery methods such as a deposition request. Whenever counsel has reason to believe the child wants to maintain a legal relationship with the parent, counsel should strive to ensure that the child is called to testify.

14.08 The Dispositional Hearing

14.08(a) Asserting the Right to a Separate Dispositional Hearing

Even if statutory grounds for termination of parental rights have been established, the court cannot terminate parental rights if it is in the best interest of the child to maintain the parent-child relationship. Because parents and children have a fundamental right to family integrity, and the state has a *parens patriae* interest in keeping families intact, the court must evaluate the long-term effect of severing the parent-child bond.

Many states permit or require inquiry into the consequences of the act of termination on the child. Several expect courts to consider the potential for the termination to do more harm than good as an independent ground upon which to refuse to terminate parental rights. *See, e.g.*, CAL. WELF. & INST. CODE § 366.26; IOWA CODE § 232.111; MINN. STAT. § 260C.312 (2014); N.J. STAT. ANN. § 30:4c-15.1(a)(4) (2014). Some states permit parents to present evidence suggesting that the child will not be harmed if termination is not ordered as support for the proposition that termination is not in the child's best interest. *See, e.g.*, KY. REV. STAT. ANN. § 625.090. Counsel should seek experts in the community who can explain to the judge why termination is too drastic an outcome in the case (usually because the child will suffer the loss of a valuable relationship with the parent).

Although the practice in most jurisdictions is that the dispositional hearing is often blended into the hearing on the grounds for termination, counsel should be careful to ensure the lines between the two determinations do not become blurred. Arguably there is a constitutional basis for a separate hearing, as the court's findings regarding the parent's failures should not create an irrebuttable presumption that the parent's only role is to care for the child in his or her home. "Psychological and sociological research over the past thirty years has confirmed (1) the importance of the biological parent-child relationship as a determinant of the child's personality, resilience and relationships with others, regardless of whether the child in fact lives with that parent, and (2) the child's ability to maintain multiple emotional bonds simultaneously." Eliza Patten, *The Subordination of Subsidized Guardianship in Child Welfare Proceedings*, 29 N.Y.U. REV. L. & SOC. CHANGE 237, 240 (2004), *citing* Marsha Garrison, *Parent's Rights vs. Children's Interest: The Case of the Foster Child*, 22 N.Y.U. REV. L. SOC. CHANGE 371, 380 (1996) (internal citations omitted).

14.08(b) Preparing for and Conducting the Hearing

Counsel's preparation for the dispositional aspect of the hearing should be done in conjunction with the methods for preparation outlined in section 14.03 regarding pretrial preparation. The focus of this aspect of the preparation should be on investigating evidence of the nature and quality of the parent and child's relationship. Despite the Agency's position that adoption is the appropriate permanency goal for the child, there may be evidence in the agency file or other documents obtained through the investigation and discovery process that contradicts this. The records may refer the positive nature of the child's relationship with the parent (e.g., notes from the foster care worker about how much the child looks forward to visits with the parent, descriptions in the therapist's progress notes of the positive memories the child has of the parent). This can be useful fodder for cross-examination.

Frequently, the Agency will rely on an expert to speak to the bond between the parent and the child, and the harm (or lack of harm) that might result if the relationship was ended forever. As discussed in section 14.07(e)(2), parent's counsel should become familiar with the standards of practice for these types of forensic evaluations and use these to cross-examine the agency expert. Parent's counsel should consider engaging an expert on behalf of the parent to counter the Agency's expert. A treating therapist, particularly a therapist who engaged in family therapy with both the parent and the child, may also be a helpful witness. Although the trend is for courts to rely on expert testimony regarding bond, most jurisdictions do not require that the finding regarding best interest be based on expert testimony. Parent's counsel should not hesitate to put on fact witnesses who can counter the expert's conclusions, such as the parent themselves, or other individuals (ideally professionals or otherwise family members) who can speak to the nature and quality of the parent-child relationship.

The dispositional hearing is also a time for parent's counsel to focus the court's attention on the Agency's failure to make an adoption plan for the child. If the child is with strangers in foster care instead of family, or if there is no adoptive resource identified for the child, all of this is evidence that should be brought before the court, because all of it speaks to whether termination is truly in the child's best interest. In some states, the child's apparent bond with foster parents should not be determinative, as the court's inquiry should be focused on the effect on the child in ending the parent-child relationship (not the benefit of maintaining the relationship with foster parents). *See* section 14.07(c). Other states, however, may permit the court to compare the homes of foster parents and birth parents at the dispositional phase of the TPR hearing.

14.09 Special Issues for Termination of Parental Rights Hearings

14.09(a) Parents with Physical or Mental Disabilities

Persons otherwise protected by the Americans with Disabilities Act, 42 U.S.C. § 12132 (2014) and/or the Rehabilitation Act, 29 U.S.C. § 794 (2014), may nonetheless lose their parental rights when they are unable to provide proper care for the child within the foreseeable future. *See* ANN M. HARALAMBIE, HANDLING CHILD CUSTODY, ABUSE AND ADOPTION CASES § 13:13 (3d. 2014). *See* Chapter 12 for more discussion on representing parents with disabilities. Courts have consistently rejected the Americans with Disabilities Act as a defense in termination cases, and have held that parents cannot wait until a termination of parental rights case has been brought to raise the need for reasonable accommodation for their disability. *See, e.g., In re Anthony P.*, 84 Cal. App. 4th 1112, 101 Cal. Rptr. 2d 423 (2000); *In re Antony B.*, 54 Conn. App. 463, 735 A.2d 893 (1999); *In re Doe*, 101 Haw. 335, 60 P.3d 285 (2002); *In re Adoption of Gregory*, 434 Mass. 117, 747 N.E.2d 120 (2001); *In re Kayla N.*, 900 A.2d 1202 (R.I. 2006), *cert. denied*, *Irving N. v. R.I. Dep't of Children, Youth & Families*, 549 U.S. 1252 (2007); *S.C. Dep't of Soc. Servs. v. Mother ex. Rel. Minor Child*, 375 S.C. 276, 651 S.E.2d 622 (Ct. App. 2007).

14.09(b) Parents Who Are Incarcerated

Parents who are incarcerated are at risk of losing their parental rights simply because they may be serving a sentence of imprisonment that runs longer than ASFA's fifteen months, or a different time period designated in state law, which mandates that foster children be freed for adoption if they have not yet reunified with their families.

See section 14.01. In addition, certain criminal convictions may form the grounds for termination. *See* section 14.07(b)(2). *See* also Chapter 5, which discusses incarcerated parents' rights in greater detail.

A separate question is whether incarceration *itself* may serve as a ground for termination. In many states, it may not. *See, e.g.*, *Michael J. v. Ariz. Dep't of Econ. Sec.*, 196 Ariz. 246, 995 P.2d 682 (2000) (en banc); *K.D. v. People*, 139 P.3d 695 (Colo. 2006) (en banc); *In re Mason*, 486 Mich. 142, 160, 782 N.W.2d 747 (2010); *In re Parental Rights to Q.L.R.*, 118 Nev. 602, 54 P.3d 56 (2002); *DYFS v. R.G.*, 217 N.J. 527, 90 A.3d 1258 (2014); *Moran v. Weldon*, 18 Or. App. 269, 57 P.3d 898 (2002); *In re R.I.S.*, 614 Pa. 275, 286–87, 36 A.3d 567 (2011).

An incarcerated parent may be able to avoid termination by making appropriate care arrangements for the child while incarcerated. *See In re Mason*, 486 Mich. at 163–64 ("[A] child's placement with relatives weighs against termination under [the statute] which expressly establishes that, although grounds allowing the initiation of termination proceedings are present, initiation of termination proceedings is not required when the children are 'being cared for by relatives.'").

Some states, however, have statutory grounds authorizing termination based solely on the length of sentence. In South Dakota, for example, courts are authorized to terminate parental rights when the parent "[i]s incarcerated and is unavailable to care for the child during a significant period of the child's minority, considering the child's age and the child's need for care by an adult." *See* S.D. Codified Laws § 26-8A-26.1(5). *See also* Mont. Code. Ann. § 41-3-609(2)(d) (when "present judicially ordered long-term confinement of the parent"); R.I. Gen. Laws § 15-7-7(a)(2)(i) (when "institutionalization of the parent, including imprisonment, for a duration as to render it improbable for the parent to care for the child for an extended period of time"); *State ex rel. G.M.F. v. W.F.F.*, 728 So. 2d 149 (Ala. Civ. App. 1998) (father's incarceration as a habitual felon justified termination of his parental rights to two-year-old child because repeated incarcerations prevented him from developing a bond with the child).

In still other states, incarceration will serve as a basis for termination, at least when the incarcerated parent (usually a father) "had little or no contact . . . or provided little or no support for the child" and is unable to care for the child for at least two years because of the incarceration. *See, e.g.*, 750 Ill. Comp. Stat. 50 / 1(D). *See also* Colo. Rev. Stat. § 19-3-604(1)(b)(III); Fla. Stat. § 39.806(d); Idaho Code § 16-2005(1)(e); Mich. Comp. Laws § 712A.19b(3)(h) (2014); Tex. Fam. Code Ann. § 161.001(1)(Q) (2014).

The question is whether there is any defense to a termination case involving an incarcerated parent serving a long sentence in a state whose statute on its face seems to leave no room for any defense. In Wisconsin, for example, the statute authorizes termination when a child has a continued need of protection or services, has been adjudged in need of protection and placed outside his home for at least six months, and where, despite reasonable agency efforts, there is a substantial likelihood that the parent will not be able to care for the child within nine months. *See* WIS. STAT. § 48.415 (2014). It would seem that a parent serving a six-year sentence has no possible defense.

But the Wisconsin Supreme Court has held that the statute would be unconstitutional if applied slavishly. *See In re Termination to Parental Rights to Max G.W.*, 293 Wis. 2d 530, 716 N.W.3d 845 (2006). First, the court explained, because the statute infringes on a fundamental right, it must be strictly construed. *See id.* at 553–60. This requires that the statute be narrowly tailored to meet a compelling state interest. *Id.* at 553–58. With this background, the court examined whether the trial court's order terminating parental rights "was constitutionally permissible when the court determined that [the parent] was an unfit parent because she failed to meet conditions of return that were impossible for her to meet because she was incarcerated." *Id.* at 558. Observing that the majority of courts that have considered the question concluded that "termination should not be based on incarceration alone," *id.*, the court held the statute would be unconstitutional as applied to an incarcerated parent unless it was interpreted to permit parents to retain their fundamental parental rights by requiring "that the court-ordered conditions of return are tailored to the particular needs of the parent and child." *See id.* at 560.

Counsel should never assume that incarceration alone is a lawful basis upon which to terminate parental rights and should seek to introduce evidence at a contested hearing showing that the parent-child relationship is worth preserving. In preparing for a termination case, counsel should meet with the incarcerated parent in person before the hearing and have all necessary exhibits available in the courtroom to offer into evidence. Counsel should also insist that the parent be allowed to appear in court in person, even though there may not be an automatic right to do so in the jurisdiction. In all events, incarcerated parents have the due process right to participate meaningfully in the proceedings.

14.10 Appeals

Because termination of parental rights has such a severe and irreversible impact, parents' counsel should always consider an appeal where legal grounds exist. If filing an appeal, parents' counsel should also ask for a stay of the termination order, and request that visits between the parent and child continue during the pendency of the appeal (though this is rarely granted). To the extent that there are legal grounds, the likely merits of an appeal will of course depend on the strength of the trial record developed by parent's counsel. For more information on appeals, *see* Chapter 15.

CHAPTER 15

Representing Parents on Appeal

Andrew Cohen

15.01 Introduction

Many attorneys reading this chapter have already handled one or more appeals. Others are trial-level lawyers who are considering adding appeals to their plate. Those who handle trial-level cases understand that parents' lawyers suffer more losses than victories. Sadly, the same is true for appellate work. Few cases raise appealable issues that are likely to change the outcome. This is particularly true in jurisdictions where parents exercise a statutory right to appeal. Finding errors at the trial level can be difficult. Even when errors did occur at trial, unless those errors were properly preserved for appeal, the appellate court will typically ignore them. And even when errors were properly preserved, the standard of review on appeal is heavily weighted in favor of affirming the judgment.

Nevertheless, appellate work is both personally rewarding and incredibly important. The parent's appellate lawyer is the last defense against the life-altering judgment calls of often-undertrained social workers. The parent's appellate attorney is the only person who can ensure that an overworked judiciary doesn't cut corners, ignore fundamental rights, or rubber-stamp decisions of child protective services ("CPS"). The appellate attorney is often in the challenging position of trying to find, pick up, and assemble the pieces to a sad, incomplete puzzle. Many parents have been treated unfairly by CPS or the judicial system. After meeting those parents and reviewing the record, counsel will commonly feel a very real indignation, if not fury, about how the client was treated at the trial level. Winning such appeals means more than just rectifying injustice for one client; it means educating the appellate court about problems in the child welfare system. In addition, every appellate victory is a not-too-subtle reminder to trial judges that they are not the final arbiter of rights and interests, and that the appellate review process is meaningful.

This chapter is intended to encourage lawyers to work on appeals in child protection cases and to inspire them to do great appellate work. But beyond inspiration, this chapter is written to help the appellate lawyer win. It is intended to teach appellate counsel to communicate effectively with parents, work cooperatively with trial counsel, identify potential winning issues, brief those issues effectively, and present a compelling oral argument.

15.02 Client Relations

Some appellate counsel in child protection cases were also counsel at the trial level. In those cases, of course, counsel already has a long-standing relationship with the client. In many cases, however, appellate counsel will be new to the case and will not have met the client before being assigned or retained to handle the appeal. For lawyers contemplating handling an appeal for a new client, the first step is to run a conflicts check to ensure that counsel does not represent, and has not previously represented, any other parties or witnesses in the case. The possibility of conflicts increases dramatically if counsel regularly accepts appeals from certain courts or counties. Many conflicts are waivable, but it is crucial that they be caught early in the process.

Assuming there is no conflict, the next step is to ascertain what the client is seeking. Counsel cannot take a position on appeal—indeed, cannot do much at all—until the client explains his or her goals. And counsel cannot expect the client to make an informed decision about appellate goals until counsel has discussed the appellate process and explained to the client all available options. An in-person meeting to start the representation works best because there is so much to discuss.

15.02(a) Locating the Client

Before discussing the case with the client, the first step is to arrange to meet with him or her. In some circumstances, the parent may contact appellate counsel; other times, counsel may meet the parent at the trial courthouse. But in many cases, appellate counsel will have to track the client down.

Depending on the jurisdiction, appellate counsel may receive contact information for the client when assigned the appeal. But if not, appellate counsel should get all contact information from trial counsel as soon as practicable. If trial counsel does not have it, or if the contact information from trial counsel (or the court or other appointing authority) is no longer accurate, appellate counsel will have to find the client him- or herself.

If appellate counsel cannot contact the client and get direction about the appeal, it is difficult to determine the next steps. It may be sufficient to rely on information from trial counsel, provided trial counsel can explain why the client appealed and what the client's last instructions were regarding the case. If those instructions were detailed and recent, appellate counsel can proceed with some comfort. But if the client "disappeared" well before trial and trial counsel filed the appeal based on stale instructions, appellate counsel is best advised to contact the appointing authority, bar counsel, or the state ethics agency for guidance. In the absence of meaningful direction from the client, or when the client's last instructions no longer make sense—for example, the client's last instructions before disappearing were to advocate for her aunt to adopt the child, but the client's aunt has passed away or no longer wants the child—appellate counsel has two options: withdraw from the appellate representation, or do nothing and wait for the client to reappear. If counsel chooses to do nothing, the case may be dismissed for failure to prosecute.

15.02(b) Communicating with the Appellate Client

15.02(b)(1) Relationship-Building

As noted above, appellate clients have the same issues as trial clients, but those issues may be worse or more deeply entrenched at the appellate stage. Some parents will have been mistreated by the system; some will believe that they have been mistreated even when they weren't. Most of them are very upset about losing at trial. Some will be angry at their trial lawyers for failing to prepare them adequately for trial or failing to present certain evidence or witness testimony, and some of those parents will be deservedly angry. Almost all of them will know relatively little about the appellate process.

Appellate counsel needs to address these matters and earn the parent's trust before beginning to try to gather the information needed to write the brief. The initial meeting with the parent is not the time to explain the rules of appellate procedure, the standards of review, or the roles of appellate judges. The initial meetings are for relationship-building. The best way to create trust is by listening closely to the parent and empathizing with him or her. The subject of meeting and getting to know the client is discussed in greater detail in Chapter 3. Empathetic listening is as important to the client as it is to counsel. Most parents at the appellate level have lived apart from their children for a significant period of time; many will never regain custody. They are often sad, angry, and scared. Appellate counsel may be their last hope. Even if counsel cannot change the outcome in the case, counsel can offer the client empathy, respect, and some answers to his or her questions.

It is also important to use an early meeting with the client to disabuse him or her of a common misconception. Many parents think of "winning" as getting their children back. Some appellate courts have, in fact, vacated trial court decisions and remanded with instructions for the trial court to dismiss the case and return children home, but that is rare. In fact, most of the time, "winning" an appeal simply means a remand for a new trial or consideration of additional evidence. This is a complicated concept for many parents, and it is important to clarify what is likely to be the best outcome in a successful appeal: the child will not be returned unless the parent wins the new trial, which is far from guaranteed. And if the parent loses again, there will be another appeal. During this time, the parent might have no visits with the child, and the child may be bonding with pre-adoptive foster parents.

This is grim news for most parents. When this news is coupled with information about how difficult it is to win an appeal, some parents decide that an appeal isn't worth the trouble. They don't want to endure a long appeal that promises little benefit, or they do not want to put their children through the process. Counsel's purpose, of course, is not to dissuade the parent from appealing; it is to avoid creating unrealistic expectations.

Parents may have other misconceptions about the appellate process. It is important to clarify that an appeal is very different from a trial. There will not be regular hearings at the appellate court; there may be none at all. Only counsel will present the case orally (if there is an oral argument); the parent will not have the chance to stand and speak his or her mind about witness credibility, fairness, parental fitness, or the child's best interests. And the parent's appeal is (in most circumstances) limited to the evidence heard by the trial court; new information about his or her progress in treatment, recently obtained restraining order, or concerns about the foster parents' alleged misdeeds are not part of the record that the appellate court will consider. It often helps to explain to the parent that counsel is merely serving as the messenger of disquieting news; counsel is not responsible for the rules.

15.02(b)(2) Ongoing Contact

Some jurisdictions or appointing authorities have rules regarding the amount and frequency of contact appellate counsel is expected to have with their clients. Regular contact with the client is important for both guidance and client relations. The client's goals may change over the course of the appeal. Even when not much is happening in the appeal, parents are entitled to know the reason for the delay and when the case is likely to proceed.

Parents are also entitled to some form of "ownership" of the appeal. Appellate counsel is authorized to make the strategic choices about which issues to brief and how to brief and organize them. But the client should know the issues and be able to weigh in on them. The simplest way to keep the parent informed is to send him or her a letter outlining the issues counsel plans to raise in the brief and why counsel chose them. In this letter, counsel may also wish to explain which issues will *not* be included and why, particularly if the parent has mentioned them before. This letter serves several purposes: it explains to the client what counsel is thinking about; it gives the client an opportunity to raise other issues counsel may not have considered; and it gives the parent an important sense of ownership of, and participation in, the appeal.

Time permitting, counsel should also consider sending a draft of the brief to the parent. This, too, shows the client that counsel is working hard and that the client is "in the loop" on the appeal. In the cover letter, counsel should ask the parent to pay particular attention to the Facts and Procedural History sections to ensure that they are correctly stated; the parent may remember important hearings, filings, or events that were omitted from the court docket. When counsel files the brief, she should also send a copy to the parent. Unless court rules prohibit it, counsel should send the client copies of all other briefs, the transcripts, and the record appendix. (Note that some jurisdictions may require court permission for parents to have access to certain records.)

15.02(b)(3) Settlement

Settlement at the appellate stage may be possible, but it is a delicate business. The parent may have already had—and turned down—settlement offers from CPS, usually in the form of an open adoption agreement, if the jurisdiction permits such an arrangement. In some cases, CPS may withdraw such offers after the parent proceeds to trial and loses. But the Agency may continue or renew the offer after trial in the hope of avoiding the long appellate process and/or a possible remand. The Agency may be concerned about eager or impatient pre-adoptive parents, or it might genuinely believe that an open adoption is best for the child. If the Agency makes or renews a settlement offer, counsel has a duty to discuss it with the parent.

15.03 Preparing for the Appeal

In every jurisdiction, there are special statutes and court rules governing the appellate process. New appellate counsel is strongly advised to master the rules. What follows is a general outline of the first steps to take in a child welfare appeal. But counsel should always consult the jurisdiction's rules and follow them faithfully.

In addition, the clerks' offices in the appellate court and the trial court have great expertise in the appellate process and are generally happy to help lawyers negotiate the process. Counsel should always contact those offices and strive to form a good working relationship with those who work in them. Clerks rarely mind when a lawyer new to the appellate process confesses to not being sure of the next steps.

15.03(a) File a Notice of Appearance in the Trial Court

In some jurisdictions, appellate counsel may need to file a notice of appearance in the trial court before being entitled to gain access to the files. File this appearance as soon as practicable.

15.03(b) Check the Notice of Appeal

Carefully review the notice of appeal to ensure that it was filed and filed timely and properly. Appeals are routinely dismissed because they were filed late. In most jurisdictions, the notice of appeal must be filed within a certain number of days from entry of the judgment on the docket (which is not the same as the judge's announcement of the decision or trial counsel's receipt of the decision). If the notice was filed late, counsel should, if possible, seek permission for it to be accepted. In some circumstances, a timely filed post-trial motion (such as a motion for new trial or motion to amend the findings) may extend the time within which to appeal. And in some jurisdictions, such motions may vitiate the notice of appeal, requiring counsel to file a new one. When filing a new notice of appeal, counsel should specify that the parent is appealing both the underlying judgment *and* the denial of the post-trial motion.

Paying attention to this first stage of the appellate process is extremely important. It is much better to address problems right away than to have them come to light—and possibly lead to dismissal of the appeal—after counsel has already briefed the case.

Note that a notice of appeal may not be necessary—or may be procedurally inappropriate—for appellate review of certain interlocutory or non-final orders. A petition, writ, or other pleading may initiate appellate review of such orders. Counsel must follow the rules carefully.

15.03(c) Check the Status of the File

In some jurisdictions, trial counsel must file certain motions along with the notice of appeal (e.g., a motion for appointment of appellate counsel, a motion to waive fees and costs associated with the appeal, a motion to proceed *in forma pauperis*). In other jurisdictions, appellate counsel must do so. If the burden lies with trial counsel, appellate counsel should ascertain that these motions were properly filed and granted. In addition, counsel should review the trial court file to ensure that all needed documents are there, including all exhibits. If the court ruled on pre-trial motions and struck (or redacted) portions of the exhibits to exclude hearsay, opinions, or privileged information, counsel should ensure that the file contains the properly redacted exhibits. In jurisdictions that require the judge to issue findings, counsel should determine that this was done. If it was not, counsel should discuss with the trial clerk what steps are needed to comply with this rule. Finally, counsel should determine whether filing the appeal automatically stays execution of the order being appealed from and, if not, whether seeking such a stay is appropriate in the case. Stays may be needed when the child is about to be adopted or moved out of state. However, some states preclude the finalization of an adoption while a termination of parental rights appeal is pending.

15.03(d) Contact the Trial Court Clerk Responsible for Appeals

After filing a notice of appearance, counsel should begin by contacting, either in person or by phone, the trial court clerk handling appeals. Few things are more important than developing a close working relationship with this clerk and his or her counterparts in other trial courts. This clerk's assistance may be invaluable in this, and future, cases. A clerk who saves counsel a trip to the courthouse by photocopying and mailing exhibits, who calls and pesters a transcriber, or who delays assembly of the record for a few weeks so that counsel can finish and file another brief, is a life-saver.

When first meeting these important allies, counsel should acknowledge his or her lack of familiarity with the appellate process (at least with respect to appeals from that court). Counsel should ask the clerk what counsel may do to make the clerk's job easier. Counsel should also inquire about the procedure for copying exhibits or making files available for copying. Some clerks will copy the entire file themselves; some will let counsel copy it at a court copy machine (for free or for a set price per page); others will let counsel take the record to a local copying business. Counsel should set a date and time to go to the court and review the file, make copies or pick them up, and get a copy of the docket sheets.

15.03(e) Order and Review the Transcripts

In some jurisdictions, appellate (or trial) counsel must order a copy of the recording of the trial (or all hearings), locate a transcriber, and order transcripts. In other jurisdictions, the clerk's office does all these things after the notice of appeal has been filed. In jurisdictions where the appellant must order them, it is important to do so expeditiously. The failure to order transcripts, or to ensure that they are completed on time, may lead to dismissal of the appeal. In jurisdictions where the clerk's office orders the transcripts automatically upon the filing of an appeal, counsel should check regularly with the clerk and/or the transcriber about their status.

Once the transcripts are ready, review them immediately to determine whether any of the testimony is missing or inaudible. If an entire day, or a substantial portion of a day, is missing, ask the clerk's office (nicely) if they have misplaced a tape or CD of the trial. Counsel may also need to ask the transcriber to look for it. If it cannot be located, or if the clerk's office knows that a portion of the recording has been lost or destroyed (or a portion of the trial was never recorded), counsel may need to reconstruct the testimony with trial counsel's help. In most jurisdictions the burden of reconstruction is on the appellant. The appellant takes the first stab at reconstruction (based on trial notes, drafts of direct and cross-examination, and other materials) and sends it to the appellee for verification and/or editing. Once the parties agree to the contents, the reconstruction is submitted to the trial court for approval. If the parties cannot agree, they submit their "competing" reconstructions to the trial judge. The judge can make his or her own changes to the reconstruction, and the judge's decision is generally not appealable. Counsel should always check the rules for the reconstruction process.

Reconstruction of missing testimony is a laborious process. But if counsel fails to do it, it usually means that arguments regarding, or relying on, the missing testimony will be deemed waived. There may, of course, be cases where the missing portions are so large, or so important to the case, that the trial testimony simply cannot be reconstructed and the appeal cannot proceed. In such cases, counsel should exhaust (and document) all efforts to reconstruct the missing portions, but then argue on appeal that those efforts have failed and due process requires a new trial.

Even when the trial transcripts are complete, counsel should ensure that they are all the *right* transcripts. Transcripts of the trial itself may be insufficient. Certain pre- or post-trial hearings may be crucial to the appeal. For example, if counsel wants to argue that the judge erred in admitting the testimony of an incompetent child, counsel must provide the appellate court with a transcript of any pre-trial hearing at which the judge addressed (or refused to address) the competency issue. If counsel wants to argue that the trial judge was biased, counsel must include a transcript of any hearing at which the judge exhibited that bias. And if the client is appealing the court's denial of a post-trial motion, some jurisdictions also require that the appellate record include the transcript of any hearings on the motion. As noted below, communication with trial counsel about potential appellate issues is crucial. Failing to consult with trial counsel may mean discovering too late that counsel is missing a crucial transcript to support the argument.

15.03(f) Get Information from Trial Counsel

Trial counsel is a very important resource who can help get the vital information below:

- The client's contact information (if needed).
- Background information about, and an assessment of, the client. For example: Did the client keep in regular contact with trial counsel? Did the client have mental health issues, developmental delays, or language issues that made communication difficult? Did trial counsel need—and will appellate counsel need—an interpreter? Did the client appear for trial? What did the client want at trial?
- Background information about the other parent, the child, the foster or pre-adoptive resources, other putative caretakers, and key CPS personnel.
- A description of the judge, the procedures and peccadilloes of the particular trial court, and whether anything out of the ordinary took place in the case.
- A brief summary of the case, from the date of filing through trial.
- A copy of all exhibits, all pleadings, and the CPS file. If trial counsel does not have time to make copies, offer to take the originals and make copies for trial counsel.
- An explanation of the judgment/disposition. For example, did the trial court terminate parental rights, enter a guardianship or permanent custody order, give custody to another parent, or some other disposition? Did the court issue any other orders that the client wanted to appeal, such as post-adoption contact, sibling visitation, or the selection of a particular adoptive resource? Ask trial counsel whether CPS or the pre-adoptive parents offered to settle the case, the terms of any settlement offer, and whether settlement remains a possibility.
- An idea of potential appellate issues, and dates of pre-trial or post-trial hearings that relate to those issues.

Appellate counsel should urge trial counsel to let her know of all developments in the case as soon as they happen.

Appellate counsel should also consider asking trial counsel for an introduction to the client. Indeed, because of mental health problems or trust issues, the client may not be willing to speak to new counsel without such an introduction. At a minimum, trial counsel should explain to the client who appellate counsel is, that the client should expect to be contacted by appellate counsel, and that the client should keep in touch with appellate counsel. At a later point, appellate counsel will want to address trial counsel's performance with the client, but that discussion should be postponed for a future meeting, alone with the client.

Too often the trial/appellate counsel relationship is strained because trial counsel is worried that appellate counsel will raise the issue of ineffective assistance of counsel. Appellate attorneys in child welfare cases rarely raise ineffective assistance. They are less likely to do so when there is open communication. Generally speaking, the actions and inactions of trial counsel cannot form the basis of an ineffective assistance claim if they were strategic (unless the strategy was manifestly unreasonable). If appellate counsel understands trial counsel's strategic reasoning—which requires frank discussion about the client and the case—appellate counsel *may* choose not to raise ineffective assistance.

Appellate counsel should never be bullied into refraining from asserting ineffective assistance. Nor should appellate counsel refrain from raising the issue out of a sense of "legal community" or fellowship with the trial attorney. But appellate counsel might decide not to raise the issue if trial counsel's missteps made strategic sense at the time and would likely be upheld as reasonable by an appellate court. For more discussion of ineffective assistance of counsel claims, *see* 15.04(k)(1).

Even when there is no issue of ineffectiveness, some trial attorneys will not cooperate with appellate counsel. They may ignore calls and letters, not send promised files, or not help identify issues or reconstruct incomplete transcripts. All appellate counsel can do in such situations is to keep a record of their efforts to speak with trial counsel and urge trial counsel to cooperate. Try to obtain needed documents and information through other means. When trial counsel's assistance is needed but not forthcoming, appellate counsel should contact the appointing authority and ask it to intervene. If appellate counsel cannot obtain help from the appointing authority in securing needed documents or assistance from trial counsel, it may be necessary to contact bar counsel or the state ethics board.

In most cases, trial and appellate counsel will act as a team, helping each other help the client. A "team" attitude in all dealings with trial counsel almost always works to everyone's advantage.

15.04 Developing the Theory of the Case

15.04(a) Theory of the Case

All appeals, like all trials, require that counsel develop a theory of the case. What, exactly, is a theory of the case? It is a story of how the parent was wronged by one or more aspects of the trial proceedings, and how those wrongs changed the result of the trial. It should be a very short story, not more than a few sentences. It is the story that will shape the brief and oral argument.

This definition makes it clear what a theory of the case is *not*. It is not the same as the story told by CPS counsel, appellee-children's counsel, or the trial judge who ruled against the parent. And unless the parent won at trial and is the appellee on appeal, the theory of the case will rarely be the same as trial counsel's theory, even if trial counsel was correct in every way. After all, trial counsel and appellate counsel are trying to prove different things. Trial counsel was trying to prove that the state's allegations against the parent were untrue or overblown and that he or she was a fit parent. Appellate counsel is trying to show that the trial judge erred and, because of that error, the case should be dismissed, remanded for a new trial, or otherwise handled differently. There is overlap, to be sure. But the stories are different and must be told in different ways.

Here is an example of the different theories of the case for trial and appellate counsel:

> Trial counsel: The parent is fit because he is not a heroin addict; he is only an occasional, recreational user, who never abused or neglected the child when he was using.
>
> Appellate counsel: The trial court erred in terminating the parent's rights because the only admissible evidence about his use of heroin showed he was an occasional, recreational user, who never abused or neglected his child. The only evidence suggesting he was an addict and neglected the child while using came from an unqualified "expert" who never interviewed the father and testified outside of her area of expertise.

Trial counsel's theory of the case focuses on the father's substance use. Appellate counsel's theory of the case focuses on the trial court's evidentiary rulings; had the judge properly excluded the expert or limited her testimony, the result of the case would have been different. The stories overlap—both suggest, as they must, that the father was fit despite his recreational drug use—but the theories of the case are different.

Appellate counsel's theory of the case is limited by the evidence, the legal issues, and the preservation of those issues by trial counsel; appellate counsel can only work with what there is. Section 15.05(b)(3) will discuss framing the issues, and section 15.05(b)(5)(B) will discuss how to tell a story in the Facts section.

15.04(b) Issue Analysis

Every trial is flawed. Trial judges admit evidence improperly and strike it improperly. They take procedural shortcuts and make procedural errors. Some of those errors are clearly insignificant; others just as clearly rise to constitutional dimensions. But trial court errors and meritorious issues are not the same things. Rather, identifying the errors is just the first step.

To determine which issues are worth briefing—and to brief them successfully—appellate counsel must answer five questions:

1. What was the error at the trial level? Section 15.04(c) below addresses how to spot the errors and provides a list of common—and not-so-common—errors to look for.
2. Did that error prejudice the parent or was it harmless? Section 15.04(g) below discusses harmless error and how to overcome it.
3. Was the error "structural" such that no prejudice need be shown? That is, was the error so fundamental that prejudice can be presumed because it calls into question the very fabric of our justice system? These issues will be addressed in section 15.04(i).
4. Was the error preserved by trial counsel? Or was it an error that did not need to be preserved to be raised on appeal? Section 15.04(j) below addresses this in more detail.
5. If the error was not preserved by trial counsel, can the issue be preserved by filing a motion for new trial, a motion to reconsider, or some other post-trial motion? Those questions will be addressed in section 15.04(j)(1).

15.04(c) Identifying Trial Errors—Methods

There are several ways to identify trial errors that may become issues on appeal:

15.04(c)(1) Ask Trial Counsel

The best way to start is to ask trial counsel. Trial counsel should know what evidence the judge (erroneously) admitted over objection, how the judge (unfairly) limited counsel's direct or cross-examination, and whether the judge (improperly) took a procedural shortcut that deprived the parent of a statutory or constitutional right. Trial counsel may not be correct; the judge's ruling might have been proper or represent a reasonable exercise of discretion. But brainstorming with trial counsel is a good way to generate ideas, ease trial counsel's anxieties about appellate counsel's role, and begin what will hopefully turn into a productive and efficient relationship.

15.04(c)(2) Ask the Client

Another important resource for error identification is the client. Clients who failed to appear for trial might explain that they did not receive notice of the proceeding or of the trial dates from the court, CPS, or their trial counsel. Clients who did appear for trial may have a "feeling" that some aspect of it was unfair. That feeling is worth exploring, not just because it is good for attorney-client relations, but because the parent's feeling may have some basis. Clients may also share their views of trial counsel's performance. Did trial counsel prepare the parent to testify? Did trial counsel secure an incarcerated parent's presence at trial or a way for the parent to participate? Did the parent tell trial counsel about any important witnesses whom trial counsel failed to subpoena? Few of these matters can be gleaned from the cold transcripts and documentary evidence. Nor are they likely to be forthcoming from trial counsel.

15.04(c)(3) Review the Findings

Trial judges are generally required to issue findings and legal conclusions that support a judgment terminating parental rights or some other final disposition, particularly if a party appeals the judgment. Those findings may not be completed at the time appellate counsel is appointed, but it is important to read them immediately after they are issued.

Often the findings themselves "reveal" errors. The judge may have applied the wrong standard for determining (or refusing to determine) the rights of a putative or "unadjudicated" father. The judge may not have addressed the correct unfitness factor or ground to support a permanent custody, guardianship, or termination judgment. The judge's findings may have scant detail. They may address the other parent's unfitness with great specificity but pay little attention to counsel's client. The judge's findings may focus on old or stale evidence and ignore evidence of current fitness. The findings may not have addressed a crucial issue that was (according to trial counsel) raised below. The judge may have cited outdated or overruled cases. Perhaps most importantly, the findings will show what the judge cared about and based his or her decision on. This is crucial in the second part of appellate counsel's issue analysis: determining whether the errors identified were prejudicial to the parent's case.

15.04(c)(4) Review the Transcripts

The transcripts are the best evidence of what took place at trial. They will reveal favorable and damaging testimony, objections to that testimony, and rulings on those objections. The transcripts may also reveal the testimony that was *not* elicited, and the objections *not* made, by trial counsel. The transcripts will reveal comments or questions by the judge that suggest bias or pre-judgment.

One thing that the transcripts will not show, however, is tone. If trial counsel or the parent indicates that the judge was biased, but there is no manifest evidence of bias in the cold transcripts, counsel may learn more by listening to the actual recording of the trial. A judge's question to a parent, "Can you tell me why you think you can safely parent this child?" may be reasonable if delivered in a flat manner, whereas it might suggest bias if the judge's voice is dripping with scorn.

15.04(c)(5) Review the Exhibits

The documentary evidence at trial is a rich source of appellate issues. Was the document properly admitted in evidence? Does it contain objectionable hearsay, opinion, or privileged information? If so, did the judge rule properly on any objections? In some jurisdictions, privileged documents may be admissible after judicial review in chambers; did the judge follow that process?

15.04(d) Identifying Trial Errors—Interlocutory or Intermediate Appeals

While this chapter primarily addresses appeals from final orders in child welfare cases, a brief note about interlocutory or intermediate appeals—that is, appeals of non-final orders—is necessary. Each jurisdiction handles such appeals differently. Some require a notice of appeal; some require a petition, an application, or writ. Some require that a full legal argument be made in the pleading that initiates the appeal; some require briefing in the same manner as a final appeal. Some permit such appeals as of right; others require trial court or appellate court permission. In some jurisdictions, interlocutory appeals are handled by a full panel of appellate judges; in others, they are handled by a single justice. And some jurisdictions require that such appeals be handled by trial counsel, whereas others assign appellate counsel. Counsel must review the appellate rules and any relevant statutory or common law procedures carefully.

The jurisdictional differences noted above render too unwieldy any in-depth discussion about procedures. But the interlocutory or intermediate *issues* counsel might face are similar across jurisdictions, and they are worth addressing. Note that certain jurisdictions might consider any of the issues mentioned below to be final orders. Common non-final orders that counsel might appeal include:

- a ruling by the trial court as to the sufficiency of the allegations in an initial petition or complaint;
- a ruling by the trial court to include a particular child on the petition when that child's parent has, prior to the petition, made alternative caretaking arrangements for the child (or that child is in the guardianship or custody of a relative);
- an order by the trial court delaying, continuing, or refusing to hold a shelter, emergency, or temporary custody hearing;
- an adverse decision by the trial court after a shelter, emergency, or temporary custody hearing;
- an order for publication notice that counsel believes is premature, because the client's address is known and/or in-hand service has not been attempted;
- an order striking counsel's appearance (as opposed to an order striking or removing a party from the case, which is generally a final order);
- a determination that CPS need not provide the client with reasonable efforts;

- an order approving a case or service plan when the parent disagrees with the contents of the plan;
- an order specifying, reducing, suspending, or terminating visitation;
- an order that a child have emergency medical treatment or be treated with anti-psychotic medication;
- an order that that the parent undergo a court-ordered evaluation against the parent's wishes;
- the denial of an order for funds to retain an expert;
- an order regarding the scheduling of, or the denial of a request for a continuance of, a permanency hearing or trial;
- a pre-trial ruling that abridges the client's privilege in medical or mental health records or communications with providers;
- a pre-trial ruling regarding the summonsing of witnesses;
- a pre-trial ruling regarding the admission of evidence.

Trial court decisions regarding privilege, evidence, and trial-scheduling may be appealable on an interlocutory basis even during the trial. But in most cases, challenges to adverse ruling on these subjects must be raised in the appeal of the final judgment.

Counsel generally must preserve interlocutory or non-final issues through motions, objections, and/or offers of proof. Counsel must also be able show that those errors prejudiced the client going forward. For a full discussion of issue preservation, *see* section 15.04(j); for a discussion of prejudice and harmless error, *see* section 15.04(g).

15.04(e) Identifying Trial Errors—Common Errors in Final Judgments

Each jurisdiction has unique procedures for evaluating allegations of parental abuse or neglect, determining that it occurred, and entering custodial orders—including orders terminating parental rights—based on this determination. In many jurisdictions, courts determine or adjudicate children as "abused," "dependent," "deprived," or "in need of care and protection," or determine that parents are "unfit," within a few months of the filing of the case. (For purposes of this chapter, we'll use the term "parental unfitness" for any determination regarding parental shortcomings or harm to the child that a court must make to give CPS permanent custody or as a predicate to termination of parental rights.) Then, at a later trial, the court determines whether to terminate parental rights or enter some other disposition. In some courts, the adjudication and termination process is combined. In some states, CPS must prove factors or grounds to establish that it is entitled to custody of the adjudicated child; other states have no factors or grounds. Regardless of the differences, many aspects of child welfare cases are common to all, or at least most, jurisdictions.

The discussion in this section will focus on final judgments terminating parental rights. Certain procedural determinations that precede possible termination of parental rights (e.g., a determination that the child is "deprived" or "in need of services") may be appealed in the same manner as judgments terminating parental rights, or they may have their own appellate procedures with shorter timeframes. Generally, appellate analysis of these prior determinations—other than those based on procedure—is the same as the analysis counsel must employ for challenging termination decisions: the errors must be identified, the errors must have been preserved for appeal, and the errors must have been prejudicial to the client's case.

15.04(e)(1) Parental Unfitness

At trial, the court must determine that the parent is "unfit" by clear and convincing evidence. *See Santosky v. Kramer*, 455 U.S. 755, 769–70 (1982). The "best interests of the child" may be a factor in the parental unfitness determination, or it may be a separate inquiry at a later termination trial. (*See* "Best Interests," in section 15.04(e)(4) below.)

Because the child protection procedures of each jurisdiction differ—and some states, themselves, have many procedural mechanisms for removing children and terminating parental rights—this section will only touch on procedural irregularities that appellate counsel might wish to challenge regarding unfitness determinations. Instead, this section will focus on challenges to unfitness determinations that apply in most, if not all, jurisdictions. For example, across jurisdictions, there are two main approaches for challenging the trial court's decision:

1. The factual findings that the trial court relied upon to support a determination of parental unfitness are clearly erroneous.
2. The factual findings as a whole do not show unfitness by clear and convincing evidence.

Appellate counsel can challenge the trial court's unfitness determination (number 2) as a stand-alone argument. But counsel cannot challenge the findings as clearly erroneous (number 1) as a stand-alone argument; counsel must also argue that the findings as a whole, *minus any deficient findings*, do not meet the clear and convincing evidence standard. Why? Because deficient findings alone constitute harmless error if the court made other, valid findings sufficient to terminate rights. For a more in-depth discussion of harmless error, *see* section 15.04(g).

15.04(e)(2) The Findings Are Clearly Erroneous

In most jurisdictions, an appellate court reviews factual findings only for "clear error." Generally speaking, a finding is clearly erroneous if (a) there is no evidence to support it, or (b) there is some evidence, but the appellate court, based on all the evidence, is left with a definite and firm conviction that an error was made.

How might a finding be clearly erroneous?

- There was no evidence to support it. For example, the judge found that the parent went *six* months during 2013 without visiting the child. But the only evidence on this point was a guardian ad litem report that said the parent went *two* months without visiting the child. The "six months" finding is clearly erroneous because there is no evidence to support it.
- It was derived from improperly admitted evidence. For example, the judge found that the parent burned the child with a cigarette. But the only evidence of this burn was an inadmissible hearsay statement by a social worker that trial counsel properly objected to. Absent the improper hearsay, there was no evidence to support the finding.
- It was against the manifest weight of the evidence; that is, the judge ignored considerably greater evidence that suggested a contrary finding. For example, the judge found that the child reacted poorly to visits with the parent. While there was evidence the child reacted poorly to two visits, the evidence also showed that the child reacted warmly to the parent at the forty other visits. The finding is clearly erroneous because, although there was some evidence to support it, the vast weight of the evidence showed otherwise.

If the court relied on several independent grounds or bases to determine parental unfitness, counsel must challenge each of them. Counsel might successfully challenge several grounds or bases of a parent's unfitness, but if a single ground or basis remains that is sufficient to support the ultimate conclusion of parental unfitness, the appeal will fail. That's why the next step, set forth below, is so important.

15.04(e)(3) The Supported or Unchallenged Findings Do Not Add Up to Clear and Convincing Proof of Unfitness

Counsel can never successfully challenge *all* of the judge's findings of fact; some of them will be supported by the evidence no matter how many errors the judge makes. But the parent can still win if the supported findings—that is, those that are not being challenged—do not prove by clear and convincing evidence that the parent is unfit.

How might the findings fall short of clear and convincing proof of unfitness?

- In a jurisdiction that does not have "grounds" for termination, the findings as a whole don't show that the parent has grievous, dangerous shortcomings (or satisfy some other definition of "unfitness"). That is, the bad facts show run-of-the-mill dysfunction, but not egregious abuse or neglect. For example, the judge's findings show that the parent let her nine-year-old watch a few R-rated movies and smoke some cigarettes. Or a developmentally delayed parent missed a few medical appointments for the child but was able to get the child to the vast majority of appointments. The parent's conduct or circumstances might not be perfect, but the dysfunction does not rise to the level of unfitness.

- If the jurisdiction has "grounds" for termination, such as abandonment, egregious harm, or failure to remedy the conditions leading to removal, the findings do not suffice to prove those grounds.
- The findings fail to show a nexus between the parent's problem and abuse or neglect of the child. If a parent's problem hasn't led, and is unlikely to lead, to abuse or neglect of a child, the parent is not unfit. For example, the findings show that the parent used cocaine several times each week and never participated in any treatment program. But she got her children to school every day, helped them with their homework, got them to medical appointments, and took care of their everyday needs.
- The findings are based on substandard parenting from years before trial, but the evidence shows no current evidence of the problematic behavior and no reason to believe that the problems persist. Stale findings should not be the basis of an unfitness finding (unless, of course, they are part of a pattern of conduct that continued up to trial).
- The findings show that the parent may be unfit as to one child, but she is adequately caring for, or is able to adequately care for, another child. Unfitness is generally child-specific. The findings must distinguish between the children based on their specific needs.

The statutory framework and common law of each jurisdiction will dictate which arguments have traction in a particular appellate court.

15.04(e)(4) Best Interests

In some jurisdictions, courts cannot terminate parental rights (or enter certain other custody orders) unless termination serves the best interests of the child. The best-interests inquiry may be part of the parental unfitness (or other predicate) determination. Or the court may only reach it after finding a parent unfit.

Whatever role best-interests determination plays in the applicable statutory scheme, it is a difficult determination to challenge on appeal. It is, by its nature, an evaluative inquiry, and appellate courts do not like to substitute their evaluation of evidence for that of the trial court. As a result, best-interests determinations are usually reviewed only for error of law or abuse of discretion. If the jurisdiction considers best interests to be a fact-finding, it is reviewed only for clear error. In either case, this is a very high hurdle.

But there are ways to attack a best-interests determination on appeal:

- Did the court make a conclusory best-interests determination without making required subsidiary findings about *why* terminating parental rights serves the child's best interests?
- Did the court determine best interests with no, or a very slim, evidentiary foundation?
- Did the court rely on inadmissible evidence, or make a procedural error, in making its best-interests determination?

- Did the court fail to consider an older child's wishes *not* to terminate in making its best-interests determination? Did it give too much weight to a child's wish to be adopted?
- Did the court make a best interests determination by inappropriately comparing the parent to the pre-adoptive parent?
- Did the court terminate parental rights without any demonstrable benefit to the child because the permanency goal or plan does not require termination? For example, did the court terminate father's parental rights even though it placed the child with the mother, and the mother is willing to give father visitation (as if it were a "standard" divorce)? Did the court terminate mother's parental rights even though the maternal grandmother is the guardian and wants the mother to have ongoing, safe contact with the child? Did termination in such circumstances provide no benefit whatsoever to the child?
- Did the court terminate the rights of a parent where the child will be a legal orphan with no hope of adoption, no desire for adoption, and no parental visitation resource other than the terminated parent? Did termination in such circumstances harm the child by depriving him or her of love and support, no matter how unfit the parent might be?

15.04(e)(5) Adoption Plan Issues

In some jurisdictions, the trial court must approve an adoption plan, or choose between two or more "competing" adoption plans. In many states, parents whose rights have been terminated have no standing to participate in this process and, therefore, no standing to appeal. But in other states, the plan approval process is a predicate to termination. In such states, parents are allowed to choose their own adoptive resource as part of the termination process; when the court chooses CPS's plan (or the child's or another parent's plan) over the parent's plan, the aggrieved parent can appeal.

Because the approval of an adoption plan is distinct from the unfitness determination, the standard of proof is usually a preponderance of evidence as to whether the plan serves the child's best interests. In some states, kin enjoy a presumption of best interests; in some, kinship is an important factor; and in others, it is irrelevant.

There are several possible appellate issues concerning the court's choice of adoption plan. Whether these issues are relevant will depend on the law of the jurisdiction. Where the court had only one plan before it:

- Did CPS proffer a plan? Where the law requires a written plan, did CPS proffer only an oral plan?
- Did the court make any findings about the plan, or did the court simply approve it?
- If the court did make findings, were those findings based on properly admitted evidence?

- Was the plan sufficiently detailed to establish that it, in fact, served the child's best interests? For example, if the plan was for recruitment of an adoptive family, did the plan discuss the child's special needs, the type of adoptive family best suited to the child's needs, and the qualifications the adoptive parents should have to deal with those needs?
- Did the plan provide for contact with biological parents, siblings, or other relatives if such contact serves the child's best interests?

Where the court had competing plans to choose from:

- Did the court consider the competing plans, or did it only consider CPS's plan?
- Did the court make findings about each plan?
- If the court did make findings, were those findings based on properly admitted evidence?
- Did the court give proper/undue weight to a plan for kinship adoption?
- Did the court fail to give proper weight to a plan that would permit the child to have sibling contact?
- Did the court favor adoption over another permanency option that would have better served the child's interests?
- Did the court give undue weight to CPS's plan because the child had bonded to the foster parents?

Trial judges usually have ample discretion when deciding which of two or more plans serves a child's best interests. It is almost impossible to argue that the judge abused her discretion by weighing the evidence improperly. Appellate courts are much more likely to reverse and remand on this issue when the trial court committed an error of law that calls into question the fairness, propriety, or legality of the weighing *process*.

15.04(e)(6) Reasonable Efforts

In some jurisdictions, statutes or cases require agencies to prove that they provided the parent with "reasonable efforts" to overcome the barriers to the safe return of their children as a precondition to terminating parental rights. In these jurisdictions, the entire appeal can rest on the Agency's failure to provide reasonable efforts, or this claim can be combined with other appellate arguments. Even in those jurisdictions where CPS's failure to provide reasonable efforts is not a defense to termination, counsel may still be able to argue that termination was premature because the parent might have overcome his or her deficiencies with proper services.

Some reasonable efforts challenges have been successful and have led to reversals of termination or permanent custody orders. *See, e.g., In re Mason*, 486 Mich. 142, 782 N.W.2d 747 (2010); *In re Adoption/Guardianship Nos. J9610436 and J9711031*,

368 Md. 666, 796 A.2d 778 (2002); *Care and Protection of Elaine*, 54 Mass. App. Ct. 266, 764 N.E.2d 917 (2002). To challenge reasonable efforts on appeal, the parent generally must show: (a) what services were needed; (b) that CPS knew about that need; (c) that needed services were available; (d) that the parent would have benefited from those services; and (e) that CPS failed or refused to access those services for the parent. In some jurisdictions, courts require that the parent prove that he or she sought help from CPS in a timely fashion. Issue preservation is often problematic. Reasonable efforts arguments brought for the first time on appeal are rarely successful.

Even when CPS's efforts are an appropriate consideration on appeal, appellate courts give considerable deference to a trial judge's assessment of "reasonableness" and whether more, or more narrowly tailored, services might have benefited a parent.

15.04(f) Identifying Trial Errors—Due Process

Parents have a substantive due process right to family integrity protected by the Fourteenth Amendment to the Federal Constitution and many state constitutions. *See Troxel v. Granville*, 530 U.S. 57, 66 (2000). "The rights to conceive and to raise one's children are "essential . . . basic civil rights of man . . . far more precious . . . than property rights." *Stanley v. Illinois,* 405 U.S. 645, 651 (1972). Before the state "deprive[s] a legitimate [*sic*] parent of all that parenthood implies," the requirements of due process must be met. *Armstrong v. Manzo,* 380 U.S. 545, 550 (1965). Procedural due process is a flexible concept; the extent of procedural protections that must be afforded varies with the circumstances. *Goldberg v. Kelly*, 397 U.S. 254, 262–63 (1970). But basic to due process is the right to be heard "at a meaningful time and in a meaningful manner." *Armstrong*, 380 U.S. at 550.

Most due process violations—like evidentiary issues—require preservation by objection or motion and some showing of harm. But some due process violations are so fundamental that they may be raised for the first time on appeal and require no showing of harm. Some of those are discussed in sections 15.04(i)(1)–(4). Whether the due process issues set forth in this section must be preserved and are subject to a harmless-error analysis depends on the jurisdiction.

15.04(f)(1) Notice

Most fundamentally, due process requires notice of the proceeding. State statutes often provide for specific types of notice—the breach of which gives rise to claims of statutory violations—but minimally adequate notice is always constitutionally required. Sometimes a parent will not appear at trial but will appear later and file a notice of appeal. Appellate counsel appointed to such a client should consider these questions:

- Did the parent receive any notice at all?
- Did CPS make any attempt to locate and serve the parent?

- Did CPS attempt to serve her by hand? Did CPS serve notice on the *wrong person* by hand? Did CPS serve notice by leaving it at the *wrong address*? Did CPS serve notice by leaving it at the correct address but in a way that the parent was unlikely to receive it?
- Did CPS make any attempt to serve an incarcerated parent? Did CPS make any attempt to determine whether the parent was, in fact, incarcerated?
- If CPS served the parent by publication, was it a publication distributed in the geographical area covering the parent's last known address? Was the publication in a language the parent understood? Were the parent's and child's names spelled correctly in the notice? Did the notice explain the nature of the proceeding accurately? Did the notice give the proper court and docket number? Did the notice give the next court date or the trial date?

If the parent appeared at court and had meaningful time to prepare for trial, the notice issue is likely waived.

15.04(f)(2) Participation

Due process also guarantees the right to be heard at a meaningful time and in a meaningful manner. Was the parent allowed to participate meaningfully in the case? There are many ways that a parent might not have been:

- Did trial start at a different time or date than was previously scheduled, catching the parent or trial counsel unaware and unprepared (or absent)?
- Was the parent given so little notice of trial that she (and her counsel) could not possibly prepare for it meaningfully?
- Was the parent kept from the trial based on circumstances beyond her control (e.g., serious illness or hospitalization, traffic jam, or accident)?
- Was an incarcerated parent brought into court on a writ of habeas corpus?
- Was an incarcerated parent denied an opportunity to participate by video, telephone, or other method?
- Was an out-of-state or out-of-country parent denied an opportunity to participate by video, telephone, or other method?

15.04(f)(3) Conduct of Trial

Due process also requires that the court conduct the proceedings in a fundamentally fair manner. Courts may violate parents' due process rights by engaging in procedures or evidence-gathering methods that deny parents the right to be meaningfully heard:

- Was the parent permitted to offer evidence and witness testimony?
- Was the parent permitted to examine the child if the child had relevant testimony to offer, or cross-examine the child if the child had offered relevant testimony?

- Did the judge interview the child in chambers without the presence of the attorneys? Was the interview recorded?
- Did the judge interview an adult in chambers or at sidebar? Was the interview recorded?
- Did the judge fail to give the parent a meaningful opportunity to rebut adverse allegations brought by CPS by cross-examination or other means?
- Did the judge so trample upon (or ignore) the rules of evidence that the proceeding was fundamentally unfair? Did the judge consider information not in evidence? Did the judge rely on his or her "familiarity" with the family based on a prior or related case?
- Was the parent permitted to retain an expert and offer relevant expert testimony?

15.04(f)(4) Right to Counsel

In many jurisdictions, parents' right to counsel is based on due process principles. Under certain circumstances, the trial court may deny a parent due process by refusing to appoint, or by striking, counsel. For a discussion of actual and constructive denial of counsel, *see* section 15.04(i)(3).

15.04(g) Harmless Error

As mentioned above, no trial is perfect. With few exceptions, appellate courts only want to hear about trial mistakes if they made a difference in the outcome. This is the principle of "harmless error," the saddest words (for appellants) in the appellate language. "Harmless error," in the broadest terms, is any mistake by the trial judge that did not prejudice the losing party and therefore does not require vacating or modifying the judgment.

There are many types of harmless error, and each requires some discussion. To illustrate, let's assume that the trial court found the parent, a father, unfit based on sexual abuse of a young child. The court relied heavily on three of the child's hearsay statements about the sexual abuse—each of which was factually similar and equally damaging—which it admitted under the jurisdiction's child sexual abuse hearsay statute. (Many states have statutes or rules of evidence that address the admissibility of out-of-court statements of children under a certain age pertaining to sexual assault or sexual abuse. *See, e.g.,* Mass. Gen. Laws. ch. 233, § 82 (2014); Ohio R. Evid. 807 (2014); Wash. Rev. Code § 91.44.120 (2014). The procedures tend to be complicated, and judges are easily tripped up.) Let's assume that the applicable statute requires that each hearsay statement be "reliable," and that the statute defines reliable to mean that the statement was detailed, the child understood the consequences of making the statement, *or* the statement was corroborated.

The trial judge in this hypothetical could make many errors, but those discussed below are not worth briefing because they are harmless:

- The judge erred in finding that the child's statements were "reliable" based on corroboration, because there was no corroboration. This error is harmless if the judge *also* found that the statements were sufficiently detailed, because that finding alone is sufficient to show reliability.
- The judge erred with respect to the child's first hearsay statement by finding it reliable even though none of the reliability factors applied. If the judge did not err with respect to the second and third hearsay statements, his error regarding the first statement is harmless; admission of the other two statements is sufficient to prove sexual abuse.
- The judge erred in admitting all of the statements under the statute. But if the statements were clearly admissible under a *different* hearsay exception—excited utterance, for example—the judge's error under the sexual abuse hearsay statute was harmless. (There may, of course, be some wiggle room with this example if the other hearsay exception does not clearly apply, if the jurisdiction requires the proponent of a hearsay statement to alert the trial court to all applicable exceptions, or the jurisdiction prohibits appellate courts from looking to alternative exceptions when reviewing hearsay errors.)
- The judge erred in admitting all of the statements under the hearsay statute, and no other exception applies. But if there is other evidence that the father sexually abused the child—such as a certified copy of the father's conviction for indecent assault and battery on the child or testimony regarding observations of improper touching—sufficient to support a finding of sexual abuse, the judge's error admitting the hearsay statements was harmless.
- The judge erred in admitting all of the statements under the hearsay statute, and no other exception applies. But the judge did not rely on the hearsay in any of his findings or conclusions of law. Or the judge specified in his findings that he did not rely on the hearsay and relied instead on other (properly admitted) evidence. Or the judge found no evidence of sexual abuse *despite* the hearsay (that is, he discredited the hearsay). In any of those cases, admission of the hearsay under the statute was harmless error.
- The judge erred in admitting all of the statements under the hearsay statute, no other exception applies, and the judge relied on the hearsay to find that the father had sexually abused the child. But the judge also found, based on properly admitted evidence, that the father had other grievous shortcomings, such as untreated mental health issues and substance abuse, which would independently support an unfitness finding. Even though the evidentiary error justifies an appellate court striking the

> sexual abuse finding, it is harmless because it would not justify overturning the ultimate finding or conclusion of unfitness. *See, e.g.*, *In re Trejo*, 462 Mich. 341, 360, 612 N.W.2d 407, 416 (2000) (reversal of TPR warranted only if trial court's finding under *every* statutory ground is clearly erroneous).

Briefing any of these issues will almost certainly be fruitless. Without a showing of harm, proving a mistake occurred below is of little value to the client.

15.04(h) Showing Prejudice

While half the battle is identifying interesting errors, the more important half is showing the harm from those errors. Evidentiary and procedural errors must matter. That is, they must be traceable to some type of harm which, in most cases, is an adverse finding of fact. But that's not the end of the matter; the erroneous, adverse finding of fact must itself be traceable to the legal conclusion that a parent is unfit or that termination of parental rights serves the child's best interests.

The Error Tracking Chart below looks complicated, but it's fairly simple. The evidence against the parent is set forth in the diagram as E1–E14. The trial court's findings of fact are set forth in the diagram as F1–F7. The legal conclusions are C1 (parental unfitness), C2 (the child's best interests), and C3 (post-adoption contact). Let's focus solely on the most damaging legal conclusion, C1, because it is relevant in all jurisdictions: the parent is unfit because his drug addiction renders him unable to meet the child's medical needs. That conclusion is supported by two factual findings, F1 (the parent continued to use illegal drugs right up until trial) and F2 (he missed several medical appointments for the child while he was using and the child was in his care). Of course, in a real case, there would be many more findings about substance abuse and the parent's inability to meet the child's needs.

Error Tracking Chart

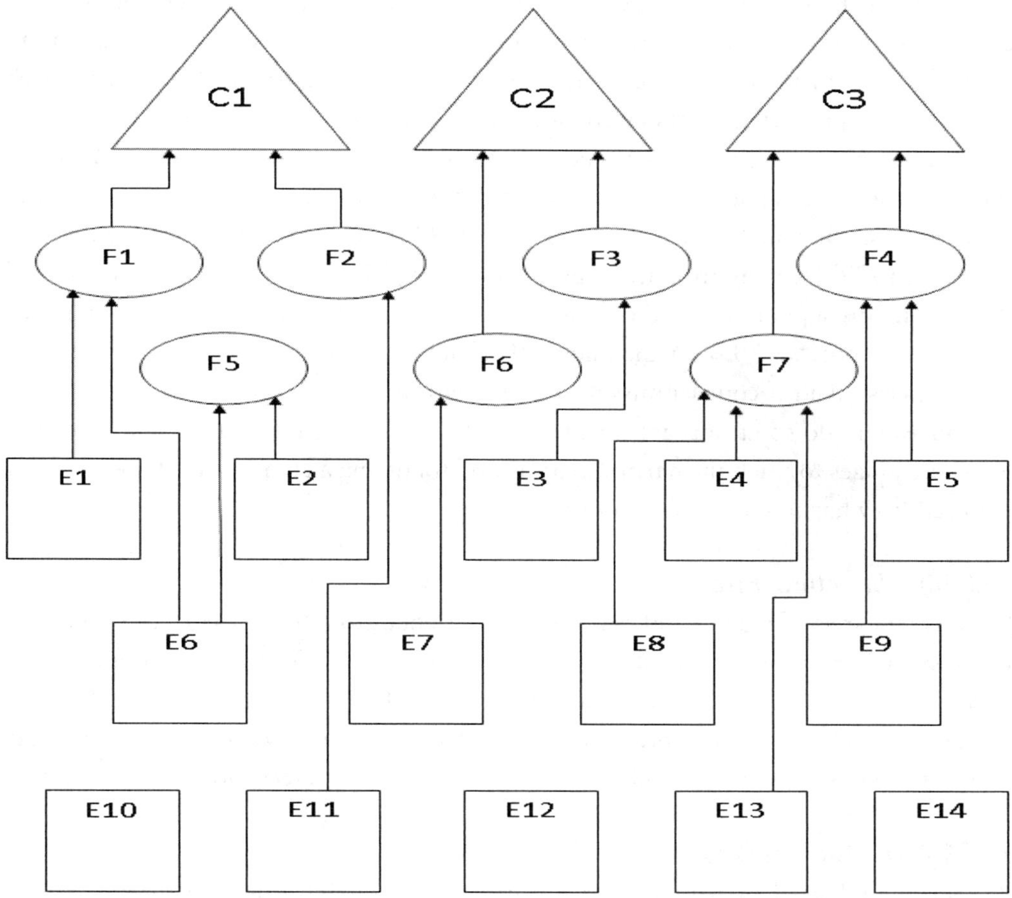

Appellate counsel's focus must be on F1 and F2, which are the only support for C1. Evidentiary errors not traceable to F1 or F2 are not worth briefing. For example, E10 is the trial court's erroneous admission of hearsay about the parent's physical abuse of the child. But the judge did not make a finding about physical abuse—that is, E10 cannot be traced to any finding—so the error is harmless and not worth briefing. Similarly, E2 is the trial court's erroneous admission of opinion testimony about the parent's verbal abuse of the mother. The court *did* make a finding about that (F5), but the court didn't rely on F5 in conclusion C1. Accordingly, it is not worthwhile to brief that error.

F1 (the parent's continued use of illegal drugs) relies on E1 (dirty urine screens) and E6 (hearsay statements by the parent's probation officer). Accordingly, any errors in admitting the dirty urine screens or the testimony were harmful, because those errors can be traced to a key finding which, in turn, can be traced to the court's conclusion of unfitness. If E1 and E6 can be knocked out, then F1 can be challenged as clearly erroneous. F2 (missed medical appointments) is only supported by E11 (hearsay statements of a social worker based on conversations with the child's pediatrician). If E11 can be knocked out, F2 can be challenged as clearly erroneous. Only by challenging both F1 and F2 can counsel challenge the conclusion of unfitness in C1. Accordingly, assuming trial counsel preserved challenges to E1, E6, and E11 by making timely objections (*see* section 15.04(j)(2)), those errors were not harmless and are worth briefing.

There are two reasons counsel is advised to create a visual aid like the Error Tracking Chart for each appeal. First, it is too risky *not* to use a visual aid to help in the harm analysis. If counsel briefs a challenge to E1 (dirty urine screens) alone, without a challenge to E6 (hearsay from the probation officer), F1 (the parent's continued use of drugs) remains supported and the evidentiary error is harmless. Without the visual aid, counsel may not "see" E6 (or the many other pieces of evidence that support findings in real cases). And if counsel misses E6, CPS will point it out in its appellee brief, or the judges will do so at oral argument. Second, counsel should make it simple for the appellate judges to track the harm. Creating and following a chart of this type will help counsel show harm in a simple manner.

15.04(i) Structural Error

Some errors are so fundamental that they call into question the very essence of our justice system. When counsel can show such errors, it may not be necessary to show harm because harm can be presumed. Some jurisdictions refer to such errors as "structural." Generally, trial counsel must preserve them. But some are so obvious or damaging that appellate courts are willing to address them even without preservation.

15.04(i)(1) Judicial Bias

A neutral, unbiased fact-finder is a basic presumption in American jurisprudence. A biased judge renders inherently unreliable decisions. Bias generally must be raised at trial by objecting to the judge's conduct or filing a motion to recuse. Few trial attorneys are brave enough to make such motions, particularly if their trial practice is solely or primarily in one court or before the same judge.

There are several ways to show bias or unreliability:

- Did the judge "pre-judge" the case by announcing a decision before hearing evidence?
- Did the judge make statements before the close of evidence that suggest he or she had already determined the result?
- Did the judge question witnesses in a biased fashion?
- Did the judge make disparaging statements about the race, religion, ethnicity, gender, or sexual orientation of a party or witness?
- Did the judge rely on information learned outside of the proceedings?
- Did the judge fall asleep during trial and miss key testimony?

15.04(i)(2) Party Status

Denial of party status to a parent may be a structural error, because the parent has not been permitted to participate at all in the proceeding. This issue usually arises in the context of noncustodial fathers, particularly those who are not on the birth certificate or whose paternity has not been legally determined. All jurisdictions handle the standing of "noncustodial," "non-resident," or "putative" fathers differently. If the court failed to properly grant the father party status under the governing statutes and common law, it may well be a structural error requiring no showing of prejudice.

15.04(i)(3) Denial of Counsel

Although the right to counsel in termination cases is not an automatic guarantee under the federal Due Process Clause, *see Lassiter v. Dep't of Soc. Servs.*, 452 U.S. 18, 31–32 (1981), it is mandated by due process in many states (and by statute in most states). The failure to provide counsel may be a structural error that requires no showing of prejudice. Trial judges (or clerks, depending on who the appointing authority is) may outright deny counsel to an indigent parent at the start of the proceeding or at the time of the parent's appearance. Or the denial of counsel may arise in other ways:

- Did the trial court allow counsel to withdraw at or near the time of trial based on lack of contact with, or direction from, the parent, leaving the parent unrepresented at trial? This is not a legitimate reason to withdraw if the parent was incarcerated and easily located or was otherwise reachable at an address or phone number in the court or CPS files.
- Did the trial court allow counsel to withdraw based on "breakdown of communication" without appointing successor counsel?
- Did the trial court remove counsel based on a parent's non-indigence without an adequate factual basis or without time for the parent to retain his or her own counsel?
- Did the trial court remove counsel based on a parent's lack of involvement in the case without a factual basis?

Trial counsel's deficient performance or late appointment may, depending on the circumstances, amount to a constructive denial of counsel:

- Did counsel fail to appear for trial or for a portion of the trial?
- Did the trial court appoint counsel the day or eve of trial such that counsel could not possibly prepare?
- Did trial counsel perform so poorly that the parent was effectively denied counsel? For example, did counsel fall asleep at trial? Did counsel fail to recognize his or her client or believe that he or she represented a different party? Did counsel fail to review any records whatsoever before trial? Did counsel say nothing at trial;

no opening, no objections, no closing? Did counsel fail to conduct any direct or cross-examination of witnesses, including the parent?

These deficiencies differ qualitatively from run-of-the-mill ineffective assistance of counsel (*see* section 15.04(k)(1)), which requires a showing of harm. They suggest that the parent never really had counsel to begin with.

15.04(j) Issue Preservation by Trial Counsel

After identifying an error and determining that it was, in fact, prejudicial to the parent, the next step is to determine whether trial counsel preserved the error. Errors that have not been preserved by trial counsel are generally waived on appeal. Some jurisdictions require that appellate counsel indicate how and where in the record trial counsel preserved an issue. There are many ways trial counsel might have preserved an issue for appeal.

15.04(j)(1) Preservation by Motion

In some circumstances, issues are preserved for appeal when trial counsel files a motion seeking relief. In many cases, the issues raised by motion must later be renewed at trial through objections. Did trial counsel file a motion to continue the trial because he or she had too little time to prepare? If so, did counsel also object to going forward at the start of trial? Did trial counsel file a pre-trial motion to exclude improper hearsay or opinion statements in exhibits? If so, did trial counsel remember to renew the motion at trial? Did trial counsel file a motion to recuse a biased trial judge prior to trial? If so, did trial counsel renew that motion at trial? Based on the law of the jurisdiction, trial counsel's pre-trial motion itself might preserve the issue.

15.04(j)(2) Preservation by Objection

Generally, trial counsel must object to improper evidentiary rulings in order to preserve the issues for appeal. Did trial counsel make *timely* objections to questions designed to elicit improper hearsay, opinions, or privileged information? Did trial counsel make timely motions to strike answers containing improper hearsay, opinion, or privileged information? Did counsel try to make, and does controlling law permit, a "rolling" or "ongoing" objection, seeking to cover a line of questions, answers, or subject matter? If the trial court admitted evidence *de bene*, did trial counsel remember to renew the objection or file a motion to strike before the close of evidence? Assuming trial counsel made timely objections, were they the *correct* objections?

In most circumstances, trial counsel must also object if the trial judge made procedural errors. Did trial counsel object when the judge insisted on beginning the trial while the parent was stuck in traffic en route to the courthouse? Did trial counsel object when the judge refused to suspend the trial when an incarcerated parent's video or telephone connection to the courthouse failed? Did trial counsel object when the trial judge refused to qualify the parent's psychologist as an expert? Did trial counsel object when the judge decided to hold the trial on a day scheduled only for a pre-trial conference?

If more than one parent opposed CPS at trial, did trial counsel make timely, proper objections, or did he or she silently "ride the coattails" of the more active attorney? In some circumstances, one party's objection *might* put the court "on notice" of an evidentiary problem sufficient to preserve it for appeal by all parties. But it might not.

15.04(j)(3) Offers of Proof

Preservation might require not just an objection but also an offer of proof. An offer of proof (sometimes called a "proffer") is usually a statement from counsel, whether oral or written, about the content of evidence the judge refused to admit. The offer of proof accomplishes two things: it allows the trial judge to change his or her mind and admit the evidence, and it provides a quasi-evidentiary basis for the appellate court to determine whether the trial court's decision prejudiced the parent. Without an offer of proof, it's often impossible for an appellate court to evaluate harm. Let's assume, for example, that the trial judge refused, on relevancy grounds, to allow the parent's expert to testify about a certain subject. Trial counsel must make an offer of proof regarding why the expert's testimony is, in fact, relevant, and what that testimony would be if the judge permitted it. If trial counsel did not do so, he or she failed to preserve the error for appeal because the appellate court cannot assess the harm.

15.04(j)(4) No Need for Preservation

Some issues do not have to be preserved by trial counsel. Depending on the jurisdiction, some "structural" errors might be reviewable without preservation. *See* section 15.04(i) above. In addition, issues of subject-matter jurisdiction generally can be raised at any time and need not be preserved at the trial level. Certain issues under the Indian Child Welfare Act of 1978, 25 U.S.C. § 1901 *et seq.*, can be raised at any time and need not be preserved at trial. *See* Chapter 11.

15.04(k) Issue Preservation by Appellate Counsel—Post-Trial Motions

As a general matter, if an error is not preserved by trial counsel through an objection, motion to strike, offer of proof, or other method, the issue is waived on appeal. Some jurisdictions may permit appellate counsel to "preserve" issues for appeal by means of a post-trial motion, such as a motion to reconsider or a motion to reopen the evidence. When the trial court denies the motion, appellate counsel may need to file a new notice of appeal from the denial of the motion and ask that the two appeals be consolidated. Many courts have held that issues raised in post-trial motions are no substitute for timely issue preservation by trial counsel. *See Publishers Res., Inc. v. Walker-Davis Publ'g, Inc.*, 762 F.2d 557, 561 (7th Cir. 1985) (motion for reconsideration should not serve as occasion to tender new legal theories for first time); *Comm'r of Revenue v.*

Comcast Corp., 453 Mass. 293, 312–13, 901 N.E.2d 1185, 1200–01 (2009) (issues raised for first time in motion for reconsideration not preserved for appeal). Even so, filing the post-trial motion may be better than doing nothing and letting the issue go completely.

15.04(k)(1) Motions for New Trial Based on Ineffective Assistance of Counsel

15.04(k)(1)(A) How and Where to File

Trial counsel is very unlikely to raise the subject of his or her own ineffective assistance; that "pleasure" will be reserved for appellate counsel. Some jurisdictions allow appellate counsel to raise ineffective assistance directly in the appellate court, without the need to file, and have the trial court deny, a motion for new trial. Other jurisdictions require that counsel first file a motion for new trial in the trial court. This gives the trial court an opportunity to grant a new trial, rendering the appeal unnecessary.

Some jurisdictions that require a motion for new trial will nevertheless permit appellate counsel to raise ineffective assistance directly in the appellate court if trial counsel's deficient performance is manifest in the record and does not need further factual development by the trial judge. For example, if the parent's trial lawyer announced at the start of trial, "My client is a drug-addicted wife-beater, and he shouldn't have any child in his custody," or concedes unfitness over the parent's objection, such misconduct is manifest in the transcript and likely requires no further factual development.

15.04(k)(1)(B) Substantive Requirements

Ineffective assistance of counsel is a two-prong test: (i) counsel's performance must fall measurably below that of an ordinary fallible attorney, and (ii) counsel's deficient performance must have deprived the parent of an available defense. *See Strickland v. Washington*, 466 U.S. 668, 688 (1984). In the child welfare context, the second prong is generally interpreted to mean prejudice to the parent. *See, e.g., Care and Protection of Georgette*, 439 Mass. 28, 34 n.7, 785 N.E.2d 357, 360 n.7 (2003). Appellate courts need not address both prongs; indeed, they usually address only the second prong, because if trial counsel's actions or inactions did not prejudice the parent, they need not evaluate trial counsel's conduct.

In most cases, filing a properly supported motion for a new trial is a labor-intensive process that requires many attachments or exhibits. To argue that trial counsel failed to call certain key witnesses, appellate counsel must establish that those witnesses were available, what they would have testified to, and how that testimony would have mattered to the parent's case. This requires contacting the witnesses, discussing the case with them, preparing affidavits about what their testimony would have been, and securing their signatures on the affidavits. To argue that trial counsel was ineffective for failing to object to hearsay, opinion, and/or privileged statements in documents, appellate counsel must show which statements were improperly admitted, why those statements were inadmissible, and how the admission of those statements affected the outcome. All of this requires attaching the documents and a detailed list of all of the objectionable statements and the objections that trial counsel should have made.

Even the simplest new trial motion requires considerable work in order to show harm. For example, trial counsel's failure to notify the parent of the trial date *seems* pretty straight-forward. But to establish a factual basis for this claim, appellate counsel must obtain an affidavit from trial counsel (explaining what he or she did or did not do to notify the parent) and an affidavit from the parent (explaining why he or she did not know about the trial date). Depending on the jurisdiction, counsel may also have to show how the client's absence from the trial affected the result.

As a general principle, trial counsel's conduct is not deficient under the first prong of *Strickland* if it was the result of strategic decision making. For example, trial counsel cannot be faulted for failing to call the parent-client's relative as a witness for the parent if trial counsel believed, after interviewing the relative, that the relative would have done more harm than good to the parent's case. If trial counsel claims a strategic reason for his or her action or inaction, appellate counsel must show that this strategy was manifestly unreasonable. For example, trial counsel's decision not to call the relative might be manifestly unreasonable if counsel:

- never bothered to interview relative to determine the content of her testimony, and she would *not* have testified harmfully about the parent.
- interviewed the relative but misrepresented what she would have testified to, because she would *not* have testified harmfully about the parent.
- interviewed the relative and reasoned incorrectly that she would have done more harm than good. For example, counsel chose not to call the relative as a witness about the client's good parenting skills because the relative would also have testified that the client relapsed a month before trial. But CPS already knew about the relapse because the client admitted it to the social worker, so the relative's negative testimony would have been merely duplicative of the social worker's, and her favorable testimony would have benefited the client.

15.04(k)(1)(C) Dealing with Trial Counsel

Nothing tests appellate counsel's ability to work cooperatively with trial counsel like an ineffective assistance claim. Trial counsel may be angry and defensive. Trial counsel may refuse to cooperate. Trial counsel may even fight the motion for new trial in an effort to defend his or her reputation. There are a few things appellate counsel can do to make the process less painful for everyone:

- Be kind, patient, and respectful. Ineffective assistance claims are emotionally taxing for trial counsel, particularly if they have merit.
- Explain to trial counsel the importance of securing an affidavit from him explaining what he did and didn't do and why he did or didn't do it. Trial counsel need not "fall on his sword" or "concede ineffectiveness" in the affidavit; he need only be truthful about what he did and why he did it (although he can admit errors if he agrees he made them). Appellate counsel can draft the affidavit for trial counsel after speaking with him, send trial counsel the draft, and encourage him to revise it to ensure that it is correct. Appellate counsel should caution trial counsel to send drafts and the final, signed affidavit only to appellate counsel, not to counsel for the other parties.
- Remind trial counsel that he has an ongoing duty of loyalty to the client, and that he cannot actively oppose the motion, help an adverse party, or reveal confidential communications. Explain to trial counsel that, after appellate counsel files the new trial motion along with his affidavit, other counsel may contact him. Trial counsel should not speak to them, nor should he send them any documents related to the representation. Trial counsel should not appear at court unless someone subpoenas him as a witness. If subpoenaed, he should appear at the courthouse, but while there he should not speak to other counsel about the case. And if trial counsel is called to testify, he must guard against (a) disclosing confidential information unrelated to the ineffective assistance allegations, and (b) intentionally undermining his former client's case.

Trial lawyers rarely "get in trouble" when appellate counsel raise ineffective assistance claims except when they refuse to cooperate with appellate counsel, reveal confidential communications that were not at issue in the new trial motion, or actively undermine the client's case. Still, no one can promise trial counsel that the motion will not have some adverse consequences. Trial counsel may have to disclose the claim to his malpractice insurer; or the client may file a malpractice claim for damages or an ethics complaint. If trial counsel is unsure how to respond to these allegations, or whether to cooperate with appellate counsel, he should be encouraged to speak to Bar Counsel, the State Ethics Commission, or the appointing authority. If trial counsel threatens to reveal confidential client communications or undermine the client's new trial motion—or has already done so—appellate counsel may need to contact Bar Counsel, the State Ethics Commission, or the appointing authority for guidance.

15.04(k)(2) Other Post-Trial Motions

There are many reasons to file post-trial motions. If trial counsel failed to preserve an issue below, appellate counsel's post-trial motion might suffice. In addition, the trial judge might be swayed to grant the motion if given the opportunity. In most circumstances, it is better to convince the trial court to give the parent a new trial or other post-trial relief than to wait for such relief from the appellate court. Delay rarely works to a parent's advantage.

A motion for new trial or some other post-trial relief may suffice to preserve issues for appeal, especially if trial counsel could not have raised those issues. For example, a motion to reopen the evidence might be appropriate if key pre-trial evidence came to light only after trial. A motion to amend the findings might be appropriate if the judge failed to include an order, or issued a vague order, in the final judgment or findings. To raise issues related to post-trial evidence, appellate counsel will likely have to file a motion for relief from judgment. Trial judges may be more willing to grant such a post-trial motion if doing so would narrow the issues on appeal.

15.04(k)(3) Timing of the Post-Trial Motion

Under the rules of civil procedure, most post-trial motions must be filed within a very short time—as little as ten days after the entry of judgment. This deadline is often impossible for appellate counsel to meet, especially in jurisdictions that take weeks or months after the final judgment to appoint appellate counsel. Fortunately, motions for relief from judgment under Rule 60 (or its local equivalent) need only be brought within a "reasonable time," or within a year for certain categories of Rule 60(b) motions. Accordingly, consider filing the post-trial motion as a "motion for relief from judgment" whatever its caption might be in an "ordinary" civil proceeding.

15.04(k)(4) Appeal of Denial of Post-Trial Motion

If the trial court grants the post-trial motion, the appeal may well be moot; the parent will be getting a new trial or the trial court will reopen the evidence as requested. But the more likely outcome is that the trial court will deny the post-trial motion. When that happens, the next step is to file a timely notice of appeal from the denial of the motion. There will then be two appeals: the appeal of the underlying final judgment and the appeal of the denial of the post-trial motion. But no one wants two appeals. The better route is a single appeal in which counsel can argue the issues raised in both proceedings. Accordingly, depending on the jurisdiction, counsel may need to file a motion in either the trial court or appellate court seeking consolidation of the appeals. In this motion, counsel should (a) explain the procedural posture of the underlying appeal and the status of the trial proceedings, and (b) argue that consolidation makes sense for judicial economy, substantial justice for the parties, and/or speedy permanency for the child.

The filing of some post-trial motions vitiates a prior notice of appeal. Be very careful in this regard. If the post-trial motion vitiates the notice of appeal of the underlying final judgment, and the trial judge denies the motion, counsel's new notice of appeal must specify that an appeal is being taken from both the denial of the post-trial motion *and* the underlying judgment. Mistakes in this context can be costly; the appellate court may rule that there is no valid appeal of the underlying final judgment.

15.04(l) Raising Issues That Should Have Been Raised by Trial Counsel but Were Not

Generally, a party must have raised an issue at the trial level to argue it on appeal. However, "in exceptional circumstances, especially in criminal cases, appellate courts, in the public interest, may, of their own motion, notice errors to which no exception has been taken, if the errors are obvious, or if they otherwise seriously affect the fairness, integrity or public reputation of judicial proceedings." *United States v. Atkinson*, 297 U.S. 157, 160 (1936). The Supreme Court's opinion in *Hormel v. Helvering* is worth quoting:

> Rules of practice and procedure are devised to promote the ends of justice, not to defeat them. A rigid and undeviating judicially declared practice under which courts of review would invariably and under all circumstances decline to consider all questions which had not previously been specifically urged would be out of harmony with this policy. Orderly rules of procedure do not require sacrifice of the rules of fundamental justice. . . . [W]hile recognizing the desirability and existence of a general practice under which appellate courts confine themselves to the issues raised below . . . such appellate practice should not be applied where the obvious result would be a plain miscarriage of justice. . . . [D]ecisions not in accordance with law should be modified, reversed or reversed and remanded "as justice may require."

312 U.S. 552, 557–58 (1941). The Court went on to state that "[t]here may always be exceptional cases or particular circumstances which will prompt a reviewing or appellate court, where injustice might otherwise result, to consider questions of law which were neither pressed nor passed upon by the court or administrative agency below." *Id.* at 557.

In criminal cases, the standard of review for unpreserved error is "plain error," and courts will grant relief only where "a miscarriage of justice would otherwise result." *United States v. Young*, 470 U.S. 1, 15 (1985); *see also United States v. Santana-Camacho*, 833 F.2d 371, 373 (1st Cir. 1987) (prosecutor's misstatement so prejudicial that it could have caused miscarriage of justice, hence there was plain error and judgment was reversed). Counsel's jurisdiction may use a standard like "substantial risk of miscarriage of justice," "substantial justice," or "exceptional circumstances" for the review of unpreserved errors in child welfare cases. Whatever the standard, counsel must be able to show that the legal error was egregious and that it clearly prejudiced the parent.

15.05 Writing a Persuasive Brief

The most important aspect of appellate practice is brief-writing. A well-written, compelling brief is a powerful tool. It's *possible* to win with a bad brief; it just requires the appellate judges to do the necessary work, and most will not. The reverse is also true, of course. One can lose with a great brief; sometimes no amount of wizardry will change the result. But every appellate lawyer's primary goal should be to write a brief that forces the appellate judges to pay attention and take the case seriously. To do that, and to give the client a meaningful chance of success, it is important to write a compelling brief.

Because every jurisdiction has different rules, this section is intended to provide a general guide for lawyers practicing in any jurisdiction. But conformity to the rules is essential. Judges (and clerks) expect briefs to conform to the appellate rules, standing orders, and other published practice standards. Appellate lawyers must study and follow them. The advice that follows is intended to help appellate counsel write a great brief, with the further understanding that each writer must find his or her own voice.

15.05(a) Formal Requirements

15.05(a)(1) Required Sections

Within certain constraints, counsel can be very creative with briefs. But those constraints are crucial. The Rules of Appellate Procedure in most jurisdictions require certain tables and sections. They require some indication that the brief was served on other counsel. They usually require that certain court orders, or a certified copy of the trial court docket or register, be appended to the brief as an addendum.

If the submitted brief fails to include required sections or addenda, the clerk's office might reject it and require that it be rewritten. Opposing parties might move to strike portions of the brief or the entire brief if it fails to conform to the rules. The appellate court might impose sanctions or even dismiss the appeal outright if the brief does not conform. The rules must be followed.

15.05(a)(2) *Formatting*

Counsel cannot be creative with formatting. Rules commonly regulate margins, text and footnote typefaces, line spacing, cover color, and many other things. As with required sections, the failure to follow all of these technical rules carries great risk. An easy way to ensure compliance with the formatting rules is to use a template, and the best template is a brief written by well-regarded counsel in a recent case before the same court.

15.05(a)(3) Terminology

Some jurisdictions have privacy or impoundment rules that forbid the use of parties' last names in child welfare appeals. Some permit first names and last initials, such as "Richard B." Some require the use of "Mother," "Father," "Child A," and "Child B." Some jurisdictions allow counsel to refer to the child by his or her first name. In some cases, the rules forbid last names or full names but do not give guidance about what the court prefers. The clerk's office can clarify this. Counsel will likely have to follow a similar rule at oral argument.

15.05(a)(4) Impoundment

It is important to follow all applicable impoundment rules. Some jurisdictions require that appellate counsel file a "motion to impound" in all child welfare appeals. Others require that the word "Impounded" be placed on the covers of briefs and on all other filings in the appellate court.

15.05(a)(5) Staying Within the Record

Most jurisdictions require that citations be made only to evidence in the "record," that is, evidence that was admitted at trial, the parties' offers of proof, and other factual information that was in some fashion presented to, and ruled on by, the trial court. Counsel who "goes outside the record" in the brief should be prepared to answer to a motion to strike those portions of the brief or the entire brief. The appellate court may even do so sua sponte. Judicial rebukes for going outside the record are embarrassing for counsel and worse for the parent.

15.05(a)(6) Citations to Facts

Most jurisdictions require that the brief contain citations to the record for every fact included, whether that fact is in the Procedural History, Facts, or Argument section. If writing a fact-rich sentence, it may be best to cite to each fact immediately. For example:

> Mother had a psychological evaluation in May 2013 (RA. 244), a parenting evaluation in August 2013 (RA. 289), and a medication evaluation in January 2014 (RA. 351).

Placing citations to these various facts at the end of the sentence will make it more difficult and time-consuming for the judges to look up a particular evaluation in the record.

15.05(a)(7) Citations to the Law

Many jurisdictions require that legal citations conform to a specific citation format. Even if counsel's jurisdiction has no such requirement, using proper citation format makes sense for two reasons. The first is readability. Improper citations are jarring to many readers, like a glaring typographical error. The second reason is persuasion. The ultimate readers of an appellate brief are the appellate judges, many of whom were editors of law journals, many of whom are older or "old school" about citation form, and appellate clerks, many of whom were very recently editors or cite-checkers for law journals. For this readership, citation format is very important. It reflects how much counsel cares about detail and about getting it right. And it reflects how accurate and trustworthy counsel is—not only in terms of the validity of case references but, more generally, as an advocate. Counsel and the client are both judged by the written product. Thus, counsel should give the appellate court the kind of written product it expects.

15.05(a)(8) Length

Most jurisdictions have a page limit for briefs. Counsel must never exceed that limit without seeking—and obtaining—permission from the appellate court. If counsel realizes at the last minute that the brief is one or two pages beyond the limit, some courts will allow counsel to file the brief along with a "Motion to File Non-Conforming Brief," seeking permission to include the extra pages. But if the motion is denied, the clerk's office might reject the brief or strike the extra pages. A good rule of thumb is not to exceed—or even approach—the page limit. In most cases, the shorter the brief is, the better. Appellate judges appreciate brevity and concision.

15.05(a)(9) Footnotes

Keep footnotes to a minimum. It may be necessary to include a few at the start of the brief to explain what certain abbreviations stand for and why the full names of the parties are not used. But no important fact or legal argument should be placed in a footnote. Include them in the text or delete them.

Bryan Garner, in his excellent treatise *The Winning Brief*, recommends putting all legal citations in footnotes in order to declutter the Argument section. *See* BRYAN GARDNER, THE WINNING BRIEF 176–99 (3d ed. 2014). Doing so does remove clutter. But it also forces the reader to look up and down many times in order to find support for the legal argument, which some judges may find too distracting. Counsel should choose a style that is comfortable for her, unless the rules require or forbid footnotes for legal citations.

15.05(a)(10) Attachments/Addenda

Many jurisdictions require that counsel attach the trial court's docket or register, the order or judgment appealed from, and/or the trial court's findings of fact. List those items in the Table of Contents of the brief for easy reference. If counsel represents an appellee parent, and only the appellant is required to attach the documents, appellee counsel should also include those documents at the end of his or her brief. That way, the judges need not put down the appellee brief (and pick up the appellant's brief) in order to check docket entries or findings.

15.05(a)(11) A Last Word on Typographical Errors

Every brief has typographical errors. Spell-check programs catch many of them, but they do not catch certain misspellings that are, themselves, real words. While some mistakes are inevitable, they must be kept to a minimum. They are distracting, and counsel's sloppiness may unconsciously be imputed to the parent. Here is one rule about typographical errors that counsel must follow at all costs: no typos in the Table of Contents. The Table of Contents is the first thing most judges read, and you only get one chance to make a first impression. Counsel must proofread the Table of Contents with a fine-toothed comb.

15.05(b) Parts of the Brief

15.05(b)(1) Introduction

The rules generally are silent on whether and where to include an "Introduction" section in the brief. An Introduction can be the first substantive portion of the brief, located before the Statement of the Case or Procedural History. It can be placed between the Facts and the Argument. It can even be the first portion of the Argument section. But the earlier it is placed in the brief, the better. A well-written Introduction will determine how the judges read the rest of the brief.

An Introduction is an explanation of why the client should win. It should be short, usually only one to three paragraphs. It can be the theory of the case, laid bare for the judges. It can be a transcript quote that relates to the theory of the case. It can be the most egregious, prejudicial error—or a list of errors—that illustrates the theory. It can even be a hypothetical that suggests the terrible harm to children, constitutional rights, or the judicial system wrought by the trial court's error or CPS's misconduct.

However done, it should be powerful, pithy, and—of course—accurate. Here is an example of an Introduction for a case involving allegations of sexual abuse:

> **Introduction**
>
> The Juvenile Court terminated Father's parental rights based exclusively on the hearsay statements of an incompetent, developmentally delayed child who has a functional age of four; a history of fabricating horrific, detailed, and untrue stories; a craving for adult attention; and a seizure disorder that causes visual delusions.
>
> The Child never testified. Father challenged her competency, CPS conceded her incompetence, and a court clinician agreed. Still, the judge admitted the Child's hearsay statements in evidence through the Child's treating clinicians who vouched for her credibility and testified that they believed Father had sexually abused her.

> That was CPS's only case against Father, a former CPS foster parent with no criminal record, substance abuse history, or mental health problems.

This Introduction sets forth the theory of the case: the only evidence of the father's unfitness was improperly admitted hearsay from an incompetent child-declarant.

Here is an Introduction from another case, this time using a quote that illustrates the theory of the case:

> **Introduction**
>
> | | |
> |---|---|
> | Judge: | I'm not going to tell you again. Sit down, counsel. |
> | Mother's Counsel: | Your honor, I'm just objecting to the social worker's hearsay. |
> | Judge: | It's not hearsay. I've already ruled on this. |
> | Mother's Counsel: | Your honor, this social worker can't testify to . . . |
> | Judge: | She can if I say she can. Now sit down and stay down. (Tr. II, p. 40). |
>
> The trial judge treated Mother's counsel like this after almost every objection. Indeed, counsel was correct here and at other times where the court abused him; the CPS social worker's testimony *was* hearsay for which there was no exception. Such ill-treatment of counsel was not just a series of evidentiary errors. It shows bias, it is a structural error, and it requires reversal of the termination decree.

The Introduction *could* have stated that this is a case about judicial bias based on the mistreatment of counsel. But a quote that perfectly illustrates the point is an even more effective start to the brief.

15.05(b)(2) Jurisdiction/Standard of Review

Statements of jurisdiction and standards of review, divorced from the facts of the appeal, are boring to read. Most judges skim or skip them because they know the law and are more interested in how it applies to the case. But if the jurisdiction requires a section on the appellate court's jurisdiction or the applicable standards, that section must be included. Keep it brief and accurate. There is no bonus for creativity.

If the rules require setting forth the standards of review but do not require that they be placed in a separate section, the better course is to weave them into the Argument. This gives the arguments context. An example is provided below in the Argument section.

15.05(b)(3) Issues Presented

The "Issues Presented" or "Questions Presented" section of the brief is an important advocacy tool. The issues or questions should be phrased to make the answers as clear as possible, because clear answers are needed for the parent to win. The following examples start with a boring "subject matter" issue—that is, an issue statement that does little more than tell the appellate court about the general subject of the brief:

> Whether CPS failed to make reasonable efforts to reunify Father and Child.
> or
> Did CPS fail to make reasonable efforts to reunify Father and Child?

These are not good issue statements because they don't call for any particular answer. The judges will have to read the whole brief to find out. Moreover, it's already clear in the Argument headers in the Table of Contents that a portion of the brief is about reasonable efforts, so issues phrased like these add nothing.

A good issue statement is not an announcement of subject matter; it's a question about how the relevant law applies to the facts of the particular case. The issue and its resolution should be comprehensible to the appellate court without resort to anything other than the issue statement itself. *See* Susan L. Bostic, *Sample Points of Error and Issues Presented in the Past Year: The Good, the Bad, and the Ugly*, *in* STATE BAR OF TEXAS, PRACTICE BEFORE THE TEXAS SUPREME COURT 4 (2003). Therefore, a good issue statement or question presented succinctly sets forth the law and the facts in a way that suggests that the law applies favorably to the parent.

Here is a better issue statement:

> Whether CPS failed to make reasonable efforts to reunify Father with his son where it failed to schedule visitation between them, failed to provide Father with parenting classes, and failed to inform him of his son's mental health needs.
> or
> Did CPS fail to make reasonable efforts to reunify Father with his son where it failed to schedule visitation between them, failed to provide Father with parenting classes, and failed to inform him of his son's mental health needs?

(Note that "whether" issues take a period, not a question mark, because they do not pose a question. Issue statements beginning with "Is/Are" or "Do/Does/Did" take a question mark.)

These issues—in "whether" or question form—are much better, because they call for the answer the appellant-father wants. But they are still not strong enough, because they do not explain the law governing "reasonable efforts." So an even better effort (using only the question format) might be something like this:

> Did CPS fail to make reasonable efforts to reunify Father with his son, as required by Mass. Gen. Law ch. 119, § 29B and the Adoption Assistance and Child Welfare

> Act, where it failed to schedule visitation between them, failed to provide Father with parenting classes, and failed to inform him of his son's mental health needs?

This issue statement is better because it tells the appellate judges—who are not usually experts in child welfare law—that CPS's actions violated specific state and federal laws. But it is still not perfect, because now the sentence is long, and long sentences are difficult to follow.

A good solution is to apply the "deep issue" method created by legal-writing guru Bryan Garner. He suggests an issue statement comprised of three or four sentences totaling fewer than 75 words. *See* GARNER, *supra*, at 94–127. Using his approach, the issue might look like this:

> Both Mass. Gen. Laws Ch.119, § 29B and the Adoption Assistance and Child Welfare Act require that CPS make reasonable efforts to reunify parents and children and provide timely services to this end. Here, CPS failed to schedule visitation between Father and his son, never provided Father with parenting classes, and never informed him of his son's mental health needs. Did CPS fail to make reasonable efforts to reunify Father with his son?

The law and key facts that pertain to the law are clearly set forth; the closing question suggests, if not demands, an answer favorable to the parent; and the sentences are easy to read. The three or four sentences are usually (1) a statement of the uncontested legal rule, (2) a statement of the facts of the case relevant to the legal rule, and (3) a final question. The final question is usually in the form of the boring "subject matter" issues addressed at the top of this section; however, given the first two or three sentences, the "subject matter" question has an "obvious" answer. Few, if any, jurisdictions prohibit a multi-sentence issue presented.

Here are a few more examples of "deep issues":

> The Juvenile Court must have clear and convincing evidence that a parent is unfit before terminating her rights. During the fourteen months after CPS removed the child because of Mother's substance abuse and homelessness, Mother obtained stable housing, graduated from a parenting program, attended every visit, and maintained her sobriety except for a single relapse five months before trial. Did the Court err in finding Mother unfit by clear and convincing evidence?
>
> Children can legally quit school when they turn sixteen. Here, the Juvenile Court found Mother unfit because her sixteen-year-old daughter missed forty days of school. Did the Juvenile Court err in finding Mother unfit because she allowed her daughter to make an attendance-related decision the daughter was legally allowed to make?

Experts and treating clinicians are not permitted to testify that a child is credible, was sexually abused, or shares characteristics with sexually abused children. Here, the CPS experts, many of whom treated the Child, vouched for her credibility, testified that she had been sexually abused by Father, and compared her to sexually abused children. Did the court err in permitting and relying on this testimony to terminate Father's parental rights?

15.05(b)(4) Procedural History

All jurisdictions require a "Procedural History" or "Statement of the Case." Unless the rules require otherwise, counsel should only include essential information:

- the petitioner, the parent(s), the child(ren) (keeping in mind any impoundment or naming rules), and the judge;
- when and where the case was filed;
- custodial changes prior to trial;
- when and where the trial took place;
- the date and nature of the judgment or dispositional order;
- the date the appellant(s) filed the notice(s) of appeal; and
- the date the trial court issued its findings of fact.

Counsel should include other events only if they are relevant to the Argument section. For example, if the parent is arguing that the court erred in admitting the report of an unqualified guardian ad litem, include the date of appointment and any hearings about the guardian ad litem and his or her report. If the parent is arguing that the court improperly removed trial counsel, include the hearing where this occurred and any other hearings relative to the issue. Otherwise, these hearings, orders, and events have no place in the Procedural History.

In a trial motion, counsel might list relevant hearings and events in numbered paragraphs, single-sentence paragraphs, or bullet points before the legal argument. Generally, these methods are not appropriate in a brief. Instead, counsel should give the case history some narrative form and recount it in multi-sentence paragraphs.

The Procedural History section must be purely factual and devoid of argument. This section does nothing more than tell the appellate court about key dates and events. If the case is *about* procedural problems (e.g., CPS gave improper notice to the parent, the court failed to grant a discovery request, or the court erred in permitting someone to intervene), key dates and events should be *mentioned* in the Procedural History section but *explained* in the Facts section. For example:

> On March 25, 2014, Mother filed a motion seeking discovery of CPS's homestudy of the foster parents and related records. (RA. 433). The court denied the motion

the next day. (RA. 3). Mother renewed her objection at the start of trial (Tr. I:12) and before her cross-examination of the foster mother (Tr. II:157).

This identifies the discovery dispute as an important event for the appellate court. There will be room in the Facts section to explain the nature of the dispute in greater detail. Of course, none of this information belongs in the Procedural History or Facts sections unless the discovery issue is relevant to the arguments.

15.05(b)(5) Facts

Everybody likes stories. We want to be entertained; we want to identify with the main characters; we pull for the underdog; we want justice done. Appellate judges are like that, too. And while they must follow the law, they want to read briefs with stories that interest them, with characters they can identify with, and with injustices they can rectify. Child welfare appellate attorneys are fortunate in this regard, because their cases are narratively rich, populated with underdogs, and rife with injustice.

Parents have their stories, the children have their stories, the CPS social worker has his or her story, and the trial proceedings themselves are a story. Some of these stories are independent, but many are shared. The sharing does not, however, mean that they are the same. In Akira Kurosawa's film *Rashomon*, the same terrible incident is told from the perspective of each of the major characters. *See* RASHOMON (Daiei Film Co., Ltd. 1950). Each sees what happened—and the importance of what happened—differently. *See id.* Child welfare cases are like that, too.

In far too many briefs, appellate counsel presents the Facts section as either a chronological recounting of events or a restatement of the trial court's findings. These methods are problematic for several reasons. First, a chronology of dates and events tells a *boring* story. Second, it tells the story of why the parent should have lost, which is not the story counsel wants to tell on appeal. Third, it fails to further the parent's theory of the case. The story to tell in the Facts section must be the story of why the parent would and should have won had he or she not been treated unfairly at the trial level.

15.05(b)(5)(A) Basic Rules

There are some important rules for telling the story. Following these rules is crucial to maintaining credibility and avoiding trouble. For example, counsel should cite to the record for each factual reference in the brief. This is often required by the rules; but, even where it is not required, it is good practice. Liberally citing to the record proves to the court that counsel is not making anything up; it also permits the judges to easily verify the information.

Be scrupulously faithful to the record. Never misstate or "fudge" any of the evidence. Giving evidence a helpful "spin" is one thing, but any spin must be supportable. Also, never hide important bad facts (although, as set forth below, counsel need not include every detail about every bad fact). When in doubt, err on the side of disclosure. Counsel's credibility and integrity are essential. The appellate judges will not always buy into the parent's theory of the case, but they must never believe that counsel is misleading the court. Section 15.05(b)(5)(C) below suggests some appropriate ways to address bad facts.

The Facts section should rarely be longer than the Argument section; it should usually be much shorter. A fact belongs in the brief only if there is a reason: it helps tell the parent's positive story; it is important background necessary to the theory of the case; it is a difficult or damaging fact that cannot be ignored; or it is needed to develop the Argument.

Counsel must never argue in the Facts section. There is often a gray area between narrative spin and argument. Counsel should stay out of that gray area. If the appellate court believes counsel is arguing in the Facts section, counsel will lose credibility.

15.05(b)(5)(B) The Big Picture—The Story

As noted above, the story told in the Facts section must be consistent with, and further, the parent's theory of the case. The story may be about a parent who has conquered a substance abuse problem (with a very minor slip up close to trial); a parent who has escaped from the cycle of domestic violence; or a parent who didn't do the awful thing alleged and whose accuser isn't credible. The story might also be about the unfair trial procedures themselves: a mother who came to court for every hearing but who was punished for missing one trial date because she was ill; a father who lived and worked in Akron for years and who never knew about the proceeding because notice was published in a Cleveland newspaper with the child's name misspelled; or a fit parent who was badgered by the biased questioning of a judge determined to terminate rights.

The story need not be, and in most cases should not be, chronological. Like a novel, it can start in the middle or even at the climax. Thus, counsel should not kill the drama by starting the story the same way the trial judge likely started his or her findings of fact—with the birth of the child, or even the birth of the parents—unless it furthers the story. And counsel should never tell the story witness by witness. That is dry, and it forces the appellate judges to create their own story from the testimony. In putting the story together, counsel must remember the principles of primacy and recency: readers tend to remember the first and last things they read and forget what is buried in the middle. So counsel should start and end the story with something memorable. She should put the bad parts in the middle.

For example, the story might begin with the parent's successful completion of substance abuse counseling, a crowning achievement after years of drug abuse. The parent goes through a graduation ceremony and gets a certificate. The head of the program writes a glowing evaluation about her progress and prospects for the future. This story might end with a discussion of all the other services the parent completed before trial.

The middle of this story might be the best place to mention the client's many relapses and the petty crimes she perpetrated while battling her demons. That placement deemphasizes the negative information.

Counsel should divide the story into sections. It is easier to read a story in smaller bites, and it is easier for judges to find key facts in labeled sections. For example, the story can be broken down into the parent's successful history of visits; her partial compliance with a case plan; her not-so-successful history of avoiding her abuser; and the trial itself, in which the court made several significant procedural errors. If the procedural errors are the "best" part of the story, counsel might choose to start the Facts section with it.

Using headers for each section of the Facts is an effective organizational tool. Because counsel cannot argue in a Facts section, the headers—unlike Argument headers—must not be argumentative. There are two ways of approaching Facts headers. The "topic" method avoids any taint of argument but does little for the story other than divide it. Topic Facts headers may look like this:

- Mother's Substance Abuse Treatment
- Father's Visitation
- The Trial
- Trial Counsel's Actions

Alternatively, counsel may use more descriptive titles:

- Mother Graduates from Residential Substance Abuse Program
- Father's Perfect Attendance at Visits
- The Trial Court Removes Mother's Counsel on Morning of Trial
- Trial Counsel's Failure to Interview Witnesses

The descriptive method is not argumentative provided everything written is uncontested, has support in the record, and includes no opinion. Whether counsel uses topic headers or more descriptive headers is a matter of style. But counsel cannot argue in the headers. These headers are *not* acceptable in a Facts section:

- Mother Proves Her Fitness by Completing Substance Abuse Treatment
- Father's Attendance at Visits Shows That He Is More Committed to the Child Than Mother Is
- The Trial Court Improperly Removes Mother's Counsel
- Trial Counsel Is Ineffective Based on Her Failure to Interview Witnesses

Use Facts headers, but keep the argument out of them.

15.05(b)(5)(C) The Little Picture—Part I: Addressing the Facts Within Each Paragraph

The record will likely be replete with "bad facts." While they must be addressed, counsel's goal is to minimize their impact. Here are some techniques:

Pair a bad fact with a good fact

Although Mother stopped seeing her psychiatrist four months before trial, she regularly took all of her medication and regularly attended her therapy appointments.

Father attended twenty out of twenty-three scheduled visits, missing only two just before trial.

Although Mother was late to ten of her visits, every one of her visits went well and the Children were always happy to see her.

"Hide" the bad fact in the middle of a paragraph

The principles of primacy and recency suggest that we remember the first and last things we read in a paragraph. We tend to forget what is in the middle. "Bury" the bad stuff in the middle of a paragraph where it is harder to see and easier to forget.

Summarize related bad events

Although bad facts must be addressed, no rule requires that every related bad fact be discussed separately. Instead of this:

> On March 3, 2014, a mandated reporter filed a report to CPS alleging that Mother brought Kim to daycare looking unwashed. (RA. 23). On March 23, 2014, another mandated reporter filed a report with CPS alleging that Mother brought Kim to the doctor's office hungry and smelling like she hadn't been bathed in a month. (RA. 34). On April 1, 2014, a non-mandated reporter filed a report with CPS alleging that Kim appeared cold and unclean in the halls of their apartment building. (RA. 56).

Try this:

> Between March 3 and April 1, 2014, three reports were filed against Mother alleging neglect of Kim. (RA. 23, 34, 56).

This is accurate without playing "hide-the-ball." It is also a much better summary of the facts from the parent's perspective.

Generalize when describing a bad event

There is no need to describe a bad fact in detail unless the details themselves are important facts. Instead of this:

> On March 5, 2014, witnesses reported that Mother and her boyfriend were screaming at each other on the sidewalk in front of the apartment. (Tr. 23; RA. 77). The screaming then continued up the stairs and into the apartment. (Tr. 24; RA. 77). Other neighbors overheard Mother yelling at her boyfriend through the open widows, and they reported that they feared for mother's safety. (Tr. 24; RA. 77). One of them called the police. The police came, and the boyfriend was removed from the apartment in handcuffs. (Tr. 25; RA. 77).

Try this:

> In March 2014, Mother and her boyfriend were overheard yelling at each other. (Tr. 23; RA. 77). Although no one was harmed, the boyfriend was arrested. (Tr. 25; RA. 77).

In the second example, counsel fairly discloses the bad fact but gives it the space that it deserves (according to the parent's theory of the case). Of course, if the details are important, disclose them. If, for example, the boyfriend had waived a machete around during the argument, counsel should probably disclose that fact.

Use detail when describing a good event

Save the details for the good stuff. This is the best opportunity to paint a favorable picture for the appellate judges. The description below fails to paint a picture:

> On July 8, 2013, Father visited with the Child. The visit went well. He visited the Child three more times in 2013 before trial. Those visits also went well.

That visits "went well" evokes no images for appellate judges who are unfamiliar with child welfare cases. Instead, if the evidence supports it, give more details:

> On July 8, 2013, Father traveled for two hours each way, taking three buses, to a visit with the Child at the Albany CPS office. The Child ran to Father and hugged him, then sat on his lap while they ate a snack that Father had brought for him. Father also brought the Child a toy truck that the Child played with, all around, and often on,

Father. They laughed and played together for the entire hour. At the end of the visit, the Child kissed and hugged Father and cried when the social worker told him the visit was over. A similar scene took place at three other visits before trial.

Details help paint a picture of mutual affection. They *show* the appellate judges that the visits went well. This is much more effective than only telling them so.

Eliminate date clutter

Counsel must include the dates of important procedural events (e.g., the date CPS filed the case, the dates of trial, the date the appeal was filed) and important events in the parent's and child's life during the case (e.g., the dates the parent entered and completed substance abuse treatment, the date of the visit where the parent slapped the child). But counsel should not clutter a brief with unimportant dates. For example, in the visitation example above, there is no need to include the dates of the father's other three successful visits because the dates are not important. Indeed, including them would interrupt the narrative flow. Instead, include (as is required) the record citations for the three visits. If an appellate judge thinks those dates are important, he or she can easily look them up.

15.05(b)(5)(D) The Little Picture—Part 2: Readability

A good brief demands that appellate judges keep their eyes glued to it; it makes them *want* to read more. Judges will not feel this way if the language is dense, complicated, or confusing; they will if the language is crisp and easy to read. Here are a few techniques for making each paragraph more readable:

Active vs. passive voice

Too much passive voice slows the narrative flow. It also creates confusion, because it is often unclear who the actor is. Active voice also makes it easier to use more powerful and descriptive verbs. Instead of this:

Family therapy was not offered to Father by CPS, although it was requested.

Try this:

CPS did not offer family therapy to Father, although he requested it.

Or better yet,

CPS *refused* to offer family therapy to Father, although he requested it.

Use passive voice only when trying to distance the parent from an act ("The Child was struck by Mother on the cheek.") or the actor doesn't matter or is unknown ("The needle was found in the crib near the baby's head.").

Verbs vs. nouns

Some perfectly good active verbs are buried in vague nouns. Replacing those nouns with their verb forms enlivens the writing and reduces the number of words. Instead of this:

> Father had visitation with the children twice per month. His attendance at parenting classes was regular.

Try this:

> Father visited with the children twice per month and regularly attended parenting classes.

Short paragraphs, short sentences

A few rules of thumb:

- No paragraph in the Facts (or Argument) section should be longer than a page. Page-long paragraphs should be broken into two or three smaller paragraphs.
- A single-sentence paragraph is fine for dramatic effect, so long as there are not too many of them.
- Long sentences try the reader's patience. If a sentence is so long that it is hard to find the verb, break it into two or three shorter sentences.
- It is important to vary sentence length, but when in doubt, shorter is better.

Use bullet points for lists

Appellate briefs in child welfare cases commonly list many things: services offered and required by CPS; case plan tasks ordered by the court; services completed by parents; conditions of custody; and much more. Lists in paragraph form give appellate judges eye-glaze. Bullet points are a great way to make lists easier to read and keep judges' eyes on the brief. Instead of this:

> The April 2014 CPS case plan required that Mother attend parenting classes, participate in a psychological evaluation and follow through with recommendations, attend

domestic violence counseling and follow through with recommendations, draft a budget of all monthly expenses, visit with Juan and Maria once each week at the CPS office, participate in therapy, and sign releases for all therapy providers. (RA. 234). Mother fulfilled all of these requirements before trial. (Tr. 23; RA. 445).

Try this:

The April 2014 CPS case plan required that Mother:

- attend parenting classes;
- participate in a psychological evaluation and follow through with recommendations;
- attend domestic violence counseling and follow through with recommendations;
- draft a budget of all monthly expenses;
- visit with Juan and Maria once each week at the CPS office;
- participate in therapy; and
- sign releases for all therapy providers (RA. 234).

Mother fulfilled all of these requirements before trial. (Tr. 23; RA. 445).

15.05(b)(6) Summary of the Argument

Many jurisdictions require a Summary of the Argument if the Argument section is more than a certain number of pages. The Summary generally must include references to the pages in the Argument, be in paragraph form, and not merely repeat the Argument headers. This last point is difficult for many attorneys to put into practice. An Argument header tells the judges what counsel hopes to prove in the text below; a Summary-of-the-Argument paragraph actually proves it, albeit in less detail than in the Argument itself.

Here is an example of a good Argument header, followed by a good paragraph from a Summary of the Argument:

Argument header:

I. The trial court erred in allowing experts and the Child's treating professionals to vouch for the Child's credibility, compare her to sexually abused children, and testify that the Child was, in fact, sexually abused.

Corresponding paragraph in the Summary of the Argument:

The trial court allowed CPS's experts and the Child's treating clinicians to vouch for the credibility of the Child, testify that she was sexually abused by Father, and compare her to sexually abused children. This Court has long held

> that the admission of such vouching and comparisons is improper. While the trial court noted that it did not credit the expert vouching, the findings show that the court relied on it extensively. Several key findings note that the experts believed that the child was telling the truth. This prejudicial error requires a new trial. See pages 33–38.

Even if the Argument is too short to require a Summary, it is a good idea to include one. It is an opportunity to give the appellate court a preview of the arguments. Why pass up an advocacy opportunity?

15.05(b)(7) Argument

The Argument, like the Facts section, must be consistent with the parent's theory of the case. It must be clear and logical. There are complicated aspects to child welfare cases, and appellate judges rarely are experts in child welfare law. They will not know where most of the arguments are going before they get there. Make no assumptions; skip no steps in the analysis.

The Argument section must also be readable. The goal is to persuade, and counsel cannot persuade the judges if their eyes glaze over for portions of the Argument section. Accordingly, whatever counsel's style, make the Argument section easy and interesting to read. The writing suggestions in the Facts section discussion above regarding paragraph and sentence structure, section 15.05(b)(5)(D), apply equally to the Argument section. Here are a few other suggestions:

15.05(b)(7)(A) Organization

If there is no separate "Introduction" section, consider using an introductory paragraph to begin the Argument section. *See* section 15.05(b)(1).

After any introductory paragraph(s), put the best and strongest argument first. There are two important exceptions to this. First, if there is a subject-matter jurisdiction argument with any heft, put it first; winning on this issue usually eliminates the need for the court to read any further. *See* Robert L. Stern, Appellate Practice in the United States 292 (2d ed. 1989). Second, logic may require putting a weaker issue before a better one. For example, it probably makes sense to argue that the court erred in permitting an unqualified expert to testify before arguing that the court erred in permitting that expert to testify outside of his area of expertise, even if the latter argument is stronger.

Counsel should not argue too many issues. Weak issues will dilute stronger ones. Thus, choosing only the three or four strongest issues will work best. But there is an important exception to this. Counsel must argue every issue that *needs* to be addressed in order to avoid losing. For example, if counsel's jurisdiction has seven independently sufficient grounds for termination and the court has found that each ground exists, counsel must argue that the court erred as to each of them.

15.05(b)(7)(B) Use of Boilerplate Legal Standards

The standards of review are extremely important. The Arguments must acknowledge and address them. But unless the rules require a section entitled "Standards of Review," it rarely makes sense to start the Argument section with pages of boilerplate standards. When judges see briefs that open with huge blocks of boilerplate standards, their eyes skip over those blocks to what matters: the particular case.

Instead, tie the legal standards to the facts. For example, instead of opening with the standard that appellate courts review findings of fact for clear error, wait until a challenge to a factual finding:

The trial court found in Finding #25 that Father punched Mother on May 5, 2010. It relied heavily on Finding #25 in determining that Father did not learn anything from his batterer's treatment program. But the only testimony regarding this incident was that *Mother punched Father* on that date, not the other way around. No other evidence supported Finding #25. A finding is clearly erroneous when it lacks any evidentiary support. *See In re Irma W.*, 228 State 455, 457 (2012).

The appellate court will read that citation rather than gloss over it in order to get to the good stuff, because the citation is *part* of the good stuff.

15.05(b)(7)(C) Use of Headers

Argument headers are an important advocacy tool. They are a road map to help the appellate court navigate the brief. A judge should be able to read only the headers to understand the arguments and agree with them. If the headers are too long, the judge will skim them. But if they only state the issue objectively (e.g., "I. Father's Unfitness"), the judge will not know counsel's argument. (Objective headers are fine, of course, in the Facts section where argument is not allowed.) Here are a few rules of thumb for effective Argument headers:

- Each header should be one sentence (as opposed to the Issues Presented, which may be longer). If the idea has several subparts, make each subpart its own header.
- The header should be declarative. Unlike the Issues Presented, it is not an inquiry. Do *not* start a header with "Whether" or "Is" or "Do/Does" and do not end it with a question mark.
- The header should advocate for the outcome sought by explaining *why* it is the correct result. Include key facts or controlling law.

For example, instead of this:

I. The Juvenile Court erred in finding that Father abandoned the Child.

Try this:

I. The Juvenile Court erred in finding that Father abandoned the Child because he paid child support and sent several letters to CPS inquiring about the Child's welfare.

Instead of this:

I. CPS provided improper notice to Father.

Try this:

I. CPS violated [statute] by publishing notice to Father in the Knoxville News Sentinel instead of serving him by hand at his long-term, well-known address in Memphis.

- Unless court rules, practices, or standing orders require it, do not use all capital letters or initial capital letters for certain levels of headers. IT IS VERY HARD TO READ A SENTENCE WHEN ALL OF IT IS IN CAPITAL LETTERS, And It Is Even Harder To Read A Sentence When The First Letter Of Each Word Is Capitalized. Normal capitalization is fine. Why make anything in the brief hard to read? If counsel must use different styles in different levels of headers, use bold-face or underlines. Those are easier to read than all or initial capital letters.
- While the entire brief should be thoroughly proofread, proofing the headers is particularly important. Argument headers must generally be included in the Table of Contents, and they are the first things most judges look at in the brief. Do not start off on the wrong foot with typos in the headers. And make sure the headers in the Table of Contents match the headers used in the Argument section.

String cites. Judges tend to gloss over a dense block of string cites. Instead, counsel should pick a recent case or the most important case to support a legal proposition. Counsel should cite several cases only if (a) each one is relevant, and then include a parenthetical to explain the relevance; (b) the point is to stress the number of cases that stand for that proposition or the length of time the court has recognized the proposition; or (c) the cases are from other jurisdictions and counsel is citing them to prove broad support for the proposition. There may be other reasons for using string cites, but use them sparingly.

Instead of blocks of cases, counsel should try using bullet points. Usually, the case name itself is not important; what is important is the case's holding. So counsel can use bullet points for the holding (or what makes the case worth citing), and then cite the case. For example, instead of this:

> This Court has held that due process requires many procedural protections for parents in child welfare cases. [case] (appointment of counsel for indigent parents);

> [case] (a hearing within 72 hours of emergency removal); [case] (notice by in-hand delivery).

Try this:

> This Court has held that due process requires many procedural protections for parents in child welfare cases:
>
> - Appointment of counsel for indigent parents. [case]
> - A hearing within 72 hours of emergency removal. [case]
> - Notice by in-hand delivery. [case]
>
> This technique focuses the judges' eyes on what *is* important—the holding.

15.05(b)(7)(D) Conclusion

The Conclusion should be short, clear, and concise. Specify the relief being sought. If the relief is procedurally complex, spell it out for the appellate court. If counsel fails to explain it carefully, any remand order may do more harm than good.

15.05(c) The Reply Brief

Many jurisdictions permit the appellant to file a reply brief after the appellee files its brief. Reply briefs must conform to all rules for principal briefs, but the page limit is usually shorter. The appellant generally does not have to file a reply brief; it is left to the appellant's discretion.

Filing a reply brief is worthwhile if the appellee has materially misrepresented the facts or the law; if the appellee points out a problem in the Facts or Argument that needs to be fixed; or if the appellee has raised an issue that the appellant's brief did not, particularly a jurisdictional or policy issue, that now needs to be addressed. It is not worthwhile if the reply brief will merely restate portions of the Argument from the principal brief. Arguments are rarely improved by virtue of repetition. Many jurisdictions do not permit raising new issues in a reply brief. *See, e.g.*, *Check Reporting Servs., Inc. v. Michigan Nat'l Bank-Lansing*, 191 Mich. App. 614, 628, 478 N.W.2d 893, 901 (1991).

15.06 Oral Argument

15.06(a) Introduction

In some jurisdictions, all child welfare appeals get oral argument; in some, counsel must request it; in others, only meritorious cases (as determined by counsel, staff at the appellate court, or an appellate judge) get it; in still others, oral arguments are rarely, if ever, granted. It is unfortunate for appellate counsel when the appellate court grants oral argument sparingly; it can be the most exciting aspect of appellate practice.

That said, oral argument—like public speaking generally—can be nerve-wracking. Experience helps; the more arguments one does, the easier they get.

Oral arguments are "directed conversations" between counsel and the appellate judges. The conversation has rules—maintaining a respectful tone, never interrupting questions from the judges, and so on—but the rules are not complicated. It is getting ready for the conversation that takes so much work.

15.06(b) Preparation

The record may be huge, comprising hundreds, if not thousands, of pages of transcripts, exhibits, and pleadings. No one wants to review a record that size more than once before the argument. Counsel's goal is to condense the appeal into a small binder of the most important information so that it is easy to master. To do this, create three outlines: important dates, key portions of the record, and arguments. These can be used both to prepare for, and for support at, the argument.

15.06(b)(1) Outlines

15.06(b)(1)(A) Outline of Key Dates

Create a list of the most important dates and events in the case: when the child was born, when CPS first got involved, when the case was filed, when key events took place (e.g., when the parent entered a residential program, when the parent obtained a divorce from her abusive spouse), when key procedural events took place (e.g., the date of the pretrial hearing on admissibility of sexual abuse hearsay, the date trial counsel withdrew without the appointment of successor counsel), when trial took place, when the court entered judgment and/or issued the findings, and the date the parent filed her notice of appeal. It is extremely important to know these dates well. The appellate judges will ask questions about the record. While it is okay not to know some of the answers, counsel should never look baffled when asked, "When did trial take place?" or, in a domestic violence case, "When was the last incident of domestic violence?" If counsel does not know those answers, the judges will not give much credence to anything else said at oral argument.

The outline of key dates and events should rarely be longer than one page. It should be at counsel's fingertips.

15.06(b)(1)(B) Outline of the Record

Counsel must be very familiar with the record. Review the briefs, exhibits, transcripts, and important pleadings. Create an outline of exhibits and witness testimony. List the favorable and unfavorable evidence in each document, noting the record appendix page numbers. List the favorable and unfavorable testimony of each witness, noting the transcript page numbers. If counsel does this thoroughly once, the outline of exhibit and witness highlights will "replace" the massive record appendix and transcript volumes.

Whether this outline is two pages or twenty, it will be easier to master (and carry) than the original source material.

The first time counsel tries this method, the outline will be huge; it will include far more information under each document- or witness-header than needed. But, with each argument, it becomes easier to focus on the key information. Remember that the goal is not to know every word in the record; perfection isn't possible (or cost-effective). The goal is to know the most important information cold and have a solid grasp on the rest. Plan to review this outline many times before the oral argument.

15.06(b)(1)(C) Outline of Arguments

Hopefully, counsel wrote the brief in accordance with a theory of the case. Ideally, but not invariably, counsel should have the same theory of the case at oral argument. If counsel has internalized the theory of the case, questions from the appellate judges will not be difficult to handle. The answers will be consistent with the theory, and when the questions stray to other topics, it will be easier to answer them and then guide the judges back to the parent's theory.

Counsel must know the arguments cold and should outline them. Counsel must not simply outline the arguments in the brief, but also the arguments counsel *could* have made in the brief but didn't, the appellees' responsive arguments, and the policy implications of those arguments. Counsel should think about all of the questions the judges *could* ask, and then outline those answers, in addition to why the errors mattered. In every jurisdiction, counsel must be prepared for this question: "Let's assume we agree with you; how did that mistake make any difference to the outcome?" The answer is crucial.

The outlined arguments will rely on case law, statutes, rules, and the record. Counsel should put key legal citations (the format here does not matter; it is for counsel's use only) and record references in the outline. Counsel can use the outline of the record to fill in the record references in the argument outline. Putting all of this information into the argument outline will make it easier to answer two other common questions: (1) "What's your best case for that?" and (2) "Where in the record can we find that?" When making a legal argument, counsel is responsible for knowing the law that supports (or refutes) it. Similarly, when making an argument that relies on the facts or procedural events in the case, counsel is responsible for knowing where in the record the judges can find those facts or events. If that information is in the argument outline, it will be at counsel's fingertips during oral argument.

The argument depends heavily on the standards of review on appeal. They are important to work into the outline for two reasons: (1) the appellate judges will ask about these standards, and whether counsel's challenges to the trial court's decision meet those standards; (2) the standards will guide the answers to all questions from the bench. If the appellate court reviews findings of fact only for clear error, the answers to questions about the trial court's adverse findings must focus on why they are clearly erroneous. If the appellate court reviews the trial court's denial of post-trial motions for abuse of discretion, counsel's answers must focus on why the judge abused his or her discretion.

Even if counsel is dividing time with another appellant, counsel should prepare outlines for all possible questions. While some courts will let lawyers "punt" certain subjects to other appellate counsel, most judges want the answers right away.

Finally, counsel should prepare for the possibility that there will be very few questions. Indeed, there may be none at all. If there is a flat, disinterested bench, counsel should deliver a "presentation argument." Counsel should pick two or three of the strongest arguments and should tell the court why the parent should win in a direct, bullet-pointed manner. Counsel should try to keep this "speech" conversational, with plenty of eye contact and should prepare it in advance, just in case.

When the outlines are done, counsel should put them in a three-ring binder. The one-page outline of key dates should be at counsel's fingertips; tape it to the inside left cover of the binder. Even if counsel never actually looks at any of the outlines during the argument, having the key talking-points, cases, and record citations readily accessible during the argument will provide confidence. The only other things that should be in the binder are counsel's brief and the trial court's findings and/or judgment. Nothing else should be brought to the lectern, because the judges will almost never ask about anything else. And if they ask about information in the record that is unfamiliar or not readily obtainable, counsel can escape gracefully with this crucial response: "I'm sorry, your honor, but I don't have that record citation/case citation handy at the moment, but I'd be happy to provide it to the court in a letter by the end of the week." The judges will be satisfied with that; they do not want to wait while counsel looks things up.

15.06(b)(2) Moot Courts

Moot-courting the argument is a great way to prepare. Counsel can ask other attorneys to help. If counsel has a solo practice, counsel can find other appellate attorneys who can trade off moot courts. To prepare for the moots, counsel should give the moot-court judges copies of all briefs and the trial court's findings and should give the judges at least a week to review the materials. The moot should be scheduled for three to seven days before the actual argument; this gives counsel time to work on the actual argument without forgetting the lessons from the moot court. At the start of the moot court, counsel should practice the opening. Counsel can ask if it grips the judges. If it doesn't, counsel can ask the moot court judges to suggest a better one. How do *they* see the case? What opening would *they* give? Their feedback will help craft the presentation. Counsel should insist that the moot-court judges ask hard questions, questions based on the record, and questions based on public policy. Counsel should urge them to attack every weakness in the argument with as nasty a tone as they wish. The tougher they are, the readier counsel will be for the actual argument. The goal is to leave the moot court with a good idea of what the real judges will ask. Hopefully, the moot-court judges will be harder on counsel than the real ones.

15.06(c) The Argument

15.06(c)(1) Inviting and Preparing the Client

Counsel should always invite the parent to the oral argument. After all, it is his or her case being decided, and the parent has a right to know what is happening. But counsel must prepare the parent for the experience. It is hard for appellant parents to watch oral arguments, because they must listen to CPS counsel recount, in gory detail, all of the reasons the trial court found the parent unfit. Worse still, the parent cannot respond. Parents generally do not sit at the appellate counsel table. They cannot whisper in counsel's ear that the CPS attorney is wrong or that the witness quoted by the CPS attorney was lying. They must sit back and take it. Some parents cannot handle this. Some know that they cannot. The point is to allow them to choose whether to come to the appellate courthouse or not.

Assuming the parent wishes to attend, counsel should ask him or her to dress as nicely as possible. Counsel should explain that the parent cannot address the judges, stand up, or grimace; strict decorum will be expected from everyone. When the argument is over, counsel should meet with the parent outside of the courtroom for debriefing. Counsel should explain the timing of a decision, and promise to keep him or her informed about it. And then do so.

15.06(c)(2) The Opening

Counsel has little control over the direction of an oral argument except at the beginning. Most of the time, counsel will be able to say at least two things before judges interrupt: the introduction and opening. The introduction should be boilerplate. Greet the judges and tell them who you are and who your client is (though not by name if the jurisdiction prohibits the use of identifying information): "Good morning. May it please the Court, my name is Robert Smith, and I represent the appellant-mother." Counsel should not overthink it.

The opening, on the other hand, requires considerable thought. It may be the most important part of the argument. The opening is where counsel must grab the judges' attention, frame the argument, and give the court the parent's theory of the case. If the opening is strong enough, the judges will listen attentively.

A good opening is *not* a recitation of the facts or the procedural history. Most "hot benches" have read the briefs and know the record reasonably well, and if counsel starts with the facts or procedural history, the court will admonish counsel to move on to other matters. A good opening is thirty seconds on why the parent should win, or why the case is so outrageous that the appellate court must remedy the injustice. Listed below are four good ways to open the argument:

- State the parent's theory of the case. "The court erred in admitting the child's hearsay about sexual abuse, and without that hearsay there was no evidence of sexual abuse. The only properly admitted evidence showed a father who provided excellent care for his children, and had no history of mental illness, substance abuse, or violence."
- Use a theme. "Shortcuts are not acceptable in termination of parental rights cases. The trial court took many shortcuts in this case, and they deprived the Mother of due process. Let me start with the most obvious shortcut . . ."
- Use an illustrative quote. Start with a "wow" quote from the transcript or an exhibit to show how it illustrates the parent's theory of the case:
  "Do you have an opinion about whether Mr. C. can parent Dontrelle?" asked the CPS attorney.
  "Yes," the CPS expert answered. "I'm not sure he can."
  "Not sure?" the CPS attorney repeated.
  "I mean, maybe not. I kind of doubt it," the expert answered.

  The trial court relied heavily on this expert testimony to terminate the Father's rights in this case. But "maybe not" and "I kind of doubt it" are not good enough to deprive a parent of the fundamental right to care for his son.

Counsel should work on the opening. The language, tone, and cadence should be perfect. Keep the tone conversational and your eyes raised (unless you are reading a quote). Counsel must practice it again and again.

15.06(c)(3) The Delivery and Presentation

Oral argument is a formal, respectful conversation. Counsel's goal is to persuade. Here are some common-sense rules and suggestions:

- Don't read the argument—make as much eye contact as possible.
- Address the judges, not the other attorneys or the ceiling.
- Use a pleasant, conversational tone. Don't speak too fast, too quietly, or in a monotone. Don't be over-dramatic or angry.
- Minor hand gestures are acceptable, but generally keep motions to a minimum. Don't wander from the lectern or gesticulate wildly.
- Refer to the judges as "your honor" or "Judge Jones" or "Justice Diaz." Don't say, "Yes, ma'am" or "No, sir."

- Don't make jokes or try to be funny. Remember that the appeal is deadly serious, and the parent certainly doesn't find any of this funny. That said, it's okay to laugh at a judge's joke.
- Don't say, "My client's position is that . . ." or "Mother believes that . . ." or "Mother argues that . . . ." Sentence-starters like these distance counsel from the argument, as if counsel does not believe it but is being forced to make a crazy argument by the client.
- Don't say, "I believe . . ." or "I feel . . . ." What *counsel* believes or feels about the case is irrelevant.
- Read the judges. Are they bored two minutes into the argument? If so segue to another issue. Are they bored toward the end of the argument? Segue right to the conclusion.
- Don't keep going when the time is up, especially if a judge says, "Thank you, your time is up." Don't say, "But I just wanted to address one more point . . . ." It's too late.

15.06(c)(4) Answering Questions

Questions from the bench are good, and experienced appellate lawyers welcome them. An inquisitive bench shows that the judges have read the briefs and record and have enough interest in the case to want more information or clarification.

Answering the judges' questions is not enough for a successful oral argument. A successful argument requires answering questions *the right way*—honestly, quickly, and directly. This is harder than it sounds. The suggestions below will illustrate:

- Never postpone an answer. Answer immediately, even if the plan was to discuss the matter later in the argument. The judges don't want to be put off and, if they have a lot of questions, "later" may never come.
- Listen carefully to the entire question. If the question isn't clear, ask for clarification. Better to have the judge rephrase the question than to give the wrong answer. There is nothing wrong with: "Your honor, are you asking what the legislature's intent was in 1997 when it enacted the statute, or what its intent was in 2008 when it amended the statute?"
- If the judge asks a yes-no question, answer it with a "yes" or "no" and *only then* explain. Trying to explain *before* answering "yes" or "no" leaves judges with the impression that counsel is not answering the question. Further, if a judge interrupts with another question before counsel answers "yes" or "no," counsel has lost the opportunity to give the more complete answer. This is the hardest oral argument skill to master—the ability to answer "yes" or "no" first and explain after.
- If asked a hypothetical question, answer it, and only then explain why this case fits or does not fit in the hypothetical.

- Never hide bad facts. The judges will find them. Acknowledge them without emphasizing or spending much time on them. Explain why the bad facts do not damage the parent's case, or are consistent with the parent's theory of the case.
- Go into the oral argument knowing what facts and legal conclusions *can* be conceded, and be willing to concede them at argument. The judges will appreciate the candor of an appropriate concession, and it will move them along to more important issues. If counsel does not concede a fact or legal conclusion that should have been conceded, precious time will be wasted in a losing battle with the judges.
- Go into the oral argument knowing what facts and legal conclusions *cannot* be conceded, and be prepared not to concede them. Do not bow to pressure. Some of the pressure may only be a "test" from the bench.
- Accept "softballs"—questions that are intended as "gifts," clarifying counsel's arguments or reframing them more persuasively. The proper response to a softball question is, "Yes, your honor, that's *exactly* what I'm arguing!" Don't assume a question is antagonistic or challenging; some are designed to help.
- Never praise a question. If a judge bothers to ask a question, he or she already thinks it's a good one.
- Never criticize a question as being the "wrong question," "not the point," or a "red herring." Answer it and then address the "correct" question without ever identifying it as such.
- Never interrupt a question or comment from the bench. Always let the judge finish before speaking.
- Never ask the judges any questions except to clarify their own questions.
- When the truthful answer to the question is "I don't know," say so. Never make the answer up.
- If the judges ask about something counsel cannot recall from the record, don't pause (or tell the judges to wait) and look it up. Instead offer to provide the court with the answer in a letter by the end of the week. Then, after the argument, do it.
- Always stay within the record. Never offer information outside the record about how the parent is doing, how the child is doing, or what the CPS social worker has said or done. Judges commonly scold lawyers who talk about matters not in the record, and sometimes even sanction them. The jurisdiction may permit counsel to refer to matters on the trial court docket that are outside the record (i.e., two months after trial, the court ordered custody transferred to the parent's sister in Vermont). When counsel is *invited* by the judges to go outside the record, do so carefully, sticking to unchallengeable facts.

15.06(c)(5) Closing

If possible, counsel should keep an eye on the timer or light and save the final 30–60 seconds for a closing. The closing should be a *short* restatement of the parent's theory of the case and an explanation of the relief sought. If time is very short, simply ask for the relief. Then smile, thank the court, and sit. If, before time is up, the judges announce, "Thank you, counsel; I think we've got it," thank them and sit down. They are done.

15.07 After the Decision

Most appellant-parents lose on appeal. That is the nature of the appellate process; it is weighted heavily in favor of appellees. Cynics might say that this is also the nature of the child welfare legal system. Either way, it is an unfortunate fact.

Appellate counsel must explain a loss to the parent as soon as possible. It is better for the parent to hear the result from appellate counsel than from the CPS social worker or the pre-adoptive parent. Even after the loss, it might be possible to resolve the case with some form of open adoption agreement. Pursue that option if the parent wishes. While most agency social workers and pre-adoptive parents are happy to wash their hands of the case after they've won on appeal, others may be more open to post-adoption contact when the parent is no longer a threat. The "best interests of the child" often look very different to CPS and adoptive parents when all legal risks are removed.

Local rules may permit further appellate review. Further review may be automatic, or the state's highest court may grant review sparingly. If granted further review, the appellate process may begin all over again, either ab initio or in some truncated fashion. This is where the fun really begins, because most states' high courts only accept cases of first impression or other legal significance.

Appellate work on behalf of parents can be frustrating, exhausting, and demoralizing. But with good appellate lawyering—and a lot of luck—appellate counsel can rectify injustice, vindicate a parent who was wrongly accused, or reunify a family. Counsel may even be able to effect systemic change for the benefit of all present and future clients. Hopefully, the suggestions in this chapter will help parents' lawyers enjoy that immense satisfaction while furthering the rights of their clients.

CHAPTER 16

The Impact of Abuse and Neglect Findings Beyond the Juvenile Courthouse: Understanding the Child Abuse Register System and Ways to Challenge Administrative Child Abuse Register Determinations

Diane L. Redleaf

> "The current flood of unfounded reports is overwhelming the limited resources of child protective agencies. For fear of missing even one abused child, workers perform extensive investigations of vague and apparently unsupported reports."
>
> —Douglas Besharov, *Child Abuse Realities: Over-reporting and Poverty*, 8 VA. J. SOC. POL'Y & L. 165, 191 (2000).

16.01 Introduction

Most of the chapters in this book focus on practices and procedures when child welfare cases are prosecuted in court. But the child welfare system operates well beyond matters that ever get to court. Indeed, the majority of work done by child welfare agencies never ends up going to court or involving lawyers. This chapter focuses on an important but relatively unknown feature of child welfare investigations: how individuals end up with their names on a state-wide child abuse register ("Register"); the potential consequences to them for being on the Register; and how to seek the removal of their names from it.

Before discussing the Register itself, however, it is important to describe the investigative function of child welfare agencies, which is an integral aspect of Registers. Investigations are the overwhelming activity in which child welfare agencies engage in the United States. The number of children brought to the attention of child protection authorities due to hotline calls in the United States is truly staggering: in 2012, 6,300,000 children were the subject of a call to a child abuse or neglect hotline. Not all of these calls were accepted for investigation, but more than 3.2 million children in 2012 alone were the subjects of investigations for abuse or neglect by a person in a caretaking role, most often a parent. This chapter will often refer to "caregivers," rather than "parents," because any person serving in a caregiving role, including day care workers, social workers, health care workers, and teachers, among many others, may become the subject of a child protection investigation. Of the investigated cases, less than 40 percent are "indicated" or "substantiated" by child protective services investigators (the rates vary widely from state to state). This chapter will use the term "indicated" to refer to all findings made by the person or Agency responsible for investigating allegations that a child was maltreated (abused or neglected), regardless of the terminology of any particular jurisdiction.

When a case is "indicated," it results in the name of the person found to have maltreated a child to be placed into the Register maintained by every state. Only a small fraction of the indicated investigated cases result in charges being brought in court. In Illinois, for example, more than 80 percent of cases in which initial investigations were indicated never result in judicial proceedings being commenced against the caregiver. An even smaller percentage of such cases result in criminal prosecutions. For example, of the 150,000 names in the Register in Illinois in 1997, only 5,000 had criminal convictions for child abuse.

In addition, a staggeringly high percentage of names in Registers are removed after an administrative review. Federal courts in Illinois and New York concluded that as many as three out of four names on the Register in those two states are removed when challenged through the administrative process. *See Valmonte v. Bane*, 18 F.3d 992, 1004 (2d Cir. 1994) (describing the system as having an "unacceptably high risk of error"); *Dupuy v. McDonald*, 141 F. Supp. 2d 1090, 1136 (N.D. Ill. 2001) (terming the 74.6 percent reversal rate a staggering rate of error), *aff'd in relevant part*, 397 F.3d 493 (7th Cir. 2005). A Missouri court found a 35–40-percent reversal rate in administrative register appeals. *See Jamison v. Mo. Dep't of Soc. Servs.*, 218 S.W.3d 399, 409 (Mo. 2007). According to the Connecticut's Department of Children and Families' website, in 2004, the Connecticut Child Welfare Agency found that half of its CPS findings of abuse or neglect got overturned on appeal. In 2013, the Illinois Supreme Court issued a ruling resulting in the expungement of more than 19,000 names on the Register. *See Julie Q. v. Dep't of Children and Family Servs.*, 2013 IL 113783, ¶ 44, 376 Ill. Dec. 294, 489, 995 N.E.2d 977, 986 (2013).

When cases end up in court, caregivers have the opportunity as defendants or respondents to defend themselves and to have the court determine after an evidentiary hearing whether or not the charges are proven. But when no court action is commenced—in other words, the vast majority of the time—unless the caregiver challenges the initial indicated finding in an administrative proceeding that the caregiver needs to commence, the caregiver's name will end up on the Register, often remaining there for many years.

Lawyers who are assigned to represent caregivers in court proceedings commonly regard the child abuse administrative register process as beyond their workload, in part because the court assignment does not go beyond the court proceeding itself. Many lawyers who represent caregivers in child protection court proceedings know relatively little about child abuse registers. To the extent lawyers have an awareness of registers generally, they are too often confused with criminal registries (including Sex Offender Registers), which are entirely different systems having no connection to the subject of this chapter. Caregivers' lawyers in child protection cases may not even realize, for example, that even when the caregiver *wins* in court, in many states, the caregiver's name may not be automatically removed from the Register. Unless removed, the person's name will stay in the Register, in some states, for as long as fifty years or until the person dies.

There are, however, important—and accessible—administrative proceedings with internal reviews and appeals that are available to all persons whose name is placed on the Register. The Register is an important aspect of the child protection system imposing very significant, long-lasting consequences on persons whose names end up on it. In some cases, challenging the decision to put an individual's name into the Register may have an immediate impact on the dependency case. Lawyers representing caregivers in child protection cases should become familiar with how the child abuse reporting, investigation, and findings system works in their state. Moreover, lawyers should know how the resolution of the court case may impact efforts to secure the removal of a caregiver's name from the Register. This chapter is written both to inform lawyers about the available processes and to encourage them to become more involved in challenging indicated findings and seeking the removal of their clients' names from the Register.

As will be shown, when someone is listed in the Register, considerably more is at stake than mere reputation. Lawyers for caregivers in court proceedings who expand their focus to the administrative process not only will come to enjoy a new practice that has considerable opportunity for success but they will be advancing the interests of their clients dramatically.

16.02 The Origins and Operation of the Child Abuse Hotline and Register System

In 1974, Congress enacted the Child Abuse Prevention and Treatment Act (CAPTA), which revolutionized and created the modern child welfare system in place in every state in the country. Child Abuse Prevention and Treatment Act, Pub. L. No. 93-247, (codified at 42 U.S.C. § 5101 (1996)). CAPTA mandates that each state maintain an active child abuse hotline that receives calls twenty-four hours a day, seven days of the week. Federal law leaves wide discretion to each state to implement the hotline as states see fit. Some are administered at the local level; others at the state level; some are maintained by the child protection system itself (Illinois); others are administered by the Justice Department (California).

Federal law also created two categories of persons who use the hotline. "Mandated reporters" are persons who work in a large variety of jobs (including all kinds of health care professionals, teachers, therapists, social workers, among many others). Still others (everyone else) are permissive reporters—individuals who are encouraged, but not required by law, to call in their suspicion of child maltreatment. What counts as a reportable act, however, is so overbroad and indefinite, that hundreds of thousands of calls are made each year in the United States that turn out to be baseless. In South Dakota, for example, reports are required by mandated reporters whenever someone concludes that the child's "environment is injurious to [his or her] welfare." S.D. Codified Laws § 26-8A-2 (2013). *See generally Julie Q., supra* (discussing the need for clear guidelines for child abuse reporters so they know what conduct is required to be reported to authorities, given potential criminal penalties for failure to report). One unfortunate cost of this over-reporting is that already underfinanced agencies are diverted from working with families in need.

Federal law requires not only that every state operate a statewide child abuse reporting system, it also requires that states promptly investigate matters that come to their attention and make a determination whether the matter is substantiated. 42 U.S.C. § 5106(a) (2013). Most importantly for the purposes of this chapter, federal law also requires states to place the names of substantiated cases in a database. Finally, federal law requires that each state develop minimum due process mechanisms with respect to the maintenance of the database, including promptly correcting and expunging records when appropriate. 42 U.S.C. § 5106(b)(2)(B)(xii) (2013). Federal dollars given to states for child welfare are conditioned on each state having procedures in its state plan that facilitate the prompt review of any records that may be used to adversely affect a person's employment. *See generally* Child Abuse, Family Rights and the Child Protective System: A Critical Analysis from Law, Ethics, and Catholic Social Teaching (Stephen M. Krason ed., 2013).

States have leeway to define the length of time for which child abuse and neglect findings are registered. In Illinois, for example, the names of individuals indicated for sex abuse will be kept on the Register for fifty years. 325 ILL. COMP. STAT. § 5/7.14 (2013). In Michigan, a person's name is kept on the Register until they die. MICH. COMP. LAWS §§ 722.627 (7); 722.628 (11) (2013). All the while, individuals whose names are on the Register are effectively barred from pursuing careers involving contact with children.

16.03 The Impact of Child Abuse Registers: Background Checks and Disclosure and Use of Registered Findings, Considerations Regarding Employment, Education, Foster Parents, and Adoption

Child abuse Registers were originally conceived for a very different purpose than they are commonly used for today. Originally, Registers primarily were to serve an epidemiological purpose. They were also conceived as a means of targeting limited state dollars to an identified group of children who were deemed to be most at risk. There is no mention in the legislative history of CAPTA of Registers having any impact on someone's employability. *See* Jill D. Moore, *Charting a Course Between Scylla and Charybdis: Child Abuse Registries and Procedural Due Process*, 73 N.C. L. REV. 2063, 2066–68 (1995). In many states today, however, that is a primary effect.

Registers are not generally accessible to the public. Depending on the state, however, some employers may, and others must, check the Register before hiring a prospective employee. The range of occupations that may be impacted by the Register is often broader than many people know. Specifics vary by jurisdiction and lawyers should learn the rules for their state.

In some states, the range of employment areas affected by the Register—requiring employers in those fields to consult the Register whenever someone seeks employment with it—is very broad. In New York, for example, "[n]umerous state agencies, private businesses, and licensing agencies related to child care, adoption, and foster care are required by law to inquire whether potential employees or applicants are on the Central Register." *Valmonte*, 18 F.3d at 995 (*citing* N.Y. SOC. SERV. LAW § 424-a(1) (2014)). *See also* CAL. PENAL CODE § 11170(b)(7)-(9) (2013) (providing information to entities making inquiries for purposes of pre-employment background investigations for peace officers, child-care licensing or employment, adoption, or child placement). States commonly tinker with these laws seeking to ever broaden the employment fields impacted by the Register. *See, e.g.*, ILL. H.R. RES. 201 WORK GROUP FINAL LEGIS. REP., 96th Gen. Assemb., at 4-5 (2011) (recommending the inclusion of employment with the elderly and persons with disabilities as jobs requiring checking with the Register.)

States use very different procedures for submission of background checks that include checks of people on the Register. Many states may notify employers who are licensed to provide child care, schools, and other entities when a child abuse finding has been registered against an employee of a licensed facility. Employers rarely are precluded by law from hiring someone listed in the Register. For obvious reasons (advice of counsel being a large one), many employees either choose not to hire the employee or to terminate the employment when they learn that an employee is listed in the Register.

In addition to this risk-averse explanation, many employers are given insufficient facts about the underlying incident to make a meaningful determination of risk to the employer. In some states, the only fact that may be disclosed from the Register is that someone's name is on it. *See, e.g.*, N.Y. Soc. Serv. Law § 424-a(1) (2014). This arrangement commonly places individuals listed in the Register in the worst of all worlds. The state agency will not release any details of the event and the caregiver's version is almost certain to be received with skepticism as coming from a self-interested source.

The rights of employees who are terminated because an employer was alerted that their name was on a Register are beyond the focus of this chapter. In some cases, an employee may be able to seek damages against the child protection investigator who wrongly placed his or her name into the Register, causing him or her to lose employment opportunities. *See Hughes v. Jones*, No. 12 C 09494, 2014 U.S. Dist. LEXIS 53181, at *39, 2014 WL 1569187, at *10 (N.D. Ill. April 17, 2014) (denying motion to dismiss, finding rights to consideration of exculpatory evidence and notice before state officials may adversely affect an individual's employment prospects to be "clearly established"). Some employees, including tenured teachers or union employees, often have contracts protecting them from losing their job without first affording them due process protections.

In virtually every state, agencies will also conduct a search of the Register before allowing someone to become a foster or adoptive parent. Foster parents who end up with an indicated report often have limited recourse to protect their ability to maintain a license in good standing. Children are often immediately removed from foster homes when foster parents are the subject of a hotline call. Foster parents who have registered findings face multiple hurdles in securing the return of children to their care, even when the findings lack merit. Indicated reports are also commonly used against someone in a custody dispute.

Currently there is no centralized or federal database for Registers. The definition of child abuse and neglect varies widely from state to state, making it difficult to determine, in some categories at least, if the decision to place someone on the Register in one state would be made under standards in operation in another state. Nonetheless, states commonly cooperate and answer out-of-state requests for information about a person's listing on the Register when asked by prospective employers. *See, e.g.*, Cal. Pen. Code §11170 (2014). States also routinely seek cooperation from other state agencies to assist in child abuse investigations.

16.04 Challenging Indicated Findings and Clearing Records in State Central Registers

Lawyers seeking to challenge the placement or retention of a client's name on the Register need to familiarize themselves with the rules of administrative hearings, a process that is obscure to many courtroom practitioners. Counsel should read the relevant state statutes and also consult carefully the administrative rules that are commonly promulgated by the relevant Agency overseeing the Register. The combination of these laws and regulations constitute the framework for substantive and procedural rules for challenges to the Register.

16.04(a) Timing of Filing Challenge

States are free to set reasonable deadlines on when a challenge may be brought. In New York, which has a relatively generous scheme, one can challenge the placement of his or her name on the Register at the time it is first placed can wait until years later and raise a challenge after he or she is informed that a prospective employer has made a request for information, thereby allowing an opportunity to individuals to expunge or seal the record before it is disclosed to the employer. *See* N.Y. Soc. Serv. Law §§ 422(8), 424-a(1)(d-1)(e)(i) (2014). In Illinois, by contrast, the right to appeal lasts for only sixty days after an individual's name is entered in the Register, assuming notice of the finding has been timely issued. *See* 325 Ill. Comp. Stat. § 5/7.14 (2014).

16.04(b) Discovery

Procedural rules regulating challenges to the Register will commonly be based on administrative law proceedings in each state. They usually include some kind of limited discovery, allowing the caregiver the opportunity to secure the written (redacted) file of the Agency before the hearing takes place. The caregiver will also commonly be required to comply with the reciprocal duty to disclose the evidence that will be presented at the hearing. This would include an exchange of witness lists and production of the child protection investigation file. Whether a caregiver would be allowed to enforce subpoenas for various records as part of the discovery process would be determined by local law.

16.04(c) Admissibility of Evidence at the Administrative Hearing

Administrative hearings challenging the placement or retention of someone's name on the Register commonly permit the introduction of hearsay and counsel should be prepared to expect that at least part of the Agency's case will be based on out-of-court statements. But some courts have insisted on limiting hearsay at these proceedings. A 1994 Pennsylvania Supreme Court decision, for example, held that uncorroborated children's statements could not be admitted at a Register expungement hearing. *See A. Y. v. Commonwealth*, 537 Pa. 116, 126, 641 A.2d 1148, 1153 (1994). The traditional rule that even admissible hearsay must contain some indicia of reliability remains. Courts will, for example, preclude as inadmissible double hearsay (repeating by an out-of-court declarant the words of another out-of-court declarant) when it is not the type of statements on which reasonably prudent persons would rely in the conduct of their affairs. *See, e.g., Julie Q. v. Dep't of Children and Fam. Servs.*, 2011 Il. App. (2d) 100643, ¶45, 357 Ill. Dec. 448, 461, 963 N.E.2d 401, 414 (2011), *aff'd on other grounds*, 2013 Il. 113783, 374 Ill. Dec. 480, 995 N.E.2d 977 (2013).

16.04(d) Standards of Evidence and Burden of Proof

At the investigation stage, most states have a low standard that has to be met before an individual can be placed on the Register. Many states require nothing more than "some credible evidence" or "probable cause" supporting the allegation. When individuals seek expungement of their name on the Register, courts uniformly place the burden of proof on the Agency to prove by a preponderance of evidence that the individual committed an act of maltreatment. *See Lyon v. Dep't of Children & Fam. Servs.*, 209 Ill.2d 264, 281, Ill. Dec. 799, 812, 807 N.E.2d 423, 436 (2004) (holding that a "credible evidence" standard at the first-stage appeal satisfies due process requirements because the second-stage appeal uses the "preponderance of the evidence" standard). Many states require this by statute. *See, e.g.*, S.D. Codified Laws § 26-8A-1 (2014).

Many state laws that have not been challenged require keeping someone's name on the Register whenever there is credible evidence to justify its retention. *See, e.g.*, 325 Ill. Comp. Stat. § 5/8.1 (2014) (report will be indicated unless there is "no credible evidence" of maltreatment); N.Y. Soc. Serv. Law § 422(5) (2014) (report is to be indicated whenever there is "any credible evidence" of maltreatment. But these laws may be found unconstitutional if challenged. *See Valmonte v. Bane*, 18 F.3d at 1004; *Cavarretta v. Dep't of Children and Fam. Servs.*, 277 Ill. App. 3d 16, 27, 214 Ill. Dec. 59, 67, 660 N.E.2d 250, 258 (1996); *see also Jamison*, 218 S.W.3d at 412 (Agency must find by preponderance of evidence that caregiver maltreated child before disseminating information about the individual outside of Agency); *In re W.B.M.*, 202 N.C. App 606, 621, 690 S.E.2d 41, 52 (2010).

Caregivers must also be allowed to present evidence not considered by the investigator when seeking the removal of their name from the Register. As the Seventh Circuit explained, child protection investigators are required to "take into account *all* of the available evidence that tends to show that abuse or neglect did *or* did not occur," including exculpatory evidence, because "[o]nly then may the investigator decide whether that totality of evidence would cause a reasonable individual to believe that a child was abused or neglected." *Dupuy v. Samuels*, 397 F.3d 493, 506 (7th Cir. 2005). This standard, requiring consideration of all of the available evidence, is constitutionally required because indicated findings may result in the deprivation individuals of a liberty interest in employment opportunity.

16.04(e) Expedited v. Non-Expedited Decision

Some states require register challenges to be expedited when they involve employees in certain fields, such as child care. In Illinois, for example, when child care workers challenge their name being placed on the Register, they must be decided within thirty-five days. *Dupuy v. Samuels*, 397 F.3d at 509. The Illinois Supreme Court held in *Lyon*, 209 Ill.2d at 275, Ill. Dec. at 808, 807 N.E.2d at 432, that if a decision on the challenge is not made within ninety days, ordinarily the record must be expunged. But in many states, there are no such time limits and cases may linger for years. A Federal District court in New York ruled that hearings must be commenced within six months from the date of request and final decisions issued no later than thirty days after the hearing is over. *See Finch v. N.Y. State Office of Children & Family Servs.*, No. 04 Civ. 1668 (SAS), 2008 U.S. Dist. LEXIS, 103413, at *12, 2008 WL 5330616, at ** 2–3 (S.D.N.Y. Dec. 18, 2008).

16.04(f) Impartiality of Hearing Officer

An important feature of due process is the right to be heard before an impartial hearing officer. *See Humphries v. County of L.A.*, 554 F.3d 1170, 1200-01 (9th Cir. 2009). Counsel should ensure that the person presiding over the hearing is impartial and free to render an independent judgment. Hearing officers or fact-finders in these reviews may be employed by the investigating agency, but it would violate due process if the decision maker was involved in the investigation of the matter at an earlier stage. *See, e.g.*, *C.C.B. v. Ark. Dep't of Health & Human Servs.*, 368 Ark. 540, 543–45, 247 S.W.3d 870, 872–74 (2007).

16.04(g) Challenges Brought Beyond the Statutory Time Frame

Few Register systems provide a means by which individuals may seek to have their names removed based on newly discovered evidence, rehabilitation, or manifest injustice once the time period within which to bring a challenge has expired. This should not prevent counsel from advocating through available channels to expunge a record, particularly when the evidence in favor of expungement is strong, or to seek new avenues for relief by amending policies that bar such review. In some cases a compelling request to expunge may persuade the Agency to expunge findings on equitable grounds, and in some jurisdictions a refusal to do so may be amenable to challenge as an abuse of discretion.

16.05 Challenges During Pending Court Proceedings

In many cases, a person's name is placed on the Register while a related court proceeding (criminal, custody, or child protection) is pending. Counsel should find out whether there is a time limit within which to begin a challenge or whether there is a right to make a challenge through the administrative proceeding after the court proceedings have been completed. Unfortunately, many caregivers do not understand that these processes are separate and learn only after the judicial process has concluded that there remains a registered finding that they did not appeal in a timely way. Even if counsel is unable to provide representation in the administrative proceeding, counsel should advise the client to pursue available administrative remedies to protect him- or herself and avoid preclusion of his or her later appeals.

Rarely are judicial and administrative proceedings pursued simultaneously. Usually, the court proceeding will take its course and the administrative proceeding would follow. Sometimes an administrative proceeding will begin and be halted by the filing of a formal court petition. If a caregiver litigates and loses the dependency case in court and the court makes a judicial finding that the caregiver maltreated a child, the caregiver is very likely estopped from relitigating that claim in any subsequent proceeding (unless the findings are significantly different: for example, a finding of assault may not estop the caregiver from appealing an indicated finding for sexual molestation). Assuming that the burden of proof in the administrative proceeding is the same or lower than the judicial proceeding, a finding against the caregiver by a court prevents the caregiver from claiming s/he did not commit an act of maltreatment. *See, e.g.*, S.D. Codified Laws § 26-8A-11 (2014).

Caregivers will not necessarily benefit in the same way from *winning* in the judicial proceeding. The caregiver may not be able to assert an affirmative claim of issue preclusion or estoppel in the subsequent administrative challenge to the Register, depending on whether the Agency has policies in effect that provide that a caregiver must go to hearing in order to overcome an indicated finding in a Register. If so, a challenge to these policies may be necessary in order to establish that preclusion extends to all matters that were actually litigated or could have been litigated in the judicial forum.

In many states, challenges to the Register may be stayed pending the outcome of the related court proceedings. As a general rule, counsel may be unable to avoid such a stay, as simultaneous litigation of the same issue in two different settings is challenging at best. If the client works with children, however, and is at risk of losing employment opportunities, pressing forward in the administrative proceeding may be advantageous and necessary.

Most importantly, counsel should know the consequences for the client of making an admission in the court proceeding or entering into any stipulated or agreed resolution of the Petition. There may be ways to structure an admission or settlement so as to track the requirements of the statute while leaving open the possibility of challenging the placement of one's name on the Register. In cases in which two parents are named in the court proceeding, it may be possible to have admissions made by one parent that will protect the employment of the parent who works with children. Generally speaking, however, admissions will result in the caregiver's name remaining on the Register for as long as state law requires. Therefore, it is essential that negotiated agreements, including admissions made in court, are entered into with full awareness of the impact of those agreements on the caregiver's rights with respect to matters involving the Register. Counsel should always include this subject as part of the issues discussed when counseling a client to settle the court case.

16.06 Constitutional Challenges to Registries

Lawyers representing someone interested in challenging the placement of their name on a Register should find out what processes for such challenges are in place in the jurisdiction. If the procedures are clear and fair, the appropriate next step is to invoke them and seek to have the name expunged. If they are inadequate, it may be necessary to file a lawsuit, either in state or federal court, to secure a fairer system for challenges. Successful suits brought in federal court pursuant to 28 U.S.C. § 1983 bring with them an award of attorney fees. *See* 29 U.S.C. § 1988 (2014).

Not all states have created a fair system for such challenges. In some states, lawsuits have been successfully brought declaring the process for removing one's name from Registers as unconstitutionally deficient. These states include California, Illinois, New Hampshire, Missouri, North Carolina, and New York. *See Humphries*, 554 F.3d at 1188, *rev'd on other grounds*, 562 U.S. 29 (2010); *Dupuy v. Samuels*, 397 F.3d at 503; *Valmonte*, 18 F.3d at 1000; *Finch v. N.Y. State Office of Children & Fam. Servs.*, 499 F. Supp. 2d 521, 529–30 (S.D.N.Y. 2007); *Jamison,* 218 S.W.3d at 406; *In re W.B.M.*, 202 N.C. App at 617, 690 S.E.2d at 49. *But see Behrens v. Regier*, 422 F.3d 1255, 1261 (11th Cir. 2005); *Smith ex rel. Smith v. Siegelman*, 322 F.3d 1290, 1297 (11th Cir. 2003); *Hodge v. Jones*, 31 F.3d 157, 164 (4th Cir. 1994). In most states, however, no challenge has ever been brought even though the procedure for challenging Registries may be inadequate.

The Supreme Court has held that individuals do not possess a constitutionally protected liberty interest when government officials merely impugn their reputation. *See Paul v. Davis*, 424 U.S. 693, 712 (1976). But, as is true in almost all child abuse Register schemes, when state action does more than affect an individual's reputation and prevents him from doing something, the individual has a constitutionally protected interest in challenging the state officials' action. *Wisconsin v. Constantineau*, 400 U.S. 433, 437 (1971) (holding that police officer's notice in liquor stores to prohibit sales to certain individual violates liberty interest). The combination of these two cases is neatly summarized by the idea that when state officials merely stigmatize someone, it is not enough to trigger a constitutionally protected interest, but if the action results in "stigma plus," then the individual's liberty interest is protected by the Constitution. Applying the principle of "stigma plus," the cases cited in the previous paragraph have held that when child abuse Registries are used as an obstacle to individuals securing a job, as is the case in many states, the Constitution requires that the state use a fair system for allowing individuals to challenge the placement or maintenance of their name on the Register.

As the Seventh Circuit explained, in many cases an indicated case implicates a protected liberty interest because state laws may require that the prospective employee's status on the Register be disseminated to all potential employers during the hiring process, resulting in "a significant, indeed almost insuperable, impediment on obtaining a position in the entire field of child care." *Dupuy v. Samuels*, 397 F.3d at 510–11. A decade earlier, the Second Circuit reached the same conclusion, holding that an indicated finding on the New York Register "places a tangible burden" on employment prospects where a state statute required child care providers to consult the central register during the hiring process. *See Valmonte*, 18 F.3d at 1001.

Not every challenge to Registers has successfully asserted that the Constitution requires a fair process for seeking its expungement. In *Behrens*, 422 F.3d at 1261, the Eleventh Circuit held that even when someone is denied the opportunity to adopt a child due to a wrongfully registered finding, there was not a "stigma plus" deprivation of liberty because there is no established liberty interest in adopting a child. Similarly, the Seventh Circuit held that not every negative cost to being on the Register counts as a constitutionally protected liberty interest. *Dupuy v. Samuels*, 397 F. 3d at 515 (foster parents do not have protected liberty interests to become or remain foster parents, which, though "noble work," is not a career).

Many states that permit challenges to placing a person's name on the Register expressly permit such a challenge *after* a person's name is placed on it, allowing an opportunity to have it expunged. But the Constitution may require an opportunity to challenge the placement of one's name on the Register *before* it is done when there are immediate consequences to being placed on the Register. *See Goldberg v. Kelly*, 397 U.S. 254, 267 (1970); *Barry v. Barchi*, 443 U.S. 55, 72 (1979); *In re W.B.M.*, 202 N.C. App. at 620, 690 S.E.2d at 51. Where the individual cannot be said to suffer any harm merely by having his or her name included in the Register, it is sufficient to allow a challenge after the fact. But *some* form of pre-deprivation process is required when there is an immediate harm from being placed on the Register. At least where individuals are employed in positions that require their discharge if they are placed on the Register, a process for an independent review of the evidence, called an "Administrator's Conference," is constitutionally required before the person is placed on the Register. *Dupuy v. Samuels*, 397 F.3d at 507–08. A second federal court went even further and held that no negative consequences may flow from being placed on the Register until the affected individual has had an opportunity to contest the propriety of the indicated report. *See Valmonte*, 18 F.3d 992 at 1004.

16.07 Conclusion

Lawyers who work in the child protection field are well-advised to become familiar with the rules and procedures governing Registers. The Family Defense Center in Chicago has a manual on its website that is available to assist lawyers in preparing for an administrative Register appeal. These Registers are ubiquitous and may drastically impair a person's life. Having one's name on the Register may mean losing all opportunity to work in a wide range of fields and may operate to prevent clients from adopting children or keeping custody of children. Each state not only maintains a Register but also must have in place a fair procedure for individuals whose names are placed on them to challenge the placement and seek expungement of their names. It also is a field of practice of great important to many individuals—not only to parents who are unfairly accused of maltreatment but many non-parents as well who work in child-related fields. Lawyers who successfully represent caregivers in child protection proceedings, but who ignore the impact of the Register on their clients' lives, may be leaving their clients with an unfair burden to bear for the rest of their lives. Hopefully, this chapter will encourage lawyers to include this area of practice in their portfolio so that parents and others who become ensnared in the Register can more easily locate competent, committed counsel to represent them.

CHAPTER 17

Reforming the System

Joanne I. Moore

17.01 The Importance of Systemic Reform Work

Many parents' attorneys went to law school to acquire the tools to seek justice in the world. Our legal system promises "liberty and justice for all," yet the media is replete with stories about poor and minority individuals receiving less than fair treatment. In dependency courts, one can see hearings in child welfare cases brought by government entities against impoverished parents who are bewildered and have little capacity to defend their families. At stake in these hearings is one of parents' most fundamental rights: the ability to raise their own children. Although most states guarantee the right to counsel to these parents, this right alone falls far short of ensuring that the system provides justice for all.

Attorneys who represent parents in child welfare cases have myriad opportunities to initiate systemic changes to improve fairness for parents and families. Parents' lawyers have profound exposure to how the child welfare system operates and how it may help some families, yet go terribly wrong for many others. They are knowledgeable of advocacy techniques and how to move legal matters forward. Perhaps most importantly, parents' lawyers understand and appreciate the strengths and value of their parent clients, which are often overlooked by other stakeholders in the child welfare system.

Uniquely, parents' attorneys have frank, direct conversations with their clients, which allow them to better understand their clients' realities. Parents involved with the child welfare system face numerous obstacles: detrimental effects of inadequate visitation rights, biased expert evaluations of parents, long periods of time between court dates, deficient services, and debilitating poverty, among many others. As cases progress, attorneys for parents learn about the challenges their clients suffer, and they witness the tireless devotion that these parents have to their children nevertheless. Importantly, parents' lawyers aim to protect parents through the difficulties in bringing their children home, especially when judges and department social workers misunderstand or disregard these difficulties.

Parents' attorneys get a direct view of injustice, which provides them with knowledge of what needs to be changed in the system—and can fuel their passion to take it on. Attorneys can access a number of paths to effect significant change in the legal system. They should assess their own skills and environment in choosing which efforts to take on and how to pursue them. Through careful planning and action, they can bring about huge changes to benefit the lives of their clients.

To diligent parents' attorneys who give 110 percent to representing their clients, tackling system reform may seem daunting. However, systemic reform is achieved most often through careful planning and fidelity to strategy that do not require a vast number of hours. In fact, the time parents' attorneys dedicate to promoting systemic reform now can make their representation of clients much more efficient in the future. For example, if the process for obtaining a specific service is improved, attorneys do not have to argue the same motion for that service over and over.

The child welfare system already provides opportunities for parents' attorneys to initiate reform at every level—including the trial, appellate, and state levels—but parents' attorneys must come to recognize and seize these opportunities. This chapter discusses some potentially successful methods for changing the legal system and ways to implement them. These methods include the promotion of parents' and parents' attorneys' voices in policymaking, participation in local and statewide court reform committees, the creation of new laws through state legislatures and court rules, strategic litigation and appeals to create new case law, and the establishment of a new parents' representation program. First, several general themes and recommendations that commonly apply to systemic reform will be discussed.

17.02 Work with Other Parents' Attorneys if Possible

An army of peers can usually accomplish far more than a single attorney working alone. Parents' attorneys should look for other like-minded professionals by joining an organized effort in the jurisdiction or area, or by organizing collective action in their area from the beginning. On the local level, enlisting colleagues to brainstorm about issues and how they might be addressed—both case issues and systemic issues—enriches understanding and strategy. Attorneys can make plans to effect change together, with different attorneys fulfilling different roles in the joint effort. Part of the strategy might involve weighing the talents available in the group. For example, some attorneys may be best suited to focus on the trial or appellate courts, others may want to tackle the state legislature, and still others may decide to join a child welfare reform committee. On a broader level, inviting judges, politicians, and social workers, among others, to join the conversation would add necessary perspective and could lead to feasible ideas for collaboration.

Meeting with parents' attorneys from other courts across the state could likewise provide opportunities for enriching reform strategy. Statewide listservs multiply each attorney's resources for case strategies, pleadings, information about experts, and case law analysis, and broaden opportunities for finding out how other courts and child protection departments work and what constructive programs or services have been implemented elsewhere. The American Bar Association (ABA) National Project to Improve Representation for Parents' listserv serves the same purpose nationally. If no listserv exists in a particular state, implementing one would be an effective start to systemic change.

17.03 Be Knowledgeable, Do Homework, and Use Data

Whichever manner of system reform one considers, maintaining factual accuracy throughout the effort is critical. Obviously, any attorney who wishes to achieve change through litigation or appellate advocacy must keep abreast of changes in the law and systemic realities to argue for change effectively. It is important to have a strong basic understanding about the state or county department. A comprehensive familiarity with case law and the statutory regime strengthens an advocate's skill set and, undoubtedly, impacts his or her persuasiveness.

Once a parents' attorney becomes reliably knowledgeable about the relevant legal framework, he or she will be regarded as a leader, whether working in a court reform committee, a legislative environment, or a more informal, grassroots environment. The more one observes and learns about the legal and child welfare systems, the better. Due to the complexity and challenge of representing parents, parents' lawyers probably already have a solid foundation of knowledge to draw on. Continuously updating one's knowledge base is as important for effective reform as it is for excellent practice in court.

Parents' attorneys who successfully achieve systemic reform should ensure the reform stays effective and strong. For example, attorneys who have effected change through a court system reform committee should continue to support the committee by volunteering to take minutes, help draft agenda, make follow-up phone calls, and so forth. Notably, the individuals who participate in planning and writing the pamphlets and messages that committees produce gain critical influence over the final product. Parents' attorneys in a North Carolina program, for example, volunteered to participate in the child protection department's production of videos for parents to ensure that the videos had a supportive tone. In many other states, including California and Washington, parents' attorneys who participate in court reform committees volunteer to assist judges in preparing agenda or materials, or conduct research on behalf of the committee. Parents' attorneys' who carry out various committee-related tasks end up rewarded by a more positive impact on the system than if they left the tasks to others. See Section 17.09 for further discussion of how court systems change committees.

Time spent gathering statistics also is well spent. An advocate's ability to research and utilize data (and in appropriate areas, to generate it) is a powerful asset in pursuing any strategy for changing the legal system. The child welfare field is rich with data: the Children's Bureau reports on the states' practices and case outcomes, and creates periodic Child and Family Service Reviews (CFSRs) for each state, and, in innumerable states and counties, statistical reports of various sorts are compiled. The child welfare and court systems, like many fields, features a culture of conventional wisdom based on "facts" that may be exaggerated or imprecise. Therefore, an advocate's knowledge of real facts and their sources provides a powerful way to persuade stakeholders.

17.04 Pursue Incremental Changes

An important concept in system reform is to pick battles carefully. Although it may be too easy to list a myriad systemic child welfare problems, no advocate or group of advocates can take them all on. Occasionally, the sustained mission and passion of one or more attorneys can fuel prompt system-wide reform (especially through litigation or appellate representation). Frequently, however, immediate big changes are elusive; a more constructive method often is to implement incremental changes. This is especially true when working with judges and system-change committees.

Part of an attorney's analysis of which changes are worth pursuing should be to review painstakingly the political and funding realities of the problem and the system, and the attorney's time and financial resource limitations. Sometimes this requires self-discipline—for example, resisting the temptation to construct a new, ideal child welfare model. An attempt to implement a wholesale makeover of the child welfare system would likely result in frustrating years of little success while families remain in distress. Most system changes evolve in gradual shifts. Simpler, more incremental changes implemented consistently can affect the overall impact sought, and usually will be much more attainable.

17.05 The Importance of Relationships, Reputation, and Tenacity

To effect system change —especially through informal changes, committee work, and legislation—it is crucial to hone a collaborative style. Aggressive, litigious language and actions almost certainly will set back the effort. This is not to say that one should not be assertive; rather, try to be pleasant *and* assertive. An effective advocate has an awareness of the culture and relevant political situations (e.g., the local power structure), a respectful attitude toward all stakeholders, good group interaction and communication skills, and a willingness to compromise to achieve important goals. *See* Shirley A. Dobbin et al., *Building a Better Collaboration: Facilitating Change in the Court and Child Welfare System*, NAT'L COUNCIL OF JUV. & FAM. CT. JUDGES TECHNICAL ASSISTANCE BULL. (Nat'l Council of Juv. and Fam. Ct. Judges, Reno, NV), Apr. 2004, at 30. Besides achieving the systemic change at hand, an attorney who has incorporated these traits—and is knowledgeable—will soon build a reputation as a credible, thoughtful advocate, which will be invaluable for future efforts.

Most system reform initiators have optimistic outlooks, and convey their optimism to stakeholders, the courts, and legislatures. They communicate not only that the system can be improved, but also that the chosen strategy can succeed. Although the child welfare system is filled with pessimism—"what you're proposing will never work"—optimism inspires hope, which many working in the system need. As effective business and political leaders know, optimism is a powerful tool for energizing the players. Some methods for inspiring hope include referring to the big picture, engaging others in creative planning, and talking about how much better the system will serve families when the reform efforts succeed.

When deciding to embark on an effort for meaningful change, one should prepare to be engaged for the long haul. Comprehensive types of systemic change take extended periods of time, and one should expect to encounter obstacles and setbacks. Achieving lasting reform usually requires an unyielding commitment to keep going until the goal is reached. This is a quality that parents in the child welfare system must also have to succeed. Like them, attorneys who want to make a difference must pick themselves up after a setback, and find another way to approach the goal. It is encouraging to remember that often, initial efforts are valuable even if they do not completely succeed, because they raise awareness and get stakeholders to think about inefficiencies and injustices in a systemic way.

Many parents' attorneys who are working to implement system reforms choose to do so in an unheralded way. They have an ability to keep their egos in check and share the credit for group successes, even when they did the lion's share of moving the project forward. Few parents' attorneys announce an intention to implement major reforms, but rather concentrate on going ahead and working with stakeholders. They derive much of their satisfaction in achievements more from knowing that their work has made a difference than from public acknowledgment. This low-key approach helps diminish competitiveness and fosters the trust of all stakeholders.

17.06 Work with Parents' Groups

Over the last decade or so, parents who succeeded in reuniting with their children after child welfare proceedings have joined together as "parent advocates" and have become a significant force for systemic change. The parent advocate movement is gaining momentum in many states. Parent advocates work with parents' attorneys and child welfare agencies to improve communication with and provide support for parents going through the system. Parent advocates who participate in system-change committees or in trainings are often profoundly influential. They usually are closely listened to by professionals working in the child welfare system, and can encourage good ideas, or help defeat bad ideas, for systemic reform. Parent advocates and parents' attorneys can partner to powerfully initiate change together.

In New York City, parent advocacy has transformed the local child welfare system. Recently, David Tobis authored a book tracing the history and phenomenal success of parent advocates there. *See* David Tobis, From Pariahs to Partners (2013). Parents who once had been accused of neglecting their children formed the Child Welfare Organizing Project, a community-based advocacy group that called for more respectful treatment of parents and a better understanding of their needs and what it feels like to be accused of child maltreatment. The Child Welfare Organizing Project eventually secured funding to train parent advocates to advise parents currently going through the child welfare system. Today it works directly with stakeholders in the local child welfare system, including the child services agencies. These veterans of the system have become, as the title of Tobis's book indicates, partners in reform efforts to improve the system.

In other states, parent advocate programs are in various stages of development. Parent advocates are organized at the county level in Washington State. Some Washington counties directly employ parent advocates as part of the court staff; in others, social service agencies employ parent advocates with the help of Court Improvement Project funds. The Washington State Parent Advocacy Network (WSPAN) is comprised of parent representatives of local parent advocacy committees and child welfare community stakeholders. It meets quarterly to network, plan, provide training, and discuss family issues in the child welfare system with policymakers. This group has successfully advocated for proposed legislation and has put on statewide conferences for parent advocates. On the individual case level, parent advocates in Washington support parents by accompanying them to case hearings to provide support, presenting trainings for parents undergoing cases, and communicating with and encouraging parents. They work with parents' attorneys and parents' social workers; in addition, some parent advocates have direct contracts with the Parents Representation Program to provide case support. In May 2013, WSPAN received a statewide honor for promoting the safety and security of children.

In a growing number of states, parent advocates are integrating into child protection departments, nonprofit organizations, and legal representation programs to provide support services for parents. Additional parents' representation programs that work with parent mentors and parent advocates include the Detroit Center for Family

Advocacy, which provides prevention representation services to families with teams comprising a lawyer, a social worker, and a parent advocate. In Iowa, a Department of Human Services program called Community Partnership sponsors a Parent Partnership in which parent advocates attend team-decision meetings and go to appointments and court appearances with parents involved in child welfare cases. *See* Tobis, *supra* at 156–60. On the national front, the strikingly positive impact of parent advocate groups and programs is heralded by the ABA National Project to Improve Representation for Parents.

Rise Magazine, which reaches 15,000 parents and child welfare practitioners nationwide, provides a national forum for parent advocates' voices. The magazine began as a collaboration between the Child Welfare Organizing Project and Youth Communication in 2005. *Rise*'s primary mission is to dispel negative stereotypes of parents involved in the child welfare system. *Rise* publishes parents' stories about their experiences with the child welfare system to support other parents and draw attention to the need for parent advocacy. *Rise* also presents training for parents on techniques for writing their stories, and partners with agencies nationwide to promote the use of parents' stories in support groups and parent and staff trainings. These stories provide parents with information about the system and are used by family support organizations and other institutions to educate and support parents. Researchers and advocates use these stories to incorporate parents' voices in movements to reform child welfare policies.

17.07 Assimilating a New Message into the System

Words and messages are a cornerstone of reform efforts. Advocates often develop several types of messages to support systemic change. These can be used interchangeably depending on who engages in the conversation and what the purpose of the conversation is. An advocate might use a different but harmonious message when speaking to a legislator than when talking to child welfare stakeholders on a court systems change committee.

Advocates can produce both lengthier descriptions about the flaws in the child welfare system and shorter sound-bite descriptions. A longer, more in-depth investigative-type report has effectively supported the proposed systemic changes made by parents' representation programs in some states. The ABA Parent Representation Project has conducted such investigative reports for Court Improvement Project committees in Wyoming, North Carolina, and Michigan, as have advocates in some jurisdictions. *See* Am. Bar Assoc. Ctr. on Children & the Law, Legal Representation for Parents in Child Welfare Proceedings: A Performance-Based Analysis of North Carolina Practice (2013); Legal Representation for Parents in Child Welfare Proceedings: An analysis of Wyoming Practice (2011); and Legal Representation for Parents in Child Welfare Proceedings: A Performance-Based

Analysis of Michigan Practice (2009). Advocates who wish to develop comprehensive analyses of their jurisdictions' legal representation systems could seek support from their state Court Improvement Projects, or seek legislative or grant funding. The resulting reports can provide powerful evidence for numerous reform efforts, including major parents' representation overhauls, in following years.

A short sound bite can effectively reset the way the public or child welfare stakeholders perceive the system. Messages are often best created through brainstorming with colleagues. One helpful way for advocates to begin developing a sound bite is to create a generalized yet pithy description of the many issues and problems that is uncontroversial. For example, one message could be that federal laws afford parents more rights than state systems. Federal laws require reunification as the preferred permanency outcome, and parents are entitled to effective services and adequate visitation. But often, state procedures do not operate in this way. Frequently, required procedural protections are not actually provided to parents, the termination rate is unnecessarily high, and the state system has a poor record of delivering services and providing family time (visitation). Messages are most useful when they embrace concepts that everyone can accept, and are general enough that attorneys can use them to develop persuasive reasoning about subtopics that flow from the message.

An effective short message might be, "We must give families a fair chance." This is a non-provocative message with which no one can disagree. It features the strongly held American value of "fair chance." It mentions "families" rather than "parents." Advocates can spin many sub-comments from a message like this by initiating conversation on (1) what federal law requires, (2) needed services, (3) brain development research, (4) how children love their parents, (5) how teens run away from foster care to return home, or (6) about the research that shows the harm children suffer when removed from their families and placed in foster care. *See, e.g.*, Joseph J. Doyle Jr., *Child Protection and Child Outcomes: Measuring the Effects of Foster Care*, 97 Am. Econ. Rev. 1583 (2007).

Consider how these messages contrast with, "Parents are not treated fairly by the system." A bluntly critical message is more likely to alienate court partners, particularly judges. It is often more productive to insist that the system must become *fairer* than that it is *unfair*. The ABA National Project to Improve Representation for Parents has created an invaluable source of information for parents' attorneys and parent advocates that can inspire messaging on its website.

Another source of effective messaging generates empathy and emotional appeal. Parents and former foster children successfully convey what is wrong with the system by telling their stories. *Rise Magazine* is a rich repository of parents' stories about how their children were taken into foster care and what obstacles they had to contend with to reunify with them. These stories can be found at *Rise*'s website. As another example of the power of families' stories, in one state, parents' attorneys wrote a series of newsletters for legislators and other political figures featuring local families' involvement with the child welfare system and what the parents had to go through to recover their children. At key times, legislators discussed these stories during floor debates.

An additional type of uncontroversial message can be developed from the underlying idea that the child welfare system needs to be modernized. The Department of Health and Human Services consistently encourages systemic development to incorporate new practices and research. People's attitudes toward policies evolve with passing time and societal changes. Alert advocates study these changes and work them into their messages. Be meticulous in accurately understanding practices and research, whether new or long-standing, and embed them into the context of the message. Commonly, judges and other court partners will find an advocate's grasp of evolving national information to be persuasive.

Effective messages can resonate powerfully when repeated in various court, meeting, and legislative settings. Instead of repeating a message over and over unadorned, the message is best artfully woven into the advocate's general persuasive statements. It is significantly more powerful if a group of advocates articulates the message jointly. When multiple people articulate a common message in multiple settings, there can be profound political shifts. A fresh interpretation of a legal concept that may be heard as uncomfortable or unpersuasive at first can gain wide credibility purely through repetition, which helps make it acceptable and current. *See* BENJAMIN N. CARDOZO, THE NATURE OF THE JUDICIAL PROCESS 58 (1921) ("[F]undamental conceptions once attained form the starting point from which are derived new consequences, which, at first tentative and groping, gain by reiteration a new permanence and certainty. In the end, they become accepted themselves as fundamental and axiomatic.") The repetition of ideas is a maxim for initiating culture changes in the court system, just as it is for public relations and advertising.

After hearing negative messages about parents for years, attorneys in various states have succeeded in changing the dialogue. They have accomplished this by creating new vocabulary which parents' attorneys and advocates have then repeated over and over. Malcom Gladwell describes how word-of-mouth practices spread ideas that become widely accepted. *See* MALCOLM GLADWELL, THE TIPPING POINT 193 (2000).

For example, in one state, all parties and stakeholders used an acronym for the dependency court that stood for "Department Court," conferring improper (and probably unintended) power on the Agency. After brainstorming, parents' attorneys renamed the acronym "DT Court" (dependency and termination court), a more neutral title. Parents' attorneys consistently used the new title statewide. Eventually everyone in the system changed their vocabulary. Here, thoughtful advocacy led to the elimination of a biased title that at one time had been absorbed and articulated multiple times each day by judges.

Another important language shift was brought about in New Jersey. There, attorneys reviewed the statutes and began quoting select parent-friendly phrases and laws, over and over. They soon were incorporated into the ongoing discourse as truisms, which they were.

Getting new information into the system challenges anti-parent biases as well. One excellent way to bring in new information is to present at court-wide or statewide trainings. Panels of parents and parent advocates telling their stories of their struggles and how they were treated make very effective presentations; parents who speak next to their teenage children with whom they have reunited are tremendously inspiring. During the planning stages of conferences, parents' attorneys and parent advocates have often successfully incorporated themselves into court training agendas.

17.08 Working with the Media

Media coverage of child welfare cases can have a huge impact of policy and practice. In Michigan, for example, a minor event at a Detriot Tigers baseball game in 2008 spiraled into a major change in the law, in large part because of media attention. After a father accidentally purchased for his son hard lemonade at the game, his son was placed in protective custody pending a further investigation. Media attention to the story, including op-eds and news coverage, led to the enactment of a new law with stricter guidelines for placing children into emergency protective services. *See* MICH. COMP. LAWS 712A.14b (2014); Tim Martin, *Accidental Drink Purchase Changing Michigan Law on Emergency Child Protective Services*, MLIVE (May 22, 2012, 3:29 PM).

Parent advocates and attorneys have been able to promote fairness to families by working with the media. In 2010, for example, after more than a decade of celebration of "Adoption Month" in the United States, the ABA National Project to Improve Representation for Parents, helped initiate "Reunification Day" or "Reunification Month" in several states. The ABA Project developed a modifiable press release that was utilized in many states. It is now commonplace for the media to publish new items celebrating Reunification Day in localities that have them. This offers an opportunity to publicize success stories as a counterweight to how child welfare stories are usually covered.

It does not take a great deal of effort to learn how to write a press release. Basic suggestions for writing press releases are available on the web. *See, e.g.*, Daniel Kehrer, *Eight Steps to Writing a Great Press Release*, DEX MEDIA (Aug. 23, 2011). Press releases are especially constructive in distributing good news, such as a favorable evaluation or good statistics about a new program or project, or expanded legislative funding. One can never predict how many news stories will result from a press release. The publication of one or two should be considered a success.

When one is contacted by a reporter for a story, it is important to remember that reporters are often not parent-friendly. They may be working on an extreme story. For example, child deaths typically are reported in excruciating detail. Parents' attorneys who are called on to comment on cases strive to maintain straightforward, legally based comments. It is helpful to have a list of two or three comments readily at hand when involved in a controversial case. For example, during a TV-news series on a case involving a child in foster care, one attorney stated, "We don't know the facts yet, and it's the American way not to judge before all the evidence is in." This message helped deflect the negative anti-parent tone.

Another form of publishing stories is to broadcast a video or audio recording of them. With YouTube, videos, and audio media, programs have fashioned their own publicity projects about parents and parents' attorneys. Advocates in Mississippi recently created a video about the need for parents' representation statewide. *See* Giving Parents a Voice (Mississippi Administrative Office of Courts 2014). In 2003, Washington State created a CD comprised of parents, parents' attorneys, and judicial officers telling stories about its pilot program, which was broadcast by public radio. *See* Audio File: The Parents Representation Program: Reuniting More Families (Marguerite Casey Foundation 2003). Perhaps the biggest advantage of creating a more-or-less complete video or CD is that the story will be told exactly as planned without the need for worries about the insertion of negative editorial slant.

17.09 Child Welfare and Court Systems Change Committees: Working with Judges and Other Stakeholders to Initiate Systemic Change

Throughout the nation, task forces and court system change committees undertake efforts to reform child welfare system problems. In 2004, the National Council for Juvenile and Family Court Judges discussed this process in detail, saying that:

> Significant systems change is not only necessary, it is imperative if juvenile and family courts, child welfare agencies, and their community of stakeholders are to meaningfully improve the lives and futures of the nation's most vulnerable children. . . . [T]he courts, child welfare agencies, and communities: *must* collaborate to improve the child protection system and ensure better outcomes for children and families; *must* bring multiple stakeholders to the table and involve them in a strategically focused collaborative process; . . . *must* become problem-solving proactive organizations that strategically and collaboratively work toward an improved child welfare system and better outcomes for children and families; and *must* undergo a fundamental paradigm shift that changes the way they work individually and in concert.

Dobbin et al., *supra*, at 1.

Whether local or statewide, court systems change committees provide excellent opportunities to work toward systemic reform, both informally and formally. Informally, parents' attorneys can bring their messages into discussions. But first, they have to be included in the committee's membership. In many localities, parents' attorneys have systematically been unrepresented, or underrepresented, on such committees. However, in recent years, in a number of states, parents' attorneys have successfully advocated for inclusion. Speaking with the committee chair privately about their absence is usually all it takes, as the fairness problems are glaring. An early suggestion to the chair should be to appoint one or more parents' attorneys and one or more parents as well, depending on the makeup of the committee.

In Washington State, the several court system change committees in large cities and statewide during the early 2000s did not appoint parents' attorneys; the committees consisted of judges, assistant attorneys general, guardians ad litem, and agency social workers only. After a parents' attorney noted this glaring absence from reading membership lists of the various committees, the attorney contacted the chairs, starting with a Supreme Court justice who was about to convene a once-a-year meeting on systems reform. The judge invited the attorney to participate. By continuing to follow the contact-the-chair method, the attorney received invitations several other dependency task forces and gradually other parents' attorneys were substituted in. As parent advocates gained visibility and political power over time, child welfare committees and task forces consistently invited parent advocates to the table.

If the "contact-the-chair" method is unsuccessful, one should ask the chair for permission to attend a meeting and make a request to add a parents' attorney to the group. However, caution should be exercised as to the tone of the request. Since committee members are there to collaborate on making improvements, it is best to stick to a message that everyone can agree on—such as, that the parents need to be there to describe how issues impact them—and to avoid dwelling on or criticizing the exclusion of parent advocates.

Other parents' attorneys have succeeded by attending open child welfare committee meetings. Los Angeles parents' attorneys began attending selected committee meetings, and subsequently were appointed as members. Today, they receive automatic appointments as members of all the systemic committees.

When working with stakeholders, it is helpful to "stand in their shoes"' by visualizing their goals and frustrations in the system. This makes it easier to better understand the motivations of agency attorneys, department social workers, other parties, and judges. As a result, one is able to fashion a more effective message and build better relationships.

During committee meetings, parents' attorneys and advocates who take a thoughtful approach to participating can influence the committee's selection of problems and issues to address, as well as committee decisions. This can be carried out by strategically stating and restating families' viewpoints and experiences, as well as legal requirements that could otherwise be overlooked during discussions. It is an excellent way to begin to emphasize and forward the underlying values of the child welfare adjudication system and strengthen attention to the need for better justice for parents and their families.

Local committees provide rich opportunities for systemic reform. Typically, communities contain dependency court committees, convened by the local judge or judges, which address process reforms. As noted by Judge Leonard Edwards, "In addition to courtroom responsibilities, the juvenile judge's role includes leadership, administrative, collaborative, advocacy, and engagement activities." Leonard Edwards, *Judicial Leadership in the Juvenile Court*, NAT'L COUNCIL ON CRIME & DELINQUENCY BLOG (NOV. 13, 2013). The judge's role on such committees is to bring stakeholders together for discussions that will lead to action plans for change. When parents' attorneys and advocates, agency attorneys, children's attorneys, and agency social workers discuss how to change local child welfare problem areas, they can "approach problems in collaborative ways, engage each other in defining the work to be done, and are able to facilitate interaction and sustain action so that goals can be reached." *See* DOBBIN ET AL., *supra*, at 33.

Numerous parents' attorneys have seen the achievements of such local court committees. A key concept for success through a court committee is "finding the common ground." There are many issues that are of concern to all stakeholders in the system, and these are the issues where one is most likely to see collaborative progress. As examples, parents' attorneys have initiated the following reforms by working with their local court committees:

- *Establishing a new procedure for distributing orders to parents.* In one court, parents were leaving hearings without copies of court orders entered. Instead, the orders were mailed from parents' attorneys' offices. Since a number of parents were not in stable housing situations, some orders were never received or were lost. Parents' attorneys worked with their local court committee to establish a copying system so parents would receive orders onsite, and their attorneys could explain them onsite.
- *Making such procedural improvements on a regular basis.* New York City parents' attorneys meet quarterly with opposing counsel, the Agency, the court, and other stakeholders to achieve collective improvements in common ground areas, without compromising their obligations to their clients. Recently, protocols were developed to improve information sharing at court conferences.
- *Shortening the time parents must wait for contested initial hearings.* In one court, four parents' attorneys persuasively challenged the routine delay of two weeks or more, and worked with the court and other parties to set up a timely procedure.
- *Negotiation of a protocol between the agency caseworkers and attorneys representing children and parents.* In New York City, parents' attorneys worked with the Agency and agency case workers to create favorable new guidelines to facilitate communication between the parties, which were issued as an official protocol by the Agency's commissioner.

- *Creating a new system for entering parenting plans in dependency court cases.* Attorneys working statewide secured a legislative amendment allowing parenting plans to be entered in dependency cases (rather than in a new family law case) where the court required a formal custody order. Subsequently, a local parents' attorney developed new forms and worked with the judicial officer and local court committee to create a new procedure allowing numerous reunifications to go forward.
- *Negotiating an enhanced visitation system that expands visitation availability (family time) for parents and their children.* Parents' attorneys in New York City co-chaired a work group with the Agency involving all stakeholders in establishing guidelines for the use of Visit Hosts. The Agency's commissioner issued official guidelines to encourage the new practice.

If there is no such committee in a local court system, judges may be receptive to the suggestion that a collaborative team of stakeholders should informally or formally convene to work on system-wide problems. When approaching a judge, the parents' attorney should suggest issues of concern to the judge and focus on court process problems or other issues of common ground.

On a statewide basis, court systems change committees can significantly influence and improve the child welfare system. Typically, these committees are called Court Improvement Program committees or Commissions on Children in Foster Care. Both types of committees resulted from national initiatives, but operate on a statewide basis. Usually, they are concerned with creating child welfare improvement projects or developing and coordinating programs. Court Improvement Project committees receive federal funding each year and typically fund selective innovative projects. These state committees provide excellent opportunities for prepared, hard-working parents' attorneys and parent advocates to promote family-support projects. The same techniques are recommended for successful participation in a statewide committee as in a local committee. Examples of recent reform projects initiated by parents' attorneys who worked with statewide committees include:

- A local parents' attorney set up a local procedure for timely paternity testing. Technology changes had made testing inexpensive, but the system in the local court, and statewide, was slow and dependent on the county prosecutor. After the success of the attorney's procedure, parents' attorneys worked with the Court Improvement Project, judges, and other stakeholders in four counties to set up a pilot program to implement quicker paternity testing, with funding provided by the Court Improvement Project.
- Parents' attorneys in Washington State worked to improve reasonable efforts statewide by working with the Commission on Children in Foster Care to publish a

best practices book. This project addressed the fact that there are more available services in urban areas than rural, and that various evidence-based services exist in some areas, but not all. A stakeholder subcommittee formed to develop a handbook on effective evidence-based services. Parents' attorneys now use the handbook to argue for enhanced services for their parent clients, and judges and stakeholders use it to gain information about the myriad services available in the state.

- During the last few years, a number of Court Improvement Projects have funded statewide and regional parents' attorney conferences, in response to parents' attorneys' requests for such conferences. One of the highest priorities of the ABA National Project to Improve Parental Representation for Parents is to support regional conferences. The Court Improvement Projects provide funding for a multi-day conference that brings together attorneys and advocates from around the surrounding States. For some, this has been the beginning of statewide and regional communication and has flourished into an active listserv and joint support and reform projects.

The impact of strategic committee participation can be substantial. Conclusions and recommendations signal stakeholder agreement on needed reforms and solutions. The recommendations may result in legislative or court rule changes (local or statewide), and they provide excellent opportunities for furthering the viewpoints and strengths of parents and their families. Once the recommendations are made, it is important to monitor them and work to implement them. Judges will usually implement procedural changes, but others may go nowhere unless someone makes the system accountable by monitoring and reminding the court systems change committee. Often this requires vigilance on the part of participating parents' attorneys. One effective way to implement recommendations is to persuade committees that they should take on the implementation of the recommendations as a practical second committee project.

17.10 Improving the Child Welfare System Through Case Law: Appeals and Litigation

Successful litigation against child protection departments has caused substantial positive changes in the system for parents. An example of a case brought on behalf of families is New York City's *Nicholson v. Scorpetta*, 3 N.Y.3d 357, 787 N.Y.S.2d 196, 820 N.E.2d 840 (2004), which condemned the Administration for Children's Services' practice of removing children who had seen domestic abuse against their mothers, without more. An earlier decision in the same case in federal court eventually pushed the New York State Legislature to increase the payment for parents' attorneys from $40 per hour for in-court work and $25 per hour for out-of-court work to $75 per hour for each hour. *See* N.Y. Jud. § 35(3) (2010); *Nicholson v. Williams*, 203 F. Supp. 2d 153, 259–60 (E.D.N.Y. 2002) (recommending a compensation rate of no less than $90 per hour for attorneys of indigent clients to protect the constitutional rights of indigent mothers). This, in turn, contributed to New York City officials' institution of the first ever multi-disciplinary institutional parental representation offices.

Many other affirmative challenges to the child welfare system have resulted in sweeping reforms. *See, e.g.*, Modified Settlement Agreement, *Charlie & Nadine H. v. Corzine*, No. 99-3678 (D.N.J. July 7, 2006) (challenge to the functioning of the New Jersey child welfare system that led to a consent decree increasing the amount of visitation and services, including mental health treatment, the development of individualized service plans built on the family's strengths and needs, the provision of services called for in case plans to families, flexible funds for families' needs, and an increase in child care slots to support families as well as increased substance abuse services).

Another effective way to impact justice for parents is by changing case law through appeals. This is an area where one attorney, working alone, can take on an unjust statute or departmental practice by contesting it in an appellate court and winning. Chapter 15 of this book describes methods for succeeding in appellate advocacy.

Over the past few years, reorganization of the parents' attorneys' appellate program has resulted in significantly improved case law in some states. Many states' indigent defense appellate programs consist of appointments to "pool" or "list" attorneys, who may or may not be knowledgeable about dependency and termination laws. Appellate parents' representation differs significantly from appellate criminal representation. To be competent, appellate attorneys who represent parents in dependency and termination cases must develop specialized skills through training and experience. Appointments should only be made to attorneys who specialize in the field.

Limiting case appointments to skilled appellate attorneys well versed in dependency and termination laws results in more wins for parents, along with an improved body of case law upon which trial attorneys can rely. In several states, including New Jersey, North Carolina, and Washington, appellate program reorganization, specifically with the coordination of trial and appellate attorneys, has produced measurably superior results for families. The results can be striking: Where parents seldom prevailed in only about 5 percent of published dependency and termination opinions a decade ago in one state, they now prevail in over 50 percent. Reorganization of the appellate appointment system can be a strikingly efficient and effective way to enhance justice.

Monitoring the enforcement of case law, established either by litigation or appellate decisions, is critical. Even when case law changes by an appellate court, a case decision, or a consent decree, some judges, attorneys, or department employees may persist in ignoring the change. Sometimes local parties may not know of the new decision. Multiple follow-up efforts to persuade judges or parties that they have to adhere to the higher court's new ruling might be necessary. It is not uncommon to appear in trial courts where judges declare after an appellate decision reversed the trial court that the higher court did not understand the case, and the trial court does not agree with the decision.

After securing a change in the interpretation of the law by an appellate court, trial lawyers need to cite to the case, be prepared to make a good record that the trial court is ignoring the new decision, and file a second appeal.

Parents' lawyers should also widely discuss the new decision at stakeholder group meetings. Listserv communication and multiple efforts are critical in upholding new case law.

17.11 Establishing New Law Through Court Rules and the Legislative Process

Getting legislation passed usually takes a lot of intensive work up front, but can create significant and long-lasting changes in the legal system. Effective legislative advocacy techniques include:

- Establishing relationships with other professionals and groups who will support the proposed legislative change.
- Establishing relationships with key legislators.
- Strategically identifying issues that can be addressed through legislation.
- Carefully and thoroughly promoting the proposed legislative change.

As discussed above, establishing relationships with parent groups, parent and family-friendly organizations, and other family-friendly groups working in child welfare provides an excellent foundation for any type of systemic reform, including legislative changes. On a national level, the ABA National Project to Improve Representation for Parents works to influence national policies and promote family-friendly bills in Congress. At the state and local levels, parents' attorneys who work with like-minded coalitions should consider collaborating on enacting legislation.

Stakeholder group work, involving all parties to the system, can be effective. Through stakeholder group collaboration, parents' attorneys and their colleagues in Georgia recently achieved a complete rewriting of the Juvenile Code, a lengthy but worthwhile process for the attorneys involved. *See Georgia's Juvenile Code: New Year for New Law*, 19 Ga. B. J., Dec. 2013, at 13. After the state bar of Georgia drafted a new model code, it was vetted through stakeholders. Through diligent cooperative work, parents' attorneys were able to achieve major gains in the discovery procedure and visitation sections of the Code—and were able to prevent regressive new sections. *See, e.g.*, Ga. Code Ann. § 15-11-112(b) (2013) (presumption that visitation shall be unsupervised).

Similarly, parents' attorneys in North Carolina participate in a legislative drafting committee initiated by the Court Improvement Program. All stakeholders are represented and actively collaborate. As a result, the bills drafted by the committee cover "common ground" areas that all stakeholders can agree upon. These have included discovery improvements and reinstatement of parents' rights bills. The committee has been very successful in getting proposed legislation enacted into law.

If the goal is to work with the state legislature to pass a bill, establishing a relationship with one or more appropriate legislator(s) is essential. Finding a legislator who believes in the cause and wants to sponsor the bill is obviously the best way to begin. Most state legislatures have topic-specific committees, and child welfare is no exception. Establishing a relationship with one or more legislators on the committee that covers child welfare is therefore a good place to start. Successful advocates study the records of legislators to determine whether they are parent- and family-friendly before approaching them. How have the legislators voted on child welfare issues previously? What are their reputations? State legislatures have detailed websites that yield a great deal of information. Since advocates will be working closely with the sponsor of a bill as it goes through the various stages of the process, it is crucial to develop and maintain a good relationship.

One shortcut for obtaining information about legislators is to communicate with legislative liaisons, or lobbyists. Many social services organizations employ liaisons, and the courts are likely to employ one or more. Contact the right person in the organization or the court, and ask about having a meeting with the liaison. Knowledge of the legislative system and the individual members is the liaisons' stock-in-trade, and they are usually friendly and open.

As a legislative advocate, one should strive to be dedicated and credible. When meeting with legislators, a thorough knowledge of all the facts surrounding the issues is critical. Most legislators are skeptical and cautious about taking on an issue unless it is supported by evidence. The more data gathered, the better. If the proposal may result in savings, be prepared to make the case. Another route for supporting proposed legislation is to characterize it as a response to a significant event that was widely covered by the media. For example, as mentioned earlier, attorneys and parents in Michigan successfully promoted legislation to limit the Department of Human Services' authority to remove children following the highly publicized removal of a middle-class boy after he became sick at a baseball game. *See* Martin, *supra*.

Remember that enacting legislation is a collaborative process. If there is opposition to the proposed bill, the chances of succeeding are greatly reduced. Usually it is better to meet with legislators who oppose it, ascertain where there is common ground, and accept compromises that do not gut one's objective.

As noted earlier, an advocate's ability to pick battles strategically will greatly enhance the chance that a reform will prove effective and lasting. Although the state laws on the books may need a wholesale overhaul, it is unlikely that parents' advocates can generate such reform in a short period of time. For the most part, parents' attorneys and parents can better achieve lasting legislative change by making progress incrementally. Dozens of less comprehensive but meaningful legal changes can be pushed forward by legislative proposals. The cumulative adoption of targeted legislation over a just a few years can implement a fairer and more effective system. Examples of potential targeted legislation include the following:

- Has a statewide or local reform committee identified a discrete procedure that operates unfairly or inefficiently? A common example is the child protection department's failure to provide parents with proper notice of hearings, which causes continuances and court delays. It also clogs the court system, raises the parties' caseloads, and prolongs children's stays in out-of-home care. A win-win procedural-change bill is a great way to work with all parties and gain credibility in the state legislature.
- Another procedural issue involves court-appointed evaluators. A basic principle of fairness is that when the court appoints evaluators or experts who will be paid by public funds to examine a parent, they should not be selected by the state alone. In Washington State, parents' attorneys successfully initiated legislation that requires that the parents' attorneys and the state agree on who the expert will be, which has helped to diminish experts' biases. WASH. REV. CODE § 13.34.370 (2009).
- What deficient practice findings resulted from the department's last Child and Family Services Review (CFSR)? One or more findings might be susceptible to legislative remedy. That there is already a clear audit, proving the problem exists, makes the legislative process easier. (But note that working collaboratively with the child protection department on developing this kind of legislation would most likely be important in terms of one's ongoing relationship with the department.)
- Some types of visitation problems can be addressed through legislation. For example, an amendment could be proposed that would establish that "visitation shall not be limited as a sanction for a parent's failure to comply with court orders or services where the health, safety, or welfare of the child is not at risk as a result of the visitation." This quote is from a Washington State provision that parents' attorneys have been able to use to protect family time (visitation) even if the parent is behind on fulfilling services orders, and so forth. WASH. REV. CODE §§ 13.34.136(2)(b)(ii)(B)–(C) (2014).

In addition to drafting and proposing bills, another way to influence the system legislatively is to watch for good bills (especially coming out of the Child Welfare Committee), and support them by talking to the sponsor and other legislators recommended by the sponsor, and testifying at committee hearings. Supporting his or her efforts through legislative advocacy is an excellent way to build a relationship with a legislator. Even when parents' attorneys do not have time to monitor legislative proposals to determine whether they constructively support families, one might be able to obtain information more easily from statewide child welfare advocacy groups.

Whether following the progress of the bill, or promoting another bill, one should be sure to track these bills closely, as they tend to move quickly through the various hearings. Although concise writings such as letters can be helpful, a particularly effective advocacy technique is scheduling personal meetings with legislators. This is how most legislative advocacy is enacted. Two years ago, a Tennessee attorney learned of a bill that would make it much easier for the state to terminate parental rights. Alarmed, she consulted with court officials and was advised there was no possibility of stopping the adoption of the bill. Rather than giving up, she made appointments with each of the legislators on the committee to talk with them personally. Through these meetings, she persuaded the legislators of the negative impacts of the bill, and it was dropped.

When testifying at hearings or meeting with legislators, it is important to speak clearly and briefly. Talking at length about theories, embellishing statements unnecessarily, or reading from notes all are turn-offs for legislators who listen to dozens of people speaking every day. Stories can be very effective. Use personal experiences and work with parents' personal experiences to illustrate the problem, but again, relate them in a concise way. Because families' stories are naturally emotional and memorable, they bring a sense of urgency and passion to advocacy efforts.

Court rules should also be considered an avenue for reform. A special committee or the state supreme court generally adopts amendments. The same basic advocacy techniques apply to court rule change efforts: Be well-versed about the rule change being sought, work with stakeholders to garner support, and figure out the procedure for proposing changes in the rules. In Washington State, children were commonly adopted out after their parents lost termination trials, even if the parents had appealed the termination. The adoption created an untenable situation when parents won their appeals, as a lengthy amount of time had passed during which the parent and child had no visitation, and the trial judge was reluctant to disrupt the adoption. To prevent these premature adoptions, the Washington State Supreme Court adopted a rule change proposed by parents' attorneys to require the Department of Social and Health Services to give notice of any pending adoption to the parents' appellate attorney, who could then object and ask that the adoption be delayed. *See* WASH. R. APP. P. 18.13A(k). Because of the rule change, premature adoptions are no longer finalized prior to the appellate decision.

17.12 Creation of a New Parents' Representation System

In Washington State and New York, organized, improved parents' representation programs have surfaced in recent years, with very positive results. Following are descriptions of their development; both started as pilot programs and have expanded to the extent that they now handle yearly caseloads of more than 1,000 parents. Although the programs each have unique organizational styles, they went through fairly similar establishment processes and share ongoing characteristics. First, in each location, there was one or more action establishing publically that the parents' representation system was in crisis. Second (as a result of advocates' work), the judiciary and legislature recognized the need for reform of parents' representation. Third, a new method for representing parents was developed based on improved standards of practice. Fourth, both programs feature continuous quality monitoring, including the measurement of case outcomes.

In 2000, the Washington State Parents Representation Program was instituted after the Washington State Legislature requested a report of parental representation conducted by the Washington State Office of Public Defense. The report found that parents' attorneys typically had excessive caseloads and low pay, and that many parents in various counties were poorly represented. In addition, continuances and case delays were endemic. Fiscally, the Washington State Attorney General's Office was funded at about two-and-a-half times to prosecute the cases as the counties were funding parents' attorneys. In short, the report exposed the crisis and created a strong foundation for advocating for a new way to represent parents.

The Washington State Office of Public Defense secured pilot program funding from the Washington State Legislature and implemented the pilot in two juvenile courts. New practice standards, including lower caseloads, were developed and the pilot attorneys were provided with training and with additional resources, including significant social worker support and sufficient funds for experts. *See* Bobbe J. Bridge and Joanne I. Moore, *Implementing Equal Justice for Parents in Washington: A Dual Approach*, 53 JUV. FAM. CT. J. 31, 33–35 (2002).

From 2001 to 2011, several favorable evaluations and studies showed greatly improved reunification and timeliness outcomes for children and parents in Washington State. *See* Mark E. Courtney and Jennifer L. Hook, *Evaluation of the Impact of Enhanced Parental Legal Representation on the Timing of Permanency Outcomes for Children in Foster Care*, 34 CHILDREN AND YOUTH SERVICES REV. 1337 (2012) (study of more than 12,000 cases found that strong parental representation greatly shortened time to permanency for children, reducing children's stay in foster care). The researchers recommended that "[j]urisdictions with poor parental representation that wish to address [ ] deficienc[ies] in their dependency court process . . . should consider implementing something akin to" Washington State's Parental Representation Project if they wished to "shorten[ ] the time children spend in foster care and [reduce] the costs associated with additional days in care." *See id.* at 1343.

Five years after the inception of the pilot program, the Washington State Legislature was convinced that the Parents Representation Program should gradually expand throughout the state, as parents and families represented by the program had increased reunifications and children had quicker permanency outcomes. The Legislature concluded that the program was producing significant foster care and adoption subsidy savings. As of 2014, in 85 percent of the state, Parent Representation Project contract attorneys represent virtually all parents. The program has represented over 30,000 parents, and handles about 8,000 open dependency and termination representations at any one time.

Resources for improved parents' representation have expanded during the duration of the program. Program attorneys in urban and medium-sized counties now work closely with the parent advocates who support parents through the process. For the most part, parent advocates operate out of a stand-alone program organized by an Agency and advised by a parent advocating council, which includes several Parent Representation Project attorneys.

A primary duty of these attorneys is to work with and hold accountable department social workers to obtain constructive services for parent clients in the case plan by tracking their clients' ability to access services and make progress. If the supervising Agency is not providing needed services, the parent's attorney enforces his or her client's rights by obtaining court orders. The Parent Representation Project contracted social worker component provides each attorney with about forty hours of social work services per month. The social workers obtain cases through attorney referrals, mostly when an attorney has concluded that a parent needs extra support.

The program is based on the right to counsel, and as such, all funding for the program is directly appropriated by the state. In 2013, the Oregon State Legislature appropriated $2.4 million for the establishment of a parents' representation pilot program, similar to the Washington State program, to reduce dependency caseloads. In 2014, the Colorado State Legislature passed a bill authorizing and funding the development of a state office to oversee parents' representation.

New York City also has undergone dramatic changes in parental representation since 2000. That year, as a result of a federal lawsuit challenging various deficiencies in child welfare practices, the federal court appointed an advisory panel of child welfare experts to investigate conditions in the system. *See Marisol A. ex rel. Forbes v. Giuliani*, 185 F.R.D. 152, 157 (S.D.N.Y. 1999). Although neither court practices nor parental representation were among the issues raised in the lawsuit itself, the panel, headed by John Mattingly of the Annie E. Casey Foundation, issued a scathing report in 2000 on the practices in Family Court. *See* ANNIE E. CASEY FOUNDATION, ADVISORY REPORT ON FRONT LINE AND SUPERVISORY PRACTICE 44–52 (2000).

This fresh, outside perspective roused an emerging parent representation community to focus on improving the legal representation afforded to parents in child welfare cases. At the time, the only lawyers assigned to represent parents in court proceedings were solo practitioners on a panel of eligible appointees. They were paid $25 per hour of out-of-court work and $40 per hour for in-court work and their ranks were being depleted. Moreover, because of their caseloads and the fact that they worked alone, they spent virtually their entire time in court. The Special Report on Family Court, included in the Advisory Report on Front Line and Supervisory Practice, found that parent clients were unable to speak or meet with their lawyers between court appearances and had to endure the intervention of the Agency in their lives alone. *See id.* at 46. Similar to Washington State's parent attorney situation at the time, the larger job of negotiating with agencies out of court, identifying and securing needed services for families, and preparing parents for various out-of-court meetings and examinations, among many other vital tasks, were beyond the sights of the court-assigned lawyers.

Shortly after the report criticizing practice in New York Family Court was issued, a consortium of advocates emerged. Through a grant from the Annie E. Casey Foundation, this consortium became the Center for Family Representation (CFR). Beginning in 2002, CFR experimented in representing parents before petitions were filed in court, shortly after families were targeted by the child welfare agency. The success of this new practice eventually led to a dramatic breakthrough in the arrangement for representing parents throughout New York City. In 2006, New York City officials placed the first-ever Request for Proposals for institutional, multi-disciplinary legal representation for indigent parents. In 2007, it awarded three contracts to three different offices, one of which was CFR.

As of 2014, there are four multi-disciplinary offices in New York City that represent the vast majority of all parents in Family Court. All of them work in teams on cases commonly consisting of social workers, parent advocates, and lawyers. Their focus is to prevent foster care placement, and when it cannot be avoided, to shorten the children's length of stay in care in order to minimize the consequences of prolonged separation on children and families. They meet with their clients on a regular basis out of court and prepare them for various agency meetings that take place between court appearances. They have a combined staff of more than 200 professionals. The practice model features intensive social work support and advocacy for parents; clients have available the services of a social worker, a parent advocate, and an attorney. Most of the money supporting the offices comes from a contract awarded by New York City officials. The offices also secure other government grants and private fundraising, including from foundations and individuals.

CFR provides training to other jurisdictions. A number of such jurisdictions have implemented pilot programs based on the CFR model, including one county in Michigan and in New Mexico and counties in Louisiana.

Other notable social-work-intensive representation programs include the Detroit Center for Family Advocacy, which works on the front-end before cases are filed by securing services for families that obviate the need to charge parents with neglect. The Detroit office creates attorney and social worker teams that aim to assist families by obtaining collateral orders regarding child support, divorce, landlord-tenant matters, housing, and so forth to prevent the child protection department from removing children into foster care. The program also represents caregivers of children to promote permanency through adoption, guardianship, and reunification with non-offending parents.

17.13 Conclusion

The long-term objective of systemic reform is to institute a *cultural* shift in the child welfare system: an altered way of thinking and acting on the part of *all* child welfare system stakeholders, one that fully reflects parents' rightful roles and the protection of families under the Constitution. The efforts of parents' attorneys and advocates have advanced this cause throughout the United States.

In 2006, participants in the first day-long meeting of what became the ABA National Project to Improve Representation for Parents wrote a Mission Statement embracing a major cultural shift in the child welfare system. Parents' attorneys from all over the United States had observed the same fundamental problems in the various states and united in their commitment to work for change. Its Mission Statement, which can be found on its website, reads as follows:

> The mission of the National Parents' Counsel Organization is to achieve procedural and social justice for all families involved with child welfare systems, through legal, legislative, and policy advocacy. Recognizing that parents and their attorneys have largely been excluded from child welfare policy discussions at the national, state and local levels, we seek to ensure that parents are more at the center of all serious conversations about child welfare matters. . . . [W]e aim to increase the focus on procedural and substantive due process issues, eliminating barriers to reunification . . . [and to] raise awareness that child welfare systems are involved disproportionately in the lives of low-income and minority families and to ensure equal treatment for all. We seek to ensure that every parent . . . is legally entitled to and actually provided with representation by zealous counsel . . . [and] [w]e believe that parents are entitled to counsel who are qualified attorneys . . . .

Today, thanks largely to a growing body of reform efforts by parents' attorneys and advocates, the child welfare culture has decidedly begun to shift. By steadily working in our child welfare system environments, separately and in concert, we can inexorably advance a cultural shift, until all working in the system embrace the laws and policies that value parents, families, and children.

BIOS OF CONTRIBUTING AUTHORS

Andrew Cohen has represented parents and children for the Committee for Public Counsel Services Children and Family Law (CAFL) Division since 1995. In his current position as CAFL Director of Appellate Panel, Mr. Cohen oversees the work of about 130 private child welfare appellate attorneys, helps to oversee the work of about eight hundred private child welfare trial attorneys, conducts trial and appellate trainings, and maintains a small trial and appellate caseload. He has argued many appeals before the Massachusetts Supreme Judicial Court and Appeals Court. He also regularly files *amicus curiae* briefs in child welfare matters on behalf of his agency. He has authored several articles and book chapters on evidence, parent representation, and child welfare trial and appellate practice. Mr. Cohen has lectured at the American Bar Association, the Massachusetts Bar Association, the National Center for Adoption Law & Policy, the International Commission on Couple and Family Relations, the American Professional Society on the Abuse of Children, and Harvard Law School. Before joining the CAFL Division, he worked for four years doing commercial and bankruptcy trial and appellate litigation and clerked for The Honorable Carolyn Dineen King of the Fifth Circuit Court of Appeals in Houston. He is a graduate of Harvard College and the University of Pennsylvania Law School. Mr. Cohen is a former chair of the Boston Bar Association Family Law Section and a former member of the Boston Bar Journal's board of editors. He currently serves on the steering committee for the American Bar Association's National Parents' Counsel Organization.

The Center for Family Representation was founded in 2002 in New York City to provide families in crisis with free legal representation and social work services to enable children to live with their parents safely. It is the major provider of legal services in New York and Queens County in New York City for indigent parents charged in Family Court with maltreating their children. Every CFR client works with a team of professionals comprised of a lawyer, a social worker, and a parent advocate—a trained professional who has experienced the child welfare system firsthand and has successfully reunited with her family. The team model ensures that families access services, get fair legal treatment, and are able to better take care of their children.

In addition to representing parents, Ms. Cortese served as a child's attorney for over a dozen years and has also represented foster care agencies in trial and appellate proceedings. She worked at the NYC Legal Aid Society Juvenile Rights Practice ("JRP"), as the

Director of Professional Development, where she coordinated and conducted training citywide for attorney, social work, paralegal, and management staff. She also served as the Attorney-In-Charge of JRP's Manhattan trial office that represented 12,000 children annually in child protective, delinquency, and PINS proceedings. Ms. Cortese has been a member of the faculty of the Practicing Law Institute, the New York State Judicial Institute and the Child Welfare League of America, and has written for the American Bar Association's Center on Children and the Law. In May of 2010, Ms. Cortese received the Kathryn A. McDonald award from the New York City Bar Association for Excellence in Service to the Family Courts. Ms. Cortese is a graduate of Columbia University School of Law and Colgate University.

Richard Cozzola is the Director of the Children and Families Practice Group at LAF in Chicago, Illinois, the largest provider of legal services to the poor in Chicago. He has represented parents, adolescents and children, foster parents, and relatives in Juvenile Court matters for over thirty years. Mr. Cozzola joined LAF in 1997.

He has been a faculty member for trial skills programs for juvenile court practitioners sponsored by the National Institute of Trial Advocacy, the National Association of Counsel for Children, and the Juvenile Law Society. He has also conducted trainings for attorneys, case workers, and medical and mental health providers working with children in Juvenile and Family Courts for over twenty years both at national conferences for the American Bar Association's Center on Children and the Law, and the National Association of Counsel for Children and for local offices such as Public Defender's offices, and court improvement programs in several states.

He has written on a number of topics including working with social workers in a legal setting, the importance of out-of-court advocacy for clients in the child welfare system, and effective trial strategies in child welfare cases, including work with expert witnesses.

Kara Finck is a Practice Associate Professor of Law at the University of Pennsylvania Law School where she directs the Interdisciplinary Child Advocacy Clinic, focusing on the legal needs of families. Prior to teaching, she was the Managing Attorney of the Family Defense Practice at The Bronx Defenders, where she created an interdisciplinary legal practice for parents involved in the child welfare system. She has presented on best practices in child welfare and dependency cases, the collateral consequences of child welfare involvement and interdisciplinary collaboration. She is the co-author of *Social Work Practice and the Law* (Springer Publishing 2011) with Dr. Lyn Slater, Ph.D. She received both her undergraduate and law degree from Columbia University and was a Skadden Fellow at The Door Legal Services Center.

Matthew Fraidin is a Professor of Law at the University of the District of Columbia David A. Clarke School of Law. He directs the General Practice Clinic and teaches Civil

Procedure, Professional Responsibility, and Disaster Law: Katrina and Beyond. Prior to joining the School of Law, he served as Legal Director of The Children's Law Center in Washington, D.C., Supervising Attorney at The Legal Aid Society of the District of Columbia, and Associate Counsel to Vice President Al Gore. Professor Fraidin's published articles include *Heuristics, Cognitive Biases, and Accountability: Decision-Making In Dependency Court*, 90 Clev. St. L. Rev. 913 (2013), *Changing the Narrative of Child Welfare*, 19 Geo. J. on Poverty L. & Pol'y 97-109 (2012), and *Stories Told and Untold: Confidentiality Laws and the Master Narrative of Child Welfare*, 63 Maine Law Review 1 (2010).

Darice M. Good-Dworak is a solo practitioner in Georgia. She is a member of the steering committee of the American Bar Association's Parent Representation Project and the President of the Georgia Parent Attorney Advocacy Committee. Mrs. Good-Dworak is nationally certified as a Child Welfare Law Specialist by the National Association of Counsel for Children. She is also a member of the CWLS section of the Georgia Supreme Court Committee on Justice for Children. Lastly, she is a certified trainer for the National Institute of Trial Attorneys. She formerly served as a Fellow for the Georgia Supreme Court Committee on Justice for Children Cold Case Project, and as the co-chair of the Juvenile Law Section of the Young Lawyers Division of the State Bar of Georgia. She obtained her Bachelor's Degree from the University of Washington and her Juris Doctorate from Mercer School of Law.

Martin Guggenheim has taught at NYU School of Law, where he now co-directs the Family Defense Clinic, since 1973. From 1998 to 2002, he was director of Clinical and Advocacy Programs. Professor Guggenheim has been an active litigator in the area of children and the law and has argued leading cases on juvenile delinquency and termination of parental rights in the US Supreme Court. He is also a well-known scholar, having published more than fifty articles and book chapters, plus six books, including *What's Wrong with Children's Rights* (2005). His research has focused on adolescent abortion, First Amendment rights in schools, the role of counsel for children in court proceedings, and empirical research on child welfare practice, juvenile justice, and family law. He is a founding member of the steering committee of the American Bar Association's parent representation project.

Diana Rugh Johnson is a Child Welfare Law Specialist and serves as a Judge Pro Tempore in the Juvenile Court of DeKalb County, Georgia. She is a solo practitioner specializing in child welfare law and Social Security Disability. She holds a Master's Degree in Biochemistry from Clemson University and a law degree from Georgia State University. She is a member of the National Association of Counsel for Children and was the 2010 recipient of their Stephen Cahn Outstanding Young Lawyer Award. Diana is a member of the Georgia Supreme Court's Committee on Justice for Children and the Parent Attorney Advocacy Committee. She serves on the steering committee of the American Bar Association's Parent Representation Project and on the Board of Directors of the Georgia Association of Counsel for Children. Diana teaches other child welfare attorneys in Georgia and across the United States on a variety of topics including trial skills, effective case planning, understanding drug tests, and due diligence in medically-complicated cases.

Joshua Kay earned his PhD in clinical psychology and his JD from the University of Michigan. Prior to law school, he was an assistant professor of physical medicine and rehabilitation at the University of Michigan Medical School, where he specialized in the neuropsychological and behavioral assessment and treatment of children with disabilities and their families. He is a Clinical Assistant Professor at the University of Michigan Law School, where he has taught extensively in the Child Advocacy Law Clinic and Child Welfare Appellate Clinic.

Sarah Katz joined the Temple Law faculty as Visiting Clinical Professor in July 2012 and became Assistant Clinical Professor of Law in July 2013. Prior to her arrival at Temple, Professor Katz was a supervising attorney in the Family Advocacy Unit at Community Legal Services in Philadelphia, PA. There, she was responsible for direct representation of parents in civil child abuse and neglect cases; management and training of new attorneys, paralegals, and certified law students; policy and advocacy work at the city and state levels; and community and continuing legal education. She also served as an Adjunct Professor at Temple Law and a Lecturer in Law at the University of Pennsylvania Law School, teaching "Parent, Child, and the State." Professor Katz began her legal career as a law clerk to the Honorable Norma L. Shapiro, Eastern District of Pennsylvania. She earned her JD at the University of Pennsylvania Law School in 2003 and her BA at Columbia University in 1997.

Kenneth Krekorian is the Founder and Executive Director of Los Angeles Dependency Lawyers, Inc., the largest parent's representation organization in the country, with 110 attorneys representing more than 22,000 parents. He is a member of the California Bar and began representing parents and children in dependency cases in 1974. He has represented thousands of parents and children at the trial and appellate levels.

David M. Meyers is the Chief Operating Officer of Dependency Legal Services, where he serves as a National Consultant, Trainer, and Attorney Advocate in child welfare cases. He previously served as a Senior Attorney with California's Administrative Office of the Courts, Center for Families Children and the Courts (CFCC), where he developed statewide curriculum for attorneys and court professionals engaged in juvenile law practice, and represented the California judiciary on a number of state and national boards and workgroups dedicated to improving attorney representation and child welfare systems. He is currently a consultant with the American Bar Association's National Resource Center for Juvenile and Legal Issues and member of their Parent Attorney Representation Project Steering Committee. Through Dependency Legal Services, he provides and oversees the representation of parents and children in Sonoma, Marin, Stanislaus, and Humboldt Counties. He is licensed to practice law in California, Arizona, and the Pascua Yaqui Nation. He holds a BA in journalism and music from the University of Florida and his JD from the University of Arizona.

Joanne Moore, Director of the Washington State Office of Public Defense, founded the Parents Representation Program, nationally known as one of the largest and most successful parent representation programs. Ms. Moore is responsible for the program's ongoing quality and oversight, as well as for a number of other state-funded public defense programs. She has received a number of awards for her establishment of lasting equal justice reforms to Washington's legal system.

Annick Lenoir-Peek is an Assistant Appellate Defender and Assistant Parent Representation Coordinator for the North Carolina Indigent Defense Services' Office of Parent Representation, a position she has held since June 2008. Ms. Lenoir-Peek is nationally certified as a Child Welfare Law Specialist by the National Association of Counsel for Children. She began representing parents in child welfare cases in 1999 in South Carolina prior to moving to North Carolina. She has practiced in this area of law exclusively since 2002. Ms. Lenoir-Peek was a Department of Social Services attorney for two years and has concentrated on representing parents at the appellate level since 2002.

In addition to representing indigent parents in appeals to the Court of Appeals and North Carolina Supreme Court, Ms. Lenoir-Peek trains parent attorneys at both the trial and appellate levels in North Carolina and nationally. She has worked on various Court Improvement Program projects in North Carolina intended to improve outcomes for families involved in the child welfare system. She has developed forms and tools to assist trial and appellate parent counsel in their representation of clients involved in court actions.

She received her Bachelor's Degree from Georgetown University and her Juris Doctorate from the Columbus School of Law at Catholic University of America.

Diane L. Redleaf is the founder and Executive Director of the Family Defense Center since 2005. From 1996 through 2005, she was a partner at the public interest law firm Lehrer and Redleaf She previously was a supervisory attorney in the Children's Rights Project of the Legal Assistance Foundation (Chicago), which she founded and led from 1984 until 1996. A child and family advocate since she graduated from Stanford Law School in 1979, Ms. Redleaf has brought more than two dozen major systemic reform cases, has led amicus briefing efforts in several cases before the United States Supreme Court, has argued or briefed many precedential appeals on behalf of families, has been involved in over sixty cases with published opinions, has spearheaded major legislative reforms in Illinois, and has represented parents in hundreds of juvenile court and administrative proceedings. She has taught child welfare law at the University of Chicago Law School. In 2014, she received the prestigious Founder's Award of the Chicago Bar Association's Alliance for Women, which recognizes excellence, leadership, and mentoring of other lawyers. She is on the Steering Committee of the ABA Children in the Law's Parent Representation Project and a founder/leader of the Illinois Parent Attorney Network.

Vivek S. Sankaran is a clinical professor of law and directs both the Child Advocacy Law Clinic and the Child Welfare Appellate Clinic at the University of Michigan Law School. Sankaran also founded the Detroit Center for Family Advocacy, which aims to safely reduce the number of children in foster care by providing families with legal and social work advocacy.

Professor Sankaran's research and policy interests center on improving outcomes for children in child abuse and neglect cases by empowering parents and strengthening due process protections in the child welfare system. Sankaran sits on the steering committee of the ABA National Project to Improve Representation for Parents Involved in the Child Welfare System. He has litigated numerous cases on behalf of parents before the Michigan Supreme Court. He also has authored scholarly pieces and practical resource guides to assist professionals working with parents in the system and regularly conducts national and statewide training on these issues.

Sankaran earned his BA, *magna cum laude*, from the College of William and Mary. He earned his JD, *cum laude*, from Michigan Law School, where he was an associate editor of the *Michigan Law Review*. After law school, he joined "The Children's Law Center (CLC)" as a Skadden Fellow and became a permanent staff attorney with the CLC in September 2003. Sankaran was named the "2004 Michigan Law School Public Interest Alumni of the Year" and in 2006 and was certified as a child welfare specialist by the National Association of Counsel for Children. In 2011, he was named the "Parent Attorney of the Year" by the Michigan Foster Care Review Board.

Lauren Shapiro is the director of the Family Defense Practice at Brooklyn Defender Services, where she is responsible for managing over fifty staff members, including lawyers, social workers, parent advocates, and administrative staff, and for coordinating the litigation and systemic advocacy efforts of the practice. After graduating from New York University School of Law in 1986, Ms. Shapiro started her career at South Brooklyn Legal Services, where she worked for over twenty years. She founded and for seven years directed the office's HIV Unit. She was the director of the Family Law Unit, which represented clients in child welfare and domestic violence cases, for ten years. She also taught an externship clinic at Brooklyn Law School for many years. She is a member of the Bar Association's Council on Children and co-chairs the ASFA Ad Hoc Task Force, a collaboration of agencies that work on areas of mutual concern involving child welfare issues. She has written extensively on child welfare issues.

Joanna Woolman is an Assistant Professor of Law and Executive Director of the Child Protection Program at William Mitchell College of Law in St. Paul, Minnesota. Professor Woolman directs a clinic where law students work with social workers and parent mentors to provide direct representation to parents in the child protection system. Her work with the Child Protection Program includes conducting statewide attorney trainings, community events, and policy work to promote best practices in the area of child protection. Professor Woolman researches, publishes, and presents on issues relating to women's experiences in the criminal and child protection systems. She also teaches criminal law. Professor Woolman received a BS from the University of Wisconsin Madison in 1998 and a JD from the University of San Francisco School of Law in 2004. Prior to coming to William Mitchell College of Law full-time in 2011, Professor Woolman worked as a Public Defender for five years.

INDEX

THE THOMAS M. COOLEY LAW SCHOOL
In corde hominum est anima legis.
1972
LAW LIBRARY